Wiley CPAexcel® Exam Review
COURSE OUTLINES

JANUARY 2016

Wiley CPAexcel® Exam Review

COURSE OUTLINES

JANUARY 2016

REGULATION

Gregory Carnes, Ph.D., CPA
Marianne M. Jennings, J.D.
Robert A. Prentice, J.D.

Wiley Efficient Learning™

Cover image: © iStock.com/turtleteeth
Cover design: Wiley

For general information on our other products and services or for technical support, please contact our Customer Care Department within the United States at (800) 762-2974, outside the United States at (317) 572-3993 or fax (317) 572-4002.

Wiley publishes in a variety of print and electronic formats and by print-on-demand. Some material included with standard print versions of this book may not be included in e-books or in print-on-demand. If this book refers to media such as a CD or DVD that is not included in the version you purchased, you may download this material at http://booksupport.wiley.com. For more information about Wiley products, visit www.wiley.com.

Library of Congress Cataloging-in-Publication Data:
ISBN 9781119236641
Edition 7.13

ISBN 9781119257035 (ebk); 9781119257042 (ebk)

Printed in the United States of America

10 9 8 7 6 5 4 3 2

Contents

Contents

About the Authors

CPAexcel® content is authored by a team of accounting professors and CPA exam experts from top accounting colleges such as the University of Texas at Austin (frequently ranked the #1 accounting school in the country), California State University at Sacramento, Northern Illinois University, and University of North Alabama.

Professor Craig Bain
CPAexcel® Author, Mentor and Video Lecturer
Ph.D., CPA
Northern Arizona University: Franke College of Business, Professor and Accounting Area Coordinator

Professor Allen H. Bizzell
CPAexcel® Author, Mentor and Video Lecturer
Ph.D., CPA
Former Associate Dean and Accounting Faculty, University of Texas (Retired)
Associate Professor, Department of Accounting, Texas State University (Retired)

Professor Ervin L. Black
CPAexcel® Author and Video Lecturer
Ph.D.
Brigham Young University—Lecturer in international accounting and financial accounting

Professor Gregory Carnes
CPAexcel® Author and Video Lecturer
Ph.D., CPA
Raburn Eminent Scholar of Accounting, University of North Alabama; Former Dean, College of Business, Lipscomb University, Former Chair, Department of Accountancy, Northern Illinois University

Professor B. Douglas Clinton
CPAexcel® Author and Video Lecturer
Ph.D., CPA, CMA
Alta Via Consulting Professor of Management Accountancy, Department of Accountancy, Northern Illinois University

Professor Charles J. Davis
CPAexcel® Author and Video Lecturer
Ph.D., CPA
Professor of Accounting, Department of Accounting, College of Business Administration, California State University-Sacramento

Professor Donald R. Deis Jr.
CPAexcel® Author and Video Lecturer
Ph.D., CPA, MBA
Ennis & Virginia Joslin Endowed Chair in Accounting, College of Business, Texas A&M University—Corpus Christi
Former Director of the School of Accountancy, University of Missouri—Columbia
Former Professor and Director of the Accounting Ph.D. Program, Louisiana State University—Baton Rouge

Professor Marianne M. Jennings
CPAexcel® Author and Video Lecturer
J.D.
Professor of Legal and Ethical Studies, W.P. Carey School of Business, Arizona State University

Professor Robert A. Prentice
CPAexcel® Author and Video Lecturer
J.D.
Ed and Molly Smith Centennial Professor In Business Law and Distinguished Teaching Professor, J.D.
McCombs School of Business, University of Texas   Austin

Professor Pam Smith
CPAexcel® Author and Video Lecturer
Ph.D., MBA, CPA
KPMG Professor of Accountancy, Department of Accountancy, Northern Illinois University

Professor Dan Stone
CPAexcel® Author and Video Lecturer
Ph.D., MPA
Gatton Endowed Chair, Von Allmen School of Accountancy and the Department of Management, University of Kentucky

Professor Donald Tidrick
CPAexcel® Author and Video Lecturer
Ph.D., CPA, CMA, CIA
Deloitte Professor of Accountancy, Northern Illinois University, Former Associate Chairman of the Department of Accounting, Director of Professional Program in Accounting Director of the CPA Review Course, University of Texas at Austin

About the Regulation Professors

Professor Gregory Carnes is the Raburn Eminent Scholar of Accounting, University of North Alabama, former dean of the College of Business at Lipscomb University in Nashville, Tennessee, and former department chair and Crowe Chizek professor of Accountancy at Northern Illinois University. He taught Partnership Taxation and Taxation of Compensation and Benefits in NIU's Masters of Science in Taxation Program. Greg has published approximately 20 articles in journals such as *The Journal of Economic Psychology; Journal of the American Taxation Association; Advances in Taxation; The Journal of International Accounting; Auditing, and Taxation; The Tax Adviser; Taxation for Accountants; Taxation for Lawyers;* and *The CPA Journal*. He is a contributing author on *Federal Taxation* (ARC Publishing). He currently serves on the board of the Federation of Schools of Accountancy and is vice-president of communication for the Accounting Program Leadership Group. He is a member of the AICPA, the Illinois Society of CPAs, the American Accounting Association, and the American Taxation Association.

   Greg received his PhD from Georgia State University, his M.S. (Tax Specialization) from the University of Memphis, and his B.S. (Accountancy) from Lipscomb University. He previously taught at Louisiana State University, and worked for Ernst & Young in Nashville, Tennessee.

Professor Marianne Jennings is Professor of Legal and Ethical Studies at the W.P. Carey School of Business, Arizona State University. In her teaching, her writing, and her consulting, Professor Jennings demonstrates how making the ethical choice is the right choice because nice people can succeed—even in business! She has developed a workplace ethical behavior 10-step action plan that can be implemented anywhere. She has consulted with Mattel, Bell Helicopter, Blue Shield/Blue Cross, and many other companies on instilling workplace ethics.

Professor Robert A. Prentice is the Ed and Molly Smith Centennial Professor of Business Law at the University of Texas at Austin and has taught both UT's and other CPA courses for fifteen years. He created a new course in accounting ethics and regulation that he has taught for the last decade. Professor Prentice has written several textbooks, many major law review articles on securities regulation and accountants' liability, and has won more than thirty teaching awards.

Welcome to Regulation

Business Law

The scope of material in the Regulation—Business Law Section that is "fair game" under the AICPA content guidelines has been changed significantly, but is still vast. Cover all the material in each subject area as thoroughly as possible, but use the new learning objectives to help you stay focused on the big picture so that you can easily compartmentalize the minutiae. Regulation topics areas have a great deal of detail. All these details are fair game for the exam questions. Going over the material just once is inadequate to fully master it. For many of you, some of these subject areas will be completely new learning experiences. Whether the subject area is new to you or you studied it in college, take the lessons one at a time and in 30-minute increments. Then take the time to go back and review. If you try to master all the minutiae in huge blocks of study time, you will not conquer the details. Do a little each day. Then go back and use the tools again to get more familiar with those concepts. When you are able to sit down and write your own outline or flow chart of each area, without referring back to the text, the flash cards, or the video, you have reached a point of mastery.

In addition, I recommend the following:

A. Review the Overview for each General Subject area. The Overview gives you my opinion of where to emphasize your study.

B. Read the lesson text and view the video—go over the examples in the text and videos carefully.

C. Go through all of the questions available to you. The more questions you do, the more knowledge you have about question patterns and the more you realize that certain themes are repeated with different fact patterns. If you are not understanding a particular question, use the discussion forum to post the question and ask for more explanation on that question and the area. Also, just going through the mentored discussions can often clear up areas that are not as familiar to you and prevent you from spending too much time on one question or issue.

D. The exam does more than test in each subject area. The exam includes questions that have cross-over material. For example, it is not unusual for an exam question to cover issues of UCC Article 2 risk of loss along with UCC Article 9 secured transaction questions. Often, the answer for a question will require you to combine contracts formation with an issue related to suretyship. The materials include many of these combined topic questions. These questions are the best form of review because they require mastery of more than one area and integration of the materials.

~ Professor Marianne M. Jennings

Federal Taxation

The challenge in the tax area is that there are so many topics that can be tested. However, once a topic is chosen for the test, the question asked is usually somewhat basic. So make sure you know the foundational concepts very well and do not be as concerned about the complex areas.

When you take the exam, you will be working problems, so that is what you must practice. Do not just read the problems and the solutions. That will not prepare you. Work as many problems as you possibly can.

~ Professor Gregory A. Carnes

Ethics, Professional, and Legal Responsibilities

In the REG section, I am initially responsible for the 15%–19% of REG that is devoted to Ethics, Professional, and Legal Responsibilities.

First, this material covers the professional responsibilities (and liabilities) of tax professionals, derived in detail from the AICPA's Statements on Standards for Tax Services (SSTSs). These were rewritten and reorganized in 2010. Particular attention should be paid to SSTS No. 1, and to the fact that it is subordinate to conflicting Internal Revenue Code Guidelines. The other SSTSs are heavily based on common sense, fortunately. Other important guidelines for tax professionals come from the IRS's rules of practice contained in Circular 230 and civil and criminal provisions that apply to tax return preparers (TRPs) and others contained in the Internal Revenue Code (IRC). Within these two areas, it might pay to give particular attention to the new rules for "covered opinions" (tax shelters) in Circular 230 and to the definition of a TRP in the IRC.

Second, this material covers licensing and disciplinary systems, the standards state boards of accountancy impose for those who wish to qualify for a CPA license and the grounds upon which those licenses might be taken away. Disciplinary processes are also covered. These are not necessarily logical, but must be learned.

Third, this material covers the common law malpractice theories (negligence, breach of contract, fraud) that might be the basis for lawsuits against accountants and also addresses federal statutory liability of accountants, including RICO and the Foreign Corrupt Practices Act. In real life, and hopefully on the exam, the most important part of this material for CPAs is the part that deals with potential negligence liability to third parties (non-clients, such as lenders, suppliers, and investors) who have relied upon audited financial statements. There are several different tests for how widely a careless auditor's liability extends, with the most popular version being the Restatement's "limited class" test.

In the REG section, I am also responsible for the Government Regulation of Business and Business Structure (Selection of a Business Entity) portions of Business Law (which comprises 17%–21% of REG.

Much important material is contained in these sections.

Government Regulation of Business is divided into two sections—federal securities regulation and all other federal regulation. That division alone should tell you how important securities regulation is.

Federal Securities Regulation can itself be subdivided (largely) into the part based on the Securities Act of 1933 (that governs the initial sale of securities in the primary markets) and the part based on the Securities Exchange Act of 1934 (that governs the trading of securities in the secondary markets). Over the years, the CPA exam has emphasized the definition of a "security," the Regulation D exemptions for registration, and the differences between the 1933 Act's Section 11 (a negligence-based statute that punishes false statements in the audited financial statements contained in registered public offerings) and the 1934 Act's Section 10(b) (an intent-based statute that punishes fraudulent statements of any type when securities are being bought and sold). Although an accountant's potential liability under Section 11 and Section 10(b) have long received much attention on the exam, recent disclosed questions indicate that the 1933 Act's Section 12(a)(1) and 12(a)(2) and the 1934 Act's Section 18(a) have received attention as well. The JOBS Act of 2012 made some significant changes to the 1933 Act material. What is an EGC? What is crowdfunding? These matters will be covered on the exam in 2013 and beyond.

Other Federal Laws and Regulations—The material in this section has traditionally not received as much attention as the securities laws have, although it covers a wide range of federal regulatory matters, including labor law, employment law, and antitrust law. It might pay to give special attention to new content areas recently added to the course content specifications, including copyrights, patents, and money laundering.

The Business Structure portion of the Business Law materials has been moved to REG from BEC and completely reorganized. The most important part is probably the introductory material, which will give you the basics of all the major forms of business organization—partnership, corporation, LLP, LLC, etc. Formerly, the organizational pattern focused on a particular form of organization (such as a partnership or an LLC), and then ran through its features (formation, operation, termination, powers, financial structure, rights, powers, etc.) before moving on to the next form. Now, the content specifications indicate that we should focus on the features (formation, operations, termination, powers, financial structure, etc.) and within those sections compare and contrast the various forms of organization. This material is organized consistently with the new content specifications, but a great way to study would be to develop your own outline that reorganizes the material within each form of organization.

~ Professor Robert Prentice

Ethics, Professional, and Legal Responsibilities

Treasury Department Circular 230

After studying this lesson, you should be able to:

1. Understand the role of Circular 230 in providing the rules of practice for federal tax practitioners.

2. Comprehend several important provisions of Circular 230 relating to such matters as proper fees, conflicts of interest, general best practices, and best practices for tax shelters.

I. Introduction

A. Circular 230 contains the IRS's rules of practice governing CPAs and others who practice before the agency. The government may censure, fine, suspend, or disbar tax advisors from practice before the IRS if they violate Circular 230's standards of conduct.

B. Subpart A of Circular 230 sets forth rules governing authority to practice before the IRS. Most importantly, Section 10.3 provides that "[a]ny certified public accountant who is not currently under suspension or disbarment from practice before the Internal Revenue Service may practice before the Internal Revenue Service by filing with the Internal Revenue Service a written declaration that he or she is currently qualified as a certified public accountant and is authorized to represent the party or parties."

C. Subpart B contains the substantive rules that govern tax practitioners, including CPAs. Our discussion will focus upon those rules.

D. Subpart C spells out sanctions for violations and Subpart D contains procedural rules for disciplinary proceedings.

II. Substantive Provisions

A. **Furnishing information**—A practitioner must *promptly* submit to the IRS any records or information that its agents and officers request properly and lawfully, "unless the practitioner believes in good faith and on reasonable grounds that the records or information are privileged." In other words, Section 10.20 requires prompt cooperation with all IRS requests for information.

B. **Client's omission**—What if you learn that your client has not complied with the laws or made an error or omission on a tax return? Consistent with AICPA ethics guidelines, Section 10.21 requires the practitioner to promptly notify the client of the error and its potential consequences, but the practitioner need not notify the IRS of the error and may not do so without the client's permission.

C. **Due diligence and reliance on others**—Practitioners must exercise *due diligence* in all aspects of their tax practice, including preparing tax returns and making representations to the IRS. Section 10.22 allows a practitioner to rely upon the work product of others, if the practitioner used reasonable care in engaging, supervising, training, and evaluating them, though there are a couple of slight limitations on this reliance contained in Sections 10.34 and 10.37.

D. **Delays**—Practitioners may not *unreasonably* delay the prompt disposition of any matters before the Service. Stalling tactics are strongly discouraged by Section 10.23.

E. **Assistance from the disbarred**—What if your former partner violated regulations and has been disbarred by the IRS? She still needs a job and wants to continue to do the same work as before, but have you sign off on everything since you are still in good standing. Section 10.24 provides that a practitioner should not knowingly accept even indirect assistance from any person disbarred or suspended from practice by the IRS.

F. **Practice by former IRS agents**—The IRS is concerned about abuses by former IRS agents who might try to exploit their former position when they leave the Service. Therefore, Section 10.25 contains extensive rules meant to prevent conflicts of interest, such as IRS employees going into private practice and working on cases they had knowledge of when they worked for the government. For example, if IRS agent Fred worked on a matter involving taxpayer Stan within one year before he left the IRS, he could not join an accounting firm and represent Stan in that matter within two years of leaving the Service.

G. Notaries—A practitioner must not act as a notary public with respect to matters before the IRS in which he or she is involved or interested (Section 10.26).

H. Fees

    1. Unconscionable fees—No practitioner may charge an *unconscionable fee* for representing a client before the IRS.

    2. Contingent fees—The rest of Section 10.27 relates to contingent fees, providing that a practitioner *may not* charge a contingent fee for providing services before the IRS, with three exceptions. A contingent fee may be charged:

        a. For services rendered in connection with an IRS *examination or challenge* to either (i) an original tax return or (ii) an amended return or claim for refund when they were filed within 120 days of receiving a written notice of examination or written challenge to the original exam

        b. Where a claim for refund is filed solely in connection with determination of statutory interest or penalties

        c. When the accountant is representing the client in judicial proceedings.
        In these three situations, the threat that the tax practitioner and client will play the "audit lottery" (taking an aggressive position because it is unlikely that the Service will substantively examine it) is small

    3. PCAOB—Remember that the PCAOB believes that a public company auditor is not independent from an audit client if it offers that client any services on a contingent fee basis.

I. Return of client records—What if you have fired the client, or the client has fired you? You still have the client's tax records, but perhaps the client has not paid you. You don't want to give the client's records back until you are paid. Section 10.28 instructs the practitioner to promptly return any and all records needed for the client to comply with federal tax obligations. The practitioner may keep a copy. The rule specifies that the existence of a fee dispute does not change this obligation, but does go on to recognize that if applicable state law permits retention in the case of a fee dispute, the practitioner need return only those records that must be attached to the taxpayer's return. However, the rule further provides, the practitioner "must provide the client with reasonable access to review and copy any additional records of the client retained by the practitioner under state law that are necessary for the client to comply with his or her Federal tax obligations." The rule broadly defines "records of the client," but states that "[t]he term does not include any return, claim for refund, schedule, affidavit, appraisal or other document prepared by the practitioner ... if the practitioner is withholding such documents pending the client's performance of its contractual obligation to pay fees with respect to such document."

J. Conflicts of interest—Section 10.29 provides that practitioners should not represent a client before the IRS if to do so would create a *conflict of interest*.

    1. Such a conflict exists if the representation of one client would be adverse to that of another, or if there is a significant risk that the representation of one client would be *materially limited* by the practitioner's responsibilities to another client.

    2. Notwithstanding the existence of a conflict of interest, however, practitioners may represent a client if they:

        a. Reasonably believe that they can provide competent and diligent representation to the client

        b. The representation is not prohibited by law and

        c. The affected client gives *informed* consent in writing. Practitioners should keep the consents on file for at least three years

K. Solicitation—Section 10.30 contains several limitations upon solicitation of clients. Among others, false advertising is, of course, prohibited. But practitioners may publish accurate written schedules of fees and hourly rates.

L. Check negotiation—A practitioner who prepares tax returns may not endorse or otherwise negotiate any check issued to a client by the IRS, according to Section 10.31.

M. Practicing law—Tax accountants, typically, learn quite a bit of tax law, but nothing in Circular 230 is meant to authorize persons who are not members of the bar to practice law (Section 10.32).

N. Best practices—Section 10.33 sets forth **best practices** for tax advisors, including:

1. Communicating clearly with the client regarding the terms of the engagement, including the purpose, use, scope, and form of the advice

2. Establishing the facts, determining which facts are relevant, evaluating the reasonableness of assumptions or representations, relating the applicable law to the relevant facts, and arriving at a conclusion supported by the law and the facts

3. Advising the client regarding the import of the conclusions reached, including whether taxpayers may avoid accuracy-related penalties if they rely on the advice

4. Acting fairly and with integrity when practicing before the IRS

5. Exercising any firm supervisory powers to ensure that firm employees act in accordance with best practices

O. Tax return standards—Section 10.34 instructs practitioners not to willfully, recklessly, or through gross incompetence sign a tax return or claim for refund that the practitioner knows or reasonably should know contains a position that: (1) lacks a reasonable basis; (2) is an unreasonable position as defined by the Internal Revenue Code (Sec. 6694(a)(2)); or is a willful attempt to understate the tax liability or a reckless or intentional is regard of IRC rules. Nor should a practitioner advise a client to take such unreasonable positions.

1. Additionally, practitioners should not advise clients to take "frivolous" positions on documents filed with the IRS.

2. Practitioners must inform clients of penalties reasonably likely to be imposed with respect to positions taken.

3. Practitioners may generally rely in good faith upon information provided by their clients but may not ignore inconsistent information in their personal knowledge or other red flags that might appear.

P. Competence—Practitioners must be competent, meaning that they possess "the appropriate level of knowledge, skill, thoroughness, and preparation necessary." They may acquire competence by studying the relevant law or consulting with experts.

1. **Compliance procedures**—Section 10.36 provides that practitioners who have or share principal authority and responsibility for overseeing a firm's tax practice may be sanctioned if they either (a) willfully, recklessly, or through gross incompetence fail to take reasonable steps to assure that the firm has adequate procedures in place to ensure that all members and employees are complying with Circular 230, or (b) know or should know that a member or employee is not complying with Circular 230, but through willfulness, recklessness or gross incompetence fail to take prompt corrective action. The obvious purpose of this provision is to prevent those officials at the top of an accounting firm from placing all the blame for inappropriate tax shelter activity upon lower-ranking members of the firm. The provision is an exception to Section 10.22's provision that allows a practitioner to rely upon the work product of others if the practitioner used reasonable care in engaging, supervising, training, and evaluating them.

2. **Other written advice**—Section 10.37 provides that tax practitioners may give written advice if the practitioner (a) bases the advice on reasonable factual and legal assumptions; (b) reasonably considers all relevant facts and circumstances that the practitioner knows or reasonably should know; (c) uses reasonable efforts to identify and ascertain relevant facts; (d) does not rely on others' representations if to do so would be unreasonable; (e) relates applicable law and authorities to facts; and (f) does not take into account the possibility that a tax return will not be audited, that an issue will not be raised on audit, or that an issue will be settled.

III. Penalties and Procedures

A. Subpart C of Circular 230 sets forth the rules and penalties for disciplinary proceedings.

    1. As a general notion, Circular 230 authorizes the IRS to punish any tax professional who is incompetent, disreputable, violates the Treasury Department's rules of practice or with intent to defraud willfully and knowingly misleads or threatens the person being represented.

    2. Section 10.50 empowers the IRS to impose a monetary penalty on practitioners who have violated practice rules. The maximum penalty equals 100% of the gross income derived from the conduct and may be added to other penalties, such as suspensions and censures. It may also be added to the 50% penalty of gross income authorized by 26 U.S.C. Section 6694, meaning that the penalty could theoretically be up to 150% of the income derived from an engagement.

B. The remainder of Subpart C, as well as Subchapter D, contains sections setting forth the procedures governing the process when the IRS takes disciplinary action against tax practitioners.

Statements on Standards for Tax Services

After studying this lesson, you should be able to:

1. Understand the AICPA's ethical expectations for tax accountants.

2. Apply the AICPA's ethical rules for tax accountants to specific situations.

I. **Introduction**—The Statements on Standards for Tax Services (SSTSs) were modified, effective January 1, 2010. Former numbers 6 and 7 were consolidated. Number 8 was relabeled as number 7; consequently the total number of SSTSs shrank slightly. The only significant change came in No. 1.

II. **SSTS No. 1—Tax Return Positions**

A. **Overview**—SSTS No. 1 begins by instructing members that they should comply with standards, if any, imposed by applicable taxing authorities. This is required because Congress has raised its standard to a higher level than the AICPA standard. In 26 U.S.C. Section 6694, Congress has provided that a tax return preparer who takes an "unreasonable position" may be punished. A position is unreasonable unless there is "substantial authority" supporting it. This provision is discussed at length in the next section on tax return preparers under the Internal Revenue Code, but it has been suggested that if after proper research a preparer concludes that there is at least a 40% chance that the IRS would accept a particular position, then it has "substantial authority" supporting it. If a tax position relates to a tax shelter, then it is unreasonable unless it is "more likely than not" (more than 50%) to be sustained on its merits. So, for federal tax work, members must be aware of Section 6694.

B. **Tax return position**—If a taxing authority has no written standards for preparing or signing tax returns, or if its standards are lower, then two AICPA standards apply:

1. "A member should not recommend a tax return position or prepare or sign a tax return taking a position unless the member has a good-faith belief that the position has at least a **realistic possibility** (generally regarded as 33% likelihood) of being sustained administratively or judicially on its merits if challenged."

2. Even if there is not a realistic possibility of a position being sustained, a member may recommend a tax return position or prepare or sign a return if he or she concludes that (i) there is a **reasonable basis** (generally regarded as a 20%–33% likelihood) for the position, and (ii) the position is disclosed to the IRS so it can be reviewed.

C. **Potential penalties**—SSTS No. 1 instructs members to advise taxpayers regarding potential penalty consequences of the tax positions they take and of potential opportunities to avoid penalties through disclosure.

D. **Prohibitions**—Members should never recommend a tax return position or prepare or sign a return reflecting a position that:

1. Exploits the audit selection process (In other words, a preparer should never be heard to say, "This is not correct, but the IRS never checks it"); or

2. Serves as a mere arguing position advanced to obtain leverage in settlement negotiations (in other words, a preparer should never be heard to say, "You're entitled to a $20,000 deduction, but the IRS will fight you on this, so we'll claim $40,000 and see if we can compromise with the Service at $20,000").

E. **Advocacy**—Unlike auditors, who are watchdogs, members recommending tax positions have both the "right and the responsibility" to advocate for their taxpayer clients if claimed positions meet the applicable standards. CPAs owe a duty both to their clients and to the tax system.

F. **Authority**—Internal Revenue Code Section 6662 and accompanying Treasury Regulation 1.662-4(d)(3)(iii) are very narrow in what it recognizes as valid authority. The AICPA allows members to consider (1) a well-reasoned construction of the applicable statute, (2) well-reasoned articles or treatises, and (3) pronouncements issued by the applicable taxing authority regardless of whether Section 6662 would recognize them.

III. **SSTS No. 2—Answers to Questions on Returns**

    A. **Reasonable efforts**—Members should make "reasonable efforts" to obtain from their clients the information necessary to provide "appropriate answers" to all questions on a tax return that they sign as preparers.

        1. **Reasons for the rule**

            a. A question may be important in determining taxable income or loss, or the tax liability so that its omission would detract from the return's quality.

            b. A request for information may require a disclosure necessary for a complete return or to avoid penalties.

            c. A member often must sign a preparer's declarations stating that the return is true, correct, and complete.

        2. **Grounds for omission**—Reasonable grounds (which need not be explained) for omitting an answer to a question or a request for information:

            a. Information not readily available **and** answer is not significant in terms of taxes.

            b. Uncertainty as to meaning of question in relation to the particular return.

            c. Answer is voluminous and return states that data will be supplied upon examination.

        3. It is impermissible to omit information for the reason that disclosure might disadvantage the taxpayer.

IV. **SSTS No. 3—Procedural Aspects of Preparing a Return**

    A. **Good faith reliance**—In preparing or signing a return, a member may in good faith rely, without verification, on information furnished by the taxpayer or by third parties. Members need not put their clients through a lie detector test to check the truthfulness of the clients' representations.

    B. **Red flags**—Members should not ignore red flags and should make "reasonable inquiries" if the information furnished appears to be incorrect, incomplete, or inconsistent either on its face or on the basis of other facts known to the member.

    C. **Check earlier returns**—Where feasible, a member should examine the taxpayer's returns for other years to check for inconsistencies.

    D. **Conditions**—Sometimes tax law imposes conditions for qualification for a deduction or other tax treatment, such as production of substantiating documentation. In such cases, a member should make "appropriate inquiries" to determine whether the conditions are met.

    E. **Others' returns**—When preparing a tax return, a member should consider information known from other taxpayers' returns. For example, a CPA preparing tax returns for both a limited partnership and one of its limited partners should note any inconsistencies. In using such information, the member should keep in mind confidentiality rules.

V. **SSTS No. 4—Use of Estimates**

    A. **General rule**—Unless prohibited by statute or rule, a member may use the taxpayer's estimates in preparing a tax return if:

        1. It is not practical to obtain exact data; **and**

        2. The member determines that the estimates are reasonable based on known facts and circumstances known to the member.

    B. **Limitation**—The taxpayer's estimates should not imply greater accuracy than exists. For example, an estimate should not read: "$1,296.19."

    C. **Disclosure**—It is usually not necessary to disclose that an estimate is being used. However, disclosure should be made if needed to avoid misleading the taxing authority as to accuracy, as where:

        1. A taxpayer has died or is ill at the time the return must be filed

2. A taxpayer has not received a Schedule K-1 for a pass-through entity at the time the tax return is to be filed

3. There is litigation pending (e.g., a bankruptcy proceeding) that bears on the return

4. Fire, computer failure, or natural disaster has destroyed the relevant records

VI. SSTS No. 5—Departures from a Previous Position

A. **General rule**—The fact that a return position was rejected by the IRS or the Tax Court last year does not mean that it is necessarily improper to take that position again this year as long as the member believes in good faith that the standards of SSTS No. 1 are met.

B. **Possible grounds for asserting the position again**

1. The position lacked documentation last year; this year, documentation is available.

2. The taxpayer simply wanted to settle the dispute last year, even though the advice met the standards of SSTS No. 1.

3. New court decisions, rulings, or other authorities have developed since the prior ruling and they support the previous position.

C. **Exception**—If, in order to settle a proceeding with the IRS or in Tax Court, the taxpayer promises in a formal closing agreement not to take the position again, then, of course, the position should not be asserted a second time.

VII. SSTS No. 6—Knowledge of Error

A. **The issue**—What should members do when they learn that a required return has not been filed or that a material error has been made in a previously filed return or a return subject to an administrative proceeding?

B. **The answer**—The member should promptly notify the taxpayer. However, the member "is not allowed to inform the taxing authority without the taxpayer's permission, except when required by law." So, tell the taxpayer, but not the IRS.

C. **The following year**—If the member has informed the taxpayer of the previous error and the taxpayer has not taken appropriate action to correct the error, the member should consider severing the professional relationship. If the member does go ahead to prepare the next year's return, he or she should take reasonable efforts to prevent the previous error from being repeated.

1. **Additional advice**

   a. Once a taxpayer has given permission to correct, the member should act promptly.

   b. If a member believes the client may face fraud or other criminal charges, he or she should advise the client to consult an attorney.

   c. A member need not inform the client of errors that have no more than an insignificant effect upon the taxpayer's tax liability.

VIII. SSTS No. 7—Form and content of advice to taxpayers

A. **Format**—No standard format for communicating tax advice is required by the AICPA, but members are urged to consider putting advice in writing when it involves important, unusual, substantial dollar value, or complicated transactions.

B. **Standards to consider**—In giving tax advice, members should remember that their advice will affect their clients' actions in filing their tax returns and should therefore consider, when relevant, (a) return reporting and disclosure standards, including SSTS No.1 and (b) potential penalty consequences of recommended return positions.

C. **No duty to update**—Finally, a member has no general duty to update tax advice when tax law later changes. There are two exceptions: (1) when changes occur while the member is assisting a taxpayer in implementing procedures or plans associated with the advice provided; and (2) when a member specifically agrees to provide updates.

Internal Revenue Code of 1986 (TRP)

After studying this lesson, you should be able to:

1. Understand the criteria for determining who is a tax return preparer under federal law.

2. Be conversant with important criminal and civil provisions in the Internal Revenue Code that apply to tax return preparers and others.

I. **Internal Revenue Code—Tax Return Preparers**

    A. **Introduction**—The Internal Revenue Code (IRC) has many provisions that relate solely or largely to *tax return preparers (TRPs).* Some also apply to tax advisors. This section surveys those provisions, both civil and criminal.

II. **Who Is a Tax Return Preparer?**

> **Definition:**
>
> *Tax Return Preparer:* A TRP, generally speaking, is "any person who prepares for compensation, or who employs one or more persons to prepare for compensation, all or a substantial portion of any return of tax or any claim for refund of tax under the Internal Revenue Code."

    A. **Coverage**—Although this provision used to apply only to federal **income** tax returns, it now also covers federal estate and gift tax returns, employment tax returns, and excise tax returns. From this definition one may conclude that people are TRPs if they:

        1. Are paid

        2. To prepare, or retain employees to prepare

        3. A substantial portion

        4. Of any federal tax return or refund claim

    B. **Subtypes**—It is slightly more complicated than this. For example, Smith is a signing TRP who bears primary responsibility for the overall accuracy of the return. Kahn is a nonsigning TRP who is responsible for that part of the return in which he played a major role. Obviously Khan might do a lot of work on a tax return that is signed by Smith. Therefore, the rules recognize two sub-types: signing and nonsigning TRPs.

        1. *Signing TRPs* are individual TRPs who bear "primary responsibility" for the overall accuracy of the return or claim for refund (Smith in our example).

        2. *Nonsigning TRPs* are those other than the signing TRP who prepare all or a substantial portion of a return or claim for refund (Khan in our example).

    C. **Substantial portion**—Under the rules, the signing TRP is always responsible for a substantial portion of the return, but what about nonsigning TRPs? Current rules indicate that if Khan (to return to our example), evaluates a corporate taxpayer's just-completed transaction and concludes that it entitles the taxpayer to take a large deduction, he has prepared a "substantial portion" unless the deduction involves either:

        1. Less than $10,000 *or*

        2. Less than $400,000, which is also less than 20% of the gross income indicated on the return

> **Example:**
> Kahn opines that the taxpayer may take a deduction of $300,000 on a return reflecting $26 million in gross income. Kahn would not be a nonsigning TRP because, although $300,000 is a lot of money for some of us, it is not a "substantial portion" of a return featuring $26 million in gross income.

D. Not a TRP—One is not a TRP merely because he or she:

    1. Furnishes typing, reproducing, or other mechanical assistance

    2. Prepares a return or claim for refund of the employer (or of an officer or employee of the employer) by whom he or she is regularly and continuously employed

    3. Prepares as a fiduciary a return or claim for refund for any person

E. Additional clarification

    1. A firm that employs a TRP is treated as the sole **signing** TRP.

    2. When there are multiple people working on a return, the one who is primarily responsible for the position giving rise to an understatement is the TRP punishable under these provisions.

    3. If it is unclear who is responsible, the one with overall supervisory responsibility for the return or for the position will be the TRP.

III. Civil Provisions—The following IRC civil provisions apply to TRPs, and often others.

  A. Understatement of taxpayer's liability—Subsection (a) of Section 6694 imposes a penalty against a TRP when an "unreasonable" position causes an understatement of tax liability.

    1. Guidelines

      a. A position is unreasonable if there is no *substantial authority* (less than 40% chance of being sustained) for the position;

      b. A position is unreasonable if it is *disclosed* yet there is no *reasonable basis* (less than 20% chance of being sustained) for it;

      c. If the position relates to a *tax shelter*, it is unreasonable unless it is *more likely than not* (MLTN) (less than 50% chance) that the position will be sustained.

    2. Fortunately for TRPs, there is a good faith defense.

    3. Whereas Subsection (a) focuses on negligent conduct, Subsection (b) of 6694 imposes a larger penalty if the understatement is due to willful or reckless conduct.

  B. Disclosure provisions—Section 6695 punishes TRPS for, among other things:

    1. Failure to furnish copy of return to taxpayer

    2. Failure to sign return and show own identity

    3. Failure to furnish preparer's identifying number to the IRS

    4. Failure to keep copy of return

  C. Abusive tax shelters—Section 6700 punishes TRPs and others who promote abusive tax shelters when they:

    1. Organize or participate in the sale of a shelter *and*

    2. Either:

      a. Knowingly or recklessly make a material false statement that affects tax liability *or*

      b. Engage in a gross overvaluation of property (twice actual value)

  D. Aiding and abetting understatement of tax liability—Civil penalties can also be imposed under Section 6701 upon TRPs and others who:

    1. Aid, assist, procure, or advise in preparation or presentation of any portion of any return or other document

    2. Know or have reason to know it will be used in matters arising under tax law

    3. Know that if the return or document is so used, an understatement of the tax liability of another person will result

E. **Confidentiality**—With obvious exceptions for court orders, peer reviews, and the like, Section 6713 penalizes both:

    1. Disclosure of any information furnished to the TRP in connection with preparation of a return *or*

    2. Use of any such information for any purpose other than to prepare the return

F. **Injunctions**—In addition to civil fines, Section 7407 authorizes the IRS to enjoin TRPs and others from committing specific violations of the IRC (narrow injunctions) and can enjoin accountants and others from serving at all as TRPs (broad injunctions).

IV. **Criminal Provisions**—The IRC also contains criminal provisions to punish TRPs and others for various tax-related wrongdoing. The burden of proof is on the government to establish the crime beyond a reasonable doubt.

A. **Tax evasion**—IRC Section 7201 punishes tax evasion. It has been used to prosecute failure to file a return, falsifying income, and falsifying amounts that reduce taxable income. It is applied very broadly. The government must prove:

    1. An affirmative act constituting an attempt to evade or defeat payment of a tax

    2. Willfulness

    3. Existence of a tax deficiency

B. **Tax fraud**—IRC Section 7206 punishes fraud and false statements, criminalizing:

    1. Willfully making and subscribing to any document made under penalty of perjury, which the accountant does not believe to be true as to every material matter

    2. Willfully aiding the preparation of any tax-related matter that is fraudulent as to any material matter

    3. Concealing client's property with intent to defeat taxes

C. **Miscellaneous tax crimes**—Although most criminal prosecutions are brought under Sections 7201 or 7206, other criminal provisions include:

    1. Willful failure to file return, supply information, or pay tax (Section 7203)

    2. Willful failure to collect or pay over tax (Section 7202)

    3. Fraudulent returns, statements, or other documents (Section 7207)

    4. Attempts to interfere with administration of the Internal Revenue laws, such as threatening IRS agents or misleading them (Section 7212)

    5. Unauthorized disclosure of taxpayer information (with obvious exceptions for court orders, peer reviews, and the like) (Section 7213)

    6. Willful disclosure or use of confidential information learned while preparing a tax return (Section 7216)

    7. Conspiracy to commit any offense or fraud against the United States, including tax offenses (18 U.S.C. Section 371)

Licensing and Disciplinary Systems

After studying this lesson, you should be able to:

1. Understand the basic criteria for gaining a CPA license.

2. Realize that it is state boards of accountancy that grant and take away CPA licenses.

3. Understand the disciplinary role served by the AICPA.

4. Be conversant with the AICPA's disciplinary processes.

I. Role of State Boards of Accountancy

A. **Authority**—State boards of accountancy license CPAs and can prohibit non-CPAs from performing attest functions.

   1. It is only state boards that can grant CPA licenses and only state boards that can take them away.

   2. While the AICPA and state societies of CPAs cannot grant or take away CPA licenses, they can grant membership, take away membership, and punish members by suspensions, etc. The AICPA's authority in this regard is covered in the AUD materials.

B. **Licensing**—To qualify to be licensed as a "certified public accountant," one must meet several requirements. In most states, three steps are the key and may be accomplished in any order:

   1. **Education**

      a. "BA + 30" (150 hours of college education).

      b. Professional ethics course (required by many states).

      c. CPE—Once certification is gained, there are also continuing professional education requirements.

   2. **Examination**

      a. Pass the CPA exam.

   3. **Experience**

      a. How long? One year of professional experience (but at least 2,000 hours).

      b. In what areas? In accounting, attest, management advisory, financial advisory, tax or consulting areas and may be while working for any employer (accounting firm, corporation, government agency, etc.).

C. **Attest-related functions**

   1. One needs a CPA license to perform attest-related functions:

      a. Any audit or other engagement to be performed in accordance with SAS (Statements on Auditing Standards)

      b. Any review of a financial statement to be performed in accordance with SSARS (Statements on Standards on Accounting and Review Services)

      c. Any examination of prospective financial information to be performed in accordance with SSAE (Statements on Standards for Attest Engagements)

      d. Any engagement to be performed in accordance with the standards of the PCAOB

D. **Nonattest services**

   1. One does not need a CPA license to perform such nonattest services as

      a. Preparation of tax returns

      b. Management advisory services (consulting)

      c. Preparing financial statements without issuing a report thereon

E. **Discipline**—State boards may revoke CPA licenses and impose other penalties (such as fines) for such acts as:

    1. Fraud or deceit in obtaining a certificate

    2. Cancellation of a certificate in any other state for disciplinary reasons

    3. Failure to comply with requirements for renewal

    4. Revocation of the right to practice before any state or federal agency, including the PCAOB

    5. Dishonesty, fraud, or gross negligence in performance of services or failure to file one's own income tax returns

    6. Violation of professional standards

    7. Conviction of a felony or any crime involving fraud or dishonesty

F. **Reciprocity**—Most states are now an active part of the "UAA Mobility" project supported by the AICPA and the National Association of State Boards of Accountancy (NASBA). When fully implemented, accountants from one state will be able to represent clients in another state without obtaining a license from or paying a fee to the latter state's accountancy board.

II. Role of AICPA

A. **Professional Ethics Division**

    1. Investigates violations of AICPA Code and sanctions minor cases.

B. **Joint Trial Board**

    1. Hears more serious cases.

    2. Has power to acquit, admonish, suspend, or expel.

    3. Initial decisions are made by a panel whose actions are reviewable by the full trial board, whose decisions are conclusive.

C. *Automatic expulsion* from the AICPA without a hearing results when a member has been convicted or received an adverse judgment for:

    1. committing a felony

    2. willfully failing to file a tax return

    3. filing a fraudulent tax return on own or client's behalf

    4. aiding in preparing a fraudulent tax return for a client

> **Rationale:** If a member has already been convicted or received an adverse judgment, then there has already been an opportunity for the member to have a full-blown criminal or civil trial. Consequently, it would be a waste of resources to have a second hearing and summary punishment is justified.

D. **Revocation of certificate** by a state board of accountancy also leads to automatic expulsion.

E. **Joint Ethics Enforcement Program (JEEP)**

    1. The AICPA and most state CPA societies have agreements to split the handling of ethics complaints.

    2. Typically, the AICPA handles:

      a. matters of national concern

      b. matters involving more than one state

      c. matters in litigation

    3. The individual states handle the rest.

Malpractice Liability

This lesson covers four main topics:

Breach of Contract: Whereas other theories of liability often involve the courts making public policy in setting up the rules, breach of contract law focuses on the parties' agreement. Remember that punitive damages may not be recovered by a plaintiff in a simple breach of contract suit.

Negligence Liability to Clients: When one hears of an accountant "malpractice" action, that suit is usually brought by a client against its accountant on a negligence theory. This section spells out the basic things that a client must prove to recover from an accountant in such a case.

Fraud: No accountant wants to be accused of fraud, but each year many are. The most important things to derive from this section are these: (a) an ability to compare and contrast the elements of fraud and simple negligence; (b) an appreciation of the difference between actual fraud and constructive fraud; and (c) the knowledge that a fraud claim can lead to imposition of punitive damages, whereas punitive damages are not available in cases involving breach of contract, simple negligence, or federal securities law claims.

Negligence Liability to Third Parties: The most important and controversial issue in the area of accountants' liability under the common law relates to auditors' exposure to liability in negligence suits brought by third parties (usually investors and/or creditors). The area is controversial and has generated at least three points of view.

After studying this lesson, you should be able to:

1. Understand the basic elements of a malpractice action against an accountant based on a breach of contract theory, a negligence theory and a common law fraud theory.

2. Understand the potential scope of an accountant's liability to third parties, such as a client's investors, lenders, and suppliers.

Breach of Contract

> **Definition:**
> *Breach of Contract:* An accountant breaches the contract when he or she fails to perform substantially as agreed under contract.

I. **Accountants' Duties**—Accountants' duties arise from:

    A. **Express agreement of the parties**

        1. In a written engagement letter

        2. An oral agreement may also be enforceable

    B. **Implied agreement**—(read in as a matter of law) To perform in a nonnegligent manner consistent with the standards of the profession.

Example:
An accountant carelessly performs a tax (or audit or consulting) engagement. When the client sues for breach of contract, the accountant points out that nowhere in the contract did he promise to perform nonnegligently. The accountant is nonetheless in breach of contract because the law implies such a promise on the accountant's behalf.

II. An Accountant Is Not a Guarantor or Insurer

    A. "Normal" audit is not intended to uncover fraud, shortages, defalcations, or irregularities in general (although it may do so), but is meant to provide auditor evidence needed to express opinion on fairness of financial statements. (Note: Juries often have difficulty grasping this concept.)

    B. An accountant is generally not liable for failure to detect fraud or irregularities, unless:

        1. A normal audit by a careful accountant would have detected them or

        2. In the engagement letter, accountant undertakes greater responsibility to detect fraud, etc. **or**

        3. The wording of the audit report indicates that the auditor does have such a duty.

    C. An accountant should follow up on "red flags" and that investigation should not accept explanations at face value.

III. Client Breaches the Contract—The client breaches the contract when it interferes with or prevents the accountant from performing.

IV. Consequences of Breach by Accountant

	Yes	No
Accountant entitled to fee:		
—if breach is major		x
—if breach is minor	x	
Client entitled to:		
—compensatory damages	x	
—punitive damages		x

V. Disclaimers—Attempts by accountants to avoid liability by disclaimers in the contract are generally ineffective.

Negligence Liability to Clients

Misconception: Two forms of disclaimers are often confused. If an accountant clearly provides in an engagement letter that s/he is not performing an audit, but merely an unaudited compilation, that provision will generally be honored. The accountant cannot be liable for not having performed a full-fledged audit. However, if the accountant in either an audit engagement or a compilation engagement (or any other) provides in an engagement letter that s/he will not be liable for any negligence s/he may commit, that attempted disclaimer will typically not be honored.

VI. Basic Elements—The basic elements apply whether the auditor has erred in audit, tax, or consulting work. The more complex issue of when accountants should be liable to third parties (nonclients) is addressed later.

VII. Negligence vs. Breach—In many jurisdictions, the proper cause of action is breach of contract if an accountant simply failed to perform a contract, but negligence if the accountant performed the contract but did so carelessly.

    A. On the other hand, in some jurisdictions a negligence claim cannot be brought for mere economic injuries. Such a theory is reserved for personal injury claims, and all claims of economic loss must be brought as breach of contract or warranty.

VIII. Elements of Recovery to Be Proved by Plaintiff in a Negligence Case

    A. Duty

    B. Breach

    C. Damages

    D. Proximate cause

IX. Duty

    A. Standard—That degree of judgment and skill possessed by a reasonable accountant under all the circumstances.

    B. Sources of standard

        1. State and federal statutes

        2. Court decisions

        3. Contract with client

        4. GAAP and GAAS (persuasive, not conclusive):

            a. Evidence of violation of GAAP or GAAS almost automatically establishes negligence.

            b. Evidence of compliance with GAAP and GAAS does not necessarily establish reasonable care.

Example:
In one famous case, an accountant had six experts testify that GAAP and GAAS had been followed in his audit. Yet, a jury found him criminally guilty because there was evidence that the accountant knew that the particular financial statements were misleading, notwithstanding the compliance with GAAP and GAAS.

---

        5. Customs of the profession (persuasive, not conclusive)

    C. The standard can be raised above that of the reasonable accountant by:

        1. An accountant being a specialist

        2. An accountant holds self out as having special expertise *or*

        3. A contractual provision in which the accountant undertakes higher duty

X. Breach of Duty by Accountant—An error of judgment or other mistake is not actionable unless it is negligent. (Accountants, like others in our society, are not expected to be perfect.)

XI. Damages

    A. Of course, a plaintiff cannot recover from a careless accountant unless the plaintiff has suffered some injury.

    B. Key point—Punitive damages are not allowed in a mere negligence action.

Damages Recoverable by Client in a Negligence Action	Yes	No
Compensatory damages for reasonably foreseeable injuries	x	
Compensatory damages for unforeseeable injuries		x
Compensatory damages for injuries caused by client's contributory negligence		x
Punitive damages		x

XII. Proximate Cause—A plaintiff must prove that the accountant's negligence directly (proximately) caused his or her injuries.

    A. Elements

        1. "But for" causation (that is, a court can say that "but for" the accountant's negligence, the loss would not have occurred), *and*

        2. Reasonable foreseeability—i.e., no "independent intervening causes" unforeseeable to, and beyond the control of, the accountant broke up the chain of causation between the accountant's careless act and the plaintiff's loss.

> **Example:**
> A CPA negligently fails to discover during an audit that diamond rings are missing from the client's inventory. In fact, an employee stole rings both before and after the audit. The CPA would not be liable for the rings stolen before the audit because it cannot be said that "but for" the accountant's carelessness the rings would not have been stolen. The CPA would likely be liable for the rings stolen after the audit, however, because successful defalcations by employees are one of the reasonably foreseeable consequences of a defective audit.

XIII. Loss with Multiple Causes—If loss had multiple causes, accountant is liable if his or her negligence was a "substantial factor" (but perhaps not the sole proximate cause) in bringing about the loss.

XIV. Defenses to a Negligence Claim—Contributory Negligence of Client—There are **two types** of client carelessness.

    A. All jurisdictions recognize that accountants can raise as a defense the client's carelessness when that carelessness interferes with the accountant's performance of his or her task.

> **Example:**
> An auditor's request for all of the client's records of a certain type is frustrated when the client carelessly overlooks several of the records. The auditor performs the audit not knowing of the existence of these records and not taking into account the extra expenses reflected therein. Perhaps the auditor was careless in not realizing that the records were missing, but it seems clear that the client's carelessness impeded the auditor's attempt to do the audit. The auditor could raise this carelessness as a defense to defeat, or at least minimize, the client's recovery in a malpractice suit.

    B. Most jurisdictions, but not all, recognize that accountants can raise as a defense the client's carelessness that contributes to a loss even when that carelessness does not interfere with the accountant's performance of his or her task.

> **Example:**
> An auditor carelessly audits a company and does not discover that one of its employees is embezzling large sums from the company. On the other hand, the company did not investigate the employee's background before it hired him (it would have discovered an extensive criminal record), did not monitor the employee after giving him access to large amounts of cash, and asked no questions when the employee (who makes $20,000 a year) buys an expensive new home and sports car. Most jurisdictions would allow the auditor to raise the company's own careless monitoring of the employee as a defense. However, a few jurisdictions would place the entire loss upon the auditor on the theory that the company discharged its obligation of due care when it hired the auditor.

XV. Summary Chart

Status of Contributory Negligence Defense	All Jurisdictions	Most Jurisdictions
Client's carelessness interferes with accountant's performance of audit	x	
Client's carelessness helps create the situation that the audit fails to detect		x

Fraud

XVI. Elements

    A. False Representation of Fact—Accountant made a **false representation of fact** (or omitted to state a fact in the face of a duty to do so).

        1. A false statement of **expert** opinion is deemed tantamount to a representation of fact.

Example:
If A sells B his car, telling B that the car gets 50 miles per gallon when, in fact, it gets only 25, this is a false statement of fact and B can sue A for fraud. If A sells B his car, telling B, "I really love this car" when, in fact, A hates the car, B cannot sue for fraud because A merely stated an opinion (even though it was a false one). However, when an accountant issues a professional opinion, for example, by certifying financial statements as accurate, the statement carries more weight by virtue of the accountant's expertise. It is treated as tantamount to a statement of fact and actionable if fraudulent.

    B. The misrepresented (or omitted) fact was *material*.

Example:
An auditor determines that a client company made a profit of $999,950 but certifies as accurate the client's financial statements, which show a profit of $1,000,000, because that is a nice, round number. This is a false statement of fact but the inaccuracy is so small that it is probably not material.

    C. The accountant *knew* or recklessly disregarded the falsity.

        1. Knowledge (scienter) = **actual fraud**

Example:
A famous rock singer gave his money to D, accountant, to invest. The accountant issued to the singer monthly reports indicating that the money was being wisely invested and that the rock singer's fortune was growing. In fact, D had invested the money in several ventures that he operated and most of it had been lost. The monthly reports were mere fictions. This is a clear case of actual fraud on the part of the accountant.

2. Reckless disregard or gross negligence = **constructive fraud**

Example
D, accountant, is hired to issue an audit report on a client company. When D shows up for the job, the client's own accountant hands him a finished audit report to sign. D signs the audit report, hoping that it is accurate. It turns out that it is not accurate and lenders who lent money to the client company based on the inaccurate financial statements sue D in fraud. The accountant is liable for fraud of the constructive type. He had no reasonable grounds to believe that the report he signed was accurate. He is guilty of reckless disregard of the truth.

D. The accountant intended to and did induce plaintiff's reasonable *reliance* on the misstatement or omission.

Example
D, accountant, certified a client company's financial statements as accurate knowing that they were not and knowing that lenders and investors would rely upon those financial statements in making lending and investment decisions. In such a case, the accountant's intent to induce reliance by the lenders and investors would be clear. The auditor's best defense would be if he could show that some of the lenders and investors knew facts about the client that should have put them on alert that the client was in financial trouble and, thus, that their reliance on the accountant's report was not "reasonable." Unfortunately for accountants, this defense seldom works.

E. The client suffered damages.

Example
Client calls D, accountant, and asks D to audit and certify 80 copies of financial statements. Client tells D that it intends to seek lenders and/or investors. D certifies the financial statements, which vastly overstate client's worth. ABC Bank makes a loan to the client based on the financial statement and later loses lots of money when the client files bankruptcy. ABC sues D for fraud, showing that D knew or was reckless in not knowing that the financial statements were inaccurate. ABC can recover from D even though D did not know before the audit that ABC specifically would be a recipient of one of the 80 copies of the false financial statements. D did know that its report would be widely circulated and relied upon by lenders or investors.

1. Fraud is an intentional tort, whereas the essence of negligence is mere carelessness.

2. A defrauder's liability runs to all foreseeable victims of the fraud, whereas a negligent accountant's liability is much more limited in scope.

3. A defrauder may be liable for punitive damages as well as compensatory damages. A defendant who was merely negligent is not liable for punitive damages.

XVII. Summary Chart

Differences Between Fraud and Negligence Causes of Action	Fraud	Negligence
Plaintiff must prove bad intent or recklessness	Yes	No
Plaintiff must prove carelessness	No	Yes
Plaintiff must prove proximate cause	Yes	Yes

Plaintiff can recover compensatory damages	Yes	Yes
Plaintiff can recover punitive damages	Yes	No
Contributory negligence is a defense	No	Yes
All reasonably foreseeable persons may recover	Yes	No

Negligence Liability to Third Parties

XVIII. Restatement View—If you can understand the table presented in this section, you should be able to answer any question that can be presented to you on the exam. Remember that the Restatement view is the majority view around the country, but that several states have adopted the privity point of view either judicially or via statute. If a question is silent as to which approach is to be used, assume that the Restatement view applies. It is the majority rule.

XIX. Three Primary Approaches

A. The Privity approach of *Ultramares v. Touche*—Accountant is liable only to those with whom he or she is in **privity of contract**, i.e., the client, or third-party beneficiaries of the contract.

   1. **Rationale**—Whereas plaintiffs suing for fraud, recklessness, or gross negligence may recover simply by being reasonably foreseeable victims of the fraud, courts adopting the privity approach are worried about accountant liability for simple carelessness extending to an indeterminate class for an indeterminate time and for an indeterminate amount. Therefore, they limit liability to the client and third parties expressly mentioned in the engagement letter.

   2. **Fact**—A substantial number of jurisdictions have adopted the privity approach either through judicial decision or by legislation.

B. The Restatement "Limited Class" approach—An accountant is liable to a limited class of nonclients where the accountant knows:

   1. The information being supplied to the client will be given to, or is for the benefit and guidance of, a limited group of third persons.

   2. The information will influence those third persons in a specific transaction or type of transaction.

> **Note:**
> *The Restatement approach is the majority approach; more states follow it than any other view.*

C. The Reasonable Foreseeability approach—An accountant is liable to whomever he or she can reasonably foresee may use the financial statements he or she certifies or prepares.

   1. This view imposes the same scope of liability for negligent accountants as applies in any other type of negligence suit. It also applies the same basic scope of liability as exists in fraud cases against accountants.

   2. Very few jurisdictions still use the reasonable foreseeability approach.

Examples:			
	Will Plaintiffs Recover Under:		
Scenarios:	**Ultramares**	**Restatement**	**Foreseeability**
1) D, accountant, contracts to do audit for client. D mishandles the job and employees steal large sums. Client sues D in negligence.	Yes	Yes	Yes

2) D contracts to do audit for client. Letter of engagement specifies that the audit is for the benefit of ABC bank, which will use the certified financial statements to determine whether to double client's current line of credit at the bank. D mishandles the job certifying financial statements that vastly overstate client's worth. ABC doubles the line of credit but loses tons of money when client goes under. ABC sues D in negligence.	Yes	Yes	Yes
3) Client calls D and asks D to audit and certify a copy of its financial statements so that it may borrow money. During audit, D learns that client will probably borrow from ABC Bank and calls ABC Bank to ask if it has any particular concerns about client's status that D should pay special attention to during the audit. D certifies the financial statements, which vastly overstate client's worth. Client sends financial statements to ABC, which makes loan based thereon. ABC sues D in negligence.	No	Yes	Yes
4) Client calls D and asks D to audit and certify five copies of financial statements that, it tells D, it intends to provide to five unidentified banks in the area in hopes of receiving a loan. D certifies the financial statements, which vastly overstate client's worth. Longhorn National Bank, which loans money to client based on the financial statements, later sues D in negligence.	No	Yes	Yes
5) Client calls D and asks D to audit and certify 80 copies of financial statements. Client tells D that it intends to seek lenders and/or investors. D certifies the financial statements, which vastly overstate client's worth. ABC Bank makes loan based on the financial statement and later sues D in negligence.	No	No	Yes
6) Client calls D and asks D to audit and certify one copy of financial statements. Client tells D that it intends to show the statements to its long- time banker in hopes of receiving an extension of current line of credit. Instead, client shows copies of the financial statements to several out- of-state banks that loan money to client and later sue D when they discover the financial statements were error-filled.	No	No	No

Federal Statutory Liability

This lesson covers four main topics:

Foreign Corrupt Practices Act (FCPA): Scandals involving U.S. companies that pay bribes to the officials of foreign governments to obtain and retain business led to the passage of the FCPA. These scandals led to the overthrow of some foreign governments. The SEC was scandalized that these companies could pay millions of dollars in bribes, sometimes tens of millions, without ever having an entry on their financial statements reading, "Bribes paid to foreign officials: $4.2 million." The SEC was also upset that the upper-level officials in these companies could get away with saying, "Golly, we didn't know this was happening." Therefore, the FCPA contains not only antibribery provisions, but also accounting provisions to ensure that such bribes do not go unnoticed.

Racketeer Influenced and Corrupt Organizations Act (RICO): Although RICO is still part of the CPA exam, its importance for accountants has been dramatically reduced by a recent Supreme Court decision and a recent statute enacted by Congress. The result is that RICO, once fearsome, can no longer be the basis for a civil damage action against accountants in a situation where the essence of the claim is securities fraud, unless the accountant has already been criminally convicted of the offense.

Mail and Wire Fraud: Anytime someone tells a lie over the phone ("The check is in the mail."), he has likely committed the criminal offense of wire fraud. Anytime someone tells a lie in a letter, he has likely committed mail fraud. These are broad criminal provisions and you should know their basics.

SOX Criminal Liability Provisions: In response to the Enron/Arthur Andersen scandal, Congress passed the Sarbanes-Oxley Act, which not only affected the regulation of the accounting profession, but also amended and supplemented the federal securities laws and added new provisions to prevent destruction of evidence.

After studying this lesson, you should be able to:

1. Comprehend the basic provisions of the Foreign Corrupt Practices Act and the Racketeer Influenced and Corrupt Organizations Act as they pertain to accountants.

2. Understand the potential criminal liability that accountants face under the mail and wire fraud provisions.

3. Be conversant with some key Sarbanes-Oxley criminal provisions.

Foreign Corrupt Practices Act (FCPA)

I. **Introduction**—The FCPA was a post-Watergate response to illegal foreign bribes paid by U.S. companies. It contains two major provisions.

   A. It contains **anti-bribery provisions** aimed at preventing U.S. companies from gaining or retaining foreign business by bribing foreign government officials. A 1998 amendment banned foreign bribery as a means of obtaining a competitive advantage;

   B. More relevant to accountants, it contains **accounting provisions** aimed specifically at preventing companies from hiding huge bribes on their financial statements.

II. **Accounting Provisions**

   A. **All companies registered with the SEC** must keep "reasonably detailed" records that "accurately and fairly" reflect the company's financial activities. The accounting portion of the FCPA does not require the company to do any business abroad.

   B. These companies must devise sufficient internal accounting controls (IACs) to provide "reasonable assurance" that:

      1. Transactions are executed in accordance with the management's general or specific authorization

2. Transactions are recorded as necessary to:

    a. permit preparation of proper financial statements

    b. maintain accountability for assets

3. Access to assets is authorized

4. Recorded assets are compared with existing assets at reasonable intervals

III. Penalties

    A. Criminal:

        1. Individual: maximum of $100,000 fine and/or five years in jail

        2. Corporation: maximum of $1,000,000 fine

        3. There will be no criminal prosecutions for inadvertent or insignificant errors.

    B. Civil: maximum civil fine of $10,000

IV. Examples

Example:

1. D bought 51% of an SEC-registered company engaged in the wholesale and retail trade in rare coins, precious metals, and the like. D was warned about the company's internal accounting controls but did nothing to remedy the problem. Inventory controls were lax. Rare coins were left unguarded, employees were allowed to take large quantities of assets off the premises, appraisals were inadequate, and the company could not even determine how much had been paid for coins in the inventory. There was no separation of duties. One employee could, without supervision, appraise a particular coin, buy it from a customer, draw a check for the coin, count the coin into inventory, value the coin for inventory purposes, and sell the coin to another. No employees were bonded. Poor control of checks caused the company to bounce more than 100 checks. $1.7 million in checks were written to D without supporting documents. Ultimately, the company went from 40 employees to just three and from $2 million in assets to less than $500,000 in just a couple of years. The SEC successfully brought FCPA charges proving violations of the accounting rules.

2. An SEC-registered company paid a large sum to bribe an infamous African dictator. The bribe payment showed up nowhere on the company's books. The company was held to have violated the FCPA's accounting provisions.

3. M, an SEC-registered company's CEO and 47% owner, received $100,000 for nonbusiness-related expenses in a period of a few years. The company had no procedure for independent review of M's expenses. Occasionally, M would sit down with the company's accountants and mark vouchers with a C (company) or a P (personal). This was held to be a violation of the FCPA accounting provisions.

Racketeer Influenced and Corrupt Organizations Act (RICO)

V. Purpose—To prevent organized crime's infiltration into legitimate business.

VI. RICO Has Two Sides

    A. Criminal—Charges can be brought by the Department of Justice (DOJ).

    B. Civil—Injured individuals can sue for treble damages and attorneys' fees.

VII. RICO Prohibits

    A. Receiving money or property through a pattern of racketeering activity and subsequently investing that money into an enterprise (Section 1962[a])

    B. Acquiring and controlling an enterprise through a pattern of racketeering activity (Section 1962[b])

C. Conducting or participating, directly or indirectly, in the conduct of an enterprise's affairs (Section 1962[c])

D. Conspiring to violate A., B., or C. (Section 1962[d])

VIII. Section 1962(c)—Most RICO cases are brought under Section 1962(c), which has four elements: (1) defendant conducted or participated in the conduct (2) of an enterprise (3) through a pattern (4) of racketeering activity.

A. Conduct or participation—Defendant conducted or participated in the conduct

  1. The Supreme Court has held that the "conduct or participation" test is met only by those who actually manage a business. If an accountant sticks to accounting and does not become involved in "calling the shots," the accountant will not meet this test. Since this case was decided, RICO has become much less fearsome to accountants.

Example:
An accounting firm provided audit, accounting, and consulting services for an insurance company that became insolvent. Investors sued the firm under RICO proving that it had issued inaccurate audit reports, provided other accounting services, and attended board meetings of the insurer. Despite this activity, the court held that there was no evidence that the accounting firm had made managerial decisions for the insurance company. Therefore, the "conduct or participation" element was not met and the firm could not be liable under RICO.

B. Of an enterprise

  1. The enterprise requirement means that the "person" being charged under RICO must be separate and distinct from the "enterprise."

    a. **Example**—The auditor could be the "person," the client could be the "enterprise."

C. Through a pattern

  1. A "pattern" is defined in the statute as two acts of racketeering occurring within a 10-year period, but the Supreme Court has held that the pattern requirement is not met unless the acts

    a. Are related *and*

    b. Threaten a continuity of racketeering activity

D. Of racketeering activity

  1. "Racketeering activity" is defined in the statute by example and includes:

    a. Mail fraud: any lie told through the mail

    b. Wire fraud: any lie told over the phone ("The check is in the mail")

    c. About 30 other listed acts that are known as RICO "predicate acts"

  2. The plaintiff usually must prove that these racketeering acts occurred but it doesn't mean that defendant has been convicted of them already.

    a. **Exception**—Any civil plaintiff bringing a RICO claim for damages in a case involving acts that could constitute securities fraud (any lie told involving the sale or purchase of securities) must prove that the defendant had already been criminally convicted of securities fraud.

    b. **Fact**—This greatly reduces accountants' exposure to liability under RICO because most RICO claims brought against accountants have involved securities fraud, and accountants are seldom criminally convicted of securities fraud.

Mail and Wire Fraud

IX. Fraud

A. Any fraud committed with use of the mail or telephones (telegraphs, Internet, etc.) is a federal crime.

X. Criminal Liability

A. The mail and wire fraud provisions are two of the most important federal provisions under which accountants can be held **criminally** liable. However, one cannot overlook the securities law, tax law, FCPA, and RICO criminal provisions.

SOX Criminal Liability Provisions

XI. Record Retention, Destruction, and Tampering Statutes—Motivated largely by Arthur Andersen's shredding of two tons' worth of documents as the SEC and the Department of Justice began looking into the Enron scandal, Congress included three criminal provisions related to document handling in Sarbanes-Oxley:

A. Willful failure to retain audit and review work papers—SOX created a new federal crime punishing a "knowing and willful" failure to retain audit or review work papers for a period of five years by up to 10 years in jail and a fine (Section 802, codified at 18 U.S.C. Section 1520). Because another provision of SOX required the PCAOB to establish rules that require auditors of public companies to maintain audit work papers for not less than seven years, that length of time remains quite important.

B. Destruction of records—SOX created a new federal crime that relates to destruction of records involved in any federal governmental matter or bankruptcy, making it a crime punishable by fine, imprisonment of up to 20 years, or both to "knowingly alter, destroy, mutilate, conceal, cover up, falsify, or make a false entry in any record, document, or tangible object with intent to impede, obstruct, or influence the investigation or proper administration of any matter within the jurisdiction of any department or agency of the United States or any case filed under the Bankruptcy Code." (Section 802, codified at 18 U.S.C. Section 1519). This provision was meant to eliminate any possible technical requirement in previous statutes that a subpoena already be issued or a grand jury indictment be issued before potential defendants were to stop shredding. Notice that it goes well beyond just audit-related documents.

C. Corrupt tampering with documents to be used in an official proceeding—SOX also created a new federal crime for tampering with documents to be used in an official proceeding, providing that any person who "corruptly" (1) alters, destroys, mutilates, or conceals a record, document, or other object, or attempts to do so, with the intent to impair the object's integrity or availability for use in an official proceeding, or (2) otherwise obstructs, influences, or impedes any official proceeding, or attempts to do so, shall be fined or imprisoned up to 20 years or both. The attempt to do these acts is also a crime. (Section 1102, codified at 18 U.S.C. Section 1512)

XII. Securities Fraud Statutes

A. Although Section 10(b) of the 1934 Securities Exchange Act has long been used to punish criminal securities fraud, it is found in the securities law title to the U.S. Code. Congress decided that a securities fraud provision should also be included in the U.S. Criminal Code. Therefore, it enacted 18 U.S.C. Section 1348, which appears to ease the prosecutor's burden. The Department of Justice need not prove as much to secure a criminal conviction under 1348 as under Section 10(b). Section 1348 punishes anyone who knowingly executes or attempts to execute a scheme or artifice (1) to defraud any person in connection with any security of a public company, or (2) to obtain, by means of false or fraudulent pretenses, representations or promises, any money or property in connection with a class of stock of a public company. The maximum term of imprisonment is 25 years.

B. Prosecutors typically find it easier to convict defendants under a conspiracy statute than under an underlying substantive statute, and SOX contains a criminal provision that punishes conspiracy to commit securities fraud.

XIII. Whistleblower Protection

A. To encourage whistleblowing in the tradition of Sherron Watkins (Enron) and Cynthia Cooper (WorldCom), SOX contained two civil provisions (one granting rewards to whistleblowers and one giving them a civil cause of action to sue under certain circumstances). A related provision created a federal crime, punishing those who wrongfully retaliated against whistleblowers who provided truthful information to law enforcement about crimes. The provision is not restricted to securities fraud situations or to public companies.

Privileged Communications, Confidentiality, and Privacy Acts

In today's high-tech information age, safeguarding client confidential information must be an extremely high priority for all CPAs. This section examines three aspects of that subject matter: (1) confidentiality responsibilities, (2) communication privileges, and (3) privacy statutes.

After studying this lesson, you should be able to:

1. Understand the limited scope of the accountant-client testimonial privilege.

2. Understand the accountant's responsibilities to keep client confidences.

3. Understand the basics of some key privacy statutes and their implications for accountants.

I. **Privileged Communications**

   A. **Introduction**—There are two broad types of privileges.

      1. **Testimonial privileges**—Classic privileged communications include attorney-client, doctor-patient, and priest-penitent. Where applicable, the protected party (client, patient, penitent) can prevent the party who received the protected communications (attorney, doctor, priest) from testifying.

      2. **Work product privilege**—This privilege typically prevents one party in a lawsuit from learning the other side's attorney's strategies for litigation.

   B. **Accountant-client testimonial privilege**

      1. The federal courts have refused to recognize an accountant-client testimonial privilege.

      2. The state courts have refused to recognize a common law accountant-client testimonial privilege.

      3. Approximately 15 states have statutorily recognized an accountant-client privilege. In those states, remember:

         a. The privilege belongs to the client, not to the accountant.

         b. The privilege can be waived by the client, either expressly or through voluntary and knowing disclosure of the relevant information.

         c. Waiver of the privilege as to part of the communication is waiver as to all.

         d. The privilege applies only in state court, where state procedural rules apply.

   C. **The work product privilege and the "lawyer's umbrella"**

      1. Assume that a lawyer handling a case hires an accountant to help with complicated financial or accounting issues. The work product of the accountant would come under the umbrella of the lawyer's work product privilege and would be privileged from discovery by the other side. However, there is no freestanding work product privilege for accountants and their clients.

      2. Similarly, the lawyer's testimonial privilege can shelter communications to an accountant when made by a client for purposes of the accountant assisting the attorney in preparing for litigation.

   D. **The tax practitioners' privilege**

      1. Section 7525 of the Internal Revenue Code extends a modest testimonial privilege to clients of all tax advisers authorized to practice before the IRS, including accountants. However, the privilege has several exceptions and has been construed narrowly by the courts.

2. **Exceptions**—The privilege does not apply to:

   a. Criminal matters

   b. Matters not before the IRS or federal courts in cases brought by or against the United States

   c. Tax advice on state or local matters

   d. Written advice in connection with promotion of a tax shelter

3. **Construed narrowly**—Courts have not been uniform in their construction or application of the Section 7525 tax practitioners' privilege, but many have held that:

   a. It does not apply to information communicated to the practitioner solely for the purposes of facilitating tax return preparation.

   b. It merely extends to tax practitioners the same privilege accorded in the attorney-client relationship.

   c. Legal advice is protected, but not general accounting advice.

   d. The exceptions to the privilege are to be broadly construed.

II. **Confidential Communications**

A. **General rule**—According to the AICPA Code of Professional Conduct, absent client consent, a CPA shall not disclose confidential information disclosed by clients.

B. **Exceptions**—Recognized exceptions include:

   1. GAAP calls for disclosure

   2. An enforceable subpoena or summons has been issued

   3. An ethical examination is being conducted

   4. A peer review requires disclosure

   5. Disclosure is to other firm members on a "need to know" basis

C. **Miscellaneous rules**

   1. CPAs may utilize outside computer services to process tax returns, as long as there is no release of confidential information.

   2. CPAs may reveal the names of clients without client consent, unless such disclosure releases confidential information.

   3. In divorce proceedings, a member who has prepared joint returns for the couple should consider both of them to be clients for purposes of requests for confidential information relating to tax returns. If given conflicting instructions, the CPA should consider the legal implications of disclosure with an attorney.

   4. New rules on outsourcing and offshoring place a responsibility upon the member who sends business, such as tax return preparation, to outside firms or to foreign shores (one million tax returns per year are prepared in India) to ensure the confidentiality of clients' tax information.

D. **Internal Revenue Code provisions**—As noted elsewhere in these materials, the IRC has several provisions dealing with confidentiality, including:

   1. Section 6713, which imposes a civil penalty for each unauthorized disclosure or use of tax information by a tax return preparer

   2. Section 7216, which imposes a criminal fine and potential imprisonment for knowingly or recklessly:

      a. Disclosing any information obtained in connection with the preparation of a return *or*

      b. Using such information for any purpose other than to prepare or assist in preparing a return

E. Violations—Violation of confidentiality obligations is also grounds for a civil malpractice lawsuit by a client.

III. Privacy Acts

A. Introduction—In addition to the provisions referred to above, there are other privacy provisions relevant to the accountant-client relationship that should not be ignored.

B. Generally accepted privacy principles

1. **Management**—An accounting firm should define, document, communicate, and assign accountability for its privacy policies and procedures.

2. **Notice**—An accounting firm should provide notice about its privacy policies and procedures and identify the purpose for which any personal information about clients is collected, used, retained, and disclosed.

3. **Choice and consent**—An accounting firm should describe the choices available to clients and obtain implicit or explicit consent with respect to the collection, use, and disclosure of personal information.

4. **Collection**—An accounting firm should collect personal information only for the purposes identified in the notice described above.

5. **Use, retention, and disposal**—An accounting firm should limit the use of personal information to the purpose identified in the notice and for which the client has provided consent.

6. **Access**—Firms should provide clients with access to their personal information for review and update.

7. **Disclosure to third parties**—Accounting firms should disclose information to third parties only for the purposes identified in the notice and only with the client's implicit or explicit consent.

8. **Security for privacy**—Accounting firms should protect personal information against unauthorized access, as identity theft is a growing problem.

9. **Quality**—Accounting firms should maintain accurate, complete, and relevant personal information for the purposes identified in the notice.

10. **Monitoring and enforcement**—The accounting firm should monitor compliance with its privacy policies and procedures and have procedures to address privacy-related inquiries, complaints, and disputes.

C. E-mails—At least two states require accountants to encrypt e-mails that contain clients' personally identifiable information, and several other states are considering it.

D. Reasonable measures—Some states also have statutes requiring firms, such as accounting firms, which have possession of individuals' social security numbers, to take reasonable measures to preserve the confidentiality of those numbers, including by taking precautions against identity theft.

E. Section 7216—As noted in the Tax Return Preparer (TRP) discussion elsewhere in these materials, Section 7216 of the IRC imposes criminal penalties for unauthorized disclosure or use of taxpayer information.

1. This provision applies not just to TRPs, but to anyone who assists in preparing a return or provides auxiliary services in connection with return preparation regardless of whether they are paid.

2. The IRS does allow TRPs to use tax return information "for the purpose of providing other legal or accounting services to the taxpayer." For example, when the tax law changes, an accountant could use client tax return information to identify affected taxpayers for purposes of informing them about the change.

3. The IRS allows tax return preparers to use client information for purposes of sending newsletters to clients containing tax, general business, or economic information, but not for purposes of soliciting business other than tax return preparation services.

4. A TRP may generally disclose to its insurance carrier tax return information considered necessary for obtaining and maintaining a professional liability insurance policy.

F. **Section 6713**—As noted in the TRP materials, Section 6713 imposes civil fines for:

1. Disclosure of any information furnished in connection with preparation of a federal tax return *and/or*

2. Use of such information for any purpose other than to prepare the return

G. **Bank Secrecy Act and foreign bank accounts**

1. Under the Bank Secrecy Act (BSA), taxpayers have an obligation to report foreign bank accounts (FBAR).

2. Evidence indicates that only about 30% of such accounts are currently being reported and the IRS has ratcheted up enforcement.

3. While FBAR penalties are aimed primarily at the taxpayer, a tax return preparer (TRP) who, perhaps not fully understanding the FBAR rules, checked the "No" box in answering the question as to whether the client has a foreign financial account, might be punished under Internal Revenue Code provisions such as:

    a. Section 6694 (Understatement of a Taxpayer's Liability)

    b. Section 7201 (Criminal Attempt to Evade or Defeat Tax)

    c. Section 7206 (Criminal Fraud and Making False Statements)

Business Law

Introduction and Classification

After studying this lesson you should be able to:

1. Explain the two sources of contract law and when they apply to particular contracts.

2. Describe what a contract is.

3. List the types of contracts.

4. Explain why which source of contract law governs is important for determining the rights of the parties.

I. Sources of Contract Law

Definition:
Contract: An agreement supported by consideration between two or more persons with competent capacity for a legal purpose.

A. **Sources of Contract Law**—The two sources of contract law are common law and Article 2 of the Uniform Commercial Code (UCC), also known as "Sales." The common law began its formulation in England through court decisions. In the United States, that body of law has continued to be refined and supplemented by court decisions throughout the fifty states. For purposes of the exam, common law is the view of the majority of the states on particular contract issues. Some common law has been codified by individual states into their statutes, but the exam focuses on the common law majority view and the UCC.

Note:
The UCC is a form of codified commercial law that was developed by business people, lawyers, and legal experts to create a system of consistent contract principles across state lines. All states, except for Louisiana, have adopted Article 2 of the UCC.

B. **Distinctions between the UCC Article 2 and common law**

1. The two sources govern different types of contract subject matter (see "Application" discussion).

2. The UCC is codified in statutory form and common law (for exam purposes) is the law developed in judicial decisions on contracts.

Definition:
Statute: An act of a legislature that declares, proscribes, or commands something; a specific law, expressed in writing.

3. Common law requires more details and precision than does UCC Article 2 for formation, terms, and damages.

4. The UCC Article 2 requires less detail than common law does from the parties to a contract and has terms that apply if the parties fail to agree on those terms. In addition, the UCC Article 2 has more flexibility than common law does when it comes to formation and performance. The goal of UCC Article 2 is to provide efficient ways for businesses to form contracts and deal expeditiously with issues that develop during performance.

Note:
Answers to exam questions are different depending on whether the subject matter of the contract is governed by UCC or common law. Be sure you know which types of contracts are under UCC and which are under common law. Study this section carefully.

II. Application of Common Law vs. UCC

A. UCC Article 2 applies to contracts that involve the sale of goods.

1. What constitutes a good? Goods are tangible personal property, such as cars, clothes, books, iPads, livestock, groceries, and trees and crops that the seller has already harvested.

2. What types of contracts involve both the sales of goods and providing services? These are called blended contracts.

> If a contract involves providing both goods and services, then the UCC applies if the purpose of the contract is primarily the sale of the goods. If, however, the primary purpose of the contract is the installation of the goods, it is governed by common law.

Example:

1. A burglar alarm system involves the purchase of alarms, wire, and monitors. However, the buyer wants the alarm installed and functioning. The contract is a service contract and governed by common law.

2. A company agrees to rebind a school district's already owned textbooks. While goods are involved, the contract is for the service of binding. If the school district contracts to purchase rebound books, the contract is governed by the UCC because the purchase of books is the purchase of goods.

B. **Common law applies to service and real estate contracts.**

1. Contracts for employment, agency agreements, lawn service contracts, car washes, and medical care are all examples of service contracts.

2. Real estate contracts include leases, mortgages, liens, and contracts for the sale and purchase of real estate.

Example:

A contract for the sale of a home is governed by common law (real estate). A contract hiring a real estate broker is also governed by common law (services). A contract for the sale of a mobile home by a manufacturer is governed by the UCC.

Caution: Before answering any questions about contracts on the exam, first determine whether the subject matter is UCC or common law. There are differences between the two sources of laws and applying the wrong law will result in choosing one of the available answers that is correct for the WRONG source of law. Look at the subject matter of the contract and ask, "Am I under the UCC or am I under common law?"

III. **Types of Contracts**—Contracts are identified and described in various ways based on their characteristics. The characteristics and names used are not all mutually exclusive. The following are major concepts associated with contracts. A given contract may fall into more than one of the following types.

A. **Express contract**—A contract formed wholly by oral and/or written words.

Example:

Over the phone, I offer to sell you my personal computer for $400. Later in the day, you send me a fax accepting my offer. The combination of the oral offer (phone) and the written acceptance (fax) creates an express contract. (Whether the contract is required to be in writing will be covered under the Statute of Frauds.)

B. **Implied or implied-in-fact contract**—A contract formed, at least in part, based on the conduct of the parties or based on the factual circumstances.

Example:
You call a tax accountant and inquire how much the accountant charges to prepare a tax return. The fee charged is given by the receptionist who answered your call. The next day, you drop off your canceled checks, W-2 forms, and other information at the accountant's office. The accountant prepares your return. Your conduct in dropping off the tax materials and the conduct of the accountant in preparing the tax return create an implied-in-fact contract.

When you go to the doctor, not all of the payment terms and costs are clear; however, there is a basic understanding that you will pay for the services the doctor renders. Some urgent care clinics have moved away from implied contracts to express contracts, as they require patients to sign an agreement to pay before treatment and require a deposit or credit card prior to beginning treatment. These medical care providers have decided to move away from implied contracts to express contracts.

C. **Quasi-contract or implied-in-law contract**—A contract imposed by the courts or by law when some performance has gone forward, even though there is no express or implied contract. The law creates a quasi-contract for the parties to prevent unjust enrichment of one party by the other.

Example:
A political campaign staff member goes to a copy center store to order posters for her candidate. She asks the copy center employee to run five hundred copies of the poster. When the campaign staffer leaves the campaign, the posters are picked up by another staff member who directs the copy center to talk to someone else on the campaign staff. Those at the campaign headquarters were not aware of the terms of the poster production so they refuse to pay without a written agreement. As a result, the copy center is not paid. The copy center would still be entitled to payment because allowing the campaign to place the large order, use the posters, and not pay would be unjust enrichment. There is no written agreement, but the cost to the copy center is great and the campaign benefited by having the posters to use.

D. **Bilateral contract**—A type of contract in which both sides make a promise. A promise is made by one party to the contract in exchange for a promise from the other party to the contract.

Example:
Most contracts are bilateral contracts. The car dealership offers to sell you a car in exchange for your promise to make monthly payments for four years. The bank offers to lend you $150,000 for the purchase of a home in exchange for your promise to grant the bank a mortgage and make monthly payments on the mortgage loan.

E. **Unilateral contract**—A type of contract in which one side makes a promise in exchange for an action or performance from the other side.

Example:
"Mow my yard, and I will pay you $50." You mow the yard and complete the performance. The yard owner is required to pay you the $50 in exchange for the act of mowing the yard. "Drive my car from New York to San Francisco, and I will pay you $1,000." If you get the car to San Francisco, you collect the $1,000. The action or performance of mowing the yard or driving the car is given in exchange for the promise to pay.

F. **Executed Contract**—A contract that has been fully performed by both parties to that contract.

Example:
I offer to sell you my watch for $200. You accept and we exchange the watch for $200 cash. Since the contractual obligations of both parties have been completed, it is now an executed contract.

G. Executory contract—A contract that has not yet been fully performed by the involved parties

Example:
I offer to sell you my watch for $200 with the payment and transfer of the watch to take place in ten days. You accept. Since no performance has taken place, but a valid contract has still been formed, it is called an executory contract.

H. Partially executed contract—A contract that has been performed in part, that is, one side has performed the contractual obligation.

Example:
If, for example, in the watch sale agreement, the buyer pays the seller the sales price of $200, but the seller has not yet delivered the watch, the contract is a partially executed contract because one side has performed but the other has not. In construction contracts, the building may be complete, but the owner has not yet paid because of loan processing time. The contract is partially executed, as the contract has been executed on the part of the contractor but not on the part of the landowner, who has not yet paid.

I. Valid contract—A contract that has been legally formed and meets all necessary requirements for formation. (For formation requirements see the "Formation—Offer and Acceptance" lesson.)

J. Void contract—A contract that lacks a legal purpose or is in violation of the law. A void contract cannot be enforced by the courts because enforcement would violate public policy and encourage illegal conduct.

Example:
You and I agree that if I pay you $10,000, you will burn down the classroom building. Since the performance required under the contract is arson (i.e., a crime), not for a legal purpose, the contract is void. When movie characters say, "There is a contract out on his life," you now know that they are incorrect. A contract for murder for hire is void.

K. Voidable contract—An otherwise valid contract that can be set aside because one party has protection under the law and the right, by choice, to be relieved of liability under the contract. Examples of these include contracts that involved fraud in formation or the protected party lacked the required capacity to form contracts.

Example:
I offer to sell you a Picasso painting, that I know is a fake for $100,000. You accept. Due to my fraud, you are relieved of any liability under this contract.

L. Unenforceable contract—An otherwise valid contract that cannot be enforced because of a statutory or other legal defense. An unenforceable contract is one that the courts will not enforce, but an unenforceable contract can still be honored by the parties if they choose.

Example:
I orally offer to sell you my real property for $125,000. You accept. This contract is unenforceable because it is not in writing as required by the Statute of Frauds. (See text discussion of "Statute of Frauds.") The courts cannot enforce the agreement because there is a legal defense of a lack of writing. However, if the buyer and seller choose to honor their oral agreement, the courts do not prohibit them from honoring it.

Formation—Offer and Acceptance

After studying this lesson you should be able to:

1. List all the elements required for the valid formation of a contract.

2. List how an offer can be terminated.

3. Explain the type of language needed for a valid acceptance.

4. Describe the timing rules for when an acceptance is effective.

5. Explain the requirements for the creation of a valid offer.

6. Describe what happens in formation when there are additional or differing terms in an acceptance of an offer.

I. Parties to a Contract

Definitions:
Offeror: Party who makes the offer.
Offeree: Party with the right to accept the offer.

II. Requirements for the Formation of a Contract

A. Offer

B. Acceptance

C. Consideration (see next lesson on "Consideration")

D. No defenses (see lessons on "Contract Form" and "Defenses to Formation")

III. Requirements of a Valid Offer

A. **Present intent**—Offer (and acceptance) must be made with serious intent (objective intent).

1. Objective intent is measured by a reasonable person's interpretation of the acts, language of the parties, and the circumstances surrounding the transaction.

2. Humor, anger, and context are used to determine intent.

Example:
A business owner who is having a tough day writes in an e-mail, "Today has been so bad that I'd sell this business in a heartbeat to anyone with $50,000 in cash." Circumstances and language indicate that there is no intent to contract.

3. Advertisements usually are not offers but rather an invitation to the reader to make an offer. An advertisement that is a unilateral offer meets the requirements.

Example:
1. Ad in newspaper from a clothier: "Dresses 50% off marked price." This is not an offer; it is inviting the reader to come to the store and offer to buy a dress for 50% of the marked price.
2. Ad by a dog owner: "I offer a $100 reward to the person who returns to me my lost dog Lasso (description)." The ad is a unilateral offer that will result in people who read it to look for the dog, thus, expending effort and time. It is a valid offer.

4. Present intent requires that the parties do something more than preliminary negotiations.

a. **Price lists**—Invites a buyer to offer to purchase at the seller's listed prices (usual notation: "price subject to change"). Price lists are not offers but invitations to buyers to offer to buy at that price.

b. **Solicitation of bids**—A solicitation invites bids (offers) to perform certain duties. The bid is the offer; the solicitation is not an offer.

c. **Auctions**—The seller, through an auctioneer, invites bids (offers) from prospective buyers. The buyer, not the seller, is the offeror.

d. **Negotiations**—Expressions of possible offers or future offers are not valid offers.

Example:
"I might consider selling it for the right amount of cash."
"When I am ready to retire, I will be selling my business."
"I will be mailing out an offer to sell my car next month."

B. **Definite terms**—Terms of the offer must be definite enough to cover the legal minimums for formation (same for acceptance).

1. Under common law, definite and certain terms require identification of the parties, the subject matter, the price stated, and the time for performance.

2. **UCC Article 2**—Article 2 relaxes the requirements of certainty and the definiteness of the terms. The UCC Article 2 requires only that the offer identify the subject matter (and quantity if more than one is being sold). Article 2 has a series of sections that supply any missing terms, including price, time of performance, delivery, and payment terms. "I will sell you some Rolex President watches" is not enough for an offer under the UCC but, "I will sell you one hundred Rolex President watches" is sufficient.

C. **Communication of offer**—The offer must be communicated by the offeror or authorized agent and received by the offeree or authorized agent.

Example:
BonTon's CEO writes a letter offer to an MBA graduate offering her a position as director of credit at the store. However, the CEO never mailed the letter. There is no offer for the MBA to accept because it was never communicated. Even if the CEO's assistant found the letter in the CEO's desk and told the MBA of the letter, there is no power of acceptance unless and until the CEO communicates the offer or authorizes its communication to the MBA.

IV. Termination of Offers

A. Revocation—general rule—An offer can be revoked at any time prior to acceptance.

1. Revocations are effective when they are received so they must be communicated.

2. Revocation must be received prior to acceptance by the offeree (see discussion below for timing rules on acceptance).

Example:
Jane offers to sell Jim her textbook for $50. That evening, Jane changes her mind and mails Jim a letter of revocation. The next morning, Jim accepts Jane's offer. That afternoon, Jane's letter of revocation is received. Jane's revocation was not effective until received in the afternoon. Jim's acceptance in the morning binds Jane to the contract.

B. **Revocation of irrevocable offers—Options and merchant's firm offers**

1. Options—Options are unique in that they are offers that are part of a contract for time. The offeror and offeree have a separate contract for time. The offeree gives consideration (see the next lesson on "Consideration"), but generally money, in exchange for the offeror's promise

to keep the offer open (no revocation or lapse) for a specified period. The offeror must keep the offer open for the period specified for the offeree who paid for it. The phrase "She has an option contract" is legally accurate because an option is an agreement that allows the offeree time to make a decision on whether to enter into the contract.

> **Example:**
> A seller of land has offered to sell a parcel of land to a school district. The school district is not sure whether it wants to buy this tract but does not want the seller to be able to withdraw the offer. The school district offers the seller $5,000 if the seller will keep the offer open for three months. If the seller agrees and accepts the payment, the school district has an option and the seller must keep the offer open (not sell to someone else) for three months.

    a. The offeror cannot withdraw the offer during the option period.

    b. The offeree has the right to accept the offer during the option period, but is not required to accept.

    c. The offeree's rejection during the option period does not end the option. The offeree has the right to that offer during the full option period.

2. Firm offers—The UCC Article 2 has its own form of options called a merchant's firm offer.

    a. The requirements for and the effect of a merchant's firm offer are that it:

        i. Is an offer in writing, evidenced by a record (see "Contract Form" lesson for more information)

        ii. Is made by a merchant (a merchant is defined, for purposes of the exam as someone who is in the business of selling the goods that are the subject matter of the contract, e.g., Best Buy is a merchant of televisions; Home Depot is a merchant of lumber)

        iii. States that it will be kept open or provides a stated time that it will be open, but the maximum length under the UCC is three months **and**

        iv. Does not require consideration

        v. Once these elements are present, the offeree holds an irrevocable offer (despite no consideration) for the time stated in the firm offer (or if none is stated, for a reasonable period) but no longer than three months—(UCC2-205)

        vi. If the parties want an offer for the sale of goods to remain open longer than three months, then there must be consideration, just as with option contracts under common law

        vii. If the offeror is a nonmerchant, the rules for common-law options apply and there must be consideration.

        viii. A valid firm offer is just like a common-law option; it cannot be revoked and it ends only upon the expiration of the stated time or three months, whichever is shorter.

> **Example:**
> 1. A rain check is an example of a merchant's firm offer. If a store runs out of an advertised product, it will give customers who ask for that product a rain check, which is something in writing that gives the customer the right to purchase the product at the sale price for the time provided on the rain check. The rain check time is its expiration date, such as "Good through 12/31/2011."
>
> 2. Sue owns a retail TV store. Sue, by a signed letter, offers to purchase from Adam, a TV manufacturer, 50 TVs at Adam's catalog price. Her letter states that her offer would remain open and not be withdrawn for 60 days. Sue's offer is irrevocable without having to pay consideration for the stated 60 days. If Sue had stated a six-month period (rather than 60 days), her offer would only be irrevocable for three months and after this period, she could revoke her offer at any time.

C. Rejection—An offer is terminated, at any time prior to acceptance, by the offeree saying or writing something as simple as "Terms are not acceptable," "No thank you," or "Funds for purchase are not available at this time."

    1. An inquiry is not a rejection. Asking, "Would you consider a lower price?" is not a rejection.

    2. A rejection is effective when it is received.

D. Counteroffer—**general rule**—A counteroffer made at any time prior to acceptance is a form of rejection. A counteroffer is made when the offeree responds with changed terms. The determination of whether the offeree has made a counteroffer is controlled by whether the subject matter is under common law or UCC.

> **Note:**
> *Common law follows the mirror image rule. That is, acceptance must be absolute, unequivocal, and unqualified. Any variation in the terms results in a counteroffer and rejection. The UCC Article 2 rules are less rigid (see the UCC discussion below).*

    1. A counteroffer is not only a rejection of the original offer by the offeree but also a new offer that makes the original offeree an offeror.

    2. Conditional acceptance is also a form of a counteroffer. A conditional acceptance is never acceptance but rather a counteroffer under both the UCC and the common law. Counteroffers are usually spotted through the use of prepositional phrases, such as "But I must," "on the condition that," or "provided that." These terms present in the offeree's response indicate conditional acceptance and, therefore, counteroffer.

Example:
David offers to sell his textbook to Doris for $60. Doris responds, "I would not buy your textbook for $60 but I will offer to pay you $50 for it." This is a counteroffer because Doris has made it conditional with the word "but," and David's offer for $60 is terminated. Doris has made a counteroffer to David to buy his book for $50. If Doris responded, "I will buy your textbook for $60, but I must take delivery right now," she has still made a conditional acceptance that is a counteroffer and a rejection even though she has agreed to pay the price.

E. Termination of offers through lapse of time by operation of law

> **Note:**
> *An offer that states that it will be kept open for a stated period can still be revoked at any time prior to acceptance unless it is a firm offer or option.*

    1. Lapse of time—**general rule**—An offer automatically terminates at the end of a stated period for its existence, or if no period is stated, it terminates after a reasonable period has lapsed.

Example:
Sally sends an offer to a real estate investor and offers to sell her house for $121,000 cash, stating that the offer will be kept open for 90 days. Sally sends another letter to the investor on Day 15 that states "Never mind. Have decided to stay in my house and not sell." The offer is revoked. It is irrevocable only if the real investor pays for the 90-day period.

F. Termination of offers by operation of the law—Certain events terminate an offer by law.

    1. Death or insanity of the offeror or offeree—The exception is options. Because options are separate contracts to hold an offer open, they do survive the death of the offeror.

    2. Destruction of the specific subject matter of the offer—general rule—If the specific object of the offer is destroyed prior to acceptance, the offer terminates automatically (perishes) with the destruction. If the items that are destroyed are fungible goods or commodities, the general rule does not apply because the offeror can easily obtain the same product to deliver to the offeree.

    3. Illegality of the subject matter—Sometimes the subject matter of the contract becomes illegal to sell. For example, in the United States, it is illegal to sell toys that contain paint with lead. When lead paint was discovered on toys manufactured in China, all offers that toy companies had made for selling toys made in China were terminated by operation of law due to illegality.

V. Acceptance of an Offer

A. Unilateral offer—**general rule**—Acceptance takes place upon completion (total performance) of the act required by the offer. Generally, no notice to the offeror is required, unless such is required by law (see UCC 2-206(2)) or the offeror would have no means to know that the act has been completed.

B. Bilateral offer—**general rule**—Acceptance (promise) must be absolute, unequivocal, unconditional, and communicated to the offeror.

1. Language of acceptance—Determination of acceptance is controlled by whether the UCC Article 2 or common law applies. Before answering any question on acceptance, be sure to ask "Is this contract governed by the UCC or common law?" Then apply the appropriate rules for acceptance according to the source of law that governs the contract.

> **Note:**
> *It is rare to find any exam that does not have a question on either the language or the timing issues in offer and acceptance.*

a. Common law and the mirror image rule—(noted earlier in discussion of rejection and counteroffer)—In common law, which applies to contracts involving real property and services (employment), any deviation in the terms of acceptance from those in the offer constitutes a counteroffer, not an acceptance.

Example:
Sally makes a written offer to buy a house for $121,000 from Bill. Bill reviews the offer and is fine with the price, closing date, and payment terms. However, Bill wants to take the Tuff Shed from his backyard with him when he moves. Bill writes back, "Will sell on your terms. Tuff Shed is not included." The Tuff Shed may seem like an immaterial and negotiable item, but Bill has made a counteroffer and rejection because under the mirror image rule under common law, the acceptance contains different terms.

2. The UCC Article 2 and language of acceptance—Under UCC 2-207, the question of whether there has been an acceptance depends on whether the parties are merchants or nonmerchants. (See discussion under "Firm offers" above for the definition of a merchant.)

a. For both merchants and nonmerchants, a definite expression of acceptance (not conditional acceptance) that does not change any terms results in a contract.

b. For nonmerchants, if there is a definite statement of acceptance (not conditional acceptance) followed by some additional terms, a contract is formed, but without the additional terms.

c. For merchants, if there is a definite statement of acceptance (not conditional acceptance) followed by additional terms, there is a contract WITH the additional terms UNLESS

i. The additional terms are material, such as a waiver of warranties.

ii. The offer specifically states, "This offer is limited to these terms." In this situation, a contract is formed, but without the additional terms in the acceptance.

iii. The offeror objects within a reasonable time after receiving the acceptance to the additional terms.

Example:
Steib is a merchant of ribbon. Bold offers, "I will buy 50 spools of grosgrain blue ribbon for $4.39 per spool." Steib responds, "Will send ribbon. No warranty on color." The two have a contract **without** the warranty waiver because a warranty waiver is a material term.

Same parties but Bold adds, "This offer is limited to these terms." Steib responds, "Will send ribbon. Terms are 2/10/ net 30." The two have a contract for the ribbon with those payment terms because these types of terms are immaterial. The two have a contract for the ribbon **without** those payment terms because despite the fact that these types of terms are immaterial, the offer was expressly limited, and that controls all terms proposed after that—whether material or immaterial.

Same parties but Bold offers, "I will buy 50 spools of grosgrain blue ribbon for $4.39 per spool." Steib responds, "Will send ribbon. Terms are 2/10/ net 30." Bold e-mails back within two hours, "No, the terms on payment are not acceptable." The two have a contract without the payment terms because Bold objected in a timely manner.

If we changed the examples and made Bold and Steib nonmerchants, then there would be a contract for the ribbon without the additional terms in all three examples.

3. Timing of an acceptance—If sent by an authorized medium, the acceptance is effective, that is, a contract is formed when the offeree delivers the acceptance to the authorized medium—even if it is never received by the offeror.

   a. An authorized medium is the same or faster method of communication used by the offeror if no method is specified in the offer. If a means of acceptance is specified in the offer, the only authorized means is that specified means. If the offeree uses the authorized means, once the acceptance to a mail-authorized offer is dropped in a mailbox, there is acceptance of the offer, regardless of any delays or nondelivery. Often called the mailbox rule, this timing applies only to acceptance communication and not to offers, counteroffers, rejections, or revocations. Offers, counteroffers, rejections, and revocations are effective only when actually received.

   b. If the offer has an authorized means that is expressly specified as the means of acceptance and the offeree uses a means other than the means specified, it is considered a counteroffer and rejection because the offeree has violated the terms of the offer and the mirror image rule.

   c. If the offer has no authorized means specified, and the offeree sends acceptance by an unauthorized means, such as using a slower method of communication than that used by the offeror, then the acceptance is effective only when received by the offeror.

 Example:
On May 1, Mary sends John a letter offering to sell her condo. John receives the offer on May 2. On May 3, Mary sends John a letter withdrawing her offer. On May 4, John sends a properly addressed letter with correct postage to Mary accepting her offer. On May 5, John receives Mary's letter of revocation. Mary does not receive John's letter of acceptance because of the destruction of the mail sack with the letter in it. Mary and John have a contract formed on May 4 when John used mail (implied authorization under all three of the above requirements) as the medium for acceptance. Her letter of revocation was not effective until received, which was after John had accepted.

C. Silence—**general rule**—Silence is not an acceptance unless the offeree's actions indicate an attempt to accept or the offeree (such as soliciting the offer) has a duty to reject.

Note:
Under common law, the same method of communication is often required. The exam tends to avoid the split on the common law rule (some states following the same means of communication requirement and other states allowing the same or faster) by using problems in which the same or stipulated means are used for acceptance.

Consideration

After studying this lesson you should be able to:

1. Explain what consideration is and why it is a requirement for forming a valid contract.

2. List the exceptions for the requirement of consideration and give examples of these exceptions.

I. Consideration/Legal Detriment—Consideration is required, along with offer and acceptance, for the formation of a contract.

> **Definition:**
> *Consideration:* Consists of the benefit promised by the offeror (promisor) and the legal detriment promised or performed by the offeree (promisee). In a bilateral contract, both the offeror and offeree are promisors (those making a promise) and promisees (those receiving the promise). Both sides must have benefit and detriment for valid consideration to be present and the detriment on one side induces the detriment on the other side. The exchange of the detriment is bargained for by the parties.

    A. Legal detriment—Often defined as doing what you are free not to do and not doing what you are free to do.

        You don't have to buy a car, but if you contract to buy one, your detriment is giving up the money.

        Likewise, you don't have to settle a lawsuit, but if you do settle it, giving up the right to have the case fully litigated is your detriment.

        Detriment is giving up money, rights, property, time—just think of what each side is giving up for what it wants under the contract.

        If you don't give anything up, you don't have detriment and are thereby missing the element of consideration, ergo, no contract.

        For example, you can't get more money for what you are already obligated to do. If you contract to do an audit for $15,000, you can't come back and say, "Oh, wow. I really underestimated the work—I am gonna need more money here." You have no new detriment. However, if you came back and said, "I think we are going to need to take a look at another factory as part of this audit," that would mean something is required in your professional opinion that was not in the original scope. If the client agrees, there is new detriment and you could be paid money for it because you have the detriment of an additional factory visit.

        1. Consists of something of legal value—Legal value can be measured by dollars and/or market value. An agreement for one side to purchase a Trek bicycle for $300 has the legal value detriment of $300 on one side in exchange for a bicycle that is worth $300 on the market. Legal value can, however, be giving up the right to file suit for damages. A promise not to file a suit against another has legal value—it is not doing what you are free to do. When two parties settle claims based on a car accident, each side is giving up the right to go to court and have a determination of damages that could be more or less than the settlement. Giving up that right to a lawsuit is legal detriment. When you buy a car you pay money—you are doing something you are free not to do, which is pay your money to the seller for the car.

>
> **Example:**
> Sam negligently runs over Jim causing injury. Sam promises in writing that if Jim will not sue Sam in tort (negligence), Sam will pay Jim for all medical costs plus $10,000. Jim's agreement (forbearance to file a tort suit) is consideration to contractually obligate Sam to pay all of Jim's medical costs plus $10,000.

        2. Consists of a legally sufficient amount (adequacy of consideration)—Courts do not generally examine the amount of consideration as long as it is actually exchanged. There can be differences in values on each side because the value of the promises is not the key—what is controlling is whether the value promised is legally sufficient so as not to be considered a gift. This element distinguishes gifts from contracts.

Example:
If your grandmother says, "Come to my house tonight and I will give you my car," you do not have legally sufficient detriment because your grandmother is not giving you the car because you came over. She is giving you the car out of love; it is a promise to make a gift and, thus, not enforceable as a contract.

B. **Bargained-for exchange**—This element of consideration means that the promise induces the detriment on each side. You are willing to sign the deed for title to your house because the buyer is willing to pay you $121,000.

Example:
Mary's offer to purchase Jim's accounting text for $50 and his acceptance constitute consideration. The text and $50 both have legal value, the book and the $50 are both legally sufficient to show that this is not a gift, and Mary's promise to pay $50 induces Jim's promise to transfer the book and vice versa. The bargained-for action of detriment and benefit is the basis of the contract.

II. Preexisting Duty and Consideration

Definition:
Preexisting Duty: A preexisting duty is one that exists under a valid contract or perhaps by law. A preexisting legal duty is an enforceable obligation.

A. **General rule**—You cannot obtain more detriment from the other party in order to perform what you are already legally obligated to do. You are not entitled to more payment (consideration) for what you are already legally obligated to do. An example of a legal obligation for which you are not entitled to more money relates to law enforcement officials. Police officers cannot collect rewards for catching a criminal because they have a legal obligation to do so as part of their work.

Example:
Able contracts to build you a home for $150,000 according to a set of specific plans and specifications. Later, Able tells you that he will lose money building your house and that he will complete the house only if you agree to pay him an additional $5,000. You agree. This agreement to pay $5,000 is without consideration and it is unenforceable. Able gave up nothing of legal value for the $5,000, as he was already legally obligated to build the same house for $150,000. Even if you agreed in writing to pay the $5,000, the agreement would not be a contract because it is missing the element of consideration. You would have offer and acceptance, but there is no contract because there must be additional consideration given by both sides. Your $5,000 is not enough to have the second agreement be a contract. Able would have to agree to do something more to be legally entitled to that price increase.

The modification of a COMMON LAW contract requires additional consideration on BOTH sides; otherwise, the modification is not a valid contract because it is missing the required element of consideration.

B. **Exceptions to preexisting duty rule**

1. **Rescission and new contract**—The mutual rejection by both parties to a contract of their existing contract (rescission) and then making a new one ($155,000 to build the house above). The consideration consists of both sides giving up their rights under the original agreement in exchange for a new one. They are doing what they do not have to do in waiving those original contract rights.

2. **UCC modification for contracts for the sale of goods**—Under the UCC, the parties are permitted to, in good faith, modify their contracts even without additional consideration (detriment) on both sides (UCC 2-209(1)).

3. **Unforeseen hardship**—If the parties to a contract have no idea about an undisclosed hardship to the accomplishment of a contractual duty then they have not necessarily bargained that risk to one party or the other of a contract. Therefore, when that hardship occurs then the promise of additional consideration to overcome the hardship is an exception to the preexisting duty rule.

> **Note:**
> *The common law and UCC rules for modification are very different. Once again, always determine the subject matter of the contract and then determine whether the contract is under UCC or common law so that you can apply the different principles and reach the correct solution.*

Example:
Clara's Cookies has a supply contract with Clarence's Chips for Clarence's to furnish chocolate and butterscotch baking chips to Clara's at a price of $2.29 per pound. Clarence and Clara have their supply contracts run for one year and they have been doing business with each other for 10 years. An increase in gasoline prices has hit Clarence's business model (one that involves personal delivery to ensure that the chips do not melt) particularly hard. Clarence asks Clara if he can increase the price per pound to $2.30. Clara does not have to agree to the price increase, but, if she does, the increase is enforceable even though Clarence has no additional legal detriment and Clara does. Because the contract is under UCC, this modification without additional consideration is valid and enforceable.

III. Consideration in UCC Requirements and Output Contracts

A. **UCC requirements contract**—The type of contract is one in which a buyer agrees to purchase all that he needs for his home or business from the seller. The quantity is left open, but under the UCC this type of agreement is enforceable in order to allow businesses and buyers to operate on an as-needed basis.

Example:
A homeowner who heats with propane gas or oil agrees to purchase all that she needs to heat her home for the winter. She does not know the amount she will need because the temperature for the winter will control that. She might need very little fuel, or she might need a great deal. But, her open-end quantity contract is still supported by consideration under the UCC.

B. **UCC output contract**—The contract is one in which a seller agrees to sell all that it produces to a particular buyer. Under the UCC, this type of open-end quantity agreement is a valid contract that is supported by consideration if the contract is based on an established production or ability to produce by the seller and the seller is required to sell its production to the buyer.

IV. Consideration in Accord and Satisfaction

Definition:
Accord and Satisfaction: An accord is an agreement to waive legal rights and release another party from legal obligations. Satisfaction is the actual payment of the amounts agreed to in the accord. The detriment on both sides of an accord is both parties agreeing to do something they are not legally required to do (settle a claim) or not doing what they could legally do (bring a lawsuit to recover on their rights).

A. **Liquidated debts and accord and satisfaction**—A liquidated debt is one in which the amount due and owing is clear to both parties. Charlie owes Fred $5,000 plus 5% interest, and the amount is to be paid in monthly payments over a two-year period. Charlie cannot write "Payment in full" on his 20ᵗʰ monthly check and have the debt discharged. He does not have detriment; only Fred would. If, however, Charlie negotiated with Fred and agreed to pay a lesser amount four months early and Fred agreed, then the "payment in full" would be the accord and Fred cashing the check would be the satisfaction because Charlie paid the full amount early and Fred got the use of his money earlier than he was entitled to have it.

B. **Unliquidated debts and accord and satisfaction**—An unliquidated debt is one in which the parties acknowledge that money is due and owed, but they disagree on the amount. An agreement (accord) between the two parties on an amount and then payment of that amount is an accord and satisfaction because both are giving up their right to have the amount due determined by a court. "Payment in full" placed on a check for an unliquidated debt would serve to discharge the debt.

Example:
Sam negligently runs his car into the rear of John's car. Sam, in a signed writing, promises to pay John $1,000 if John will release Sam from any further property liability due to the accident. This accepted release by John is binding and bars John from any further recovery. Sam is giving up his right to have a court determine his level of liability and John is giving up the right to have the court possibly determine that his damages are greater than $1,000.

Example:
Joe, in his most recent will, leaves all of his assets to his son, Able, and nothing to his two married daughters who both were unaware of Joe's heart condition. It is learned that Able had not informed his sisters of their dad's condition and Joe has told friends that Able had said that his daughters did not care about him. The daughters have indicated they would contest the will. Able and his sisters agree that if the sisters do not contest the will, he will give each $15,000 from monies he will receive under the will. This (giving up the legal right to contest the will for $15,000) is a covenant not to sue (contract) and enforceable.

Example:
1. Jim borrows $100 from Joan payable back without interest. Jim sends to Joan a check clearly marked as "payment in full" for $90. Such an action would not serve to discharge the debt. Jim owes Joan $100, the debt is liquidated and Joan can still legally pursue recovery of $10 from Jim.

2. Jim contracts to purchase from Joan a new file cabinet for $250. Upon delivery, Jim discovers that the cabinet is scratched. Jim tenders to Joan a check clearly marked "payment in full" for $200. Joan has no idea as to the cost of damage due to the scratches. She can avoid the issue and return the check (no accord), but if she cashes it (since reasonable persons could disagree as to the cost of damage), the purported debt is canceled because their agreement on what to do about the defective file cabinet (the scratch) is open for debate. It could cost $50 to fix it or $10 or something greater. The amount due is not liquidated even though the original purchase price was because they are now dealing with goods not delivered as promised. Joan does not have to accept the $200, but once she does, Jim's obligation is satisfied.

V. **Past consideration**—A promise to pay for an act already completed is without (not bargained-for) consideration.

Example:
An employer states, "In consideration of the 20 years of loyal service you have given the company, I promise to pay you $10,000." The promise is unenforceable because it is for an event that has already taken place.

VI. Exceptions to the Consideration Requirement

Definition:
Estoppel: A legal principle that bars a party from denying or alleging a certain fact owing to that party's previous conduct, allegation, or denial.

A. **Promissory estoppel**—A promise, which induces another party to rely on that promise and results in the party materially changing their position, estops the other party from refusing to honor that promise based on a claim of no valid consideration.

Example:
Jim pledges (promises) $50,000 to the church to add a childcare room to the church. In reliance (induces church to change its position) thereon, the church contracts for the addition (changes substantially their position). In the interest of justice, the church can hold Jim to his pledge denying his claim that his pledge lacked consideration.

B. **Promises barred by the statute of limitations**—The statute of limitations is the time the law imposes by statute for bringing a suit to enforce legal rights. For example, the general statute of limitations under the UCC is four years. Parties to a contract have four years from the time the contract is formed or from the time of the breach (depending on the reason for the suit) to enforce their rights. Once that time allowed under the statute passes, the contract is unenforceable. If, however, the party who owed money on that contract agrees to pay the amount due, the renewed promise to pay is enforceable because the party is agreeing to do something he was not required to do by law since the statute of limitations discharged the debt. Although the detriment is one-sided, these agreements are enforceable.

C. **Promises to pay debts discharged in bankruptcy**—A debtor need not assume responsibility for debts that could be discharged in bankruptcy, but if those debts are exempted prior to the discharge, their payment can be enforced.

Statute of Frauds and Records

I. **The Statute of Frauds**—Originally, at common law, called the Statute for the Prevention of Frauds and Perjuries, this law (codified in most states) requires certain types of contracts to be in writing (be evidenced by a record, as discussed below) to be enforceable. The types of contracts that must be in writing are those that folks are most likely to lie about in order to secure the benefit. If the Statute of Frauds requires a contract to be in writing and it is oral, then it is unenforceable (See the "Introduction and Classification" lesson for discussion of the types of contracts).

II. **Types of Contracts That Must Be in Writing under the Statute of Frauds**

  A. Guaranty of debt contracts

  B. Contracts involving an interest in real property

  C. Contracts impossible to perform within one year of formation

  D. Contracts for the sale of goods priced at $500 or more

  E. Promises of executors for personal liability for debts of the estate

III. **Contracts That Promise to Pay the Debt of Another**

  A. A contract that promises to pay the debt of another must be in writing under the Statute of Frauds:

    1. This requirement does not apply to original promises, i.e., where you borrow money for yourself and agree to repay that money (although such an agreement might be under another provision of the Statute of Frauds—see below).

    2. A promise to pay the debt of another is illustrated by the following example that is shown in the triangle diagram: "If PD does not pay and is in default, then I (G) will pay." This is a collateral promise—the party who is promising to pay the debt of another is not the original promisor for the loan.

Note:
If you own a business and are guaranteeing a loan to that business, it is not a promise to pay the debt of another. It is an original promise then. For example, if A and B are general partners and A agrees to personally guarantee a loan to the partnership, it is not a promise to pay the debt of another. It is an original promise and need not be in writing. On the exam, this type of problem has appeared, where you are tested not only on your knowledge of the Statute of Frauds but also on your knowledge of individual and personal liability under certain business structures.

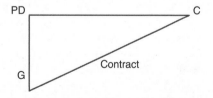

Definition:
Guarantor: A person who guarantees to pay for someone else's debt if he or she should default on a loan obligation.

Example:
Able is a commission agent selling Peter's products. Peter has a rule that his agents only sell to customers for cash. Able knows she can sell more, and thus make more commissions, if she can also sell to customers on credit. Able orally contracts with Peter allowing Able to sell to customers on credit, and if any customer does not pay when due, she agrees she will pay Peter. Some customers who were sold Peter's products on credit fail to pay Peter. Peter demands Able pay.

Question: Does the Able-Peter contract allowing Able to sell on credit come under the Statute of Frauds?

Answer: Yes. It is a contract (formed by words) between a guarantor (Able) and a creditor (Peter) creating a secondary debt obligation. Able is liable only if customer, the principal debtor, fails to pay. In order to enforce the guaranty by Able, Peter must have a written agreement (record) signed by Able.

IV. **Contracts Involving an Interest in Real Property**

A. **General rule**—Any contract involving an interest in real property, to be enforceable, must be in writing (unless one of the exceptions in B, below, applies), including:

1. Real property purchase contracts

2. Leases of real property. Exceptions in most states apply to leases less than one year in length

3. Real property mortgages

4. Easements

5. Creation of any other real property interests

6. Real estate broker contracts

B. **Exception to writing requirement for real property rule**—This exception applies when the parties have behaved in such a way and provided evidence beyond their own words that there was some kind of contract relationship between them. The partial performance exception requires the following:

1. Payment of some part or all of the purchase price has been made

2. The buyer in possession of the land by living there (residential) or proceeding to develop it (commercial land)

3. The buyer has made valuable improvements

See the following example.

Example:
Mary orally contracts to purchase Jim's house and lot. Mary sends Jim a check for 5% of the purchase price, which Jim cashes. The closing (passage of deed and payment) will not take place for two months. Mary's lease has expired and Mary and Jim agree that Mary can move in to the house and pay Jim a rental payment. Mary moves into the house, plants a number of trees, and adds a deck to the back porch. Just before closing, Jim is offered $20,000 more than Mary's purchase price. Jim tenders return of Mary's down payment and claims the oral contract is unenforceable.

Question: Does this contract come under the Statute of Frauds?

Answer: Yes. A purchase of real property contract is an interest in real property.

Question: Can Jim successfully claim that the oral contract is unenforceable under the Statute of Frauds?

Answer: No. The partial performance rule applies (in all states) because there was a payment, possession, and valuable improvements, which will not allow Jim to use the Statute of Frauds as a defense to the contract.

Question: What if only the payment had been made (no possession or valuable improvement)?

Answer: This exception requires more than just payment to apply. Without more than payment, the exception does not apply.

V. Contracts That Cannot be Performed within One Year of Formation—General Rule

A. Any contract that is objectively impossible to perform within one year from the date of contract formation (date of acceptance) without breaching the terms must be in writing or have written evidence of it to be enforceable.

B. If the contract COULD be performed within one year, it need not be in writing to be enforceable. For example, ABC orally agrees to do an internal controls audit for XYZ Company. ABC does not know how long the audit will take. The oral agreement is valid because the audit could be done in less than a year. However, if ABC accepts a three-year engagement to do internal control audits each year, that contract must be in writing to be enforceable.

C. The one-year mark is measured from the date of acceptance; the time frame is not just the period of performance. For example, suppose Helen agrees to perform a nine-month consulting contract with Framery Inc., to run from June 1, 2011 until March 31, 2012. Helen agrees to do so on February 1, 2011. While the contract term is less than a year, Helen's acceptance is longer than a year out from completed performance so the agreement must be in writing.

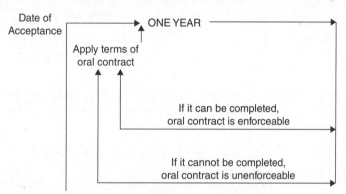

VI. Contracts for the Sale of Goods—General Statute of Frauds Rule

A. Any contract for the sale of goods priced at $500 or more must be in writing or record (memorandum), or an applicable exception—UCC 2-201(1)(2)(3).

1. With the passage of the E-sign law, all states are required to accept electronic and fax communications as evidence of a written agreement.

2. The writing requirement is now referred to as a "record" because a writing includes the E- sign forms of communication. When these materials use the term "writing" or "written agreement," they are including "record," which can be electronic as in an e-mail, a click agreement, a faxed document, or a PDF agreement.

> **Note:**
> *You must determine whether the subject matter of the contract is under common law or UCC before you answer questions about whether the contract must be in writing in order to be enforceable. The rules for written contracts are different under UCC and common law.*

Caution:
Do not mix together the provisions of the Statute of Frauds. The UCC Statute of Frauds applies only to contracts for the sale of goods. So, a contract for the purchase of an option in real estate for $450 must be in writing because it is a real property interest. But, a contract for the sale of a refrigerator for $450 need not be in writing because it is covered by the UCC. The amount of the purchase price is irrelevant for real property contracts, which are covered under common law Statute of Frauds provisions. Under UCC, the amount involved determines whether the contract must be in writing.

B. **Exceptions to the UCC General Statute of Frauds Rule**—UCC-201(2)(3)

   1. **Merchant's confirmation memorandum**—**between merchants (only)**—If two merchants have an oral agreement that must be in writing under the UCC Statute of Frauds, that writing requirement is met through a process referred to as a merchant's confirmation memorandum. If one merchant sends the other merchant a written confirmation, and the other, after receipt, does not object in writing within 10 days, the oral contract is enforceable by either party even though only one party actually signed the memorandum. The memorandum can be given via letter, e-mail, or fax.

> **Example:**
> S and B have an oral agreement for the sale of 500 pounds of T-bone steak at a price of $3.89 per pound. S sends B 200 pounds of T-bone steak and B resells the steaks. B is liable for that amount of their agreement (200 × $3.89), but courts will not enforce the remainder of their alleged oral agreement. Likewise, if B sends S a check for 200 pounds of T-bone steaks (200 × $3.89) and S cashes the check, S must deliver 200 pounds of T-bone steak, but the remaining 300 pounds under their alleged oral agreement cannot be enforced.

   2. **Special ordered goods**—Goods that a seller cannot resell in his/her ordinary course of business are special ordered goods. An oral contract for special ordered goods is enforceable if the seller has substantially begun performance, or has made an irrevocable commitment to do so, before the buyer cancels the order claiming the Statute of Frauds. An order for a custom-made suit would be an example.

   3. **Admission under oath**—Any admission under oath (deposition, interrogatory, signing of answer, or on the stand during trial) that an oral contract was made removes the Statute of Frauds as a defense.

   4. **Performance by buyer**—If the buyer takes possession or makes a payment accepted by the seller, the Statute of Frauds is removed (oral contract enforced), at least to the quantity accepted or paid for.

> **Example:**
> By telephone, Joan orders 300 backpacks from Bertha's Backpacks at a price of $20 each, to be delivered on the first of each month over the next three months in lots of 100. After Joan sends a check for the first 100 backpacks (which Bertha cashes), Bertha refuses to deliver the backpacks because she says the contract needed to be in writing to be enforceable. The contract can be enforced for the first 100 backpacks. Likewise, if Bertha delivered 100 backpacks and Joan accepted them, she would be required to pay for those 100 backpacks. However, neither situation would allow them to demand performance for the full 300 backpacks, only for what has been paid for or for what has been delivered and accepted.

VII. **The Requirements for a Valid Writing/Record of a Contract**—**General Rule**—A record is tangible evidence of the existence of an oral contract and, if the record meets all the standards and includes the necessary information, the requirements of the Statute of Frauds are met.

A. **Criteria for a valid writing/record**

   1. Signature (authentication) of the party to be held liable on the oral contract.

   2. Exception: Merchant's confirmation memorandum allows one party's signature to bind both parties (both are merchants) to the agreement.

   3. A writing/record need not be in one document or formal. E-mails, letters, and faxes can be grouped together to establish the written/record requirement for a valid contract.

VIII. **Interpretation of Terms in Contracts**

A. **Meanings of terms**—Terms are assumed to have their ordinary meaning; if technical, their technical meaning.

B. **Ambiguities**—Any ambiguity will be construed against the party who drafted the contract.

C. **No contradictions**—Under the UCC (UCC 2-202) a written contract can be explained, but not contradicted, by usage of trade, course of performance, or course of dealing.

IX. Parol Evidence Rule and How It Affects Contracts

A. The parol evidence rule applies to fully integrated contracts. A fully integrated contract is one that is complete and unambiguous.

    1. **Ambiguous terms**—If the record of a contract has ambiguities, it is not fully integrated and parol evidence can be introduced only to clean up the ambiguity.

    2. **Obvious clerical or typographical error**—In reducing oral contract into a record, parol evidence can be used for obvious typos and clerical errors because, again, it is not fully integrated.

    3. **Incomplete contracts**—Parol evidence can be admitted to "fill in" the gaps because an incomplete contract is not a fully integrated contract.

B. Under the parol evidence rule, a fully integrated contract (one that is complete, unambiguous, and without defenses in formation) cannot be contradicted, varied, or altered by evidence of the parties' prior negotiations, prior agreements, or contemporaneous oral agreements. Once the parties reduce their agreement to a record, they are bound by those terms and cannot use the courts to rewrite their agreement. Without this rule, courts would always be dealing with who said what and when and whether what they said should be part of the contract. Remember the parol evidence rule by thinking, "If what you wanted is not in the contract but promised as an aside in negotiations, you can't bring that up later and expect to get it."

Example:
Tenant leased a commercial warehouse from Landlord for three years. Landlord orally agreed to replace the elevator in the warehouse but did not want to put the replacement clause in their written agreement. Landlord didn't want other tenants to know and begin demanding new elevators. The lease agreement is fully integrated. If Landlord does not replace the elevator, Tenant cannot enforce the agreement because it was not part of the contract.

C. **Exceptions to the parol evidence rule**

    1. **Subsequent modification**—If the parties to a contract later agree to modify their contract, evidence of the modification is admissible. If the modification is required to be in writing, the parties will need that record as proof of the modification.

    2. **Defenses to the formation of the contract**—Oral evidence can be introduced to show any of the defenses to formation (covered in Defenses to Formation). For example, if the seller used fraud or mistake or the duress to get the acceptance by the buyer, then the buyer can have evidence admitted to show that there is no valid contract.

Defenses to Formation

After studying this lesson you should be able to:

1. Explain what happens when one party has a defense to the formation of a contract.

2. Define fraud and misrepresentation and explain their effect on a contract.

3. Describe the circumstances that would lead to duress being present in the formation of a contract.

4. Define undue influence and explain its effect on a contract.

5. List the defenses to formation of a valid contract.

6. Explain what capacity to form a contract is and discuss the forms of incapacity and explain what happens under each type of incapacity when it is present during formation.

7. Explain the two types of contracts that are void; i.e. lack legal purpose and discuss what happens when a contract is void.

8. Describe the types of mistakes that result in a contract being rescinded.

I. **Five Types of Defenses to Formation**—Some actions during the formation stage of a contract result in the creation of defenses to formation of a valid contract. Offer, acceptance, and consideration must occur in a forthright atmosphere in which the parties agreed on a contract based on full and accurate information. If that voluntary and open atmosphere did not exist, there is a defense to the formation. The following are types of defenses that can be used to invalidate the formation of a contract:

   A. Mistake

   B. Fraud (also called fraud in the inducement) or misrepresentation

   C. Duress

   D. Undue influence

   E. Illegality

II. **The Types of Capacity Required for Formation of a Contract**

   A. Each party must be of legal age (minors are limited in the types of valid contracts they can make).

   B. Each party must have the mental capacity to enter into a contract and mental capacity includes being free from a level of intoxication that results in mental incapacity.

III. **Age Capacity Requirement—Minors**

   A. **General definition of a minor**—In most states and for most contracts, a minor is any person under the age of 18. A minor is not prohibited by law from entering into contracts, except for contracts that are illegal (e.g., contracts for liquor or cigarettes). However, the law does provide protections for minors who do enter into contracts based on the public policy of protection of those who may not have developed the judgment or experience to enter into fairly negotiated contracts.

   B. **Minor's right to disaffirm**—A minor who enters into a contract has the right to disaffirm the contract and avoid liability at any time before reaching majority and for a reasonable time thereafter.

   C. **How a minor disaffirms**—If a minor wishes to avoid liability (disaffirm), the minor must show intent to do so and must return any consideration derived from the contract that the minor still possesses or controls.

   D. **Inability to return consideration**— The minor does not lose the right to disaffirm despite an inability to return the consideration. If the minor does not possess or control the consideration, the minor still has the right to disaffirm the contract. The minor need only return what he or she still has left of the consideration. If all a minor has left of a car that he or she purchased is a hubcap, the minor can return the hubcap and be entitled to recoup any money paid to the seller. The minor is entitled back any consideration that he or she has paid and cannot be held further on the contract.

E. Exceptions to the minor's right to disaffirm—Necessities

1. To be a contract of necessity, the following criteria must be met:

    a. It must be an item of necessity (e.g., food, clothing, shelter, etc.)

    b. It must be in value of what the minor is accustomed (standard of living)

    c. Minor must not be under the care of a parent or guardian

2. If all three criteria are met, the minor may disaffirm the contract but the minor is liable for the reasonable value of the goods used. Note: The contract remains voidable because of the lack of capacity but the courts allow recovery by the seller on the basis of reasonable value, not necessarily the negotiated contract price.

F. Ratification—Any minor's contract that is affirmed by the minor after reaching the age of majority (now an adult), is fully liable.

1. **Express ratification**—The minor notifies the other party that he or she intends to honor the contract after reaching the age of majority.

2. **Implied ratification**—The minor continues to perform on the contract beyond reaching the age of majority and what would be a reasonable time for disaffirming.

Example:
Able, a minor age 17 is fully supporting his way through college (parents deceased). Able leases an apartment from Sue for one year with rental payments of $400 per month. Able makes five payments, turns 18, and makes one more payment before Able and Sue have a dispute followed by Able turning the apartment back to Sue upon moving. What are the possible claims and results of liability for Able?

Possible Results:

If Able can disaffirm (within a reasonable time after becoming 18), Able (by majority rule) is entitled to the return of all six payments made to Sue and has no further liability (remaining six months' rent).

If a court determines that this is a contract for a necessity, Sue can keep the six payments made (reasonable value based on use) but cannot collect for the remaining six months' rent.

IV. The Requirement of Mental Capacity

A. Mentally incompetent persons—general rule—Contracts made by a mentally incompetent person, but before a court has adjudged that person incompetent, are voidable by the person or legal guardian (the same as with a minor) during the period of incompetency and for a reasonable time after regaining his or her competency. To avoid liability, however, the mentally incompetent party must be able to return the consideration received under the contract. If the contract is made after the person has been adjudged incompetent by the court, the contract is void (can only be made by a legal guardian), not voidable. Laws on necessity and ratification on voidable contracts after regaining competency are the same as for a minor.

B. Intoxicated persons and capacity—general rule—Any person who becomes intoxicated can avoid any contract made while intoxicated if the intoxication was to such an extent that the person did not understand the binding nature of the contract and did not understand what was actually being conveyed or purchased by the terms of the contract. The person must be so drunk that their state is one of being mentally incompetent (not yet court adjudged) at the time the contract was made in order to have the contract be voidable. Courts are generally stricter on restitution for contracts voidable by intoxication.

V. Types of Mistakes

   A. Unilateral mistake—general rule—If only one of the parties makes a mistake, the mistake is binding on the mistaken party, unless:

     1. The other party knows or should know of the mistake or

     2. The mistake is material and obvious, as when there is a transposition of numbers, e.g., $501.20 vs. $5012.00. If the mistake is immaterial, e.g., $501.20 vs. $502.10, then the mistake is binding *or*

     3. The error was due to a mathematical calculation (addition, subtraction, division, or multiplication) and the mistake was made inadvertently and not through gross negligence.

Example:
Jim is going to offer to sell Mary his laptop computer for $550. That evening when Jim is typing up his offer to Mary, he inadvertently types the price at $500 rather than $550. Upon receiving Jim's letter, Mary writes back a simple "I accept" message.

Question: Do Jim and Mary have a contract?

Answer: Yes.

Question: What is the price in the contract?

Answer: Even though Jim intended to sell Mary the laptop computer for $550, he made a unilateral mistake, which Mary did not know had been made. Thus, the mistake falls on Jim and the contract is for $500.

Question: Would your answer be different if Jim had typed $5.50?

Answer: Yes, because here Mary would know Jim had made a mistake and such cannot be held against Jim.

   B. Bilateral (mutual) mistake—general rule—If both parties are mistaken and the mistake is one that involves the identity, existence, or quantity of the subject matter, the contract cannot be enforced by either party.

Example:
John and Mary have negotiated an agreement for Mary to purchase John's office building for $787,000. Unbeknownst to both of them, the office building (which is located in another city) has burned down following a gas pipe explosion. Both parties are mistaken as to the existence of the subject matter and have the defense of mistake to the contract.

VI. Innocent Misrepresentation

   A. Elements

     1. Deception about the subject matter of a contract that involves facts or promises of performance.

     2. The misrepresentation must be based on fact-based statements, not sales puffing (the use of superlatives to describe products or property).

Statements of fact	Puffing
"These bottles are made of 100% recycled materials."	"These bottles mean you are helping the environment."
"These shirts are 100% cotton."	"These shirts are soft and comfortable."
"You will lose two pounds per week on this diet."	"You will feel and look better on this diet."
"This ranch gets 41 inches of rain per year."	"This ranch gets plenty of water."
a. Expert opinions on the contract subject matter are statements of facts (e.g., an audit opinion or an appraisal). b. The opinions of nonexperts are treated in the same manner as puffing, e.g., a non-accountant who says, "This company's earnings are on track."	

3. The deception involves something material: Would the information affect the party's decision to enter into the contract? In all of the above examples, the information is material.

4. One party has relied on the deception. Parties in negotiations are permitted to rely on the factual representations and promises of performance made by the other parties.

B. **Damages**—The basic difference between fraud and innocent misrepresentation is intent and for innocent misrepresentation the remedy is usually limited to rescission.

VII. Fraud or Fraud in the Inducement

A. Elements

1. Just as with misrepresentation, the deception involves a material fact about the contract subject matter.

2. Just as in misrepresentation, one party has relied upon and been deceived by the other party's false representations.

3. Intentional deception—is the factor that distinguishes misrepresentation from fraud.

Example:
Jill is selling her home to Tanner. Tanner has required a termite inspection as a condition precedent (see Performance and Remedies for more information on conditions precedent) to closing on the purchase of the home. The first termite inspection by AAA Termite, Inc. results in a report that finds termites in the house. Jill does not turn the report over to Tanner; instead, she hires BBB Termite, Inc. to do a second inspection. BBB's report concludes that the house is clean, no termites. Tanner is pleased with the BBB report and closes on the house. Shortly after moving in, Tanner sees what he believes to be termite tracks. Tanner happens to call AAA, and AAA discloses the report. Because Jill withheld the AAA report from Tanner, there is intentional deception, not misrepresentation. The defense of fraud or fraudulent misrepresentation applies here.

If Jill hired BBB first and BBB found no termites even though there were termites, then there would be misrepresentation. Jill did not intend to mislead Tanner; she just hired a company that missed finding the termites.

B. **Damages**—If all three elements are present, the deceived party is entitled to damages (including punitive damages) or can rescind (cancel) the contract. Fraud in formation is one of the few times that punitive damages are available in contract suits.

VIII. Undue Influence

A. Undue influence arises when there is a special relationship, often called a confidential relationship, whereby one party, because of this relationship, can exercise undue influence over the free will of the other in rendering decisions. Examples include lawyer/client; priest/parishioner; child/elderly parent.

B. Undue influence exists when there is a relationship of trust and dependence and one party takes advantage of the other party because of the dependence.

C. Contracts entered into under undue influence are voidable. The party who is unduly influenced is able to set aside the contract if he or she wishes to do so.

Example:
A sister, upon whom a disabled brother heavily relies for his care, talks her brother into contracting to sell his only asset, his house, to her at 50% of its market value. This relationship of dependence allowed the sister to overcome her brother's free will and, thus, the brother can set aside this contract or sale.

IX. Duress

A. Duress is a defense when one party in the formation stage is deprived of his or her free will or choice for entering into the contract.

B. **Forms of duress**

1. Physical force or threats of physical force (that rise to level of criminal assault or battery) to the party or to their family

2. Threats to disclose private information

3. Economic pressure—if a party does not enter into a contract the other party threatens to ruin his or her business

Example:
An employer threatens to fire and have an employee "black-listed" in an industry the employer controls unless the employee contracts to sell the employer mineral rights to a piece of land the employee has just purchased. This threat of economic sanctions, loss of job, plus not being able to work and apply his or her industry skills to earn a living, is economic duress.

X. **Illegality**

A. **Contracts in violation of statutes**—Contracts in violation of a statute are void. There may be offer, acceptance, consideration, and capacity, but if the subject matter is illegal, the contract is void, which means that neither side can enforce the agreement.

1. **Usury**—This means charging a higher interest rate than permitted by law (maximum rate). Contracts for usurious loans are void. The remedy may be the entire contract is void, the interest is void, or the interest charged above the usurious rate is void.

2. **Gambling contracts**—These contracts are illegal and void but payment of the gambling debt may be only voidable.

3. **Licensing statutes**—If the purpose of the licensing law is mainly revenue generation, the contract with the unlicensed person may be enforceable. If the purpose is to regulate public welfare (e.g., a doctor or lawyer), the contract with the unlicensed person is null and void.

Example:
Real estate agents are required to be licensed in all states in which they are working. Even if an unlicensed agent has a listing agreement in writing, there will be no commission paid nor will the listing contract be enforced by the courts because the licensing statutes are qualification statutes. To allow unlicensed agents to collect commissions would defeat the public purposes of having knowledgeable and trained agents.

B. **Contracts contrary to public policy**—Contracts may be void not because they violate a statute but rather because enforcing them would undermine public policy goals and standards.

1. Unconscionable contracts or clauses in consumer contracts.

Example:
A consumer credit contract under which the consumer is never able to repay the seller for the goods because the payments are spread among all the contracts instead of paying off the debt one item at a time to provide the consumer with some paid-off debts. It would be unconscionable to impose such a credit payment standard.

2. **Exculpatory clauses**—A clause in a contract, that disclaims any liability regardless of fault.

Note:
This concept has been on the exam in the past.

Example:
A clause in a sale of goods contract that eliminates all liability for personal injuries caused by a product is void.

3. **Contracts in restraint of trade**—Covenants-not-to-compete.

    a. A covenants-not-to-compete is enforceable if it is:

        i. Ancillary—a part of a larger contract *and*

        ii. Reasonable in restraint in length of time and geographic scope

Example:
Charles contracts to sell his Italian restaurant to Susan. In the contract is a clause that prohibits Charles from starting an Italian restaurant in the city for six months. This is probably an enforceable covenant-not-to-compete because it is ancillary—part of the sale of business contract and the restraint is reasonable in length and geographic scope.

Performance and Remedies

After studying this lesson you should be able to:

1. List the types of remedies available for breach of contract.

2. List the types of damages and explain when they are available for recovery.

3. Explain when performance is due under a contract.

4. Describe when performance is due and how it is completed.

5. List the circumstances under which the obligations of performance under a contract are discharged and how discharge occurs.

I. **When is Performance Due?**—A contract is a legal obligation to perform a given promise. However, implied in every contract are certain conditions that must transpire for performance to occur. Likewise, the duty to perform can be discharged if other conditions occur. The presence or absence of conditions controls the duty to perform the promises under a contract.

   A. **Types of conditions for performance**

      1. **Precedent**—A precedent condition is something that must be present or occur before a party has a duty to perform.

Example:
Jane signs a contract for the purchase of her first home. The condition precedent for the purchase is that she must qualify for a home mortgage loan at a rate not to exceed 6%. If Jane cannot secure financing, the condition precedent is not met and Jane is not required to perform under the contract.

      2. **Subsequent**—A condition subsequent is something that must be present or occur after a duty to perform has arisen. This condition subsequent must be present in order to hold a party liable on the contract, i.e., required to complete the contract duties.

Example:
A fire policy has a provision, that requires the policyholder to submit a proof of loss by filing with the insurer, within 60 days after the fire, in order for the policyholder to recover for the fire loss. The requirement of the filing of a proof of loss after the fire to receive payment for the fire loss covered by the policy is a condition subsequent. If the condition subsequent of filing a proof of loss (also known as a proof of claim) is not met, then the insurer is discharged of its duty to perform, i.e., pay the insured for the loss.

      3. **Concurrent**—Each party's duty to perform under a contract is dependent upon the other party's absolute duty to perform at the same time. All contracts have some form of condition concurrent.

Example:
A buyer of oranges promises to pay for the oranges only upon seller's delivery. The seller's duty to deliver is conditioned upon the buyer's tender or payment, and buyer's duty to tender or pay is conditioned upon seller's tender or delivery of the oranges. You also do the same thing when you are checking out at the grocery store. You and the store have conditions concurrent of payment and the store bagging the groceries for you to take with you as it passes title. (See the lesson on "Title and Risk of Loss" for more information on the passage of title.)

   B. **Discharge of duty to perform**—When is your duty to perform under a contract discharged? There are several types of actions, events, and legal provisions that provide a discharge for your contract duties.

1. **Discharge by failure of conditions**—If the condition precedent does not occur, then the duty to perform is discharged.

Example:
1. DTR public accounting firm agrees to perform an audit of the Xanadu Publishing House, Inc. within six months of the signing of the engagement letter. An implied condition precedent is Xanadu giving DTR access to its records so that DTR can conduct the audit. If Xanadu never provides access to those records, DTR's duty to perform never arises because it cannot complete an audit without access to records and the ability to question employees. DTR would be discharged from its obligations under the audit agreement for the failure of the condition precedent.

2. If an author failed to complete a manuscript by the deadline provided in the publishing agreement, the author would be in breach of contract. However, the publisher must file suit within the statute of limitations (generally four years for breach of contract) in order to recover the advance paid to the author under the contract for the manuscript. If the publisher does not file suit within the four years, then the author's duty to return the advance is discharged.

2. **Discharge by agreement or party action**

    a. **Release**—A release is a discharge of a party's obligations under a contract. A release usually must be in writing, it must be given voluntarily and in good faith, and it usually requires consideration.

    b. **Waiver**—A waiver by the nonbreaching party is a relinquishment of rights related to the other party to a contract and his or her breach.

    c. **Mutual rescission**—A mutual rescission is an enforceable mutual agreement to discharge all contract obligations and restore the parties to their precontract positions.

Example:
Able contracts with you to sell her accounting book for $70. Later, both of you change your mind about the sale and you both agree to cancel the contract. This is mutual rescission. If you already paid the $70, then Able must return to you the $70 paid upon agreement of mutual rescission.

    d. **Novation**—By agreement between the original parties to a contract and through a valid subsequent contract, a new party is substituted for one of the original parties thereby discharging the duties of the parties under the original contract.

Example:
Son Able will not be able to pay the debt on a loan from West Bank when it comes due. Able's mother, Sue Able, and West Bank agree that if West Bank will release Son Able and provide a 30-day extension, Sue will pay the loan. In this novation, Able is discharged (released) from the loan, terminating the old contract, and a new contract is created by substituting Sue as the debtor. Notice that all parties must agree to a novation—the original parties to the agreement as well as the new third party who is being substituted through the novation.

    e. **Discharge by accord and satisfaction**—This is an agreement whereby the original contract can be satisfied either by completion of the original performance or by a different performance. (See also the lesson on "Consideration.")

Example:
Green owes you $5,000 due on May 1. On April 20, Green tells you he is not sure he can pay you the $5,000 but, if not, offers to deed to you a lot Green owns. You agree (which is the accord). On May 1, Green can satisfy the debt by either paying you $5,000 or by transfer of the deed to the lot.

3. **Discharge by operation of law**

   a. **Statute of limitations**—If a suit for breach of contract is not filed in a court of law or equity within a statutory period of time, the nonbreaching party is barred from pursuing a remedy. This effectively discharges the contract. The statutory periods of time vary from state to state and depend on the type of contract. For the sale of goods, it is a four-year period from date of cause of action but this period can be reduced to one year by agreement (see UCC 2-725). The time period for the statute of limitations starts when the cause of action arises. For example, the statute of limitations on a sales contract would run from the time the seller failed to deliver the goods.

   b. **Bankruptcy decree**—Most obligations of a bankrupt debtor can be fully discharged by a decree in bankruptcy. (See the lessons on "Prebankruptcy Options and Introduction to Bankruptcy" and "Bankruptcy Process" materials for more information on dischargeable and nondischargeable debts.)

   c. **Discharge by impossibility or impracticability of performance**—This type of discharge of performance occurs when it has become objectively impossible for the contract obligations to be completed.

   d. **Death or insanity** of a person whose performance is essential to completion of a contract.

Example:
For $500, Able contracts with Sue to sing at her party on Friday. On Thursday, Able dies. Because one party is no longer alive, this contract is objectively impossible to perform, discharging the contract.

   e. **Destruction of the specific subject matter** of the contract is an automatic discharge of the contract.

Example:
Able contracts to sell you her boat *Flying Cloud*. Before she can deliver the boat specified, the boat is destroyed through no fault of Able. This contract is automatically discharged at the time of destruction.

   f. **Illegality**—If legal changes occur that now render the contract illegal, the contract is automatically discharged upon the change in the law.

Example:
You have a contract with Able to build an apartment complex on your lot. Before construction, but after the contract has been formed, laws are changed so that only single residences may be built.

   g. **Commercial impracticability**—For the doctrine of commercial impracticability to apply, the failed performance must meet an objective standard and not be merely more difficult to perform. Extreme difficulty or cost may meet the objective standard test.

Example:
1. Able contracts to move hazardous waste 10 miles through a city to a hazardous waste site for $50 per load ($5 per mile). The city now prohibits hazardous waste to travel through the city. The only other safe route to the site is around a series of mountains for a distance of 300 miles. The new cost to travel far exceeds the contracted price per load. This contract would probably now be rendered commercially impractical.

Chapter 1: Able has a contract to sell peanuts to Planter's Inc. Able's peanut crop is destroyed. There are peanuts available on the open market, but it would cost Able much more than the price Planter's is paying in order to buy the peanuts. The additional cost would not be commercial impracticability because, objectively, peanuts are available to satisfy the contract. Able could get around such an issue by contracting to sell the output from his peanut farm. If the crop is destroyed, it is objectively impossible for him to sell his output and his duty would be discharged.

4. **Discharge by performance**

    a. Each party has completed the obligations negotiated under the terms of the contract. With some contracts, performance is easily determined; the seller either delivered the food for the catered lunch or did not. With other contracts, the complexity of the contract or the time required makes performance a more difficult question.

Example:
Able contracts to sell Baker his car for $2,000. Able delivers his car to Baker and Baker gives Able $2,000. The fully performed contract discharges both parties. A contract is automatically discharged when both parties fully perform.

    b. **Doctrine of substantial performance**—Some contracts are complex in terms of determining whether performance has occurred, such as in the construction of a home. There can be variations from the contract and the builder can still be paid as long as there is substantial performance. Substantial performance means that any deviation from the terms was done in good faith and for practical purposes (i.e., whatever was substituted is just as good as the original plan).

Example:
Specifications for the building of a house call for Kohler plumbing fixtures. The contractor installs American Standard, a comparable value fixture. Unless the contract payment was conditioned upon installation of only Kohler plumbing fixtures, the specification is a promise and the installation of a comparable fixture is substantial performance rather than a material breach.

    c. **Contracts that require personal satisfaction**—If a condition is precedent, it requires the actual satisfaction or approval for discharge of the contract.

Example:
1. The president of the United States hires you as an artist to paint his or her official portrait to his or her personal satisfaction. This is a condition and any real dissatisfaction causes a failure of the condition and no liability for the president.

2. Smith is hired to clean the lobby of an office building to the personal satisfaction of the building manager. This is merely a promise for satisfaction and a reasonable person test would be used to see if substantial performance had been achieved. If so, there is no material breach even if the building manager claims dissatisfaction.

    d. **Discharge by anticipatory breach**—If either party repudiates a contract prior to the time of performance, the nonbreaching party may treat the repudiation as an anticipatory and immediate material breach. This doctrine permits a party to pursue remedies prior to the stated date for performance (see UCC 2-610 and 2-611).

5. **Discharge by material breach**—If one party has materially breached the contract, the other side is no longer obligated to perform and the other party's duties under the contract are discharged. A material breach is one in which the nonbreaching party's circumstances are affected by the other party's breach. For example, an airline catering firm that fails to deliver meals on time for flights has materially breached that supply contract because there is no way to obtain other sources of food in those circumstances.

II. Remedies for Breach

A. Types of remedies

1. Damages—monetary recovery

    a. **Nominal**—There is a breach but no financial loss has been suffered. Court awards a nominal amount ($1 or some other small amount).

b. **Compensatory**—These are all costs or loss actually suffered and proved caused by the breach.

c. **Incidental damages**—Incidental expenses are incurred by the nonbreaching party due to the breach (see UCC 2-715(1)).

d. **Consequential damages**—These include any foreseeable loss known by the breaching party (UCC 2-715(2)). These types of damages include penalties for delay in performing a contract because a party has been tardy in delivering goods or performance on a contract. To recover consequential damages, the breaching party must be aware that time is of the essence in the performance of the contract.

Example:
1. Able contracts to purchase 100 transmissions for $40,000 from Sallar Inc. The transmissions are to be installed in custom-made recreational vehicles to be driven in the mountains. Delivery is to be on or before May 1. On April 20, Sallar tells Able that Sallar cannot deliver on time. Able immediately, with notice to Sallar, purchases the transmissions from Green Inc. on the open market at a price of $42,000. Able can collect from Sallar all expenses incurred in the making of the new contract, such as additional shipping charges and those incurred from Sallar's breach, such as delays in his work, and the actual increase in price of $2,000.

2. Able contracts with Sallor Inc. to deliver on or before May 1 parts for a special oil field valve that Able is making for Oiltax. Able's contract with Sallor specifically states "time is of the essence" and "any delay in our production and delivery will result in Able paying Oiltax liquidated damages of $1,000 per day." Sallor does not deliver on time and by the time that Able can purchase the parts elsewhere, the delivery to Oiltax is five days late. Here Able can recover from Sallor not only all expenses and the increased parts price purchase costs, but also the foreseeable liquidated damages ($5,000) caused by Sallor's breach.

e. **Punitive damages**—Damages awarded to punish a wrongdoer. Punitive damages are rarely given in breach of contract cases, with the example covered on the exam being in the case of fraud in the inducement in formation of the contract. (See "Defenses to Formation" for more information on this topic.)

f. **Liquidated damages**—The parties agree in their contract that a specific sum is to be paid in the event that the contract is breached. Liquidated damage provisions are enforceable as long as (a) at the time of formation of the contract it is apparent that damages would be difficult to estimate in the event of breach, and (b) the amount stated is a reasonable sum estimate. The provision cannot be constituted as a penalty (see UCC 2-718).

Example:
Able has agreed to construct a 100-unit apartment complex for Green. The completion date is agreed to be May 1 or earlier. Since Green will be preleasing the apartments with one-year leases to begin on May 1, it is agreed to include a liquidated damage clause to cover breach of lease actions and costs incurred in housing by the affected tenants if the apartments are not completed on time. The liquidated damage amount is based upon average occupancy for new apartment buildings when first available in the community and the estimate that at least 70% of the tenants would require substitute housing and storage. This is broken down on a daily basis to create the liquidated damage amount per day for late construction. This clause would probably be enforceable because of the difficulty in estimating damages and the reasonable amount per day (determination).

B. **Mitigation of damages**—When a breach takes place, the law usually imposes on the nonbreaching party the duty to take actions to mitigate (reduce) the amount of damages owed. Some states require such in breach of real estate lease cases.

Example:
Able has a one-year lease with Green for $1,000 per month. After six months, Able breaches the lease and abandons the property. If mitigation is required, Green must use reasonable means to find and lease the property to a suitable tenant. Able is still liable for any difference and, if no tenant can be found, for the balance of the lease.

C. Remedies in equity

1. **Specific performance**—Requiring the other party to perform the contract; available when there are rare goods (antiques) or for buyers of land (land is unique);

   a. If the object of the contract is unique and damages are inappropriate as a remedy, by court order, the nonbreaching party (usually a buyer) can force the breaching party to perform the contract. This is not applicable to personal service contracts.

Example:
Able contracts to sell his lake lot to Green for $10,000. Able now has a better offer and refuses to deed the lot to Green. Because land is unique (no two parcels have the same legal description) and damages would hardly satisfy Green who wants the lot, specific performance is an appropriate remedy.

2. **Rescission and restitution**—In rescission, the parties, in effect, go back to their corners and are restored to the same positions they were in before the contract was entered into (see discussion of misrepresentation in Defenses to Formation for more information).

   a. Rescission is the undoing of a contract to return the parties to their original position. Generally, both parties must make restitution (i.e., returning anything each has received). As a remedy, this is where one party is in breach and the nonbreaching party with notice rescinds the contracts. (Remember that in mutual rescission there is no breach but discharge of the contract.) The breaching party must restore the nonbreaching party to his or her original position, but the nonbreaching party cannot retain the benefits that he or she has received as unjust enrichment.

3. **Reformation**—A contract rewritten to address an issue that affects the parties. Reformation is used by the court to correct an imperfectly expressed contract. It is applied most often to correct clerical errors, errors in reducing a valid oral contract into a written form, or to make a covenant-not-to-compete reasonable in time or area—all to reflect the true intentions of the parties.

4. **Quasi-contract recovery**—Remedy given when there is no contract (see discussion of types of contracts in the "Introduction and Classification" lesson). A remedy to give a reasonable value benefit to one party and avoid an unjust enrichment received by the other party.

Example:
Able has a one-year $50,000 employment contract with Green. The contract contains an option to cancel clause "at any time" which renders the one-year contract unenforceable because of a lack of consideration. Able works for 15 days and is dismissed for no reason. Although there was no one-year contract for $50,000, Able has given Green valuable services. Green must pay Able a sum equal to the reasonable (market) value of those services. Not to be required to do so would give Green an unjust benefit.

Third-Party Rights

After studying this lesson you should be able to:

1. Explain the requirements for creating a valid assignment and/or delegation.

2. Describe the rights of the parties in an assignment and/or delegation.

3. Define a third-party beneficiary relationship.

4. List the types of third-party beneficiary relationships and explain the rights of the parties.

5. List and give examples of the types of third-party contractual relationships.

I. **General Rule**—Unless a party is in privity (a party thereto) to a contract, that party (called a third party) has no enforceable rights to or obligations under the contract. However, contract law does provide for certain types of third-party relationships that do give rights under the contract to third parties.

II. **Assignments and Delegations**

A. **Terminology**

1. **Rights**—Rights (or the benefits under a contract) can be assigned. For example, a contractor who owes money to Home Depot can assign his payment from a customer to Home Depot so that he can pay off his Home Depot bill. (See the "Consideration" lesson for discussion of benefits.)

2. **Duties**—Duties are the detriment under a contract and they can be delegated. For example, XYZ Corporation may be getting out of the business of home dry-cleaning pick- up and delivery, but it still has contracts with 45 customers. XYZ can delegate the duties to ABC Company, a small local dry cleaner to complete performance under the contracts. (See the "Consideration" lesson for discussion of both benefit and detriment as elements of consideration.)

3. **Assignment and delegation parties**

a. **Assignor**—Party (usually one of the original contracting parties) who makes the assignment (the contractor in the above example)

b. **Assignee**—Party to whom rights are assigned (Home Depot in the above example)

c. **Delegator**—Party who makes the delegation (XYZ Company in the above example)

d. **Delegatee**—Party to whom the duties are delegated (ABC Company in the above example)

e. **Obligor**—Name given to party in the contract for the party's detriment; every party to a contract has an obligation—the duty to perform; in a contract for the sale of a car, the buyer is the obligor for payment and the seller is the obligor for delivery of the car

f. **Obligee**—Name given to party in the contract for the party's benefit; every party to a contract has a benefit; in a contract for the sale of a car, the buyer is the obligee for the car and the seller is the obligee for the money to be paid for the car

B. **Assignments**

1. Any right can be assigned or delegated unless an exception applies.

2. The assignment of rights is a contract separate from the original agreement.

3. **Assignment exceptions**

    a. **Prohibited by contract terms (anti-assignment clause).**

Example:
In a typical term lease, the lease contract terms do not allow the tenant to assign the lease without the landlord's consent. Most fire insurance policies prohibit assignment of the policy without the insurer's consent, but the policyholder can assign a money claim for a loss sustained covered by the policy.

    b. **Prohibited by statute**

Example:
Future social security or workers' compensation benefits, in many states future wages, and some rights that are intended only for a particular person, such as alimony or child support, are not assignable by statute.

    c. **Prohibited by personal contracts**—Contracts unique to the person receiving services.

Example:
You contract to tutor Green's children after observing them. Green assigns her right to your services to Hope for the tutoring of her children. This assignment is prohibited without your consent because Hope's children may have different needs or temperaments.

    d. **Prohibited due to increased material risks to the obligor**

Example:
Green owns a restaurant and has a fire insurance policy (contract) with ABC Insure. Green cannot assign the policy to Able to cover a restaurant that Able owns on the other side of the city without ABC Insure's consent. The reason is that ABC Insure's policy was made based on risks assumed on ABC's evaluation of Green's circumstances. Able's circumstances and resulting risks could be quite different and thus could substantially increase ABC's risks.

C. Delegations—Duties under a contract can be delegated unless

    1. **Contract terms prohibit delegation**

Example:
Green wants to have her products locally delivered to her customers' front porches. Any local delivery carrier can make these deliveries. Green contracts with ABC Del Inc. to make her deliveries and places in the contract that the contract cannot be delegated to any other carrier. This clause prohibits delegation.

    2. **Contract is based on the personal skill of the obligor (personal services contracts)**—or a special trust has been placed in the obligor.

Example:
You hire a famous heart specialist to perform a heart transplant. This doctor cannot delegate the surgery to any other doctor—even one with equal skills—because your contract was made dependent upon this doctor's skill and the trust that you have placed in him or her.

3. **Contract performance will materially vary from that expected by obligee**

Example:
Green contracts with Smith to clean a surface by use of sandblasting. Green delegates the duty to Able who specializes in cleaning the same type of surface with hot water. Even though the result is the same, Green's expectation of sandblasting is materially different from that of hot water.

D. **Rights of the parties upon assignment**—(applies equally to delegation)

1. An assignee (delegate) can acquire no better rights than those possessed by the assignor (delegator) (but can acquire lesser rights); the third party steps into the shoes of the original contracting party.

2. An assignment is not binding on the other party to the contract until the obligor has notice of the assignment:

   a. Between two assignees to the same contract, the one with the most rights is the one who

      I. Is first in time of assignment (U.S. Rule) *or*

      II. Is first to give notice of the assignment (English Rule).

   b. Until given notice, the original party to the contract can discharge the contract by completing performance to the assignor.

Example:
1. John owes Jane $100. Jane assigns her right to the money to Sam. Until John has notice of the assignment, John can discharge his obligation by payment to Jane. If John has notice, John can only discharge the debt by payment to Sam. If Jane had also assigned, the next day after her assignment to Sam, the payment to Mary, and Mary gave John notice, as between Sam and Mary's priority, it depends upon whether the U.S. rule (Sam gets priority by first in time) or the English rule (Mary gets priority by first to give notice) applies.

2. Jane has her mortgage through Fourth Second Bank. Fourth Second Bank assigns Jane's mortgage to CDO Mortgage Company. Neither Fourth Second Bank nor CDO Mortgage notifies Jane of the assignment. Jane continues to pay Fourth Second Bank. Jane has completed her monthly obligations by continuing to pay Fourth Second and she is not required to pay CDO Mortgage until she knows of the assignment.

3. Any defenses that the original contracting party had now belong to the third party assignee (delegate). Likewise, any defenses waived by the original party to the contract remained waived with respect to the third party.

Example:
ABC Appliance store contracts to sell Jones a TV, model X, for $1,450. Jones, through fraud, gives ABC false credit information. ABC is to make delivery at the end of the week on Friday. On Wednesday, ABC discovers that it had sold its last model X TV earlier. ABC assigns its contract for delivery and sale to XYZ Appliance who has model X TVs in stock. On Thursday, ABC learns of the fraud and notifies XYZ. ABC's defense of fraud (avoid the contract) is also a defense available to XYZ, who does not have to deliver the TV set to Jones.

4. An assignment does not waive or eliminate the contract rights of the original party to the contract. Unless released, the assignor remains liable to the other contracting party. If the assignee (delegatee) fails to perform the obligations under the contract, the assignor (obligor) is still responsible.

> **CAUTION:** The only way an assignor can be released is if the original party to the contract agrees to a release. A novation is required to substitute parties to a contract. A novation requires the assent of both original parties to the contract as well as the assent of the substituted party. This concept of novation is often tested on the exam.

> **Example:**
> Assume a tenant is allowed to assign the balance of a five-year lease with a landlord to an assignee. Unless the assignor (tenant) is released by the landlord, the assignor is still liable for any default by the assignee. Therefore, if the new tenant fails to pay rent, the original tenant remains liable for it. If, however, the landlord and tenant execute a novation, the assignee is substituted under the lease and the tenant is released from liability. A novation requires that all three parties agree to the substitution and release of the assignor (the original tenant).

III. Third-Party Beneficiary Contracts

A. Types of third-party beneficiaries

1. **Donee (intended) beneficiary**—The contract must be made for the direct benefit of the beneficiary and the donee's rights must be given in the contract (i.e., the donee beneficiary has a legal right to what is given by the two parties to the contract).

> **Example:**
> You contract with ABC Life Insurance Company for a $25,000 policy on your life with your spouse as the named beneficiary. The named beneficiary has no rights in the policy until you are dead. At that time, the life insurance company must honor its contract with you by paying the benefits according to the terms of your policy. Both the named beneficiary and your estate have the right to enforce the agreement against the insurance company upon your death. However, the beneficiary would not have the right to recover from your estate if the life insurance company did not pay.

2. **Creditor beneficiary**—There must be a debtor-creditor relationship, and the debtor must make a contract that befits the creditor with a third person.

> **Example:**
> 1. ABC is the mortgagee (creditor/mortgage lender) on a home owned by Green (debtor). Green contracts to sell the home to Able (third person), with Able agreeing to assume the mortgage (become personally liable to make payments to ABC). Although ABC is not a party to the purchase contract, ABC is a creditor beneficiary and can enforce mortgage payments against Able. Creditor beneficiaries can enforce their rights against both parties to the contract.
>
> 2. You have a medical insurance policy and require emergency room treatment at a hospital. The hospital is a creditor beneficiary of your insurance policy because you owe the hospital for the emergency room treatment even if your insurance does not pay. The hospital has the right to bring suit to collect from either the insurance company or you because the hospital is one of your creditors.

3. **Incidental beneficiary**—A third party who receives an unintended benefit has no legal rights in a contract between two parties.

> **Example:**
> A contractor has a contract with the city to build a swimming pool in a small neighborhood park. The swimming pool will increase the value of the homes in the neighborhood. The contractor breaches the contract. The city decides not to sue. The homeowners wish to file suits against the contractor as a beneficiary of the contractor-city contract. Since the homeowners are only incidental beneficiaries, they have no legal rights in the contractor-city contract. Incidental beneficiaries have no rights of enforcement against either party to the original contract.

Application and Formation (AFTPDT Formula)

> **After studying this lesson you should be able to:**
>
> **1.** Explain when the UCC Article 2 applies to contracts.
>
> **2.** Explain the requirements for formation under the UCC and be sure to list the differences between UCC and common law formation.
>
> **3.** Give the definitions for the basic terms of UCC Article 2 including goods and merchant.

I. **About the Uniform Commercial Code**—This unit of the review focuses on one portion of the UCC—Article 2 Sales. However, you will also be studying other portions of the UCC:

> Article 3—Negotiable Instruments
> Article 5—Letters of Credit
> Article 7—Documents of Title
> Article 9—Security Interests

    A. **UCC Article 2**—This article covers the sales of goods (see "Introduction and Classification" under "Contracts" for discussion of application).

        1. When studying Article 2, use the AFTPDT formula:

> Application—When do I apply the UCC Article 2 to a contract? This question often controls the answer to questions you will have on the exam. Understanding when to apply the UCC determines whether you will get your answer correct!
>
> Formation—When is a contract formed under the UCC Article 2?
>
> Terms—What are the terms of a UCC Article 2 contract?
>
> Performance—What is required for performance under a UCC Article 2 contract?
>
> Damages—What damages are available to buyers and sellers under UCC Article 2?
>
> Title and Risk of Loss—What are the issues of title and risk of loss under UCC Article 2?

        2. In this section you are covering application and formation as well as some of the terms in a UCC Article 2 contract.

    B. When the contract involves **both service and the sale of goods**—use **the predominant purpose test;** was the primary purpose of the transaction the sale of goods or the provision of a service?

    See the following example.

Example:

1. You contract with an artist to paint a portrait of you for a Christmas present. Is this a contract for a good—the finished portrait—or a contract for a service—the painting of the portrait? Obviously, the predominant feature of the contract is the artist painting (service) your portrait.

2. You order food to be cooked at a restaurant. Are you purchasing the cooking (preparation) of the food or the food itself? Here, the food itself is the predominant feature and a sale of goods (See UCC 2-314(1)).

    C. When a contract involves both realty and the sale of goods, use the UCC (UCC 2-107) and common law on fixtures (real property).

Example:

1. The sales of minerals, oil, gas, or structures on earth to be moved are considered goods if they are to be severed by the seller; if severed by the buyer, real estate law governs.

2. Sales of growing crops or timber are the sale of goods regardless who severs.

3. "Things" attached but not deemed fixtures, which can be severed without material harm to realty, are goods.

    D. **Article 2 applies to merchants and non-merchants alike**—There are certain sections that apply only when a seller, buyer, or both are **merchants**.

II. Article 2—Basic Definitions

Definition:
Sale of Goods: Passage of title of goods from a seller to a buyer for a price.

Study Tip:
Before answering any contracts questions on the exam be sure to determine whether the subject matter puts you under the UCC or common law. Many exam questions on contracts will have both the UCC and the common law answer among the choices. You must look at the subject matter to know whether you should answer under UCC or common law.

    A. **Bailments**—The transfer of personal property but not title. Article 2 does not apply to bailments.

Example:
You rent a rollaway bed for use by your visiting relatives. Your rental of the bed is not a sale of goods.

Definitions:
Merchant: A person who deals in goods of the kind being sold, or a person who holds himself or herself out as having knowledge or skill specific to the purchases or goods involved in the transaction.

Goods: All movable and tangible personal property other than money, investments, or securities and things in action. Notice that Article 2 does not apply to all forms of personal property. Intellectual property rights are not covered under Article 2.

Example:

Merchant: (Deals in goods of the kind being sold)

A manufacturer of washing machines

A retail seller of washing machines

A farmer who regularly sells crops

A university that sells used and obsolete equipment five times a year

Merchant: (Holds self out as having knowledge or skill by occupation) A restaurant owner who purchases a large oven for the restaurant

A computer division of the IRS that buys a new computer

A university purchasing department that purchases chemistry laboratory equipment

---

B. **Good faith**—Good faith is the obligation of both parties to an Article 2 contract to act with forthrightness and fairness in the formation, performance, and modification of their contracts. The UCC's goal is to produce smooth transactions and minimize unnecessary expenses in performing contracts and handling failures to perform. Both parties have an obligation to act in good faith.

III. Contract Formation—Article 2

A. **Review the Formation**—Review the Offer and Acceptance portion of Contracts in order to understand how contracts are formed under Article 2. This section simply highlights the distinctions between common law contract formation and formation of contracts under Article 2.

B. **The certainty and definiteness of terms standard is less stringent under the UCC than under common law**

1. A contract for sale of goods is formed as long as the subject matter and quantity of goods (if there is more than one) are agreed upon—UCC 2-204(3).

2. Terms of agreement— The UCC supplies the terms in absence of agreement. For an:

   a. **Open price term**—A reasonable or market price at the time of delivery will apply, or if price is to be fixed by either party, good faith is required in doing so—UCC 2-305.

Misconception: A contract can be formed if the price for the sale of goods is not stated in the contract or the price is to be determined in amount at the time of shipment. This statement is correct under the UCC because the UCC specifically allows prices to be determined at time of shipment (sometimes referred to as an "escalation clause"), and the price can be what is a reasonable or a market price at time of either contract, shipment, delivery, or payment.

---

   b. **Open payment term**—Payment is due at time and place buyer is to receive the goods—UCC 2-310.

   c. **Open place of delivery term**—Delivery is at seller's business or, if the seller does not have a place of business, at seller's residence—UCC 2-308.

Misconception: Buyer Green is from New Orleans and Seller Smith is from Dallas. Smith offers to sell Green a watch for $100. Green accepts Smith's offer. The contract is silent as to the place of delivery, so delivery is at the buyer's place in New Orleans. No, in absence of agreement, it is at Smith's residence in Dallas. Green is required to "pick up" the watch or be in breach of contract.

---

    d. **Open time for contracted performance**—In absence of agreement it is a reasonable time—UCC 2-309.

C. **Firm offer**

    1. The offer is made by a **merchant** (can be either the seller or buyer making the firm offer).

    2. The offeror states that it will be kept open or gives **assurance** that the offer will not be withdrawn for a stated period of time (the maximum length is three months unless there is consideration). If no time is given, the offer is kept open for a reasonable time, an amount of time that is determined by the nature of the goods. Produce firm offers that are left open-ended could be just days long whereas firm offers for computers that are left open could be up to three months long.

    3. The offer is in a **signed writing (record)**—UCC 2-205.

Example:

Green, a retail seller of TVs, offers in a letter to purchase 500 Model X TVs from Vision Inc. (a manufacturer of TVs) at the current Vision Inc. price list. In the letter, Green states that time is of the essence and that the offer is only good for 30 days from the date of the letter and will not be withdrawn during that time. A week later, Green decides to withdraw the offer and mails a revocation of the offer. Even if Vision receives the letter of revocation, Vision can accept Green's offer and bind Green to a contract during the 30-day period. Green's offer as a merchant, in a letter as a signed writing, gave Vision assurance that the offer would not be withdrawn for 30 days. Thus, Green made a firm offer, which was irrevocable without payment of consideration for the 30-day period, and cannot legally revoke the offer.

D. **Acceptance by shipment of goods**—A seller can form a contract through action, i.e., shipment of goods—UCC 2-206(1)(b).

    1. The seller delivers conforming goods (goods that fulfill the buyer's order or offer) to a carrier.

    2. The seller can also accept an offer by promising to ship promptly.

    3. If the seller is shipping goods that are different from what the buyer ordered or offered to buy, i.e., nonconforming goods, the seller must notify the buyer *before* shipping that the shipment is offered only as an accommodation. If the seller ships *without advance notification* of the nonconforming goods, then there is an acceptance and automatic breach at the same time.

E. **Additional terms in acceptance—Battle of the Forms**

    1. **Common law**—Follows the mirror image rule (see the "Formation—Offer and Acceptance" lesson for more details). Acceptance must be absolute, unequivocal, and unconditional or it is treated as a counteroffer, not an acceptance.

    2. **The UCC—UCC 2-207**—Modifies the common law based on a definite expression of acceptance. A definite expression of acceptance followed by additional terms may or may not form a contract with the additional terms. (Review the "Formation—Offer and Acceptance" lesson and remember that whether the terms become a part of the contract depends upon whether the parties are merchants and whether the terms are material, the offer is limited, and if the offeror objects upon receiving the additional terms.)

Study Tip:
Remember that conditional acceptance is never acceptance, whether under UCC or common law. If an offeree uses language such as, "I'll take it but. . .," "I'll take it provided that . . .," "I'll take it but I must . . .," or "I'll take it on the condition that . . ." there is a conditional acceptanc. Conditional acceptance is never acceptance, it is a counteroffer. Watch on the exam for those prepositions in attempted acceptances (e.g., *but, provided, if, and only if*).

Example:
A seller offers to sell to the buyer 5,000 pounds of a "specific type" of chicken at 50 cents per pound. The buyer responds "I accept your offer for 5,000 pounds as certified by a public scale weight certificate the specific type of chicken at 50 cents per pound." Since this is a sale of goods (chicken), and the buyer gave a definite expression of acceptance ("I accept") without conditional assent to the modification, a contract is formed even though the buyer's acceptance with additional terms (public weight certificate) modified the terms of the seller's offer.

Example:
In the above sale of 5,000 pounds of chicken, with the offeree's additional terms of a public scale weight certificate, since both parties are obviously merchants, the contract is formed on the offeree's (buyer's) terms unless the seller objects with notice to the buyer within a reasonable time. If the seller does object, the contract is formed on the seller's terms (delivery without a required public scale weight certificate).

F. Other Article 2 differences in formation

1. Consideration

    a. An agreement to modify the existing terms of a contract is unenforceable unless the modification is supported by consideration. You cannot get more money for what you are already contractually obligated to do.

    b. Under UCC (UCC 2-209)—"An agreement modifying a contract for the sale of goods needs no consideration to be binding." The modification may have to be in writing (evidenced by a record) if either the original contract or the modification places the contract under the Statute of Frauds. The modification must also be in good faith. That is, one side cannot threaten the other side to stop performing on the contract unless there is a modification. No one MUST agree to a modification to an existing contract. However, if they do agree to a modification under the UCC, the modification is enforceable despite the lack of new consideration.

Example:
ABC Gas Inc. has a requirement contract to furnish Green Industries with all the gas it needs to run its plants for 10 years at 50 cents per cubic foot of gas. Exploration and transportation costs will triple in the next three years and ABC is starting to lose money on the contract. The present market price is 80 cents per cubic foot. ABC and Green agree in writing to raise the price of the gas supplied to Green to 60 cents per cubic foot for the rest of the term of the contract. Even though no consideration is given by ABC for the increase in price, the 60 cents price is now binding on both parties.

2. Unconscionable contract or clause

    2. Unconscionable contract or clause— The UCC (UCC 2-302) follows the common law rule that any contract or clause that "hurts the conscience of society" is illegal, and either just the clause or the entire contract is unenforceable.

Example:
Some rent-to-own contracts result in the buyers paying seven times as much for a washer as what they would have paid if they had purchased the washer outright or on credit terms.

3. **Statute of Frauds**—Contracts for the sale of goods priced at $500 or more must be in writing to be enforceable (UCC 2-201) except:

   a. **Between-merchants (merchant's confirmation memorandum)**—If one merchant sends the other a written confirmation and the one receiving the confirmation, with knowledge of its contents, does not object in writing within 10 days of receipt of the confirmation, the oral contract is enforceable by either party. (See the "Statute of Frauds and Records" lesson for more examples and details.)

   Example:
   ABC is an auto parts store. ABC orders by phone $10,000 worth of parts from Auto Warehouse. Auto Warehouse immediately sends ABC a fax covering the contract made on the telephone. ABC receives the fax and reads it. Twelve days later, ABC learns it can buy all of the parts it ordered from another parts warehouse company for $9,500. ABC calls Auto Warehouse and tells Auto Warehouse not to ship the parts because it is claiming the Statute of Frauds as a defense. ABC and Auto Warehouse have an enforceable contract, even though it is an oral contract, for the sale of goods priced at $500 or more because both parties are merchants and Auto Warehouse sent by fax a written confirmation of the oral contract, which ABC read. Since ABC did not object to the contents of the written confirmation within 10 days of receipt, the oral contract is fully enforceable by Auto Warehouse.

   b. **Special ordered contracted goods**—Goods that a seller could not resell in his or her ordinary course of business are removed from the Statute of Frauds only if the seller has made a substantial beginning of manufacture or commitment for procurement to make the goods. (See the "Statute of Frauds and Records" lesson for more examples and details.)

   c. **Admission under oath**—If a party admits under oath (disposition, interrogatory, in pleadings, or on the "stand") the existence of the oral contract, that person cannot claim the Statute of Frauds as a defense.

   d. **Buyer's performance**—By either making a payment or taking possession of the goods, Buyer removes the Statute of Frauds as a defense, at least to the amount of goods covered by the payment or the goods possessed.

   Example:
   Green, owner of ABC Television, orally offers to sell Red a TV for $600. Later, Red calls Green and accepts Green's offer. Later yet, Red changes his mind and does not wish to buy the TV. Because Red has not signed a written contract for the sale of goods priced at $500 or more, and Red has neither taken possession of nor made a payment for the TV, Red can claim the Statute of Frauds, and Green cannot enforce the oral contract against Red.

   e. Article 2 permits a record of a contract to be pieced together from various memos, documents, and correspondence if the writings/records show that a contract was formed and the necessary terms are included.

Title and Risk of Loss

After studying this lesson you should be able to:

1. List and define all the terms used in shipping goods.

2. Describe when title passes from the seller to the buyer.

3. Explain why passage of title is a significant event in a sales-of-goods transactions.

4. Describe when risk of loss passes from the seller to the buyer.

5. Explain why passage of risk of loss is significant to both buyers and sellers.

6. Discuss the rights of third parties in title.

I. General Background on Title and Risk of Loss

A. Title and risk of loss under UCC Article 2 have very detailed and nuanced rules.

> **Misconception:**
> In the sale of goods, title and risk of loss always pass at the same time. This statement is incorrect because (1) the parties can expressly determine the exact moment when title and risk of loss pass and the two can differ; and (2) even in absence of agreement UCC Article 2 has rules that can have them pass at the same time in one situation and at different times in another situation.

> **Study Tip:**
> The exam nearly always has a question on title, risk of loss, or both. One reason is that many of the financial frauds during the 2000–2010 period involved issues in which title and risk of loss passed for purposes of financial reporting.

B. Passage of Title is found in **UCC 2-401** and passage of risk of loss in **UCC 2-509**.

II. Identification—A Prerequisite to Passage of Title and Risk of Loss

A. Before any interest in goods (title or risk of loss) can pass from a seller to a buyer, the goods must be in **existence** and **identified** to the contract—UCC 2-105(2).

B. **General rule on identification**—For goods in existence at the time the contract is entered into, identification occurs at the time the parties enter into the contract. If, for example, you are buying goods that have to be altered, they are not technically in existence at the time of the contract. A suit that you are having altered is not in existence at the time of the contracting. Once the goods are in existence, i.e., alterations for you have been completed, then title can pass because the goods are identified.

> **Study Tip:**
> The key in most CPA exams is whether identification has taken place because, in most cases, whether goods are in existence, is obvious. Some questions are tricky because they ask when risk or title has passed when the key to the question is knowing that the goods have not yet been identified.

C. **Fungible goods**—Fungible goods are those that either cannot be distinguished because of homogenous qualities or that are so mixed together that they cannot be distinguished by individual units, e.g., grains, fruit, cases of canned goods. Identification occurs when the goods are shipped, marked, or otherwise designated for the buyer, i.e., set aside in the warehouse. (See the lesson on "Remedies" to also understand how identification is important in determining the remedies available to buyer and seller in cases of manufactured and fungible goods.)

D. **Future goods**—For goods to be manufactured, such as when a company is manufacturing rocking chairs for a furniture store, identification occurs when those rocking chairs are shipped, marked, or otherwise designated for the buyer.

Example:
1. Green has 1,000 cases of peas in the warehouse and Beyer has contracted to purchase 100 cases. Since the goods are fungible, the 100 cases must be identified (marked or separated from the mass) before title or risk of loss can pass.

2. Green and Smith have deposited wheat in a silo. Green's deposit is 5,000 bushels and Smith's deposit is 10,000 bushels. Smith sells 2,000 bushels to Beyer. The wheat is fungible (mixture of like kind goods with intent to become tenant in common owners) and is identified under the contract when it is shipped, marked, or otherwise designated for Beyer. Until then the risk remains with the sellers, Green and Smith. If the wheat were destroyed, the loss would be prorated based on ownership (pro rata shares).

E. Once goods are in existence and identified, title and risk of loss can pass at the time the parties **expressly agree** or, if there is no agreement, they pass according to UCC Article 2 rules (covered in the following section).

III. **Delivery Terms**—How and when risk of loss and title pass depend upon the shipping/delivery terms in a contract.

A. **F.O.B.**—(free on board)—Place of shipment (seller's city, business, or warehouse, or "shippoint."). Title and risk of loss pass upon **delivery (possession) of conforming goods to the carrier**—UCC 2-319(1)(a), 2-509(1)(a).

> **Note:**
> *THIS IS A KEY ISSUE ON THE EXAM. First determine whether there are shipment terms in the language the exam provides for you, then determine risk of loss and title. Many questions in the past have focused on the distinction in passage of title and risk of loss in shipment vs. non-shipment contracts.*

Example:
Seller contracts to sell 100 personal laptop computers to Buyer at a given price with the FOB being the seller's warehouse via ABC Truck Lines. Until ABC Truck Lines picks up the 100 laptop computers, risk is on the seller. Once ABC Truck Lines has possession of the 100 laptop computers, the risk of loss is on the buyer.

B. **F.A.S**—(free alongside vessel)—Place of shipment. Title and risk of loss pass upon seller's delivery of conforming goods alongside the vessel in the manner usual in that port, or on a dock designated and provided by the buyer—UCC 2-319(2).

C. **C.I.F.**—(cost, insurance, freight)—Title and risk of loss pass from seller to buyer when the seller delivers (possession) identified conforming goods to the carrier, obtains a negotiable bill(s) of lading covering transportation to a named destination, procures an insurance policy, and forwards to buyer all documents—UCC 2-320(2)(a).

D. **C&F**—(cost and freight)—This follows the same rule as in C.I.F., except procurement of an insurance policy is not required on seller's part.

E. **COD**—(cash on delivery)—This term requires the buyer to pay cash upon tender of the goods. If goods are shipped COD, then the timing of the buyer's right to inspection is affected (see lesson on "Performance").

IV. **Passage of Title—REMEMBER:** When title passes is important for purposes of determining the rights of third parties with respect to the buyer and seller. For example, suppose that the IRS is about to levy a lien on the buyer's property. If the buyer has a contract that is FOB place of shipment and the goods are in transit, the IRS can seize the goods. If, however, the contract was FOB place of destination, title to the goods still rests with the seller during transit. The IRS cannot seize the goods from the seller's warehouse or from the carrier. Title does not pass until the goods are tendered at their destination.

A. Determine whether the contract is a delivery (shipment) or non-delivery (non-shipment) contract.

1. In the absence of an agreement, delivery is at the seller's place of business or, if the seller has none, at the seller's residence. In other words, without an agreement, no delivery is provided for under Article 2. (See lesson on "Application and Formation (AFTPDT Formula)" for more information on contract terms under Article 2.)

2. Passage of title occurs at different times depending on whether the contract is non-delivery or delivery.

> **Note:**
> *You must be sure that identification has occurred regardless of whether the contract is delivery or non-delivery. Without identification, title cannot pass.*

B. Passage of title in non-delivery (non-shipment) contracts

1. Determine whether there is a document of title involved with the goods and the contract. (See the lesson on "Article 7—Documents of Title" for more information.)

2. If there is no document of title, title passes at the moment the contract is made. Note that in nonshipment contracts for goods, identification and passage of title occur at the same time.

3. If there is a document of title, and the document of title is nonnegotiable, then title passes to buyer upon buyer's receipt of the document—UCC 2-401(3)(a).

4. If there is a document of title, and the document of title is negotiable, then title passes to the buyer upon the buyer's receipt of the document—UCC 2-401(3)(a), 2-509(2)(a).

C. Passage of title in delivery (shipment) contracts

1. If delivery is FOB place of shipment or FOB seller's place of business, warehouse, or residence, then title passes at the time and place of shipments or when the goods are delivered to the carrier.

2. If delivery FOB place of destination or FOB buyer's city, business, warehouse, or residence, then title passes upon the seller's tender of conforming goods at place of contract destination—UCC 2-509(1)(b).

a. Tender is the key—A proper tender is the seller's holding out to the buyer the goods in a reasonable manner, for a reasonable time, to allow the buyer to take possession of the goods—UCC 2-503(1). Tender means the goods have arrived, they are available for the buyer to pick up, and the buyer has been notified that the goods are there and available for pick-up.

See the following example.

> **Example:**
> Bradford, a buyer in Norfolk, owes $210,000 to the IRS. The IRS has obtained a lien that allows it to seize any real and personal property owned by Bradford. Sanford, a seller from Los Angeles has agreed to ship 100 cases of plastic travel bottles to Bradford. The shipment term is FOB Norfolk. The 100 cases of plastic travel bottles have arrived at the loading dock at Norfolk and Bradford's receiving department has been notified. The IRS seizes the 100 cases of travel bottles from the loading dock. Bradford objects on the grounds that the bottles still belong to Sanford, that title has not yet passed, and that the IRS could not seize the goods. Bradford is incorrect. The 100 cases had been tendered and title passed to Bradford. The IRS could seize the goods.
>
> Change the situation a bit to understand FOB place of shipment. Suppose that Sanford is the party subject to an IRS lien and Sanford is shipping the 100 cases to Bradford under an FOB Los Angeles contract. The IRS seizes the 100 cases at Norfolk. This time, Sanford objects, claiming it was too late for the IRS to seize the goods. Sanford is correct. Title passed to Bradford when the goods were delivered to the carrier in Los Angeles. The IRS could not seize the 100 cases as property belonging to Sanford because title had already passed.

D. Delivery "Ex-ship"—Title and risk of loss do not pass until the ship arrives at a port of destination and not until the goods leave the ship's "tackle" or are otherwise properly unloaded. This is the converse of a delivery F.A.S., previously described—UCC 2-322.

E. Deliver—If contract merely calls for the seller to deliver at the buyer's destination and there are no other delivery terms, title passes from the seller to the buyer upon tender of conforming goods at buyer's destination—UCC 2-509(1)(b).

V. Passage of Risk of Loss

A. Remember—the goods must be identified or risk of loss cannot pass.

B. Passage of risk of loss in non-delivery contracts

1. Determine whether the contract is a delivery or non-delivery contract. Unless the parties provide for shipment/delivery, there is no delivery provided under Article 2.

2. Determine whether the seller is a merchant or nonmerchant (the lessons in "Contracts: Formation and Acceptance" and "Article 2 Sales: Application and Formation" cover the definition of merchants).

   a. If seller is a merchant, risk of loss does not pass until buyer actually gets possession. For example, when you buy a sofa at The Room Store but agree to pick it up yourself, you do not assume the risk of loss until that sofa is in the back of your pick-up truck.

   b. If seller is a nonmerchant, risk of loss passes upon seller's tender of the goods to the buyer. If you buy a sofa at a garage sale and leave to go get your truck to pick it up, the risk of loss has already passed to you. If the sofa is destroyed while you are procuring your truck, you absorb the loss.

3. **REMEMBER**—In most cases the determination of risk of loss is important because it controls which of the parties' insurers will be responsible for reimbursement for the loss.

C. Passage of risk of loss when there is delivery (shipment contract)

1. If delivery is FOB place of shipment (or ship point) or FOB seller's place of business, warehouse, or residence, then the risk of loss passes at the time the goods are delivered to the carrier.

2. If the delivery is FOB place of destination, or FOB buyer's place of business, warehouse, or residence, then the risk of loss passes at the time of tender.

D. Passage of risk of loss when there is a negotiable document of title and no delivery. Risk of loss passes—to the buyer upon the buyer's receipt of the document—UCC 2-401(3)(a).

Example:
Able Corp. sells 500 boxes of copy paper to Green company. The 500 boxes were shipped to the Fox Warehouse Co. earlier and Fox issued to Able a negotiable warehouse receipt representing the 500 boxes. Able indorses and delivers the warehouse receipt to Green at 4:00pm on Friday. During the weekend, the warehouse burns down and the 500 boxes are completely destroyed. Green suffers the loss because risk of loss passed to Green upon Green's receipt of the negotiable document of title.

E. Passage of risk of loss when there is no delivery and a nonnegotiable document of title—Risk of loss passes to buyer after receipt of the document and buyer has had a reasonable time to present the document, to receive the goods, or to give directions to the bailee.

Example:
Able Corp. sells 500 boxes of copier paper to Green Company. The 500 boxes were shipped to the Fox Warehouse Co. earlier and Fox issued a nonnegotiable warehouse receipt representing the 500 boxes. The warehouse is only open Monday through Friday from 7:30 a.m. to 4:30 p.m. On Friday at 4:00 p.m., Able delivers the warehouse receipt to Green. Over the weekend, the Fox warehouse burns down and the 500 boxes are completely destroyed. Able suffers the loss because, although Green had title, risk of loss would not pass until Green has had a reasonable time to present the document to Fox, or to give directions to the bailee Fox. Most courts would hold that 30 minutes is not a reasonable length of time and the risk of loss over the weekend was still with Able.

F. Passage of risk of loss when the goods are held by a third party (bailee, warehouseman, someone other than the seller) and there is no document of title— Risk of loss passes to the buyer when the bailee acknowledges the buyer's right to the possession of the goods. The risk of loss, in effect, passes upon the equivalent of tender by the warehouseman.

> **Example:**
> Seller contracts to deliver 1,000 cases of beans to the buyer FOB buyer's warehouse. The beans are shipped by ABC Truck Lines. The truck arrives at buyer's warehouse at 1:00pm on Monday. Buyer cannot unload the truck until Tuesday morning and asks the carrier to leave the truck at the buyer's warehouse dock until it is unloaded in two hours on Tuesday morning. Carrier agrees. During the night, through no fault of the buyer, the beans are destroyed by fire. The risk of loss has passed to the buyer and the buyer must pay the seller for the beans. This is a destination delivery contract and the seller's tender by the carrier began at 1:00 p.m. on Monday. This was a holding out to the buyer in a reasonable manner and, certainly, if the truck could be unloaded in two hours, the load was held out (the entire afternoon) for a reasonable time to enable buyer to take possession. Risk passed to the buyer Monday afternoon.

G. Summary of rules on passage of title and risk of loss:

Delivery Situations	Delivery Terms	Law
Delivery by shipment	Ship, FOB origin or seller's place of business—FAS, CIF, C&F	Title and risk of loss pass to buyer upon carrier's **possession** of conforming goods
Delivery to destination	Deliver, FOB buyer's place of business—Delivery ex- ship	Title and risk of loss pass to buyer upon **tender** of conforming goods to the buyer
Delivery by seller without physical movement of the goods	Delivery without a document of title	Title passes to buyer upon **formation** of the **contract**. Risk of loss passes to the buyer (a.) upon the buyer's **receipt** of the goods if the seller is a merchant or (b.) upon the seller's **tender** of the goods if the seller is a nonmerchant.
	Delivery with a document of title—Nonnegotiable document	Title passes upon buyer's **receipt** of the document. Risk of loss passes to buyer after buyer receives the document **and a reasonable time has lapsed**.
	Delivery with a document of title—Negotiable document	Title **and** risk of loss pass upon buyer's **receipt** of the document

VI. Effect of Breach on the Passage of Title and Risk of Loss (Nonconforming goods)

A. If goods are nonconforming due to **seller's breach** and the buyer has a right to reject the goods, risk of loss does not pass to the buyer until the defects are cured or buyer accepts goods despite their nonconformity—UCC 2-510 (1). The buyer does not hold the risk of loss for nonconforming goods in his/her possession or for their return to the seller.

B. In addition, if the goods are accepted and acceptance is revoked, risk of loss goes back to the seller to the extent that the buyer's insurance did not cover the loss—UCC 2-510 (2).

C. If the **breach is due to fault of the buyer** and risk has not passed, risk shifts immediately to the buyer for a commercially reasonable period after seller learns of the breach, but only to the extent not covered by seller's insurance—UCC 2-510 (3).

D. Breach affects risk of loss, but not title. Title passes according to the rules DESPITE the breach.

VII. Special Issues in Title and Risk of Loss

A. **Sale on approval**—Until the buyer accepts the goods, **title and risk of loss remain with seller**. Cost of proper return (rejection of offer) falls on the seller—UCC 2-327 (1). Buyer can accept by:

1. Due notification ("I accept") .

2. Failure to reject within the time of trial period (keeps goods beyond trial period).

3. Does any act inconsistent with seller's ownership. (Buyer takes home lawn mower to try it out for two weeks. During the two weeks buyer mows 15 yards for fees.)

B. **Sale or return**—An actual sale with title, risk of loss, and possession with the buyer subject to the condition that buyer can restore title and risk upon the seller by a proper return of the goods. Cost of return is on the buyer. Failure to timely return finalizes the sale—UCC 2-327(2). The UCC treats a consignment as a sale or return.

VIII. Third-Party Rights and Title

A. Article 2 has special provisions to deal with situations in which a third party is affected by title issues related to the conduct of the original parties to the contract, that is, there is some problem with perfect title as it relates to a third party.

B. The problems results from there being an innocent third party known as a bona fide purchaser (BFP) for value, defined by Karl Llwelyn (the main author of the UCC) as "a pure heart and an empty head." In third-party right issues, who has the best title—the original owner or the BFP?

C. **Rights of a BFP when void title has been transferred**—A void title cannot be passed to anyone. The original owner has the best title—UCC 2-403 (1).

 Example:
Thomas, a thief, steals your bicycle and sells it to Smith. Smith has no knowledge that Thomas is not the owner or that the bike has been stolen. You discover Smith has the bike. You are entitled to return of your bicycle from Smith because Thomas had a void title (no title) to pass to Smith. Smith, however, can legally recover from Thomas if Smith can find Thomas.

D. **Rights of a BFP when there is a voidable title**—A title, that even though passed to a buyer, can be recovered. There is one exception—if the buyer in turn passes title to a BFP— UCC 2-403(1).

 Example:
Mary is a minor who contracts to sell her bicycle to an adult, Jim, for $250. Mary transfers the bicycle and title to Jim. Since Mary is a minor, Jim receives a voidable title and Mary can disaffirm the sale and recover her bicycle. If Jim sells the bicycle to Judy (a BFP for value) before Mary disaffirms the sale, Mary can still disaffirm the contract with Jim but cannot recover the bicycle from Judy. Judy's title is absolute and cuts off Mary's voidable title.

IX. Rights of a BFP with Entrusting of Goods

A. Entrusting of goods to a **merchant** (person who deals in goods of that kind) by a buyer gives the merchant the power to transfer all rights (including title) to a buyer in the ordinary course of business—UCC 2-403(2)(3).

> **Example:**
> Harry took his TV set to ABC TV Inc. for repairs. ABC sells both used and new TVs. The set is repaired but, by mistake, is sold to a customer of ABC without knowledge of Harry's ownership rights. Since ABC is a merchant (in the business of selling used TVs), ABC passed good title to Harry's set to the customer and Harry cannot recover the set from the customer. ABC has committed a tort of conversion, however, and is liable to Harry in a civil suit.

B. When entrusting goods to a **nonmerchant**, delivery is a mere bailment. Unless the original owner has given some indicia of ownership to the bailee to lead a buyer to believe that the bailee either is the owner or has authority to sell, there can be no passage of title (treat as a void title).

Terms—Warranties and Products Liability

After studying this lesson you should be able to:

1. Describe if and how each of the warranties can be disclaimed.

2. Explain product liability requirements under tort law, including both strict tort liability as well as negligence.

3. List and give examples of the express and implied warranties that exist under UCC Article 2.

I. **Products Liability Consists of Warranty Terms under the UCC and Tort Liability**

   A. You are studying terms under the AFTPDT (Application, Formation, Terms, Performance, and Damages) outline for Article 2. The warranty terms are a critical part of contract terms under contracts for the sale of goods. These warranty terms provide contract protections for defective products and are a form of product liability.

   B. In addition to the contract protections for product liability, tort law provides some rights and remedies for defective products. Referred to as strict tort liability, the remedies under tort law protect more people, allow for greater damage recovery, and are less stringent in requirements for recovery than under the UCC.

   C. **Caveat Emptor**— Prior to the Article 2 warranties and strict tort liability, a policy of *Caveat Emptor* or "Let the buyer beware" was followed.

      1. Article 2 warranties moved this public policy to one of seller responsibility.

      2. Strict tort liability moved the buyer protection to a point of shifting almost all responsibility for defective products to sellers, even when they were not aware of defects in their products.

II. **Warranty Product Liability Protection under Article 2**—There are **four types** of warranties that can exist in a contract for the sale of goods under Article 2.

   A. **Express warranties—UCC 2-313**

      1. **Affirmations of fact or promises of performance**—"This suit is 100% wool," or "this pump will not overheat even with continuous use." Sales puffing is not an affirmation of fact or promise of performance, e.g., "This is the best suit money can buy." Review the "Defenses to Formation" lesson for more discussion and examples of statements of fact and promises of performance to understand the type of language that constitutes an express warranty.

         a. Statements of value or opinion (seller huffing and puffing) are not express warranties.

      2. **A description of the goods under an Article 2 contract is an express warranty**—In a contract with a buyer for a camel's hair coat, the seller must deliver a camel's hair coat.

      3. **Samples or models are express warranties under Article 2**—Bulk or finished product must conform exactly to sample or model.

      4. The statement of fact, the promise of performance, the description, or the sample or model must be what is known as a basis of bargain or sale—UCC 2-313(1), which means that the express warranty, given in any of the forms discussed, was something that was important to the buyer in making the decision to purchase the goods.

      5. **Nature of Express Warranties**

         a. Can be oral or written

         b. Can be in **brochures, advertisements,** etc. of seller

         c. Can be created without using words like warranty or guaranty

         d. Can be given by merchants and nonmerchants alike

6. **Disclaimer of express warranties**—For purposes of the exam, it is impossible to disclaim a written express warranty. A seller cannot put samples, models, or descriptions and promises out there to attract buyers and then revoke those warranties. Disclaimer of oral express warranties must be specific, unambiguous, and clearly and conspicuously called to the attention of the buyer. Oral express warranties must be consistent with written express warranties—UCC 2-316 (1).

   a. Definition of conspicuous: type is larger, type is in a different color, disclaimer is not buried in any written document but it called out for the buyer to see.

B. **Implied warranty of title—UCC 2-312**

1. An implied warranty of title is given in every sale of goods by merchants and nonmerchants unless it is disclaimed or the buyer knows that no warranty of title is being given. For example, purchasing goods at a pawnshop is a situation in which there is no expectation of a warranty of title.

2. **Content of warranty**

   a. Seller has a **good title** and its transfer is rightful.

   b. No outstanding liens, encumbrances, or security interests against the goods are hidden from the buyer.

   c. If **seller is a merchant,** the goods shall be delivered **free from third-party infringement** (patent/copyright, etc.) claims.

3. **Disclaimer of warranty of title—UCC 2-312(2)**

   a. Can be accomplished by specific language or buyer's knowledge of title problems. The language must include a reference to the warranty of title. Any general disclaimers of warranties do not disclaim the warranty of title. See discussion below of implied warranty disclaimers.

   b. Can also be disclaimed if the buyer purchased the goods under circumstances where he or she should have been aware there would be no warranty of title (purchasing designer goods from the trunk of a car).

Example:
A sales contract states "Seller conveys only such title as he or she has." This would effectively disclaim the implied warranty of title. A statement that "seller disclaims all warranties" would not be a sufficient disclaimer of title.

C. **Implied warranty of merchantability—UCC 2-314**

1. This warranty can only be made by a merchant.

Example:
Able purchases a ham from ABC Meat Market. Unknown to Able or ABC Meat Market, the ham is tainted and Able becomes seriously ill after eating it. Able can recover from ABC Meat Market because it is a merchant seller and the ham was not fit for human consumption (ordinary use) and not of the proper quality.

4. To specifically disclaim the Implied Warranty of Merchantability:

   a. Must mention word merchantability

   b. Can be oral or in writing; if in writing, must be conspicuous—UCC 2-316(2).

D. **Implied warranty of fitness for a particular purpose**—UCC 2-315

1. To create this type of warranty, **two** criteria are needed:

   a. The seller must expressly or by implication know the purpose or buyer's use of the goods *and*

b. The buyer must rely on the seller's selection or recommendation in making the purchase.

2. This warranty is sometimes referred to as the salesperson's warranty because the warranty results when salespersons make recommendations to buyers about the type of product/good they should use for their described needs.

Example:
Beyer tells Sallor he needs a water pump that will pump 100 gallons a minute of muddy water out of a mine shaft. Sallor tells Beyer the company has the ideal pump, its Z model. Beyer purchases the pump and, although the pump is not defective and runs to its full capacity, it can only pump 75 gallons per minute. Beyer can hold Sallor liable for breach of the implied warranty for a particular purpose because Beyer made Sallor aware of his needs and Beyer purchased in reliance of Sallor's recommendation that Z model would fulfill Beyer's needs.

3. Disclaimer of implied warranties of fitness for a particular purpose

a. Must be in writing and must be conspicuous.

Example:
1. "THERE ARE NO WARRANTIES THAT EXTEND BEYOND THE DESCRIPTION ON THE FACE HEREOF."—UCC 2-316(2)

2. Green Inc. contracts to sell Able Industries a piece of equipment. In the contract, the following clause is in bold type:

"THERE ARE NO IMPLIED WARRANTIES OF FITNESS FOR A PARTICULAR PURPOSE OR MERCHANTABILITY THAT ACCOMPANY THIS SALE."

This clause disclaims both implied warranties because it is in writing, conspicuous, and mentions the word merchantability.

b. General disclaimer words—Both the implied warranty of merchantability and implied warranty of fitness for a particular purpose can be disclaimed by words such as:

i. "Sold as is"

ii. "Sold with all faults"

iii. "As they stand"

iv. Other language, which is called to the buyer's attention and makes plain that there is no implied warranty—UCC 2-316(3)(a).

c. Other ways to disclaim warranties

i. Disclaimer by custom or usage—In certain industries, it is a long established custom that sales do not carry implied warranties. For example, in a few states sales of used goods carry no implied warranties.

ii. Disclaimer by examination

1. If the buyer actually examines the goods prior to the sale, the buyer is bound for all defects found (patent or obvious, and latent or hidden), and all defects buyer should have found (patent).

2. If seller offers buyer the opportunity to examine the goods and the buyer refuses to do so, the buyer is bound by all defects he or she should have found (patent defects) if buyer had examined the goods.

> **Note:**
> **Misconception:** *The terms of a sale "as is" disclaims all express warranties and the implied warranty of title. This is incorrect. Only the implied warranties of merchantability and fitness for a particular purpose are disclaimed in an "as is" sale.*

E. Strict tort liability

   1. Why strict tort liability?—Limitations of Article 2 warranty protections

   a. The privity issue—(not being a party to the sales contract)—Article 2—UCC 2-318 does not require privity (direct contract relationship) as a precondition for recovering under a breach of warranty. For example, you buy a truck from a car dealer and have privity of contract with the dealer, but you do not have privity of contract with the truck manufacturer. Still, if the truck fails to meet the requirements for the warranty of merchantability, you have breach of warranty claims against both the dealership and the manufacturer.

   b. UCC 2-318 extends, in most states, warranty protection, despite lack of privity to, third parties who could be expected to use or consume the product.

Example:
You invite a friend to dinner and to afterward watch a sporting contest on TV. You purchase a frozen turkey for the dinner and cook the turkey without negligence or knowledge that the turkey is tainted. Your friend becomes ill from eating the turkey. Under early common law, your friend could not recover from the store or the turkey processor under contract law (breach of warranty) because your friend was not a party to the purchase contract. Today, your friend can file an action against either or both because privity is no longer required under Article 2 warranty protections. If you became ill you can also recover because you obviously are in privity to the store (breach of implied warranty of merchantability) and lack of privity does not eliminate the processor's liability.

   2. Strict tort liability requirements

   a. The product is in a defective condition that makes it unreasonably dangerous.

      i. Defective in its design—the slats in baby cribs had to be changed to be narrower than previous slats because of infants getting stuck in between the slats and choking.

      ii. Defective in its manufacture—for example, a car manufacturer fails to install several bolts on the car chassis and the result is an accident that injures the buyer of the car.

      iii. Defective in the lack of warnings—for example, the seller fails to warn that oven cleaner should be used in well ventilated areas and buyer is overcome by fumes from the spray.

   b. The seller is in the business of selling and/or manufacturing the defective product.

   c. The product has reached the buyer in the same condition it was in when it left the manufacturer, i.e., the product has not been tampered with or altered. For example, if a box of cereal has been opened and in your home for a time, the cereal manufacturer is not liable for foreign matter found in the cereal that makes you ill because there is no way to know if the cereal left the manufacturer with the foreign matter or if it got into the cereal after it was opened.

   3. Negligence basis for product liability

   a. Negligent product liability has the same elements as those for strict tort liability (2.a, b, and c mentioned above).

   b. It also includes the fourth element of knowledge—the seller or manufacturer was aware of the defect in the product.

   c. The distinction is that knowledge of the defect allows for recovery of punitive damages.

Performance

After studying this lesson you should be able to:

1. Define anticipatory repudiation and explain the rights of buyer and seller when this occurs.

2. Explain what perfect tender is and list the buyer's option when the goods do not meet the perfect tender standard.

3. Explain when the seller has the right to cure and what the seller must do to "cure."

4. List the steps the parties to a contract can take if the other party is not performing according to the contract terms.

5. Describe what the seller must do to complete performance.

6. Describe when performance under a sales contract is either excused or completed.

I. **Overview**—In the AFTPDT (Application, Formation, Terms, Performance, Damages, and Title) study model, performance covers the rights of buyers and sellers after the contract has been formed. When is performance due? What if it looks like performance may be unlikely? What is performance? What are steps that buyers and sellers can take to encourage performance?

II. **Problems between the Time of Contracting and Actual Delivery**

A. At times, there are problems that arise between the time the parties have their contractual obligations related to purchase and sale of goods and the actual delivery of the goods (performance of the contract). Article 2 has specific rights and steps for the parties during this interim period.

B. **Heading off nonperformance with assurances**—The goal of Article 2 is to have the parties do all that is possible to get the contract performance completed. To do that, both buyers and sellers have the right of assurance and the duty of cooperation.

   1. **Right of assurance**—If a party has "reasonable grounds" to believe that the other party will not perform as contracted, he or she may demand in writing that the other party give adequate assurance of due performance—UCC 2-609. If the party does not provide reasonable assurance as demanded within 30 days, this failure is a repudiation of the contract and can be treated as an anticipatory breach.

      a. Once a party is entitled to and demands reasonable assurance, that party can suspend performance without liability until he or she receives the assurance requested.

      b. Reasonable grounds for insecurity depend on the facts. Between-merchants commercial standards may be used.

      c. The actions of assurance that can be requested also depend on the facts, and, again, between-merchants commercial standards can be used.

      See the following example.

Example:
Smith Inc. has contracted to buy a specific piece of equipment from ABC. Smith believes that if it runs this piece of equipment at a certain speed it will increase Smith's productivity by 5%. Smith learns from another buyer (Green) who has previously purchased a similar piece of equipment from ABC, that, although Green seldom ran the equipment at that speed, whenever Green did the equipment broke down. ABC's literature had indicated the equipment could be run at a variety of speeds including the speed Smith anticipated running the equipment.

Question:
Is Green's experience sufficient (reasonable) grounds for Smith to believe that ABC's equipment will not perform as contracted?

Answer:
Most probably, yes.

Question:
What can Smith do before the equipment is delivered?

Answer:
In writing, ask for reasonable assurances that the equipment will perform as contracted and for protection if it does not.

Question:
What are reasonable requests for assurance that Smith could seek?

Answer:
Smith could ask for express warranties, money-back guaranty, or, perhaps, even replacement equipment if such is available. The point is that ABC must satisfy Smith's insecurity, as long as it is reasonable.

Example:
Smith has two contracts with ABC. One is to sell ABC 100 washing machines with delivery on May 1 with ABC's payment to be made on or before June 1. The second is to sell ABC 100 dryers with delivery on July 1 with ABC's payment to be made on or before August 1. The washers are timely delivered and accepted by ABC. On June 15, Smith still has not been paid despite two phone calls requesting payment. Smith has reasonable grounds to ask for some assurance for payment of the dryers to be delivered on July 1. Smith, in writing, can demand reasonable assurance (perhaps the washing machine payment plus some other dryer payment, such as cash on delivery). Pending ABC's assurance, Smith can suspend the delivery of the dryers without liability and, if assurance is not forthcoming within 30 days, treat the dryer contract (washer contract already breached) as breached.

C. **When assurances fail: Rights of parties in nonperformance—Goods not delivered**

1. **Anticipatory repudiation or breach in advance of contract performance date**—This type of nonperformance occurs when either the seller or the buyer repudiates the contract prior to the required contract date of performance. Key is whether there is repudiation—UCC 2-610.

2. Upon anticipatory breach, the non-breaching party can:

   a. Await performance for a commercially reasonable period *or*

   b. Treat the breach as final and resort to remedies *and*

   c. Suspend their own performance without liability for breach

3. Unless the non-breaching party has "canceled" (given notice of breach and intent to pursue remedies), materially changed their position based on the breach, or given notice that the anticipatory breach is considered "final," the breaching party can retract (by any method or notice) his or her repudiation, which restores the parties back to their original obligation—UCC 2-611.

Example:
1. A seller and buyer have a contract with the seller to deliver 200 Fun CDs on or before May 1. On April 15, the seller sends a fax to the buyer stating that the seller cannot deliver by May 1, but would do so on May 15. The seller requests the buyer

to agree to the May 15 delivery date by return fax. If the buyer sends the fax agreeing to the May 15 delivery date, there is no breach and the contract has been modified (without consideration). If the buyer does not consent to the May 15 delivery date, the buyer can treat the repudiation (cannot delivery by May 1) as a material breach and pursue remedies. If the buyer does not consent to the May 15 date and merely states that the buyer expects the seller to deliver on time or be held in breach if not delivered by May 1, the seller can (with notice) retract its repudiation. This restores the parties back to the May 1st delivery date.

2. Great Falls School District School Board has decided to put computers in all the classrooms in four of its 10 high schools. Great Falls contracts with ABC Computer Inc. for the sale of these computers with delivery to be made by August 1 at the four schools to be designated later by the school board. It will take ABC four days from the date of shipment to deliver the computers. The contract has the school board's address on it. Because of various PTA oppositions, the school board has not designated the four schools for ABC delivery as of July 26.

Question:
What are ABC's options due to the school board's failure to cooperate?

Answer:
ABC could suspend making any shipment and, at ABC's option, hold the school board in breach and pursue remedies, or ABC could deliver all the computers to the school board's address and then, if not paid, sue for the purchase price.

III. Delivery of Goods, Determining Performance, and Buyer's Responsibilities Upon Delivery

A. **Inspection**—Upon delivery of the goods, the buyer has the right of inspection.

1. Unless agreed to the contrary or provided under Article 2 (i.e., a C.O.D. shipment does not allow buyers the right of inspection before payment), a buyer has a right, before paying for the goods, to inspect the goods at any reasonable time, place, or manner—UCC2-513.

2. Inspection need not be immediate. The buyer may receive the goods on a busy Friday afternoon and is not required to inspect them at that time—the buyer would have a reasonable time (at least through Monday) to conduct the inspection.

3. Inspection allows the buyer to open boxes, examine goods, and even conduct tests to see if the goods meet the buyer's needs that were specified in the contract.

B. **Right of rejection**

1. Under Article 2, the seller has an obligation to deliver goods that conform to the contract specifications. This requirement is sometimes called "the perfect tender rule."

2. If the seller delivers goods that fall short of the contract requirements in any way (the shortfall need not be material because the perfect tender rule requires 100% compliance with the contract terms, including the correct goods, the correct color, and the correct amount) then the buyer has the following options:

   a. Reject the entire shipment

   b. Accept the entire shipment

   c. Accept any commercial unit and reject the rest. A commercial unit is determined by industry practices and custom for the particular good involved in the contract. For example, candy is often shipped in bags of one gross—144 pieces. The buyer would reject a shipment of candy by the bag, not by individual pieces of candy. The purpose of rejection in commercial unit is to reduce confusion with partial packages and the breaking up of units.

Example:
Seller's contract calls for delivery of 100 cases of carrots. Seller tenders to the buyer 200 cases of carrots, a nonconforming goods tender. The buyer could reject the entire 200 cases, accept the 200 cases paying for the additional 100 cases, or accept 100 cases and reject the other 100 cases.

3. For information on the seller's obligations for delivery and proper contract for carriage, refer to the lesson on "Title and Risk of Loss."

C. **Buyer's responsibilities for rejection of nonconforming goods—UCC 2-601**

1. To reject and pursue remedies, the purchaser must do so properly:

   a. Rejection must be within a reasonable time after tender of or delivery—UCC 2-602.

   b. Rejection is not effective until known by seller—UCC 2-602.

   c. Specific reasons for rejection should be given. If not given, buyer cannot pursue remedies if seller could have cured, or if seller made a request in writing for a written statement of reasons—UCC 2-605.

   d. If buyer has possession of the nonconforming goods, the buyer must act as a bailee (use reasonable care over the goods)—UCC 2-602, and if buyer is a merchant, the buyer must follow any seller's reasonable instructions at seller's cost (buyer's reimbursement) concerning the disposition of the nonconforming goods—UCC 2-603.

   e. If the goods are perishable or threaten to rapidly decline in value, buyer must make a reasonable effort to sell, and he or she is entitled to reimbursement for all costs in caring for and selling the goods, plus a 10% sales commission, out of the proceeds of the sale—UCC 2-603.

   f. If seller does not give buyer instructions (and the goods are not perishable or rapidly declining in value), the buyer can store the goods for seller's account (storage charge), reship back at seller's expense, or sell the goods deducting costs and sales commission from the proceeds—UCC 2-604.

D. **Seller's rights upon rejection**

1. The reason that the buyer is required to follow certain steps in rejecting goods is because Article 2 provides sellers with the opportunity to fix or "cure" the problems that the buyer has found upon inspection of the goods.

2. **Fixing nonperformance—right to cure**—A seller who tenders nonconforming goods may still have the ability to cure and not be in breach of contract. Sometimes there is a casualty, partially or completely, to identified goods, or the seller is able to perform once the seller is made aware of the error.

   a. **Cure—UCC 2-508**

      i. If a seller tenders delivery of nonconforming goods prior to the contract date, and buyer rejects the goods, the seller can, with notice, indicate an intent to cure (i.e., fix whatever problem the buyer has pointed out as the reason for rejection). The seller always has until the time that contract performance is due to get conforming goods to the buyer who has rejected the initial delivery.

      See the following example.

Example:
Contract terms call for the seller to delivery on or before June 1 100 model Z washing machines. On May 16, the seller tenders 100 model A washing machines and the buyer rejects the shipment. The buyer sends the seller a fax stating that the seller made an error and the nonconforming shipment has been rejected. The seller immediately sends the buyer a fax apologizing for the error and tells the buyer that a corrected shipment will be made in two days. The seller has now shown an intent to cure and if the washing machines are delivered before June 1, the seller is not liable for breach of contract.

    ii. Sometimes the seller tenders nonconforming goods to the buyer but it is a tender that a reasonable buyer would be expected to accept (does not require a money allowance, but frequently this is the case). If the buyer rejects the reasonable tender, the seller, with notice of intent to cure, can tender conforming goods to the buyer within a reasonable period (even if after the contracted date of delivery) without being in breach.

Example:
Contract terms call for seller's delivery of 100 model Z tape recorders at $800 per unit on or before June 1. On May 25th, seller discovers that, due to a computer error, seller does not have 100 model Z tape recorders in stock but does have model A tape recorders, which sell for $950 per unit. On May 29, sellers tenders 100 model A tape recorders but only invoices buyer at $825 per unit price. Because of budget limitations, buyer rejects the model A tape recorders. If the seller notifies buyer that a corrected shipment will be made and such is tendered within a reasonable time (even after June 1), seller has made a cure of the contract delivery, is not in breach, and buyer must accept and pay for the goods.

    b. Substituted performance—UCC 2-614(1)

        i. If, without fault of the seller, the agreed facilities or type of contract carrier is not available or delivery is impractical but a commercially reasonable substitute carrier is available, seller must use substitute carrier and buyer must accept delivery and pay. (Usually, any additional costs incurred by buyer must be borne by the seller.)

Example:
Contract terms call for shipment via ABC Truck Lines. ABC Truck employees are on strike and no other drivers will cross the picket line. If XYZ Railroad is available and a reasonable substitute, seller must ship by this rail carrier and such shipment is not a breach of contract.

IV. When Does Acceptance of Performance Occur? Buyer's Acceptance

  A. Once buyer accepts, the buyer loses right to reject (and certain remedies). However, the buyer then steps into the Article 2 rights of revocation of acceptance (discussed below) and acceptance of nonconforming goods with proper notice to the seller does not preclude all remedies.

  B. Acceptance occurs under UCC 2-606 when any of the following have occurred:

> **Note:**
> *Revocation of acceptance is a different remedy from rejection. Loss of the right of rejection does not also waive the right of revocation of acceptance.*

    1. After opportunity to inspect the goods the buyer either notifies the seller that the goods are conforming or that the buyer will accept even if nonconforming goods. Payment for the goods in and of itself is not acceptance;

    2. If the buyer fails to reject the goods after inspection or after a reasonable opportunity to do so;

3. The buyer engages in any act that is inconsistent with seller's ownership (such as knowingly using nonconforming goods).

C. **When can a buyer revoke acceptance?**

1. Under the following conditions, a buyer can revoke his or her previous acceptance—UCC2-608:

   a. Buyer was given reasonable assurance seller would cure a nonconforming shipment, and cure has not taken place.

Example:
A buyer orders 100 barrels of Brand 52 cleaning solvent. The seller delivers Brand 50 cleaning solvent, a weaker but still usable solvent. The seller tells the buyer to use what it can of the Brand 50 solvent, and an immediate corrected Brand 52 shipment (cure) will be made. The buyer's use of the Brand 50 cleaning solvent is technically an acceptance. If, however, the seller does not immediately deliver the corrected Brand 52 solvent, the buyer can revoke his or her acceptance and hold the seller liable for breach (same as if the original nonconforming shipment had been rejected).

   b. Seller has assured buyer that goods are conforming, and it is later discovered the goods are nonconforming.

Example:
A buyer orders 20 cardboard boxes of red pens. Each cardboard box has 100 small boxes with a dozen pens in each. The cardboard boxes arrive with the words "Green Pens" on each cardboard box. Without opening the boxes, the buyer calls the seller and tells the seller of the "Green Pen" notation. The seller assures the buyer that the labeling is a mistake and inside the cardboard boxes are red pens. The buyer stores the cardboard boxes and pays the seller for the pens. When the buyer opens the cardboard boxes six months later, the buyer discovers that there are, in fact, only green pens inside, not the red pens that the seller had assured the buyer. In this case, the buyer can revoke the acceptance.

   c. **The nonconformity was difficult to detect.**

Example:
Buyer purchases a back-up generator. Buyer has no facility to test the generator and stores it. Six months later, the present generator malfunctions and when the back-up generator is placed into service buyer discovers it is defective. Buyer can revoke its earlier acceptance of the generator.

2. **Revocation timing**—Revocation must take place within a reasonable time of discovery or time in which the buyer should have discovered the defect, and revocation is not effective until the seller has notice of it.

Article 2 Remedies

After studying this lesson you should be able to:

1. List and describe the remedies available for the seller.

2. Explain when the seller has the right to reclaim goods from a carrier or the buyer.

3. List and describe the remedies available for the buyer.

4. Describe when buyer can pursue remedies.

5. List the types of buyer's remedies.

6. Explain when each remedy is appropriate.

I. **Overview**—If one of the parties to an Article 2 sales contract does not meet the standards of performance, then sections of Article 2 provide for remedies for both buyers and sellers.

II. **Seller's Remedies**

A. **Remedies for sellers who still have the goods under the contract**—The seller still has possession of the goods.

1. **Identify goods to the contract**—The seller can set aside the goods for the contract. If the seller is still in the process of manufacturing the goods when the buyer repudiates the contract or fails to respond to assurances, the seller can proceed to complete the manufacturing and resell the finished product rather than sell the unfinished goods as scrap (UCC 2-704). The seller can then proceed with the other remedies discussed below.

2. **Withhold delivery**—If the buyer has repudiated the contract, failed to provide assurances, or if the buyer is insolvent, the seller can demand full payment in cash and withhold delivery if the assurances or payment are not given—UCC 2-702, 2-703(a). The seller can then proceed with the other remedies discussed below.

3. **Cancel and/or rescind contract**—If the buyer is not performing or has failed to provide assurances, the seller can cancel or rescind the contract. The seller must notify buyer of cancellation promptly and either proceed with remedies below, or, if rescission is chosen, seller is entitled to be indemnified to return to the original position before the contract was made—UCC 2-703(f).

   Note:
   Important: *Any profit goes to seller, but if there is a deficiency (proceeds of sale do not cover breach and sales costs plus contract price) seller is entitled to the amount not obtained through sale, (i.e., obtain a deficiency judgment against the buyer)—UCC 2-706.*

4. **Resell goods**

   a. The sale must be conducted in a reasonably commercial manner (public or private sale).

   b. The seller must always give the buyer notice of private and public sale (except for perishable or rapidly declining value goods).

   c. The sale must be conducted at a reasonable time and place.

5. **Sue for breach of contract**—Used mostly if breach takes place before delivery or buyer improperly rejects goods.

   a. **Measure of damages is difference between market price at time and place of tender and the unpaid contract price plus incidental (costs of breach) damages—UCC 2-708.**

6. **Retain buyer's deposit**—Where the seller justifiably withholds delivery of goods and the buyer has made a deposit or payment and there is no liquidated damage clause, the seller may keep $500 or 20% of the purchase price, whichever is less. (NOTE: The exam has tested on this concept.)

B. **Remedies for seller if the goods are in transit**—Neither seller nor buyer has possession—UCC 2-705.

1. **If buyer is insolvent**—(not paying debts when due or in ordinary course of business, or insolvent under the Bankruptcy Act) the seller (upon buyer's repudiation) can stop any quantity shipped and can also recover goods from the buyer within 10 days after delivery. In addition, if the buyer misrepresents solvency within 90 days prior to delivery of goods on credit, there are no time limits on the seller's ability to recover the goods. Note that the rights for the seller to reclaim the goods when there is insolvency continue through delivery to the buyer (with the time limitations noted for insolvency events).

Example:
Stratford sold 300 flat-screen TVs to Kelvinator Appliance on a line of credit. There were rumors around the retail appliance industry that Kelvinator was struggling financially. Stratford demanded assurances from Kelvinator that it would be able to pay for the TVs. Kelvinator sent an audited financial statement to Stratford on September 1 that indicated Kelvinator was in good financial condition and had a steady cash flow. Stratford shipped the 300 TVs to Kelvinator on October 1. While the TVs were in transit, Kelvinator filed for bankruptcy (on October 14). Stratford would occupy a position of priority above Kelvinator's secured creditors because of the misrepresentation of solvency, even though the goods would be reclaimed after 10 days. There is no time limit on a seller's right to reclaim the goods when there is a misrepresentation of solvency.

NOTE: This detailed concept has been tested on the exam a number of times. See the lesson on "Distribution of Debtor's Estate" for further illustrations of this priority of sellers.

2. **If the buyer is not insolvent**—the seller can stop large shipments (carloads, truckloads, planeloads of goods). While we allow sellers to stop any size shipment for insolvency (to prevent having the seller lose the goods when there can be no payment), we only allow stoppage of large shipments for other reasons because large shipments are easier to track and stop. Stopping any size shipment for any reason would result in a slowing of commerce.

Example:
Contract calls for seller's delivery of five cases of peas to buyer's place of business. The five cases are loaded on ABC Truck carrier's truck. The truck is also hauling five other seller's products. Buyer repudiates the contract claiming that seller's peas are of poor quality. Seller cannot stop the goods in transit because buyer's repudiation is not due to insolvency and the shipment (five cases) is not a truckload.

3. Seller can **stop shipment** at any time (under the insolvency and repudiation rules just discussed). Until buyer actually takes possession of the goods, there is a negotiation to buyer of a negotiable document of title, (see the "Definition, Forms, Negotiation, and Rights" lesson in the Article 7 Documents of Title unit) or notification by a third party such as a warehouseman or carrier (see the lesson on "Title and Risk of Loss" for more information) to the buyer that the goods are available for pick-up.

C. **Remedies for seller if the buyer has possession**

1. If buyer received the goods on credit while insolvent, seller may reclaim the goods within 10 days of receipt by buyer. Remember, if there has been misrepresentation of insolvency, then the 10-day time limitation does not apply.

2. Seller can seek to recover damages noted—the compensatory damages of the contract purchase price plus any incidental damages incurred because of the buyer's failure to pay.

III. Buyer's Remedies

A. Remedies when the seller fails to deliver the goods

1. **Cancel and rescind with notice**—The contract is rescinded by the buyer with the effect of restoring both buyer and seller back to the positions they would have been before entering the contract—UCC 2-711.

2. **Cover**—Permits the buyer to make a reasonable substitute purchase (e.g., on the open market) in good faith and within reasonable time. The buyer can then recover the difference between the cost of cover and the contract price plus incidental damages (costs of breach) and consequential damages (foreseeable loss) less expenses saved in consequence of the seller's breach—UCC 2-712. (See the "Performance and Remedies" lesson in the Contracts unit for discussion of incidental and consequential damages.)

3. **Sue for breach of contract**—The buyer can treat the nondelivery as a breach of contract and pursue a lawsuit to recover damages. The damages can include the difference between the market price at the time that the buyer learned of the breach (this time is changed to place of tender if goods are rejected or time of revocation of acceptance and at place of arrival) and contract price plus incidental and consequential damages—UCC 2-713.

4. **Specific performance**—Available when the goods are unique, or in other proper circumstances such as where the remedy to cover is not available (e.g., rare goods; antiques). Specific performance is available for land under common law, but is rare under Article 2 UCC. Rarely will specific performance be granted where damages are appropriate as a remedy—UCC 2-716.

Example:
Seller agrees to sell to buyer an original painting by Picasso. Later, seller refuses to deliver the painting even though buyer has tendered fully the contract price. Buyer can in a court in equity file an action for specific performance (painting is unique—one of a kind) requiring the seller to transfer the painting to buyer.

---

5. **Replevin**—If seller refuses to tender delivery of identified goods to the buyer, and the buyer cannot cover, the buyer can file a suit in equity requiring the seller to deliver the goods to the buyer—UCC 2-716(3). Replevin is also rare and would occur in those types of contracts where cover is not possible.

B. Remedies for buyers if the seller tenders nonconforming goods—(buyer rejects)

1. Some remedies that are available to buyers in the case of seller nondelivery are also available to buyers when sellers ship nonconforming goods, including:

   a. cancellation;

   b. cover; *cover* means that the buyer goes out and finds substitute goods for what the seller failed to deliver or as a substitute for the wrong goods the seller delivered. If the seller was to deliver three-speed blenders, the buyer can go out and purchase substitute blenders to "cover" the breach by the seller. If all the buyer can find in the short time afforded for cover is five-speed blenders, that would be considered reasonable cover.

   c. treat as breach of contract and pursue suit for damages;

   d. replevin possible for substituting for goods that are damaged or not delivered if the goods meet the equitable standards of uniqueness.

2. Seek substitute goods (cover) for those damaged or nonconforming goods that have been rejected.

3. Buyer may also keep the goods and recover damages for the value of the goods as delivered and as they should have been (i.e., seller has delivered nonconforming goods); a price reduction for damages is typical.

a. **If buyer accepts nonconforming goods**—The buyer can with notice pursue the following remedies: (Notice is important because failure to give notice bars buyer from any remedies.)—UCC 2-607(3)(a)

    i. **Recover ordinary damages**—Incurred in the ordinary course of business and in a proper case receive incidental and consequential damages—UCC 2-714(1).

    ii. **Recover for breach of warranty**—Buyer can recover the difference between the value of the goods accepted and the value the goods would have been, had they been as warranted (unless special circumstances show proximate damages of a different amount) plus, if appropriate, incidental and consequential damages—UCC 2-714(2).

> **Example:**
> An accounting firm purchases a computer warranted to be a $40,000 value for $30,000. Upon delivery, the computer (although usable) is found to be worth only $20,000 due to a defect. Unless special circumstances would show proximate damages of a different amount, the buyer should recover $20,000, the difference between the value as warranted, $40,000, and the value of the computer as delivered, $20,000.

    iii. **Deduction of damages from purchase price**—(Called the "self-help" remedy) Buyer can deduct all or any part of the damages from the price still due and payable to the seller—UCC 2-717. Buyer should note clearly to seller that the amount tendered is in "Full Accord and Satisfaction" or "Payment in Full," and seller's acceptance of the deducted amount is full satisfaction of the debt.

> **Example:**
> A buyer has contracted for 10 new file cabinets priced at $300 each. The new file cabinets are tendered but two are scratched, though still fully usable. With notice, the buyer can accept all 10 file cabinets and tender to the seller a check for $2,900 ($50 per scratched cabinet deduction to cover refinishing costs) and a letter, indicating clearly on both the check and the letter that the check is intended as final payment and it is in full accord and satisfaction of the contract price. If seller cashes the check, the buyer has fully paid and has no further liability.

b. **Liquidated damages**—The parties by agreement in the contract can predetermine the amount of damages in case of a future breach. The amount must be reasonable in anticipation of what the actual loss would be. This is useful if there would be difficulties in the proof of loss and other adequate remedies would probably not be available. If the court holds the amount to be a penalty, the liquidated damage provision is void. If valid, the parties are limited to the liquidated damages stated— UCC 2-718.

> **Example:**
> Seller agrees to deliver certain inventory to the buyer knowing that failure to deliver timely could result in buyer having to shut-down or limit production at its factory. Seller and buyer agree, that for every day seller delays in making delivery, it will cost the buyer a loss of somewhere between $4,000 and $8,000. The contract contains a liquidated damage clause of $5,000 per day for each day's late delivery. This is a liquidated damage clause and is valid because it appears to be a reasonable amount in expectation of buyer's loss, the proof of loss would be difficult to ascertain, and no other adequate remedy would be available.

c. **Buyer can seek recovery of payment**—If the buyer makes a payment and seller is or becomes insolvent within 10 days of receipt of the payment and the goods are identified (see lesson on "Title and Risk of Loss"), then the buyer can tender the balance owed and is entitled to the goods—UCC 2-502.

IV. Limitations on Remedies

A. **Contract limitation**—Parties can agree to limit (or even add) remedies otherwise available under the UCC. For example, by agreement a buyer's remedies can be limited to a seller's repair or replacement of defective goods—UCC 2-719(1).

B. **Installment contract**—Unless a breach of one or more installments substantially impairs the value of the whole contract, or the contract so provides, breach of an installment by a seller is not a breach of the whole contract, and a buyer's remedies are limited to that installment—UCC 2-612.

> **Example:**
> If you have an installment contract, you have a relationship, not just a one-time delivery. For example, if a seller is to send 100 5x7 picture frames each month for six months, and the first shipment has 50 of the frames that lack a hanging hook, the seller can simply send 150 the next month, complete with the hanging hook, if the buyer can wait that long. If not, the full contract is not breached and the buyer just gets the damages from that installment, for example, or what it cost the buyer to get substitute frames or attach the hooks to the frames the seller sent. For there to be a breach of the full installment contract, you have to have the kind of breach where it is clear the seller cannot perform going forward.

C. **Statute of limitations**—Time period from date of cause of action in which the party must file or be barred from recovery—UCC 2-725.

1. Complaint must be filed within four years of the cause of action.

2. Parties can agree to lessen the period to not less than one year, but they cannot extend the period.

3. For breach of warranty, the cause of action begins at time of tender of delivery, not when the breach is discovered by the buyer.

Introduction to Negotiable Instruments and Negotiability

After studying this lesson you should be able to:

1. Explain why negotiable instruments are important and what they do in commerce.

2. List the types of negotiable instruments and give examples of each.

3. Define all of the parties to the various forms of negotiable instruments.

4. Discuss what affects negotiability.

5. Explain the requirements for negotiability.

I. **Why Do We Need Negotiable Instruments?**

    A. They are used as a method of payment that allows ease of transfer of funds and payment rights.

    B. A contract's rights to payment can be assigned (see the "Third-Party Rights" lesson), but the original parties still have defenses and rights that interfere with payment rights under the contract.

    C. Negotiable instruments are a way to separate the payment rights from the contract rights.

        1. Payment rights are subject to limited defenses with negotiable instruments if the transferee (assignee) of the negotiable instrument is a holder in due course (HDC).

        2. The contract issues are left to the original parties to work out and the funds from the contract can flow freely through commerce.

II. **The Law That Governs Negotiable Instruments**—Negotiable instruments are governed primarily by Article 3 of the **UCC**, which has been adopted by all 50 states. Article 3 has recently been revised and the revision has been adopted by almost all of the states. Article 4 covers the rights and responsibilities of banks with respect to negotiable instruments.

    A. Nonnegotiable instruments are governed by **contract law.**

    B. You can still call a nonnegotiable instrument by its name under Article 3—for example, you can have a nonnegotiable promissory note.

III. **Types of Negotiable Instruments**—There are two types of negotiable instruments:

    A. Orders to pay

	Order to pay
Drafts—UCC 3-104(c)	Three party instruments consisting of a **drawer**, who
Checks—UCC 3-104(f)	orders a **drawee**, to pay a **payee**.
	Promises to pay

    B. Promises to pay

Notes—UCC 3-104(e)	Two party instruments consisting of a **maker**, who promises
Certificates of Deposit—UCC 3-104(j)	to pay a **payee.**

IV. **Classifications of Negotiable Instruments under Promises and Orders to Pay**—Within each "type," instruments can be classified depending on certain features or functions.

A. Drafts—A three-party instrument drawn by one party as a means of ensuring payment. In a sale-of-goods transactions, the seller is the drawer, the buyer is the drawee, and the payee is either the seller or the seller's bank.

1. **Sight draft**—A draft payable on demand immediately upon issue by the drawer and presentment (sight) to the drawee.

2. **Time draft**—A draft payable by the drawee at a specific time.

3. **Trade acceptance**—A draft drawn by a seller-drawer on the buyer-drawee for the buyer-drawee's agreement (acceptance) to pay the amount of the purchase price of the sale plus interest upon presentment to the drawee-acceptor. If the draft is drawn on the buyer's bank, it is referred to as a banker's acceptance.

   a. **Example—TRADE ACCEPTANCE**

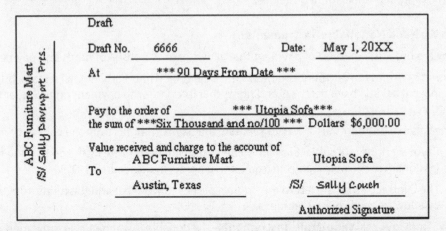

Example:
Grayson's Digital Computer World, a retail store, agrees to purchase from Samstone, a new laptop computer company, 500 model Z laptop computers. Grayson's payment policy is to pay 90 days after receipt of the merchandise, giving the store time to sell the majority of the purchased inventory. Being a new company with cash flow problems, Samstone signs, as drawer, a 90-day trade acceptance, naming itself as payee and Grayson as drawee, and requests Grayson to sign (accept) the instrument and send the trade acceptance back to Samstone. If Grayson signs (accepts), Grayson has agreed to be primarily liable for payment at the end of the 90-day period. In the meantime, Samstone can take the signed trade acceptance and sell it with a discount to its bank giving Samstone instant cash.

B. Checks—A draft drawn on a bank (including savings bank, savings and loan associations, credit unions, and trust companies), payable on demand.

1. **Cashier's check**—A draft in which the drawer and drawee are the same bank or branches of the same bank—UCC 3-104(g)

2. **Teller's check (the old bank draft)**—A draft drawn by one bank on another bank (or payable at or through another bank)—UCC 3-104(h)

3. **Traveler's check**—A draft payable on demand drawn on a bank or through a bank that requires as condition of payment a countersignature by a person whose specimen signature appears on the instrument—UCC 3-104(i)

4. **Certified check**—A check drawn by a drawer on which the drawee bank accepts (by its signature) a primary and absolute obligation to pay the check upon presentment

> **Note:**
> *A **money order** that is payable on demand and drawn on a bank is a check.*

> **Misconception:** There is a belief that a drawee bank is required to certify a check if the drawer presently has sufficient funds to cover the check in the bank. This is in error. Certification is a voluntary act by the drawee bank and the bank's refusal to certify a check is not an act of dishonor.

C. **Notes**—A written promise by a maker to pay money to another party or to bearer.

  1. **Promissory note**—A note payable on demand or within a definite time to a specific payee (or order) or to the bearer.

    a. **Example: PROMISSORY NOTE**

```
$ 6,000 .                                    2 May        20XX

    Ninety (90) days         after date  the undersigned  promise to pay to

the order of Utopia Sofa Corporation

Six Thousand and no/100  --------------------------------------------
Dollars

at  ten percent interest per annum

Value received                        ABC Furniture Mart

NO. 62636              by  Sally Davenport      President
```

    b. **Allonge**—Additional paper firmly attached to commercial paper, such as a promissory note, to provide room to write endorsements.

D. **Certificate of deposits (CDs)**—A note made by a bank acknowledging that it has a deposit of funds payable to the holder (usually payee) —UCC 3-104(2)(c)

  1. Most CDs are time-interest instruments but some can be demand CDs.

    a. **Example: CERTIFICATE OF DEPOSIT**

```
BANK OF WEST AUSTIN               22-1        13992
NEGOTIABLE CERTIFICATE OF DEPOSIT   960

        AUSTIN, TX.  February 15   20XX
THIS CERTIFIES to the deposit in this Bank the sum of $ 6000.00

---------------- Six thousand and no/100---------------DOLLARS

which is payable to bearer on the 15th day of August ,20 XX against
presentation and surrender of this certificate, and bears interest at the rate
of 5 1/2% per annum, to be computed (on the basis of 360 days and actual
days elapsed) to, and payable at maturity.  No payment may be made prior
to, and no interest runs after, that date.

                BANK OF WEST AUSTIN

            By  John Vault, Pres.
                SIGNATURE
```

E. **Nonnegotiable instruments**—While the following are all enforceable contracts, they are not negotiable instruments covered under Article 3 of the UCC:

   1. Letters of Credit (see the "Purpose, Requirements, and Payment" lesson)

   2. Warehouse Receipts (see the "Definitions, Forms, Negotiation, and Rights" lesson)

   3. Bills of Lading (see the "Definitions, Forms, Negotiation, and Rights" lesson)

   4. Stocks and Bonds

   5. Contracts (see Contracts unit)

V. **Negotiability**

   A. **Importance**—The special transferability ease and rights of HDCs are not available unless an instrument is negotiable. If an instrument is nonnegotiable, it is covered by contract law. If an instrument is negotiable, the special rights and protections of Article 3 apply to the parties to the instrument and any transferees of the instrument.

   > **Misconception:** A nonnegotiable instrument is totally unenforceable. This is incorrect. A nonnegotiable instrument is a simple contract and is totally enforceable unless the person or persons responsible to pay have a legal defense against having to do so.

   B. **Requirements to Be a Negotiable Instrument—UCC 3-104**

      1. **Written**—The instrument must be in **writing**. It can be written on anything providing the matter has a degree of permanence and is readily transferable.

      > **Example:**
      > A promissory note written on a blackboard in chalk is not a negotiable instrument, and has neither permanence nor transferability.
      > A promissory note written in ink on the back of test paper is negotiable because it meets both tests.

      2. **Signed**—The instrument must be signed by the maker or drawer.

         a. **Signature to authenticate**—Any symbol, mark, or signature executed or adopted by a party with the intent to authenticate a writing is a signature—UCC 1-201(39).

         b. **Other legal signatures**—A person's initials, rubber stamp, nickname, and even a person's X (usually must be accompanied by a signed witness) is a signature.

      > **Example:**
      > A typewritten name is not a signature but handwritten initials (M.M.J) for Marianne M. Jennings would be.

         c. The signature can appear any place on the instrument.

      3. **Unconditional promise or order**—The instrument must contain an **unconditional promise or order to pay**—UCC 3-106.

         a. **Definite promise**—A note or CD must contain a **definite promise** to pay, not a mere acknowledgment of a debt.

      > **Example:**
      > "I/We promise to pay ..." is a definite obligation to pay.

      > **Misconception:** A drawer or maker's signature must appear in the lower right hand corner. This is totally in error—signature could even be in the body of the instrument.

b. A draft or check must contain language that **orders** the drawee to pay.

Example:

The word "Pay" on a check is an order to the drawee meeting this criteria.

C. Conditional instrument—Instruments **expressly** conditioned on the happening of an event or **subject** to a holder having to read another instrument or document to see whether or on what terms payment will be made renders the instrument conditional and nonnegotiable.

    i. An instrument is not made conditional simply because it references the underlying contract transaction.

        1. Purpose of payment stated (on check "May rent")

        2. Consideration received ("payment is for 10 bales of cotton received")

        3. Reason for instrument or mere "reference" to another writing ("note is in accordance with security agreement #222 of even date")

        4. Account to be debited ("charge to petty cash")

        5. Reference to security for the instrument ("This note is secured by a mortgage on the property located at   ."

    ii. An instrument is conditional, and therefore not negotiable, if its payment is tied to a specific event or any conduct external to the instrument itself.

> **Note:**
> *This clause is more than a reference. This clause makes payment subject to the security agreement. The exam has tested on this fine point of grammatical distinction.*

        1. Payment is expressly conditioned ("upon my daughter getting married");

        2. Payment is subject to another instrument or document ("payment of this note is subject to a security agreement of even date").

4. Sum certain in money—The stated amount of the instrument must be a **sum certain** (fixed) **payable in money**—UCC 3-10.

    a. The general rule is that the **sum is certain** if a holder can calculate the amount owed at time payment is due or any time thereafter.

        i. Thus, the instrument can be payable:

            1. With a stated interest rate or by stated installments;

            2. At different rates of interest before and after maturity; and

            3. At a stated discount for early payment.

        ii. Also, a sum is certain even though:

            1. Tied to a variable interest rate (such as tied to a consumer price index). However, the variable interest rate must be tied to a third-party index and not be subject to the discretion of any party to the instrument or a particular individual's decision.

            2. The instrument provides for costs of collection and/or attorney fees upon default.

    b. Money—is any medium of exchange recognized by a government as its currency (not goods or services).

i. An instrument is not negotiable if it is payable in a combination of money and property. For example, payable in cash plus real estate, or payable in cash and securities would be nonnegotiable instruments because they are not payable exclusively in money. They would be governed under contract law.

> **Note:**
> **Misconception:** *A note payable in U.S. gold is a payment in money. This is not correct because, in and of itself, gold is not a currency recognized by the United States government as a medium of exchange.*

ii. (2) The parties need not be in a particular country to have a negotiable instrument payable in the currency of that country. As long as the payment is in some form of currency recognized by some country, the instrument meets this requirement of negotiability.

Example:
A check payable in Mexican pesos is negotiable because the peso is recognized by the Mexican government as its medium of currency.

5. **Payable on demand or at a definite time**—The instrument must be payable on **demand or at a definite time**—UCC 3-108.

   a. **Types of instruments**

      i. **Demand instruments**—Those that are payable immediately upon issue, such as "payable at sight" or "payable upon presentation," or those which no time period is specified (such as a check or sight draft).

      ii. **Time instruments**—Those payable at a specific time after issue:

         1. A time instrument allows the maker or drawer to pay before a specific date ("On or before Oct. 1, 20XX, I promise ...");

         2. An acceleration clause (for any reason), which permits a holder to demand full payment upon the happening of an event does not affect this requirement of negotiability because most promissory notes, for example, do have an acceleration clause upon default so that the lender can collect the full amount of the note, not just the payments that have been missed;

         3. Extension clauses to extend for a specific definite time by the maker, drawer, or the happening of a specified event also do not lose this requirement of negotiability.

6. **Words of negotiability**—To be negotiable, an instrument must be either payable to **order** or **bearer**—UCC 3-109.

   a. **Order** instruments are payable to the order of:

      i. An identified person (pay to order of M.M. Jennings);

      ii. An agent, trust, estate, office, or organization (pay to Travis County Tax Assessor);

      iii. Specific rules for order instruments:

         1. The "person" must be identified with certainty (so a person can tell who must indorse instrument);

         2. Can be payable to the order of persons jointly or alternatively;

         3. "Pay to" is not a phrase that qualifies for words of negotiability (except on a check and when written on the back of the instrument as part of an indorsement).

   b. **Bearer** instruments are payable to:

      i. Bearer;

      ii. An identified person or bearer (payable to John Smith or bearer);

iii. Cash or some nonidentified person—for example, a check may be made "Payable to cash." This instrument is still a check, but it is a bearer check.

C. Whether an instrument has bearer or order words of negotiability on the front of the instrument controls how the instrument will be transferred (see the "Transfer of Negotiable Instruments and Holders in Due Course" lesson). The following list helps you to learn to classify instruments as bearer or order paper, a step that helps you determine how an instrument can be transferred. See the following table.

WORDS OF NEGOTIABILITY	TYPE
Pay to the order of cash	bearer
Pay to the order of Joan Smith	order
Pay to Joan Smith	nonnegotiable unless used on a check order on a check
Pay to Joan Smith or cash	bearer
Pay to Joan Smith or bearer	bearer
Pay to the order of Joan Smith or cash	bearer
Pay to the order of Joan Smith or bearer	bearer
Pay to the order of Joan Smith and cash	order
Pay to cash	bearer
Pay to bearer	bearer

C. **Important summary—memorize**—Six elements for a negotiable instrument must be:

> **Note:**
> *The exam nearly always has sample instruments on it that require you determine what type of instrument it is and whether it is negotiable.*

1. In **writing**;

2. **Signed** by maker or drawer;

3. **Unconditioned** promise or order;

4. **Sum certain** in **money**;

5. Payable on **demand** or at a **definite** time; and

6. Words of negotiability (i.e., payable to **order** or **bearer**—except for a check).

VI. Factors not Affecting Negotiability

A. **Contradictory terms**—Typewritten words prevail over printed and handwritten words prevail over both typewritten and printed. Written word amounts prevail over numerical amounts unless written amount is ambiguous—UCC 3-114.

Example:
A check is written for five hundred twenty-five dollars and the numerical amount is $505. This contradiction does not affect the negotiability of the instrument and the sum certain is the written amount of $525.

B. **Omission of date**—Unless necessary to determine a definite time for payment for a time instrument, no date on a check (a demand instrument) does not affect the check's negotiability—UCC 3-113.

C. **Postdating or antedating**—Neither affect negotiability—UCC 3-113 (See the "Presentment, Payment, and Dishonor of Negotiable Instruments" lesson for more information on this issue). A bank does not have to abide by the postdate on a check. Unless you have something similar to a stop-payment order in place, the bank can process a postdated check as if it had the current date.

D. **Collateral**—Additional promises to maintain, give additional, or the notation that collateral has been given as security do not affect the negotiability of the instrument.

E. **Presence of a guaranty**—A guaranty of payment on an instrument does not affect negotiability.

Transfer of Instruments and Holders in Due Course

> **After studying this lesson you should be able to:**
>
> **1.** Explain how bearer instruments are transferred.
>
> **2.** Explain how order instruments are transferred.
>
> **3.** List the requirements for becoming a holder in due course.

I. Nonnegotiable Instruments—Transfer of a nonnegotiable instrument, or a negotiable instrument without a required proper indorsement, is by assignment (see the "Third-Party Rights" lesson).

II. Negotiable Instruments—Transfer of a negotiable instrument is by negotiation allowing the holder (if criteria is met) to become an HDC—UCC 3-201.

    A. Bearer instruments—are negotiated by mere **delivery** to a holder.

    B. Order instruments—are negotiated only by a **delivery plus an indorsement**.

III. Indorsements

    A. There are **four** types of indorsements: blank, special, qualified, and restrictive.

        1. Blank indorsements—Specify no particular holder to receive payment.

> **Example:**
> A check payable "to the order of Erin Marie" is negotiated by Erin Marie to Able Red by Erin's signature on the back of the check and delivery of the check to Able Red—UCC 3-205(b).

           a. Legal effects of a blank indorsement

                i. Converts an order instrument into a bearer instrument and Able Red can negotiate the check to Robin Orange by delivery only.

                ii. Transfer warranties (further discussed in Liabilities and Discharge of the Parties) are extended to Able Red and any subsequent holders such as Robin Orange mentioned above—UCC 3-416.

                iii. Blank indorser has a (**signature**) **secondary liability** to pay to all subsequent holders (Able Red and Robin Orange in example)—UCC 3-415.

        2. Special indorsements—Specify a person to whom payment or to whose order payment is to be made. A special indorsement requires the signature indorsement of the person specified plus delivery to negotiate the instrument further.

> **Example:**
> A check is payable "to bearer" or "to order of Erin Marie." Erin Marie will negotiate the instrument to Able Red by delivery plus she will indorse the instrument "Pay to Able Red" signed "Erin Marie"—UCC 3-205(a).

           a. Legal effect of a special indorsement

                i. Converts a bearer instrument into, or continues an order instrument as, an order instrument for further negotiation. To further negotiate the instrument, Able Red can indorse in blank, converting the instrument to a bearer instrument, or Able Red can indorse the instrument to a specific person such as Robin Orange by special indorsement.

    ii.   **Transfer warranties** are extended to Able Red and any subsequent holder such as Robin Orange—UCC 3-416.

    iii.   Special indorser has a (**signature**) **secondary liability** to pay all subsequent holders (Able Red and Robin Orange in illustration)—UCC 3-415.

3. **Qualified indorsements**

    a.   Usually, indorsement includes the term "without recourse" or similar words.

Example:
A check is payable to Able Red. Able Red indorses the check "without recourse /s/ Able Red" and transfers the check to Robin Orange. This is a bank qualified indorsement.

    b.   **Legal effect of a qualified indorsement**

        i.   **Disclaims** contract signature (secondary party) liability—UCC 3-415 (b).

        ii.   **Transfer warranties** are extended to Robin Orange and all subsequent holders—UCC 3-415.

4. **Restrictive indorsements**

    a.   **Three types of restrictive indorsements**—UCC 3-206.

        i.   **Conditional**—Payment is conditional upon the happening of an event.

Example:
Indorsement states "Pay to Able Red upon her delivery of a laptop computer as per our contract of January 15. /s/ Erin Marie."

        ii.   **Prohibitive**—Purports to prohibit further transfer of the instrument.

Example:
Indorsement states "Pay to Able Red only. /s/ Erin Marie."

Misconception: A restrictive indorsement, which states that further negotiation is prohibited, does in fact stop further transfer by negotiation preventing subsequent holders from becoming HDCs. This statement is incorrect—the UCC specifically provides that such an indorsement does not prevent further transfer or negotiation of the instrument.

        iii.   **For deposit or collection**—Makes the indorsee (usually depositary) bank a collection agent of the indorser—UCC 3-206(c).

Example:
A check is made payable to Erin Marie drawn on Green Bank. Erin Marie indorses the check "For Deposit /s/ Erin Marie" and deposits the check with her bank (West Bank). West Bank is now the collecting agent for Erin Marie and must so act (not binding on an intermediary bank or the drawee bank—Green Bank).

    b.   **Legal effect of a restrictive indorsement**

        i.   Restrictive indorsement **does not prohibit further negotiation** of the instrument and subsequent holders can become HDCs—UCC 3-206 (e).

        ii.   **Except** for the **conditional restrictive indorsement**, the indorser's liability to subsequent holders is subject to the restriction being met. If a conditional indorsement or restriction is met, the indorser can be held secondary (contract) liable—UCC 3-206(b)(f).

B. Other indorsement issues

1. **Misspelled name**—A payee or indorsee whose name is misspelled can indorse with the misspelled name, the correct name, or both—UCC 3-204(d).

2. **Multiple payees**

   a. If payable to two or more **jointly**—all must indorse. U.S. Treasury checks (income tax refunds) require the signature of both spouses.

   b. If payable to two or more **in the alternative**—any of the parties can indorse.

   c. If there is no space left for indorsements on the back of an instrument, additional space can be used through attachment of more paper, known as allonge.

IV. Holder in Due Course (HDC)

A. HDC status

1. **Importance**—An HDC has greater rights than an assignee in seeking payment (see Third Party Rights under Contracts to review the rights of assignees). An HDC course can take free from most defenses to contracts and be paid regardless of underlying contract disputes.

   a. **Important**—A party can still be a holder of an instrument even though he or she does not qualify for HDC status. A party who does not meet HDC requirements has the rights of a holder only. The transfer to someone as a holder is NOT invalid. The transfer to someone as an HDC simply gives him or her greater rights and protections than a holder would have.

   > **Example:**
   > Erin Marie has contracted for $500 to purchase 10 chairs from Able Red. Erin Marie makes out a check payable to Able Red for $500. Able Red negotiates the check to Robin Orange. Able Red never delivers the chairs to Erin Marie. If Robin Orange is an HDC, Robin Orange can recover $500 from Erin Marie. If Robin Orange is an assignee, any defense (such as breach of contract) that Erin Marie has against paying the check to Able Red is also a defense against having to pay Robin Orange (contract law—assignment).

2. **Time of determination**—HDC status is usually determined at time HDC receives the instrument.

3. **Requirements for becoming an HDC**—The following criteria must be met to become an HDC—UCC 3-302:

   a. Must be a **holder**;

   b. Must take the instrument for **value**;

   c. **In good faith**; and

   d. **Without notice** that the instrument is:

      i. **Overdue**;

      ii. **Been previously dishonored**; or

      iii. **Of any claim or defense** on the part of any person.

B. Elements examined

1. **Holder**—A holder is someone in possession of an instrument that runs to them. An instrument runs to them if it is bearer paper (because bearer paper runs to anyone), if the instrument is payable to their order, or if the instrument is indorsed to them—UCC 1-201(20).

   a. **Simply**, the holder is anyone who takes possession of a negotiable instrument through issue or negotiation. A holder is someone who is in possession of an instrument that is made payable to him or her, the bearer, or is negotiated to him or her.

2. **Value**

    a.   Consideration—A holder takes value if the holder gives consideration (see Contracts Consideration). However, the holder is only an HDC to the extent that the agreed-upon consideration has **actually been paid, or in the case of actions required, actually been performed**. If what has been performed is *all* that the parties have intended to be done, the holder is an HDC for the **face value** stated on the instrument—UCC 3-303.

Examples:

1. A check is drawn payable to Erin Marie for $500. Erin Marie negotiates the check by blank indorsement to Robin Orange with Robin Orange paying $300 and promising to pay Erin Marie $200 next week when she gets her pay check. Robin Orange is presently only an HDC for the amount paid (performed) $300.

2. Erin Marie negotiates the above check by blank indorsement to Robin Orange with Robin Orange paying $450 for the $500 check. Robin Orange has no further obligation to pay. Robin Orange has fully performed the consideration promised and she is an HDC for $500..

Chapter 1: Erin Marie presently has $1,000 in her checking account. She has received a $500 check drawn by Robin Orange on West Bank and immediately deposits the check in her bank—East Bank. The same day, Erin Marie drafts checks amounting to $1,200 and all of these checks are paid by East Bank. Three days later, Robin Orange's check is received back by East Bank with the notation that it was dishonored by West Bank because of insufficient funds in Robin Orange's account. East Bank is an HDC of the $500 check because East Bank paid value (its own funds in the amount $200) but it is only an HDC against Robin Orange to the amount it has paid. This is referred to as the FIFO rule.

    b.   **Antecedent debt**—A holder takes value if the holder takes the instrument in **payment** of, or as **security for, an antecedent debt** (a debt already in existence at the time the instrument is transferred to them as a holder).

Example:

Chapter 2: A check is issued to Erin Marie for $500. Erin Marie owes Robin Orange $500 for legal services Robin Orange had previously provided Erin Marie. Erin Marie gives the check to Robin Orange to satisfy her debt. Robin Orange has taken the check for value.

    c.   **Negotiable instrument**—The holder takes value if the holder gives a negotiable instrument in payment for it.

Example:

A check is issued to Erin Marie for $500. Erin Marie negotiates the check to Robin Orange with Robin Orange paying Erin Marie $200 in cash and giving Erin Marie a negotiable promissory note for $300. Robin Orange is an HDC having given value ($200 cash plus the $300 negotiable note). Had this been a nonnegotiable promissory note, Robin Orange would have been an HDC for only $200—the consideration paid.

3. **Good faith**

Definition:
Good Faith: "Honesty in fact and the observance of reasonable commercial standards of dealing" (a pure heart and an empty head)—UCC 3-103(a)(4).

    a.   **Assumed**—Good faith is generally assumed unless taken under very unusual circumstances.

Example:

A holder who paid $250 for a $1,000 negotiable CD in an alley at 2:00 a.m. most probably did not take in good faith.

b. A holder cannot take in good faith if the circumstances would cause a reasonable person to raise questions—substantial discount on value of an instrument in a situation that is not the ordinary course of business and it is transferred under rushed circumstances.

4. Without notice

  a. Overdue

   i. An instrument that is payable at a definite time (one of the requirements for negotiability) in the future or, a **time instrument**, is overdue if taken one minute after its due date—UCC 3-304.

Example:
A promissory note is due and payable on May 1. The payee tries to transfer it to one of his creditors at 12:01 a.m. May 2. The creditor cannot be an HDC because the transfer occurred AFTER the due date for the note.

   ii. A **demand instrument** is overdue if taken after the instrument has been outstanding for an unreasonable period of time after its date, or the instrument is taken on the day after the day a demand for payment has been duly made—UCC 3-304(a).

   iii. A **check** is overdue if taken more than 90 days after its date—UCC 3-304(a)(2).

   See the following example.

Example:
A check drawn by Erin Marie is dated May 1 but not issued to Robin Orange until May 30 because Robin Orange was out of town. Robin Orange misplaces the check but finds it on August 3 and she indorses the check to her landlord for her August rent. Unknown to the landlord, Erin Marie and Robin Orange had a dispute over services rendered for the check and Erin Marie stopped payment because of the personal dispute. If the landlord is an HDC, the landlord can collect fully from Erin Marie on the check. If not, assuming Erin Marie's defense is a legal defense, the landlord's claim is subject to Erin Marie's defense. Here, the landlord is not an HDC. Although the landlord took the check within 90 days of issue, it was not taken within 90 days of its May 1 date. The landlord is not an HDC.

   iv. If an instrument is **payable in installments,** any nonpayment of an installment or lack of full payment of the installment principal (not interest) is notice that the instrument is overdue.

  b. Previously been dishonored—To disqualify a holder from becoming an HDC, the holder must have actual knowledge that the instrument has been dishonored—UCC 3-302(a)(2).

Example:
"Insufficient Funds" has been stamped on the face of a check by the drawee bank. No subsequent holder can be an HDC.

  c. Claim or defense—Again, the holder must have actual knowledge that a claim or defense exists to be disqualified from HDC status. It requires actual knowledge UCC 3-302(a)(b). That actual knowledge can come from direct disclosure of the claim or defense by the parties involved or through unusual or irregular circumstances.

   i. Irregular—Holder has notice if the instrument is so incomplete, bears such visible evidence of forgery or alteration, or is otherwise so irregular or incomplete as to call into question its authenticity—UCC 3-302(a)(1).

Example:
An instrument's amount in which the sum of $25 is crossed out and a different colored ink is used to raise it from $25 to $2,500 would be a visible alteration and a holder taking this instrument would not be an HDC. However, an instrument originally payable as $7.00 (seven), and in which the same color ink is used to add a zero and a 'ty' ($70.00 and seventy) would not be a visible alteration and subsequent holders could qualify as HDCs.

    ii. Prior notice—Holder has notice if holder has knowledge that the obligation of any party is voidable or that all parties have been discharged.

Example:
A note is payable to the order of Erin Marie, a minor. Erin Marie indorses the note in blank to her father Harry Marie. Harry Marie cannot be an HDC because Harry Marie knows his daughter is a minor and that she can disaffirm her liability as an indorser and transferor of the note.

    iii. Close connection doctrine—The holder has notice if the holder is connected with the transferor and there has been a history of problems, claims, and defenses on the notes transferred on a regular basis between the transferor and the holder. This restriction generally applies when those affected are able to show that the transferor and the holder were working together, i.e., in cahoots on questionable transactions and trying to use HDC status to get around taking care of underlying contract problems.

C. Holder through an HDC—Shelter Rule (Provision)—Any holder who cannot qualify as an HDC but took the instrument through an HDC, has the same rights as if an HDC. For example, someone who receives an instrument as a gift is not a holder in due course because he or she did not give value. But if the donor was an HDC, then the donee is an HDC because of that standing and despite having given no value.

1. The Shelter Provision protects those who receive an instrument from an HDC. This law gives the holder the same rights as the transferor (this section of the code incorporates the simple law of assignments from contracts—you get the same rights as an assignee that the assignor holds; see the Third-Party Rights lesson for more information).

Example:
A and B are special indorsers and C is the holder of a note. A is qualified as an HDC, but B is not because B did not take the note for value, and C is not an HDC because C took the note with notice the note is overdue. Although C is not an HDC and did not take the note from an HDC (B), C has the rights of an HDC.

    a. Bond fraudulently induced Teal to make a note payable to Wilk, to whom Bond was indebted. Bond delivered the note to Wilk. Wilk negotiated the instrument to Monk, who purchased it with knowledge of the fraud and after it was overdue. If Wilk qualifies as a holder in due course (HDC), then Monk has the standing of a holder in due course through Wilk.

    b. Under the Shelter Provision, even though Monk was not an HDC, he obtained the instrument from Wilk who was a HDC. Therefore, Monk qualifies as a holder through an HDC and thus obtains all of the rights of an HDC.

2. Shelter Provision limitation—A holder cannot improve his or her position under the Shelter Provision by a negotiation of an instrument to an HDC and the subsequent reacquirement of it.

Example:
Erin Marie acquires a note by fraud and negotiates the note to Robin Orange, who qualifies as an HDC. Later, Erin Marie repurchases the note from Robin Orange. Here, the Shelter Provision would not apply and Erin Marie does not have the rights of an HDC.

3. Shipping—through exception—This allows a holder to transfer an instrument to an HDC and then have it transferred back, thus, improving his or her status to HDC. For example, suppose H is only a holder because he or she did not give value. H can ship through to an HDC and then take back from the HDC to become an HDC. Again, shipping through cannot cure the problem of only being a holder due to having notice that there are defenses to the instrument, that it has been dishonored, or that it is overdue.

Presentment, Payment, and Dishonor of Negotiable Instruments

After studying this lesson you should be able to:

1. Explain the requirements for presentment for payment of a negotiable instrument.

2. Describe the requirements for dishonor, and notice of dishonor, and explain the time limits for each.

I. **Proper Steps—Sequence and Requirements**—Payment of an instrument and by whom are conditioned on a proper sequence of steps, each with requirements and time limits.

A. **Presentment**

> **Definition:**
> *Proper Presentment:* To properly present an instrument, the holder must present the instrument to the right person for the correct reason in the right manner timely—UCC3-501.

1. **Who presents what and to whom?**

   a. The holder (or HDC, if so qualified) presents the instrument to the primary party for payment.

   b. Primary parties are makers of CDs and notes and drawees of drafts and checks.

   c. The holder is required to present the instrument and the party paying the instrument is permitted to ask for appropriate proof of the transaction (identification, receipts, etc.).

   > **Note:**
   > *On a draft, a drawee can only be a primary party if the drawee has accepted liability. A drawee of a draft accepts liability if the drawee signs the drafts.*

   d. Presentment is the contractual obligation of the holder (or Holder in Due Course (HDC) of the instrument. All other rights under the instrument and with respect to other parties are contingent upon this first step of presentment.

2. **Who are the primary parties to negotiable instruments?**

   a. For notes, the primary party is the payor/debtor.

   b. For CDs, the primary party is the bank that agreed to accept the CD deposit and that bank will pay that amount plus the contracted-for interest.

   c. For checks, the drawee bank is the party to whom the check is first presented. However, the bank does not occupy the role of primary party for purposes of liability because the bank's payment of the check is always conditioned upon the customer having sufficient funds in his or her account. A bank is a primary party only if it has agreed to certify the check. If the bank certifies a check, the bank has accepted primary liability on that check and it is absolutely obligated to pay the check.

   > **Note:**
   > *Refusal to certify a check is NOT dishonor. A bank is not required to certify a check, but if it does so, it becomes primarily liable.*

   d. For drafts, the primary party is the drawee of the draft.

3. **There are time restrictions on presentment for checks.**

   a. A check must be presented to the drawee bank for payment either at the drawee bank or by deposit in the depositary bank within 30 days after date to hold drawer liable and within 30 days after indorsement to hold an indorser liable—UCC 3-414(f), 3-415(e). A bank can still honor a check after that time period but there are certain liability limitations that apply (see below on failure to present within 30 days and issues on liability).

   b. Note—postdating a check has no effect on the time for presentment—bank need not honor the postdate unless the customer has filed a request in a manner similar to a stop payment order.

    c. The bank enjoys a presumption of paying in good faith for six months after the date of the check.

    d. Bank can still pay a check after the six-month period but probably would not do so without verifying with the drawer.

4. Time for presentment on other types of instrument is controlled by the type of instrument.

    a. Time draft—can be presented when time for payment arrives.

    b. Note—can be presented as of due date. (Note—when note is overdue, there are risks of losing HDC status and ability to transfer free from defenses. See study text on Transfer of Instrument and Holders in Due Course.)

    c. Sight draft—can be presented at any time.

B. Dishonor

> **Definition:**
> *Dishonor*: Generally, any refusal to pay or accept (where required) is a dishonor, except where the holder refuses to show identification, show evidence of authority to receive payment, exhibit the instrument, or sign a receipt (anywhere on the instrument) that the holder has received payment—UCC 3-501, 3-502. It is not dishonor for the party who is required to pay to ask for identification and other steps that are generally part of establishing proof that the proper party was paid.

C. To whom is notice of dishonor given?

    1. Notice of dishonor is given to:

        a. Secondary parties on the instrument. If the primary party does not pay the instrument, then the holder (HDC) has the right to turn to the secondary parties who have contractual liability under the instrument according to the terms of Article 3;

        b. Secondary parties for checks;

            i. Drawer of the check;

            ii. Any indorsers of the check as it has moved through commerce (Note: qualified indorsers have a different sort of secondary liability (see lessons on Liability of the Parties);

            iii. Payees of the check (who could also be indorsers).

        c. Secondary parties for notes/CDs:

            i. Any indorsers of the note as it has moved along through commerce;

            ii. Indorsers include those parties who have signed allongers, which are separate pieces of paper that are affixed to an instrument in order to allow further negotiation after the space on the instrument is exhausted;

            iii. Payees of the note (may also be an indorser).

        d. Secondary parties for drafts:

            i. The drawer of the draft;

            ii. Any indorsers of the draft;

            iii. Payees of the draft (may also be an indorser).

D. Notice of dishonor is received—Notice can be given by any reasonable means and, once received, is effective notice for all subsequent holders—UCC 3-503(b).

> **Definition:**
> *Notice of Dishonor:* Must be given within 30 days of dishonor or within 30 days after notice of dishonor is received. For banks, notice of dishonor must be given by midnight of the next banking day or the bank can be held accountable for the instrument.

E. **Presentment and notice can be excused**—Generally, if presentment cannot be made with reasonable diligence, the drawer or indorser waives such, or by the instrument terms (such as adding the words "payment guaranteed"), excuses such. In addition, presentment is waived if drawer instructed drawee not to pay or accept instrument, maker or acceptor is deceased, or drawer disclaimed contract liability (such as signing "without recourse")—UCC 3-304.

F. **Failure to present properly or give timely notice of dishonor**

   1. **Indorser's secondary** (contract signature liability) is **completely discharged**—UCC 3-415(e). The time for non-bank indorser notice of dishonor is 30 days.

   2. Drawer's secondary (contract signature) liability is excused from liability **only to extent that the drawer is deprived of funds** due to such failure—UCC 3-414(f).

Example:
Green has $150,000 in her checking account. On May 1, Green issues a check for $110,000 to Smith for the purchase of an expensive lake lot. Smith negotiates the check to a land development company on May 20. On June 15, the land development attempts to cash the check only to learn that Green's drawee bank was closed on June 12 due to financial reasons. The FDIC Insurance only covers $100,000. The land development company wants to hold Green for the full $110,000. However, due to improper presentment (more than 30 days from date), Green's liability is excused to extent that he or she was deprived of funds (here, $10,000) because, had there been proper presentment, the check would have been fully honored. If you present a check (presentment within 30 days from the date of the check), then you have the liability of the primary and secondary parties on the instrument (drawer and drawee). However, if, as in this case, you present it late and the bank fails, we have a problem. Bank failures used to not be an issue, but, 2008 taught us differently, and so now we must be prepared for exam questions. When there is late presentment, there is always FDIC recovery—the $100,000. We are left with $10,000 unpaid. Ordinarily we would go to the drawer (Green), but under this insolvency provision, we are prohibited from doing so because had the check been timely presented, the bank would not have been insolvent. Drawers are not held secondarily liable for their bank's failures unless there is timely presentment.

Liabilities and Discharge of Duties

After studying this lesson you should be able to:

1. List and explain the types of defenses and which ones apply to HDCs.

2. Define a material alteration and describe what happens when an instrument has been materially altered and how liability is affected.

3. List the primary and secondary liability obligations under negotiable instruments.

4. Explain the differences and requirements of contract and warranty liability of the parties.

I. **Contract Liability of Parties**—Contract liability of parties under an instrument depends on the role that they play with regard to the instrument. Article 3 outlines their payment responsibility and order of payment according to the role that they play under the instrument.

   A. **Primary party liability**—As discussed in the "Presentment, Payment, and Dishonor" lesson, there are certain parties who have primary liability.

      1. **Makers of CDs and notes;**

      2. **Drawees of drafts or checks**—UCC 3-409. Remember: A drawee of a draft cannot be held liable on that instrument until he or she "accepts" (i.e., signs, that instrument). When the bank is the drawee of a check, there is an interesting distinction that is important. We must first turn to the bank for payment of a check, although the bank does not have primary liability because the bank always holds the right to dishonor the check for lack of sufficient funds. So, the check must be presented to the bank first as the primary party in order to attach liability of the secondary parties on the check. But, the bank always has a valid reason for refusing to pay—insufficient funds. We do not, however, skip the bank. Presentment and dishonor are required.

   B. **Secondary party liability**

      1. Drawers of an ordinary check or draft

      2. Indorsers (unqualified)

   C. **Accommodation party liability**

      1. An **accommodation party** signs an instrument to lend his or her name to guaranty the liability of the accommodated party.

      2. The accommodation party has the same level of liability as the party for whom he or she is accommodating. An accommodation party who signs for a maker has primary liability and an accommodation party who signs to accommodate a drawer has secondary liability—UCC 3-410.

      3. The accommodation party is treated as a surety or guarantor (see Debtor-Creditor Relationships). A holder or HDC who is seeking payment does not have to demand payment from the accommodated party before turning to the accommodation party for payment.

> **Note:**
> *There is no such thing as a "maker" of a check. There is a drawer of a check. The exam has had questions whose answers depend on your understanding of this critical distinction. The distinction is important because a maker of a note has primary liability and the drawer of a check has secondary liability.*

II. **Warranty liability**

   A. **Transferor warranty liability**—This liability results from the role the party plays in transferring the instrument.

      1. **General and qualified indorsers**—who receive consideration make the following transfer warranties to all subsequent holders—UCC 3-416:

         a. Transferor is entitled to enforce the instrument (has good title).

         b. All signatures are authorized and genuine.

         c. Instrument has not been altered.

d. Instrument is not subject to a claim or defense by any party that can be asserted against the transferor.

e. The transferor has no knowledge of any insolvency proceeding commenced with respect to the maker, acceptor, or drawer.

2. Nonindorsers—These are those in the chain of commerce who transferred bearer paper. They make the same transfer warranties, but these warranties are given only to the bearer transferor's immediate transferee.

> **Note:**
> **Misconception:**
> *Nonindorsers have no liability on an instrument. This is true for contract liability but even nonindorsers who receive value do make to their immediate transferee the transfer warranties.*

Example:
A check is made payable to Erin Marie. Erin Marie indorses (blank indorsement) the check to Megan Orange as a gift. Megan Orange transfers the check without indorsement to Eric Edward for value. Eric Edward then transfers the check (by special indorsement) for value to you as a holder. Megan Orange has no transfer warranty liability to you because, as a nonindorser, you are not her immediate transferee. Eric Edward does pass all five transfer warranties to you.

B. Presentment warranties

1. Anyone who obtains payment or acceptance of a draft or check warrants to the party who pays or accepts—UCC 3-417.

a. The person obtaining payment or acceptance is authorized to do so and is entitled to enforce the instrument.

b. The instrument has not been altered (does not apply to an HDC).

c. The person obtaining payment or acceptance has no knowledge that the signature of the drawer is unauthorized (does not apply to an HDC).

2. Cannot be disclaimed—These warranties cannot be disclaimed by presenters of checks. Remember the 30-day time restriction on turning to secondary parties on checks (see lesson on "Presentment, Payment, and Dishonor").

III. Defenses of Primary and Secondary Parties to the Obligation to Pay

A. Personal defenses—These can be asserted against ordinary holders but not against an HDC or a holder with rights of an HDC under the Shelter Provision or Shipping-Through Exception.

1. Mistake

2. Misrepresentation

3. Fraud in the inducement

Example:
Erin Marie contracts to buy Eric Crook's "race horse" for $10,000. Erin Marie gives Eric Crook a check for this amount not knowing that the horse has a condition that will not allow the horse to race. Eric Crook knew of the condition. Crook has negotiated the check to Megan Orange who is not an HDC. If Erin Marie refuses to pay the check (has stopped payment), Megan Orange cannot enforce payment. If Megan Orange had been an HDC, Erin Marie would be liable to Orange on the check for $10,000.

4. Lack of consideration

Example:
Erin Marie issues a $1,000 note to Megan Orange as a gift. There is no consideration for the note and thus the note is unenforceable; but this is only a personal defense.

5. Breach of contract

6. Product warranty issues

B. Real or universal defenses—These can be asserted against all holders, including HDCs and holders with rights of an HDC.

1. **Forgery**—Only those whose authorized signatures appear on an instrument can be held liable (but see discussion of types of forgery later in this study text).

> **Example:**
> Erin Marie's blank check is stolen by Eric Crook and Eric Crook forges Erin Marie's name as drawer of the check. Erin Marie would not be liable on the check even to an HDC of the check.

2. **Fraud in execution**—(also known as fraud in factum). A person is deceived into signing a negotiable instrument believing that what is being signed is some other document. This does not apply if the person signing should know the nature of the document that they are signing.

> **Note:**
> *Fraud in the inducement is NOT a real defense. Fraud in the inducement is the defense grounded in misrepresentation of fact about the contract subject matter.*

> **Example:**
> Robert Gonzalas is a single male from Mexico and does not read English. Eric Crook, a deceitful neighbor, delivers a small package to Gonzalas asking him to sign a "receipt," which, in fact, is a $10,000 negotiable promissory note. Gonzalas signs what he believes is a receipt. This is fraud-in-execution. This would not apply to you, as an accountant, because you obviously can read English and have the intelligence to understand what you are signing.

3. **Minority**—This is a universal or real defense only to the extent that state law recognizes minority as a defense to a simple contract (voidable right) (see Contracts; Defenses to Formation).

> **Example:**
> Erin Marie is a minor who purchases by check an $800 CD player. Since this is not an item of necessity, Erin Marie can disaffirm (avoid) the purchase and her obligation to pay the check claiming her minority as a real defense.

4. **Inability to pay (lack of solvency) and/or discharge decree in bankruptcy**—The petition into bankruptcy is not a real defense, but the discharge decree issued by the bankruptcy court discharging the obligation to pay the instrument is a real defense. We all take our contracts and negotiable instruments with the risk that the parties obligated to pay simply cannot pay. Being an HDC does not guarantee payment. The rights of an HDC only guarantee that, if the party liable is solvent, payment will not be withheld based on certain defenses.

5. **Void events**—Any event that renders an obligation or instrument void is a real or universal defense.

   a. **Illegality**—Any law that renders an instrument void because it was executed in connection with illegal conduct. If the law merely makes the instrument voidable, it is a personal defense.

> **Example:**
> In state X, it is illegal to gamble but the payment of a gambling debt is merely unenforceable (voidable). In this state, a check written to pay off a gambling debt would be unenforceable by the payee-winner, but the drawer would be fully liable to an HDC of the check.

b. **Mental incapacity**—Any instrument drawn, made, or indorsed by a person who has been adjudicated (declared) by a court as mentally incompetent is a void instrument and it cannot be enforced by an HDC. If the person has not yet been adjudicated mentally incompetent, but is mentally incompetent, it is a personal defense.

c. **Duress**—Any person who signs an instrument under "extreme" duress (threat or force that would result in death or serious injury, for example) has a real defense because the instrument is void.

IV. The Effect of Material Alteration on the Contractual and Warranty Duties to Pay

A. Changing the contract terms or obligations in any way between any two parties—such as adding clauses, changing dates, amounts, or interest, deleting clauses, completing an instrument in an unauthorized manner—is a material alteration.

B. Material alterations can be:

1. **Complete defense**—against both an ordinary holder and an HDC (as when a holder crosses out the qualified indorsement of a indorser—that cross-out changes materially the obligations of the indorser).

2. **Partial defense**—where the original tenor of the instrument is altered cleverly (changing $7.00 to $700.00), the altered amount is a real defense for the altered amount ($693), but an HDC can enforce the instrument for its original tenor ($7).

3. **No defense**—If an original instrument is incomplete but later completed in an unauthorized manner, this alteration is no longer a defense against an HDC and the HDC can enforce the instrument as completed.

> **Example:**
> Erin Marie has contracted with Eric Crook to repair her damaged car. Erin Marie is leaving town and drafts a check payable to Eric Crook leaving the amount blank. It is agreed that Eric should fill in the amount upon completion of the repairs but the amount would not exceed the $1,000 estimate. Instead, Eric fills in the amount $3,000 and negotiates the check to Emily Elizabeth, an HDC. Emily Elizabeth can fully hold Erin Marie on the check for $3,000.

V. Unauthorized Signatures and Forgeries

A. **Unauthorized signature liability**

1. **Unauthorized signatures**—include those that are forged and those made by persons knowing that they are not entitled to payment.

a. **The agency issues**—How an agent signs an instrument controls whether the principal or agent will be liable on the instrument and whether additional evidence (parol evidence—see Contract Form: Statute of Frauds for more information on parol evidence) can be used to establish liability.

Principal/Agent Liability		
Signature	**Liability?**	**Parol?**
A. Agent	Agent	No
A. Agent, VP	Agent	Yes
P. Prince, A. Agent	Principal	Yes
P. Prince by A. Agent	Principal	No
P. Prince	Principal	No

B. **A forged signature**—(general rule) with whom liability on the instrument for the forged indorsement ultimately rests when there is a forgery depends on the role the forger played in that forgery.

1. **Forgery of drawer's signature**—liability ultimately rests with the drawee, because the drawee is presumed to know the signature of the drawer.

2. **Forgery of payee/indorser's signature**—liability ultimately rests with the first party to accept the instrument AFTER the forged indorsement because that party had face-to-face contact and could have checked identification.

3. **Exceptions to the general rule—Impostor**—A person who procures an instrument impersonating that he/she is someone else by mail, telephone, in person, etc., and indorses the instrument in the name personated; (although fraudulent) the indorsement is effective. The drawer or maker cannot treat the indorsement as unauthorized and is liable to any person who, in good faith, pays the instrument or takes it for value or collection—UCC 3-404(a).

> **Example:**
> Eric Crook calls Erin Marie and tells her he is Jerry Lewis and is soliciting funds in his (Jerry Lewis's) own name for a charity. Erin Marie makes out a check payable to "Jerry Lewis" and sends it to the address Crook gives her over the phone. It is Crook's address. Crook indorses the check "Jerry Lewis," transfers the check to a co-conspirator, Jeff Slug, and Slug cashes the check at Erin Marie's bank. Erin Marie cannot claim that her bank paid a "forged" instrument and recover the funds from her bank.

4. **Exceptions to the general rule—Fictitious payees**—Important for exam. This generally involves a dishonest employee who either drafts checks for the employer's signature or has the authority to draft and sign checks for the employer. The employee takes advantage of his position to make out checks to persons not entitled to payment. Indorsements by these payees (although fraudulent) are effective in favor of any person who pays the instrument or takes it for value or collection in good faith—UCC 3-404 (b).

> **Example:**
> Sly Green is a bookkeeper for Able Cook's restaurant. Green drafts all checks for Cook's signature, distributes the signed checks, and reconciles Cook's bank statement. Unknown to Cook, Green is a compulsive gambler and owes money to a number of bookmakers. Green drafts checks payable to the bookmakers telling Cook these are suppliers of food products for the restaurant. Cook signs the checks. The bookmakers indorse the checks in their own names and cash the checks. All are paid by Cook's bank. An audit reveals the fraudulent payments. Cook claims the indorsements are unauthorized and wants reimbursement from his bank. Unfortunately for Cook, the fictitious payee rule is applied, the indorsements are effective, and Cook suffers the loss (but can still sue Green and bookmakers, however).

Purpose, Requirements, and Payment

After studying this lesson you should be able to:

1. Define "letter of credit" and explain the roles of the parties to a letter of credit.

2. Explain the obligations of banks on letters of credit and their liability for failure to pay.

3. Describe how a letter of credit is created.

I. Basic Definitions—UCC 5-102

Definitions:

Applicant: The person at whose request or on whose account a letter of credit is issued.

Beneficiary: The person under the letter of credit terms who is entitled to have the letter honored upon presentation.

Issuer: A bank or person that issues a letter of credit.

Correspondent bank: A bank that is designated to handle the payment under an authorized letter of credit.

Nominated Person: A person or bank whom the issuer designates or authorizes to pay, negotiate, or give value under a letter of credit.

Presentation: Delivery of a document to an issuer or nominated person to honor or give value under a letter of credit.

Record: Letters of credit require a record. As under Article 2, a record is defined as a tangible, electronic, or other medium that is retrievable in perceivable form.

II. How the Letters of Credit are Created and Used—A letter of credit is a means that sellers use to provide themselves with assurance that they will be paid for delivering goods. The following steps should help you to understand the letter of credit process in an international setting:

A. Buyer and seller make a sales contract, included in the terms are provisions for a letter of credit to be used to finance the sale.

B. Buyer makes an application to its bank for a letter of credit.

C. The buyer's bank (issuer) forwards the letter of credit (record) to a correspondent bank (nominated person) in the seller's country.

D. The correspondent bank sends the letter of credit to the seller (beneficiary).

E. The seller, upon receipt, prepares the goods for shipment and prepares the documents required under the letter of credit delivering the documents to the correspondent bank.

F. The correspondent bank, if it deems the documents are in order (see discussion below on rights and obligations for more information on everything being in order for payment), sends the documents to the issuer (buyer's bank) and pays the seller according to the terms of the letter of credit.

G. The issuing bank, if the documents are in order, charges the buyer's account, forwards the documents to the buyer (or a custom broker), and reimburses the correspondent bank.

H. The buyer (or custom broker) takes the documents to the carrier and picks up or has the goods delivered to the buyer.

III. Creation of Letters of Credit and General Right

A. A letter of credit can be issued in any form that is a record and is authenticated by a signature, or in accordance with the agreement of the parties, or standard practice of financial institutions—UCC5-104.

B. Consideration is not required for the issuance of a letter of credit—UCC5-108.

C. A letter of credit can be revocable, if so provided in the letter—UCC5-106. In an international sale of goods where shipment is overseas, the letter is irrevocable, unless otherwise agreed—UCC2-325.

D. Letters of credit, unless stated to the contrary, expire one year after its stated date of issuance or date of issue. If the duration is stated to be "perpetual," the letter expires five years after its stated date or date of issue—UCC5-106.

E. There is a one year statute of limitations for bringing suit under a letter of credit—UCC 5-115.

IV. Duties, Rights, and Obligations of Parties under Letters of Credit

A. An issuer must honor a presentation, that appears on its face to strictly comply with the terms of the letter. An issuer has seven business days to either honor or give notice of a defect in presentation—UCC5-108. This obligation to honor the terms of the letter does not apply when there has been fraud or forgery involved in its issuance.

> **Note:**
> *A typical exam question focuses on this issue. The correspondent bank cannot substitute its judgment on performance of a contract for the terms of the letter of credit. Parties who want performance-based issues to be satisfied prior to payment must provide for those requirements in the letter of credit.*

    1. There is little room for discretion in the letter of credit.

    2. The buyer's issues with the goods cannot be raised as objections to payment if the terms require payment upon delivery.

B. If the correspondent bank wrongfully dishonors payment under the terms of the letter of credit, the issuer is liable for the amount that is the subject of dishonor, or damages for its breach, or, sometimes, specific performance plus incidental (but not consequential) damages, and reasonable attorney fees and other expenses of litigations—UCC5-111.

C. If presentation is honored, the beneficiary warrants to the issuer that there is no fraud or forgery and warrants to the applicant that there is no violation of any agreement between the parties intended to be augmented by the letter of credit. Note: These are additional to other warranties if documents or instruments are also part of the transaction—UCC5-110.

D. Generally, a letter of credit may not be transferred, unless so stated in the letter of credit, or by operation of the law—UCC5-112, 5-113. Proceeds, however, from a letter of credit are generally assignable—UCC5-114.

E. A letter of credit is independent of the underlying contract between the seller and buyer. Other laws, such as the sale of goods (UCC Article 2 or International Convention on International Sales of Goods (CISG)) or the secured transactions laws (Article 9 UCC9-306, 9-312), apply to the rights of the buyer and seller with respect to the sale of the goods, as well as any security interests that the seller may take in addition to using the letter of credit.

> **Example:**
> A bank obligated to issue payment under a letter of credit "when the goods are delivered" must honor that obligation even if the buyer has complaints about the goods.

Definitions, Forms, Negotiation, and Rights

After studying this lesson you should be able to:

1. List and define the types of documents of title.

2. List the requirements for a negotiable document of title.

3. Discuss the rights and liabilities of the parties to a document of title.

4. Explain how documents of title are transferred.

I. Definitions and Types of Documents of Title

    A. Documents of title are governed by Article 7 of the UCC

        1. Defined as any document that, in the regular course of business proves that the person in possession has title to and is entitled to receive the goods—UCC 1-201(15).

        2. Documents of title offer a means for transferring title to goods without physically moving the goods.

    B. Types of documents of title

        1. *Bill of Lading:* A document evidencing the receipt of goods by a carrier for shipment—UCC 1-201(6).

            a. *Warehouse Receipt:* A receipt issued by a person engaged in the business of storing goods—UCC 1-201(45).

        2. Parties to a document of title

            a. *Issuer:* A person who is a bailee and issues (delivers) the document to the bailor or a third person—UCC 7-102(1)(g). Does not apply to unaccepted delivery order.

            b. *Delivery Order:* An order by the bailor or a third person for the bailee to deliver goods—UCC 7-102(1)(d).

            c. *Consignor:* A person who delivers goods to a carrier named in a bill of lading—UCC 7-102(1)(c).

            d. *Consignee:* A person named in a bill of lading to whom or whose order the goods are to be delivered—UCC 7-102(1)(b).

II. Creating a Negotiable Document of Title

    A. Language required

        1. Must have words of negotiability; that is, the document must be made out to the bearer or to the order of the consignee or person to whom delivery is to be made.

        2. If there is not language of negotiability, the parties have rights under the document, but those rights are contractual rights and not covered under Article 7.

            a. Warehouse receipt: Need location of goods, date of issue and number, whether order or bearer, rates, description, any liens, signature of warehouseman, and a statement if warehouseman is owner.

            b. Bill of lading: Must be in writing and adequately describe goods shipped.

        3. International documents are negotiable if they run to a named person or his or her assigns—UCC 7-104(1).

        4. Article 7 requires that documents of title be in record form.

III. Duty of Care with Respect to Goods under a Document of Title

    A. Common Carriers—Have absolute or strict liability for loss or damage to the goods except in these circumstances:

1. An act of God, meaning a natural phenomenon that is not reasonably foreseeable;

2. An act of a public enemy, such as the military forces of an opposing government, as distinguished from ordinary robbers;

3. An act of a public authority, such as a health officer removing goods from the carrier;

4. An act of the shipper, such as fraudulent labeling or defective packing;

5. The inherent nature of the goods, such as those naturally tending to spoil or deteriorate.

This topic of carrier liability has been a frequent one on the exam, generally involving a truck accident and the resulting liability. Often appearing in combination with an Article 2 question on risk of loss, you are asked to determine who has ultimate liability. If, for example, an earthquake results in destruction of the goods, the carrier is not liable (Act of God) and you return to your Article 2 Sales rules on passage of risk of loss to determine who is liable. If the goods are seized by an army, the carrier is not liable, and you return to Article 2 risk of loss rules.

B. **Warehouse company**—Has high degree of care (See the "Title and Risk of Loss" lesson in the Article-2 Sales unit).

C. Both warehouse company and carrier have a right to place possessory liens on goods for any storage or carrier charges and costs not paid by the bailor.

1. Lien is the same as any other creditor lien.

2. Enforcement is by private or public sale, but such must be commercially reasonable with proper notice—UCC 7-209, 7-210, 7-307, 7-308.

IV. Transfer and Negotiation of Documents of Title

A. **A nonnegotiable document of title**—Goods are transferred by assignment. Use basic assignment law discussed in contracts and negotiable instruments; assignee acquires only title and rights of the transferor-assignor and is subject to all defenses and claims against the assignor—UCC 7-504.

Example:
Through fraud, Green has purchased 1,440 cases of Green Valley Peas from Fraser. Green deposits the cases into lots (144 cases of peas per lot) with the Able Warehouse Company. Able issues ten nonnegotiable warehouse receipts to Green. Green sells one of the warehouse receipts to Beyer. Before Beyer can pick up the lot, Fraser, by court order, repossesses the cases of peas held by Able. Beyer received a voidable title to the goods through the nonnegotiable warehouse receipt. Thus, Beyer has no title or rights to the goods repossessed by Fraser.

B. **A negotiable document of title**—Through negotiation, the holder can acquire better rights than the transferor-assignor—UCC 7-501, 7-502.

1. Due negotiation for bearer documents requires delivery only.

2. Order document require delivery plus an indorsement.

C. Negotiation becomes duly negotiated to a holder if the holder takes the document in good faith, without notice of defense or claim of a person to the document or goods, for value, and in the ordinary course of business. (Note: Except for the latter, these requirements are the same as those for becoming a holder in due course of a negotiable instrument.)

1. **Shelter principle is applicable**—(see the "Transfer of Instruments and Holders in Due Course" lesson in the Article-3 Negotiable Instruments unit.)—UCC 7-504(1). Even though holder cannot qualify as a holder through due negotiation, the holder can have the rights of a holder through due negotiation if the holder took through a holder with due negotiation.

D. **Rights of a duly negotiable document**

1. A duly negotiated holder acquires title to the goods.

2. A duly negotiated holder has a right to have delivery or possession of these goods according to the terms of the document contract.

3. Indorser warrants that the negotiable document is genuine, that the indorser has no knowledge of claims or facts that would impair the goods or documents value, and that the transfer is rightful—UCC 7-502.

4. We all take subject to the risk of nonperformance under all UCC articles. There is no guaranty of performance under Article 7.

V. Limitation of Rights

A. Forgery of the document or any indorsement defeats rights of any holder to either the document or the goods. (Forgery of a document of title is treated as Real Defenses are handled in the "Liabilities and Discharge of Duties" lesson.)

Example:
Able, via ABC Truck Lines, ships 100 model Z personal computers to Beyer. Able sends a negotiable bill of lading to Beyer. Before the bill of lading reaches Beyer, it is stolen by Theef. Theef forges Beyer's name as an indorsement on the bill of lading and transfers the bill to you. Able, upon learning that Beyer had not yet received the bill of lading, orders ABC to stop delivery. Able can legally do so because the forged indorsement is a real defense to delivery of the goods, and the forged indorsement defeated any rights you had to the goods.

B. Stolen goods and documents of title.

C. Title does not pass—UCC 7-503(1).

Introduction and Creation of Security Interests

After studying this lesson you should be able to:

1. Explain why a security interest is important for creditors.

2. Describe the forms of collateral available under Article 9.

3. List the requirements for the creation of a security interest.

I. Importance and Application

A. Creditors want additional security if the debtor defaults.

   1. An Article 9 security interest gives the creditor the right to specific collateral that the debtor owns, or has rights in, in order to satisfy the debt.

   2. Article 9 also gives creditors a way to have priority to that collateral, through a step known as perfection of the security interest.

B. Article 9 of the UCC is the uniform law that governs the rights of creditors and debtors for security interests in personal property and fixtures.

C. Article 9 security interests apply to personal property or fixtures including goods, documents, instruments, general intangibles, chattel paper, and accounts), agricultural liens, sales of accounts, chattel paper, and promissory notes, and commercial consignments of $1,000 or more—UCC 9-109.

   1. Transactions excluded from secured transactions law (other laws apply):

      a. Landlord's liens;

      b. Mechanic's liens;

      c. Artisan's liens;

      d. Assignment of wage;

      e. Tort claims;

      f. Insurance (except proceeds from policies covering covered collateral);

      g. Judgments;

      h. Leases;

      i. Real estate mortgages.

II. Basic Terminology

A. **Definitions**—Important for creation and perfection by filing

Secured Party: The creditor who has a security interest in the debtor's collateral. Can be a seller, or lender, or a buyer of accounts or chattels—UCC 9-102(a)(72).

Debtor: The "person" who owes payment or other performance of the secured obligation—*UCC 9-102(a)(28).*

Security Interest: The interest in the collateral (personal property, fixtures etc.), that secures payment or performance of an obligation—UCC 1-201(37).

Security Agreement: An agreement that creates or provides for a security interest—UCC *9-102(a)(73).*
Collateral: The personal property or intangible interest that is the subject of the security interest—UCC 9-102(a)(12).

Financing Statement: Referred to as a UCC-1 form, is the instrument usually filed to give public notice to third parties of the secured party's security interest—UCC 9-102(a)(39).

B. Collateral definitions and classifications

1. Tangible goods

Consumer Goods: Used or bought primarily for personal, family, or household purposes—UCC 9-102(a)(23).

Equipment: Used or bought primarily for use in a business, and not part of inventory or farm products—UCC 9-102(a)(33).

Farm Products: Crops (including aquatic goods) and livestock, or supplies produced in a farming operation such as ginned cotton, milk, eggs, maple syrup, etc.—UCC 9-102(a) (34).

Inventory: Held by a person for sale under a contract of service or lease, or raw materials held for production and work in progress—UCC 9-102(a)(48).

Fixtures: Personal property, that become so attached or so related to realty that an interest in them arises under real estate law—UCC 9-102(a)(41).

Accessions: Personal property that is so attached, installed, or fixed, to other personal property (goods) that it becomes a part of the goods (other personal property) i.e., installing a compact disk-tape recorder radio in an automobile—UCC 9-102(a)(1).

2. Intangibles

Chattel paper: A writing or writings (records) that evidences both a security interest in goods and/or software used in goods and a monetary obligation to pay—such as a security agreement, or a security agreement and a promissory note.

Instrument: A negotiable instrument (e.g., check, note, CD, or draft) or other writing that evidences a right to the payment of money and is not a security agreement or lease, but a type that can ordinarily be transferred (by endorsement if necessary) by delivery—UCC 9-102(a)(47).

Account: Any right to receive payment for any property (real or personal) sold, leased, licensed, assigned, or otherwise disposed of, including intellectual licensed property; services rendered or to be rendered, such as contract rights; incurring surety obligations; policies of insurance; use of a credit card; winnings of a government sponsored or authorized lottery or other game of chance; health-care -insurance receivables (defined as an interest or claim under a policy of insurance to payment for health-care goods or services provided)—UCC 9-102(a)(2), (a)(46).

Deposit account: Any demand, time savings, passbook, or similar account maintained with a bank—UCC 9-102(a)(29).

Agricultural lien: A nonpossessory statutory lien on a debtor's farm products—UCC 9-102(a)(5).

Commercial tort claim: A claim arising out of a tort in which the claimant is an organization, or arose in the course of a claimant's business or profession, and does not include damages for death or personal injury—UCC 9-102(a)(13).

General Intangibles: Any personal property other than goods, accounts, chattel paper, deposit accounts, commercial tort claims, investment property, letter of credit-rights, documents, instruments, and money (i.e., oil royalties, copyrights, patents, etc.)—UCC9-102(a)(42).

3. Payment intangibles—a general intangible under which the principal debtor's obligation is to pay money (such as a loan without an instrument or chattel paper)—UCC 9-102(a) (61).

4. Software is a good, if the software is so embedded in a computer that it is considered a part of the computer, but if it is independent from the computer or a good, it is a general intangible—UCC 9-102(a)(44), (a)(75).

III. Creation of Security Interest

A. Requirements for a security interest to attach—UCC 9-203

1. A writing

   a. Unless the collateral is in the possession of the secured party, there must be a written or authenticated security.

   b. The writing must be signed or authenticated by the debtor. (Authenticated includes any agreement or signature inscribed on a tangible medium or stored in an electronic or other retrievable medium—UCC 9-102(a)(7)(69).)

   c. The security agreement must describe the collateral. Revised Article 9 (which is covered on the exam) also gives examples of what constitutes a sufficient description of the collateral—UCC 9-108(b)—such as "specified listing, category, quantity, UCC defined collateral, etc." and states that super-generic descriptions, such as "all the debtor's assets," or "all the debtor's personal property," or words of similar import are not a sufficient description. See UCC 9-108(c).

2. The secured party must give to the debtor something of value (such as a binding commitment to extend credit, or security, or satisfaction of a preexisting debt, or consideration to support a simple contract)—UCC 1-201(44). Note: The creation of a security interest does not require consideration because a security interest can be given in order to secure an already existing debt and still be valid.

3. The debtor must have "rights" in the collateral.

   a. Be sure to refer to Article 2 and the lesson on Passage of Title because these two areas of UCC Article 2 and UCC Article 9 are often combined on the exam. A debtor may be advanced a credit line by a creditor with the creditor taking a security interest in the equipment the debtor is buying with the credit line. Suppose that the debtor and creditor sign the credit line agreement and security agreement (which meet all of the requirements listed above) on December 1. The equipment is to be delivered FOB seller's place of business on December 15. The security agreement will attach on December 15 when the seller sets aside and ships the equipment to the debtor/buyer.

B. When these three requirements are ALL met, the security interest attaches, which means that the creditor has rights in the collateral, including the right to repossess the collateral in the event the debtor defaults.

See the following note.

Misconception 1: To create a security interest for the secured party, there must be a written security agreement and the agreement must be signed by both the debtor and secured party. Both are incorrect. A security interest can be created by the secured party taking possession of the lateral under an I agreement, and if the security agreement is in writing or authenticated, only the debtor's signature is required to create the security interest.

Misconception 2: The debtor must be the "owner" (have title) of the lateral before the secured party can have a security interest in the lateral. For example, suppose that the debtor has given a security interest in goods that are to be manufactured. Once those goods are identified under the contract, the debtor has rights in them and the security interest attaches even though title will not pass until later.

C. **Rights of the creditor upon security interest attachment**

   1. Creditor has the right to repossess the collateral (see Rights of Secured Parties and Debtors).

   2. Creditor can sell the repossessed collateral (see Rights of Secured Parties and Debtors).

   3. Creditor is a secured creditor and has priority over other unsecured creditors (see Priorities in Security Interests).

   4. Creditor has priority in bankruptcy above unsecured creditors (see Distribution of Debtor's Estate).

   5. Creditor has the right to perfect the security interest in order to stand first in line among secured creditors (see the "Priorities in Security Interests" lesson).

Perfection of Security Interests

After studying this lesson you should be able to:

1. Define perfection and explain its purpose.

2. List the ways a creditor can obtain perfection.

I. What Is Perfection?

Definition:

Perfection: A means by which a secured party gains priority to a debtor's collateral over other third parties who also claim to have an interest in the same collateral. Types of third parties who may claim a conflicting interest are unsecured creditors, other secured parties (unperfected) including lien holders, perfected secured parties, trustees in bankruptcy, and purchasers of the collateral.

II. Methods of Perfection—Filing; Possession; Automatic; and Temporary

A. Filing

1. **What is filed?**— Either a UCC-1 form or the security agreement.

2. **Filing requirements**—UCC 9-502

   a. A filing must state names of both the debtor (for registered organizations, estates, and trusts, the sufficiency of the debtor's name must meet certain criteria—UCC 9-503(a)) and secured party.

   b. There are two different standards for financing statements versus security agreements. The standards for financing statements can be generic—UCC 9-504. The standards for security agreements require specificity—UCC 9-108.

   c. A filing must contain a description of the collateral subject to the security interest. The description can be a generic description, such as "all assets" or "all personal property." For land-related security interests, a legal description of the land is required and the security interest is filed in real property records—UCC 9-504.

   > **Note:**
   > *Debtor's signature is not required and a uniform national form is provided in UCC 9-521. In addition, addresses of the debtor and secured party must be stated or the filing officer will reject the filing because these addresses will prove to be critical for the notifications required for priorities—UCC 9-516b(4)(5), 9-520(a) (see Priorities in Security Interests).*

3. **Where is it filed?**

   a. **Filing location for perfection**—For all classifications of collateral, except those listed below or where perfection is limited to possession, or control, or specified in a statute, perfection is known as a central filing or in the designated offices for filing in the state where the debtor is located—UCC 9-301.

   b. **Exceptions**

      i. For fixtures, timber to be cut, and collateral to be extracted (such as oil, coal, gas, minerals) filing is in the jurisdiction where the collateral is located and the filing must include a description of the realty—UCC 9-301(3)(4), 9-502(b).

      ii. For possessory security interests, perfection (and priority) is in the jurisdiction where the collateral is located—UCC 9-301(2).

      iii. For certificated securities perfection is where the security certificate is located, but for uncertificated securities it is the location of the issuer—UCC 9-305(a)(1) (2).

4. **Timing issues with perfection**

   a. **When can a financing statement be filed?**

      i. Before a security agreement is made or a security interest attaches;

      ii. Before debtor authorization is required—UCC 9-502(d), 9-509;

      iii. Before the authentication of a security agreement constitutes the debtor's authorization for the filing of a financing statement—UCC 9-509(b).

   b. Perfection occurs upon communication (allows electronic filings, if so authorized) of a financing statement (or security agreement) and tender of the filing fee to the filing officer—**OR**—acceptance of the financing statement by the filing officer—UCC 9-516(a).

      i. A filing is effective even if filing officer refuses it unless, generally—UCC 9-516(d):

         1. The proper filing fee is not tendered.

         2. The name of the debtor is not provided (which would prevent indexing).

         3. The record filing is communicated in an unauthorized (as set by the filing offices) medium.

         4. Where required, there is not a sufficient description of the realty—UCC 9-516(b).

   c. **Time of perfection**

      i. **A financing statement**—can be filed before a security agreement is made or a security interest attaches, but debtor authorization is required—UCC 9-502(d), 9-509, and the financing statement is not effective until all requirements are met. Authentication of a security agreement constitutes the debtor's authorization for the filing of a financing statement—UCC 9-509(b).

      For example, creditor files a financing statement on November 1 for a security interest in inventory of the debtor. They have agreed to the Article 9 financing arrangements and the paperwork is complete, but the debtor has not signed the paperwork. Debtor signs the paperwork on November 15. The perfection is not effective until November 15—all requirements for attachment must be met for the financing statement to be effective.

      ii. **A security interest**—is perfected upon communication (allows electronic filings, if so authorized) of a financing statement (or security agreement) and tender of the filing fee to the filing officer—**OR**—acceptance of the financing statement by the filing officer—UCC 9-516(a).

         1. A filing is effective even if filing officer refuses it unless, generally—UCC 9-516(d):

            a. The proper filing fee is not tendered.

            b. The name of the debtor is not provided (which would prevent indexing).

            c. The record filing is communicated in an unauthorized (as set by the filing offices) medium.

            d. Where required, there is not a sufficient description of the realty—UCC 9-516(b).

      iii. Generally, a person (such as the debtor) can file a correction statement if it is believed that the original financing statement is inaccurate or wrongfully filed, but this does not affect the effectiveness of the initial financing statement—UCC 9-518.

5. **A filed financing statement**—is effective for five years from date of filing, and can be extended for another five years if a continuation statement is filed (only) during the six-month period prior to the expiration of the five-year period—UCC 9-515.

Example:
The five-year period for a perfected (by filing) security interest will expire on December 1. If the secured party wants to extend its perfection for another five years, the secured party must file a continuation statement at anytime from June 1 to December 1 (the six months before the expiration). Should the secured party file the continuation before the six-month window, the continuation would not be effective and its perfection would expire on December 1.

B. Perfection by possession

1. **Generally**—Article 9 requires filing for perfection, but it also allows perfection by either possession or another method of perfection—UCC 9-310, 9-312(a), 9-313. For example, instruments (whether negotiable or nonnegotiable) can be perfected by filing or possession.

   Note:
   For public-finance transactions or manufactured home transactions, the effective period is 30 years—UCC 9-515(b).

2. **Possession**

   a. Creditor has physical possession of the goods.

   b. Pawn of goods is possession.

   c. Transfer of instruments or chattel paper from debtor to creditor is transfer of possession.

   d. Field warehousing—The creditor has an agent at the debtor's place of business (warehouse), and the creditor's agent's signature is required before the buyer can sell, pledge, or do anything with the goods subject to the field warehousing arrangement that might affect the creditor's rights and/or priority in those goods.

3. **Special rules on possession and perfection**

   a. **Letter of credit rights**—Perfection is by control unless it is a supporting obligation—UCC 9-308(d), 9-312(b)(2). Control means that the debtor cannot do anything with regard to the letter of credit without the approval of the creditor

   b. **Electronic chattel paper**—Perfection is by filing or control unless it is a supporting obligation—UCC 9-310(a), 9-313(a), 9-314(a).

   c. **Deposit accounts**—Used as original collateral; can be perfected only by control—UCC 9-312(b)(3).

   d. **Money**—Can only be perfected by possession—UCC 9-312(b)(3).

   e. **Investment property**—(such as securities, security accounts, security entitlements, etc.)—May be perfected by filing—UCC 9-312(a)—or control—UCC9-314. For priority purposes, perfection by control prevails over perfection by filing—UCC 9-328(1).

C. Automatic Perfection—Perfection is automatic upon creation of the security interest (no filing or possession required). Applies only in a few situations. Two most important are:

1. A purchase money security interest (PMSI) in consumer goods—UCC 9-309(1).

   a. Consumer goods are goods used or bought primarily for personal, family, or household purposes—UCC 9-102(a)(23).

   b. PMSI is created when the interest is taken or retained by the seller of the collateral to secure the price—UCC 9-103(a)(2). In other words, the creditor is advancing the funds for the purchase of the collateral.

Example:
Beyer wants to purchase a large-screen TV from Sallor TV Inc. for $1,500. Beyer pays $200 down, and signs a security agreement giving Sallor TV a security interest in the set being purchased until the balance of $1,300 is paid. Sallor has a PMSI.

    c. This special perfection rule has a practical basis. If every consumer credit purchase had to have a filed, perfected financing statement, the records would be impossible to manage.

    d. The creditor need not be the merchant seller of the collateral. A bank can be an automatically perfected PMSI creditor if the debtor does indeed buy the goods that are listed in the security agreement.

Example:
Beyer wants to buy a large-screen TV from Sallor TV Inc. Beyer goes to West Bank seeking a loan to buy the set. West Bank loans Beyer the money and Beyer signs a security agreement giving West Bank a security interest in the to-be- purchased TV set. If Beyer does purchase the set, West Bank has a PMSI in the set. Note: If Beyer purchases a large refrigerator-freezer instead of the TV, West Bank would be an unsecured creditor.

    2. Other collateral subject to automatic perfection are:

      a. a sale of payment intangibles;

      b. a sale of promissory notes;

        i. an assignment of health-care-insurance receivables to the health care provider;

        ii. supporting obligations such as letter-of-credit rights, secondary obligations (guarantees, etc.) that support payments on accounts, chattel paper, instruments, general intangibles, etc.—UCC 9-308(d), 9-309.

D. Temporary perfection—UCC 9-312(e)(f)(g)

    1. Without filing or possession

      a. For 20 days from creation of the security interest by authenticated security agreement;

      b. Certificated securities, negotiable documents, and instruments if new value is given.

    2. If perfected—Remains perfected for 20 days without a filing:

      a. for goods in possession of a bailee or a negotiable document where the secured party makes the goods or documents available to the debtor for sale, exchange, loading, shipping, etc.;

      b. for a certificated security or an instrument where the secured party delivers the security certificate or instrument to the debtor for sale, exchange, collection, presentation, etc.

    3. When a debtor moves out of state—(debtor moved to a new jurisdiction)—UCC 9-316.

      a. If collateral is perfected in one jurisdiction (for example, in state A) and the debtor moves into another jurisdiction (state B), the perfected secured party (state A) has priority over a subsequent perfected secured party in the new jurisdiction (state B) for a period of four months (or for the period of time remaining under the original perfection, whichever is earlier) from the date the debtor changes his/her location into the new jurisdiction (state B). Where there is a transfer of the collateral to another debtor, who then becomes the debtor and is located in another jurisdiction, the priority period is one year—UCC 9-316(a)(3). If the perfected secured party in the original jurisdiction perfects in the new jurisdiction within the four-month period, its priority continues until the perfection expires.

> **Example:**
> West Bank has a perfected security interest in Wisconsin on Able's equipment. (Able is a sole proprietorship located in Wisconsin.) Able has built a new plant in Illinois and on May 1, without West's consent, transfers some of the Wisconsin plant equipment to the Illinois plant and installs the equipment with some newly purchased equipment there. On June 1, Able gets a loan from East Bank in Illinois putting up all the Illinois plant equipment as collateral. Before making the loan, East Bank had checked for prior filings on the equipment in Illinois. If Able goes into default to both West Bank and East Bank on August 1, West Bank has priority over East Bank as to the equipment moved to Illinois because West Bank's perfection in Wisconsin still has priority over the equipment transferred to the Illinois plant until September 1.

4. Automatic perfection in proceeds

a. **Proceeds**—UCC 9-315—Not only does a security interest continue in the collateral even after its sale or exchange, but it also applies to any proceeds (usually payments) payable to the debtor from the sale or destruction (assuming an insurance policy with the debtor as beneficiary) of the collateral. If perfection by filing includes proceeds, perfection also gives the secured party priority to proceeds. If proceeds are not perfected by filing, priority only extends for 21 days after the debtors receipt unless the secured party perfects the proceeds by filing within the 21-day period.

> **Example:**
> West Bank has a filed perfected security interest in all of Ralph's TV present inventory, any after-acquired inventory, and the proceeds from any of these TVs. Able purchases a TV from Ralph signing a security agreement in which she is to make monthly payments. Ralph goes into default to West Bank. Although West Bank cannot repossess the TV sold to Able (Able is a buyer in the ordinary course of business.), West Bank is entitled to the monthly payments by Able as proceeds.

III. Rights of Secured Parties on Filing for Perfection

A. **Release**—A secured party can release all (used as a termination statement) or part of any collateral described in the filing thereby terminating its security interest in that collateral. Record of the release is by filing a uniform amendment form—UCC 9-512, 9-521(b).

B. **Assignment**—A secured party can assign all or any part of the security interest to a third party assignee, and the assignee can become the secured party of record if the assignment is filed by use of a uniform amendment form—UCC 9-514, 9-521(a).

C. **Amendment**—If debtor and secured party so agree, the filing can be amended (such as, by adding new collateral if authorized by the debtor) by filing a uniform amendment form, that indicates by file number the initial financing statement—UCC 9-512(a). The amendment does not extend the time period of perfection, but, if the amendment adds collateral, the perfection date (for priority purposes) for the new collateral only begins at date of the filing of the amendment—UCC 9-512(b)(c).

D. **Information request**—Any person, such as a prospective creditor, can request from the filing officer "information" on previously filed security interests of a specific debtor. For a fee, a certificate or copies of the previous filings can be furnished—UCC 9-523(c), 9-525(d).

Priorities in Security Interests

I. General Rules

A. A perfected secured party's interest has priority over the following parties—UCC 9-317, 9-322:

1. **Unsecured Creditors**—perfected secured creditor vs. unsecured creditor: Perfected secured creditor has priority.

2. **Unperfected Secured Parties**—perfected secured party vs. unperfected secured party: Perfected secured creditor has priority.

3. **Lien Creditors**—perfected secured creditor vs. lien creditor: First to attach has priority. If the perfected secured party perfected before the lien attached, the perfected secured party has priority, and if the lien attached prior to perfection, the lien creditor has priority.

4. **Judgment creditors**—perfected secured creditor vs. judgment creditor: First to attach has priority. If the perfected secured party perfected before the judgment lien attached, the perfected secured party has priority, and if the judgment lien attached prior to perfection, the lien creditor has priority.

5. **Trustees in Bankruptcy**—See priority rules in the "Distribution of Debtor's Estate" lesson.

II. Priority of Perfected Secured Parties over Buyers

A. **Buyers in the ordinary course of business**—A buyer in the ordinary course of business takes free of a secured party's security interest, even if it is perfected, and buyer knows of the security interest at time of sale—UCC 9-320(a). Perfected secured creditor v. buyer in the ordinary course of business: Buyer in the ordinary course of business wins and gets the goods/collateral.

Definition:
A Buyer in the Ordinary Course of Business: A buyer who buys goods from a merchant (a seller who deals in goods of that kind)—UCC 1-201(9).

B. **Buyer not in the ordinary course of business**—perfected secured party vs. buyer not in the ordinary course of business: Perfected secured party takes priority because buyers not in the ordinary course of business need to check for creditors' interests before buying in less-than-ordinary transactions.

C. **Buyer not in the ordinary course of business**—secured creditor vs. buyer not in the ordinary course of business: Buyer will have priority unless the buyer is aware of the creditor's secured interest.

See the following example.

Example:
West Bank has a perfected security interest in a tractor owned by a farmer. After the harvest season, the farmer sells the tractor to a farm implement dealer (one who sells and buys used and new tractors). The farmer goes into default and West Bank claims priority to the tractor purchased by the farm implement dealer. The farm implement dealer claims it is a buyer in the ordinary course of business because it buys and sells used tractors. Here, West Bank has priority because the farm implement dealer is not a buyer in the ordinary course of business. The reason is the farmer (the seller) does not regularly sell tractors, thus, does not deal in goods of that kind.

Example:

On July 8, Ace, a refrigerator wholesaler, purchased 50 refrigerators. This comprised Ace's entire inventory and was financed under an agreement with Rome Bank that gave Rome a security interest in all refrigerators on Ace's premises, all future acquired refrigerators, and the proceeds of sales. On July 12, Rome filed a financing statement that adequately identified the collateral. On August 15, Ace sold one refrigerator to Cray for personal use and four refrigerators to Zone Co. for its business. Because Ace is a wholesaler and the purchase made by Zone, although for use in its business, it was still a purchase in the ordinary course of business. All buyers in the ordinary course of business are protected.

D. Buyer not in the ordinary course of business of consumer goods—A buyer not in the ordinary course of business of consumer goods will prevail over a previously perfected secured party by attachment (automatically; without filing) if the buyer can prove the four requirements—UCC 9-320(b)(e). If the buyer cannot establish all four of these requirements, the perfected secured party has priority.

1. Buyer must give **value** to the seller-debtor;

2. Buyer must **not know** of secured party's security interest;

3. Buyer must buy for **personal use** (as consumer goods);

4. Buyer must buy **before** the **secured party perfects by filing**.

> **Note:**
> *A consumer seller/creditor's automatically perfected security interest gives that seller/creditor over all other creditors, but the failure to file makes that seller/creditor subject to the buyer who is not even in the ordinary course of business.*

Example:

Beyer purchases a large-screen TV for personal use from Ralph's TV store. Beyer cannot pay the full purchase price and, upon making a down payment, signs a security agreement giving Ralph a security interest in the set purchased. Ralph has a perfected PMSI without a filing (perfection by attachment). Later, while still making payments to Ralph, Beyer sells the set to her next-door-neighbor Sally Hawks. Hawks is not a buyer in the ordinary course of business. Due to some financial reverses, Beyer goes into default to Ralph's TVs. If Hawks did not know of Ralph's security interest at the time of sale and Hawks purchased the TV as a consumer good (for her personal, family, or household use), Ralph cannot repossess the set from Hawks. Had Ralph's TVs perfected its security interest (also) by filing before the sale to Hawks, Ralph's TVs could have repossessed the TV from Hawks to satisfy the balance of Beyer's debt.

E. Buyers of negotiable instruments, documents, or securities—Buyers who are HDCs of instruments, holders to whom a negotiable document has been duly negotiated, or BFPs of securities have priority over a previously perfected security interest—UCC 9-330(d), 331(a).

III. Priority between Two Perfected Security Interests in the Same Collateral

A. General rule—Priority between two perfected secured parties in the same debtor's collateral, including agricultural liens unless a state statute states otherwise, is first in time of perfection is first in priority right—UCC 9-322(a)(1).

B. Exceptions

1. **Inventory**—A PMSI in a debtor's inventory will have priority over a previously perfected non-PMSI providing these two events take place before the debtor takes possession of the collateral.

   a. The PMSI secured party perfects; **and**

   b. The PMSI secured party sends (and the non-PMSI party receives) written notice of the PMSI—UCC 9-324(b). This requirement is why addresses are required in the financing statements. The filed financing statement is where creditors obtain names and contact information so that they can exercise their priority rights under Article 9.

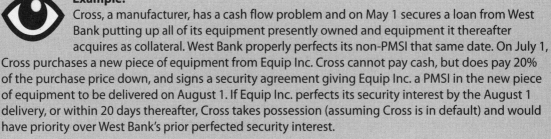

Example:
Ralph's TV Inc. has a cash flow problem. On May 1, Ralph secures a loan from West Bank putting up Ralph's entire present inventory and any inventory thereafter acquired. This is a non-PMSI and West Bank properly perfects its security interest with a filing on that same date. On August 1, Ralph learns that it can purchase 100 TV sets directly from one of its suppliers, Inter TV. Ralph cannot pay cash but does pay 20% of the purchase price as a down payment and signs a security agreement giving Inter TV a security interest in the 100 TV sets that Ralph is purchasing. Delivery of the 100 TV sets is to be on or before September 1. Inter TV has a PMSI. On August 2, Inter TV perfects its security interest with a proper filing, and, on August 20, sends West Bank a fax, which is received, notifying West Bank of Inter TV's security interest. If Ralph goes into default to both West Bank and Inter TV, Inter TV would have priority over West Bank's after-acquired collateral interest in the 100 sets purchased by Ralph. This is because Inter TV has a PMSI properly perfected, and West Bank was sent and it received written notice of Inter TV's security interest prior to Ralph's possession of the 100 TV sets.

2. **Collateral other than inventory**—For any other types of collateral, a PMSI will have priority over a previously perfected non-PMSI provided that if the PMSI secured party perfects before or within 20 days after debtor takes possession of the collateral. No notice is required—UCC 9-324(a).

Example:
Cross, a manufacturer, has a cash flow problem and on May 1 secures a loan from West Bank putting up all of its equipment presently owned and equipment it thereafter acquires as collateral. West Bank properly perfects its non-PMSI that same date. On July 1, Cross purchases a new piece of equipment from Equip Inc. Cross cannot pay cash, but does pay 20% of the purchase price down, and signs a security agreement giving Equip Inc. a PMSI in the new piece of equipment to be delivered on August 1. If Equip Inc. perfects its security interest by the August 1 delivery, or within 20 days thereafter, Cross takes possession (assuming Cross is in default) and would have priority over West Bank's prior perfected security interest.

3. **Software**— Applies only to a purchase-money security in software if used in goods subject to a purchase-money security interest. Priority is determined the same as if the goods are inventory (if the goods are inventory), or if not as if the goods are other than inventory—UCC 9-103(c), 9-324(f).

IV. Perfection and the Floating Lien

A. **Floating lien concept**—The floating lien concept allows the (perfected) secured party to have a security interest in collateral not in existence at time of its creation, apply to payments made on sale or destruction or exchange of the collateral, to apply to future advances of funds, to commingled goods, and even continues when collateral is moved into a different jurisdiction. In short, a perfected secured party could have a single security interest in raw materials to be used in the manufacture of goods, and this interest would continue during the manufacturing process to the finished goods, continue during shipment to another state jurisdiction, and to the proceeds from the sale or exchange of these goods.

B. **Floating lien types**

1. **After-acquired collateral clauses**—A security agreement can provide for not only a security interest in the present collateral of the debtor, but it can also be applied to any collateral the debtor acquires in the future—UCC 9-204. (This includes consumer goods when given as additional collateral if debtor acquires rights in them within 10 days after the secured party gives value.)

Example:
West Bank has a perfected security interest in the present and after-acquired inventory of a retailer. The retailer purchases for cash some new inventory. West Bank's prior perfection also applies to the new inventory just purchased.

2. **Future advances**—A perfected security interest in collateral of the debtor can also be applied to future loans made by the perfected secured party using the same collateral as security without a new perfection for the new loans—UCC 9-204.

Example:
On May 1, West Bank has a perfected security interest (for a loan of $200,000) in $1,000,000 worth of the debtor's collateral. The security agreement includes a future advance clause that allows the debtor to borrow up to $400,000 using the same million dollars of collateral. On August 1, the debtor borrows $100,000 from East Bank giving East Bank a security interest in the same collateral. East Bank is treating its loan like a second mortgage. On September 1, the debtor, through the future advance clause, borrows another $200,000 from West Bank. West Bank does not perfect this loan. On October 1, the collateral has rapidly depreciated in value to $400,000 and the debtor goes into default on all three loans. In this case, because of the future advance clause, West Bank is entitled to the full $400,000 even though its last loan was subsequent to East Bank's $100,000 loan.

Rights of Secured Parties and Debtors

After studying this lesson you should be able to:

1. Describe the rights of the debtor upon full payment of the debt.

2. Describe the rights of the creditor upon the debtor's default.

3. Explain the duties that creditors have on the repossession and sale of collateral.

4. Explain how proceeds from the sale of collateral are distributed.

I. Creditor's Options Upon Debtor Default

A. Upon debtor's default, the secured party can proceed under the UCC, or can proceed with any existing judicial remedy. For example, a creditor could simply file a suit to reduce debt to judgment and levy on the debtor's nonexempt property—property other than the collateral, or garnish etc.—UCC 9-601.

B. **Creditor's right to require the debtor to assemble the collateral**—If the security agreement so provides, the secured party can require the debtor to assemble the collateral upon debtor's default and place the collateral at a location reasonably convenient to both parties—UCC 9-609(c).

C. **Creditor's right to render collateral unusable**—Upon default, the secured party can, without removal of the collateral, render the collateral unusable (not damaged) to the debtor—UCC 9-609(a). (Some states prohibit this.)

Example:
A lumber saw mill owner is in default and the secured party has a security interest in the huge machine that saws timber into lumber. Under this law, the secured party could remove the saw blades from the huge machine rendering the machine unusable.

D. **Creditor's right to pursue the self-help remedy of repossession**

1. Upon debtor's default, the secured party is entitled to take peaceful possession of the collateral without the use of judicial process—UCC 9-609(b).

2. The UCC does not define peaceful possession. General rule is if secured party can take possession without committing any of the acts listed below the collateral has been taken peacefully.

    a. Trespass onto realty;

    b. Assault and/or battery; or

    c. Breaking and entering.

E. **Creditor's right to pursue judicial process**—If the collateral cannot be taken peacefully or secured party does not wish to try, the secured party can secure possession through a judicial petition and hearing—UCC 9-609(b)(1), (c).

F. **Creditor's rights on disposal of the repossessed collateral**

1. **Keep collateral**—In full or partial satisfaction of the debt (always with debtor's consent)—UCC 9-620(a)(1),(c). In order to keep the collateral, the following steps are required:

    a. Secured party sends notice to the debtor and junior security interests, who gave notice of their claim or have filed a statutory security interest—UCC 9-620(a), 9-621; and

    b. The secured party has not received notification or objection from any of the above parties within 20 days after notice was sent.

2. **When the creditor must sell the collateral**—If the collateral is consumer goods and 60% or more of the purchase price (or debt if the collateral was not fully financed by the creditor) has been paid, the creditor must sell it—UCC 9-620(e).

3. **Creditor's right to sell collateral**—Secured party can always sell—UCC 9-610(a).

    a. **Time requirement for sale**—If objection is received or secured must sell, the secured party must dispose of the collateral within 90 days after taking possession.

    b. Otherwise the secured party can be held liable for tort of conversion, or, if the collateral is consumer goods, for any loss and an amount not less than the credit service charge plus 10% of the principal amount of the debt, or the time price differential plus 10% of the cash price—UCC 9-620(f), 9-625(c).

    c. **Reasonable manner**—The UCC only requires that sale, lease, or license be conducted in a commercially reasonable manner—UCC 9-602(7), 9-603, 9-610(a).

> **Note:**
> *The reason notice is not required in consumer goods transactions is because there might not be financing statements filed on the goods that would let the creditor know who the junior lienholders are. PMSIs are perfected without filing, so the selling creditor would have no way of determining all the junior lien holders in the transaction.*

    i. Sale can be public or private;

    ii. Secured party must give debtor notice of time and place of disposition, and, except for consumer goods junior lien holders who have given notice of their claims (Notice is not required if collateral is perishable, rapidly declining in value, or to be sold on a recognized market.), to junior lien holders of record 10 days before notification date; (Contents of notification are stated—UCC 9-613 for commercial transactions and UCC 9-614 for consumer transactions.)

    iii. Disposition must be at a reasonable time and place;

    iv. Secured party can disclaim disposal warranties;

    v. Secured party can "buy" if a public sale, goods are sold on a recognized market or one where there are widely distributed price quotations—UCC 9-610, 9-611.

    d. **Distribution of proceeds**

        I. **Expenses** incurred by secured party in repossession, keeping, and resale;

        II. **Balance of debt** owed to the secured party;

        ill. **Junior lien holders** who have made written demands;

        iv. Debtor (unless the collateral is accounts or chattel paper, then to secured party unless, to the contrary, provided to the debtor in the security agreement)—UCC 9-608(a), 9-615(a).

    e. If the secured party receives noncash proceeds from the disposition, the secured party is required to make a value determination and apply this value in a reasonably commercial manner—UCC 9-608(a)(3), 9-615(c). The amount received from a disposition does not in and of itself give grounds that the sale was not conducted in a reasonable manner, however, the price may suggest the need for judicial scrutiny—UCC 9-627(a), but see Official Comments 10 to UCC 9-610 and Comment 6 to UCC 9-615.

    f. **Creditor's rights to collect deficiency of sale funds from debtor**—Unless the collateral is accounts, chattel paper, payment intangibles, or promissory notes, if the proceeds are insufficient to cover the expenses and balance of the debt, the secured party is entitled to a deficiency judgment, which enables the secured party to get a writ to levy on other property (nonexempt) of the debtor. If the collateral is accounts, chattel paper, payment intangibles, or promissory notes, the secured party is only entitled to a deficiency judgment, if it is provided for in the security agreement—UCC 9-615(d)(e).

g. Failure of the secured party to conduct the disposition in a reasonable manner or give proper notice, the deficiency of the debtor is reduced to the extent such failure affected the price received at the disposition—UCC 9-627(a)(3).

h. **Debtor's right of redemption**—If the secured party is not allowed to keep the collateral in possession in full satisfaction of the debt, the debtor or any other secured party has a right of redemption and by doing so can regain possession of the collateral until there is a sale—UCC 9-623.

i. **Waiver**—The debtor can waive the compulsory requirement of the secured party to dispose, and the debtor's right of redemption only after default—UCC 9-624.

II. **The Soldiers and Sailors Civil Relief Act (1940) (as amended 2012)**— Prohibits a secured party (whose security interest has been previously created) from repossession if the debtor (in default) has enlisted or has been called into active duty in the military after the security interest was created. This protection does not apply if the debtor is in the active military service at the time the security interest is created. This prohibition from repossession extends the entire period the debtor is in active service and can extend up to six months thereafter.

Misconception: Upon a debtor's default, only the secured party with priority has rights to the debtor's collateral. This is incorrect because junior lien holders, who have given the secured party written notice of their claims, are entitled to notice (except for consumer goods) if the secured party wants to keep the collateral in full satisfaction of the debt and can object forcing a sale. If there is a sale, the secured party must turn over to them any proceeds remaining after the expenses of default and balance of debt owed the secured party are satisfied.

Suretyship—Introduction, Creation, and Types

After studying this lesson you should be able to:

1. Explain the type of surety and guarantor relationships and their purpose.

2. Describe the rights of co-sureties and show how their shares of liability in the event of a default are computed.

3. Define all the terminology used for the rights of the parties in a surety relationship.

4. Define and distinguish the guarantor of collection.

5. Describe how a surety relationship is created.

I. Introduction

A. Definitions and terms

1. A guarantor or a surety is someone who agrees to stand liable for a debt of another. A guaranty or suretyship is a way for a creditor to have another form of backup for payment of the obligation owed. A surety or guarantor can be in addition to any collateral the debtor might pledge to the creditor.

B. The parties

1. The creditor;

2. The principal debtor;

3. The surety or guarantor.

 Example:
A surety or guarantor is liable to the creditor for the debt of the principal debtor. Frank owes money to June. Dallan agrees to serve as a surety for Frank. Frank is the principal debtor. June is the creditor, and Dallan is the surety or guarantor.

C. In a straight surety or guaranty relationship, the surety or guarantor must pay the creditor when the debt is due (unless there has been a discharge of the debt). The creditor can turn to the surety or guarantor for payment.

D. In a guarantor of collection relationship, the guarantor is responsible for the debt only after the principal debtor has defaulted because the guarantor is secondarily liable.

II. Creation

A. Because the suretyship relationship is one in which a third party agrees to stand liable for the debt of another, the suretyship contract (or a written memo) must be in writing and signed by the surety (guarantor) for it to be enforceable against the surety.

B. **Consideration is not required**—A surety relationship is created even when the surety is not compensated. However, certain differing rights result when there is a compensated vs. an uncompensated surety (see the "Suretyship—Rights of Parties" lesson).

C. **Creation of a multiple surety relationship**

1. Creditors can request that the debtor provide more than one surety.

Note:
The exam tends to use the terms surety and suretyship when dealing with most issues related to this topic. For the most part, the exam is testing the straight surety relationship. The exam has moved away from using the terms guaranty and guarantor. If the terms guarantor and guaranty are used alone (with no qualifying language), then they equate with surety and suretyship. If the exam is addressing an issue related to the differing order of liability for a guarantor of collection, the term "guarantor of collection" is used. The exam uses this approach to avoid confusion on the use of the term "guarantor." Most questions use only the terms suretyship, surety, and cosurety.

2. Creditor could ask for a sub-surety. A sub-surety is a surety for the surety, a party who agrees to be liable to the creditor if the principal debtor and the first surety fail to pay. A creditor cannot turn first to a sub-surety. The creditor must approach sub-sureties in the order in which they agreed to stand liable.

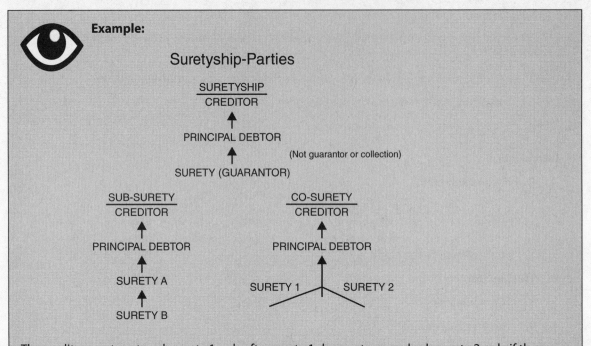

Example:

Suretyship-Parties

<u>SURETYSHIP</u>
CREDITOR
↑
PRINCIPAL DEBTOR
↑   (Not guarantor or collection)
SURETY (GUARANTOR)

<u>SUB-SURETY</u>   <u>CO-SURETY</u>
CREDITOR   CREDITOR
↑   ↑
PRINCIPAL DEBTOR   PRINCIPAL DEBTOR
↑   ↑
SURETY A   SURETY 1   SURETY 2
↑
SURETY B

The creditor can turn to sub-surety 1 only after surety 1 does not pay and sub-surety 2 only if the surety and sub-surety 1 have failed to pay.

3. A creditor could ask for more than one surety on the same level of liability, known as cosureties. Cosureties agree to stand jointly and severally liable to the creditor for the principal debtor.

   a. Cosureties can be sureties for the full amount of the debt.

   b. Cosureties can be sureties for certain percentages of the debt.

   See the following example.

Example:
1. CREDITOR (owed $60,000)

DEBTOR (agreed to pay the creditor $60,000)

Cosurety 1   Cosurety 2

($60,000)   ($60,000)

The creditor can turn to one or both of the sureties for payment. If one surety has to pay the full amount due, then the other cosureties are liable for paying their share (see right of contribution in the "Suretyship—Rights of Parties" lesson).

2. CREDITOR (owed $60,000)

   DEBTOR (agreed to pay the creditor $60,000)

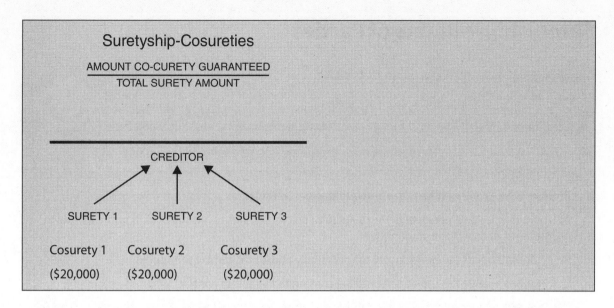

4. **Rights of creditors and sureties on amount paid toward principal debt**—In the absence of an agreement, the contribution of each cosurety (if the principal debtor does not pay) is determined on a pro rata basis computed by a ratio of the proportionate maximum liability of each cosurety to the total amount that all cosureties have pledged to stand liable.

Formula:
(Max Liability of Cosurety / Total Max. Liability of All Cosureties) × Amount Paid by Cosurety Seeking Contribution = Amount of Contribution Entitlement

Example 2 from above: 3 cosureties with $20,000 pledged

The principal debtor has defaulted. The creditor is still owed $45,000. Each of the cosureties is liable for $20,000/$60,000 or 1/3 of the amount due. Each would be required to pay $15,000 of the remaining debt.

Suppose that there were two cosureties, one for $45,000 and one for $15,000, and the debt remaining after the principal debtor's default is $45,000. Again, the maximum amount each would pay would be 15,000/60,000 or 1/4 and 45,000/60,000 or 3/4. Therefore, the $15,000 surety would pay $11,250 and the $60,000 surety would pay the remaining $34,750.

Example:
Able, Baker, and Carl are cosureties on a $50,000 debt owed by Daniel. Able's maximum liability is $10,000, Baker's maximum liability is $16,000, and Carl's maximum liability is $24,000. Daniel is in default and still owes $40,000. The creditor collects the full amount from Carl and Carl seeks rights of contribution from Able and Baker. Carl has these rights because Carl has paid more than his proportionate share. Using the formula above:

Able: $10,000/$50,000 x $40,000 = $8,000

Baker: $16,000/$50,000 x $40,000 = $12,800 which means Carl's proportionate share owed is:

$24,000/$50,000 x $40,000 = $19,200

Suretyship—Rights of Parties

After studying this lesson you should be able to:

1. Explain what defenses are available for sureties.

2. List those defenses that do not excuse a surety from payment.

3. Describe the circumstances that will release a surety from payment.

I. Rights of the Creditor When the Principal Debtor Defaults

A. Generally, upon a principal debtor's default, the creditor has several choices in terms of how to proceed to collect the amount due.

B. Proceed against the principal debtor personally and/or the debtor's property.

C. Proceed against the surety personally according to the surety contract.

D. Proceed against collateral of the debtor held either by the creditor or the surety. Creditor can sell the collateral to satisfy the debt and default costs, and any balance must be turned over to the principal debtor.

II. Rights of the Surety or Guarantor

A. **Exoneration**—This equitable right permits a surety to petition the court to order the creditor by court decree to exhaust recovery against the principal debtor before holding the surety liable.

Example:
Phillip is in default on a guaranteed loan made by West Bank. Phillip has numerous assets but these are located in another state. Evans, the surety, presently has most of her assets tied up (such as long-term CDs) to the extent that if she is required to pay now she will suffer severe financial losses. Under these circumstances, Evans could petition a court of equity for exoneration, which the court may grant.

B. **Reimbursement and indemnity**—Whenever the surety has fully or partially fulfilled the debtor's obligation to the creditor, the surety has a right to seek reimbursement from the principal debtor.

1. Right of reimbursement covers all costs that the guarantor has incurred because of surety agreement.

2. If principal debtor has a defense against paying the creditor, the surety's right of reimbursement is correspondingly reduced.

C. **Subrogation**—Upon payment, the surety succeeds to any rights the creditor has (stands in the shoes of the creditor). These include the following.

1. Creditor's rights against the principal debtor, including right to file a claim in bankruptcy.

2. Creditor's rights to the principal debtor's collateral held by the creditor or the surety.

3. Creditor's rights against third parties; for example, those who damage the principal debtor's collateral held by the creditor.

4. Creditor's rights against a cosurety.

Example:
Evans has guaranteed a loan made to Phillips by West Bank. West Bank has in its possession collateral owned by Phillips, of which some has been damaged due to the negligence of a third party, Green. Phillips files for bankruptcy and the bankruptcy court, upon West Bank's petition, allows West Bank to collect from Evans.

Question: What are Evans's rights in this situation?

Answer: Evans has the right of subrogation. This allows Evans to file West Bank's creditor's claim against Phillips's bankruptcy estate, to sue Green for damage to the collateral due to Green's negligence, and to take possession of any remaining collateral held by West Bank.

D. **Right of contribution**—Applies when two or more sureties or guarantors are liable on the same obligation to the same creditor and, upon debtor's default, one cosurety pays more than his or her proportionate share of the obligation. The right of contribution entitles this cosurety to recover the amount paid above his or her share owed from the other cosurety.

   1. **Generally**—Cosureties are jointly and severally liable. They can become cosureties by contract, can be bound as cosureties for different amounts, and can become cosureties even without knowledge of each other's existence (see the "Suretyship—Introduction, Creation, and Types" lesson for a discussion of allocation of amounts).

   2. **Release of cosurety**—If the creditor releases a cosurety without the other cosureties' consent (or reserving rights in the release in the remaining cosureties), the remaining cosureties' liability is released to the extent that the right of contribution cannot be obtained.

   3. **Reimbursement**—If a cosurety is fully reimbursed, there is no right of contribution.

   4. **Collateral**—In absence of agreement, cosureties are entitled to share in proportion to their liability a debtor's collateral in the hands of the creditor or acquired by a surety after the cosuretyship relationship was created.

III. **Defenses of the Parties—Events that DO NOT Release the Surety from Liability**—There are certain events than can occur as the principal debtor, the creditor, and the surety perform their obligations and exercise their rights. This section covers the events that do not result in a release of a surety.

   A. **Insolvency of the principal debtor**—Problems with the principal debtor's ability to pay is the reason for the surety's agreement.

   B. **Bankruptcy of the principal debtor**—Financial problems that the debtor might experience are among the reasons for having a surety agreement.

   C. **Fraud or misrepresentation by the debtor**—The debtor fraudulently misrepresents his financial status in order to convince the surety to act as a surety for the debtor's obligation to the creditor. Unless the creditor participated with the debtor in perpetrating the fraud, the surety is not released because of the fraud. The surety has the usual contract defenses and resulting damage rights against the debtor, but the surety must still pay the obligation to the creditor.

   D. **The principal debtor's incapacity**

   See the following example.

Example:
Daniel is the minor son of Emily and Emily is the surety of a loan West Bank made to Daniel. Daniel, being a minor, has legally disaffirmed his liability on the loan. Although West Bank cannot hold Daniel liable, Emily cannot escape her surety liability by claiming her son's minority as a defense.

   E. **Death of the principal debtor**—The death of the principal debtor does not discharge the surety. The surety is there as a backup for payment to the creditor when unforeseen events occur.

F. Release—Release by the creditor of the principal debtor, without the surety's consent and with the creditor reserving rights against the surety, does not result in a release of the surety.

G. Changes or modification—Changes or modification of the loan terms when there is a compensated surety.

>
>
> **Example:**
> Phillips wants a loan to start a restaurant. West Bank will not make the loan to Phillips unless she can secure a satisfactory surety. Evans, a financial entrepreneur, agrees with Phillips to be a surety if Phillips will turn over to Evans 5% of all gross proceeds for three years. Phillips agrees and the guaranteed loan contract is made with West Bank. Later, Phillips and West Bank make a material, binding modification of the loan without Evans's consent. Upon Phillips default, because Evans is a compensated surety, Evans can only escape surety liability to the extent of loss Evans can prove he suffered due to the modification.

H. The creditor's failure to give the surety notice of the principal debtor's default does not result in a discharge. Unless the creditor agreed to give notice of the default, the creditor is not required to do so. The creditor is entitled to payment from the surety when there is default.

I. Failure of the creditor to first resort to the collateral in order to satisfy the debt does not result in a discharge of the surety because it is the creditor's choice as to proceed against the surety, the collateral, or through litigation against the principal debtor.

IV. Defenses of the Parties—Events that DO Result in the Release of the Surety

A. Principal debt paid—Once the principal debtor has satisfied his obligation to the creditor, the surety is released from his suretyship obligation.

B. Surety's incapacity—Note that in some states a minor does not have capacity to contract as a guarantor.

C. Guarantor's discharge decree in bankruptcy—With certain exemptions discussed in the bankruptcy lessons, bankruptcy discharges all the debts of the bankrupt's estate, including surety obligations.

D. Statute of limitations expires—All contractual obligations are enforceable only if actions to enforce them are brought within the statute of limitations that applies to contracts. In a surety relationship, the statute of limitations for the creditor to run on the date upon which the surety's liability kicked in, i.e., when the creditor had the right to turn to the surety for payment.

E. Fraud or misrepresentation by the creditor—A surety is released from payment obligations to the creditor if the creditor participated with the principal debtor in committing fraud or misrepresentation that resulted in the surety's willingness to sign as a surety for the principal debtor. To be released for this reason, the surety must be able to show that the principal debtor and the creditor were in cahoots to use false information to convince the surety to act as a surety.

> **Example:**
> Creditor, by fraud, induces a principal debtor to incur a large debt guaranteed by Jones for the purchase of land from the creditor, which later proves to be worthless. The principal debtor can avoid the loan due to the creditor's fraud. Jones also can avoid his/her payment as a surety because of the creditor's fraud on the principal debtor.

> **Note:**
> *If the creditor, in the release to the principal debtor, reserved rights against the guarantor, this is no longer a release but a covenant not to sue, which does not discharge the guarantor from liability.*

F. **Release**—Release of the principal debtor without the guarantor's consent is also a release from liability of the guarantor. Collateral of the principal debtor held by either the creditor or the guarantor can still be used by the creditor to satisfy the debt.

G. **Refusal of principal debtor's tender**—If the principal debtor tenders payment to the creditor under a surety contract, and the creditor refuses the proper tender, the surety is completely discharged from liability.

> **Note:**
> *The principal debtor is not discharged if the proper tender is refused, but the surety is discharged and the principal debtor is not liable for future interest or other charges.*

 Example:
Peter has a loan from West Bank that is fully guaranteed by Susan. Peter sends a check for the full amount of the debt, including interest, to West Bank. Peter has more than sufficient funds on deposit to cover the check and the check clearly states that payment is in full accord and satisfaction of the loan. However, a bank officer mistakenly believes that the amount of the check is insufficient to cover both the principal and interest owed and sends the check back to Peter. Under these circumstances (proper tender refused), Susan is discharged from her surety liability and only Peter remains liable to West Bank.

H. **Material alteration by creditor**—When there is an uncompensated surety, any material alteration of the written loan or surety contract, such as the amount of the debt, by the creditor is a complete discharge of the surety's liability. The material alteration release includes situations in which the creditor substitutes a different principal debtor. A surety contract is personal to the principal debtor, and there cannot be substitution or assignment without consent of the surety. Without consent, the surety is released from liability.

I. **Creditor's failure to disclose**—A creditor's failure to disclose material facts that affect the risks of liability to a prospective surety is, in most states, presumed to be the defense of fraud and permits the guarantor to disaffirm the surety contract (complete discharge of liability).

 Example:
Peter seeks a loan from West Bank. After a careful credit analysis, West Bank denies the loan because of two factors that West Bank feels would make the loan too risky to make. The next day, Peter comes to West Bank with a prospective surety, Gloria, a wealthy customer of West Bank. Gloria tells West Bank that if it will make the loan to Peter, she would sign a surety contract. In this case, if West Bank is willing to make the loan with Gloria as surety, West Bank must tell Gloria of the material risk factors, that caused it to deny the loan. Failure to do so is presumed fraud and this allows Gloria, at any time, to disaffirm her surety liability. Note: To avoid a violation of privacy, West Bank must have Peter's permission for disclosure.

Example:
Gloria is the mother of Phillip and she has guaranteed a loan made to Phillip by West Bank. Later, Phillip and West Bank, without Gloria's consent, raise the amount of the loan's interest rate and extend the loan period. This is a binding (with consideration) and material modification of the loan contract. Since Gloria is a gratuitous (uncompensated) guarantor, this modification completely discharges her surety liability.

Example:
Evans is a gratuitous guarantor on a loan made to her daughter by West Bank. The loan is due in one month. Without Evans' consent, her daughter and West Bank agree to extend the loan period for one month without interest or other fees charged. After the one month, the daughter goes into default. It is not a change in the loan terms, it is simply an extension of time for the original terms (immaterial). The extension made no difference in amount due or even the ability of the debtor to pay. We discharge guarantors/sureties when they are affected by a change—i.e., collateral is released, loan is restructured. But an added month on a loan that is already due does not change the loan contract in amount, interest, or terms.

J. Changes and modifications where there is an UNCOMPENSATED surety—A material and binding modification of the loan contract made between the principal debtor and the creditor without the consent of the surety results in a release of the uncompensated surety.

K. Surrender or impairment of debtor's collateral—If the creditor surrenders the debtor's collateral held in the creditor's possession without the consent of the surety or commits acts that impair the value of the collateral, the surety is discharged to the extent of loss suffered by the surety due to the surrender or impairment. The surety's obligation is reduced ONLY by the amount of the collateral lost or released.

Example:
West Bank made a $100,000 loan to Phillip with Phillip transferring to West Bank 5,000 shares of stock (value $25,000) and having Evans as a surety. Later, without Evans's consent, West Bank releases back to Phillip the 5,000 shares. Upon Philip's default, Evans' surety liability on the $100,000 surety will be reduced by the value of the shares released to Phillip (or $25,000).

L. Special release for guaranty of collections—Any failure of the creditor to give the guarantor of collection proper notice of the principal debtor's default, or any material delay in attempting to collect first from the principal debtor, discharges the guarantor of collection from liability to the extent of loss suffered by such failure.

1. Remember: a guaranty of collections is different from a surety or simple guaranty so this failure to give notice is different from an ordinary guaranty relationship where the failure to give notice does not result in a release.

M. Statute of Frauds—Surety contracts must be in writing. A surety is always released from liability under an oral suretyship agreement.

Real Property

After studying this lesson you should be able to:

1. Define and differentiate between freehold and nonfreehold estates.

2. Explain nonpossessory interests.

3. Define liens.

4. Explain real property acquisition.

5. Define different methods of holding title.

I. **Types of Real Property Interests**

  A. **Freehold estates—possessory interests**

    1. **Fee simple estate**—A person has complete ownership for an unlimited duration to do with the property as he or she legally chooses.

    2. **Fee simple defeasible estate**—An estate in which ownership is automatically terminated upon the happening of a particular event, and the property reverts back to the grantor or a third party.

Example:
Green conveys the property to Smith, subject to the condition that should alcoholic beverages ever be sold on the property, the property would revert back to Green.

    3. **Life estate**—Title is held by the grantor or a third party but subject to a holder of a life estate to the possession, use, and ordinary profit (not to waste estate assets) derived from the property for the duration of the life tenant's life or the life of another party. Absolute title passes to the third party or grantor upon the life tenant's death.

      a. Life estate interests are taxable as a gift or inheritance and can be mortgaged. Life estates can be created by law, such as dower or courtesy rights (upon a husband or wife's death).

      b. Life tenant is required to maintain the property and pay the real estate taxes.

Example:
Smith owns a large lake house. Smith conveys the lake house to his two children, but reserves a life estate in the lake house to his elderly mother. Title passes to his two children, but Smith's mother has the right to the exclusive possession and use during her lifetime. If, instead of a lake house, it were an apartment building, Smith's mother could take possession and use of an apartment and could collect rent on the occupancy of the other apartments. She could not, however, demolish the building (waste the property) without the children's consent.

    4. **Future interests**—(not covered in depth on CPA exam)—A future interest is a nonpossessory interest where the right to possession and use is postponed to a possible future time.

      a. **Reversion interest**—Owner of a fee simple interest transfers an interest which, when terminated, reverts to the owner. For example, Green conveys a fee simple defeasible title to Smith in which should Smith ever divorce Green's daughter, title would revert to Green.

      b. **Remainder interest**—Owner of a fee simple transfers a lesser estate, such as a life estate, to his son with title to his grandchildren. The grandchildren have a remainder interest, with full title passing to them upon the expiration of the life estate interest.

B. **Nonfreehold estates—possessory interests**

1 **Leasehold estates—four types**

A. **Tenancy for years**—A lease for a specified duration (can even be one day or a month). The lease automatically terminates at the end of the period and no notice to the tenant is required. If a year or longer, a tenancy for years must be in writing. To create a valid lease, the lease agreement must name the parties, include identification of the property, and include any lease term that the parties wish to have. Without the lease term, however, the lease could still be valid but it would be a periodic tenancy or tenancy from period to period.

Note:
The names are important! A remainder is the future interest with a life estate. A reversion goes with a fee simple defeasible interest.

B. **Tenancy from period to period** (periodic tenancy)—A lease that is automatically renewed for the same fixed period until the lease is terminated. Usually, the period is the same as the rent period. For example, a month-to-month tenancy begins with a one month lease with the rent paid for the month, and then the lease continues until terminated on a month-to-month basis. To terminate, tenant or landlord must receive written notice of termination, usually prior to payment of the last month's rent. For example, on a month-to-month tenancy with rent payment due on the first of each month, the tenant or landlord would have to give written notice sometime prior to the January 1 rent payment to terminate the lease on January 31 (at least a month notice).

C. **Tenancy at will**—A tenancy that simply continues with permission of the landlord. Until treated as a periodic tenancy, a tenancy at will can be terminated by either party without notice.

Example:
Smith has a one-year lease (tenancy for years). It expires on May 31, which is when Smith is supposed to move into his or her newly built home. Due to the weather, Smith's home is not yet finished, but it is expected to be completed in 10 days. Since Green does not yet have a tenant to replace Smith, Green tells Smith to continue to occupy the premises. This is a tenancy at will.

D. **Tenancy at sufferance**—A tenancy without consent of the landlord. Since the tenant is technically a trespasser, the landlord can terminate the tenancy by eviction. (In some states, landlord can remove tenant and place the tenant's possessions "on the curb" after serving of the eviction notice.)

Example:
A tenant under a tenancy for years refuses to leave after the lease's termination despite the landlord's request. This is a tenancy at sufferance.

2. **Types of nonpossessory interests**

a. **Easements**—The right of a person to make limited use of another's realty, usually without taking anything from it, or possession of it.

   i. **Appurtenant**—An easement created especially for use in connection with an adjacent piece of realty. For example, Able and Smith own adjoining tracts of land, and Able grants Smith the right to cross Able's land to reach a county road.

   ii. **In gross**—An easement created specifically for use in connection with a single tract of land. For example, Able gives the Inca Power Company an easement to run power lines on towers across his or her property.

     iii. **Profit**—An easement for a party to go upon another's realty and take part of the land or product of the land. For example, Able contracts with Gravel Inc. to come upon his property and remove 500 tons of sand and gravel.

     iv. **Grant**—A conveyance by contract or deed.

     v. **Implication**—This is created when parties demonstrate, by circumstances that indicate implied consent, that an intent to create an easement exists. For example, Able and Smith have been neighbors for years. Smith always drives his tractor across Able's pasture to reach a field that Smith owns without any objection from Able.

     vi. **Necessity**—This is created by law to allow a party access to a use of another piece of property or part of the realty. For example, if you lease the third floor of an office building, you automatically have an easement to use the stairs or elevator to reach the third floor. The same is true if you bought a land-locked piece of realty and the only way to reach a highway is to cross another's realty.

  b. **License**—A revocable right to come upon another's land, usually to enjoy it or perform a function. For example, an electric meter reader has a license to come upon your property to read the meter, or you, as a ticket holder to a sporting event, have a license to enter upon the realty to watch the event.

C. Fixtures

1. All fixtures are initially personal property. Trade fixtures, such as store coolers or glass display cases, remain personal property.

2. Once personal property is attached to the realty, it becomes a part of the realty and a fixture if:

  a. The person who attached the personal property intends it to be a fixture. The best indication of intent is the parties' agreement. If there is no agreement, intent is frequently based on whether removal would cause substantial damage to the realty.

  b. The property is so attached to the realty that its adaptation becomes a permanent part of the realty itself.

> **Misconception:** *Statues and fountains placed in your yard are personal property because they can be removed without substantial damage to the realty. This is in error, because the statues and fountains are intended to be a part of the yard (land) and are an adaptation as a permanent part of the land.*

Example:

1. A two-ton statue placed on a piece of land with the intent of it to be a part of the land and its placement to be an adaptation as a permanent part of the land.

2. A mobile home with the axles and tires removed sitting on top of a cement foundation.

3. A built-into-the-wall refrigerator—cannot be removed without substantial damage to the wall, plus adaptation to become a part of the realty.

D. Liens

1. **Judicial liens**—(judgment liens) can be placed on real property (see the "Prebankruptcy Options and Introduction to Bankruptcy" lesson).

2. A **mechanic's lien** (sometimes referred to as a materialman's lien) is a statutorily filed lien by a creditor when he or she has rendered services, labor, or material to repair or improve real estate but the purchaser has not paid him or her.

  a. To create a mechanic's lien, the person furnishing the labor or materials **must file the lien, usually within 60 to 120 days of the last date the services or materials were furnished**.

   b. The **creditor** can be:

      i. A materials supply store (such as a lumber yard, plumbing supply store, etc.);

      ii. A subcontractor;

      iii. A general contractor;

      iv. Or any employee of either of the latter two.

   c. The lien is upon the entire realty and, if the homeowner does not pay, the lien can be foreclosed (same as a real estate mortgage).

   d. In most states, the mechanic's lien and real estate mortgage have equal dignity, thus one does not have priority over the other.

   e. Upon foreclosure, only surplus goes to the former owner.

> **Example:**
> Sue has owned her home for 25 years. She contracts with Joe's Remodeling to completely remodel the guest bathroom in the house. Joe's Remodeling contracts with Ace Plumbing Fixtures for the purchase of a new bathtub, which is installed by John Pool, a sole proprietorship plumber. Upon completion of the remodeling, Sue pays fully Joe's Remodeling. Joe's Remodeling did not pay either Ace Plumbing Fixtures or John Pool. In this situation, either or both (if they have properly filed) have a lien on Sue's house and can foreclose (have the house sold) to satisfy their claims.

II. Real Property Acquisition

  A. General—same as an acquisition of personal property for the following:

   1. Gift

   2. Will or inheritance

   3. Sale—Contract

    a. Contract must generally be in writing with a legal description of the land, the parties identified, price stated, and signed. Broker (real estate agent) contract must also be in writing and signed.

      i. Broker's listing of the property is usually open (available to any agent to "sell" the property) or exclusive (only the broker can "sell" the property).

    b. Most contracts require buyer to pay an amount upon the signing of the contract called **earnest money**. Upon default of buyer, this money is usually treated as liquidated damages.

    c. Seller agrees in the contract to give the buyer a **marketable title**. This is a title that does not contain serious defects.

    d. The seller agrees to furnish the buyer either an **abstract** (a history of the title of the property) or **title insurance**, a policy which insures the good title and will compensate the buyer for any loss due to title defects.

    e. Modern law gives the buyer an **implied warranty of habitability**, which requires the seller to disclose to the buyer material property defects.

    f. All monies paid by the buyer are usually placed in an **escrow account** held by a third party as escrow agent, such as a title company.

> **Note:**
> *These types of issues are easily remedied if Sue structures the payments to her general contractor correctly. You do not pay unless and until you have lien waivers from subcontractors. All states have notice requirements for subcontractors so that the homeowners are aware of who is working on their property. Also, the homeowner can do a hold-back on payment to the general contractor until the lien waivers are all supplied.*

g. Contracts are assignable unless expressly prohibited in the contract.

h. **Closing** is the final settlement of the contract (payment by buyer and passage of title by the seller).

B. How the transfer occurs—by deed

1. **Warranty deed**—highest level of protection; grantor guarantees title and his right to transfer.

2. **Special warranty deed**—(bargain and sale deed) guarantees no problems with title only for the period owned by the grantor.

3. **Quitclaim deed**—grantor transfers only what title he has, if any. There are no warranties or guarantees on the title.

4. **Requirements for a valid deed**

    a. It must be in writing.

    b. It must be signed by the grantor.

    c. It must include a description of the land.

5. **Recording statutes**

    a. Recording the deed is not required to pass title to land, but protects the grantee/transferee from possible loss of title.

    b. There are three types of recording statutes that determine priority as to who owns land.

        i. Race—First person to record the deed holds title to the land and takes possession clear of any subsequently recorded liens or transfers.

        ii. Notice—The last BFP (a buyer who does not know of any problems with the land) to take title from the grantor holds the actual title.

        iii. Race/notice or notice/race—The first BFP to record the deed takes title.

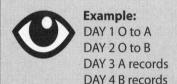

Example:
DAY 1 O to A
DAY 2 O to B
DAY 3 A records
DAY 4 B records

Race—A—First to record, regardless of time of taking or BFP status wins title.
Notice—Last BFP to take title because it is the failure to record that caused the problems for those earlier in the chain of title—so B.
Race/Notice—First BFP to record, which would be A because there is no indication that A knew of any troubles with the property since his was the first and the B transaction followed.

DAY 1 O to A
DAY 2 O to B (bfp)
DAY 3 O to C
DAY 4 C records
DAY 5 B records
DAY 6 A records

Race—First to record, regardless of BFP status, so C.
Notice—Last BFP to take title, so B.
Race/Notice—First BFP to record B.

DAY 1 O to A
DAY 2 O to B (bfp)
DAY 3 O to C
DAY 4 C records
DAY 5 A records
DAY 6 B records

Race—C because it is the first to record
Notice—Last BFP to take title—so B
Race/notice—First BFP to record, so it would be A—no indication that A knew anything and A was the first in the line of transactions and so, is by definition, a BFP—There were no prior transactions to have notice of.

Under Race—pure race to the courthouse to record—so C wins.

Under Notice—last BFP to take title—which is B because B is the last BFP to take title.

Race/Notice—first BFP to record—So B because C is not a BFP—you have to have both—you have to be the first to record who is also a BFP.

Note: The timing for these recording statutes also applies to the timing for the recording of mortgages.

Example:
The grantor conveys title to real property to A, who neglects to record the deed. The grantor then conveys the same real property title to B, who records the deed. B knew nothing about the conveyance to A when he bought the property. Under a race statute, B takes title. Under a notice statute, B is a BFP and is the last buyer to take title, so B holds valid title and A is left to pursue remedies for fraud against the grantor. Under race notice, B would also hold title because he is a BFP and recorded first.

If we change the facts just a little and have B aware of the grantor to A transaction, he is not a BFP. In that situation, the answer to who would take title looks like this:

Race—B takes title because BFP status is not an issue in race recording statutes.

Notice—A takes title because A was the last BFP.

Race Notice—A takes title. Although B recorded first, he is not a BFP and cannot qualify to take the property. B would be left to take his remedies against the grantor and A gets the land.

C. **Financing real property acquisition by sale**

1. **Mortgage**—A nonpossessory security right, that upon default of the mortgagor (debtor realty owner) allows the mortgagee (creditor holding the mortgage) to foreclose (sell or take title) on the property.

2. A mortgage is a security interest in realty that the landowner voluntarily grants to a lender to secure payment of a debt. If the mortgage is given to purchase the realty, it is called a purchase money mortgage and this "lien" is usually given priority over other liens and claims.

3. Mortgages must be in writing, signed by the mortgagor, containing a legal description of the property, and delivered to the mortgagee to be enforceable.

4. Mortgages are recorded (like deeds) to give purchasers and others notice of the mortgagee's lien, and that they take the property subject to the mortgagee's interest.

5. **Mortgage Theories**

   a. **Title theory**—Mortgagee takes title.

   b. **Lien theory**—Mortgagor has title.

   c. **Deed of trust theory**—Title is held by a third party, such as an abstract company.

6. The latter two mortgage theories are the most common and treated very similarly upon mortgagor's default.

7. **Mortgagor has the right**

   a. To possess realty and have reasonable use;

   b. To lease or sell the realty, unless prohibited by mortgage, without mortgagee's consent;

   c. To right of redemption upon default before foreclosure sale.

8. **Mortgagee has the right**

   a. To freely assign the mortgage;

   b. To collect mortgage payments;

   c. To foreclose upon default. Most common foreclosures are by judicial sale or by a power pursuant to the mortgage.

9. **Sale to a buyer**

   a. **Subject to the mortgage**—Title to the realty passes to the buyer with the buyer making payments to the mortgagor. The mortgagee still has a lien on the realty, and can hold the mortgagor liable on the mortgage note (unless released by mortgagee) if there is a default, but the mortgagee cannot hold the buyer personally liable.

   b. **Assumption of mortgage**—The buyer takes title and makes mortgage payments to the mortgagee. The mortgagee still has a lien on the realty, can hold the mortgagor liable on the mortgage note (unless released by mortgagee), and, as a creditor beneficiary, can hold the buyer personally liable upon default.

D. **Adverse possession**—The obtaining of title without a contract or deed through continuous hostile possession contrary to the true owner rights.

1. For title to pass, the possession must meet the following requirements:

   a. **Actual and open**—Must not be secretive or hidden. Possessor must "live" on the premises.

   b. **Continuous**—The possession must be continuous for the required statutory period (10 to 20 years).

   c. **Exclusive and hostile**—The possession must be adverse to all, including the owner, and the party claiming title by adverse possession is on the property without the owner's permission.

Example:
Green operates a 360-acre farm. Green fences in the boundaries of the farm and, by mistake, fences in a strip of land owned by his neighbor. For 25 years Green has plowed and grown crops on the land and paid taxes on the land, including this strip. Green has in the past removed hunters and others from his land, including those found on the strip. Green's neighbor is now selling the land and a survey discovers Green's error. The neighbor wants the land back, which he or she claims is included in the deed. In this situation, Green gets to keep the land because of his adverse possession. (His ownership was actual, open, continuous, and it was exclusive and hostile for the 25-year period.)

III. **Methods of Holding Title**

A. **Tenancy in common**

1. Ownership is held by two or more individuals—can be 1/2 and 1/2 or 1/3 and 2/3 or four owners can hold any portion.

2. Tenants in common can sell, will, or mortgage their interests.

B. **Joint tenancy**

1. Ownership is held in equal shares by two or more individuals.

2. Joint tenancy requires unity in time, title, interest, and possession—the joint tenancy interest is created in equal shares at the same time with the same title and equal rights of possession.

3. There is a right of survivorship. When one joint tenant dies, title vests in the remaining joint tenants.

4. If one tenant transfers an interest, the joint tenancy is severed and the transferee becomes a tenant in common.

 Example:
A, B, and C are joint tenants with right of survivorship in a building. C transfers his ownership rights in the building to D. D is a tenant in common while A and B remain joint tenants. If B dies, A would own 2/3 and D would own 1/3. If D dies, his interest would pass through his estate.

Prebankruptcy Options and Introduction to Bankruptcy

After studying this lesson you should be able to:

1. List the options for creditors who have a non-paying debtor.

2. Explain the differences between voluntary and involuntary bankruptcy.

3. Discuss the structure of each type of bankruptcy.

4. Describe how a bankruptcy begins and who can begin the process.

5. Describe the purpose of liens and the process of foreclosure.

6. Discuss the process of a creditor obtaining a judgment and how the judgment is executed for collection of the debt through attachment and garnishment.

7. Explain the options for creditor agreements, such as composition and assignment, to try to avoid debtor declaration of bankruptcy.

8. Discuss a debtor's rights for wrongful declaration of bankruptcy.

I. When the Debtor Does Not Pay—Options for Creditors

A. Creditors may execute rights under Article 9 secured transactions and/or suretyship agreements.

B. Creditors may foreclose on liens.

Definitions:

Bailee's Lien: A bailee, such as a warehouse company, a common carrier, or an innkeeper, has a right to compensation (by contract) or reimbursement (for expenses incurred in the keeping of the bailed property). To enforce this right of payment from the bailor, the bailee has a lien on the bailed property and can sell the property to satisfy the lien.

Artisan's Lien: (Sometimes referred to as a worker's lien.) A contract bailee who improves or repairs bailed property to increase its value. Failure of bailor to pay as contracted allows the bailee to place a possessory lien on the bailed property, and the bailee, with proper notice, can sell the property to satisfy the lien.

Example:

Mary takes her car to Jim's Auto Shop to have some major repairs. A sign and a notice above her signature authorizing the repairs states clearly "All Repairs Are For Cash Payment." Mary authorizes Jim to repair the car for an estimate of $900. When she comes to pick up her repaired car, she does not have sufficient cash to pay the $900 repair bill. Jim refuses to give Mary her car until she tenders $900 in cash. Jim has met both criteria above to create an artisan's lien on the car. Following any statutory procedure, he may sell the car and deduct from the proceeds the cost of sale, costs suffered due to default, and the $900. Any balance would be turned over to Mary.

---

1. **Relationship of liens to other creditor security interests**—In most states, an artisan's lien has priority over a previously perfected statutorily filed lien (such as a filed UCC-1 financing statement under Article 9).

Example:
To purchase a tractor, farmer John signed a security agreement with West Bank and put up the tractor as security for the loan. West Bank has properly perfected its security interest by filing a UCC-1. Later, Farmer John takes the tractor to I.M. Implement and has some engine repairs made. All repairs are for cash. Having fallen on hard times, farmer John cannot pay cash for the repairs and is in default to West Bank. In this case, even though West Bank's lien is first in time, it is a filed lien and I.M. Implement's artisan's lien, being a possessory lien, has priority over West Bank's perfected secured interest. I.M. Implement can "foreclose on its lien," and satisfy all of its costs and repair charges from the proceeds before West Bank has any entitlement.

C. Obtain a judgment against the debtor and execute that judgment

    1. Attachment—An action taken by a creditor for a court-ordered seizure for the taking into custody the debtor's nonexempt property prior to the creditor getting a judgment.

    2. Writ of execution—After receiving an unsatisfied judgment, a creditor can seek from the court a writ to levy (possess and sell) on nonexempt property of the debtor. The order usually directs the sheriff or an official of the court to seize and sell the nonexempt property.

    3. Garnishment—A court order requiring third parties (garnishees) to deliver a debtor's property held in their possession, or to pay debts they owe to the debtor to the creditor to satisfy a debt or judgment.

        a. Property typically garnished includes:

            i. Bank accounts;

            ii. Wages—The garnishment of wages is usually limited by federal or state law to 25% of take-home pay. (Only two states prohibit garnishment of wages, except for child support.) An employer must pay to the court 25% and 75% to the debtor and employee, respectively. Some states permit continuous garnishments (i.e., one court order covers all wages owed by a particular employer without the creditor having to file for each period the wage is paid). An employer cannot discharge an employee because of a garnishment.

        b. Cannot garnish certain payments such as Social Security, and employers cannot fire an employee because of garnishment.

D. Other creditor collection methods

    1. Composition of creditor's agreements—A contract between the debtor and his or her creditors whereby the creditors agree to discharge the debtor's debts upon a payment (usually a lesser sum).

        a. Creditors who do not contract are not bound by the composition agreement.

        b. The advantage, however, of composition agreements is an immediate payment and it avoids costs and delay of bankruptcy proceedings; plus, many times the payments made exceed those a creditor would receive through bankruptcy.

    2. Setting aside fraudulent conveyances—Transfers by a debtor of property to a third party, by gift or contract, done to defraud creditors can be set aside. In these cases, title reverts to the debtor subject to remedies of the creditors. There are two types of fraud.

Note:
Misconception: *The term "judgment proof" is a misnomer. With a proper claim, the plaintiff can almost always get a judgment. The problem is collecting the amount of the judgment. Many believe this is easy if the debtor has assets. The problem is that frequently many of the assets of individuals are exempt from collection of a judgment. Assets such as homesteads, cars, household furniture and appliances, farm animals, cemetery plots, clothing, books, and even tools of one's trade are exempt and not subject to a writ of execution. Thus, instead of being "judgment proof," it might be better to use the term "execution proof."*

Example:
Creditor Smith is about to get a judgment against debtor Jones, whose major nonexempt asset is a boat. Just before the judgment is issued, Jones transfers the boat to his 10-year-old son as a gift. This transfer is made strictly with the intent to deny Smith a writ to levy execution on Jones's boat, thus to defraud Smith. Smith can have title of the boat to the son set aside and then secure a writ of execution and levy on the boat.

3. **Assignment for the benefit of creditors**—This usually involves an insolvent debtor who voluntarily transfers certain assets to a trustee or assignee. The trustee or assignee liquidates the assets and tenders a payment on a pro rata basis in satisfaction of that debt to each creditor.

   a. The amount of property turned over to the trustee or assignee, and thus pro rata share is entirely at the discretion of the debtor.

   b. Creditors can accept or reject amount tendered.

      i. Referred as a "cram-down" or "take-it-or-leave-it" choice of the creditor.

      ii. Acceptance by the creditor is a complete discharge of the debt.

      iii. Rejection eliminates a creditor's right to the property assigned, but creditor can then pursue other remedies including involuntary bankruptcy petition against debtor.

Example:
Debtor Smith has come upon difficult financial times and has not found his 20 creditors willing to accept a lesser sum in a creditors' composition agreement. Smith's debts amount to $100,000. Smith turns over to a trustee (Jones) $20,000 worth of property, and instructs Jones (for a fee) to sell the property and pro rate the proceeds among his 20 creditors. Jones sells the property and then on a pro rata basis offers each creditor a sum. Creditors who accept the lesser sum discharge their debt. If all creditors accepted the sums offered by Smith, the entire $100,000 in debt is discharged. If none of the creditors accepted or only some, Smith could petition himself into bankruptcy.

II. Before You Begin to Study Bankruptcy

Author's advice for studying bankruptcy—The text is detailed and the law on bankruptcy is complicated. Add to this the fact that the percentage of the value of the subject has been reduced substantially but the content coverage has not been reduced and has even been expanded with the enactment of the 2005 Bankruptcy Act, and you have a dilemma. That dilemma is how much time should you spend on detail when there will only be a few questions on the exam.

Here are some suggestions—Prefaced by the fact that the text is detailed for those who want or need some in-depth knowledge. Even limiting your study for the test to the basics under the nine recommendations below is a lot to chew. Good luck.

A. **Do not** memorize numerical **amounts** in the text. You will never remember them and these will change every three years. If you feel you need to know a few of the numerical amounts, I suggest the following:

   1. The amount of the debt required for the filing of an involuntary Chapter 7;

   2. The monetary limits for the filing of Chapter 12 and Chapter 13 petitions; and

   3. The maximums for the categories in priority of payment (distribution of liquidated estates).

B. Know the five different petition filing Chapters, 7, 9, 11, 12, and 13, who cannot file under each, and the requirements for filing under each.

C. **Generally**, what a debtor is required to file beside the petition to commence the bankruptcy proceedings.

D. What **basically** constitutes the debtor's estate, including gifts etc., acquired after petition is filed.

E. **Generally**, know what the federal exemptions are, and, if the debtor elects the state exemptions, what the limitation is on the homestead equity amount.

F. What constitutes a **preference** for trustee avoidance of the transfer.

G. Know a **summary** of the order of priorities among creditors. Note, on unsecured creditors, that the top priority is domestic support obligations and tax claims are low priority.

H. What debtors or debts will **not be discharged**. For example, partnerships and corporations cannot get a Chapter 7 discharge; only one Chapter 7 discharge every eight years; no discharge for domestic support obligations, student loans, and generally due to conduct of the debtor.

I. **Requirements** of reaffirmations.

Note: The three types emphasized most often on the exam are 7, 11, and 13.

IMPORTANT—The law on bankruptcy will be constantly changing. There are a number of reasons. First, the 1994 amendments to the Bankruptcy Act created a Bankruptcy Review Commission of nine members to review and make recommendations for possible yearly legislative reform. Recent recommendations have resulted in passage of the Bankruptcy Abuse Prevention and Consumer Protection Act of 2005 (referred to as the Bankruptcy Reform Act of 2005). Second, beginning on April 1, 1998, and every three years thereafter, almost all dollar amounts will be adjusted automatically to reflect the Consumer Price Index rounded off to the nearest $25. The following text has the April 1, 2013 adjustment figures and the Bankruptcy Reform Act of 2005 (the most recent adjustments).

III. Commencement of Bankruptcy—Types of Bankruptcy *Very Important*

    A. There are **five** types (the three emphasized on the exam are 7, 11, and 13).

        1. Chapter 7—Referred to as **"straight bankruptcy"** or **liquidation**

            a. Permits **voluntary and involuntary petitions**;

            b. Permits individuals and businesses to file;

                i. Under the 2005 reforms, consumers generally cannot go directly to a Chapter 7 liquidation bankruptcy.

                ii. The consumer must establish that he or she does not have the means to repay his or her debt.

                iii. Known as the "means" test, this test is a formula that takes the debtor's monthly income, subtracts out allowable expenses provided for under the bankruptcy law and then determines whether the consumer debtors has the means to pay off his or her debts.

                iv. Consumers can be held responsible for bankruptcy abuse if they do not qualify under the means test.

                v. If there has been bankruptcy abuse, both the consumer and the consumer's lawyer can be held liable for costs.

            c. Trustee is appointed. (Note: Some questions on the exam deal with whether a trustee is required under the various chapters.)

            d. Not eligible for Chapter 7:

                i. Railroad

                ii. Domestic insurance company

        iii. Savings bank

        iv. Savings and loan

        v. Cooperative bank

        vi. Certain SBA entities

2. **Chapter 9**—Allows for the adjustment of debts of an insolvent municipality—a rehabilitation of municipalities, defined as any political subdivision, public agency, or instrumentality (includes any taxing unit) of a State.

    a. Permits **voluntary petitions** by the municipality.

    b. This chapter is rarely addressed on the exam.

3. **Chapter 11**—Allows for the **reorganization** of a debtor to pay debts—a rehabilitation of a debtor.

    a. Permits **voluntary and involuntary petitions**;

    b. Allows companies to restructure and be discharged from certain debts;

    c. Generally, no trustee;

    d. Reorganization plan approved by 1/2 of the creditors with 2/3 of the total claims (includes shareholders);

    e. Court must approve.

4. **Chapter 12**—Allows for the **adjustment of debts of a family farmer and family fisherman**—a rehabilitation of a person (including a corporation or a partnership) who meets **the definition of a family farmer or fisherman** (rarely tested on the exam).

    a. Permits only **voluntary petitions** by the family farmer or family fisherman.

5. **Chapter 13**—Allows for the adjustment **of debts of an individual with regular income**—a rehabilitation of only individuals (not partnerships or corporations) with limited total secured and unsecured debt amounts.

    a. Permits only **voluntary petitions**;

    b. Less than $383,175 in unsecured and less than $1,149,525 in secured debt;

    c. Always has a trustee;

    d. Applies only to individuals (debt limits);

    e. Debtor's plan;

    f. Court confirmation;

    g. Three to five years for plan—discharged if payment is made.

> **Note:**
> **IMPORTANT!** *Prior to commencement of a filing, the clerk of the bankruptcy court is required to give "consumer" debtors detailed notice of each chapter available under which the debtor may proceed and the clerk must provide informational materials on the types of services available from credit counseling agencies.*

IV. Requirements for Bankruptcy

A. Chapter 7 (Voluntary)

1. Any **person** (individual, partnerships, or corporations) may voluntarily petition themselves into a Chapter 7 bankruptcy (spouse can jointly file).

2. Exceptions to Chapter 7 eligibility:

    a. Banks;

    b. Savings (buildings) and loan associations;

    c. Credit unions;

    d. Railroads;

    e. Insurance companies;

    f. Governmental units (usually);

    g. Small business investment companies licensed by the Small Business Administration.

  3. Special consumer debtor requirements—Before debtors (consumers) can file a petition, they must receive credit counseling from an approved nonprofit agency within 180 days prior to the date of filing.

B. Chapter 7—Involuntarily petition into a Chapter 7 bankruptcy

  1. Same persons eligible as under voluntary Chapter 7 declaration except:

    a. All of the above exclusions from a voluntary Chapter 7 petition;

    b. Nonprofit (not for profit) corporations;

    c. Farmers (those that receive 80% or more of gross income from a farming operation and family farmers who meet that definition under a Chapter 12 bankruptcy).

  2. Requirements for creditors' involuntary petitions of a debtor into bankruptcy

    a. If the debtor has **12 or more unsecured creditors with noncontingent claims,** the petition must be signed by three or more of these creditors whose aggregate claims are $15,325 or more;

    b. If the debtor has less than **12 unsecured creditors with noncontingent claims,** the petition requires only one (more can sign) of these creditors with an aggregate debt of $15,325 or more to sign the involuntary petition.

  3. Debtor's challenge involuntary petitions—requires creditors to prove:

    a. Debtor has not been paying debts as they become due; or

    b. Debtor's property has been placed in receivership, or debtor has made an assignment for the benefit of creditors within 120 days of the filing of the involuntary petition.

    c. Notice that the standard for involuntary bankruptcy is not proving that liabilities are greater than assets; i.e., insolvency in the accounting sense is not the test for the validity of an involuntary petition. The standard is the inability to pay debts as they become due.

> **Note:**
> *If a court dismisses the creditor's petition due to the debtor's successful challenge, the bankruptcy court can assess all costs against the petitioners (including reasonable attorney fees and any damages). If the petition was filed in bad faith, recovering could include punitive damages. This would also be a form of bankruptcy abuse.*

V. Effect of Bankruptcy Petition

A. Upon the filing of a **voluntary petition** or the filing or **granting of an involuntary petition**, the court will grant an **order for relief** or a stay.

B. Order for relief or stay means that creditors must stop collection and all pending credit proceedings (lien foreclosure; judicial liens, etc. as discussed in the earlier sections of this lesson) are stayed (stopped) and the debts and payments will be handled through the bankruptcy court.

C. This sets in motion proceedings that lead to the discharge of the debtor's debts.

D. Upon filing of an involuntary petition, and following the determination that the debtor is insolvent (with insolvency being defined as the inability to pay debts as they become due), the order for relief is entered.

E. There are some proceedings that are not affected by the order for relief or stay including paternity determinations, child support hearings, and marriage dissolutions.

Bankruptcy Process

After studying this lesson you should be able to:

1. List the responsibilities of the debtor upon a bankruptcy filing.

2. Summarize the duties of the trustee in bankruptcy.

3. Describe what property is included in the bankrupt's estate, including the meaning of the 180-day limitation.

4. Discuss what types of claims are valid.

5. Explain how a bankruptcy trustee can set aside payments and security interests as voidable preferences and the time limits for doing so.

6. Describe what constitutes a fraudulent conveyance by a debtor prior to declaration of bankruptcy.

7. Discuss the purpose of the means test for consumer bankruptcies.

8. List the property exemptions from the debtor's bankruptcy estate.

I. **Overview**—At this point, either the voluntary petition has been accepted by the bankruptcy court or the involuntary petition has been held to be valid. No matter how the parties got into bankruptcy court, the court follows a similar process in handling the debtor's estate. The steps outlined here occur **after** the order for relief has been entered (see lesson on "Prebankruptcy Options and Introduction to Bankruptcy").

II. **Debtor's Obligation to Provide Information**

   A. The debtor is required to **file** the following (under oath and signed as being complete and accurate).

   1. List of all creditors with addresses and amounts owed;

   2. Schedule of assets and liabilities;

   3. Schedule showing current income and expenses;

   4. Statement of financial affairs;

   5. Statement of intention to retain or surrender any property (which secures a consumer debt), and to specify property claimed exempt from bankruptcy proceedings;

   6. Certificate from an approved credit-counseling agency (for consumers);

   7. Statement of the amount of monthly income itemized to show how the amount is calculated;

   8. Copy of debtor's federal income tax return for most recent year prior to filing;

   9. Proof of payments received from employers during last six months.

   10. The debtor is also required to cooperate fully and to respond truthfully during examinations by the trustee or creditors, appear at all hearings, and to surrender to trustee all property, books, and records subject to the bankruptcy proceedings. Failure by the debtor is grounds for denial of discharge of debts.

   B. Failure to cooperate may also be grounds for the court to dismiss the bankruptcy petition.

III. **Appointment of the Trustee and Initial Duties**

   A. In those proceedings where a trustee is required (Chapter 7) and after an order for relief is entered, the trustee (a government-appointed official) takes charge of the process that must be followed under the jurisdiction of the bankruptcy court.

   B. Basic **trustee duties** include:

   1. Collecting the debtor's property;

2. Accounting for all property received and making a final report to account for the administration of the debtor's estate;

3. Investigating the financial affairs of the debtor to determine what valid debts exist and whether the debtor has;

4. Furnishing information and reports concerning the debtor's estate; and

5. Providing notice information to domestic support creditors.

IV. **Collection of Assets—The Debtor's Estate**—Debtor's estate includes:

A. **All tangible and intangible property**—(all legal and equitable interests) of the debtor held at the time the bankruptcy proceedings began.

B. The following **after-acquired property** that the debtor acquired within 180 days after the petition is filed:

1. Property by **inheritance or gift**;

2. Property by **divorce, separation, or property settlement**;

3. **Beneficiary proceeds from a life insurance policy.**

C. Any property appreciation, income, etc. from existing property but excludes withholdings for employee benefit plan contributions.

D. Property reacquired by trustee's avoidable powers such as preferences, fraudulent transfers, transfer by mistake, under duress, etc. (See the "Distribution of Debtor's Estate" lesson.)

V. **Property that is Exempt from Bankrupt's Estate**

A. Only **individuals**, not partnerships or corporations, **can claim** exemptions.

B. Two lists of exemptions: state and federal. Congress has authorized states to limit exemptions to those of the state and a majority of the states have done so. However, if the homestead is acquired within three and a half years preceding the date of filing, the maximum state homestead equity exempted is $155,675 and the debtor must have domiciled in the state for two years.

C. For the other states, the debtor can choose either the state or the federal exemptions below:

1. The debtor's interest in a homestead used as a residence up to a value of $49,950; (states exemptions vary significantly—up to $155,675);

2. The debtor's interest in a motor vehicle up to $3,675;

3. The debtor's interest up to $575 per item in household furnishings (includes one computer, one television, one videocassette recorder, and educational materials and equipment, but excludes items such as works of art, antiques over $500 in value, and electronic entertainment equipment with a fair market value of over $500), appliances, wearing apparel, animals, crops, or musical instruments that are owned primarily for personal uses, subject to a total of $12,250 for all such;

4. The debtor's interest in any kind of property ("wildcard" exemption) up to a limit of $1,225 plus up to $11,500 of any unused homestead exemption;

5. Any unused portion of the $49,950 homestead exemption, subject to a limit of $10,825;

6. The debtor's interest in implements, tools, or professional books used in his or her trade, not to exceed $2,300 in value;

7. Any unmatured life insurance policies owned by the debtor (except for credit life policies) plus interests in accrued dividends and interest up to $12,250;

8. Professionally prescribed health aids;

9. The debtor's right to receive various government benefits, such as unemployment compensation, social security, veteran's benefits, etc.;

10. The debtor's right to receive various private benefits, such as alimony, child support, pension payments, disability benefits, etc.;

11. The right to receive damages for bodily injury up to $22,975; and

12. The debtor's interest in jewelry up to a total of $1,550, that is owned primarily for personal purposes.

> **Note:**
> *The exam just tests generally on exempt property and does not ask specific dollar amounts. However, questions could require your knowledge that the exemptions do have limitations.*

VI. Bringing Transferred Property Back into the Bankruptcy Estate

A. The trustee has the power to set aside transfers of the debtor's property.

B. These set-asides of transfers of property by the debtor are called voidable preferences.

1. Trustee can set aside transfers due to the usual contract defenses such as **duress, mistake, undue influence**, **failure of consideration**, **debtor's incapacity**, etc.

Example:
The debtor was a minor at the time of transfer. The debtor, now in bankruptcy, still has the right to disaffirm the transfer due to his or her minority. The trustee can set aside this transfer.

2. Trustee can set aside fraudulent transactions. Note that there are no time limits here when fraud is involved.

Example:
Debtor, three days before the filing for bankruptcy, transfers a boat (nonexempt property) to his daughter retaining possession and use, and converts nonexempt property into cash, buying a $100,000 life insurance annuity contract. The debtor already has substantial amounts of life insurance. Both the transfer of the boat and the purchase of the $100,000 policy can be set aside and become property subject to the bankruptcy proceedings.

3. Trustee can set aside any transfer of property of the estate made by the debtor **after the debtor became subject to the bankruptcy proceeding**, except those made with permission of the trustee or the court.

4. Trustee can set aside any transfer that results in a **legal preference**.

a. There are two types of legal or voidable preferences: those for creditors and those for insiders. Note: time lengths vary for the two different categories.

b. **Elements for All Transfers by Debtors to Creditors**

i. A transfer of **debtor's property to a creditor**;

ii. For an **antecedent or preexisting debt**;

iii. Made within **90 days of the filing of the petition**;

iv. Made while the debtor was insolvent (insolvency presumed for any transfer made within 90 days of the petition being filed).

c. **Elements for All Insiders**

i. An insider is an individual or business, that has a close relationship with the debtor. For example, a relative, a partner, a corporation (board of directors of which the debtor is a member or as an officer of the corporation);

ii. A transfer of debtor's property to an insider;

iii. For an antecedent or preexisting debt;

iv. Made within **one year** from date **of the filing of the bankruptcy petition**;

v. Made while the debtor was insolvent—There is a presumption of insolvency for any transfer made during the **90-day window** that precedes the date of filing of the petition. To set aside a transfer made during the one-year period beyond the 90-day window, the trustee must actually **prove that the debtor was insolvent at the time of transfer**.

C. **EXCEPTIONS**—to the trustee's authority to do a set-aside

1. A **contemporaneous exchange** between the debtor and a creditor for new value.

Example:
Debtor retailer purchased new inventory and paid two days later in cash.

OR

Debtor purchases new inventory to be delivered on May 1 with the seller-creditor taking a **PMSI** in the new inventory to be delivered. If the secured seller-creditor perfects its security interest within **20 days after the debtor takes possession**, the security interest is not a preference.

2. The payment of a debt incurred in the ordinary course of business or financial affairs of the debtor.

Example:
Debtor pays its utility bills upon receipt.

3. A **consumer debtor's payment** of up to $6,225 is not a preference.

4. Payments for **paternity, alimony, maintenance, and child support** are not preferences.

VII. Creditors' Meetings

A. The first creditors' meeting is called by the U.S. Trustee on behalf of the Court (not less than 10 days nor more than 40 days from the order for relief). The judge does not attend.

B. **Creditors**—may elect a permanent trustee by majority vote if at least 20% of total unsecured claims filed are in attendance. If not, the trustee is appointed (usually the interim trustee).

C. **Debtor**—is usually required to appear and may under oath be examined about his or her assets and any matter relevant to a discharge. Failure to answer truthfully is grounds for denial of discharge.

Distribution of Debtor's Estate

After studying this lesson you should be able to:

1. Take a list of available property and allowable claims and distribute the property to the creditors according to statutory priorities.

2. Develop a list for the order of distribution of the bankrupt's estate and include limits on the priority for each level in the priority list.

I. **Determining the Debtors: The Filing of a Proof of Claim**—Any creditor, equity security holder, co-debtor, surety or guarantor may file proof of any legal claim or interest on behalf of a creditor, or trustee.

   A. **Time for filing**—Determined by Rules of Bankruptcy Procedure. (Must be filed within 90 days from first meeting of creditors. Same for Chapter 12 and Chapter 13 bankruptcies.) Taxing and governmental units have 180 days.

   B. All legal obligations of the debtor are claims—Thus, there is no need to prove a claim. This includes **disputed and unliquidated claims** for which the court may estimate value.

II. **Trustee's Evaluation of Claims**—Any claim filed is deemed allowed unless a party in interest objects. Generally, the following claims will be disallowed, at least to the amount held unenforceable:

   A. Claims unenforceable due to fraud, usury, being illegal (unconscionable), failure of consideration, etc.;

   B. For **unexpired leases of the debtor**, the trustee can:

      1. Assume and perform the lease;

      2. Assume and assign or sublease;

      3. Reject the lease (if not assumed within 60 days, lease is rejected).

III. **Distribution of Estate**

   A. **Perfected secured parties**—Perfected secured parties have priority to the collateral or proceeds over general creditors and the trustee. Unperfected secured parties are treated in bankruptcy as general creditors.

      1. If the security agreement so provides, the secured party has priority of the collateral to cover costs of default plus reasonable attorney fees.

      2. If there is insufficient collateral or value to cover the perfected secured creditor debt entitlement, the creditor can file a claim as a general creditor. Any amount that exceeds the secured creditor's entitlement is available for general creditor distribution. The secured creditor has priority only for the amount provided by the collateral. Once that is received, the creditor takes his or her position with the other unsecured general creditors.

> **Note:**
> The priorities of distribution for the bankrupt's estate are tested frequently on the exam. You will need to know the order of this list for priorities upon distribution. When there are insufficient proceeds to cover any particular group, the funds are prorated among the members of that group, and subsequent groups receive nothing. The bankruptcy trustee keeps going down the priority list for distribution until reaching a point of insufficiency for that class of creditor. At that point, the remaining funds are prorated and the distribution is complete with the inevitable result that some creditors receive nothing from the bankruptcy estate because it was insufficient to satisfy all creditors.

Example:
West Bank is a perfected secured party on a loan balance of $10,000 with a security interest in $14,000 of the debtor's equipment. The debtor is in default. West Bank has repossessed the equipment and stored it for $500 pending its sale. West Bank also has $1,000 in attorney fees due to debtor's default. If the equipment is sold for $11,000 by either the debtor or trustee, assuming West Bank's security agreement also covers default costs and attorney fees, West Bank would receive the entire $11,000 and would have to file a claim as a general creditor for $500.

B. **Claims for domestic support obligations**—such as child support and alimony.

C. **Administrative costs**—including all the costs and expenses of the bankruptcy proceedings. Trustee, attorney, appraisal, and accountant fees fall into this category.

D. **Claims arising in the ordinary course of business**—after bankruptcy petition is filed but before the order of relief is entered (involuntary bankruptcy proceeding). If an involuntary petition has been filed but the trustee has not yet been appointed (such as when the debtor challenges the involuntary petition), any expenses incurred by the debtor in the ordinary course of business from date of filing to the appointment of the trustee or order of relief (called "gap creditors"). The reason for this priority is so that the debtor is not shut down in the time it takes to get the bankruptcy process moving forward.

> **Example:**
> Three creditors whose aggregate unsecured, noncontingent claims are $50,000 sign an involuntary petition putting Elizabeth, sole owner of a clothing store, into bankruptcy. Elizabeth immediately challenges the petition. A hearing is held two weeks later when the court rules in favor of the creditors, an order of relief is issued and a trustee is appointed. During the two-week period, Elizabeth has continued to do business and has incurred debts to ABC Wholesale Clothes and XYZ Janitorial Services. When distribution of Elizabeth's estate is to take place, ABC and XYZ will be third in line of general creditors to be paid.

E. **Employee wages**—Employee claims for back wages, salaries, or commissions (including vacation, severance, sick leave, and other benefits) but limited to those earned within 90 days of the filing of the petition or cessation of business (whichever is first) to a maximum amount of $12,475.

1. **IMPORTANT**—Any amount of back wages, etc., owed, regardless of when owed or amount owed above the $12,475 during the 90-day period, is still a claim but for priority purposes goes to the last category—general creditors.

> **Example:**
> Clara is employed as the manager of a clothing store. She is paid $5,000 per month. The clothing-store owner suffers financial reverses and, based on promises, Clara manages the store for four months without pay. The owner now goes into a Chapter 7 bankruptcy. Clara will file a claim for her entire $20,000 owed in back salary, with $11,725 (earned during the last 90 days) as a priority. The remaining $8,275 will be treated as a last general creditor priority. If Clara had worked one month without pay, quit, and the owner continued to manage the store for three months, before she shut down the business and filed for bankruptcy, Clara would get no employee priority (earned outside the 90-day window) and her entire claim would be treated last with the general creditors.

F. **Contributions to employee benefit plans**—Any claim for contributions to an employee benefit plan arising from services performed within 180 days before the filing of the petition or cessation of business (whichever comes first) up to $12,475 per employee (less the aggregate amount paid to employees under the fourth priority above). Any amount above is treated as a general creditor claim.

G. **Claims of farm producers and fishermen**—against debtors who own or operate grain storage facilities or fish storage or processing facilities up to the amount of $6,150 per creditor. Any amount above is treated as a general creditor claim.

H. **Consumer creditors**—who deposit or prepay for the purchase, lease, or rental of goods or services for personal, family, or household use up to an amount of $2,775 per creditor. Any amount above $2,775 is treated as a general creditor claim.

> **Example:**
> John contracts with a yard fertilizer and maintenance company to mow his home yard weekly and fertilize it eight times during the coming year. The price is $3,000 less 10% if paid in advance. John pays $2,700 to the company. Before any services are performed, the company goes into Chapter 7 bankruptcy. John has a priority claim of $2,600 if there are funds remaining for this category and a general creditor priority claim of $100.

I. **Claims of governmental units for various taxes**—These are subject to time limits that vary on the type of tax.

J. **Claims for death or personal injury**—resulting from operation of a vehicle or vessel because debtor was intoxicated from use of alcohol, drugs, or other substances.

K. **All general unsecured creditors**.

L. **If any amount is left, it goes to the debtor.**

> **Example:**
> Knox operates an electronics store as a sole proprietor. On April 5, 1988, Knox was involuntarily petitioned into bankruptcy under the liquidation provisions of the Bankruptcy Code. On April 20, a trustee in bankruptcy was appointed and an order for relief was entered. Knox's non-exempt property has been converted to cash, which is available to satisfy the following claims and expenses as may be appropriate:
>
> *Claims and Expenses*
>
> | | |
> |---|---|
> | Claims by Dart Corp. (one of Knox's suppliers) for computers ordered on April 6, 1988, and delivered on credit to Knox on April 10, 1988 | $20,000 |
> | Fee earned by the bankruptcy trustee | $15,000 |
> | Claim by Boyd for a deposit given to Knox on April 1, 1988, for a computer Boyd purchased for personal use but that had not yet been received by Boyd | $1,500 |
> | Claim by Noll Co. for the delivery of stereos to Knox on credit. The stereos were delivered on March 4, 1988, and a financing statement was properly filed on March 5, 1988. These stereos were sold by the trustee with Noll's consent for $7,500 for their fair market value | $5,000 |
> | Fees earned by the attorneys for the bankruptcy estate | $10,000 |
> | Claims by unsecured general creditor | $1,000 |
>
> The cash available for distribution includes the proceeds from the sale of the stereos.
> What amount will be distributed to the trustee as a fee if the cash available for distribution is $15,000?
>
> a. $6,000
>
> b. $9,000
>
> c. $10,000
>
> d. $15,000
>
> Secured creditors go first with the $5,000. Then you have $25,000 TOTAL administrative expenses for lawyers and trustees, and the trustees are $15,000 of that, so you take the $15,000/25,000 × the $10,000 remaining and 3/5 of $10,000 which is $6,000.

Discharge and Reaffirmation Agreements

After studying this lesson you should be able to:

1. List the reasons a debtor can be denied a discharge.

2. List the debts that a debtor cannot have discharged in bankruptcy.

3. Describe the types of consumer debts that cannot be discharged.

4. Explain what reaffirmation agreements are and the requirements for them to be enforceable.

I. **Generally**—After the estate has been distributed, the court will grant the debtor a discharge decree (at a hearing), that releases the debtor from further liability of his or her debts. This decree is revocable for one year.

II. **Conditions under which Discharge May Be Denied**

   A. A **partnership** or **corporation cannot get a discharge decree** under Chapter 7 (can under other chapters), **only individuals can**.

   B. **A debtor will be denied a discharge** if he or she received a discharge within eight years before the filing of the current petition.

   C. **Grounds for denial**—Any of the following acts by the debtor is a ground for denial of the discharge decree:

      1. Any intentional concealment, distribution, or transfer of assets or records to the detriment of creditors or the trustee (without justification);

      2. Any fraudulent claims, statements, oaths, or receipt or transfer of property;

      3. Any refusal to obey lawful orders, failure to file required or requested tax documents, failure to testify after grant of immunity, or explain loss or deficiency of assets;

      4. Failure of debtor to complete the required consumer education course.

   D. **Consumer debts**—(can be rebutted by debtor):

      1. Any consumer debt incurred within 90 days of filing of petition (order of relief) of more than $575 to a single creditor for luxury goods or services;

      2. Any cash advance more than $925 by the debtor using a credit card or other open-ended consumer credit if incurred within 70 days of the filing of the petition (order of relief).

III. **Debts Not Discharged (by Statute) under Any Circumstances—(the most important ones):**

   A. **Unpaid taxes (two years)**—includes charges incurred to pay U.S. taxes;

   B. **Debts**—incurred through fraud, larceny, or embezzlement (i.e., obtaining money by false pretenses);

   C. **Judgments for willful and malicious injuries**—(i.e., something more than an accident or negligence);

   D. Debts incurred (judgments) as a result of driving while intoxicated;

   E. **Unscheduled debts**—(those not listed by the debtor upon filing of bankruptcy and not actually known to trustee) (see lesson on Bankruptcy Process);

   F. Alimony, maintenance, and child support;

   G. Debts resulting from fraud as a fiduciary (embezzlement);

   H. **Fines and penalties**—payable to a governmental unit;

   I. **Student loan debts or benefits**—(exception if debtor can demonstrate undue hardship);

J. **Sarbanes-Oxley bonuses and incentives**—awarded to executives of companies based on fraudulent financial statements—their obligation to repay these amounts cannot be discharged;

K. **Consumer debts**—Debts incurred within 90 days of the filing for bankruptcy by the debtor. $575 and below gets exempted from this non-discharge. Anything that you spend over the $600 on luxury goods would be a nondischargeable debt—you would still owe that amount to that creditor.

IV. Tax Claims Discharged—If trustee requests a tax audit (determination of unpaid taxes) and the taxing authority does not notify the trustee within 60 days that the audit has been commenced, or if the audit is not completed within 180 days, both the trustee and debtor are discharged from tax liability.

V. Reaffirmations—Agreements between a debtor and creditor that a debt will not be discharged in bankruptcy.

A. **Rules for a reaffirmation to be enforceable**

1. The agreement must be entered into prior to the granting of the discharge decree in bankruptcy;

2. The agreement must be signed and filed with the court;

3. If debtor is represented by an attorney, no hearing or court approval is required if the attorney files an affidavit or declaration that the debtor has been fully advised of the legal consequences of the agreement and such is not a hardship on the debtor or the debtor's family. If not represented by an attorney, a hearing and approval is required;

4. The agreement must include a statement for debtor's right to rescind the agreement at any time prior to the discharge decree being granted or within 60 days of the filing of the agreement, whichever is later. This statement must be clearly and conspicuously stated.

B. **The Bankruptcy Reform Act of 2005 added the following:**

1. If debtor's monthly income less debtor's monthly expenses is less than scheduled payments on reaffirmed debt a rebuttable presumption of discharge due to hardship is presumed. To rebut (because the debtor wishes to pay the reaffirmed debts), the debtor can file a written explanation and debtor's attorney must certify that in his or her opinion the debtor is not unable (i.e., is able) to make the payments on the reaffirmed debts.

2. The debtor must receive several disclosures before signing a reaffirmation. These disclosures include notice that debtor is not required to affirm any debt, liens on secured property (such as real estate mortgages and liens on cars) will remain in effect even if debt is not reaffirmed, state the amount of debt affirmed with rates of interest and when payments begin, and the right to rescind. These disclosures must be signed by the debtor, certified by the debtor's attorney, and filed with the court with the reaffirmation agreement.

Types of Agency Relationships and Creation

After studying this lesson you should be able to:

1. List the types of agency and explain the differences.

2. Define an agency relationship and tell who the parties are.

3. Explain how an agency relationship is created and list the requirements for creation.

4. Discuss how agency relationships are terminated and the requirements for termination of all types of authority.

I. Agency Relationship and Parties

    A. One party designates another to act on his, her, or its behalf.

Example:

1. A corporation authorizes its CEO to negotiate a merger.

2. A storeowner hires a clerk to receive payments and sell goods.

3. A college athlete hires a professional sports agent to represent him in negotiations with professional sports teams.

    B. Two parties—There are two parties in an agency relationship—Principal and Agent.

Definitions:

Principal: The party who delegates authority to another in order to accomplish a task or consummate a transaction.

Agent: One who acts on a principal's behalf to accomplish a task or consummate a transaction for the principal.

II. Types of Agents

    A. Special agent—One authorized to conduct a single transaction or series of related transactions on the principal's behalf.

Example:

1. A real estate agent is authorized to sell only the principal's house.

2. The executor of an estate (principal) hires an estate liquidating company (special agent) to sell all the personal property for the estate.

3. A bankruptcy trustee (principal) hires a company (special agent) to liquidate the assets of a company in Chapter 7 bankruptcy.

    B. General agent—One authorized to conduct all necessary personal or business transactions for the principal.

Example:
A restaurant owner (principal) who owns a restaurant in another city hires a manager (general agent) to run that restaurant.

C. **Universal agent**—One authorized to do all acts that can be legally delegated to an agent.

Example:
A soldier (principal) who is to be stationed abroad for three years appoints his sister (universal agent) to handle all his business affairs during his absence.

D. **Power of attorney**

Definition:
Power of Attorney: A formal written creation of an agency relationship that lists the authority granted.

    1. A power of attorney must be signed by the principal (but need not be signed by the agent to be valid).

    2. A power of attorney is generally construed narrowly.

E. **Independent contractor**—An independent contractor is someone who acts on behalf of a principal, but that principal does not control the agent's day-to-day activities and the scope of the independent contractor is limited.

Example:
You hire a lawyer to create a living trust for you. The lawyer is working for you on that limited activity, but you do not control the lawyer's work hours or have liability for the conduct of the lawyer toward third parties (see the "Tort Liability of Agents and Principals" lesson for more information about the unique limitations of independent contractors).

III. **Creation of an Express Agency Relationship**

A. An express agency relationship is one in which the principal orally or in writing delegates authority to another.

B. **Requirements for the creation of an express agency relationship.**

    1. A writing or record is not generally required for a valid agency relationship, except when the contract that the agent is entering into is under the Statute of Frauds (see Contracts for more information on the Statute of Frauds):

        a. The contract the agent is authorized to enter into must be in writing under the Statute of Frauds, such as a real estate contract.

        b. The agency relationship cannot reasonably be completed within one year.

    2. **Capacity of the agent**

Example:
A minor agent can bind an adult principal, and vice versa (although the minor agent can quit at any time and the minor principal can disaffirm any contract negotiated by the adult agent). As a practical matter, using a minor may not show the best business judgment, but the CPA exam has, in the past, had questions that required you to distinguish between the need for capacity of the principal vs. no requirement of capacity on the part of the agent.

    3. **Consideration**—An agency relationship can be created with or without consideration and is called a gratuitous agency relationship. However, an agent who serves without consideration in a gratuitous agency can quit at any time.

C. Accompanying implied authority that goes with express authority:

  1. When a principal creates an express agency relationship, the agent holds whatever authority is provided for in the agreement.

  2. In addition, the agent has whatever authority is customary for his or her position—whatever authority can be implied because of the position.

Example:
An apartment manager has the implied authority to receive rent, make minor repairs around the apartment building, and have tenants sign lease agreements because those types of actions are customary for most apartment managers.

IV. Creation of an Apparent Agency Relationship

A. **Apparent agency**—This is an agency relationship in which the agent does not have an express agreement but still has authority to act as an agent for a principal because of the appearance of having that authority.

Example:
Agent is not an employee of Principal but in the presence of Principal, Agent tells X that she is such an employee. If Principal does not object, X may justifiably assume that Agent is indeed an employee of Principal and enforce subsequent contracts negotiated by Agent against Principal.

B. **Lingering apparent agency**—This type of agency exists when the principal fires an agent (ends the actual or express agreement), but the agent continues to act as an employee. The agency continues until properly terminated (see the "Contract Liability of Agents and Principals" lesson for more discussion of the liabilities of the parties in this type of agency relationship).

Example:
XYC Corporation sells its custom-home division to Randy Eggerton, a former VP of XYZ. Eggerton continues to use office space at XYZ and even uses XYC's custom- home plans and letterhead. By not stopping Eggerton from using its name and office space, XYZ has allowed Eggerton to remain as an agent.

C. **Agency by estoppel or ostensible authority**—For the purposes of the exam, this agency relationship is another form of apparent authority agency that is created when the principal acts as if another is his or her agent.

V. Creation of an Agency Relationship by Ratification

A. In this situation, the agent does not have express, implied, or apparent authority, but he or she enters into a contract on behalf of an assumed principal. The principal is not bound, but ratification gives the principal a choice.

B. If another enters into a contract for you without authority, you, as the principal, can choose to be bound by the agreement.

Example:
Hollywood Star P hires Ace Talent to handle public relations for her. Ace Talent books a personal appearance for Hollywood Star P. P need not honor the contract but she could decide to do so for goodwill or because the publicity is so good.

Duties of Agents and Principals

After studying this lesson you should be able to:

1. Describe the duties of agents.

2. Describe the duties of principals.

I. Duties of Principal to Agent

    A. To comply with agency agreement—As with any other contract, a principal must follow the terms of the agency contract.

> **Example:**
> Paula Prentice (principal) hired Alex Reger (agent) to serve as her driver for two years. Prentice agreed to pay Reger $1,500 per month for that period. As the principal, Prentice has the duty to pay Alex the $1,500 per month compensation that he was promised under the agency agreement.

    B. To reimburse reasonable expenses—The principal must reimburse the agent for expenses incurred in carrying out the agency agreement.

        1. Absent contrary agreement, the principal is responsible for expenses the agent incurs in reasonably performing his or her activities on the principal's behalf.

> **Example:**
> Alyssa (agent) is a truck driver who delivers furniture for Pruitt's Furniture Store (principal). While doing deliveries for Pruitt, Alyssa uses all of her gas and refills the truck with gasoline so that she can complete the deliveries. Absent agreement to the contrary, Pruitt should reimburse Alyssa for the expense.

II. Duties of the Agent to the Principal—A Fiduciary Relationship

    A. Fiduciary duty.

        1. The agency relationship is a fiduciary relationship.

        2. Because an agent is a fiduciary, the agent owes a supreme duty of loyalty to his or her principal. The agent cannot make a profit at the principal's expense.

> **Example:**
> Rand Turner is the trainer for Cheshire Farms. Rand does not have an exclusive arrangement with Cheshire and he also trains for Hillsbrook Farms. Rand arranged to have Cheshire sell two of its mares to Hillsbrook for a discounted price. Rand had already prenegotiated the sale of those mares by Hillsbrook to a third party for twice the amount Hillsbrook paid to Cheshire. Rand breached his fiduciary duty because he profited on the second sale without disclosing to Cheshire that the second sale, for twice the amount, was already pending.

    B. Duty to follow instructions (duty of obedience)—The agent should follow the principal's instructions unless those instructions call for illegal or immoral acts.

    C. Reasonable care—The agent should discharge all responsibilities carefully and is theoretically liable in negligence to the principal for damage caused by carelessness.

Example:
An agent hired by an estate to sell the personal property of the estate should make sure that the buyers have the ability to pay for those goods.

D. **Accounting**—The agent has a duty to provide the principal with an accounting for all funds of the principal.

E. The agent should always keep any of the principal's funds in the agent's custody separate from agent's own funds and should always be able to tell the principal exactly where the funds are located.

F. **Duty of disclosure**—The agent should immediately inform the principal of any important information that the principal would want to know.

Example:
Agent, a sales representative, learns that a long-established credit customer is on the brink of bankruptcy. Agent should inform principal so that principal can evaluate whether to continue selling to the customer on credit.

G. **Duty of loyalty**—As a fiduciary, an agent acts in the best interest of the principal and does not make profits on transactions at the principal's expense.

   1. **No competition**—Agents' duty of loyalty means that they cannot compete with their principals.

Example:
Agent (accountant) siphons tax business away from his or her accounting firm (the principal) by telling small clients to come to his or her house on weekends where he or she will do their taxes for much less than the firm charges.

   2. **No conflict of interest**.

Example:
Agent is a buyer for a major retailer and begins buying goods from a company that the agent had established in a friend's name.

   3. **No appropriation of business opportunities**.

Example:
Two partners are in the oil and gas business and one learns of a fabulous oil and gas opportunity in Mexico. He or she invests in that opportunity for himself or herself only.

   4. **No disclosure of confidential information**.

Example:
Agent learns trade secrets, such as customer lists and preferences, while working for principal. Agent should not sell or give those trade secrets to anyone.

Misconception: Many believe that trade secrets can be disclosed and used for the agent's benefit unless the agent has signed a covenant-not-to-compete. This is erroneous. The common law of agency imposes a duty of nondisclosure of confidential information that extends beyond the existence of the agency relationship regardless of whether the agent has signed a restrictive covenant. Even in those states that do not recognize covenants-not-to-compete as valid there is protection for the trade secrets of principals.

III. **Duties of the Parties upon Termination**—Agency relationships require special steps on the part of principals and agents when the relationship terminates in order to be certain third parties are not affected adversely.

  A. **Termination of agency relationships by act of the parties**.

   1. **Termination by fulfillment**—An agency relationship is terminated when the conduct authorized under the agency relationship is complete.

Example:
Paul Purcell hired Alice Anderson (agent), a real estate broker, to sell his home. Once Alice has found a buyer and the sale closes, Paul's agency relationship with Alice terminates.

   2. **Termination by lapse of time**—If an agency relationship is restricted in length and the authorized length of time ends, then the agency relationship ends.

Example:
Most real estate listing agreements, in which a homeowner (principal) hires a real estate broker (agent) to sell her house, are limited in length to 90 days. When the 90 days have ended, the listing agreement also ends.

   3. **Termination by a specified event**—An agency relationship established to accomplish an event ends when that event is done.

Example:
A wedding planner (agent) hired to negotiate contracts for venues, cakes, flowers, etc. for a wedding has no further authority once the wedding takes place.

   4. **Termination by mutual agreement**—An agency relationship ends when the principal and agent agree that they wish to end their relationships.

Example:
When a company (principal) and an advertising agency (agent) agree that they no longer wish to work with each other, they have reached a mutual agreement and the agency will no longer have the authority to negotiate ad contracts for the company.

   5. **Termination by unilateral act of one party**—("You're fired" or "I quit")—When the principal or agent fails to perform the duties under the agency agreement, the agency relationship ends, just as in the case of any breach of contract.

Example:
Paula Prentice (principal) hires Alex Reger (agent) to serve as her driver for two years. Prentice agrees to pay Reger $1,500 per month for that period. Either Prentice or Reger can end the relationship at any time. However, the termination of the agency does not resolve the underlying issues of damages for breach of contract to the other party.

   a. **Exception to the grounds for termination**—A principal cannot (that is, has neither the right nor the power to) terminate an *agency coupled with an interest*.

   b. An **agency coupled with an interest** is a unique agency relationship created by a writing, that gives the agent some interest vested in the property that is the subject matter of the agency relationship.

> **Example:**
> Pat Page (principal) borrows $5,000 from Alice Akers. To secure the loan, Pat grants Alice a security interest (a property interest for the sole purpose of securing a debt—see the UCC segment) in Pat's antique store inventory. To protect her status as a lender, Alice inserts in the agreement a provision whereby Pat makes Alice his agent for the sale of the inventory in the event that Pat defaults on the loan. Since Alice has an interest in the subject matter of the agency (the inventory), the arrangement is an agency coupled with an interest and Pat cannot terminate Alice's authority to sell without Alice's consent. Of course, if Pat repays the loan, then Alice will no longer have an interest in the subject matter and the agency will terminate.

B. **Termination by act of parties**—terminates ONLY express and implied authority, not apparent authority.

    1. Principal has a duty to notify third parties about the termination in order to halt the agent's authority.

    2. Agent has a duty to honor the termination and not use apparent authority to continue benefiting from the relationship.

    3. Lingering apparent authority that exists after termination by act of the parties can be ended as follows:

        a. Actual notice to third parties that the agent no longer has authority.

        b. Constructive notice—publication or general mailings that indicate the agency relationship has been terminated.

C. **Termination by operation of law**.

    1. **Termination by death of either principal or agent**

        a. Death of the principal means that there is no longer a party to the contract.

        b. Death of the agent speaks for itself.

    2. **Termination by insanity of the principal**

        a. The insanity of the principal means that there is no party with capacity (see the Contracts discussion for more information on capacity) to enter into contracts.

        b. As a result, the agency terminates by the way the law operates.

>
> **Example:**
> Pam Poly hires Arnold Ashforth to sell Pam's house. Pam dies. The agency terminates at the moment of Pam's death.

    3. **Termination by bankruptcy**

        a. Bankruptcy of the principal is another event that can trigger an operation-of-law termination of an agency, if the principal's bankruptcy would cause the agent to realize that P would no longer wish A to enter into transactions on P's behalf.

        b. Bankruptcy of the agent terminates an agency relationship only if the agent's bankruptcy would impair A's ability to act as an agent.

> **Example:**
> Anissa (agent) has been working as the on-site leasing agent for Premiere Properties' (principal) apartment complex, Las Sendas. Premiere has declared bankruptcy. Anissa can continue with the day-to-day activities of Las Sendas, including signing leases and accepting rent. If, however, Anissa had been hired by Premiere to sell off some of its properties, the bankruptcy means that further sales would not be proper until the trustee has a chance to determine creditor rights and property transfers (see the Bankruptcy segment for more discussion of the rights of parties once bankruptcy is declared).

4. **Termination by change of law**—As with all contracts, if the law makes the conduct of the agent or the subject matter of the contract illegal, the agency relationship ends (see Contracts for more discussion of the effect of illegality on a contract).

Examples:

1. Alan is hired to buy a dog race track for Peter and dog racing is declared illegal.

2. Chiquita Banana hires a mercenary group to provide protection for its employees in Colombia. The U.S. government passes a law that makes it illegal for U.S. companies to compensate groups that are listed as terrorist groups by the U.S. Department of Justice. Chiquita's agency relationship with the group terminates.

5. **Termination by circumstances such as loss or destruction of subject matter**—The loss or destruction of the property that is the subject matter of the agency relationship terminates the agency relationship.

Example:
Anna is hired by Pepe to sell Pepe's warehouse, which is destroyed by a tornado before she can sell it. Anna's agency relationship ends because the subject matter is destroyed.

D. Termination by operation of law ends ALL authority: express, implied, and apparent. The duty of notice does not apply because the law has ended the agency relationship.

Contract Liability of Agents and Principals

After studying this lesson you should be able to:

1. Describe the authority and liability of agents with regard to contracts entered into with third parties.

2. Describe the authority and liability of principals for contacts entered into on their behalf by their agents.

I. **Contract Relationships of Principals, Agents, and Third Parties**—The liability of the principal and agent to third parties for contracts and the ability of third parties to enforce contracts against principals and agents depend on two factors: the type of authority the agent had and whether the principal was disclosed to the third party.

II. **The Liability of a Disclosed Principal**

    A. **Disclosed principal**—In this situation, the third party is aware that the agent is acting for a principal and the third party knows whom that principal is.

Example:
A sports agent who is negotiating a contract for an NBA free agent is an example of a disclosed principal situation. The third party (the team) knows the identity of the player and knows that the sports agent is authorized to act on his behalf.

    B. **Disclosed principal with actual authority (express or implied)**—In this situation, the principal ONLY is liable to the third party.

Examples:
1. Antique dealer (agent) is hired by an estate executor (principal) to sell an armoire from the estate. The agent discloses the executor's name to the buyer (third party), explains her role, and negotiates a sale of the armoire for $1,700. The executor thinks the price is too low and refuses to honor the contract. The buyer can require the executor to convey title to the armoire and the executor is liable for damages to the buyer for failure to deliver. The antique dealer has no liability to the buyer even if the executor breaches the contract.

2. Principal hires agent to sell P's house for at least $90,000. The express authority is for the agent to find a buyer to buy the house for $90,000. Agent finds a ready, willing, and able buyer for $100,000. The principal is bound to sell the house to the buyer because the agent had express authority to sell the house.

3. Principal hires Agent to manage Principal's restaurant. Principal does not spell out Agent's authority. The law implies that Agent has the authority customarily exercised by managers of comparable businesses in the area (this is implied authority), which likely includes the authority to hire and fire employees, to open bank accounts, to purchase supplies, to sell to customers, etc.

4. Principal instructs Agent to deliver a truckload of furniture to a customer. The truck has a flat tire as the delivery is being made. Although Principal did not instruct Agent to do so, Agent has the authority to replace the tire if it is incidental (necessary) to completion of the assigned task.

5. When Principal is out of town, a flash flood threatens his retail store. The manager of the store (Agent) incurs substantial bills in a good faith effort to protect the store from the flooding, even though Agent has never been expressly authorized to do so by Principal. Principal would be liable for payment of these funds because Agent's exercise of emergency authority.

III. **Disclosed Principal with Apparent Authority**—There must always be a disclosed principal under apparent authority because the authority exists due to the principal holding out someone as an agent.

    A. In this situation, the principal ONLY is liable to the third party, but the agent is also liable to the principal for acting as an agent without express or implied authority.

B. **Apparent authority**—Even if the agent lacks express or implied authority (both being types of "actual authority"), the principal may still be liable for contracts negotiated by the agent if:

1. Principal held Agent out as Principal's agent; that is, a third party reasonably believed that the agent worked for the principal and had the authority to enter into contracts;

2. Agent acted within scope of apparent authority; and

3. Third party reasonably relied on the appearance in entering into a contract.

Examples:

1. Principal and Principal's brother work together running a construction firm that builds single-family homes, townhomes, and custom homes. Principal's brother wants to take the custom-home contracts and operate his own building company that focuses on custom homes only. Principal agrees to transfer all the pending custom home contracts to his brother. Principal's brother continues to use office space in the Principal's building, shows customers the floor plans with Principal's name on them, and uses his old business cards that reflect the Principal's business. If Principal's brother does not finish the homes or absconds with the deposits for new homes, the Principal would be liable for allowing his brother to continue to appear to be a part of his business.

2. Agent is a traveling sales representative for Principal for 10 years. Principal then fires Agent for dishonesty. Agent goes to long-time customer X who has not heard of the firing and negotiates a contract to sell Principal's goods to X and accepts a downpayment, which he then steals. X can bind Principal to the contract because it appeared to X that Agent still had authority to work for Principal. The terminated agent has what is known as lingering apparent authority, or authority that comes from the failure to let third parties know that the agent no longer works for you.

C. **Terminating agent's authority**—The means for terminating an agency relationship depends upon the type of authority (See also the lesson on "Duties of Agents and Principals" for more information).

1. **Terminating actual authority**—To effectively terminate an Agent's actual authority, the Principal must end the relationship. Termination of the relationship ends all actual authority, including express and implied authority.

2. **Terminating apparent authority**—The termination of actual authority ends express and implied authority, but not apparent authority. In the previous example about the terminated sales agent, the Principal should have first given direct notice (phone, mail, or e-mail) to all of Agent's regular customers that Agent no longer worked for Principal. Second, the Principal should have given constructive notice to all potential customers by publishing in a newspaper of general circulation a notice that the Agent no longer worked for the Principal. In the Principal's brother example, the Principal would need to collect all the old business cards and building plans and structure and label the office so that the customers would understand that his brother's business is different from his business.

3. **Limitation—operation of law agency terminations**—When agency relationships end by operation of law, as when the principal dies, such a termination ends all actual and apparent authority. The notice procedures discussed above are required in cases of termination of the agency by act of the parties; "You are fired," or "I quit."

D. **Liability of disclosed principal—agent has no actual or apparent authority**—In this situation, the agent only is liable to the third party; the principal has NO liability.

Example:

Alex goes to a new town and represents to a hotel manager that he is there to book the hotel for the upcoming convention of the National Association of Realtors (NAR). Alex presents no authority, the manager does not check with the NAR, and the manager reserves the hotel for the NAR. The NAR is not liable to the hotel for the deposits and damages for no convention, but Alex is (if the hotel can find Alex!).

IV. Contract Liability of Partially Disclosed, and Undisclosed Principals under Actual Authority

    A. Partially disclosed principals—If an agent is acting for a principal under actual authority, but does not identify the principal, then both the principal and the agent are liable to the third party. Real estate agents disclose that they are acting for a buyer but do not want the seller to know who the buyer is because the seller might increase the price if the buyer is a wealthy individual or a developer. The agent's principal would be unable to obtain a fair price for the property if the seller knew his or her identity.

 Example:
Agent negotiates to buy a house on behalf of a principal but does not tell the seller (the third party) who the principal is. Both the agent and the principal are liable to the seller (the third party) for damages if the agent, acting with authority, agrees to purchase the house but then the principal refuses to go through with the contract. A contract entered into with authority on behalf of a principal is the same as a contract that the principal actually enters into on his or her own. As a result, the undisclosed principal is liable on the contract along with the agent. Of course, the agent can identify the principal if the seller/third party pursues the claim for breach of the contract and would be entitled to reimbursement from the principal if the agent ends up paying the seller the damages.

    B. Undisclosed principals—If an agent with actual authority does not disclose to a the third party the fact that he or she is acting on behalf of a principal, and the third party believes the agent is acting on his or her own behalf, the agent and principal are BOTH personally liable on the contract. However, the agent can identify the principal (unless there was an agreement of confidentiality), and the third party can choose to pursue the principal for any damages. The agent is entitled to reimbursement from the principal if the agent has to pay the third party any damages.

Example:
Agent negotiates to buy a house on behalf of a principal but tells the seller that she is buying for herself.

Be sure to distinguish between the third party's right to enforce the contract and the liability of the agent and principal to the third party.

In the undisclosed principal situation, the agent is functionally a party to the contract and may enforce it against the third party. If the agent reveals the identity of the principal or the principal decides to disclose his or her identity, then the principal can enforce the contract against the third party.

The principal could face three situations under which the third party can refuse to perform for the previously undisclosed principal. If the third party has already performed the contract for the agent, then the third party is not required to perform the same contract again for P; and—if the contract is the type that cannot typically be assigned (e.g., it calls for personal service by the agent) or the third party's decision was based on the agent's personal credit standing, judgment, or skill and those factors were the bases for the third party contracting with A then the third party can refuse to perform.

Tort Liability of Agents and Principals

After studying this lesson you should be able to:

1. Discuss when agents and principals are liable for the torts committed by agents.

2. Diagram the tort liability between and among principals, agents, and third parties.

I. Agent's Liability—Agents are liable for the torts they commit.

> **Misconception:** Many people believe that agents are not liable for the torts they commit if they were ordered to commit the torts by their boss. However, the agents *are* liable notwithstanding their obedience to their boss's instructions. We are always liable for our own torts, regardless of whom we were working for at the time.

II. Principal's Liability through Conduct

    A. A principal is liable for his or her agent's torts if the agent was doing as the principal instructed or ordered.

> **Example:**
> Principal tells Agent that X owes him or her money and Agent should beat on X until he pays. If the Agent does so, the Principal is liable for assault and battery because he directed the commission of the tort.

    B. A principal is liable if the principal hires an agent who is not qualified to perform the job assigned (sometimes called negligent entrustment).

> **Example:**
> Principal owns a construction company and entrusts Agent, a high school student without a driver's license, with a large dump truck. Agent drives the vehicle carelessly and causes injury to X. X can recover from Principal because Principal negligently entrusted the truck to an agent incapable of handling it.

    C. A principal is liable for the torts of the agents if the principal failed to supervise properly (tort of negligent supervision).

> **Example:**
> Principal hires Agent who has a known history of violence as a door-to-door sales representative. While on a sales call, Agent assaults a customer in the customer's home. Principal is generally liable for not supervising the Agent.

    D. A principal is liable for the torts of the agent if the principal was negligent in hiring the agent (failure to screen agent applicants properly) and/or negligent in retention (i.e., the principal had reports of negligent conduct by the agent but took no action to stop those actions or terminate the agent).

> **Example:**
> **1.** Principal hires Agent as a truck driver without checking Agent's driving record, which would have disclosed multiple arrests for DUI. Agent causes an accident while driving under the influence. Principal is liable for negligent hiring.
>
> **2.** Principal hires Agent as a truck driver. Agent has a good driving record but later develops a drinking problem of which the Principal is aware. Agent causes an accident while driving under the influence. Principal is probably liable for negligent retention.

III. Principal's Liability for Negligent Torts of the Agent or Acts of the Agent

A. Vicarious liability—Even if the principal has not done anything wrong personally, he may be vicariously liable under the doctrine of respondeat superior.

B. Requirements for vicarious liability

1. **Existence of a master-servant relationship**—A master-servant relationship is determined by the ability of the principal to control the activity of the agent. This relationship is different from an independent contractor relationship.

> **Example:**
> If ABC Welding hires lawyer X from the XYZ law firm to handle its commercial litigation, X is an independent contractor. If ABC Welding hires X as its general counsel, X is in a master-servant relationship. If X is an independent contractor, ABC does not have vicarious liability for X's torts, even when X is driving to depositions for ABC. However, if X is a general counsel for ABC, ABC would have liability for X's torts when he is driving to depositions on ABC litigation.

    a. **Agent is a servant**—The key to determining whether the agent is a servant for whose torts the principal is liable, or an independent contractor for whose torts the principal usually is not liable, is this question: Does P have the right to control the method and manner of A's work?

        i. If the answer is yes, then it is a master-servant relationship.

        ii. If the answer is no, then it is an independent contractor relationship.

    b. **Additional factors**—In determining whether an agent is a servant or an independent contractor:

        i. Does A work regular hours for P (e.g., 9–5)?

        ii. Does P provide A's tools?

        iii. Is A paid by the hour or week rather than by the job?

        iv. Is P A's major source of income, rather than being simply one of A's many customers?

            1. If the answer is yes, then it indicates a master-servant relationship.

            2. If the answer is no, then it indicates an independent contractor relationship.

2. **Scope of Employment**—Scope of employment means that the agent commits the tort while the agent is doing something for the principal.

    a. The principal is less likely to be held liable for an agent's intentional torts than for an agent's mere negligence because it is more likely that the agent is not acting within the scope of employment when committing intentional torts. However, if the agent is authorized to commit the tort or motivated in any important way by a desire to serve the principal, then the principal is liable.

>
> **Example:**
> **1.** Agent is a bouncer at Principal's bar. X, a customer, walks in and Agent exclaims: "That's the guy who stole my girlfriend!" Agent beats up X. Principal is not liable because Agent acted for purely personal motives.
>
> **2.** Agent is a bouncer at Principal's bar. X, a customer, becomes unruly. Agent uses excessive force in ejecting X, even though Principal has warned Agent to be careful. X is seriously injured and sues Principal. Principal is probably liable.
>
> Remember also that when an intentional tort is committed by an agent and the principal was aware or should have known that the agent had a tendency to commit those kinds of torts, the principal is liable (negligent hiring and negligent supervision).

b. **Within authority**—An agent will be held to have acted within the scope of employment when committing the tort if these three questions are answered affirmatively:

   i. Was this the type of work agent was hired to do?

   ii. Did it occur substantially within normal time and space limitations?

   iii. Was it done to serve the principal in some way?

   1. While delivering furniture for his employer, P Furniture Co., Agent carelessly drives the truck through a stop sign injuring X. P is liable to X.

   2. While on vacation from his job at P Furniture Co., Agent carelessly drives his family car through a stop sign injuring X. P is not liable to X.

Example:
If an administrative assistant takes her car and goes to the bank for the company with which she works (the Principal), the company is liable for the torts the administrative assistant (the Agent) commits while on her way to and from the bank. If the administrative assistant runs a red light during this journey, she is liable for any injuries that her running the red light causes, but the company is also liable for those injuries.

c. **Deviations from the scope**—of employment will not alter the principal's liability if:

   i. They are minor; or

   ii. After deviation, A is returning and "reasonably close" to the point of departure.

   iii. Frolic and detour—agent is completing personal tasks while working on principal's business—no liability for principal during the frolic and detour.

   iv. Return from frolic and detour—agent gets back to the business of the principal after personal business is complete; liability returns.

Examples:
1. While delivering furniture for his employer, P Furniture Co., Agent leaves the highway to get a soda at a fast food restaurant that he spotted just off the highway. Agent drives his car carelessly in the fast food restaurant's parking lot and injures customer X. P is liable to X.

2. While delivering furniture for his employer, P Furniture Co., Agent leaves the highway to visit an old friend several miles away. After the visit, Agent is returning to the highway in order to complete the delivery and carelessly causes an accident on the on-ramp injuring X. P is liable to X.

Misconception: Many people believe that a principal cannot be liable unless he or she has done something morally blameworthy. However, a completely innocent principal can have the best motives in the world and be very careful but may still be liable for his or her agents' torts within the scope of authority. The rationale is based in part on the notion that the principal profits when the agent does things right and therefore should incur the costs when the agent errs. The rationale is also based in part upon a natural desire to compensate the innocent victims of the agent's torts.

3. When "extra-hazardous activity" is involved (e.g., use of explosives, radioactive material, etc.), then the principal has strict liability, even in the case of an independent contractor.

Example:
Principal wishes to "implode" a downtown office building to make way for new construction and he or she hires the independent contractor A Construction Co. If A botches the job, Principal is liable.

4. Where a statute imposes a "nondelegable duty" (e.g., the duty of a railroad to maintain railroad crossings, the duty to repossess cars without breach of the peace).

Defining a "Security"

The first step in mastering securities regulation is to understand logically what a "security" is. The definition is rather broad.

After studying this lesson, you should be able to:

1. Understand which instruments and arrangements are treated as "securities" by the law and therefore come within the scope of securities regulation.

I. Definition

   A. The statutory definition (1933 Act) contains a laundry list, plus catch-all terms, broadly defining a **security** to mean:

   > "Any note, stock, treasury stock, bond, debenture, evidence of indebtedness, certificate of interest or participation in a profit-sharing agreement, collateral-trust certificate, pre-organization certificate of subscription, transferable share, **investment contract**, voting-trust certificate, certificate of deposit for a security, fractional undivided interest in oil, gas, or other mineral rights, any put, call, straddle, option, or privilege on any security, certificate of deposit, or group of index of securities (including any interest therein or based on the value thereof), or any put, call, straddle, option, or privilege entered into on a national securities exchange relating to foreign currency, or, in general, any interest or instrumentality common known as a 'security,' or any certificate of interest or participation in, temporary or interim certificate for, receipt for, guarantee of, or warrant or right to subscribe to or purchase, any of the foregoing."

   B. The 1934 Act's definition is quite similar.

   1. A share of corporate stock is the prototypical security. It is always a security and any other investment interest that seems to share most of its features, especially an investment of money to be managed by others with an expectation of profit, is probably a security.

II. The Investment Contract—The most important of the catch-all categories is the investment contract.

   A. Elements of an investment contract:

   1. Investment of money;

   2. In a common enterprise;

   3. With an expectation of profit;

   4. To be earned primarily by the actions of others.

Example:
Promoters seeking to develop an orange grove could have incorporated and sold stock in the corporation to raise funds. Instead, they sold the actual trees to investors. If an investor put in 1/20th of the money, then he was deemed owner of 1/20th of the trees. All oranges were tended, harvested, and sold by the promoters. The owner of 1/20th of the trees would receive 1/20th of the profits. Although the promoters insisted that they were selling trees, the court held that they were actually selling "securities" in the form of an investment contract. The investors invested money in a common enterprise (if the weather was good all could profit; if there was a serious freeze, all investors would lose money). They did so hoping to make money primarily by the planting, cultivating, harvesting, and marketing efforts of the promoters.

III. Key Distinctions to Remember

   A. Passive investors need legal protection more than investors who are actively involved in the enterprise and their investments are more likely to be deemed securities.

Examples:
1. General partners invest money in a common enterprise (the partnership business) with an expectation of profit. However, because they are general partners, they can protect themselves by being actively involved in the enterprise. General partnership interests usually are not securities.

2. Limited partners invest money in a common enterprise (the partnership business) with an expectation of profit. Additionally, because they must sit on the sidelines in order to protect their limited liability and may not take an active role in directing the enterprise, they, unlike general partners, hope to profit by the efforts of others (the general partners). Limited partnership interests usually are securities.

B. A transaction involving an investment purpose is more likely to create a security than a transaction involving a purpose of consumption.

Example:
A loans $50,000 to B so that B can start a business. B signs a note promising to pay the money back with interest. This is more likely to be a security than if B had borrowed the money (and signed the note) in order to buy a luxury boat that he wanted to cruise around in during his spare time.

The Registration Process

After studying this lesson, you should be able to:

1. Understand the background reasons for requiring companies to register securities with the SEC.

2. List the basic registration exemptions that exist.

3. Comprehend the traditional rules that govern the registration process.

4. Understand the recent reforms to the process and be able to explain what a WKSI and an FWP are.

I. **Requirements and Basic Procedure**

   A. **The 1933 Act's requirements cover**

      1. Initial public offerings, wherein companies sell to the general investing public for the first time;

      2. Seasoned offerings, wherein public companies print and sell new securities to the public;

      3. Secondary offerings, wherein persons controlling or closely affiliated with public companies sell their securities under circumstances where it is appropriate to treat the transaction as if it were being made by the company itself.

   B. **Basic procedure**

      1. Issuer files registration statement with SEC;

      2. Issuer waits 20 days for SEC approval, during which time preliminary "red herring" prospectus is disseminated, and oral offers and limited types of written offers can be made;

      3. Registration statement is deemed "effective" and sales can begin.

II. **The Distribution Process for Securities Is Similar to That for Products**

   A. **Product**—Manufacturer–Wholesaler–Retailer–Customer.

   B. **Security**—Issuer–Underwriter–Broker–Investor.

III. **Basic Legal Framework**

   A. **The process breaks down into three periods**:

      1. The prefiling period, before the registration statement is filed with the SEC;

      2. The waiting period, after the issuing company has filed but before the SEC has given permission for selling to begin (the effective date);

      3. The post-effective period.

   B. **During the prefiling period**—A company can neither offer to sell securities nor sell them.

   C. **During the waiting period**—A company may make oral offers and certain types of written offers but cannot sell the securities.

   D. **Elaboration**—During the waiting period, oral offers are permitted along with certain specified types of written offers, most importantly:

      1. The preliminary or "red herring" prospectus, and

      2. The "tombstone" ad, a black-bordered advertisement usually placed in the *Wall Street Journal* that would contain only:

         a. The name of the issuer;

         b. The full title of the security and the amount being offered;

         c. A brief description of the company's business;

      d. The price range of the security;

      e. The name of the managing underwriter;

      F. The contemplated date of the issuance;

      G. A few other minor items.

    3. Both the red herring prospectus and the tombstone ad will contain cautionary words that they constitute neither offers to sell nor solicitations of offers to buy and that no binding contract can be entered into until after the registration statement becomes effective.

  E. **During the post-effective period**—An issuer may both offer and sell the securities.

IV. Contents of Registration Statements—The registration statements include, among other items:

  A. Financial Statements audited by independent CPA;

  B. Names of issuer, directors, officers, underwriters, etc.;

  C. Risks;

  D. Description of issuer's business;

  E. Description of security and intended use for proceeds.

V. Disclosure to Investors—Much of the registration statement's contents go into the prospectus, a part of the registration statement that must be delivered to buyers.

  A. The preliminary ("red herring") prospectus is used during the waiting period, but cannot be used thereafter; it contains most of the information that the final prospectus will contain, except for information such as the final price to be charged and fees to underwriters that cannot be determined until the effective date.

  B. The final prospectus is used after the effective date.

  C. The final prospectus must be delivered to investors before, or along with, the purchased securities (or written confirmation of purchase).

  D. The final prospectus may be supplemented by written advertising material called "free writing" that is not permissible during the waiting period.

VI. SEC Review

  A. **Theoretically**—The SEC reviews the registration statement during a 20-day waiting period and the registration statement becomes effective on the 20th day after filing.

  B. **Fact**—The SEC usually does not review the registration statements of seasoned issuers and often allows them to "accelerate" their registration statements and sell before the theoretical 20-day waiting period has expired. When the SEC does review registration statements, such as for all companies going public for the first time, it usually takes much longer than 20 days, typically 60–80 days. Nonetheless, the AICPA tests the theoretical legal framework rather than the actual practice.

  C. **Key point**—The SEC does not review the merits of the securities being offered nor make any guarantees to investors as to the quality of the securities. Issuers can sell the worst securities imaginable so long as they fully disclose how bad they are. Nor does the SEC guarantee the thoroughness and accuracy of the registration materials. When it allows a registration statement to become effective, the SEC is simply indicating that it has not found anything wrong with the disclosures contained therein. Nothing prevents the SEC from finding problems later and acting on them.

VII. Shelf Registration—Before shelf registration, a company that had two or more offerings in a relatively short time frame would have to go through the entire registration process for each offering, which was very duplicative and wasteful. The SEC realized that this was somewhat wasteful and began allowing the largest 2,000 or so companies to file a single registration statement that would cover the securities they expected to sell during the next three years. Then, whenever an advantageous "market window" presented itself, these firms could pull the securities "off the shelf" and begin selling them within just a day or two.

VIII. Securities Offering Reform Program (SORP)

A. In December 2005, through the Securities Offering Reform Program (SORP), the SEC expanded the "shelf registration" concept to what might be considered "company registration." The largest firms, which are widely followed in the marketplace, are allowed to file a registration statement covering three-year periods. They can then largely ignore the traditional rules covering permissible activities in prefiling and waiting periods. The notion is that these firms are so widely followed in the market every day that a registration statement really does not add much in the way of meaningful information. Therefore, they can talk about their companies and even their companies' stock, largely without restriction.

B. **Two particular concepts should be noted**.

1. **First**—The SORP rules divide issuers into several categories, the largest of which are called *well-known seasoned issuers* (WKSIs—pronounced "wicksees"). These are firms that have been reporting regularly to SEC for at least a year, (b) eligible to use Form S-3 or F-3, and (c) have either (i) $700 million of worldwide public common equity float, or (ii) have issued $1 billion of registered debt in the previous three years. These firms make up only 30% of listed firms but they control 95% of listed firms' assets. It is only these firms that are allowed to take full advantage of the new SORP rules, although more limited benefits flow to many smaller issuers.

2. **Second**—It is important to know the concept of a *free writing prospectus* (FWP). Traditionally, after the effective date, firms were allowed to supplement the final prospectus with additional literature called "free writing." WKSIs are now allowed to use additional material (FWPs) at any time with few restrictions other than the material usually has to be filed with the SEC. Some of the other categories of issuers are allowed to use FWPs on a more restricted basis (typically only after filing a registration statement).

C. The JOBS Act of 2012, which will be discussed in subsequent lessons, made additional significant changes to the traditional registration process, primarily by allowing firms that declare themselves to be *emerging growth companies* (EGCs) to receive certain breaks from the traditional rules.

Exempt Transactions and Securities

Because registration is expensive and time-consuming, companies seeking to raise capital would generally prefer to avoid it. They may avoid it if they sell exempt securities or sell nonexempt securities through exempt transactions. This lesson addresses exempt securities.

After studying this lesson, you should be able to:

1. Identify securities that are exempt from SEC registration rules.

2. Understand the basic rules that can exempt certain offerings from the SEC registration process.

3. Understand the motives and benefits for issuers of qualifying for these exemptions.

4. Comprehend that these are exemptions from the registration process but not from the antifraud rules.

5. Understand the (subordinate) role of state securities regulations (blue sky laws) in the overall securities regulatory scheme.

I. Bank and Government Securities

   A. Rationale—Bank and government securities are heavily regulated by other federal and state laws.

   B. Limitation—Public utilities are not exempt.

II. Short-Term Notes—Commercial notes (not notes for investment purposes) are exempt if carrying maturity of less than nine months.

III. Charitable Organizations' Securities—Nonprofit educational, religious, benevolent, fraternal, or charitable organizations.

IV. Others

   A. Regulated savings and loans

   B. Federally regulated common carriers

   C. Receivers or trustees in bankruptcy (with court approval)

   D. Insurance and annuity policies (but not regular securities issued by insurance companies)

      1. Limitation—Regular securities issued by insurance companies are not exempt.

Example:
Prudential Insurance Co. sells annuities. These carry many of the same characteristics of securities but are exempt from registration. Prudential Insurance Co. decides to have a public offering of its own securities to raise capital. This transaction is not exempt from registration on grounds that the offeror is an insurance company.

   E. Domestic governmental organizations

V. Offerings That Are Exempt from Registration

   A. Three major types—Congress has authorized three major types of transaction exemptions wherein the securities need not be registered with the SEC even though they are not exempt securities.

      1. "Small offering" exemptions—(authorized by Sec. 3(b) of the 1933 Act).

         a. Rationale—These offerings need not be regulated because of the relatively small threat to the public posed by small offering.

Example:
Regulation A, and Rules 504 and 505 of Regulation D.

2. **Private placement exemptions**—(authorized by Sec. 4(2) of the 1933 Act).

   a. **Rationale**—These offerings need not be regulated because of the sophisticated nature of offerees who can protect themselves.

   b. **Key concept**—Accredited Investors (AIs) who can look out for themselves and therefore do not need the protection of the 1933 Act's disclosure provisions, include: millionaires; persons who make $200,000/yr (or $300,000/yr with spouse); institutional investors; insiders of the issuer; and charitable, educational, or religious organizations worth at least $5 million.

Example:
Rule 506 of Regulation D.

3. **Intrastate offering exemptions**—(authorized by Sec. 3(a)(11) of the 1933 Act).

   a. **Rationale**—These offerings need not be federally regulated because they happen primarily inside a single state's borders and can be adequately regulated by that state.

Example:
Rule 147 under Sec. 3(a)(11) of the 1933 Act.

B. **Characteristics of Key Transaction Exemptions**

   1. **Rule 504 of Regulation D**

      a. **Nature of issuer**—Rule 504 can be used mostly by small companies, not by 1934 Act reporting companies or investment companies.

      b. **Limit on amount**—Rule 504 can be used to raise only $1 million in any 12-month period.

      c. **Manner of offering**—General solicitation and advertising are not allowed unless either (a) the securities are registered under a state law requiring public filing and delivery of a substantive disclosure document to investors before sale, or (b) the securities are issued under a state law exemption that permits general solicitation, as long as sales are made only to accredited investors.

      d. **Purchaser requirements**—There are no such requirements; Rule 504 securities may be sold to anyone.

      e. **Information requirements**—There are none.

      f. **Filing requirements**—The issuer need only file a Form D with the SEC within 15 days of the first sale of securities under the exemption. Even failure to comply with this requirement will not disqualify the offering from the exemption, but the SEC may prevent the issuer from using Reg D again in the future.

      g. **Resale restrictions**—Resale is restricted unless the conditions mentioned for the manner of offering are met.

   2. **Rule 505 of Regulation D**

      a. **Nature of issuer**—Cannot be used by investment companies or companies that have recently been in trouble with the SEC ("bad boys").

      b. **Limit on amount**—Can be used to raise only $5 million in any 12-month period.

      c. **Manner of offering**—Cannot use general solicitation or advertising, unless sell only to AIs.

    d. **Purchaser requirements**—Can sell to an unlimited amount of accredited investors but no more than 35 unaccredited investors.

    e. **Information requirements**—Same as Rule 506.

    f. **Filing requirements**—Form D within 15 days.

    g. **Resale restrictions**—To prevent easy circumvention of the rule's restrictions, the shares' resale is restricted for a year and the issuer must take steps to ensure that buyers know that they are restricted, such as by printing a legend on the securities.

3. **Rule 506 of Regulation D**

    a. **Nature of issuer**—Cannot be used by companies that have recently been in trouble with the SEC ("bad boys").

    b. **Limit on amount**—None.

    c. **Manner of offering**—Cannot use general advertising or solicitation, unless sell only to AIs.

    d. **Purchaser requirements**—Can sell to an unlimited number of accredited investors but no more than 35 unaccredited investors. Furthermore, all of the unaccredited investors must either be "sophisticated" in their own right or act through "purchaser representatives" who have the skill to evaluate the investments for them.

    e. **Information requirements**—No particular information must be disclosed if sales are exclusively to accredited investors, but if some sales are made to unaccredited investors, there are certain minimal disclosure requirements. The more funds are raised, the higher the disclosure requirements.

    f. **Filing requirements**—Form D within 15 days.

    g. **Resale restrictions**—To prevent easy circumvention of the rule's restrictions, the shares' resale is restricted for a year and the issuer must take steps to ensure that buyers know that they are restricted, such as by printing a legend on the securities.

4. **Regulation A** (also known as Reg A+ after recent amendments)

    a. **Nature of issuer**—Cannot be used by 1934 Act reporting companies, investment companies, non-Canadian foreign issuers, or "bad actors."

    b. **Limit on amount**—

        i. Tier 1—$20 million in 12-month period

        ii. Tier 2—$50 million in 12-month period

    c. **Manner of offering**—Unique "testing the waters" provision allows offeror to make some preliminary offers to determine whether there is sufficient interest in the securities and to cancel the offering completely without violation if there is not.

    d. **Offeree and purchaser requirements**—

        i. Tier 1: None

        ii. Tier 2: Non-accredited individual investor cannot buy stock constituting more than 10% or greater of his or her annual income or net worth (unless the stock is also listed on a national stock exchange). Non-accredited firm cannot buy more than 10% of the greater of annual revenue or net assets.

    e. **Information requirements**—

        i. Tier 1: Offering circular, 2 years unaudited F/S

        ii. Tier 2: Offering circular, 2 years audited F/S, *and* limited periodic reporting to SEC

    f. **Filing requirements**—

        i. Tier 1: Simplified Form 1-A and offering circular

        ii. Tier 2: Simplified Form 1-A, offering circular, and 2 years audited F/S.

   g. **Resale restrictions**—None

   h. **Other**—

   Tier 2 offerings are exempt from state blue sky review, though states' regulators may continue to require mere "notice" filings and to punish fraud in connection with such offerings.

Type of Offering	Nature of Issuer	Limit on Amount	Manner of Offering	Offeree and Purchase Requirements	Info Req.	Filing Req.	Resale Restrictions
Reg. A	No '34 Act reporting co's, inv. co's, non-Canadian foreign issuers, or "bad actors"	Tier 1: $20m/12 mo. Tier 2: $50m/12 mo.	"Testing the waters" permitted before filing Form 1-A	Tier 1: no requirements Tier 2: non-accredited individual investors can't buy stock worth more than 10% or greater of annual income or net worth	Tier 1: offering circular Tier 2: 2 yrs audited F/S, limited periodic reporting to SEC	Tier 1: simplified Form 1-A and offering circular Tier 2: simplified Form 1-A, offering circular, and 2 yrs audited F/S	None
Rule 147	Issuer must be organized and doing bus. in-state (80% test) and use 80% of proceeds in state	No limit	No limit, but must state intrastate	All offerees must be residents of state	None	None	Limited to other residents for 9 mo.

5. **Rule 147 Intrastate Offering**

   a. **Nature of issuer**—Issuer must be organized and doing business in the state in which it plans to do the offering. To be safe, should meet "80%" test, including having at least 80% of its assets in-state, making 80% of its revenue in-state, and using 80% of the proceeds of the offering in-state.

   b. **Limit on amount**—No limit.

   c. **Manner of offering**—No limitation, except that the offering must stay intrastate.

   d. **Offeree and purchaser requirements**—All offerees and purchasers must be in-state residents; offer to even one out-of-state resident can disqualify the exemption.

   e. **Information requirements**—None.

   f. **Filing requirements**—None.

   g. **Resale restrictions**—For nine months can resell only to other residents of the state.

C. **The Exemptions in Table Form**

   1. **The exemptions in table form—Reg. D**

      See the following table.

Type of Offering	Nature of Issuer	Limit on Amount	Manner of Offering	Offeree and Purchaser Requirements	Info. Req.	Filing Req.	Resale Restrictions
Rule 504	No. '34 Act reporting co's or inv. co's	$1m/12m o.	No general solicitation or advertising(*)	No requirements	None	Form D w/in 15 days of first date	Restricted resale (*)
Rule 505	No "bad boys" or inv. co's	$5m/12m o.	No general advertising or solicitation(**)	35 non-AIs unlimited AIs	None if all AIs. If sell to non-AIs, disclosure requirement varies with whether issuer is reporting co. and amount of offering.	Form D	Restricted; take reasonable care to prevent resale
Rule 506	No "bad boys"	No limit	No general advertising or solicitation(**)	35 non-AIs unlimited AIs, but all non-AIs must be "sophisticated" or act thru "purchaser reps"	Same as 505	Form D	Same as 505

(*) Under Rule 504, the limitations on general solicitation and resale are lifted if either (a) the securities are registered under a state law requiring public filing and delivery of a substantive disclosure document to investors before sale, or (b) the securities are issued under a state law exemption that permits general solicitation and advertising, so long as sales are made only to AIs.
(**) Can use general solicitation if sales are to only AIs.

2.   The exemptions in table form—Non-Reg. D

Type of Offering	Nature of Issuer	Limit on Amount	Manner of Offering	Offeree and Purchaser Requirements	Info. Req.	Filing Req.	Resale Restrictions
Reg. A	No '34 Act reporting co's, inv. co's or "bad boys"	$50m/12 mo.	"Testing the waters" permitted before filing Form 1-A	No requirements	Simplified disclosure; financials (current BS and 2 yrs) need not be audited	File Form 1-A, any sales materials, and Form 2-A report to SEC of sales and use of proceeds	None
Rule 147	Issuer must be organized and doing bus. in-state (80% test) and use 80% of proceeds in-state	No limit	No limit, but must stay intrastate	All offerees must be residents of state	None	None	Limited to other residents for 9 mo.

D. **Key Point**—Reg A, Reg D, and Rule 147 are issuer exemptions. Additionally, Section 4(1) exempts everyone except issuers, brokers, and underwriters so that "Joe Blow" investors can resell their shares at any time without registering (unless they are "restricted resale" shares).

VI. Blue Sky Laws

A. **Preempted regulations**—Much state regulation, except for anti-fraud rules, was preempted by Congress in 1996.

> **Note:**
> **Misconception:** *Many people do not realize that these exemptions are simply exemptions from registration, not from federal antifraud rules. Therefore, if in the course of an exempt offering an issuing company makes any misrepresentations, it can be sued by the SEC or by investors.*

1. The National Securities Markets Improvement Act (NSMI) preempts state regulation of "covered" securities, including:

   a. Those listed on any national exchange;

   b. Those issued by registered investment companies;

   c. Those sold to "qualified purchasers";

   d. Those sold pursuant to federal exemptions authorized by Sec. 4(2) (e.g., Rule 506).

2. The NSMI did not preempt state regulation of securities issued under Sec. 3(b), so issuers selling pursuant to Regulation A and Rules 504 and 505 must still follow individual blue-sky laws, but the JOBS Act of 2012 preempts state regulation of Reg A offerings if they are made only to "qualified purchasers."

B. **Merit regulation**—In particular, the NSMI ends state "merit regulation."

C. **The NSMI allows states to continue to**

1. Enforce antifraud statutes; and

2. Require "notice" filing.

D. **The Securities Litigation Uniform Standards Act of 1998**—Provides that any class action securities fraud suits must be brought in federal, not state, court.

The JOBS Act of 2012

After studying this lesson you should be able to:

1. Explain the rationale underlying passage of the JOBS Act of 2012.

2. Explain the key provisions of the JOBS Act of 2012.

3. Demonstrate how the JOBS Act of 2012 fits into the overall scheme of federal securities regulation.

I. The JOBS Act of 2012

A. Introduction

1. The JOBS Act is not really a "jobs" act. It is a securities law that amended federal law with the goal of making it easier for small companies to raise capital with the hope that this would eventually lead to job creation.

2. The acronym stands for: Jumpstart Our Business Startups.

3. The Act did five major things, which we will study:

   a. Created a new category of firms called *emerging growth companies* (EGCs) that can go public via an initial public offering (IPO) yet avoid most of the burdens of being public for five years.

   b. Encouraged "crowdfunding."

   c. Increased the Regulation A exemption's ceiling from $5 million to $50 million.

   d. Allowed firms doing private placements to engage in general solicitation and advertising in situations where they could not do so before.

   e. Changed the definition of a "public company" in order to allow firms to grow bigger before being forced to go public and thereby be saddled with all the regulatory burdens that go with that status.

B. Emerging Growth Companies (EGCs)

1. Until JOBS was passed, companies that held IPOs immediately became "public companies" or "reporting companies" that had to file continuous financial reports with the SEC (10-Ks, 10-Qs, 8-Ks) and meet many other expensive regulatory requirements. Hoping to lower small firms' regulatory costs substantially, this provision allowed relatively small firms to declare themselves EGCs and then go public but delay complying with all these regulatory burdens for a period of five years.

2. To be an EGC, a firm must meet the following criteria:

   a. Have less than $1 billion in annual gross revenues during its most recently completed fiscal year,

   b. Have been publicly traded for less than five years,

   c. Have a public float of less than $700 million, and

   d. Have not issued $1 billion in non-convertible debt in the prior three-year period.

3. An issuer will remain an EGC until the last day of the fiscal year following its five-year anniversary of its IPO or until the EGC fails to meet the EGC criteria, whichever occurs first. During that time, it is not a reporting company and will bear substantially fewer regulatory burdens than public companies traditionally have.

4. Among other benefits firms that declare themselves EGCs enjoy are:

   a. Include only two years (instead of three years) of audited financial statements in its equity IPO registration statement.

    b. Reduced disclosure requirements regarding their executives' pay.

    c. Right to submit to the SEC a draft equity IPO registration statement for confidential **review** prior to a public filing. This allows firms to get SEC guidance before they go public without their competitors getting a chance to examine the filed information as happens in regular IPOs. However, any submission, as amended, must be filed publicly with the SEC no later than 21 days before the issuer starts conducting roadshows for the offering.

    d. Exempt for five years from complying with:

        i. Section 404(b) of the Sarbanes-Oxley Act regarding the auditor attestation report of the company's internal control over financial reporting (still need SOX 404(a) certifications by CEO & CFO).

        ii. New PCAOB rules requiring things like mandatory audit firm rotation, unless the SEC determines that such rules are necessary and in the public interest.

        iii. Various executive compensation provisions, including: (1) the say-on-pay vote requirement that gives shareholders the right to cast an advisory vote on top executives' pay, (2) the advisory vote on golden parachute payments requirement, and (3) the requirement to disclose the relationship between executive compensation and the financial performance of the company.

5. JOBS also allows more publicity regarding a company that is going public than has traditionally been allowed. It eliminated key restrictions on publishing analyst research and on communications between securities analysts, investment bankers, management, and prospective investors while an EGC's IPO registrations are underway. For example, investment bank analysts may now publish research reports on EGCs while their IPO registration statements are pending, even if the banks are members of the underwriting syndicate.

6. Note that foreign companies can be EGCs and that there is no requirement that an EGC actually create any jobs to take advantage of these provisions. It is estimated that 90% of companies going public will qualify for EGC status.

C. Crowdfunding

1. *Crowdfunding* is a process by which entrepreneurs and business owners can use the Internet to raise capital, typically from large numbers of people who invest small amounts with little federal regulation.

2. JOBS allows firms to raise up to $1 million in a 12-month period from individual investors through the Internet, subject to certain requirements and limitations. Before JOBS, these companies couldn't offer securities (ownership interests) due to federal securities laws and were therefore limited to giving out t-shirts and the like in exchange for donations.

3. Although JOBS allows crowdfunding, Congress was sufficiently concerned about frauds against unsophisticated investors that it imposed several major limitations. Plus, the SEC will issue additional rules that may further constrain use of this new mechanism for small firms to raise capital.

4. With crowdfunding, investors will likely find it easier to invest in small companies, but they will receive less disclosure than under previous rules and will not be able to transfer the shares they buy for at least a year after purchase (other than transfers to the issuer, an accredited investor, or to family members upon death or divorce).

5. Other requirements for use of the crowdfunding exemption from registration are:

    a. Foreign companies (that can be EGCs) cannot use the crowdfunding exemption.

    b. The crowdfunding exemption is capped at $1 million in any 12-month period.

    c. To minimize the potential damage that might occur if a fraudster used crowdfunding, the JOBS act limits the amount any single investor can invest in all crowdfunded investments (not just in a single company) in any year to an amount not to exceed:

        i. The greater of $2,000 or 5% of the investor's annual income or net worth if both of these are less than $100,000, and

      ii. 10% of the investor's annual income or net worth not to exceed $100,000 if the investor's annual income or net worth is $100,000 or more.

  d. Investors can invest only through a broker or a "funding portal" that is registered with the SEC and FINRA. So, instead of regulating the company raising funds, Congress provides some level of investor protection by registering the entities through which the companies raise money. The funding portal or broker must:

      i. Provide investors with information regarding risk of investment loss and risk of investing in start-ups;

      ii. Do due diligence by obtaining background checks and securities enforcement regulatory history for officers, directors, and 20% securities owners of the issuer;

      iii. Ensure that proceeds put into escrow and given to issuers only when the targeted offering amount is obtained and permit investors to cancel commitments.

  e. Companies must make certain disclosures that vary with the amount of funds they raise through crowdfunding:

      i. If a company raises $100,000 or less it is required to file only its most recent tax return, if any, and financial statements certified by the company's CEO.

      ii. If a company raises between $100,000 and $500,000, it must also have the financial statements reviewed by an independent public accountant.

      iii. If a company raises between $500,000 and $1 million, the financial statements must be audited.

  f. Companies raising capital through crowdfunding may not compensate promoters, finders, or lead generators for providing the broker or funding portal with the personal identifying information of any potential investor.

  g. There is a "bad actor" prohibition that bans certain issuers that have been in legal trouble.

  h. State securities laws are preempted and may not block crowdfunding.

D. General Solicitation

  1. In recent years, most firms have been raising their money not through IPOs but through private offerings of $1 million or less, typically with 30 or so investors, pursuant to Regulation D. Reg D contains restrictions on advertising and other general solicitations and JOBS relaxes those restrictions with the goal of giving more clarity to the rules and more freedom to issuers. In search of investors, firms may cast a wide net, so long as they throw the minnows back into the pond. The JOBS Act substantially relaxes the ban on general solicitation by:

    a. Eliminating the ban so long as all purchasers of the securities in an offering are "accredited investors" (millionaires, big institutional investors, etc.) under Regulation D, and

    b. Requiring the issuer to take "reasonable steps" to confirm the accredited investor status of all such investors.

E. Regulation A and Mini-IPOs

  1. Regulation A has been a hybrid between a private placement and an IPO. It has allowed firms to raise money by filing a stripped down offering document yet evading most traditional IPO requirements regarding publicity limitations in a sort of "mini-IPO." Regulation A even allows companies to "test the waters" by approaching investors to see if they would be interested in buying its shares and having the right to abandon the offering if investor interest is insufficient. This would be illegal "jumping the gun" under traditional rules.

  2. However, Regulation A had a ceiling of $5 million in any given year and most issuers did not view that amount to be worth going to the trouble of trying to get SEC approval for their offering document. Plus they had to go through state blue sky review, which was often slow and difficult.

  3. The JOBS Act raises the ceiling to $50 million, leading some to call it "Regulation A+."

4. State blue sky regulation is preempted, but only if the shares are listed on a national exchange or sold only to "qualified purchasers" (to be defined by the SEC).

F. Private Company Flexibility and Growth Act

1. In 2012, Facebook was approaching 500 shareholders because it had issued shares to many of its employees as compensation. Because firms became "public companies" (or "reporting companies") when they had an IPO or reached 500 shareholders and $10 million in assets, Facebook was facing all the burdens of being a public company without enjoying the benefits of an IPO. Therefore, it held an IPO, even though it didn't really want to.

2. The JOBS Act gives companies such as Facebook more control over when they go public by (a) raising the shareholder count ceiling from 500 to a maximum of either 2,000 persons in total or 500 persons who are not "accredited investors," and (b) excluding from the count investors who became shareholders through the issuer's employee compensation plan and investors who bought through crowdfunding.

Liability Provisions—1933 Act

The 1933 Act contains three explicit liability provisions: Sec. 11, Sec. 12(a)(1), and Sec. 12(a)(2). For exam purposes, Sec. 11 is the key. It is based upon common law fraud provisions, but dramatically relaxes some of the requirements of a common law fraud claim in a pro-plaintiff way.

After studying this lesson, you should be able to:

1. Understand the basic liability provisions of Section 11.

2. Understand the basic liability provisions of Section 12(a)(1).

3. Understand the basic liability provisions of Section 12(a)(2).

I. **The 1933 Act**—Because the 1933 Act focuses on the initial sale of securities, accountants' liability arises primarily due to inaccurate audited financial statements contained in the registration statement that must be filed with the SEC (unless an exemption applies). The Securities and Exchange Commission (SEC) can bring civil actions alleging 1933 Act violations, and injured investors can also bring lawsuits for civil damages.

II. **Three Primary Causes**—There are three primary causes of action for violation of 1933 Act provisions:

   A. **Sec. 11**—remedies misleading statements and omissions contained in the registration statement as of its effective date.

   B. **Sec. 12(a)(1)**—remedies violations of Sec. 5.

      1. Offering a security before filing a registration statement;

      2. Selling a security before the registration statement becomes effective;

      3. Selling a security without providing a prospectus;

      4. Providing a prospectus that does not comply with Sec. 10 requirements.

   C. **Sec. 12(a)(2)**—remedies misstatements or omissions in the initial sale of securities that occur outside the registration statement.

      1. Until 1996, 12(a)(1) and 12(a)(2) were known as 12(1) and 12(2), respectively.

   D. **Section 11 is the most important of these provisions, but here are a few things to keep in mind regarding Section 12(a)(1):**

      1. Accountants are deemed "experts" with special responsibility.

      2. Only "sellers" of securities are liable under Secs. 12(a)(1) and 12(a)(2), so unless accountants "solicit" sales, they should not be liable under those sections.

Example:

1. Only "sellers" of securities are liable: ABC Accounting Firm certifies financial statements included in a registration statement. The financial statements are materially inaccurate. Additionally, the issuer sent out prospectuses that did not conform to Sec. 10 requirements. ABC may well be liable under Sec. 11 as an expert, but it will not be liable under Sec. 12(a)(1) if all it did was certify the financial statements.

2. Only "sellers" of securities are liable: ABC Accounting Firm was asked by its tax clients for investment advice. ABC advised the clients to invest in a company that was owned in large part by partners of ABC. The clients lost a large amount of money and sued ABC under Sec. 12(a)(2). The clients were able to win because ABC's partners had gone beyond their role as accountants and actually solicited investments by the clients.

III. Elements that Plaintiffs Must Prove to Win a Sec. 11 Claim

A. A false statement or omission of fact appeared in a registration statement.

    1. The accounting firm is liable only for that part of the registration statement (financial statements) that it prepared.

Examples:

1. ABC Accounting Firm certifies the financial statements for a registration statement filed by XYZ Computer Co. The financial statements are accurate but some of the textual portion of the registration statement describing XYZ's business history is inaccurate. ABC is not liable for these inaccuracies.

2. Chapter 1: ABC Accounting Firm certifies the financial statements for a registration statement filed by XYZ Computer Co. The financial statements are accurate as of the effective date of the registration statement, but soon thereafter, the company suffers severe business reverses. The financial statements no longer accurately reflect XYZ's status. ABC cannot be liable under Sec. 11 for these problems.

B. The misstatement or omission was **material**.

Example:

ABC Accounting Firm certifies the financial statements for a registration statement filed by XYZ Computer Co. The financial statements indicate that XYZ's earnings in the previous year were $3.2 million, when really they were only $3.18 million. The $20,000 error is probably immaterial to any investor's decision and ABC is not liable for the inaccuracy.

C. Plaintiff bought securities that were issued under the defective registration statement.

    1. Need not be first purchaser, but must be able to "trace" shares to registration statement.

Example:

1. ABC Accounting Firm certifies the financial statements for a registration statement filed by XYZ Computer Co., a company going public for the first time. The financial statements are materially inaccurate and Joe, who bought his shares from Sam, sues ABC under Sec. 11. Joe can maintain the action despite not being the first purchaser. Because XYZ has just gone public for the first time, these shares were necessarily issued under the defective registration statement.

2. Chapter 1: ABC Accounting Firm certifies the financial statements for a registration statement filed by XYZ Computer Co., a company that went public a few years ago and is now making this seasoned offering. The financial statements are materially inaccurate. Joe read about the offering in the paper, called his broker, and said that he wanted to buy $10,000 worth of XYZ shares. Unless Joe can prove that the shares he bought were issued under the defective registration statement and were not previously issued shares, he cannot recover under Sec. 11.

D. Plaintiff suffered damages.

IV. Defenses for Accountant Under Sec. 11

A. Due Diligence

    1. Elements of Due Diligence:

        a. Reasonable investigation;

        b. Reasonable basis;

        c. Good faith belief.

B. Special burden on accountants who are "experts." Other individual defendants are allowed to rely upon "expertised portions" of registration statement.

> **Note:**
> *A Sec. 11 plaintiff need not prove that the accountant defendant (or any other defendant) acted in bad faith with what the law calls scienter. Indeed, a Sec. 11 plaintiff need not even prove that the accountant defendant (or any other) acted negligently. Negligence is the standard under Sec. 11, but the burden of proof is upon the defendant accountant to prove that he or she did not act negligently.*

C. The issuing company itself has no due diligence defense; it is strictly liable for errors in the registration statement.

Example:
ABC Accounting Firm certifies the financial statements for a registration statement filed by XYZ Computer Co. Notwithstanding the fact that ABC ensured that GAAP and GAAS were complied with and that ABC believed in good faith that the financial statements were accurate, it turns out that they contained materially misleading errors. Injured investors sue ABC, XYZ, and XYZ's officers and directors. ABC and all of XYZ's officers and directors who believed the financial statements were accurate have due diligence defenses and will not be liable. However, XYZ itself has no due diligence defense nor do any of its officers and directors who knew, or should have known, that ABC was making errors.

D. Lack of Reliance by P

Example:
ABC Accounting Firm certifies the financial statements for a registration statement filed by XYZ Computer Co. The financial statements were materially erroneous, a fact that was later discovered and reported in the newspaper. Joe bought XYZ shares after having read the newspaper articles. Joe could not recover against ABC under Sec. 11 because he did not rely on the false statements.

E. Alternative causation

Example:
ABC Accounting Firm certifies the financial statements for a registration statement filed by XYZ Computer Co. The financial statements were materially erroneous. The price of XYZ stock dropped 15% following the announcement of the errors. However, the entire stock market declined an average of 15% during this same time frame, and computer stocks declined, on average, even more. ABC has a very good chance of convincing a jury that the decline in XYZ shares was not caused by the errors it made in certifying the financial statements.

F. Statute of limitations: P must sue.

   1. Within one year from when s/he discovered (or should have discovered) the false statements or omissions;

   a. Inquiry notice: If P is put on notice that there is a problem, most courts start the one- year period running; they do not wait until P knows the full dimensions of the problem.

   2. Within three years after the security was bona fide offered to the public (usually the effective date).

Example:
On May 1, 1997, XYZ Computer Company's registration statement became effective. ABC Accounting Firm had certified the financial statements contained therein.
In June of 1997, rumors began to circulate that XYZ had been claiming revenue from sales that were not final. Several financial publications published articles regarding these rumors. In August of 1998, investors filed a Sec. 11 lawsuit against ABC and XYZ seeking to prove that the financial statements contained in the registration statement had been materially misleading. Because the plaintiffs had been put on notice of the potential errors in June 1997, yet they waited 14 months to file the lawsuit, they are probably barred by the statute of limitations. They filed within the three-year of the offering deadline but missed the one-year of notice deadline.

V. Damages Under Sec. 11

A. Defendants, including accountants, are jointly and severally liable under Sec. 11, except for:

    1. Outside directors (who are only severally liable), and

    2. Underwriters (whose liability is capped at the amount of securities they underwrote).

Example:
ABC Accounting Firm certifies the financial statements for a registration statement filed by XYZ Computer Co. The financial statements were materially erroneous. Investors sued for $1,000,000. Defendants included ABC, XYZ, Sam (XYZ's CEO), Ed (an outside director on XYZ's board), and Big Chief Co., an underwriter that handled $100,000 of the offering. A jury found Ed to be 5% at fault because he had ignored some red flags indicating that the financial statements were inaccurate. All other defendants were also held to be potentially liable. Ed's maximum liability is $50,000 because he is an outside director. Big Chief's maximum liability is $100,000 because that is the amount of the offering that it underwrote. All of the other defendants, including the accounting firm, could be held liable for the full $1,000,000 if their co-defendants are insolvent.

B. Calculation of Sec. 11 damages

    1. First, calculate the "amount paid," which is the lesser of:

        a. The amount actually paid by P; or

        b. The price at which the security was offered to the public.

Example:
LMN Corp. files a registration statement and sells its stock to the public at $18/share. On the second day of public trading, P buys on the secondary market at $20/share. The "amount paid" is $18/share.

    2. Apply the proper formula.

    3. When P sells the shares prior to filing suit:

Damages = "Amount paid" – Sale price

Example:
P bought LMN shares at $10/share, the public offering price. After disclosure of errors in the financial statements contained in the registration statement, LMN shares dropped to $6/share. P sold at that price and soon thereafter filed a Sec. 11 lawsuit against Longhorn and its auditor. At the time the lawsuit was filed, LMN shares were trading at $4/share. P won the suit. Damages would be $4/share.

    4. When P still owns the shares at the time of judgment:

Damages = "Amount paid" – Value at "time of suit"

Example:
P bought LMN shares at $10/share, the public offering price. After disclosure of errors in the financial statements contained in the registration statement, LMN shares dropped to $6/share. LMN shares were trading at $7/share on the day that P filed a Sec. 11 suit against LMN and its auditor. The shares were trading at $4/share on the day a jury rendered a verdict in favor of P against Ds. Damages would be $3/share.

5. When P sells the shares during the litigation at a price higher than the price "at time of suit," price:

> Damages = "Amount paid" – Sale

Example:
P bought LMN shares at $10/share, the public offering price. After disclosure of errors in the financial statements contained in the registration statement, the price of LMN shares dropped to $5/share on the day that P filed a Sec. 11 suit against LMN and its auditor. During the course of suit, the market rallied and P sold the shares at $9/share. LMN shares were trading at $4/share on the day a jury rendered a verdict in favor of P. P's damages would be $1/share.

6. When P sells during litigation at a price lower than the price "at time of suit":

> Damages = "Amount paid" – Value "at time of suit"

Example:
P bought LMN shares at $10/share, the public offering price. After disclosure of errors in the financial statements contained in the registration statement, P filed a Sec. 11 suit against LMN and its auditor. On the day suit was filed, LMN shares were trading at $7/share. During the lawsuit, P sold the shares for $2/share. A jury later returned a verdict for P. P's damages would be $3/share.

7. Key point—Punitive damages are not allowed under Sec. 11 or any other federal securities law provision.

VI. Charts Summarizing 1933 Act Civil Liability

A. Elements of recovery

See the following example.

Cause of Action?	Wrongful Act?	Scienter?	Reliance?	Causation?	Damage?	Potential Ds
Sec.11	Misleading statement or omission in RS	No; nor must P prove negligence	No, but must be able to "trace" shares to defective RS	No	Yes	Issuer and its insiders, underwriters, auditors, and other experts. Privity not necessary.
Sec.12(a)(1)	Illegal offer or sale (usually sale w/o registration where no exemption applies)	No; virtual strict liability	Same as Sec.11	No	Yes	All "sellers"—those who transfer title or who "solicit" the transaction. Privity not necessary.
Sec.12(a)(2)	Misleading statement	No; nor must P prove negligence	Same as Sec.11	No	Yes	Same as Sec.12(a)(1)

B. Defenses

Cause of Action	Statute of Limitations	Due Diligence	No Reliance by P	Alternate Causation
Sec.11	1 yr. from date misstatement was or should have been discovered and 3 yrs. from first bona fide offer to public.	Yes; all Ds except issuer	Yes, if P knew of error or 12-mo. earnings statement sent	Yes
Sec.12(a)(1)	1 yr. from date of violation and 3 yrs. from first bona fide offer to public	No, but Rule 508 protects unintentional and incidental violation of Reg.D.	No	No
Sec.12(a)(2)	1 yr. from date misstatement was or should have been discovered and 3 yrs. from sale to P	Yes	Yes, if P knew of error	Yes

Purposes, Requirements, and Provisions of the 1934 Act

The average company files a registration statement under the 1933 Act only once every nine years or so. If 1933 Act registration statements were the only source of public information about companies, investors would be in trouble. The 1934 Act is aimed at ensuring that the more important companies deliver a stream of steady information to the investing public via annual reports, quarterly reports, etc.

After studying this lesson, you should be able to:

1. Understand the wide coverage and great importance of Section 10(b).

2. Comprehend the essence of Section 10(b)'s liability provisions.

3. Comprehend the essence of Section 18(a)'s liability provisions.

4. Understand the essential purposes and basic provisions of the 1934 Securities Exchange Act.

5. List the key documents that make up the 1934 Act's periodic disclosure system.

I. **Regular Disclosure**—Provide regular disclosure by major companies even when they are not raising capital by filing registration statements.

II. **Punish Fraud**—In communications regarding the purchase and sale of securities of corporations of any size.

   A. Corporate disclosure cases

   B. Insider trading cases

III. **Created SEC**—This Act created the Securities and Exchange Commission to enforce all federal securities laws. Among other things, the SEC:

   A. Enforces the 1933 Act's registration and anti-fraud provisions;

   B. Enforces the 1934 Act's continuous disclosure and anti-fraud provisions;

   C. Registers and regulates broker-dealers;

   D. Registers and regulates investment-advisors;

   E. Enforces rules regarding proxy solicitations and tender offers;

   F. Enforces criminal provisions of the federal securities laws by investing fraud and referring cases to the Department of Justice for prosecution.

IV. **Disclosure Requirement Under the 1934 Securities Exchange Act**

   A. **Who are reporting companies who must file documents regularly with SEC?**

      1. All companies whose shares are traded on national exchanges, such as the NYSE.

      2. All companies that have registered their shares with the SEC, unless they have fallen below the following thresholds:

         a. 300 shareholders; or

         b. 500 shareholders and less than $10 million in total assets for each of the last three fiscal years.

      3. Even companies that have not registered with the SEC if they have more than **$10 million** in assets and more than **2,000 shareholders** in a single class.

      4. A company that made a registered public offering during the year.

      5. NASDAQ "Bulletin Board" companies.

      6. Remember that under the JOBS Act of 2012, firms that declare themselves to be Emerging Growth Companies (EGCs) need not comply with these filings for five years after their IPO (or until they no longer comply with the EGC requirements).

B. What documents must they file?

1. An initial registration form—(Form 10) disclosing such information as:

   a. Names of officers and directors;

   b. Nature of business;

   c. Financial structure of firm;

   d. Bonus and profit-sharing provisions for officers and directors.

2. Continuous disclosure forms

   a. 10-Ks—annual reports (containing certified F/S);

   b. 10-Qs—quarterly reports (F/S need not be certified);

   c. 8-Ks—interim reports covering important developments to be filed within four business days of when the development occurs.

C. Other 1934 Act filing requirements

1. Concentrations of shares (Sec. 13(d))

   a. Any one individual (or group working in concert) who acquires 5% of a class of equity securities of a 1934 Act reporting company must within 10 days file a Schedule 13D, disclosing:

     i. The purpose of the purchase;

       1. The key question is whether they are merely investing in the company or have acquired this block of shares as a prelude to takeover.

     ii. Amount and source of funds;

     iii. Name and background of acquirer.

   b. Purpose of requirement: to alert shareholders to potential changes in control of their corporations.

2. Tender offers

   a. If an acquirer makes a tender offer to shareholders of a target corporation for control of the target, the 1934 Act imposes substantial filing requirements on both parties.

   b. Acquirer filings must disclose much the same information required by Schedule 13D and should include a discussion of plans for change if the acquisition succeeds.

   c. Target filings must include the target management's position regarding whether target shareholders should tender their shares or resist the takeover.

   d. Purpose of requirement: So that shareholders of target corporation can make an informed judgment as to whether they should tender or retain their shares.

3. Proxy solicitations (Sec. 14)

   a. Virtually all reporting companies must solicit proxies from shareholders in order to achieve the necessary quorum to hold their state law mandated annual meetings to elect directors and special meetings to approve transactions that shareholders are entitled to vote on, including mergers.

   b. The 1934 Act mandates that such solicitations must be accompanied by proxy statements containing SEC-mandated disclosures including:

     i. All material facts about matters to be voted on;

     ii. Extensive background on nominees if it is a Board of Directors' election;

     iii. Extensive information on the advantages and disadvantages of a transaction if it is a special election for matters such as mergers or sale of major assets.

c. All issuer proxy statements must include:

    i. Proper shareholder proposals, which are proposals for corporate action suggested by the shareholders themselves to be voted on at the annual or special meeting of shareholders.

        1. Can be omitted on various grounds, including:

            a. Matters of personal grievance;

            b. Matters of "ordinary business" within the discretion of management;

            c. Matters "not significantly related" to the issuer's business; and

            d. The fact that they call for violation of state or federal law.

    ii. Two years' audited F/S.

4. Insider trading

    a. Sec. 16(a) of the 1934 Act provides that three classes of persons must disclose their transactions in their own company's stock.

        i. Officers;

        ii. Directors;

        iii. Holders of at least 10% of the company's registered equity securities.

            1. Rationale—These three categories of persons have significant control over their company and could abuse it by engaging in insider trading; disclosure of their trades to the world should minimize any abuses.

            2. In addition to filing with the SEC an initial report regarding their holdings when they attain the status of officer, director, or 10% holder, these persons must report any significant transactions in their company's shares within two days of the transaction.

    b. If a reporting company's officers, directors, or 10% holders do not comply with the Sec. 16(a) reporting requirements, the company itself must disclose these violations in its proxy statements and Form 10-Ks.

    c. Sec. 16(b) of the 1934 Act provides that any officer, director, or 10% holder must disgorge any profits derived from "shortswing" transactions in their company's stock.

        i. A "short-swing" transaction occurs almost any time the insider buys within six months of selling or sells within six months of buying.

Example:
If a director of A Corp. buys 100 A shares on July 1 for $60 and sells 100 A shares on December 10 for $70, a "short-swing" profit of $1,000 has been gained and must be disgorged.

D. Any **intentionally misleading statement** in any of these 1934 Act documents is actionable.

V. Sec. 10(b) and Rule 10b-5—of the 1934 Act apply to all securities, no matter how big or small the company is, whether it is registered or unregistered with the SEC, and whether an initial offering or secondary trading is involved. The Sarbanes-Oxley Act of 2002 made some important changes to the 1934 Act.

A. Key points

    1. If there is a false statement in a registration statement, such as erroneous financial statements certified by an accounting firm, plaintiffs can sue under both Sec. 11 of the 1933 Act and Sec. 10(b) of the 1934 Act. However, whereas the standard of liability under Sec. 11 is mere negligence (and the burden of proof is on the defendant), the standard of liability under Sec. 10(b) is scienter (bad intent) and the burden of proof is upon the plaintiff.

2. The SEC can bring civil charges alleging violations of Sec. 10(b) and injured investors can also bring civil suits for damages.

VI. **What Plaintiffs Must Prove to Win a 10b-5 Claim**

A. **False statement or omission of material fact.**

B. **Scienter by defendant**

1. "Recklessness" is sufficiently similar to bad intent to satisfy the requirement.

Example:
Recklessness - ABC Accounting Firm certified the financial statements of XYZ Computer Co. that were included in XYZ's 10-K filing with the SEC. ABC did not comply with GAAP. Indeed, it cut corners in several respects and ignored several "red flags." Nonetheless, ABC thought the financial statements might be accurate and truly hoped that they were. ABC's actions are sufficiently reckless that, if the financial statements turn out to be inaccurate, they will probably be liable under Sec. 10(b).

2. Unlike under Sec. 11, mere negligence will not suffice.

C. **Reliance by plaintiff**

1. **Omission case**—Plaintiff need not prove reliance.

a. In an omission case, plaintiff is not claiming that any affirmative lies were told, only that material facts were omitted.

Example:
Omission Case—ABC Accounting Firm certified the financial statements of XYZ Computer Co. that were included in XYZ's 10-K filing with the SEC. ABC did comply with GAAP. However, XYZ had some unusual financial considerations not covered by GAAP that, when omitted, rendered the financial statements materially misleading. Plaintiff investors suing under Sec. 10(b) and Rule 10b-5 would not have to prove reliance for it is very difficult to prove that you relied on something that was hidden from you.

2. **Active misrepresentation case**—Plaintiff must prove reliance.

a. May satisfy by proof of "fraud on the market," i.e., by P showing that although s/he did not read the particular false statement (i.e., a faulty financial statement contained in a 10-K), market professionals did and their reaction established a market price upon which P relied when purchasing the securities.

See the following example.

Example:
Active Misrepresentation Case—ABC Accounting Firm certified the financial statements of XYZ Computer Co. that were included in XYZ's 10-K filing with the SEC. The financial statements reported earnings of $10,000,000. This was surprisingly good news and the stock market reacted by boosting XYZ's share price by $10/share. It turned out that the financial statements were inaccurate having overstated XYZ's earnings by 50%. Plaintiff investors under Sec. 10(b) need not show that they read the 10-K in order to sue. Rather, they relied upon the accuracy of the market price as established by the professional analysts and institutional investors who did read the 10-K and whose activities largely establish the market price. The investors were indirectly misled.

D. **Causation**

1. **Transaction causation**—To establish transaction causation, plaintiff must show that the false statements or omissions caused him to enter into the transaction (overlaps reliance element).

Example:
Sam bought ABC shares from his girlfriend who had just become a stockbroker and was assigned the task of pushing ABC shares. It turns out that ABC's financial statements as contained in its most recent 10-K were inaccurate. Because Sam had not read those financial statements and did not really care what they said—he was buying to help out his girlfriend— he cannot establish transaction causation. Whatever misstatements were in the financials statements are not what caused him to buy the shares.

2. **Loss causation**—To establish loss causation, plaintiff must show that the false statements or omissions are what actually caused his financial loss; alternative causation may doom P's claim.

Example:
Seeking a tax shelter, Paul wished to invest in an oil and gas limited partnership in the early 1980s. He invested in ABC LP. Unfortunately for Paul, the entire oil and gas industry crashed just after he invested and he lost lots of money. He sued ABC proving that ABC had not disclosed that its promoters were not entirely honest and not very experienced in the oil and gas business. Paul may be able to show transaction causation ("I would not have bought ABC shares had I known the truth.") but he cannot show loss causation. Even if he had not invested in ABC, he would have invested in another oil and gas limited partnership and would have lost money there due to the industry-wide crash.

3. The fraud occurred in connection with a purchase or sale of securities.

    a. P must have bought or sold shares in order to have "standing" to sue.

Example:
Connection with a purchase or sale of securities—A has held ABC shares since 1980. He proves that defendant officers and directors of ABC have manipulated its shares for their own personal goals causing its value to drop. Shares A bought in 1980 at $30/share are now worth only $20/share. Nonetheless, A cannot successfully sue under Sec. 10(b) because he cannot prove that he bought or sold shares in connection with the false statements. He merely held the same shares.

    b. SEC can always sue.

4. Plaintiff suffered damages.

VII. Sec. 10(b) Defenses

A. **Statute of Limitations**—plaintiff must sue:

1. Within two years of when the fraud was or should have been discovered, and

2. Within five years of the fraud.

Example:
Statute of Limitations—On May 1, 2002, XYZ Computer Company's registration statement became effective. ABC Accounting Firm had certified the financial statements contained therein. In June of 2003, rumors began to circulate that XYZ had been claiming revenue from sales that were not final. Several financial publications published articles regarding these rumors. In August of 2005, investors filed a Sec. 10(b) lawsuit against ABC and XYZ, seeking to prove that the financial statements contained in the registration statement had been materially misleading. Because the plaintiffs had been put on notice of the potential errors in June 2003, yet they waited 26 months to file the lawsuit, they are probably barred by the statute of limitations. They filed within the five-year violation deadline but missed the two-year notice deadline.

B. Fraudulent or reckless conduct by plaintiff

> **Example:**
> Plaintiff is an officer of XYZ Computer Corp. and buys some of its shares. The shares plummet in price when it is learned that XYZ's most recent 10-K contained inaccurate financial statements. Plaintiff sues XYZ's accounting firm, ABC, under Sec. 10(b). ABC may avoid liability if it can prove that plaintiff, as an officer of XYZ, was in a position to see red flags that should have alerted him as to XYZ's troubles.

C. Bespeaks caution doctrine—If in a forward-looking statement, such as a prediction of earnings for the upcoming year, a company clearly identifies specific risk factors that might occur to prevent the prediction from coming true, that cautionary language which "bespeaks caution" will likely prevent recovery in any securities fraud suit based on a failure of the company to realize its predicted earnings. This defense was developed by the courts, but has been codified in the PSLRA of 1995.

D. Secondary liability

1. **Note**, that in a recent and very important decision, the Supreme Court held that there is no such thing as "aiding and abetting" liability under Sec. 10(b).

2. This recent decision should limit such liability for accountants who formerly have often been held liable just for "standing around" the clients who happened to be crooks; henceforth, accountants will probably be liable only for their own false statements or omissions, although this is unsettled.

3. In 1995, Congress restored the SEC's authority to bring "aiding and abetting" claims, but private damage plaintiffs still cannot use this theory.

E. Damages—(assuming P is a buyer)

1. **If P still owns shares**—Amount paid minus market value at time of suit.

2. **If P has sold shares**—Amount paid minus sale price.

3. **Punitive damages**—are not allowed in any federal securities law case, including Sec. 10(b).

VIII. Chart summarizing Sec. 10(b) Elements

Cause of Action or Omission	Sec.10(b)
Misstatement	Yes
Materiality	Yes
Scienter	Yes (recklessness will suffice)
Causation	Yes, transaction (lie made me trade) and loss (lie caused stock price decline) both needed
Reliance	Omission: No active misrep: Yes, but can satisfy by "fraud on the market"
Privity	No
Damages	Yes

IX. Section 18(a)

A. Although Section 10(b) is the most significant antifraud provision of the 1934 Securities Exchange Act, accountants are occasionally sued under Section 18(a) as well.

B. The statute reads, in part

"Any person who shall make or cause to be made any statement in any application, report, or *document filed* pursuant to (this Act), which statement was at the time and in light of the circumstances under which it was made false or misleading with respect to any material fact, shall be liable to any person (not knowing that such statement was false or misleading) who, *in reliance upon such statement*, shall have purchased or sold a security at a price that was affected by such statement, for damages caused by such reliance, *unless the person sued shall prove that he acted in good faith and had no knowledge that such statement was false or misleading.*" (emphasis added)

C. Among the key points to remember regarding Section 18(a) are:

1. It applies only to false statements in "filed documents"—documents filed with the SEC. Thus, it would not remedy false statements in press releases or interviews with the press. On the other hand, accountants often certify financial statements that are filed with the SEC and therefore become potentially liable under Sec. 18(a).

2. The courts have interpreted Sec. 18(a) to require plaintiffs to establish "eyeball reliance," that they saw, read, and believed the false statements. Because most investors do not read most documents that are filed with the SEC, this requirement definitely limits the usefulness of the provision to plaintiffs. The "fraud on the market" theory of reliance that is so important in Section 10(b) litigation is not available to plaintiffs suing under Sec. 18(a).

3. Section 18(a) assumes liability if filed documents contain materially false statements and it shifts the burden of proof to defendants, such as accountants, to establish that they "acted in good faith and had no knowledge that such statement was false or misleading."

4. As with Section 10(b), privity of contract (as direct contractual relationship) is not an element of the right to sue. Therefore, investors may file 18(a) lawsuits against accountants who did not buy or sell securities but who certified materially inaccurate financial statements that are filed with the SEC.

D. Courts hold that plaintiffs establish a prima facie case for recovery by showing

1. Defendant made or caused to be made a false or misleading statement or omission;

2. In a filed document;

3. Materiality;

4. Plaintiff's purchase or sale of securities;

5. Plaintiff's "eyeball" reliance;

6. Causation; and

7. Damages.

E. Key defenses that can be established by defendant are

1. D acted in good faith and without knowledge that the statement was false or misleading; and

2. Statute of limitations (plaintiffs must sue both within one year of discovering the facts constituting the cause of action and within three years of when the cause of action accrued (which is upon plaintiff's purchase or sale).

X. Private Securities Litigation Reform Act

A. PSLRA of 1995

1. In 1995, in response to lobbying by accountants, Congress passed the PSLRA which, in general, made it harder to bring securities fraud class action lawsuits by:

    a. Putting in procedural hurdles for plaintiffs seeking to bring class actions, and

    b. Raising the bar regarding some procedural and substantive matters regarding the causes of action.

    c. The most important procedural hurdle was a requirement that discovery be stayed in actions after defendants filed motions to dismiss. Plaintiffs' class action attorneys evaded this bar on discovery by filing parallel securities fraud actions in state court. This ploy was ended when Congress passed the Securities Litigation Uniform Standards Act of 1998, which requires all class action securities fraud suits to be brought in federal, not state, court.

  2. Interestingly, the most important part of this generally pro-accountant law is a provision that imposes upon accountants an arguable duty to "blow the whistle" on their clients to the SEC when illegal activity is discovered.

B. New rules for auditors

  1. Each audit required by the 1934 Act shall include:

    a. Procedures designed to provide reasonable assurance of detecting illegal acts that would have a direct and material effect on the determination of financial statement amounts;

    b. Procedures designed to identify material related-party transactions;

    c. An evaluation of whether there is substantial doubt about the issuer's ability to continue as a going concern.

  2. If, during the audit, the accountant becomes aware of information indicating that an illegal act (whether or not material) has occurred, then the accountant shall:

    a. Determine whether it is likely that an illegal act has occurred;

    b. If so, determine the possible effect on the issuer (in terms of fines, penalties, damages, etc.);

    c. As soon as practicable, inform the appropriate level of management of the issue and assure that its audit committee or board of directors is adequately informed.

  3. If, after the audit committee or board of directors is informed, the accountant concludes that:

    a. The illegal act has a material effect on the financial statements;

    b. The senior management has not taken timely and appropriate remedial action regarding the illegal act;

    c. The failure to take such action is reasonably expected to warrant departure from a standard report of the auditor or, when made, warrant resignation from the audit engagement.

  4. The accountant shall directly report its conclusions to the board. When the board receives such a report of an illegal act, it shall inform the SEC within one business day and provide a copy of the notice to the accountant. If the accountant fails to receive a copy of this notice, within one business day, s/he shall:

    a. Resign from the engagement, or

    b. Furnish to the SEC a copy of its report not later than one business day.

  5. If an auditor resigns, it shall, within one business day following the issuer's failure to inform the SEC, furnish the SEC with a copy of the illegal act report.

  6. "No independent accountant shall be liable in a private action for any finding, conclusion, or statement expressed in a report made to (the issuer or the SEC)."

  7. If an auditor willfully violates these requirements, the SEC may impose a civil penalty under Sec. 21C.

Criminal Liability

The SEC has the authority to refer to the Department of Justice for criminal prosecution ANY intentional violation of ANY provision of the 1933 or 1934 Acts.

After studying this lesson, you should be able to:

1. Understand that an intentional violation of any provision of the 1933 or 1934 Act is a crime.

I. 1933 Securities Act

    A. Accountants are liable for any "willful" violation of any provision of the 1933 Act.

    B. Penalties: Up to $10,000 fine and/or five years in jail.

II. 1934 Securities Exchange Act

    A. Accountants are liable for any "willful" violation of any provision of the 1934 Act.

    B. Penalties: Up to $2,500,000 fine and/or 20 years in jail (up to $25 million fine if defendant is a firm).

    C. These criminal penalties are cumulative; they may be imposed on top of the civil liability discussed elsewhere.

    D. The SEC cannot bring criminal charges itself; rather, it refers these cases to the Department of Justice, which actually files and prosecutes the cases, often based on evidence provided by the SEC.

III. Sarbanes-Oxley Criminal Provisions

    A. SOX added several criminal provisions to the U.S. Code that accountants must be aware of.

    B. Although it was already a crime to intentionally violate any provision of the 1933 and 1934 securities acts, Congress added a new securities fraud provision to the U.S. criminal code, 18 U.S.C. Sec. 1348, that is not as complicated as Section 10(b) and may eventually become nearly as important (although that certainly has not yet happened). That provision reads:

        1. "Whoever knowingly executes, or attempts to execute, a scheme or artifice shall be fined under this title, or imprisoned not more than 25 years, or both."

            a. To defraud any person in connection with any security of (a public company); or

            b. To obtain, by means of false or fraudulent pretenses, representations, or promises, any money or property in connection with a class of (a public company).

    C. In addition, SOX contains several criminal provisions for document retention and destruction that are covered elsewhere in these materials. They look like this:

        1. **Willful failure to retain audit and review workpapers**—SOX also creates a new federal crime punishing a "knowing and willful" failure to retain audit or review work papers for a period of **five years** by up to 10 years in jail and a fine. (Sec. 802, codified at 18 U.S.C. §1520). The five-year period is functionally overridden by a different SOX provision that requires public company auditors to retain their working papers for seven years.

        2. **Destruction of records**—SOX creates a new federal crime relating to destruction of records involved in *any* federal governmental matter or bankruptcy, making it a crime punishable by fine, imprisonment up to 20 years or both to "knowingly alter, destroy, mutilate, conceal, cover up, falsify, or make a false entry in any record, document, or tangible object with intent to impede, obstruct, or influence the investigation or proper administration of any matter within the jurisdiction of any department or agency of the United States or any case filed under (the Bankruptcy Code.)" (Sec. 802, codified at 18 U.S.C. §1519)

            a. This statute is meant to eliminate any technical requirement that a subpoena already be issued or a proceeding be imminent before it is improper to destroy documents the government wants.

            b. It goes well beyond audit-related documents.

3. **Corrupt tampering with documents to be used in an official proceeding**—SOX also creates a new federal crime for tampering with documents to be used in an official proceeding, providing that any person who "corruptly" (1) alters, destroys, mutilates, or conceals a record, document or other object, or attempts to do so, with the intent to impair the object's integrity or availability for use in an official proceeding, or (2) otherwise obstructs, influences, or impedes any official proceeding, or attempts to do so, shall be fined or imprisoned up to 20 years or both. The attempt to do these acts is also a crime. (Sec. 1102, codified at 18 U.S.C. §1512)

The Dodd-Frank Act of 2010

I. Dodd-Frank Act of 2010

    A. Following the subprime mortgage crisis and financial meltdown, it is unsurprising that new regulations were enacted. In 2010, Congress passed and President Obama signed the Dodd-Frank Wall Street Reform and Consumer Protection Act ("Dodd-Frank"), which at more than 2,000 pages has been called the most sweeping change to financial services regulation since the Great Depression. Because so many portions of Dodd-Frank will be enacted over a period of years, it is difficult to know exactly (or even generally) what its ultimate impact will be.

    B. It is clear that Dodd-Frank's impact upon the accounting profession is relatively minor. Whereas the last major federal financial legislation (Sarbanes-Oxley in 2002) largely remade the public accounting profession and its regulation, Dodd-Frank generally gave accountants a pass. For example, it exempted accountants from the sweeping consumer protection legislation that will be administered by an entire new federal agency.

II. General Overview—Broadly, Dodd-Frank seeks to strengthen financial market performance by (a) improving financial institutions' accountability and transparency, (b) protecting taxpayers from being saddled with future bailouts, and (c) protecting consumers from a plethora of abusive practices. In pursuit of these goals, Dodd-Frank does at least five major things.

    A. First—Dodd-Frank seeks to limit the risk posed by existing financial institutions and by contemporary financial activities. Regarding the risk stemming from financial institutions, Dodd-Frank creates a new Financial Stability Oversight Council (FSOC) to monitor activities posting a systemic risk to U.S. financial stability. The FSOC is made up of the heads of a number of regulators (Fed, FDIC, SEC, etc.) that, it is envisioned, will coordinate the planning and assessment.

        1. The FSOC will first attempt to prevent big institutions from failing. It has authority to provide greater oversight of those firms than has existed in the past and can require that they hold extra reserves that would not be required of other financial institutions. It also has authority to order liquidation of such firms in an orderly fashion if they do happen to fail. The Federal Reserve would carry out that process.

        2. What sort of a firm is "too-big-to-fail?" Dodd-Frank focuses on bank holding companies that have at least $50 billion in assets and nonbank financial institutions (insurance holding companies, investment banks, etc.) that are systemically important. As authorities attempt to flesh out the specifics of these rules, unprecedented lobbying is occurring as interested parties attempt to shape the law to their own benefit. Because Dodd-Frank left so many rules unspecified, post-legislation lobbying is probably more critical for Dodd-Frank than any other statute in modern memory.

    B. Second—Regarding risk deriving from modern financial practices, Dodd-Frank places limitations on proprietary trading by banks and their support of hedge funds (the "Volcker rule"). These limitations are to be phased in over the next few years. It is unlikely that the SEC will get all the rules rolled out without creation of a number of loopholes.

C. Third—Dodd-Frank requires increased transparency in the over-the-counter (OTC) markets. Abuse of derivative securities, such as credit default swaps, was arguably at the core of the financial meltdown of 2008. Dodd-Frank seeks to reduce the likelihood of a repeat of these abuses by, among other things, requiring that all "standard" derivatives be traded and cleared via clearinghouses, so that prices are more transparent. (The first such electronic trade occurred in late November 2010.) Dodd-Frank also requires that the clearinghouses not be controlled by the big banks and requires traders to put up "adequate" capital against losses they might sustain. Due to heavy lobbying, loopholes again abound.

D. Fourth—Dodd-Frank requires SEC registration of hedge funds. Increased disclosures by hedge funds and their advisers, which have in the past operated in an extremely opaque fashion largely ignored by regulators, is now required.

E. Fifth—Dodd-Frank seeks to protect consumers from a broad range of fraudulent and predatory practices. It creates the Consumer Financial Protection Bureau (CFPB), which consolidates most federal regulation of financial services. Most creditor providers (including mortgage lenders, payday loan outfits, and other nonbank financial companies) and banks and credit unions with assets over $10 billion will be subject to new regulation by the CFPB. Accounting firms will not.

F. Other significant features include:

1. Creating a major reward system for people who blow the whistle on financial fraud. The first reward under the new legislation has already been given out (to an accountant). In May 2011, the SEC adopted final rules implementing the whistle-blower program. The program promises to pay rewards of 10% to 30% of monetary sanctions over $1 million obtained after an investigation advanced by a whistleblower's tip. The rules encourage, but do not require, whistleblowers to report suspected violations internally to their employers before going to the SEC.

2. Additionally protecting whistleblowers who are punished by their employers for bringing fraud to light by providing a new private right of action for reinstatement, double back pay, and other relief. To be eligible, they most provide "original information" relating to a violation of the securities laws to the SEC that is derived from their own independent knowledge or analysis and not previously known by the SEC and that is not derived exclusively from external, publicly available information.

3. Amending the Commodities Exchange Act to punish insider trading by agents or employees of the Federal government who learn information that may affect the price of any commodity, option or swap.

4. Authorizing the SEC to increase shareholder access to the proxy process to tip the balance of power in public corporations away from boards of directors and officers and toward shareholders. Shareholders of public corporations are also granted a "say-on-pay" vote regarding their corporations' top officers' salaries and golden parachutes. Although the shareholder vote is not binding on the board of directors, it is expected to have a meaningful impact.

5. Requiring public companies to implement mandatory clawback systems for executive performance pay where there is an accounting restatement *whether or not fraud or other misconduct is a factor*. In other words, if executives received bonus payments for meeting certain earnings targets and it later turns out that those targets were not actually met and it only appeared so due to accounting errors, those bonuses should be "clawed back" into the corporate treasury, even if the errors were innocent.

6. Amending SOX to make a permanent exclusion from Sarbanes-Oxley's Sec. 404 internal control provisions for smaller firms—those with less than $75 million in market capitalization.

7. Authorizing the SEC to punish those who aid and abet securities fraud (and controlling persons), reducing the legal standard from "knowing" to "knowing or reckless." Dodd-Frank did not reinstate a right for injured investors to sue for aiding and abetting. Only the SEC may pursue that claim.

8. Creating a new federal insurance regulator. Previously, insurance regulation had been almost exclusively within the jurisdiction of the states.

9. Changing the rules that require pension funds and other entities to buy securities certified as investment grade by *credit rating agencies* in an attempt to reduce the importance of those agencies (which performed so abysmally during the sub-prime crisis).

10. Requiring the Federal Reserve Board to direct publicly traded nonbank financial institutions and bank holding companies with at least $10 billion in assets to establish a separate "risk committee" of the board of directors to oversee the institution's financial risk management practices. Many believe that risk management practices at major financial institutions must be improved to avoid repeats of the 2008 debacle.

11. Increasing the SEC's authority to punish bad guys, such as rogue stock brokers, administratively (on its own authority, without seeking a court order).

III. Impact on Accountants

A. As noted, Dodd-Frank's hits the accounting profession only a glancing blow. Accounting errors were not at the core of the subprime mortgage scandal and subsequent credit crisis. However, Dodd-Frank does contain less significant provisions that do have a direct (if minor) impact on accountants. Among these are provisions:

1. Increasing the jurisdictional authority of the SEC and PCAOB to force production of audit work papers by foreign private accounting firms.

2. Requiring U.S.-registered public accounting firms to secure agreement of foreign accounting firms upon which they rely in their audits to produce the work papers of that firm. Foreign firms may produce through foreign regulators.

3. Containing confidentiality provisions aimed at reducing foreign firms' objections to PCAOB inspection and document production requests.

4. Authorizing the PCAOB to monitor auditors of nonpublic broker-dealers. Because these broker-dealers are nonpublic, their auditors had previously been outside the PCAOB's scope of authority. Auditors may thank Bernie Madoff for this provision.

5. Shifting approximately 4,000 registered investment advisers (some of whom are CPAs) who have between $25 million and $100 million in assets from federal regulation under the Investment Advisers Act of 1940 (IAA) to state regulation. Those handling more than $100 million will stay under the federal regulatory regime.

6. Eliminating the private adviser exemption under the IAA, meaning that many investment advisers (some of whom are CPAs) who advise private funds will now have to register with the SEC. "Family offices"—those set up by a single wealthy family to handle its investments need not register with the SEC.

Anti-Discrimination

After studying this lesson you should be able to:

1. List the types of employment discrimination that are banned by Title VII.

2. Understand basic defenses available to employers in Title VII lawsuits.

3. Understand the essence of the Age Discrimination in Employment Act.

4. Understand the essence of the Americans with Disabilities Act.

I. **Title VII of the Civil Rights Act of 1964**

1. **Forbids discrimination in employment based on:**

Race	Three employees, one black and two white, were caught stealing from the employer. The employer fired only the two white employees. There was no apparent basis for the distinction other than race. This is impermissible discrimination under Title VII, which protects all races from racially-based discrimination.
Color	A light-skinned person of African-American descent fired all the dark-skinned persons of African-American descent in the department. This could easily constitute discrimination prohibited by Title VII.
Religion	Title VII protects both religious beliefs and religious practices. An employer's responsibility is to "reasonably accommodate" the employee's need, although the courts have not construed this responsibility in too onerous a fashion.
Religion Limitation	A Lutheran church had an opening for a pastor. Plaintiff, a Jewish rabbi, applied for the job. Here is an exception to the protection accorded by Title VII. Naturally, an accounting firm could not refuse to hire someone because they were Jewish, but the Lutheran church could in this instance.
Sex	Plaintiff, a male, wished to be a flight attendant but defendant airline had a "women only" policy. This was held to be a Title VII violation. The law protects men as well as women from gender discrimination.
National Origin	Plaintiff was fired because he was from London and had a British accent that annoyed his boss. This was prohibited discrimination under Title VII.

See the following table.

Chart of Protected and Unprotected Discriminations		
	Protected Against	Not Protected Against
Discrimination against African-Americans	x	
Discrimination against Asian-Americans	x	
Discrimination against Polish-Americans	x	
Discrimination against American Indians	x	
Discrimination against Hispanics	x	
Discrimination against whites	x	
Discrimination against white employee because of interracial marriage	x	
Discrimination against the elderly		x (but see ADEA)
Discrimination against women	x	
Discrimination against men	x	
Discrimination against Jews	x	
Discrimination on basis of pregnancy and childbirth	x	
Discrimination on basis of sexual preference		x
Discrimination in form of quid pro quo sexual harassment	x	
Discrimination in form of hostile environment	x	
Discrimination against the disabled		x (but see ADA)

1. **Title VII applies to**

   a. **Employers**

      i. Having 15 or more employees for at least 20 weeks; and

      ii. Whose business affects interstate commerce.

         1. (Virtually every business affects interstate commerce in some way, so this is not an especially burdensome requirement for plaintiffs.)

   b. **Employment agencies**

   c. **Labor unions**

   d. **Federal, state, and local government employees**

      i. **Fact**—Charitable organizations are not generally exempt, nor are religious employers (though they may hire on the basis of religious belief and practice).

2. **Title VII covers virtually all employment practices, including:**

   a. **Hiring**

   b. **Promotion**—(Including promotion to partnership in an accounting firm)

   c. **Transfers**

   d. **Firings**

   e. **Compensation**

   f. **Job assignments**

3. **Title VII is enforced by:**

   a. **Equal Employment Opportunity Commission (EEOC)**—and/or

      i. If EEOC cannot resolve a Title VII case initiated by employee complaint, it issues a "right to sue" letter to the complaining party.

   b. **Civil actions**—By individual plaintiffs

      i. Suits must be against the employer, not the offending individual supervisor.

4. **Title VII does not preempt similar state laws**—Virtually every state has laws comparable to Title VII, and some provide even greater levels of protection in terms of the practices they prohibit, the classes of persons they protect, and the size of the employers they regulate.

5. **Types of discrimination**

   a. **Intentional**—(disparate treatment)

      i. An employer assigned Hispanic customers to Hispanic employees and white customers to white employees. This was held to be intentional discrimination.

      ii. In a "mixed motive" case, P wins if illegal criterion was a "motivating factor" in decision, even if other factors were present.

Example:
Employer fired plaintiff partly because he was male and partly because he was somewhat slow in carrying out his duties. If the plaintiff would not have been fired solely on the basis of his performance, then he has a plausible Title VII claim.

   b. **Discriminatory impact**—(disparate impact)

      I. Disparate impact cases arise primarily in situations where facially neutral job criteria such as height, weight, strength, or education standards have a discriminatory impact on protected groups; such discrimination is often proved by statistical evidence.

Example:
Employer requires a high school diploma of employees seeking to be custodians. This requirement eliminates 10% of all white applicants from the applicant pool, but knocks out 40% of all African-American applicants in the area. Because it is unlikely that one needs a high school diploma to be a custodian, this requirement is probably discriminatory.

6. **Defenses for employer**

   a. **Bona Fide Occupational Qualification**—(BFOQ)

      i. If a requirement that has a discriminatory impact is a bona fide occupational qualification pertaining directly to the needs of the job, then it is not a Title VII violation.

   Example:
   Plaintiff was a Sikh whose religion prohibited him from shaving. He worked as a machinist for defendant. Unfortunately, his beard prevented the achievement of an airtight seal on the respirator that federal safety regulations required all machinists to wear. Defendant offered him a number of similar positions for which he was qualified that would not require him to wear a respirator, although all were slightly lower paying. The safety regulations provided defendant employer with a legitimate BFOQ defense.

   b. **Bona Fide seniority or merit system**

      i. No affirmative action plan can override such systems.

   Example:
   A city fire department was all white for many years. Only recently did it begin to hire African-Americans. Then budget cutbacks necessitated layoffs, which were done on a seniority basis. Naturally, most of those laid off were African-Americans because they had not had the opportunity to gain much seniority. Nonetheless, the layoffs are not a violation of Title VII if they are based on a valid seniority system.

   Misconception: Although many people seem to believe that it is improper to ever fire members of protected classes, it is always permissible to fire employees on the basis of merit criteria.

   C. **Professional-developed ability test**

      i. **Purpose**—To prove that standards or requirements serve a legitimate business purpose.

7. **Sexual harassment**—Although Congress probably did not have sexual harassment in mind when it passed Title VII, the courts have come to recognize two forms of sexual harassment that are prohibited under the Act.

   a. Quid pro quo ("this for that") has these elements:

      i. Boss (or someone for whom boss is responsible) makes unwelcome request for sexual favors; and

      ii. Compliance is reasonably seen as term or condition of employment.

   Example:
   Plaintiff worked for a fast food company. He received good evaluations and consistent promotions until he refused to sleep with his new supervisor. She began giving him poor evaluations and soon fired him. He had a valid Title VII claim.

   b. Hostile environment harassment has these elements:

      i. The employer creates or tolerates an intimidating, hostile, or offensive working environment.

> **Example:**
> Plaintiff was one of the first females to be employed at a shipyard. She was often subjected to comments by coworkers about her body and coworkers displayed "pin-ups" of naked women. Plaintiff complained to her supervisor who laughed at her and put up his own pin-ups. Plaintiff had a legitimate hostile environment sexual harassment claim.

  c. A series of important Supreme Court decisions in 1998 established that:

    i. Same-sex sexual harassment is prohibited by Title VII;

    ii. Employers may be liable for sexual harassment by their employees and supervisors even though that harassment does not aid the employer in any way; and

    iii. If victims of sexual harassment suffer an adverse job result (firing, demotion, etc.), the employer is strictly liable;

    iv. If a sexual harassment victim does not suffer an adverse job result, employers can avoid liability by establishing, communicating, and enforcing a zero-tolerance policy;

    v. Employees who do not take advantage of their employer's internal procedures for handling complaints will probably be barred from pursuing court litigation.

II. Age Discrimination in Employment Act (ADEA)

 A. Purpose—To supplement Title VII, which did not address age discrimination, by eliminating discrimination against older workers.

 B. Protects—Individuals 40 years and older.

  1. Main Effect: Prohibit mandatory retirement.

   a. Exemption for executives 65 or older;

   b. Former exemption: tenured professors.

  2. Also protects from discrimination in all other areas of employment practice.

  3. There is no cause of action for "reverse age discrimination" against the young.

 C. Applies to:

  1. Businesses employing at least 20 people;

  2. State and Local Governments;

  3. Unions (with at least 25 members);

  4. Employment Agencies.

 D. Procedures, remedies, and defenses are generally the same as under Title VII

III. Americans with Disabilities Act (ADA)

 A. Purpose—Ensure our economy takes advantage of the skills and abilities that disabled persons have to offer.

 B. Applies to

  1. Employers with 15 or more employees;

  2. All state and local governments;

  3. Most private businesses that provide accommodations, goods, or services to the public;

  4. Public services and transportation.

C. **Enforced by**—EEOC and private suits, like Title VII.

D. **Forbids discrimination against "any qualified individual with a disability," defined as:**

1. A physical or mental impairment that substantially limits one or more "major life activities" of such individual;

2. A record of any such impairment; or

3. Being regarded as having such an impairment.

4. Note: In 2008, Congress made several important changes to the ADA, including:

   a. Providing a non-exhaustive list of major life activities, including: "caring for oneself, performing manual tasks, seeing, hearing, eating, sleeping, walking, standing, lifting, bending, speaking, breathing, learning, reading, concentrating, thinking, communicating, and working."

   b. Providing that the determination whether an impairment substantially limits a major life activity must be made "without regarding to the ameliorative effects of mitigating measures" such as medication, artificial aids, assistive technology, and reasonable accommodations. There is an exception for eyeglasses and contact lenses. If they can improve a person's vision sufficiently, the person is no longer considered "disabled," even if s/he is unable to see without them. However, a person who can walk with prosthetic legs or can function at work when taking antidepressant medication, is still "disabled" if s/he cannot walk without the prosthetics or cannot work without the medication.

E. **The ADA protects (or does not) against discrimination based on**

	Protected	Not Protected
Muscular dystrophy	X	
HIV infected	X	
Mental retardation	X	
Alcoholism	X	
Emotional illness	X	
Homosexuality		X
Bisexuality		X
Transvestitism		X
Transsexualism		X
Pedophilia		X
Exhibitionism		X
Voyeurism		X
Sexual behavior disorders		X
Compulsive gambling		X
Kleptomania		X
Pyromania		X
Psychiatric substance disorders resulting from current illegal use of drugs or abuse of alcohol		X

F. Employers must:

1. Not discriminate in hiring or other employment practices.

Example:

1. Employee informed employer that he had been diagnosed with brain cancer and would have to undergo chemotherapy. The employer promptly fired the employee without determining whether or not the employee would be able to continue to perform his responsibilities. This was held as an ADA violation.

2. Employee informed his supervisor that he had tested HIV-positive. The supervisor told the employee's coworkers and had them vote on whether or not they wished to continue to work with him. He lost by an 18–14 vote and was fired. This was an ADA violation.

2. Establish nondiscriminatory hiring standards by:

   a. Identifying the "essential functions" of the job;

   b. Ensuring that any employment standards that might exclude a disabled person is "job related and of business necessity;"

   c. Determining if a "reasonable accommodation" would permit the disabled person to meet the standard.

3. Make reasonable accommodations by, among other things:

   a. Making facilities accessible;

   b. Providing adaptive hardware;

   c. Hiring readers or interpreters;

   d. Providing part-time or modified work schedules.

Employee Welfare

After studying this lesson you should be able to:

1. Understand how workers qualify for social security benefits.

2. Understand that the social security tax funds Medicare but not Medicaid.

3. Understand the scope of the Federal Insurance Contributions Act.

4. Understand the circumstances under which an accountant (or others) might be liable to pay a corporate payroll tax when the corporation itself did not do so.

5. Understand the rules for social security taxes in the self-employment setting.

I. **Federal Social Security Act—Social Security Benefits**

    A. **Purpose**—To provide **partial** replacement of earnings when a worker retires.

    B. **Mechanism**—Monthly benefits are paid to retired insured worker from age 62 onward.

    C. **Insured worker**—A **"fully insured" worker** is entitled to some benefits, although the amount payable changes often.

        1. To be "fully insured," one must accrue a minimum of 40 quarters (10 years) of contributions.

        2. A "fully insured" worker is eligible for these benefits:

            a. Survivor benefits for widow or widower and dependents;

            b. Disability benefits for worker and family;

            c. Old age retirement benefits to worker and dependents;

                i. Benefits can be reduced by:

                    1. Early retirement before age 65:

> Retire at 62 = 80% of benefits.
> Retire at 63 = 87% of benefits.
> Retire at 64 = 93% of benefits.

                    2. For most of Social Security's existence, workers were entitled to full benefits at age 65. However, for reasons of fiscal solvency, the "full benefits" threshold has been changed and is sliding later and later. For example, someone born in 1937 or before was entitled to full benefits at age 65. Someone born in 1938 is entitled to full benefits at age 65 and two months. Someone born between 1943 and 1954 is, or will be, entitled to full benefits at age 66. Someone born after 1960 will be entitled to full benefits at age 67.

                ii. Lump-sum death benefits.

        3. A "currently insured" worker is eligible for:

            a. Limited survivor benefits (usually limited to dependent minors or those caring for dependent minors);

            b. Benefits for disabled workers and dependents;

        c.   Lump-sum death benefits.

D. Medicare

    1.   Covers portion of costs of hospitalization and medical benefits of insured workers and spouses 65 and older.

    2.   Can cover younger disabled workers in some cases.

E. Disability benefits

    1.   Covers worker who suffers a severe physical or mental impairment preventing that person from working for a year or more or expected to result in the victim's death.

    2.   The disability need not be work related, but must be total.

    3.   After 24 months of disability, Medicare is made available.

        a.   Unlike Medicare, Medicaid payments are separate from the Social Security system.

II. Federal Insurance Contributions Act (FICA)

A. Imposes Social Security tax on

    1.   Employers;

    2.   Employees;

    3.   The self-employed (under the Self-Employment Contributions Tax Act).

B. Application—The tax applies only to that part of compensation that is deemed "wages."

Example

Compensation deemed "wages:" salary, commissions, bonuses, fees, tips, fringe benefits, etc. (generally: active income).

Compensation not deemed "wages:" reimbursed employee expenses, interest on bonds owned, dividends on stock owned, investment income (generally: passive income).

C. Features of FICA

    1.   Rates generally the same for employer and employee.

    2.   Rates change often. (Currently 7.65%, which breaks down to 6.2% for Social Security and 1.45% for Medicare.)

    3.   Social Security taxes are paid on only a base amount of income that is adjusted annually for inflation ($117,000 in 2014); income levels for taxes for the Medicare component are not similarly capped.

        a.   Maximum amount—After tax is deducted from maximum amount of taxable income (for Social Security purposes only), no more will be deducted until the next calendar year.

        b.   Refund—An employee who works for more than two employers may have a total higher than the base amount deducted by employer; employee is entitled to a refund.

    4.   Additional Medicare Tax. As of Jan. 1, 2013, employers are responsible for withholding a 0.9% Additional Medicare Tax (AMT) on an individual's wages in excess of $200,000. The employer need not match the AMT.

D.   Medicare—FICA is also used to fund Medicare (not Medicaid).

E.   Employers' responsibilities

1. Pay own share;

2. Withhold employee's equal share and remit it in a timely fashion;

3. Pay employee's share if fail to withhold ("double tax");

4. Furnish employee with written statement of wages paid and contributions withheld;

5. Supply Taxpayer Identification Numbers when filing returns.

F. Employers' rights

1. Collect employee's share from employee (though employer may voluntarily pay employee's share and deduct that amount as additional compensation, making it taxable to employee).

2. Deduct as a business expense the contributions made on its own behalf to FICA.

III. Payroll Tax Liability

A. Introduction

1. Certain corporate taxes are treated as "trust fund" taxes and must be remitted to tax authorities.

2. Failure to remit may lead to penalty of 100% of the tax not paid being imposed on "any responsible officer and director" who willfully fails to pay the tax.

3. The key section is 6672 of Title 26 (Internal Revenue Code).

B. Who is a "responsible person?"

1. The statute imposes liability on "any person required to collect, truthfully account for, and pay over any tax" who willfully fails to do so.

2. Many courts look at seven factors, none of which is alone determinative:

   a. Is the person an officer or director?

   b. Does the person own part of the company?

   c. Is the person active in management of day-to-day affairs?

   d. Does the person have the ability to hire and fire?

   e. Does the person have discretion to decide which, when, and in what order debts or taxes will be paid?

   f. Does the person exercise control over daily bank accounts and disbursement records?

   g. Does the person have check-signing authority?

3. Some courts say the key question is whether the person had the actual authority or ability, given his or her role within the corporation, to pay the taxes owed.

4. Accountants have been held not to be responsible persons where:

   a. They were bookkeepers who were neither officers nor managed day-to-day affairs of company.

   b. They performed part-time accounting duties with check-writing authority, but were not officers and wrote checks only as directed by sole stockholder.

   c. They performed financial services and had signatory power for checks, but signed such checks only at the request of an officer.

      d. Their authority ran solely to preventing double payment of invoices by the corporate employer.

      e. They served for several weeks as controller of their normal employer's subsidiary and had the authority to sign checks but would have needed cosigner for checks over $2,000 and were told they would be fired if they wrote a check to IRS without superiors' authorization.

    5. Accountants have been held to be responsible persons where:

      a. They cosigned corporate employer's checks as representative of a third party and exercised third party's authority to choose which creditors corporation should pay.

    6. More than one person may be a "responsible party."

  C. What is "willful failure?"

    1. Conduct that is accidental or inadvertent is not willful.

    2. However, willful need not include an intent to defraud the government.

    3. Willfulness means the awareness of the obligation and a conscious and voluntary payment of someone else with funds that should have been used to pay the tax owed.

IV. Self-Employment Contributions Act

  A. Self-employed persons—Must pay social security tax on their own self-employed taxable earnings.

    1. Self-employed income—Net business profits, director's fees.

    2. Not "income"—Gifts.

  B. Features of self-employed tax

    1. Base rate = that of FICA rate for employer and employee combined (currently 15.3%).

    2. Base rate reduced by any "wages" earned during the year, because of the FICA paid on the wages.

    3. Self-employed can deduct 50% of FICA from taxes.

Federal Unemployment Tax Act (FUTA)

A key part of our country's social safety net is unemployment compensation, a temporary bridge of support for those who have involuntarily lost their jobs. As with many areas of the law, this one is mandated by the federal government, but substantial responsibility to administer the system is placed upon the states.

After studying this lesson, you should be able to:

1. Understand the basics of the Federal Unemployment Tax Act.

I. **Purpose**—Provide unemployment compensation benefits to workers who lose jobs and can't find new ones.

II. **Mechanism**

   A. Federal unemployment tax—must be paid by employer who employs persons covered by the act.

      1. Deductible by Employer, not employee.

   B. State unemployment tax—must also be paid.

      1. State tax is credited against employer's federal tax up to a maximum of 90% of the federal tax.

      2. State tax may go up or down depending on claims against employer.

      3. Additional credit against federal tax is created by good claims record.

 Example:
ABC Co. has an excellent record and under its state's system is entitled to pay unemployment tax of only 4% as contrasted to the general state rate of 5%. ABC is entitled to take a credit of 5% against the federal unemployment tax rate of 6.2%.

   C. Only the first $7,000—paid to each covered employee is taxable under FUTA, although many states require that the state tax be paid on a higher amount than that.

   D. The maximum federal rate—fluctuates, but was 6.0% in 2013 with a maximum state tax offset credit of 5.4%, so many employers pay a federal tax of only 0.6% after receiving credit for state unemployment tax.

   E. Though federally mandated, the system is administered primarily by the states.

   F. Employer must file—If paying $1,500 or more in wages during any calendar quarter, or having at least one full or part-time employee during at least 20 weeks during the year.

III. **Coverage is Mandatory for Qualifying Employees**—Employees usually must have worked for a minimum specified period and earned a minimum amount of wages to be eligible for benefits.

IV. **Eligibility for Unemployment Benefits Usually Requires**

   A. That employee was terminated involuntarily.

   See the following table.

	Eligible	Not Eligible
Fired because of business reverses.	X	
Quit because of boredom with job.		X
Fired because of refusal to accept transfer to new department.		X
Fired for embezzling from client.		X
Laid off because of temporary decline in boss's contracts.	X	
Seasonal worker paid on yearly basis (e.g., baseball player).		X
Quit due to sexual harassment by co-employees.	X	
Fired because of carelessness on the job.	X	
Fired for repeatedly and vehemently arguing with boss.		X
Quit because firing was imminent and didn't want bad mark on record.		X

Example
Employer and employee got into a screaming match. The employee stalked toward the door, stopped then stomped and turned around. The employer told him: "Keep on walking." This was held to be a termination, so the employee was entitled to recover unemployment compensation. If the employer had kept quiet, it probably would have been a "voluntary quit" and the employee would not have been entitled to unemployment compensation.

B. Employee is currently available for and looking for work, **and**

	Eligible	Not Eligible
Refused suitable job offer.		X
Has not looked for new job.		X
Enrolled full time in school.		X
Is taking a few night school classes.	X	

C. Employee is not receiving disqualifying income.

	Eligible	Not Eligible
Receiving disability benefits.		X
Receiving pension income.		X
Receiving holiday, vacation, and back pay from earlier job.		X

D. In some states, such income does not disqualify from benefits, but simply requires dollar-for- dollar reduction in benefits.

Fair Labor Standards Act (FLSA)

The most difficult thing about the FLSA is its multidimensional aspect. We often hear about overtime, minimum wage, and child labor rules. All these are aspects of the FLSA and all employers and employers' CPAs should be familiar with their basic rules. Additionally, the FLSA has an equal pay provision that supplements Title VII's rules against general discrimination in employment.

After studying this lesson, you should be able to:

1. Understand the basic mechanics and broad coverage of the Fair Labor Standards Act regarding minimum wage rules.

2. Understand the basic mechanics and broad coverage of the FLSA regarding overtime rules.

I. Introduction

   A. Applies to all businesses that affect interstate commerce.

   B. Four major sections:

      1. Minimum Wage;

      2. Overtime Standard;

      3. Child Labor Restrictions;

      4. Equal Pay Provision.

II. Four Major Sections

   A. Minimum wage rules

      1. "Covered employees" must be paid the minimum wage (currently $7.25/hr, and higher in some states and cities).

      2. The minimum wage is determined on the basis of each work week, so year-end bonuses and the like are not factored in.

Example:
ABC Co. pays Tom $4.00/hour during the year and on December 31 writes him a check for his share of a profit-sharing plan. The profit-sharing bonus, when added to what Tom has been paid during the year, makes his total compensation more than he would have received had he been paid the minimum wage all year. Nonetheless, this is a violation of the rules.

Due to a stalemate in the legislature, the State of California did not pay wages until 15 days after they were due because there was no budget and no state funds appropriated for payment of salaries. Highway workers sued, arguing that because they were paid zero, they did not receive the minimum wage . . . in violation of the FLSA. The court agreed, holding that FLSA wages are "unpaid" unless they are paid on the employees' regular payday.

---

      3. Potential problem: **Interns**, who must be paid minimum wage, if:

         a. Their work gives the company an "immediate advantage," or

         b. They displace a regular worker.

      4. Independent contractors are not covered.

   B. Overtime standard

      1. Employees working more than 40 hours per week must be paid 1-1/2 times their hourly wage for extra hours.

         a. Public employers, such as states and counties, are allowed, under limited circumstances, to compensate employees who work overtime with extra time off instead of overtime pay.

2. There is no "offset" for weeks in which employees work less than 40 hours.

Example:
Sam, an eligible employee, works 45 hours one week and 35 the next. Although this averages out to an even 40 hours/week, there is no offset for the short week. Therefore, Sam is entitled to receive five hours worth of overtime for the first week.

3. An employer may utilize an hourly, weekly, or monthly pay base for a covered employee provided the minimum hourly rate of pay and overtime pay standards are met.

4. When an employee is "on call" in circumstances that s/he cannot spend his/her time in the way s/he would choose to do, this is viewed as "working time" rather than "waiting time" and must be counted for determining overtime compensation.

Example:
Plaintiff was a physician's assistant at a state correctional facility. She worked 40 hours per week and, in addition, was required to provide emergency medical services to inmates in several area facilities after regular working hours. She was compensated time-and-a-half for the time she actually spent at the facilities, but not for the "on-call" periods when she had to stay at home in order to be able to respond within 20 minutes to any call for services. The court found that plaintiff was unable to use the "on-call" time as her own and therefore should be compensated for it at time-and-a-half.

5. Employees not covered by either minimum wage or overtime:

    a. Key point—Minimum wage coverage is broader than overtime coverage.

	Not Covered by Either	Covered by Min. Wage but Not by Overtime
Professionals, like CPAs	x	
Executives	x	
Administrative Employees	x	
Outside Salespersons	x	
Taxi Drivers		x
Railroad Employees		x
Commercial Fishing Workers	x	
Child Actors	x	
Some Agricultural Workers	x	
Air Carrier Employees		x
Sailors on American Vessels		x

C. FLSA also has **"child labor" provisions**

1. Excluding those under 18 years of age from certain occupations designated as "hazardous," including mining, logging, and excavation work.

2. Sixteen is the basic minimum age for employment for any nonhazardous work.

3. Fourteen- and 15-year-olds are limited to certain occupations, such as sales and clerical work; they cannot work in manufacturing, or mining, or other occupations that would interfere with their schooling or their health.

4. Children under 14 cannot work except for their parents or pursuant to court-approved contracts for entertainment (child actors) or athletic contracts.

D. Equal pay

1. Prohibits an employer from discriminating between employees on the basis of sex by paying unequal wages for the same work.

2. Allows pay variance based on:

   a. Seniority;

   b. Merit;

   c. Quality or quantity of work.

3. Unlike the rest of the FLSA, the equal pay provisions:

   a. Cover executive, administrative, and professional employees.

   b. Cover state and local government employees.

III. Enforcement

A. The FLSA is enforced by the Department of Labor's Wage and Hour Division and private lawsuits.

Employee Benefits

After studying this lesson, you should be able to:

1. Understand the basic purpose of the Employee Retirement Income Security Act.

2. Explain the difference between defined-contribution and defined-benefit plans.

3. Understand the basic parameters of liability under ERISA rules.

4. Realize that accountants will seldom face such liability.

I. **Employee Retirement Income Security Act of 1970 (ERISA)**

    A. Purpose

        1. Protect employee rights in existing pension plans.

        2. Offer tax incentives to employers and employees to fund employee benefit plans by providing that if the plans meet IRS requirements:

            a. Employers get a current tax deduction for contributions, and

            b. Employees are able to defer taxation of benefits until they actually receive them.

    B. Characteristics

        1. ERISA broadly preempts state laws regulating pensions.

        2. ERISA applies to two types of plans:

            a. Employee pension benefit plans;

            b. Employee welfare benefit plans.

        3. ERISA prohibits plans that discriminate against lower-level employees.

        4. ERISA set up the Pension Benefit Guaranty Corporation (PBGC) to administer plan termination insurance for defined benefit pension plans; employers are required to purchase pension termination insurance.

    C. ERISA does not require—employers to set up pension plans.

        1. If employers do set up pension plans for employees, they **must meet these standards**:

        2. Employee contributions must "vest" (that is, the employee acquires the right to the contribution) immediately;

        3. Employees' rights to their employers' contributions generally fully vest after 5 years of employment;

        4. ERISA also provides for partial vesting.

Example:
Partial vesting—A plan may provide that partial vesting of employers' contributions begins at 20% in the third year and escalates at 20% per year until full vesting occurs in the seventh year. So, if after five years in such a plan Sam left having matched his employer's contribution of $10,000 with $10,000 of his own, Sam would be entitled to his own $10,000 (of course) and to $6,000 of his employer's contribution.

5. Standards on investment of funds must be followed to avoid mismanagement.

    a. Every plan must provide written procedures specifying means of funding the plan;

    b. Every plan must designate a fiduciary with authority to manage and control the plan's operation and management.

Example:
Fiduciaries must invest funds in accordance with the "prudent person" standard, must not engage in "self-dealing," etc.

6. Certain disclosures must be made to employees and to the government.

D. Coverage—ERISA does not apply to:

    1. Federal, state, and local government pension plans;

    2. Church plans.

E. Enforcement—ERISA is enforced by:

    1. Departments of Labor and Treasury;

    2. Private lawsuits.

F. Types of pension plans

    1. Defined-benefit plans—Ensure eligible employees and their beneficiaries a specified monthly income for life; in other words, they start with the benefits to be provided and then attempt to calculate what will be needed in the way of contributions to provide those benefits.

        a. Such plans are insured by Pension Benefit Guaranty Corporation (PBGC);

        b. Some plans are "integrated" with Social Security benefits.

Example:
Integration of SS taxes—Employer can offset benefits with the employee's anticipated benefits from Social Security, since employer is already contributing to the employee's retirement income by paying Social Security Taxes.

    2. Defined-contribution plans—Specify annual fixed-share contributions to be made by an employer into a retirement account; in other words, they focus on the contributions to be made and then hope that wise investing will provide generous benefits.

        a. Employer contributions may be tied to employee contributions or may be separately calculated.

        b. These funds are invested on behalf of the employee who receives proceeds upon retirement.

        c. Unlike in a defined-benefit plan where the investment decisions are made exclusively by the plan's fiduciary's in a defined-contribution plan, the employee typically has discretion to allocate the investment among a number of mutual funds.

        d. There is no PBGC insurance for defined-contribution plans.

    3. Under a 401(k) plan—An employee can reduce his/her reportable income by making pretax contributions to the plan (but cannot withdraw contributions prior to termination of employment absent exceptions such as death, disability, or perhaps hardship).

II. Pension and Retirement Plan Liability

A. Introduction

    1. The Employee Retirement Income Security Act of 1974 (ERISA) imposes a fiduciary duty upon retirement plan "fiduciaries."

2. The purpose is to protect plans by establishing standards of responsibility and conduct upon plan fiduciaries.

B. Who is a fiduciary?

    1. Fiduciaries include:

        a. Anyone named in a benefit plan as a fiduciary, and

        b. Anyone who:

            i. Exercises any discretionary management or control over management of the plan;

            ii. Renders investment advice for a fee; or

            iii. Has discretionary authority or responsibility in administration of the plan.

        c. Accountants who merely audit plans will not be fiduciaries.

        d. Accountants might become fiduciaries if:

            i. A management accountant who has responsibility to calculate plan benefits also has authority to authorize or disallow benefit payments when a dispute exists about the meaning of plan provisions.

            ii. A management accountant who provides advice about interpretation of the plan and knows that the trustee is almost certain to follow the advice.

            iii. An accounting firm that offers benefit consulting services to a client on a regular basis.

            iv. An accountant with authority to make withdrawals from a bank account holding ERISA plan assets exercises discretionary control over the funds.

C. Duties of fiduciaries

    1. Act with reasonable care; and

    2. Discharge duties solely in the interests of plan's participants.

D. Participating in a fiduciary breach

    1. It appears that accountants can also be liable, even if they are not fiduciaries themselves, if they participate in a fiduciary's breach of duty.

    2. Accountants, actuaries, attorneys, benefits consultants, and other non-fiduciaries may yet be liable under ERISA Section 502(1)(3), which does not limit the world of ERISA defendants to fiduciaries, if they:

        a. Participate in a fiduciary's breach of fiduciary duty in violation of Section 404 of ERISA; or

        b. Participate in an illicit transaction with a "party in interest" in violation of Section 406(a) of ERISA.

            i. "Parties in interest" include entities such as accountants, lawyers, banks, and brokers who provide services to a plan.

            ii. Prohibited transactions include those in which a plan fiduciary causes the plan to loan money to a party in interest, pay excessive compensation for accounting or other services, or transfers assets to a party in interest.

        c. Section 402(a)(3) authorizes a civil penalty of 20% of the recovery amount.

    3. Accountants and others may also be liable for assisting such breaches or for other errors under common law malpractice causes of action that most courts hold are not preempted by ERISA.

        a. Thus, a plan administrator was allowed to pursue against an accountant a malpractice action alleging faulty auditing with respect to loans approved by the plan's investment advisory committee.

III. **Federal Consolidated Budget Reconciliation Act (COBRA)**

   A. COBRA—As amended by the Health Insurance Portability and Accountability Act of 1996. COBRA amended ERISA to provide health insurance in some circumstances after a job loss.

   B. Qualifying events—For an employee, there are two "qualifying events" that give rise to COBRA coverage:

      1. Termination (including quits, firings, and layoffs) causing loss of health insurance.

         a. Unless it is for "gross misconduct" (in which case the employee is not protected).

      2. Reduction of hours causing loss of health insurance.

   C. Previous coverage—Upon the occurrence of a qualifying event, an employee may retain his previous group health insurance coverage:

      1. If s/he pays for it.

      2. Coverage:

         a. Ex-employee;

         b. Spouse;

         c. Dependent children.

      3. Length of Extra Coverage:

         a. Usually 18 months after the qualifying event.

         b. Exception—The period is 29 months if insured was "disabled" at the time of the qualifying event.

            i. The extra 11 months applies to any beneficiary, not just the employee, who has a disability any time within the first 60 days of continuation coverage.

            ii. There are a few circumstances where COBRA coverage can last up to 36 months. For example, if an insured spouse becomes entitled to Medicare, but his or her spouse is not yet so qualified, the latter may gain COBRA benefits for 36 months. Similarly, if divorce, legal separation, or death of the employee are the "qualifying events" for a spouse, he or she may enjoy 36 months of coverage. Finally, when a dependent child loses dependent status, as when a child graduates from college, he or she may purchase group health benefits under COBRA for up to 36 months.

            iii. Also, if an employee moves from one group plan to another, the new plan cannot impose a preexisting conditions exclusion that exceeds 12 months for conditions for which medical advice, diagnosis, or treatment was received or recommended within the previous six months. So, assume that X was covered by an employer group plan at Company A for two years. X then went to work for Company B and elected to join its group health care plan. Because the new plan cannot impose a preexisting exclusion that exceeds 12 months and because X had two years of coverage at Company A that Company B must credit, Company B's health plan cannot apply the preexisting condition limitation. However, under the rules, if there were a gap between X's leaving Company A's plan and joining Company B's plan that exceeded 63 days, then Company B would not have to credit X's coverage at Company A and could apply its preexisting condition exclusion.

            iv. Important, COBRA applies only to companies with 20 or more employees.

IV. **The Family and Medical Leave Act of 1993 (FMLA)**

   A. Purpose—Balance employee's workplace demands with needs of family.

      1. The first real federal requirement that an employer provide government-mandated benefits.

   B. Provisions

1. Unpaid leave—An **eligible employee** is entitled to 12 weeks of unpaid leave without losing his/her job. (Up to 26 weeks of unpaid, job-protected leave is allowed to care for a covered servicemember with a serious injury or illness.)

2. Leave is provided for:

   a. Birth of a son or daughter;

   b. Placement with the employee of a son or daughter for adoption or foster care;

   c. A personal serious health condition;

   d. Care of a son, daughter, spouse or parent with a serious health condition; and

   e. Impending order to active duty of employee's spouse, son, daughter or parent.

C. Eligibility

   1. To be eligible, an employee must have worked for employer a. For at least 12 months; and

      b. At least 1,250 hours during the previous 12 months.

   2. Employee must request—such leave; employers need not volunteer it.

D. FMLA covers

   1. Employers with over 50 employees in a 75-mile radius, and

   2. State and local government agencies.

Health and Safety

After studying this lesson, you should be able to:

1. Understand the basic provisions of the health insurance portability provisions of the Consolidated Budget Reconciliation Act (COBRA).

2. Understand the basic provisions of the Family Medical Leave Act.

3. Understand the rules for workers' compensation benefits.

I. **Workers' Compensation Act**

    A. Purpose—Provide nearly automatic compensation for employees who suffer work-related injuries or diseases.

        1. Many people think of workers' compensation as remedying only on-the-job injuries, but it also provides compensation for work-related diseases, such as asbestosis.

        2. Independent contractors usually are not covered by workers' compensation.

    B. Mechanism

        1. Employers carry workers' comp insurance, which provides established levels of benefits that are given automatically to workers for job-related injuries or diseases.

        2. Employer's liability is strict: Employee need not prove negligence or other fault by the employer.

            a. The employer's common law defenses to lawsuit are eliminated.

                i. Assumption of risk.

Example:
Assumption of risk—Sam is a roofer and is injured on the job. Sam knows, of course, that it is dangerous up on those roofs and that workers occasionally fall off roofs and are seriously injured. At common law, Sam's employer could often have successfully raised the defense that Sam "assumed the risk" by taking a dangerous job like roofing. Under workers' compensation systems, this is no defense. Sam is entitled to recover his workers' comp benefits.

                b. Negligence of fellow employee.

Example:
Negligence of fellow employee—Sam works on an assembly line and is seriously injured when Roy, who works right beside him on the line, carelessly drops a piece of heavy equipment on Sam's leg. At common law, Sam's employer could often have successfully raised the defense that the real fault lay with Sam's co-worker. Under workers' compensation systems, this is no defense. Sam is entitled to recover workers' comp benefits.

                c. Employee's contributory negligence.

Example:
Employee's contributory negligence—Sam works on an assembly line and one day his mind wanders slightly and he allows his clothes to become caught in some moving parts. He is injured. At common law, Sam's employer could often have raised the defense that the real fault lay with Sam because his own carelessness caused his injury. Under workers' compensation systems, this is no defense. Sam is entitled to recover workers' comp benefits.

3. Chart—Effect of Elimination of Employer Common Law Defenses

	Covered	Not Covered
Injured due to own negligence on the job	X	
Injured due to failure to follow boss's safety rules	X	
Injured because of intoxication on the job		X
Injured self intentionally to "get a chance to catch up on *Oprah*"		X
Injured by negligence of fellow employee	X	
Injured while working on machine known to be defective	X	

4. In exchange for having to pay benefits automatically, employer is given immunity from civil damage suit by employee.

    a. If coverage exists, employee cannot decline benefits and claim right to sue.

Example:
Sam is seriously injured while on the job. He thinks that he can prove both that his boss was negligent and that his injuries are so serious that a jury would award him many times what the workers' compensation scheme allows as recovery. Sam rejects proffered workers' compensation benefits and sues his boss for negligence. Sam will not recover if the boss was in compliance with the workers' compensation system requirements.

    b. Exceptions to immunity: Boss guilty of intentional tort or gross negligence.

Example:
Ed's supervisor, Sandy, loses her temper over an incident of incompetence by Ed and hits him with a hammer. Ed's recovery is not limited to workers' compensation because Sandy's tort is an intentional one.

    c. Mandatory versus elective coverage:

        i. Most states require all employers to carry workers' comp plans.

        ii. In some states it is elective, but those who elect not to carry benefits can be sued by injured employees.

C. Workers are covered—if they are injured on the job or in the course of employment, i.e., within the scope of authority to advance the employer's purposes (which is broadly construed in this context).

Scope of Authority	Covered	Not Covered
Injured while doing assigned task	X	
Injured while commuting to work in the morning		X
Injured while making a delivery for boss on way home	X	
Traveling sales rep injured while driving from motel to first call	X	
Injured while doing something the boss requires although it's not employee's ordinary job	X	

D. Procedure—The employee reports the injury or disease to the employer and then files a claim with the state workers' compensation board or the insurance carrier administering the plan.

E. Actions against third parties

   1. Availability of workers' comp benefits bars injured employees' suits against employer and co-employees, but not against third parties.

Example:
X is injured on the job in part because his boss told him to operate a complicated machine without giving X adequate training, in part because X's co-employees were careless, and in part because the machine was defectively designed and manufactured. X's employer is in compliance with the state's workers' compensation statute.

Injured Employee's Remedy	WC Benefits	Civil Damages
Against Employer	X	
Against Co-Employee	X	
Against Manufacturer		X

Example:
Actions against third parties—A is an employee of X Co. B is an independent contractor for Y Co. Both drive trucks and are involved in a collision that is A's fault. A was speeding. Additional evidence shows that X Co's faulty maintenance of the brakes on A's truck also contributed to the accident. Both X Co. and Y Co. are in compliance with workers' compensation statutes.

	Yes	No
A can recover workers' comp benefits from X Co.	X	
A can sue X Co. for its negligence		X
B can recover workers' comp benefits from Y Co.		X
B can sue X Co. for its negligence	X	
B can sue A for A's negligence	X	

   a. Any recovery against a third party achieved by employee that compensates injuries for which s/he has already received workers' comp is subject to claim by employer or employer's insurance carrier.

      i. If employee had chosen not to sue manufacturer, the employer or its insurance carrier could have obtained and pursued that right of action.

F. Benefits—Employees who file timely claims are usually entitled to these benefits:

1. Medical care expenses;

2. Disability protection (payment of partial wages);

3. Death benefits (to be paid to widows/widowers and minor children);

4. Retraining expenses (where necessary);

5. Scheduled payments for various losses (finger, arm, leg, etc.).

II. **OSHA**

  A. Purpose—To promote safety standards and job safety.

   1. Employer need not guarantee a 100% safe work place.

   2. Employer must:

> **Note:**
> *OSHA supplements, but does not replace, state safety rules.*

   a. Provide a workplace free from "recognized hazards" likely to cause death or serious physical harm (injury or disease).

      i. A workplace should be free of toxic substances, asbestos dust and the like; the work environment should be adequately lit, ventilated, and heated; and tools and equipment should be in proper working order.

   b. Comply with OSHA standards for safety and health.

  B. Mechanism—OSHA has broad powers to:

   1. Develop standards.

   2. Require employers to keep records of job-related injuries and report them to OSHA.

   3. Investigate complaints and inspect workplaces.

   a. If employer resists search, OSHA usually must obtain a search warrant from a court.

   b. Need not show probable cause, but only a "reasonable basis."

   c. A reasonable basis can be provided by:

      i. A higher-than-usual accident rate;

      ii. Employee complaints;

      iii. Proof of a fair, random surprise search system needed to keep employers on their toes because OSHA lacks funds and employees to do continuous and thorough searches.

   d. Warrantless searches are authorized:

      i. In cases of extreme emergency;

      ii. Where employer consents (most cases);

      iii. Inspector is merely observing what is open to public view, for there can be no expectation of privacy in such a place.

   4. Determine whether violations have occurred.

   5. Assess remedies by:

   a. Ordering correction of unsafe conditions;

   b. Imposing civil fines (per violation);

   c. Referring case to the Department of Justice for criminal prosecution, if willful violation caused death of one or more employees.

C. Employee rights

1. If a violation threatens physical harm or imminent danger, employee may:

   a. File a request for an inspection;

   b. Refuse in good faith to work if there is no time to wait for inspection.

2. Employees may not be punished by employers for exercising these rights.

3. Employees themselves may be fired for failing to comply with OSHA rules.

Union and Employee Relations

Although unions are not as powerful an influence in the American economy as they once were, it is wise to be familiar with the essential rules governing union and employee relations.

After studying this lesson, you should be able to:

1. Be familiar with the basic statutes that shape the relationships between unions and employers.

2. Understand the key collective bargaining and other responsibilities of unions and employers.

I. **Introduction**

    A. Much strife accompanied early attempts of workers to organize in unions when bargaining with their employers, causing Congress to pass several important laws, including:

        1. The Norris-LaGuardia Act—It prohibited court injunctions against many union organizing activities, particularly peaceful strikes.

        2. The National Labor Relations Act of 1935—(NLRA or the Wagner Act), which is the most important law today. Its primary purpose is to protect employees':

            a. Right to form, join, or assist unions;

            b. Right to bargain collectively through their chosen union; and

            c. Right to engage in concerted activities (such as strikes) for the purpose of collective bargaining or other mutual protection.

        3. The Labor-Management Relations Act of 1947—(Taft-Hartley Act), which tilted federal labor policy toward a more neutral (less pro-labor) perspective by prohibiting union coercion of employees and secondary boycotts.

        4. The Labor-Management Reporting and Disclosure Act of 1959—(Landrum-Griffin Act), which responded to corruption in unions by protecting workers from unfair treatment by their unions and requiring certain union reforms such as financial disclosure by union leaders.

    B. The National Labor Relations Board (NLRB) enforces the NLRA.

II. **NLRA coverage**

    A. The NLRA applies to all employers involved in or affecting interstate commerce, a concept that is broadly construed.

    B. Several categories of workers are exempt from NLRA coverage:

        1. Independent contractors;

        2. Government employees;

        3. Managerial and supervisory employees;

        4. Airline and railway employees who are covered by other statutes.

III. **The Right to Organize**

    A. Once 30% of eligible employees in an appropriate job category sign authorization cards, an employee group may petition for an election to certify a union as their bargaining representative.

        1. Management may voluntarily recognize the union as the workers' representative, but if it does not do so an election must be held.

    B. The NLRB monitors the election to ensure fairness.

    C. Employers who resist the election must avoid committing "unfair labor practices," because that would result in automatic certification of the union via an NLRB "bargaining order."

   D. Employer "unfair labor practices" include:

      1. Interfering with union organizing efforts:

         a. Employers should not bribe workers to vote against a union.

         b. Employers should not threaten workers who wish to vote for a union.

      2. Dominating or interfering with the union;

      3. Discriminating against a union member; or

      4. Refusing to bargain collectively.

   E. Unions also must refrain from "unfair labor practices," such as:

      1. Coercing employees; or

      2. Requiring employers to agree not to do business with nonunion companies that the union is trying to unionize ("hot cargo clause");

      3. Refusing to bargain collectively;

      4. Engaging in an illegal strike or secondary boycott.

   F. Lockouts: Employers may bar workers from coming to work, sometimes in anticipation of a threatened strike. The legality of such a lockout depends upon an employer's intent, and is illegal if the employer locks out employees in order to:

      1. Destroy the union;

      2. Punish workers for organizing; or

      3. Avoid its good faith bargaining responsibilities.

   G. Federal law prohibits "closed shops" (an employer's agreement to hire only members of a union, effectively giving unions a veto power over hires).

   H. Federal law does allow states to enact "right-to-work laws" (and about half have done so) that prohibit two types of agreements that are otherwise legal:

      1. "Union shops" (agreements requiring newly hired employees to join the union within a specified period after beginning employment), and

      2. "Agency shops" (agreements allowing employees not to join the union but to pay fees to cover union services).

   I. Employers may take bankruptcy in order to discharge their contractual obligations, including those under a collective bargaining agreement. The employer is required to provide a plan that treats all its creditors, including workers, "fairly and equitably," and unions are to be kept informed so that they may evaluate the proposed plan.

IV. Collective Bargaining

   A. Negotiations between management and a union are called collective bargaining.

   B. Once a union is certified, management cannot bargain with anyone else purporting to represent the employees regarding "mandatory subjects of bargaining," including:

      1. Wages;

      2. Hours; and

      3. Other conditions of employments, such as discharge, seniority rights, retirement and pension plans, insurance plans, and grievances.

   C. The NLRA imposes a duty on both sides to bargain in good faith.

      1. Withholding information important to fair bargaining is probably acting in bad faith.

      2. Presenting "take it or leave it" ultimatums is probably acting in bad faith.

3. The requirement of bargaining in good faith does not include an obligation to actually reach an agreement.

D. Unions may strike to support their rights.

1. To be legal, strikes must be supported by a majority of members.

2. Once a union has agreed to a collective bargaining agreement, it must give the employer 60 days' notice before it strikes seeking modification or rescission.

3. So-called "wildcat" strikes by a disgruntled minority of workers are illegal.

4. Secondary strikes (secondary boycotts) against third parties to coerce them to oppose management are illegal.

5. Workers on strike at a multi-employer work site, like a construction site, must picket just the relevant part of the site and not the entire work place, because that puts pressure on third parties.

6. Workers, generally, have no right to picket on the employer's private property.

E. Characteristics of a collective bargaining agreement:

1. Union usually agrees not to strike and the company agrees not to lock;

2. Employer agrees to submit disagreements and grievances that arise during the term of the agreement to binding arbitration;

3. Matters such as pay scales, seniority, overtime pay, insurance, vacation holidays, etc. are addressed.

V. Replacement Workers

A. During a strike, management may hire "replacement workers."

B. Following settlement of an authorized "unfair labor practice strike" protesting unfair management practices, management must reinstate the strikers.

C. Following settlement of a typical strike over wages and related matters ("economic strikes"), management need not lay off the "replacement workers," but cannot discriminate against the strikers if it rehires more workers.

Antitrust

After studying this lesson, you should be able to:

1. Be familiar with the basic federal antitrust statutes.

2. Understand the key provisions of these statutes and how they shape business practices in the U.S.

I. Overview

    A. The main goal of antitrust law is to promote economic competition.

    B. Among the most important antitrust statutes are:

        1. The Sherman Act (1890)

            a. Section 1 prohibits "contracts, combinations, and conspiracies in restraint of trade." It requires at least two actors.

            b. Section 2 prohibits "monopolization, attempts to monopolize, and conspiracies to monopolize." It looks at the conduct of a single economic actor.

        2. The Clayton Act (1914)

            a. Section 2 prohibits price discrimination.

            b. Section 3 prohibits some tying and exclusive dealing arrangements.

            c. Section 7 forbids anticompetitive mergers.

            d. Section 8 prohibits interlocking directorates among large corporations that compete with one another.

        3. Federal Trade Commission Act (1914)

            a. Created the Federal Trade Commission (FTC) to enforce antitrust laws.

            b. Section 5 prohibits "unfair methods of competition."

        4. Robinson-Patman Act (1936)

            a. Section 2 amends the Clayton act to make the law against price discrimination more effective.

    C. Antitrust laws cover business activity, including that of foreign companies, that either directly involves or substantially affects interstate commerce.

    D. Remedies

        1. The Department of Justice's Antitrust Division can bring criminal or civil lawsuits against violators.

        2. The FTC can enforce the Clayton, Robinson-Patman, and FTC Acts.

        3. Private parties can file civil lawsuits claiming a violation of the Sherman, Clayton, or Robinson-Patman Acts and seek treble damages (three times the actual damages).

    E. Exceptions

        1. Labor union collective bargaining activity is generally exempt from the antitrust laws.

        2. Public utilities and common carriers are generally exempt as well because they are subject to separate regulation.

        3. Activity that did not affect interstate commerce would also be exempt, but that term is so broadly construed that this exception virtually never applies.

II. Monopolization

    A. Section 2 of the Sherman Act forbids monopolization, defining a monopoly as "a firm having such an overwhelming degree of market power that it is able to control prices or exclude competition."

    B. Elements of a Section 2 violation include:

        1. Overwhelming market power; and

        2. Intent to monopolize.

    C. Market power—is the ability to raise prices without losing most customers.

        1. Market share is the key component in measuring market power, and less than 50% is usually insufficient to monopolize; and a 75% share is often sufficient.

        2. Other structural factors besides market share include:

            a. Relative size of other firms in the market;

            b. Size and power of customers;

            c. Entry barriers that prevent competitors from entering the market, such as high costs of capital for potential competitors; and

            d. Dynamics of the market—does it change rapidly?

        3. Markets are defined in terms of:

            a. Product market, including cross-elasticity of demand (could consumers switch to buttons if zippers were priced too high?), and cross-elasticity of supply (could button makers respond quickly to such an increase in demand?);

            b. Geographic market-consumers might drive quite a ways to avoid buying an overpriced car, but not so far to avoid an overpriced loaf of bread.

    D. Intent to monopolize

        1. Because monopolists must willfully acquire or maintain a monopoly, there can be legal monopolies, such as those that exist because a firm owns a patent or trade secret. One famous case noted that a business that acquires a monopoly position "merely by virtue of its superior skill, foresight, and industry" has not violated Section 2.

        2. Typically, intent to monopolize is inferred from:

            a. Predatory (below cost) pricing with intent to drive out competitors; or

            b. Nonprice predation via such means as:

                i. Tying up customers with long-term contracts that are not justified by cost savings;

                ii. Taking away key employees from a small competitor;

                iii. Falsely disparaging the products of competitors;

                iv. Forcing smaller firms into unjustified lawsuits and administrative expenses; and

                v. Sabotage.

> **Note:**
> *Some practices that do not alone violate the antitrust laws may do so in the presence of overwhelming market power.*

        3. Attempts to monopolize are also illegal if they present a dangerous probability of success.

III. Mergers

    A. Section 7 of the Clayton Act prevents one company from acquiring another if the acquisition is likely to diminish competition in a substantial way in the relevant market.

        1. Horizontal mergers—Between competitors are especially likely to diminish competition and will likely draw regulatory attention if the combined market shares of the companies exceeds

30%, although that number is scarcely hard and fast and is affected by numerous other factors, including the number of competitors in the market.

2. Vertical mergers—Between companies in a distribution chain (e.g., a steel manufacturer acquires a key ore supplier or a manufacturer of products made of steel) are less likely to diminish competition and are unlikely to be successfully challenged unless the vertically combined market is already highly concentrated and both companies have a large market share.

3. Conglomerate mergers—That have neither horizontal nor vertical characteristics (e.g., a steel manufacturer buys a chain of ice cream stores) are very unlikely to face serious antitrust challenge.

IV. Horizontal Restraints of Trade—Section 1 of the Sherman Act bans "contacts, combinations, or conspiracies in restraint of trade."

A. Collusion—Is the key to such violations, and may be evidenced by communications between the parties, opportunity to conspire, uniformity of action, etc.

Example:
When 69,000 members of the National Society of Professional Engineers voted for an ethical rule that prohibited competitive bidding by all members, the Supreme Court found illegal collusion among the members.

B. Rule of reason—Collusion violates Section 1 only if it "unreasonably" restricts competition. Defendants may raise a "rule of reason" defense focusing on the purpose and effect of the conduct.

1. Purpose—If the predominant purpose of the conduct is to restrain competition, it will probably be viewed as illegal even if the effect on competition is rather slight; but if the primary purpose of the conduct is not to restrain competition, then a violation will be found only if competition is diminished in a substantial way.

2. Effect—The most important factor affecting competition is the collective market power of the group. If the group could have achieved the claimed legitimate goal with a less restrictive alternative, a court is more likely to find a Section 1 violation.

C. Per se illegality—Certain types of activities are automatically (per se) illegal and cannot be saved by a "rule of reason" defense.

1. Price fixing—When competitors agree to charge a specific price, or establish a floor price, or agree not to submit competitive bids, or to rotate bids among a group, etc.

2. Market division—When competitors agree to divide markets by territory, customer allocation, or product line.

3. Boycotts—Company A can choose not to deal with Company C, usually. But if competitors Company A and Company B agree to boycott Company C for anticompetitive reasons (for example, they are worried that Company C is thinking about a vertical acquisition, which would allow it to compete with them), a per se violation occurs.

V. Vertical Restraints of Trade

A. Resale Price Maintenance (RPM)—(Vertical price fixing) Occurs when a seller and a buyer agree on the price at which the seller will resell to its own customers. Usually, a manufacturer tells its dealers or distributors the minimum price at which they may resell its product. This practice inhibits intrabrand competition, preventing dealer A from underpricing dealer B. Section 1 of the Sherman Act forbids RPM.

B. Until recently, RPM was per se illegal, but the Supreme Court recently held that it should now be judged by a rule of reason analysis.

VI. Vertical Nonprice Restrictions

    A. Vertical Nonprice Restrictions (VNRs) also violates Section 1 of the Sherman Act by restricting intrabrand competition.

> **Example:**
> **Territorial Restrictions:** Manufacturer guarantees its dealers that they will have the exclusive right to market its products in their geographic territory.
>
> **Customer Restrictions:** Dealers agree to resell only to particular customers.

    B. VNRs are analyzed via a rule of reason.

VII. Tying Arrangements

    A. Tying occurs when Co. A agrees to sell a desirable computer (the tying product) to Co. B only if B will also purchase a software package (the tied product) that Co. A sells that is not nearly as popular.

> **Example:**
> In the early days of business machines, IBM was found guilty when it required customers who leased its tabulating machines to also use its tabulating cards.

    B. Tying may violate both Section 1 of the Sherman Act and Section 3 of the Clayton Act, although the latter is usually redundant.

    C. Tying can occur only if the defendant has substantial market power in the market for the tying product. (Again, 30% market share is an extremely rough guide.)

    D. Courts also usually require that the tying arrangement generate a substantial amount of business in the tied market.

VIII. Exclusive Dealing

    A. Section 1 of the Sherman Act may ban illicit use of "requirements contracts" and "output contracts."

    B. Assume that a customer makes a "requirements contract" with a supplier, promising that it will purchase a particular product only from the supplier. Widespread use of such agreements could make it hard for new competitors to enter the market, because all potential customers would be locked up.

    C. Assume that a seller agrees in an "output contract" to sell only to a particular buyer and not to the buyer's competitors. This arrangement is not as worrisome as a requirements contract, but could prevent the buyer's competitors from obtaining products they need to compete.

    D. Exclusive dealing is unlikely to be illegal unless a dominant share (roughly 30% or more) of the market is locked away from competitors.

IX. Price Discrimination

    A. The Robinson-Patman Act's prohibition on price discrimination is violated if:

        1. Seller charged different prices to two or more different customers;

        2. The transaction involved tangible commodities (not land or services);

        3. The transactions were sales rather than leases, or consignments;

        4. The goods were essentially the same;

        5. Likelihood of a substantial injury to competition resulted.

B. Defenses

1. Cost justification—It is okay to charge more to Customer A than Customer B if the former is located farther away, necessitating higher shipping costs;

2. Meeting competition—If defendant charges $100 to Customer A and then learns that a competitor is charging $90, defendant can lower his price to Customer B to meet the competition.

3. Changing conditions—If defendant charges $100 to Customer A and then defendant's suppliers cut their prices, defendant could pass the savings on to Customer B.

Copyright

After studying this lesson, you should be able to:

1. Understand the basic rules of copyright, including comprehending what is copyrightable, the requirements of copyrightability, and the basic protections afforded by federal law.

I. **Overview**—There are four primary types of intellectual property.

    A. First, *trademarks* are any distinctive words, phrases, symbols, or designs adopted for the purpose of identifying the origin of goods being offered for sale. The Nike "swoosh" is an example.

    B. Second are *trade secrets*, such as the secret Coca-Cola formula. A trade secret is any type of knowledge that is not generally known and is not readily available through legal means, if the knowledge gives its owner a competitive advantage over rivals who lack the knowledge.

    C. The other two major types of intellectual property are *copyrights* and *patents*, which are the subject of this lesson and the next lesson.

II. **Introduction to Copyrights**—Copyrights are designed to protect "original works of authorship." They protect a wide range of expressions of creativity, including, among others:

    A. Books

    B. Music

    C. Drama

    D. Graphics

    E. Choreography

    F. Jewelry designs

    G. Computer programs

    H. Speeches

III. **Elements of Copyrightability**—An expressive work is protectable under copyright law if it is:

    A. Fixed in some tangible medium of expression;

    B. Creative; and

    C. Original.

> **Example:**
> If Joe has the basics of a novel floating around in his head, but has not yet written any words on paper or computer screen, the novel is not yet protectable. If Sam alphabetizes a list of important chemicals, the list may be useful but it is not copyrightable because it is not a creative work but, instead, only an unprotectable product of Sam's "sweat of the brow." Facts are not protected, but creative expressions of them can be. Finally, if Tilly writes a song that turns out to be nearly identical to a song written earlier by Chan, Tilly's song is not original.

IV. **Copyright Procedure**—Copyright procedure is self-executing. Once an expression is reduced to a tangible medium, e.g., words are written on paper or sounds are recorded, the author is entitled to copyright protection. No filing is needed. However, registering a copyright with the U.S. Copyright Office may be a good idea because it protects authors in countries that have not signed the Berne Convention and wards off "innocent infringement" claims.

V. **Length of Protection**

    A. Currently, copyright law in the U.S. protects a work for the life of the author, plus 70 years.

    B. A work-for-hire is protected for the shorter of: 95 years from the date of publication or 120 years from the date of creation.

Example:
A work-for-hire occurs when ABC Co. hires musician Jan to write a jingle to advertise its new product, intending to own the copyright itself.

VI. Elements of a Copyright Infringement Claim—An author of a book, for example, may sue the author of a similar book by showing:

    A. Ownership of a valid copyright; and

    B. Unauthorized copying of original elements of P's work by D.

        1. Intent to copy is not an element of the tort of copyright infringement.

VII. Fair Use Defense—There are several defenses to a copyright infringement claim, including the "fair use" defense, which may protect uses for purposes such as criticism, comment, news reporting, teaching, scholarship, or research. Thus, a copyright is not necessarily infringed if a teacher makes multiple copies of an article in today's newspaper for purposes of facilitating classroom discussion or a literary critic quotes some lines from a novel for purposes of illustrating his point about how good or bad the author's writing is. The factors considered in the fair use defense are:

    A. The purpose and character of the use; (An educational purpose is more likely to be protected than a commercial purpose and parody and satire are strongly protected by the First Amendment.)

    B. The nature of the copyrighted work; (A novel receives more robust protection than a textbook.)

    C. The amount and substantiality of the portion used (the more used, the weaker the defense); and

    D. The effect of the use on the potential market value of the copyrighted work.

Patents

After studying this lesson, you should be able to:

1. Understand the basic rules of patent law, including comprehending what matters are patentable, the patent process, the requirements of patentability, and the basic protections afforded by federal patent law.

I. **Introduction**—A patent is a government-granted exclusive right to make, use, or sell an invention. Governments protect patents in order to encourage inventive activity, just as they protect copyrights to reward creative expression.

II. **Patentable Subject Matter**

   A. The law recognizes patents for:

      1. Processes;

      2. Machines;

      3. Products;

      4. Compositions of matter;

      5. Any improvements upon these; and

      6. New plant varieties.

   B. The law does not patent:

      1. Printed matter (which is the subject of copyright law);

      2. Naturally occurring substances;

      3. Ideas; or

      4. Scientific principles.

   C. In recent years, methods of doing business (such as Amazon's "one-click" purchasing system) have been protected.

   D. There are all "utility" patents, although the law also recognizes "design patents" for non-functional ornamental design elements in a functional product.

III. **Elements of Patentability**—An invention may be patented if:

   A. It involves patentable subject matter;

      1. Thus, for example, a new idea may not be patentable, but a tangible application of the idea, say to create a new process, might be.

   B. It is useful;

      1. This notion is construed broadly; even a "whoopee cushion" is useful for creating a few cheap laughs. However, if a product doesn't work, is a hoax, or is merely an abstract idea, it is not patentable.

   C. It is novel;

      1. Thus, the invention must be new and created by the inventor seeking the patent.

   D. It is nonobvious (to a person with ordinary skill in that area).

      1. A creation is not patentable if it is the next obvious development from a previously patented item; thus, if A invented a "transporter" of the type that we see in science fiction movies that scrambles a person's molecules at one location and puts them back together almost instantaneously at another, B could not gain a second patent by making the same device out of slightly more durable material.

IV. Patent Filing—Unlike a copyright, which is self-executing, a patent requires filing with the U.S. Patent and Trademark Office (PTO). With some exceptions, the application must be filed within one year after the invention was created. If Sam invents a new machine before Mary independently invents the same machine, but Mary files her patent application with the PTO before Sam does, Mary will own the patent. The U.S. in 2013 joined most of the rest of the world in giving priority to the "first-to-file" over the "first-to-invent."

V. Length of Protection

    A. A utility patent lasts 20 years from the date of filing.

    B. A design patent's duration is 14 years from the date of filing.

Money Laundering

I. Introduction

> **Definition:**
> *Money Laundering*: This is the process by which one conceals the existence, illegal source, or illegal application of income, and disguises that income to make it appear legitimate.

A. Background—Money-laundering statutes originally targeted primarily drug activity by organized crime, but now aim at a wider range of illicit activities ranging from terrorism to income tax evasion.

II. Key Statutes

A. The *Bank Secrecy Act of 1970*, **31 U.S.C. 5313**—The BSA requires record keeping and reporting by banks and other financial institutions to trace the movement of currency into and out of the U.S. or deposited into banks. It requires banks to (a) report cash transactions over $10,000, (b) identify persons conducting all transactions, and (c) maintain a traceable paper trail.

B. 31 U.S.C. §5324—This statute helps prevent evasion of the BSA by making it illegal to break large transactions down into pieces smaller than $10,000 each in order to evade these reporting requirements.

C. *Money Laundering Control Act of 1986*—In the criminal area, the key statute is the *Money Laundering Control Act of 1986*, which has been amended repeatedly over the years, but remains composed primarily of two provisions—Sections 1956 and 1957 of Title 18 of the United States Code. These two sections are treated separately.

III. Money Laundering—Prohibited Transactions and Transportation

A. Section 1956 contains two primary prohibitions. First, it prohibits *transaction money laundering* where the prohibited act is the financial transaction itself. Four primary examples are financial transactions conducted with intent to (a) promote unlawful activity; (b) engage in violations of Sections 7201 or 7206 of the Tax Code; (c) attempt to conceal the nature, location, source, ownership or control of proceeds from specified unlawful activity; and (d) attempt to avoid state or federal reporting requirements.

> **Example:**
> Defendant stole a suitcase containing nearly a million dollars in cash. He then gave chunks of cash, usually in amounts less than $10,000 to several friends and had them buy cashier's checks. He then used those checks to buy a house which he leased for a year, and then sold, pocketing the cash. His tax returns did not report either the million dollars in cash or the rental income. Defendant was guilty of money laundering for purposes of concealing the source of the million dollars he had stolen.

B. Second, Section 1956 prohibits *transportation money laundering*, the transportation of criminally derived funds into or out of the United States with the intent to (a) promote illegal activity; (b) transport illegal proceeds in an attempt to hide them; or (c) transport illegal proceeds to avoid reporting requirements.

> **Example:**
> A trucker who hid duffel bags full of cocaine and cash in his truck and transported them across the country for a crime organization violated this provision.

C. A conspiracy to violate these money-laundering provisions is a separate punishable offense.

D. Penalties—Section 1956 carries a $10,000 maximum civil penalty and a maximum criminal penalty of 20 years in jail and a $500,000 fine or twice the value of the laundered money (whichever is greater).

IV. Money Laundering—Property Transactions

A. Section 1957 addresses monetary transactions in criminally derived property over $10,000. The property might be derived from unlawful activities such as drug dealing, gambling, mail fraud, wire fraud, or any of an exceedingly long list of offenses. The recipient need not know the specific unlawful activity. Nor need he or she further launder the money in order to violate the statute. A legitimate store selling legitimate goods could violate the statute. However, to be liable, the recipient must "knowingly" engage in a transaction involving criminally derived property.

Example:
A CPA who filled out false tax returns that his clients mailed to a bank in order to receive a mortgage loan to which their real income would not have entitled them, commits a money laundering violation of Section 1957. He knowingly engages in unlawful activity (mail fraud) that yielded proceeds (the loans) over $10,000 that were used in monetary transactions (the bank's wiring of the funds to the closing agent for purposes of purchasing a home).

B. Penalties—Section 1957 carries a maximum $10,000 civil penalty and a criminal punishment of up to 10 years in jail and a fine.

V. Role of Accountants
Some have proposed that accounting firms have the same reporting responsibilities as financial institutions where potential money laundering by their clients is concerned, but this policy has not been enacted. Auditors are not specifically charged with detecting and reporting money laundering activities during their audits. Only the PSLRA's provision regarding detection of illegal actions that have a direct and material impact on financial statements seems to apply, and money laundering by corporations seldom has such an impact.

Selection of a Business Entity

After studying this lesson, you should be able to:

1. Describe the basic features of important forms of business entities, such as partnerships, corporations, and LLCs.

2. Understand the advantages and disadvantages of the different forms of business entity when compared and contrasted with one another.

I. Introduction

A. Businesses may be structured in numerous ways to attain various benefits. Ranging from a simple sole proprietorship (one-owner business) to large multinational corporations, firms are structured to gain various operational efficiencies and competitive advantages.

B. Business organizations date back to ancient times. Many early forms resembled today's partnerships. This form works well for small businesses, but is not optimal for accumulating large amounts of capital. Because general partners are personally liable for all of their firm's debts, so they generally wish to do business only with close friends and relatives whom they know and trust.

C. Eventually, limited liability was invented for the corporate form, which encouraged investors to take more risks with their money, because the most they could lose was their investment in the enterprise.

D. While corporations have the advantage of limited liability, but they suffer the comparative detriment of "double taxation" in that the firm pays corporate income tax on its earnings and then its shareholders pay individual income tax on the dividends they are paid from corporate profits. Partnerships, on the other hand, enjoy single, pass-through taxation. Although the partnership files an informational return, it pays no income tax.

E. For most of the 1900s, the major forms of business organization in the United States were the corporation, general partnerships, limited partnerships, and sole proprietorships. However, around 1990, states began authorizing the creation of new forms of business organizations to encourage economic development. These organizations allow entrepreneurs and investors to enjoy both limited liability and single taxation without leaving even a single person exposed to general liability. The first form of these organizations was called the limited liability company (LLC). LLCs were made popular by IRS decisions to allow these new entities to elect ("check-the-box") partnership taxation, even though they embodied so many corporate characteristics that could have subjected them to double taxation under previous law.

F. Then "copycat" business forms were created to spread this "limited liability + single taxation" formula to the general partnership form through limited liability general partnerships (LLPs) and even to the limited partnership form through limited liability limited partnerships (LLLPs).

G. Most accounting firms today are either LLPs or LLCs.

II. Types of Business Organization

A. Sole Proprietorship—A sole proprietorship is a single-owner business. The firm's liabilities and assets belong solely to their owner. If Matt starts a cupcake catering business out of his home and takes no formal legal action to organize in another form, his business will be a sole proprietorship.

B. General Partnership—A general partnership is an association of two or more persons to carry on as co-owners of a business for profit. If Matt finds that his cupcakes often show up at catered dinners along with Adelita's salads, he may propose to Adelita that they join forces to offer a catering service with a full menu and to split the profits. If Matt and Adelita take no formal legal action to organize in another form, their new business will be a general partnership. If the partnership suffers financial reverses, Matt and Adelita are both potentially responsible to pay its debts out of their own individual pockets. If the business makes a profit, it will "pass through" to Matt and Adelita for income tax purposes. Whether distributed or not, profits are allocated and taxable directly to the partners. Although previous law treated partnerships as merely an aggregation of partners, current law generally recognizes partnership as an entity for most purposes.

C. Joint Venture—A joint venture is a term often used to denote a one-shot general partnership-type relation. Thus, if Matt and Adelita join forces to provide an ongoing full-menu catering business, they have a general partnership. However, if they agreed to work together to provide full-menu service for just a single, big dinner, they might be said to have formed a joint venture. Joint ventures are governed by general partnership law, so the distinction between the two is generally unimportant for legal purposes.

D. Limited Partnership—A limited partnership is a partnership with at least one general partner and at least one limited partner. It is distinguished from a general partnership in that its limited partners give up some of the general management rights that partners in a general partnership would have in exchange for limited liability. Thus, if Matt and Adelita need financing for their new catering business, they might ask their wealthy friend Jess to become an investor. Jess does not intend to be active in the business and certainly does not wish to become generally liable for the debts of the catering business. If certain legal steps are taken, a limited partnership can be formed that will protect Jess from liability and thereby encourage him to invest his capital. However, if Jess takes an active role in managing the firm, he will forfeit his limited liability regarding those who see his activities and believe him to be a general partner. It bears repeating that a limited partnership must have at least one general partner who will be generally liable for the firm's obligations.

E. Limited Liability Partnership (LLP)—A limited liability partnership (LLP) is a relatively new form of business organization that carries greater protection from liability than exists in either general or limited partnerships. It was created primarily to protect professionals, such as accountants, physicians, and attorneys, from undue malpractice liability arising from the errors of their partners. Thus, if Tad and Todd are CPAs who practice as general partners, Tad is personally liable for any malpractice committed by Todd. A limited liability partnership (LLP) form can shield Tad from personal tort liability caused by Todd's malpractice. In LLPs, partners are generally liable only for (a) their own malpractice, and (b) the malpractice of those they directly supervise. Most (but not all) state provisions also protect partners from personal liability for LLP *contractual* obligations. In exchange for providing this extensive liability protection, many states require LLPs to carry minimum levels of malpractice insurance to help ensure that clients harmed by malpractice will have a viable remedy.

F. Limited Liability Limited Partnership (LLLP)—A limited liability limited partnership (LLLP) is a relatively new form of business organization that allows the general partner(s) of a limited partnership to enjoy limited liability, just like limited partners. It places the burden upon third parties who deal with LLLPs to protect themselves contractually because they will not be able to dip into the pockets of either limited partners or general partners to be compensated for the firm's debts. All a limited partnership needs to do to elect to be an LLLP is to include a one-line statement to that effect in its certificate of limited partnership. While the other forms of organization mentioned in this lesson are ubiquitous, as of 2014, only about 25 states had authorized LLLPs. Note that both general and limited partners in such partnerships will remain liable for the consequences of torts they personally commit while conducting partnership business. No form of business organization shields people from personal liability for the torts they personally commit.

G. Corporation—A corporation is an artificial legal entity. Its owners (shareholders) typically enjoy limited liability. The creation of the notion of an artificial legal entity in order to encourage people to invest in others' business ideas is one of the great advances in Western legal thought. Kay may buy General Motors stock because she is secure in the notion that even if General Motors goes bankrupt, she will not be liable for its obligations. Her potential loss is limited to the amount she invested when she bought GM stock. Typically, corporations are theoretically burdened by double taxation, meaning they pay corporate income tax on their profits, and then when they distribute their gains to shareholders in the form of dividends, these shareholders pay individual income tax on their dividend income. By intelligent tax planning, however, there are ways to minimize the impact of double taxation.

H. Subchapter S—A Subchapter S corporation can eliminate the double taxation that most corporations (called Subchapter C corporations) face by meeting certain requirements of Subchapter S of the Internal Revenue Code, including having no more than 100 shareholders who unanimously agree to choose Subchapter S status.

I. Professional Corporation (PC)—A professional corporation (PC) is formed pursuant to special statutory accommodations that typically aim at allowing accountants, doctors, lawyers, and some other professionals to gain some of the benefits of the corporate form, particularly various advantages related to offering benefits to employees. Typically, the shareholders in PCs enjoy limited liability (except for their own malpractice, of course), but are subject to double taxation. The corporation is a legal entity, separate and apart from its shareholders. PCs have lost popularity with the creation of LLPs (mentioned earlier) and LLCs (see the next paragraph).

J. Limited Liability Company (LLC)—A limited liability company (LLC) is a relatively new form of business organization that allows owners of businesses to gain the liability-limiting advantages of the corporate form while enjoying the single, pass-through tax benefits of the partnership form of business. While most very large businesses are corporations and the corporate form probably remains the most important type of business organization, more LLCs are formed in the U.S. every year than any other form of business organization.

III. Advantages and Disadvantages

A. Sole Proprietorships

1. Advantages

a. Total control—The owner needs answer to no other owner; he or she may make all decisions. Other persons, such as creditors, might of course have something to say about how the business is run.

b. Simplicity—No formal documents need be filed to form a sole proprietorship, although even a sole owner of a business will ultimately have to deal with legal formalities such as tax forms, licenses to undertake a particular activity, and permission to do business in foreign jurisdictions.

c. Taxation—All income from the business accrues to the sole owner who is responsible for paying the individual income taxes on that amount.

2. Disadvantages

a. General liability—The owner is the business and the business is the owner in a sole proprietorship. Therefore, the owner is personally liable for any debts incurred by the business.

B. General Partnerships (and Joint Ventures)

1. Advantages

a. Pass-through taxation—Partnerships enjoy single taxation because the partnership entity pays no taxes (although it files an informational return). Rather, partnership income passes through to the individual partners who pay individual income tax on their share.

b. Simplicity—No formal documents need be filed to form a general partnership. If two persons associate with the goal of carrying on as co-owners of a business for profit, the law will treat their relationship as a general partnership regardless of whether they have filed any legal documents. They may, however, file such documents if they choose.

2. Disadvantages

a. General liability—All general partners are personally liable for the obligations of the business. Thus, if Sal and Pal each put $100,000 into a partnership, but it lost all that money and $100,000 more, Sal and Pal could each be personally liable for the extra $100,000 in losses.

C. Limited Partnerships

  1. Advantages

    a. Pass-through taxation—Like general partnerships, limited partnerships enjoy single taxation.

    b. Limited liability for the limited partners exists, so long as they do not take part in the management of the firm.

  2. Disadvantages

    a. Formality—Legal documents must be filed with a state office (typically the Secretary of State, or perhaps the State Corporation Commission) in order to form a limited partnership. The firm's name must reflect its limited partnership status, as by using the term "Ltd" or "LP."

    b. Authority—A limited partner must forfeit the right to manage the business in order to be entitled to limited liability. In truth, the law does allow a fair amount of direct involvement in the business (e.g., as employee, lender, guarantor) for a limited partner without imposing general liability.

    c. General liability—A limited partnership must have at least one general partner that will be generally liable to creditors for the obligations of the partnership. However, that general partner can be a corporation whose artificial entity will shield any individual owners from personal liability for business debts.

D. Limited Liability Partnerships

  1. Advantages

    a. Pass-through taxation—Like partnerships, LLPs enjoy single taxation.

    b. Limited liability—Like limited partners, LLPs are not liable for the general obligations of the partnership, although they typically remain liable for the tort liabilities generated by their own actions and the actions of those they supervise. Therefore, if Todd and Tad are partners in a CPA LLP and Todd commits malpractice, Tad will not be personally liable for that wrong. Tad is liable only for torts that he and the employees in the firm whom he supervises commit. In most states (full-shield states), this protection extends to the firm's tort *and contract* obligations. In some states (partial-shield states), the protection extends only to tort obligations.

    c. Authority—LLPs may be actively involved in managing the partnership without forfeiting the limited liability that partners in an LLP generally enjoy.

  2. Disadvantages

    a. Formality—Legal documents must be filed with a state office (typically the Secretary of State) in order to form an LLP.

    b. Insurance requirement—In many states firms must maintain a minimum level of liability insurance (for example, $1 million) in order to entitle partners to liability protection.

E. Limited Liability Limited Partnerships

  1. Advantages

    a. Pass-through taxation—Like all partnerships, LLLPs enjoy single taxation.

    b. Limited liability—As in limited partnerships, limited partners enjoy limited liability. Furthermore, in LLLPs, even general partners enjoy limited liability. (Remember, neither general nor limited partners in LLLPs may escape liability for torts they personally commit.)

  2. Disadvantages

    a. Only about 25 states authorize the formation of LLLPs.

3. Formality—Legal documents must be filed with a state office (typically the Secretary of State) in order to form an LLLP. However, a limited partnership can easily become an LLLP by simply amending its filing with the state to so indicate.

F. Corporations

1. Advantages

   a. Limited liability—All shareholders are entitled to limited liability, but two things should be kept in mind. First, occasionally rare circumstances exist that justify "piercing of the corporate veil" (making shareholders pay corporate debts from their own pockets). Second, especially with small corporations third parties may refuse to loan money to a corporation or to sell to it on credit unless its owners co-sign or otherwise guarantee the obligation, in which case the benefit is more theoretical than real.

   b. Legal personality—The corporation is viewed as a legal entity, separate and apart from its owners. It can own property, enter into contracts, and do pretty much any legal act that an individual can. This was formerly a distinct advantage over partnerships, which were viewed as mere aggregations of their owners. But modern partnership law increasingly treats partnerships in all their manifestations (GPs, LPs, LLPs, etc.) as entities for many purposes. This is true of LLCs.

   c. Perpetual duration—A traditional advantage of the corporate form has been its perpetual duration. The corporate entity is viewed as a separate legal entity, so it can last for a long, long time. If the five owners of ABC Corporation stock are all killed in a plane crash, ABC Corporation keeps on going in legal contemplation. Its new owners are the heirs of the five deceased owners. Under older laws, partnerships are dissolved upon the death or departure of individual partners so this is an important advantage for corporations. Under more modern partnership laws, however, arranging for partnerships to survive the death or departure of partners is generally easy.

2. Disadvantages

   a. Double taxation—The corporation is subject to corporate income tax, and shareholders are subject to individual income tax liability on dividends and other distributions. Therefore, double taxation has traditionally been viewed as a disadvantage of the corporate form. With proper tax planning, however, the effect of this disadvantage can be minimized.

   b. Formality—Legal documents must be filed with a state office (typically the Secretary of State) in order to form a corporation.

G. Subchapter S Corporations

1. Advantages

   a. Limited liability—Subchapter S shareholders enjoy limited liability.

   b. Single taxation—Subchapter S corporations do not pay income tax, thereby avoiding double taxation.

2. Disadvantages

   a. Formality—Legal documents must be filed with a state office (typically the Secretary of State) in order to form a Subchapter S corporation.

   b. Individual taxation—Corporate profits are considered as if they were distributed to shareholders, so an S-Corporation shareholder might be taxed on income he or she has never received, whereas a C-corporation shareholder is taxed on dividends only when these are actually received.

   c. Subchapter S requirements—To take advantage of the tax benefit offered by Subchapter S, a corporation must meet certain requirements, including:

      i. It is a domestic corporation;

   ii. All shareholders must consent to the S-Corporation election;

   iii. The firm can have no more than 100 shareholders, although all members of a family can be treated as a single shareholder;

   iv. All shareholders must be individuals, estates, certain exempt organizations, or certain trusts; and

   v. The corporation has only one class of stock. (That is, all outstanding shares confer identical rights to distribution and liquidation proceeds.)

H. Limited Liability Companies

 1. Advantages

  a. Pass-through taxation—LLCs enjoy the single taxation of a partnership without having to meet the criteria required for Subchapter S status. (However, LLCs may choose to be taxed as corporate entities if they so desire.)

  b. Limited liability—All LLC members enjoy limited liability without forfeiting management rights as limited partners would have to.

 2. Disadvantages

  a. Formality—Legal documents must be filed with a state office (typically the Secretary of State) in order to form an LLC.

Formation

After studying this lesson, you should be able to:

1. Understand the basic formation process for most forms of business organizations, such as partnerships, corporations, and LLCs.

2. Know the basic rules that govern the authority and liability of business entity promoters.

I. **Formation**

    A. Sole Proprietorships

        1. No formal filing is required for the creation of sole proprietorships.

        2. However, to do business, a sole proprietorship, like other forms of organization, may need to acquire a tax number and a license to, for example, sell fresh produce or operate a restaurant.

    B. General Partnerships—No formal filing is required to create a general partnership either. All that is needed is an intention by two or more people to enter into a relationship that the law deems a partnership, which is generally co-ownership of a business for the purpose of making profit.

        1. Governing law—General partnerships are governed by the Revised Uniform Partnership Act (RUPA).

        2. RUPA is functionally a form contract that provides default rules in case partners in a general partnership have not formed a partnership agreement as to all issues.

        3. By agreement, partners may vary (most) RUPA provisions to meet their business needs, but they may not prejudice the rights of third parties.

        4. A written partnership agreement is always a good idea, but this is not required unless the partnership is to last for a specified period longer than one year.

        5. Although no written filing is required, partners may file a *Statement of Partnership Authority* with the Secretary of State which is often useful in dealing with third parties who might wish to know, for example, which partners' signatures need to be on a document of sale for the partnership to be bound.

    C. LPs, LLPs, LLLPs, and LLCs

        1. A filing with a state agency, typically the Secretary of State, is generally required to form the other forms of business organizations discussed in this section—limited partnerships (LPs), Limited Liability Partnerships (LLPs), Limited Liability Limited Partnerships (LLLPs), and Limited Liability Companies (LLCs), as well as corporations.

        2. Governing law

            a. Limited partnership law is generally governed by the Revised Uniform Limited Partnership Act (RULPA).

            b. Although most states have enacted their own idiosyncratic version of an LLC statute, meaning that there is great variety in LLC laws from state to state, a revised model act does exist—the Revised Uniform Limited Liability Company Act (RULLCA).

            c. LLPs are generally provided for within states' RUPA or RULPA provisions.

            d. LLLPs are generally provided for within RULPA.

    D. Corporations

        1. Many states have adopted some version of the Revised Model Business Corporation Act (RMBCA) to govern the operation of corporations.

        2. The Delaware Corporate Code is a model for many other states' corporate laws.

3. RMBCA requires that those forming a corporation file Articles of Incorporation that must include the following data:

   a. The corporate name (indicating corporate status by use of "Corp.," "Inc.," etc.);

   b. Number of authorized shares;

   c. Address of the initial registered office of the corporation and the first registered agent at that address; and

   d. Names and addresses of the incorporators.

4. The general process for forming a corporation includes:

   a. Filing articles of incorporation with the Secretary of State;

   b. Holding an organizational meeting in which a board of directors is elected, and the contracts entered into by promoters are adopted or rejected;

   c. Drafting and adopting by-laws to govern the inner workings of the firm; and

   d. Obtaining certificates of authority to do business in other jurisdictions.

5. Promoters and their contracts—Before a corporation is officially formed, it often needs to hire employees, rent office space, and buy equipment, among others. A promoter is a person who takes the initiative to found and organize a business, often by doing such acts.

   a. Because of their unique position, promoters may take advantage of others and therefore have been held to owe a fiduciary duty of loyalty to:

      i. The proposed corporation;

      ii. Other promoters; and

      iii. Contemplated investors.

   b. Promoters are usually forbidden from profiting at all from pre-incorporation contracts (even if the contract is fair to the corporation) unless they:

      i. Make full disclosure to an independent board of directors and gain their approval; or

      ii. Make full disclosure to all original shareholders and gain their approval.

   c. Promoter liability on pre-incorporation contracts.

      i. Promoters are liable on the contracts they negotiate on the prospective corporation's behalf unless the contract clearly and explicitly indicates that the third party is looking only to the corporation for performance.

      ii. Even if the corporation is formed and adopts the contract, the promoter remains liable, absent a novation (an express release from the third party).

   d. Corporation liability on promoters' contracts. A corporation is liable on contracts negotiated by its promoters if it comes into existence and adopts the contract:

      i. Expressly (e.g., via the board of directors' resolution), or

      ii. Impliedly (e.g., via knowing and voluntary acceptance of the benefits of the contract).

   e. Right to enforce—Once it adopts the promoter's contracts, the corporation has the right to enforce them against third parties.

Operations

After studying this lesson, you should be able to:

1. Understand the essential rules governing the operation of important types of business entities.

2. Know the key rules that govern piercing the corporate veil in order to impose firm liability upon firm owners.

I. Operations

A. Sole Proprietorships—The sole owner of a sole proprietorship makes all important decisions or delegates these decisions to someone of his or her choosing.

B. General Partnerships

1. *Absent agreement to the contrary*, all partners have equal rights in the management and conduct of business affairs.

Example:
If A and B each contributed $50,000 to form ABC partnership, and C contributed $200,000, the partners might agree to give C more votes than A and B. Absent agreement to the contrary, however, each partner will have an equal vote notwithstanding their unequal financial contributions.

2. *Absent agreement to the contrary*, majority vote governs all ordinary course-of-business matters.

Example:
A, B, and C are partners. A and B vote to borrow money from the bank. C votes against. A and B prevail. The loan is valid and C is potentially liable to repay it along with A and B, even though C voted against the transaction.

3. *However*, unanimity is needed to take actions contrary to the partnership agreement or to take action regarding "extraordinary matters," which might include such actions as:

a. Admitting a new partner to the partnership;

b. Assigning partnership property;

Example:
Creditor X is owed money by ABC partnership. X wishes to have the partnership assign its trucks to X so that X can sell them to raise money to pay ABC's debt. Partners A, B, and C must all agree.

c. Disposing of goodwill; or

Example:
A, B, and C own an ice cream store with the name "ABC Creamery." X wishes to buy the store and to operate it under the name "ABC Creamery." All partners must agree to the sale.

    d. Doing any other act which would make it impossible to carry on the ordinary business of the partnership.

Example:
A, B, and C own a furniture store in a small town. There is only one building in town suitable for housing the business. D wishes to buy the building. A, B, and C, must unanimously agree.

C. Limited Partnerships, LLPs, and LLLPs

    1. In these forms of limited partnerships, one or more general partners make management decisions, whereas limited partners generally sit on the sidelines playing the role of passive investors.

    2. As noted elsewhere, if limited partners in limited partnerships (not LLLPs) leave the sidelines and become actively involved in the control of the limited partnership, they may forfeit their limited liability as to creditors who rely upon their apparent role as general partners.

D. Corporations

    1. Shareholders elect directors; directors select officers; and officers make the day-to-day decisions needed to operate the corporation.

    2. In small corporations, the same people may of course be the primary shareholders, directors, and officers.

    3. Piercing the Corporate Veil: Corporations are distinct legal entities, so their obligations are typically not visited upon their shareholders personally. In other words, the most a shareholder can lose when investing in a corporation is the amount he or she spent to purchase the shares. If Ford Motor Corporation went bankrupt tomorrow, its shareholders might lose their investment, but unlike general partners in a general partnership, they would not be personally liable for any outstanding obligations of Ford. However, when small, closely held corporations are involved, courts might possibly "pierce the corporate veil" and reach into shareholders' pockets to satisfy corporate obligations. This act would be unusual but can happen when courts believe such is necessary to prevent the corporate form from being used to defeat public convenience, justify wrong, protect fraud, or defend crime.

    4. Factors—The following considerations (usually in combination) may induce a court to pierce the corporate veil:

        a. Commingling of funds and other assets of the corporation with those of individual shareholders;

        b. Diversion of the corporation's funds or assets for the personal use of shareholders;

        c. Failure to maintain the necessary corporate formalities;

        d. Failure to adequately capitalize the corporation for the reasonably foreseeable risks of the enterprise;

        e. Use of the corporation as a mere shell or conduit to operate a single venture or some particular aspect of the business of an individual shareholder;

        f. Absence of separately held corporate assets;

        g. Formation and use of the corporation to assume the existing liabilities of another person or entity.

E. Limited Liability Companies

    1. LLCs may be operated in one of two primary ways:

        a. Owner-managed—LLC members may choose to run the business themselves, as if they were general partners (unlike general partners, however, they enjoy limited liability).

    b. Manager-managed—LLC members may also choose to delegate managerial powers to one or more members or non-members.

2. The choice of one of these forms and a number of other decisions regarding the operations of the LLC can be set forth in an "operating agreement" that will be filed with the Secretary of State.

3. Remember that although there is a revised uniform act for LLCs (RULLCA), relatively few states have adopted it. Most states have adopted their own version of an LLC law, meaning that legal uniformity is greatly lacking across the nation.

4. In virtually every state, one person may form an LLC. Only a few states prohibit single-member LLCs.

Termination

After studying this lesson, you should be able to:

1. Understand the basic rules that govern the termination of important types of business entities.

2. Understand the procedures and rules used to protect shareholders and other owners when business entities terminate.

I. Termination

A. Sole Proprietorships

1. A sole proprietorship naturally terminates when the sole owner dies or otherwise departs the business.

B. General Partnerships

1. Under RUPA, the fact that partners are added to or removed from the partnership does not automatically lead to the dissolution of the partnership (as was formerly the case).

   a. Rather, the causes of "dissociation" of a partner from the partnership include:

      i. Notice of a partner's express will to dissolve the partnership;

      ii. Death of a partner;

      iii. Bankruptcy of a partner;

      iv. Expulsion of a partner.

2. RUPA lists a few situations in which a partnership *must* be wound up; in all other situations, a buyout of a partner must occur. Thus, a partner's dissociation (through death, bankruptcy, etc.) must lead to either a buyout by the remaining partners or the dissolution of the partnership. The former (buyout) is preferred over the latter (dissolution).

3. If dissolution does not occur, the partnership shall purchase the interest of the dissociating partner at the amount that would have been distributable to the dissociating partner from his or her partnership account if, on the date of dissociation, the assets of the partnership were sold at the greater of liquidation or going-concern value (offset by damages caused if the dissociation was wrongful).

4. RUPA provides a 90-day "cooling off" period between dissolution and liquidation in order to give the parties an opportunity to negotiate an amicable buyout.

5. In winding up the partnership business, creditors (including partners) must be paid first. If there are insufficient assets to pay off creditors, then the partners (including the estates of the deceased partners) will have to contribute to the partnership to satisfy the obligations. If funds are left over after paying creditors, then the partnership shall make a distribution to partners in amounts equal to any excess of credits over charges in their partners' accounts.

C. Limited Partnerships

1. The process of dissociation, winding up, and liquidation (termination) for the various forms of limited partnerships (including LLPs and LLLPs) is sufficiently similar to that of general partnerships that it need not be separately treated.

2. The departure of a limited partner will not result in the dissolution of a limited partnership, and the departure of a general partner need not do so either with proper planning.

D. Corporations

1. Corporations may be voluntarily dissolved upon the approval of their directors and shareholders.

   a. Typically, a majority of directors vote to propose dissolution and a majority of shareholders vote to approve the proposal.

2. Corporations may be involuntarily dissolved *administratively* by the Secretary of State for such reasons as:

   a. Failure to pay franchise taxes;

   b. Failure to file annual reports; or

   c. Failure to properly establish and maintain a registered agent or office.

3. Corporations may be involuntarily dissolved *judicially* in:

   a. An action by the attorney general, where:

      i. The corporation fraudulently obtained approval for its articles of incorporation, or

      ii. The corporation has abused its legal authority.

   b. An action by *shareholders*;

      i. If management is deadlocked;

      ii. If those controlling the corporation are acting in an illegal or oppressive way, such as by looting the corporation or wasting its assets; or

      iii. If the shareholders are deadlocked and cannot elect directors.

   c. An action by creditors; or

   d. An unsatisfied judgment creditor's claim and the corporation is insolvent, or if the corporation admits in writing that the creditor's claim is due and owing and that it is insolvent.

4. Other major organic changes (in addition to dissolution) include sale of all or substantially all of a corporation's assets (not in the ordinary course of business) and mergers or consolidations with other corporations. Shareholder interests are protected in such transactions that can so fundamentally alter their interests by:

   a. Procedures—Directors owing a fiduciary duty must propose and shareholders must approve in a vote; and

   b. Appraisal rights—Dissenting shareholders may request that their shares be purchased at a court-valued rate pursuant to their appraisal rights (also called dissenters' rights).

E. LLCs

1. LLC law varies more from state to state than do most other forms of business organization. However, the process commonly follows the dissociation-winding up- termination approach of RUPA for general partnerships.

2. Among the events that cause a person to be dissociated as a member from an LCC, according to RULLCA, are the following:

   a. The person gives notice of express will to withdraw;

   b. An event listed in the operating agreement as causing dissociation occurs;

   c. The person is expelled pursuant to the operating agreement;

   d. The person dies; and

   e. The person is a corporation, partnership, or other organization that has been dissolved.

3. Among the events that cause the LLC to dissolve, according to RULLCA are the following:

   a. An event that causes dissolution based on the operating agreement;

   b. Consent of all members;

   c. Passage of 90 consecutive days during which the company has no members;

d. Court order, upon application of a member, dissolving the LLC on grounds that the conduct of its activities is unlawful or that carrying on the company's activities is not "reasonably practicable" in conformity with the operating agreement; and

e. Court order, upon application of a member, dissolving the LLC on grounds that those in control of the company are illegally or fraudulently acting or are oppressively behaving to harm the applicant.

4. RULLCA contains detailed provisions regarding winding up of an LLC's business by gathering together its assets and paying its obligation to creditors (including members who are creditors). If any surplus remains, it should be distributed to (a) each person whose contributions have not been repaid; if any money remains, it should be distributed to (b) members and dissociated members in equal shares.

Financial Structure

After studying this lesson, you should be able to:

1. Understand the key financial issues in partnership law.

2. Understand the key financial rules governing issuance of corporate stock.

3. Understand the key financial rules governing corporate distributions.

I. Introduction—Because all the partnership forms (GPs, LPs, LLP, LLLPs) automatically allocate income to partners or members and can elect single (pass-through) taxation, the key more complicated financial issues tend to relate to corporations. Therefore, this section discusses primarily corporation law pursuant to the RMBCA. However, this section begins with a discussion of general partnership rules on important financial matters that may generally be deemed to apply to other forms of partnerships. It concludes with a brief description of LLC issues relating to financial structure.

II. Partnerships—Financial Structure

   A. Capital accounts

      1. Under RUPA, each partner is deemed to have an account that is:

         a. Credited with an amount equal to the money plus the value of any other property, net of the amount of any liabilities, the partner contributes to the partnership, and the partner's share of the partnership profits;

         b. At the same time, this account is charged with an amount equal to the money plus the value of any other property, net of the amount of any liabilities, distributed by the partnership to the partner and the partner's share of partnership losses.

      2. Partners are to be reimbursed for payments made and indemnified for liabilities incurred in the ordinary course of the partnership business.

Example:
An emergency arises and partner Sandy pays $10,000 out of her own pocket in order to preserve partnership property worth many times that amount. Sandy is entitled to be reimbursed from partnership funds.

      3. Partners are to be reimbursed for advances to the partnership made beyond agreed capital contributions. These are loans and the partners are creditors generally on par with outside creditors.

      4. As noted elsewhere, absent agreement to the contrary, partners equally share profits and losses. If they have agreed to a non-equal sharing of profits but have not made any provision for the sharing of losses, losses will be shared in proportion to profits.

   B. Interest

      1. Under RUPA, partners, absent agreement to the contrary, should receive interest on advances made to the partnership beyond the amount of capital they agreed to contribute.

   C. Right to profits

      1. Absent agreement to the contrary, profits and losses are to be equally shared by the partners.

Example:
A contributes $100,000 to a partnership with B, who contributes $10,000. Although the partners have made unequal contributions, absent agreement to the contrary they will equally share profits.

2. If the partners agree to share profits in some proportion other than equally, but make no agreement regarding losses, losses will be shared in the same proportion as profits.

> **Example:**
> A, B, and C are partners. A contributed more to the partnership than B and C, so the partners agree that A will receive 50% of the profits and B and C will each receive 25%. The partners never even consider losses. Unfortunately, the business does not go well and the partnership loses $200,000. A is responsible for 50% of the losses, and B and C are responsible for 25% each.

D. Distributions in kind

    1. Partners have no right to receive, and may not be required to accept, a distribution in kind(rather than in cash).

> **Example:**
> Sam dissociates from a partnership and the remaining partners wish to continue the partnership and buy out Sam's interest. Calculations indicate that Sam is owed $50,000. The partners would like to give him a partnership tractor that is worth $50,000. Sam would prefer cash. Sam is entitled to insist on cash, even though it might inconvenience the partnership.

III. Corporate Financial Structure and Shareholder Distributions—Introduction and Definitions

A. Types of corporate securities—There are several types of corporate securities.

    1. Equity securities

        a. Common stock—The owners of common stock are the true owners of a corporation. They bear the most risk and have the most to gain. They have the right to vote for directors, to share pro rata in the profits of the corporation when paid out as dividends and to share in the surplus of assets over liabilities, if any, when the corporation dissolves.

        b. Preferred stock—Preferred shareholders may have economic rights that are superior to those of common shareholders in terms of either dividend rights or assets upon dissolution. Preferred shareholders are entitled to have their preferences respected. Preferred shares are usually cumulative, meaning that if the board chooses not to declare any preferred dividends in a given year, the right to receive them accumulates and in a subsequent year the board must pay both that year's preferred dividends and those that have cumulated unpaid **before any dividends are paid on common shares**. There is no right to payment of preferred dividends. There is only a right to be preferred to common shares if dividends are paid. If there's no money for dividends, then there's no money for dividends. However, if there is SOME money for dividends, holding preferred shares is good because you will be in line ahead of the common shareholders if insolvency threatens. If the preferred shares are noncumulative, no arrearages arise from one year's non-declaration and nonpayment. Once dividends are declared, the receiving shareholders are unsecured creditors of the corporation for that amount until they are actually paid.

        c. Treasury stock—Common stock that, once issued to shareholders, has now been repurchased by the corporation is called treasury stock. Such stock is often distributed to shareholders pro rata as a **share dividend**.

    2. Debt securities—These are issued to creditors who, functionally, loan money to the corporation. They are not shareholders and do not have the rights to vote, to inspect, etc. that belong to shareholders. However, like other lenders and unlike common shareholders, they do have the right to be repaid and to be paid specified interest whether the corporation is prospering or not:

    a. Notes—short-term unsecured debt instruments

    b. Debentures—long-term unsecured debt instruments

    c. Bonds—debt instruments secured by corporate property

B. Other terms

    1. Redeemable—redeemable shares must be repurchased by the corporation under specified conditions and at specified prices if the shareholder so desires.

    2. Callable—shares that are redeemable at the corporation's option.

    3. Convertible—debt securities that are convertible to equity securities at specified ratios at the request of the holder.

    4. Warrants, rights, and options—legal entitlements to purchase equity (not debt) securities at a specified price and time at the request of the holder. Until exercised, these entitlements carry no dividend, inspection, or other rights.

C. Consideration—Shares should not be simply given away for corporate fiscal soundness and the prevention of fraud. Therefore, shares must be issued only in exchange for consideration that meets both quality and quantity tests.

    1. Quality tests

        a. Traditionally, proper consideration included only money paid, services performed, and property received.

        b. Traditionally, improper consideration included unsecured promissory notes, promises to perform future services, and promises to transfer property.

        c. However, the modern trend is to recognize as valid consideration: "Any tangible or intangible benefit to the corporation, including cash, promissory notes, services performed, contracts for services to be performed, or other securities of the corporation,"

            i. The board of directors can adequately protect the corporation by issuing the shares only where there is a good chance it will benefit because the promissory notes will probably be paid, the services will probably be performed, etc.

    2. Quantity tests

        a. Par Value: This means **face value**.

            i. The RMBCA has abolished the concept, but its use persists in many states.

            ii. The issuance of **no par** is also permitted.

            iii. Par value is not always a gauge of a corporation's solvency, because watered stock (stock issued in exchange for consideration that is less than the par value of the shares) is sometimes issued.

            iv. In states that still require that consideration be at least equal to the par value, corporations use the **nominal** par value.

        b. Today, if stock is issued for less than par (in states where that concept is still recognized) or less than the authorized (by the board of directors) purchase price, then the liability to creditors and other stockholders may be placed upon:

            i. The board who allowed the sale;

            ii. The buyer who paid too little; and

            iii. Transferees of the original buyer who both know that he or she paid too little and who pay too little themselves.

> **Note:**
> **Treasury stock** *may be purchased at less than the par value; if the company's share prices have dropped since the shares were originally issued, that may be the only way the company can resell them.*

Example:
The board of directors authorizes the issuance of 10,000 shares of $1 par value stock for $20/share. The board allows 1,000 shares to be sold to Sue for $10/share. Sue sells 500 of the shares to Sam for $10/share. She sells the other 500 shares to Ace for $10/share. Sam knows that Sue did not pay the authorized sale price; Ace does not know it. If creditors of the corporation go unpaid, they may sue the board and Sue for $10,000 and Sam for $5,000 (the total recovery cannot exceed $10,000). Ace, however, is not liable because he did not know that Sue did not pay the authorized price.

    c. Valuation of consideration received

    d. General rule: Absent a showing of bad faith, the board's valuation of consideration received in exchange for stock is presumptively valid.

Example:
The board of directors of ABC Corporation wishes to purchase a tract of land from X so that it can build a factory thereon. X likes ABC's prospects and wishes to receive 10,000 ABC shares as the sale price for the land rather than cash. The board authorizes the transaction. Disgruntled shareholder Z challenges the transaction on grounds that the shares issued to X were worth more than the land received from X. To prevail, Z must prove not only that the land was worth less than the shares but also that the directors acted in bad faith.

D. A primary purpose of most corporations—To provide income for owners through a stream of dividend payments

    1. Types of dividends

        a. Cash

        b. Stock

            i. A **stock dividend** might be issued by a corporation that has no readily available funds for cash dividends. Such a dividend does not reduce the assets in the corporate till nor transfer anything but paper to shareholders. Typically, shareholders are issued one new share for each 50 or so that they already hold.

            ii. Related is the **stock split**, which involves a greater increase in outstanding shares than does a stock dividend. Typically, shareholders are issued two or three shares for each one that they already hold. Again, the transaction has no effect on the net worth of the corporation, which has no more or fewer assets. Only paper has been transferred to the shareholders.

            iii. Difference: Dividend and Split. The primary difference between a stock dividend and a stock split is an accounting difference. In a stock split, a division of the shares of stock, not of the earnings or profits of the corporation, takes place without any change in or impingement upon the existing status on the corporate books of the earned surplus and capital accounts. However, in a stock dividend, an addition of shares of stock and a division of, at least, some of the earnings or profits of the corporation take place, with such division being reflected on the corporate books by an irreversible allocation of corporate funds from the earned surplus to the capital account.

        c. Property

Example:
One company in England that operates a crematorium occasionally delivers a certificate for a free cremation as a dividend to its shareholders. More typically, property dividends are in the form of shares of stock of other corporations that the distributing corporation has acquired.

2. To be proper, dividends must be paid:

   a. Only out of legally available funds; and

   b. Only in accordance with applicable preferences.

3. Repurchase of shares has the same effect as a dividend payment (taking money out of the corporate treasury and putting it into shareholders' pockets) and must meet the same standards.

4. A distribution may not be made by a corporation if:

   a. After giving effect to the distribution, the corporation would be insolvent; or

      i. Key is bankruptcy solvency: Can the corporation meet its debt obligations as they come due?

   b. The distribution exceeds the **surplus** (defined as the "excess of the net assets of a corporation over its stated capital") of the corporation.

      i. Key is **equity solvency**: Do the corporation's assets exceed its liabilities?

5. Board discretion

   a. General rule—The board of directors' decision to pay or not pay dividends and the choice of amounts is presumed legitimate.

   b. Exception—To overcome this presumption and to force a board to pay more dividends, shareholders must prove that:

      i. The board acted in bad faith; and

      ii. Funds to pay dividends existed in a legally available source.

IV. LLC Financial Structure

A. The key LLC financial provisions tend to reflect comparable corporate (or partnership, occasionally) provisions.

B. Contributions to an LLC, as with a corporation or partnership, may be made in cash, property or services.

C. Obligations to contribute to an LLC are not excused by death, disability, or inability to perform and are enforceable by the creditors of the LLC who have relied upon them.

See the following example.

Example:
1. If member A agrees to contribute $50,000 to an LLC but dies before doing so, A 's estate is liable to pay the amount.

2. If an LLC operating agreement describes member A's contribution of $50,000 to the LLC and A does not actually contribute that amount, creditor X of the LLC who loaned it money based on the belief that that amount had been contributed by A could force A to make the contribution.

D. Like corporations, LLCs may not make distributions to members if after doing so the firm would be insolvent (either in the sense that it cannot pay its bills as they come due or in the sense that its total liabilities exceed its total assets).

   1. Reasonable compensation for present or past services or payments made in the ordinary course of business under bona fide benefits or retirement plans are not "distributions" for this purpose. Therefore, an LLC could pay a reasonable salary to a member without complying with this solvency limitation.

   2. If a distribution is improperly made, the member or non-member managers who approve it are personally liable to creditors, as are members who receive distributions they know to have been improperly made. Liability is limited to the amount above what could have been properly distributed.

E. If an LLC commits to make a distribution to members but does not make the distribution, the members become general, unsecured creditors of the LLC for purposes of that amount.

Rights and Duties

After studying this lesson, you should be able to:

1. Understand the basic rights and duties that are owed by and to various business entity constituents, including owners and managers of LLCs and shareholders and officers of corporations.

I. General Partnerships

A. As noted earlier, absent agreement to the contrary partners are entitled to:

1. Equal management rights; and

2. To have their capital contribution repaid and to equally share in profits.

B. Partnership property belongs to the partnership. Partners are entitled to use or possess partnership property, but only on behalf of the partnership.

Example:

1. Sam is entitled to use a partnership truck for partnership purposes, but not to move his sister's furniture on a weekend (unless his partners agree).

2. Sue owes money to Fred. Sue is a partner in the STD partnership. Sue may not assign partnership property to Fred in order to satisfy her debt to him. Sue may assign her partnership interest to Fred, but this does not make him a partner or give him partnership rights in any way. It only allows him to collect payments the other partners choose to make that Sue would be entitled to as a partner.

C. Creditors of individual partners may not seize partnership property to satisfy the individual debts of partners. Rather, they may go to court to obtain a charging order in which the judge orders the other partners to pay any distribution due to the debtor partner to that partner's creditor instead. Creditors of an individual partner may even purchase that partner's partnership interest at auction, but they gain only the right to receive distributions due the partner. They do not become real partners for any purpose (voting, access to information, etc.).

D. As noted elsewhere, general partners are not entitled to compensation for work performed for the partnership, except for "reasonable compensation" rendered in winding up the business of the partnership.

E. Partners may veto the admission of potential new partners because new partners may be added only upon the unanimous consent of the existing partners.

F. Information rights

1. Partners and their agents are entitled access to partnership books and records during ordinary business hours.

2. Each partner and the partnership shall furnish to partners and their legal representatives:

    a. Without demand: any information concerning the partnership's business and affairs reasonably required for the proper exercise of partners' rights;

    b. Upon demand: any other partnership information reasonably requested.

G. Standards of Conduct: The only fiduciary duties a partner owes to the partnership and other partners are the:

1. *Duty of Loyalty*, which includes:

    a. Accounting for any benefit derived;

    b. Avoiding conflicts of interest; and

    c. Refraining from competing with the partnership business.

2. *Duty of Care*, which includes refraining from engaging in grossly negligent or reckless conduct, intentional misconduct, or a knowing violation of the law.

H. Naturally, in a limited partnership the general partners who manage the firm owe these duties of care and loyalty to the passive limited partners.

II. Corporations

A. Shareholders have few duties, but they have several important rights, such as the following:

1. To vote for corporate directors;

2. To inspect corporate records for proper purposes at proper times and in proper locations;

3. To have their financial priorities respected; e.g., if they hold preferred shares, their preferences should be respected;

4. To exercise appraisal rights when they dissent from major organic changes;

5. To file derivative lawsuits against officers, directors, and others who have committed wrongful acts that have injured the corporation;

6. To exercise preemptive rights to buy their proportional share of new issuances of securities in order to maintain their relative voting strength in the corporation (although articles of incorporation often eliminate these rights).

B. Directors have several important duties, including:

1. Duty of Attention—"Directors must direct." They must not be mere figureheads, meaning that they should, at a minimum:

   a. Attend most board meetings;

   b. Gain a basic familiarity with the company's business; and

   c. Study the company's financial statements.

2. Duty of Care—Directors are not expected to be perfect, but must act:

   a. In good faith;

   b. With the care of an ordinarily prudent person in a like position; and

   c. In a manner reasonably believed to be in the best interests of the corporation.

3. Duty of Loyalty—Directors owe a fiduciary duty to shareholders. They must be loyal to the corporation and its shareholders, meaning:

   a. They should avoid conflicts of interest;

   b. The transactions between a director and the corporation are not automatically void but will be carefully scrutinized. Such transactions are permitted if (1) they are approved by an affirmative majority of disinterested directors, (2) they are approved by a majority of knowledgeable shareholders, or (3) they are "fair" to the corporation;

   c. They should respect the *corporate opportunity doctrine* by not appropriating for themselves business opportunities that rightfully belong to the corporation.

C. Directors' rights

1. Right to rely—Directors have the right to rely upon the reports of officers and other directors unless they have some reason to be suspicious.

2. Business judgment rule—Courts are not business experts, so they normally do not second-guess the business decisions of directors or officers. Rather, they apply the "business judgment rule," which states: "In the absence of a showing of bad faith on the part of the directors or of a gross abuse of discretion, the business judgment of the directors will not be interfered with by the courts. The acts of directors are presumptively acts taken in good faith and inspired for the best interests of the corporation, and a minority stockholder who challenges their bona fides of purpose has the burden of proof."

3. Liability protection—Additionally, most states allow shareholders to amend articles of incorporation to eliminate director (and officer) liability for errors of judgment or even carelessness (although not for acts of fraud or dishonesty).

D. Officers

1. Officers run the day-to-day operations of the corporation under the supervision of the board of directors, so they are very powerful and have the opportunity to abuse that power.

2. Officers are constrained by the same duties of care and loyalty that constrain directors.

III. Limited Liability Companies (LLCs)

A. Whether an LLC is managed by members or by non-member managers, those managing the firm generally owe duties of care and loyalty to the (other) members.

B. Despite the fact that LLCs are generally intended to be more "contractarian" in nature (e.g., governed by the agreement of the members rather than by default statutory provisions), RULLCA prohibits an operating agreement from totally eliminating the duty of loyalty, the duty of care, or any other fiduciary duty.

C. RULLCA also provides that the members in an LLC shall consistently discharge their duties under the act and under the operating agreement with contractual obligations of "good faith and fair dealing."

D. However, RULLCA also provides that those duties that would typically be owed by either members managing the firm or managers managing the firm may be limited in various ways if the limitations are not "manifestly unreasonable." For example, the operating agreement may:

1. Identify specific types of activities that do not violate the duty of loyalty;

2. Alter the duty of care, except to authorize intentional misconduct or knowing violation of law; and

3. Eliminate a member or manager's liability to the LLC for money damages, except for such actions as breach of the duty of loyalty, intentional infliction of harm on the firm, or intentional violation of criminal law.

E. Additionally, courts protect members by:

1. Allowing them to escape an operating agreement by convincing a court that its provisions are "manifestly unreasonable;" and

2. Providing a judicial remedy dissolving an LLC if the managers or members controlling the firm are guilty of "oppressive conduct" directly harmful to a member.

F. The business judgment rule will generally apply when managers' good faith business decisions are challenged.

Authority of Owners and Managers

After studying this lesson, you should be able to:

1. Understand the authority of managers of various forms of business entity—especially managers of LLCs, partners in partnerships, and officers and directors in corporations—to bind the entity.

I. Partnerships

A. Agency law—In partnerships, agency law tends to govern regarding the authority of partners to bind the partnership.

B. General principles—As a general rule, agency law provides:

    1. An act of a partner for apparently carrying on in the ordinary course the partnership business binds the partnership, unless (i) the partner had no authority to act for the partnership in the particular matter and (ii) the person with whom the partner was dealing knew or had received notification that the partner lacked authority.

    2. An act of a partner that is not apparently for carrying on in the ordinary course the partnership's business binds the partnership only if the act was authorized by the other partners.

C. A partner binds both the partnership and the other partners if he or she acts with:

    1. Actual authority (expressed or implied); or

    2. Apparent authority, which cannot exist where:

        a. The third party knows of a partner's lack of authority, or

        b. The partner's action is one that requires unanimity, such as an agreement to admit a new partner.

D. Ratification—An act lacking both actual and apparent authority may still bind a partnership that ratifies the action expressly or by knowingly accepting the benefits of the agreement.

E. Tort liability—Consistent with agency law, partnerships are generally liable for the torts committed by their partners or other agents within the scope of their employment or authority.

    1. Intentional torts—A partnership is usually liable if a partner commits an intentional tort while trying to advance partnership interests, even if he or she does so in a wrongful way.

    2. Misapplication of funds—RUPA imposes virtually strict liability on a partnership for the misapplication of money received by the partnership "in the course of its business." Between the innocent partners who had nothing to do with the misapplication and the innocent customer or client of the partnership, RUPA provides that the innocent customer or client deserves the most protection.

    3. Joint and several liability—Under RUPA, contract and tort liability are typically joint and several, meaning that a creditor may sue any general partner and hold that partner completely liable without suing the others. However, RUPA usually provides that the assets of the partnership must be exhausted before the partnership creditor proceeds against the individual assets of the general partners.

    4. Late arrivers—If a general partner joins an existing partnership, he or she is personally liable for all subsequently-incurred debts, but is liable for preexisting debts only out of his or her partnership contribution.

II. Corporations

A. The corporate pyramid—The corporation is typically viewed as a pyramid. Shareholders are passive investors whose input into corporate management is their vote for directors. Directors then set overall corporate policy and select officers. Officers are at the top of the pyramid, making the day-to-day decisions that bind the firm.

B. Directors—Most state corporate codes provide that "the business and affairs of a corporation shall be managed under the supervision of a board of directors." Directors have broad authority to:

1. Borrow money;

2. Sell corporate property;

3. Hire and fire officers and other employees;

4. Declare or refuse to declare dividends;

5. Make or refuse to make other distributions to shareholders;

6. Set the salaries of employees, officers, and even themselves; and

7. Propose for shareholder approval:

    a. Sale of major corporate assets;

    b. Mergers or consolidations with other firms;

    c. Dissolution; and

    d. Amendments to the articles of incorporation.

C. Officers run the firm's day-to-day operations and typically have various types of authority to bind the firm, including:

D. Express authority, derived from:

1. Articles of incorporation;

2. By-laws;

3. Directors' resolutions;

4. Statutes.

E. Implied authority, derived by virtue of their offices—The general trend is to find broad authority inherent in the offices of CEO, CFO, etc., but in questionable situations the other party may always demand a board of directors resolution to provide proof of express authority, and of course even top officers would not have authority to bind the corporation in truly extraordinary transactions, such as mergers, sales of major corporate assets, and borrowing unusually large sums of money.

F. Ratification—Even if an officer acts without either express or implied authority, the board of directors could always bind the corporation by ratifying the contracts.

III. Limited Liability Companies (LLCs)

A. The operating agreement should indicate whether the LLC will be member-managed or manager-managed. Absent provision to the contrary, an LLC is assumed to be member-managed.

B. If member-managed, an LLC will operate much like a general partnership:

1. Each member has equal rights in management;

2. Ordinary business issues are decided by majority vote;

3. Acts outside the ordinary course of business require unanimous approval; and

4. The operating agreement may be amended only with the consent of all members.

C. If manager-managed, an LLC will operate much like a limited partnership, with the managers assuming the role of a general partner:

1. Except as otherwise provided in RULLCA, matters related to the activities of the company will be exclusively decided by the managers;

2. Managers have equal rights in the management and conduct of the firm;

3. Issues arising in the ordinary course of business are decided by a majority vote of the managers;

4. The consent of all managers is required to engage in extraordinary transactions, such as the sale of all or substantially all firm property, approval of a merger, or amendment of the operating agreement.

5. Managers may be removed at any time, with or without cause, by a majority vote of the members.

D. Whereas partnership law generally provides for "statutory apparent authority," indicating that a partnership will generally be bound whenever a general partner acts to carry on the business of the partnership in the usual way, RULLCA provides to the contrary—that "a member is not an agent of the limited liability company solely by reason of being a member." An LLC may be manager-managed, so "statutory apparent authority," which still exists in several individual states' LLC statutes, has been eliminated in RULLCA.

E. The vast majority of interactions between LLCs and third parties will involve LLC employees; general agency law will govern these transactions, and no surprises should occur.

F. An LLC, like a general partnership, may (but need not) file a statement of authority with the state that will expressly spell out the managerial authority of its managers (whether or not they are also members).

Federal Taxation

Introduction to Tax Review

I. **Federal Taxation Content**—The AICPA provides a brief listing of the subject areas that are considered for inclusion in the tax portion of the Uniform CPA exam.

> **Note:**
> *The lesson outline that is shown in Section B below has 53 tax lessons.*

A. AICPA outline—The AICPA provides an outline of the tax contents (and their approximate weights) for the REG portion of the exam. The formatting shown for this outline is as shown in the AICPA content specifications.

III. **Federal Tax Process, Procedures, Accounting, and Planning (11%–15%)**

A. Federal Tax Legislative Process

B. Federal Tax Procedures

   1. Due dates and related extensions of time

   2. Internal Revenue Service (IRS) audit and appeals process

   3. Judicial process

   4. Required disclosure of tax return positions

   5. Substantiation requirements

   6. Penalties

   7. Statute of limitations

C. Accounting Periods

D. Accounting Methods

   1. Recognition of revenues and expenses under cash, accrual, or other permitted methods

   2. Inventory valuation methods, including uniform capitalization rules

   3. Accounting for long-term contracts

   4. Installment sales

E. Tax Return Elections, Including Federal Status Elections, Alternative Treatment Elections, or Other Types of Elections Applicable to an Individual or Entity's Tax Return (throughout applicable material)

F. Tax Planning

   1. Alternative treatments

   2. Projections of tax consequences

   3. Implications of different business entities

   4. Impact of proposed tax audit adjustments

   5. Impact of estimated tax payment rules on planning

   6. Role of taxes in decision-making

G. Impact of Multijurisdictional Tax Issues on Federal Taxation (Including Consideration of Local, State, and Multinational Tax Issues)

H. Tax Research and Communication

   1. Authoritative hierarchy

   2. Communications with or on behalf of clients

IV. Federal Taxation of Property Transactions (12%–16%)

    A. Types of Assets

    B. Basis and Holding Periods of Assets

    C. Cost Recovery (Depreciation, Depletion, and Amortization)

    D. Taxable and Nontaxable Sales and Exchanges

    E. Amount and Character of Gains and Losses, and Netting Process

    F. Related Party Transactions

    G. Estate and Gift Taxation

        1. Transfers subject to the gift tax

        2. Annual exclusion and gift tax deductions

        3. Determination of taxable estate

        4. Marital deduction

        5. Unified credit

V. Federal Taxation of Individuals (13%–19%)

    A. Gross Income

        1. Inclusions and exclusions

        2. Characterization of income

    B. Reporting of Items from Pass-Through Entities

    C. Adjustments and Deductions to Arrive at Taxable Income

    D. Passive Activity Losses

    E. Loss Limitations

    F. Taxation of Retirement Plan Benefits

    G. Filing Status and Exemptions

    H. Tax Computations and Credits

    I. Alternative Minimum Tax

VI. Federal Taxation of Entities (18%–24%)

    A. Similarities and Distinctions in Tax Treatment Among Business Entities

        1. Formation

        2. Operation

        3. Distributions

        4. Liquidation

    B. Differences Between Tax and Financial Accounting

        1. Reconciliation of book income to taxable income

        2. Disclosures under Schedule M-3

    C. Corporations (Lessons 26–34)

        1. Determination of taxable income/loss

        2. Tax computations and credits, including alternative minimum tax

3. Net operating losses

4. Entity/owner transactions, including contributions and distributions

5. Earnings and profits

6. Consolidated returns

D. S Corporations

1. Eligibility and election

2. Determination of ordinary income/loss and separately stated items

3. Basis of shareholder's interest

4. Entity/owner transactions, including contributions and distributions

5. Built-in gains tax

E. Partnerships

1. Determination of ordinary income/loss and separately stated items

2. Basis of partner's/member's interest and basis of assets contributed to the partnership

3. Partnership and partner elections

4. Transactions between a partner and the partnership

5. Treatment of partnership liabilities

6. Distribution of partnership assets

7. Ownership changes and liquidation and termination of partnership

F. Trusts and Estates

1. Types of trusts

2. Income and deductions

3. Determination of beneficiary's share of taxable income

G. Tax-Exempt Organizations

1. Types of organizations

2. Obtaining and maintaining tax-exempt status

3. Unrelated business income

II. Course Structure—To facilitate preparation for the exam, the review materials are divided into the following sections and lessons:

Introduction

Introduction To Tax Review

Property Transactions

Sales and Dispositions of Assets

Capital Gains and Losses

Section 1231 Assets

Sections 1231 Assets—Cost Recovery

Like-Kind Exchanges and Involuntary Conversions

Other Nonrecognition Transactions

Income

Gross Income—Concepts, Interest, and Dividends

Gross Income—Other Inclusions

Gross Income—Exclusions

Accounting Methods and Periods

Taxation of Employee Benefits

Taxation of Retirement Plans

Deductions

Deductions—Basic Principles

Deductions for AGI

Itemized Deductions—Medical, Taxes, Interest

Itemized Deductions—Other

Employee Business Expenses

Deductions—Losses and Bad Debts

Limitations on Business Deductions

Individual Tax Issues

Personal and Dependency Exemptions

Filing Status

Alternative Minimum Tax and Other Taxes

Tax Credits

Personal Tax Credits

Business Tax Credits

Corporate Taxation

Formation of a Corporation

Corporate Income

Special Corporate Deductions

Corporate Alternative Minimum Tax

Penalty Taxes

Taxation of Related Corporations

Distributions from a Corporation

Corporate Redemptions and Liquidations

Corporate Reorganizations

Multijurisdictional Tax Issues

State and Local Taxation

Taxation of Foreign Income

Tax-Exempt Entities

Tax-Exempt Organizations

Partnership Taxation

Formation and Basis

Flow-Through of Income and Losses

Transactions with Partners

Distributions

Sales and Terminations

S Corporation Taxation

Eligibility, Election, Termination

Income and Basis

Distributions and Special Taxes

Estate and Gift Taxation

Federal Gift Tax

Federal Estate Tax

Fiduciary Taxation

Income Taxation of Fiduciaries

Tax Research and Practice

Sources of Tax Authority Research

Tax Practice and Procedure

Compliance Responsibilities

Other Tax Issues

Tax Planning

Business Entity Choice

III. **Exam Preparation**—The AICPA provides a brief outline of the skills candidates should possess for the exam.

    A. AICPA indicated tasks—In addition to demonstrating knowledge and understanding of these topics, candidates are required to demonstrate the skills required to apply that knowledge in providing tax preparation and advisory services and performing other responsibilities as certified public accountants. To demonstrate such knowledge and skills, candidates will be expected to perform the following tasks:

        1. Evaluate the tax implications of different legal structures for business entities.

        2. Apply analytical reasoning tools to assess how taxes affect economic decisions related to the timing of income/expense recognition and property transactions.

        3. Consider the impact of multijurisdictional tax issues on federal taxes.

        4. Identify the differences between tax and financial accounting.

        5. Analyze information and identify data relevant for tax purposes.

        6. Identify issues, elections, and alternative tax treatments.

7. Research issues and alternative tax treatments.

8. Formulate conclusions.

9. Prepare documentation to support conclusions and tax positions.

10. Research relevant professional literature.

B. AICPA-recommended publications—The AICPA recommends that candidates study the following publications:

1. Internal Revenue Code of 1986, as amended, and Regulations

2. Treasury Department Circular 230

3. Other administrative pronouncements

4. Case law

5. Public Law 86-272

6. Uniform Division of Income for Tax Purposes Act (UDITPA)

7. Current federal tax textbooks

C. Advice for preparation

1. Use review materials strategically.

> **Note:**
> *I am certain that a thorough examination of the Internal Revenue Code and Regulations will prepare a candidate for the exam. Unfortunately, most of us have other things to do over the next 20 years. The CPAexcel® materials are designed to help you focus on the tax issues that we feel are most likely to be tested on the exam since you will not have time to review the publications listed here.*

a. Use review material to organize preparation for thorough coverage.

b. The review materials can be used to briefly review familiar topics (refresh the memory) or focus on new material.

c. Use review problems and questions as a mechanism for calibrating study efforts.

d. Watch the multimedia portions of the review course, then read all text materials, and finally complete all problems.

2. Keep the ultimate objective in mind—To pass the exam. Study topics strategically.

a. Tax topics constitute only 60% of the REG portion of the exam. Integrate the study of taxation with an overall strategy on the REG. This strategy minimizes the risk that a poor score on one topic will cause a failure on this portion of the exam.

Example:
A risky strategy is to ignore a topic because of a relatively strong understanding of other topics in the same part of the exam. This strategy is risky because the topical coverage is approximate and it may be difficult to score high enough in one topic to offset a poor score in another topic.

b. The initial time invested in understanding new topics may have a higher payoff than additional time invested in perfecting comprehension in other topics.

Example:
If individual taxation is relatively clear, but corporate taxation is confusing, a good strategy would be to concentrate on corporate topics. A relatively superficial understanding of corporate topics could result in immediate gains because some of the questions on corporate topics are likely to be relatively easy.

D. Preparation for tax questions

1. No essay questions will be given on the tax portion of the exam.

a. Tax questions are objective and will likely have unambiguous answers. Hence, the questions will probably avoid uncertain interpretations of the law.

Example:
The determination of whether an activity qualifies as "hobby" is quite uncertain because this determination is based on numerous factors. Hence, objective questions are unlikely to ask about the determination of hobby status.

b. "Nitpicking" questions are likely because details are unambiguous.

Example:
While the determination of hobby status is uncertain, the hobby loss presumption is unambiguous. A profit in three of five consecutive years results in the presumption that an activity is not a hobby. Hence, a question is more likely to be asked about this detail rather than the more ambiguous determination of hobby status.

2. How much detail should be studied?—There are over 2,000 pages in the Internal Revenue Code, so it is difficult to say. A few suggestions follow:

a. The scope of the exam is limited to the law in effect as of six months before the beginning of the testing period in which you take the exam. More recent changes should be ignored.

b. Besides changes in the law, the tax code is replete with transition rules (temporary rules existing until a change in the law becomes permanent). Questions about temporary changes are unlikely, but questions about phase-in rules are possible.

  i. Note that in recent years many new tax provisions have been passed that are intended to be in effect for only one or two years. Only the temporary changes that are the most important have been included. However, note that the likelihood that these provisions will be tested is not as high as for other material due to their temporary status.

c. A focus on specific numbers is also unlikely because there are too many specific numbers in the law and many are indexed to change each year. Any figure that is indexed to inflation does not have to be memorized. These figures are included in the materials so you will be aware of them, but generally include a date after the number to indicate the year for that particular number (e.g., exemption amount is $4,000 (2015)).

  i. Examples of important phase-out amounts that are not indexed for inflation are:

    1. Contributions to Coverdell Savings Accounts (*Taxation of Retirement Plans*): Contributions to a Coverdell Education Savings Account are limited to $2,000 per beneficiary, per year. The contribution is phased out proportionately if the taxpayer's AGI exceeds $190,000 for married filing jointly (a $30,000 range) or $95,000 for single taxpayers (a $15,000 range).

    2. $25,000 Loss Deduction for Rental Real Estate (*Limitations on Business Deductions*): The exception is phased out for taxpayers with an AGI over $100,000 at the rate of 50% ($1 of deduction for each $2 of AGI over $100,000).

    3. Child Tax Credit (*Personal Tax Credits*): The credit is phased out for married taxpayers with AGI in excess of $110,000 ($75,000 for unmarried). The credit is reduced $50 for each $1,000 (or portion) over the trigger AGI amount.

    4. American Opportunity Tax Credit (*Personal Tax Credits*): The credit is phased out ratably for single taxpayers with AGI in excess of $80,000 ($160,000 in the case of a joint return). The credit is phased out over a $10,000 range ($20,000 for joint return) and, thus, is completely gone when AGI reaches $90,000 ($180,000 joint return).

3. Remember to work as many problems as you can. Do not just read the problems and then read the solutions. On the exam you will have to WORK the problems, and the best way to improve on that skill is to work, work, work as many problems as you can.

4. The most important tax forms that you should be familiar with are included in the videos and in the appropriate lessons. You do not need to memorize anything other than the form/schedule number and the general type of information reported on the form. You may be given a short portion of a form to complete. If so, input the information requested on each line of the form based on the tax law you learned in the lessons.

IV. Test-Taking Tips

A. Educated guesses are a critical part of an exam strategy. An "educated" guess is made by eliminating all incorrect alternatives and then using general concepts (or principles) to select between the remaining alternatives.

> **Example:**
> A question several years ago asked if a taxpayer is entitled to deduct jury pay that the taxpayer had to give to his employer because the employer paid the employee during the time the employee spent on a jury. There is an obscure provision that covers this situation, but who would have studied it (given its obscurity)? An educated guess would be a deduction for adjusted gross income because the employee must include the jury pay in income, but should not be taxed on it because he or she was forced to remit it to his or her employer. An itemized deduction would have not been fair because the limits placed on these deductions might have caused the employee to be taxed on the jury pay.

B. Should you anticipate specific topics (e.g., new provisions)? With the exception of a few disclosed questions, the exams have been closed since 1996. The questions on disclosed exams indicate that exams do not stress new provisions, perhaps because of the ambiguity involved with the application of new law.

C. The AICPA examines the validity of proposed questions by including "trial" questions on the exam. These questions are not scored, but they are interspersed with actual test questions. Hence, an inability to answer some tax questions should not be cause for concern—these questions could be trial questions.

D. Advice for exam performance

1. Stay cool and do not be hasty.

2. Budget your time.

3. Eliminate alternatives.

4. Use your common sense.

5. Think positively and be confident.

Sales and Dispositions of Assets

After studying this lesson, you should be able to:

1. Classify an asset as ordinary, capital, or Section 1231.

2. Compute the realized gain/loss from a property transaction.

3. Apply the basis rules for gifts and compute the gain/loss from the sale of gifted assets.

4. Determine the proper tax basis for assets converted from personal use to business use.

I. **Categories of Assets**—Assets can be divided into three mutually exclusive categories: ordinary, Section 1231, and capital.

   A. Ordinary assets

   1. Inventory and accounts/notes receivables are ordinary assets.

   2. Depreciable property used in a trade/business and realty that have been owned for a year or less are ordinary assets.

   3. Generally, copyrights and musical, artistic, and literary works are ordinary assets if held by the person who created the work. A composer can elect to have his or her musical work treated as a capital asset.

   B. Section 1231 assets—Depreciable property used in a trade/business and realty that have been owned for more than one year are Section 1231 assets.

   C. Capital assets

   1. Capital assets do not include the items listed above as ordinary and Section 1231 assets.

   2. Most other types of property, including property held for investment use and personal use, are capital assets. Goodwill of a corporation is also a capital asset.

II. **Sales and Dispositions**

   A. **A realized gain or loss** must be computed any time there is a sale or disposition of property.

   1. The term **sale or disposition** includes sales, exchanges, trade-ins, casualties, condemnations, thefts, and retirements.

   2. Realized gain or loss is computed as follows:

   > Amount realized
   > – Adjusted basis
   > Realized gain/Loss

   B. Computing amount realized is a four-step process:

   1. Cash received;

   2. Fair market value of any property and services received;

   3. Liabilities assumed by the buyer;

   4. Less selling expenses.

   C. Adjusted basis—This equals the cost or other acquisition basis of the property,

   1. Plus capital improvements,

   2. Minus depreciation, amortization, and depletion.

   3. Cost includes any liabilities or expenses connected with the acquisition.

D. A **recognized gain/loss** is the amount of realized gain/loss that is included in the taxable income of the taxpayer.

III. Special Basis Issue

A. Basis Issues for Gifts

1. If property is gifted to a taxpayer, the donee's basis is:

   a. **Gain basis** = adjusted basis of the donor.

   b. **Loss basis** = lower of:

      i. Fair market value (FMV) at date of gift, or

      ii. Adjusted basis of the donor.

   c. **Depreciable basis** = gain basis.

   d. The basis is **increased** for the portion of any **gift tax paid** by the donor due to appreciation in the property:

$$\text{Adjustment to basis} = \frac{\text{Unrealized appreciation}}{(\text{FMV at date of gift} - \text{Annual exclusion})} \times \text{Gift tax paid}$$

> **Note:**
> Not all realized gains/losses will be recognized. If not recognized, they are either excluded or deferred. The recognized gain/loss will never exceed the realized gain/loss. Assume that all realized gains/losses are recognized unless you are aware of a tax law that provides otherwise.

B. Tax effects of basis for gifts

1. A **gain** is recognized only if the donee sells property for more than the gain basis.

2. A **loss** is recognized only if the donee sells property for less than the loss basis.

3. If the property is sold by the donee for an amount in-between the gain and loss basis, **no gain or loss is recognized**.

> **Note:**
> Only losses of sales from investment and business assets are deductible. Hence, while personal assets are capital assets, losses of these assets are not deductible.

> **Note:**
> The gain and loss basis differs only when the FMV of the property is less than its basis. The law allows a built-in gain to be transferred to another individual, but does **not** allow a transfer of a built-in loss.

Example:
TP receives a used auto from his father as a gift. The father bought the auto for $10,000 several years ago and the auto is worth $15,000 at the time of the gift. TP will take his father's basis ($10,000) in the auto.

If the father had a basis of $20,000 in the auto, in TP's hands the auto would have a gain basis of $20,000 and a loss basis of $15,000. Loss can only be recognized to the extent that the auto is sold for less than $15,000. Gain can only be recognized to the extent that the auto is sold for more than $20,000. If the automobile is sold for an amount between $15,000 and $20,000, no gain or loss is recognized.

C. Holding period of gifted property

1. If the **gain basis** is used to compute realized gain or loss, the holding period of the property for the donee **includes the holding period of the donor**.

2. If the **loss basis** is used, the holding period of the donee **begins on the date of the gift**.

D. Inheritances—Basis and holding period

1. The basis of property acquired from a decedent is the fair market value at the date of death, or the FMV on the alternate valuation date (six months after the date of death) if that date is selected by the executor as the valuation date.

2. Holding period is deemed to be long-term.

> **Note:**
> These rules prevent a nondeductible personal loss from being converted into a business loss.

E. Property converted from personal to investment/business use

Gain basis = Adjusted basis.
Loss basis and depreciable basis = Lower of 1) adjusted basis, or 2) FMV at date of conversion.

Capital Gains and Losses

After studying this lesson, you should be able to:

1. Distinguish between long-term and short-term gains and losses.

2. Identify collectibles and be able to apply their special capital gain rules.

3. Net capital gains and losses in the proper order.

4. Summarize the differences in the capital gain/loss rules for individuals and corporations.

Tax Forms for this Lesson: Form 8949, Form 1040 Schedule D (available for download and printing from the lesson overview of your software).

I. Eligibility—Only a "sale or disposition" of a "capital" asset is eligible for capital gains netting.

Definition:
Capital Assets: Include all assets except inventory, accounts receivable, depreciable assets and realty used in a business, creative works (in the hands of the creator), or certain miscellaneous assets (such as government publications or obligations). Self- created musical works are treated as capital assets even though these are creative works.

    A. Investment assets and personal use assets are capital assets. Common capital assets include stocks, bonds, real estate, and goodwill of a corporation.

II. Long-Term versus Short-Term—Each capital gain and loss is classified according to whether the asset is long-term or short-term.

    A. Long-term assets are those held over one year.

    B. Definition—The holding period begins and ends on the date title passes. The holding period for stocks and securities acquired by purchase begins on the trade date that the stock or security was acquired, and ends on the trade date on which the stock or security was sold or exchanged.

    C. For transactions where the basis of a new asset is determined by the basis of an old asset, the holding period of the old asset "tacks" onto the holding period of the new asset.

Example:
TP's pickup was destroyed in a storm and he replaced it with a similar pickup. If TP elected to defer the gain as an involuntary conversion, then the holding period of the old pickup will tack onto the holding period for the new pickup.

    D. There are automatic holding periods for nonbusiness bad debts (short-term) and inheritances (long-term).

    E. If a taxpayer has short-term capital gains **distributions**, from a mutual fund, these are reported and taxed as ordinary income. That is, these are not included in the netting process described below—they are always taxed as ordinary income.

III. Netting Process—Individuals and Corporations—The first step of the netting process is to net all short-term capital gains and losses, and net all long-term capital gains and losses.

Definitions:
Net Short-Term Gain or Loss: Is the accumulation of all short-term capital gains and all deductible short-term losses.

Net Long-Term Gain or Loss: Is the accumulation of all long-term capital gains and all deductible long-term losses.

IV. Rules for Individuals

A. If the combination of net short-term and net long-term gains and losses is negative, then individuals can deduct this **net capital loss** up to $3,000 per year. The deduction is for AGI and is limited to taxable income.

    1. Any excess capital loss for an individual can be carried forward, indefinitely, but cannot be carried back. Short-term capital losses are used first, and then long-term capital losses.

    2. If an individual dies with unused capital losses, these cannot be transferred to his estate (but can be used in the year of death subject to regular limitations).

B. The losses that are subject to the carryforward retain their character as short-term or long-term in future years. Long-term capital losses that have been carried forward offset capital gains in the following order:

> **1.** Capital gains taxed at 28%
>
> **2.** Capital gains taxed at 25%
>
> **3.** Capital gains taxed at 20% (or 15% for some taxpayers)

> **Definition:**
> *Net Capital Loss:* Occurs if a net loss results from combining net short-term gains and losses with net long-term gains and losses.

> **Example:**
> This year TP realized a net short-term gain of $2,000 and a net long-term loss of $3,000. TP can deduct a net capital loss of $1,000 for AGI.

C. If the combination of net short-term and net long-term gains and losses results in long-term capital gain, then this is labeled "net capital gain." If the combination results in short-term capital gain this is taxed as ordinary income.

D. **Net capital gain** is the portion of capital gain net income (if any) that is eligible for a reduced tax rate.

See the following example.

> **Example:**
> This year TP realized a net short-term gain of $5,000 and a net long-term loss of $3,000. TP's capital gain net income of $2,000 is comprised of net short-term gains and, accordingly, is taxed at the regular income tax rates. There is no net capital gain in this instance to tax at preferential rates.

E. Note that even though qualified dividend income is taxed at the same tax rate as long-term capital gain, the dividend income is not included in the netting process for capital gains and losses.

V. Individuals—Preferential Tax Rates—The special tax treatment accorded a net capital gain for individual taxpayers is a lower tax rate.

A. The tax calculation is done by computing the regular tax on income without the net capital gain plus the preferential tax rate times the net capital gain.

B. The preferential tax rate depends on the composition of the net long-term gain.

1. Net capital gain is taxed at a **maximum** rate of 20% for taxpayers whose ordinary income is taxed at the 39.6% rate. If the taxpayers regular tax rate is 15% or lower, then the maximum tax rate on long-term capital gains is 0%. For all other taxpayers the rate is 15%.

> **Note:**
> The 39.6% rate was added in 2013. In 2013 it applied for taxable income greater than $450,000 if married filing jointly, $425,000 if head of household, and $400,000 if single. These brackets are indexed for inflation in 2014 and beyond.

2. 3.8% net investment income tax

   a. A 3.8% net investment income tax applies to taxpayers whose modified AGI exceeds $250,000 if married filing jointly and $200,000 if single or head of household. The 3.8% tax applies to the lesser of (a) net investment income, or (b) the excess of AGI over the AGI thresholds. Capital gains are included in net investment income, so the highest tax rate on regular capital gains is 23.8% (20% + 3.8%). These thresholds are not indexed for inflation.

   b. Net investment income (NII) includes income from:

      i. Interest, dividends, annuities, and royalties, unless such income is derived from a trade/business activity;

      ii. Other passive income; and

      iii. Gain from the sale of assets generating such income.

Example:
A single filer has active income of $160,000 and net investment income (NII) of $100,000. The 3.8% tax will be paid on $60,000 of income. The excess of AGI ($260,000) over the AGI threshold ($200,000) is $60,000 versus the NII of $100,000. Because the tax applies to the lesser of these two amounts, it will be 3.8% of $60,000, or $2,280.

3. Net capital gain attributable to straight-line depreciation claimed on real estate is taxed at a maximum rate of 25%.

4. Net capital gain from "collectibles" is taxed at a maximum rate of 28%.

> **Note:**
> Unless provided otherwise, assume throughout this course that the 15% rate applies to capital gains rather than higher rates.

Definition:
Collectible: A tangible personalty such as coins, art, and antiques purchased for investment purposes. Gold and silver are also classified as collectibles subject to the 28% rate.

Example:
In 2015, TP has a 25% marginal tax rate on regular taxable income. He realized the following gains:

$9,000 gain on the sale of art held five years.

$20,000 gain on the sale of securities held 15 months.

$15,000 gain on the sale of securities held three years.

$7,000 gain on the sale of long-term rental realty attributable to depreciation.

The $9,000 gain is taxed at a maximum of 28%, while the $15,000 and the $20,000 gains are taxed at a maximum of 15%. The $7,000 gain is taxed at a maximum rate of 25%.

C. Special rules exist for netting losses against various categories of long-term gains.

   1. Capital losses offset capital gains in the following order:

1. Capital gains taxed at 28%

2. Capital gains taxed at 25%

3. Capital gains taxed at 20%/15%

See the following summary.

Summary of Preferential Long-Term Capital Gain Rates (Individuals)

Ordinary Income Rate	Regular LTCG Rate	Maximum Rate for 25% Gain	Maximum Rate for Collectible Gain	Could 3.8% NII Tax Apply?
10%	0%	10%	10%	No
15%	0%	15%	15%	No
25%	15%	25%	25%	No
28%	15%	25%	28%	Possibly
33%	15%	25%	28%	Likely
35%	15%	25%	28%	Yes
39.6%	20%	15%	28%	Yes

Note: The preferential rates are the maximum rates that will be applied to a source of income. If the ordinary income rate for the taxpayer is less than the preferential rate, then the ordinary rate is used to tax the long-term capital gain.

D. Tax Computation

1. The tax on net long-term capital gains is computed after the non-long-term capital gain potion of taxable income has been taxed.

2. As shown in the chart above, each net long-term capital component is taxed at the lower of the regular tax marginal rate or the capital gains rate that applies to that component.

Example:

TP has the following income:

Gain from stock sale taxed at maximum of 15%	$12,000
Ordinary income	$20,000

The $20,000 is taxed first using the individual tax table. The $12,000 net capital gain is then taxed. Note that the $20,000 of ordinary income places the taxpayer in the 15% tax bracket, so the net capital gain is taxed at 0%.

If TP had $60,000 of ordinary income, which would place him in the 25% bracket, the net capital gain would be taxed at 15%.

See the following examples.

Example:

1. In 2015, TP has a net short-term capital loss of $20,000. He has also realized a net long-term gain of $50,000 that comprises the following net gains and losses:

$10,000 gain on the sale of coins held three years.

$25,000 gain on the sale of securities held three years.

$15,000 gain on the sale of realty (attributable to depreciation).

TP has a net capital gain of $30,000. The short-term capital loss first offsets the gain on the collectibles, and then offsets $10,000 of the gain attributable to depreciation. Hence, the net capital gain of $30,000 comprises a $5,000 gain taxed at 25% (the realty) and a $25,000 gain taxed at a maximum rate of 15%.

2. In 2015, TP has a net long-term gain of $20,000 comprised of the following capital gains and losses:

$5,000 loss on the sale of coins held three years.

$15,000 gain on the sale of securities held three years.

$10,000 gain on the sale of realty (attributable to depreciation) held four years.

The long-term capital loss from the collectibles first offsets part of the long-term gain attributable to depreciation. Hence, the net long-term gain of $20,000 comprises $5,000 gain taxed at 25% (the realty) and a $15,000 gain taxed at a maximum rate of 15%.

E. Special situations—Some special rules exist for certain capital gains and losses.

1. For gains and losses incurred by partnerships and S corporations, the determination of the maximum tax rate is made at the entity level.

2. Special rules apply for preferred stock issued by financial institutions and sold to the federal government as part of the economic stabilization process. Gain from the sale of this specific type of preferred stock is treated as ordinary income.

3. Qualifying small business stock

   a. Gains from the sale of qualifying small business stock by noncorporate taxpayers are eligible for a 50% exclusion (2014). The remaining gain is taxed at a maximum rate of 28%. Thus, the average tax rate on the entire gain is 14%.

   b. **Qualifying small business stock** is stock of a small business corporation (less than $50 million in capital) held for more than five years.

   Study Tip:
   Note that the date of purchase of the stock, not the date of sale, determines whether the 50%, 75%, or 100% exclusion will potentially apply in the future.

   c. The maximum gain eligible for the exclusion is the lower or greater of 10 times the taxpayer's basis in the stock or $10 million in aggregate.

   d. The exclusion percentage was higher than 50% for the following time periods:

      i. 100%—after September 27, 2010 and before January 1, 2015. At the time of this writing Congress has not extended this provision to 2015.

      ii. 75%—after February 17, 2009 and before September 28, 2010.

Example:

ABC corporation, a qualified small business corporation, issued 100 shares of stock to TP for $20,000 on March 1, 2009. On September 25 of 2015, TP sold the stock for $300,000 and realized a gain of $280,000. Since the stock was held for more than five years the gain is eligible for this special treatment. The gain eligible for the exclusion cannot exceed the greater of $200,000 (10 times TP's basis) or $10 million. Hence, 75% of the qualifying gain of $280,000 is excluded from income, or $210,000. The remaining $70,000 of the excluded gain is taxed at 28%.

4. Section 1244 Stock

    a. Special rules also apply for Section 1244 stock sold by individuals. Gains from the sale of Section 1244 stock are treated as regular long-term capital gains, but losses are treated as ordinary losses (maximum characterized as ordinary is $100,000 for married filing jointly and $50,000 for others).

    b. Section 1244 stock is stock of a domestic small business corporation meaning that the capital receipts of the corporation do not exceed $1,000,000 at the time the stock is issued. Also, at least 50% of the corporation's gross receipts have to be generated from sources other than investment income during the previous five tax years.

    c. Additionally, the seller of the stock had to be the original holder of the stock for Section 1244 to apply.

F. If a nondealer, noncorporate taxpayer subdivides real property into at least two lots for resale, the gain from the sale of the lots will be treated as capital gain as long as the taxpayer had held the property for at least five years and no substantial improvement had been made to the lots by the taxpayer. All gain on the first five lots sold will be capital gain. For all lots sold over five, 5% of the selling price will be treated as ordinary income.

G. Options—Special rules apply, if a taxpayer incurs a loss on an option which he holds to buy or sell property due to the lapse of the option:

    1. If the optioned property would have been a capital asset in the taxpayer's hands, the loss is a capital loss.

    2. If the optioned property would be a Section 1231 asset in the taxpayer's hands, the capital gain/ordinary loss rules for Section 1231 assets applies.

    3. If the optioned property would have been an ordinary asset in the taxpayer's hands, the loss is an ordinary loss.

VI. Rules for Corporations

A. Corporations use the same netting process but can only use a "net capital loss" to offset capital gain net income. That is, no deduction is allowed if the net capital loss exceeds net capital gains.

B. However, the loss can be used in other tax years. Net capital losses are carried over as short-term capital losses, and these losses are carried back three years and forward five years.

C. For corporations, all capital gains, both short-term and long-term, are taxed at the regular ordinary income rates. Corporations do not have a preferential tax rate for long-term capital gains.

Example:
This year ABC Corporation began operations and realized taxable income of $36,000. ABC also recognized the following gains and losses.

Short-term capital gains	$8,500
Short-term capital losses	($4,500)
Long-term capital gains	$1,500
Long-term capital losses	($3,500)

Question: What is ABC corporation's taxable income?

Answer: ABC is taxed on $38,000, which comprises ordinary income of $36,000 and $2,000 of short-term capital gains. Net short-term capital gains are $4,000 and net long-term capital losses are ($2,000). These are netted again to produce the $2,000 short-term capital gains.

VII. Information on Sales of Capital Assets

A. Proceeds from the sale of stocks facilitated by a broker are reported to the taxpayer on Form 1099-B. The form includes the date of sale and acquisition, sales price, basis, and tax withheld.

B. Sales of real estate, including a principal residence, are reported to the taxpayer on Form 1099-S.

C. Sales of capital assets are reported on Form 8949 and the totals are then transferred to Form 1040 Schedule D.

    1. Capital gains and losses are reported by the taxpayer on Schedule D.

    2. Short-term capital gains and losses are reported in Part II and long-term gains and losses in Part III. Capital loss carryforwards are also included.

    3. Note that capital gain distributions from mutual funds (reported on Form 1099-DIV) are reported as long-term gains on Schedule D. If a mutual fund distributes short-term capital gain, that is shown as dividend income on Form 1099-DIV.

    4. Part III works through the netting process of capital gains and losses.

Section 1231 Assets

Tax Form for this Lesson: Form 4797 (available for download and printing from the lesson overview of your software).

I. Section 1231—Section 1231 is designed to provide capital gain treatment to a net gain generated from transactions involving involuntary conversions and the disposition of business assets.

    A. The scope of section 1231 is determined by the nature of the asset and the type of disposition.

        1. Section 1231 applies to the sale or exchange of "section 1231" assets.

Definition:
Section 1231 Assets: Assets used in a business and held for over 12 months (long- term). Section 1231 assets include realty and depreciable property but exclude capital assets, inventory, accounts receivable, copyrights, and government publications.

        2. Section 1231 also applies to all involuntary conversions of business assets.

    B. Recapture—*First stage of netting is recharacterization of a portion of gains attributed to accumulated depreciation (called recapture of depreciation).*

        1. Recapture of depreciation reduces the amount of gains eligible for Section 1231 treatment by **recharacterizing** the gain as ordinary income. There are two types of recapture: Section 1245 and Section 1250.

        2. "Section 1245 recapture" recharacterizes gains on **personalty as ordinary income** to the extent of accumulated depreciation.

        3. "Section 1250 recapture" is recapture of accumulated accelerated depreciation on buildings in excess of straight-line depreciation as **ordinary income**.

        4. For buildings owned by individuals "unrecaptured Section 1250 gains" recharacterizes gains on realty as eligible for a special (25%) tax rate to the extent of accumulated straight-line depreciation.

Definitions:
Section 1245 Recapture: Refers to depreciable personalty (assets other than buildings).

Section 1250 Recapture: Applies to depreciable real estate (buildings).

          a. Shortcuts

             i. Recapture does not recharacterize losses.

             ii. Gains on the sale of land held long-term in a business are always 1231 gains since land is not depreciable.

    iii. Gains on the sale of business personalty held long-term are ordinary income, unless sold for an amount greater than the original purchase price.

    iv. Gains on the sale of buildings held long-term in a business are 1231 gains but will be taxed as ordinary to the extent of accelerated depreciation in excess of straight-line with the straight-line depreciation being taxed at a 25% rate.

Example:

1. Section 1245 Recapture, all gain is ordinary—TP sells a machine held long-term with an original cost of $10 and accumulated depreciation of $7. If the machine is sold for $5, then TP will have a realized gain of $2 (TP's adjusted basis is $3). TP would characterize this gain as ordinary to the extent of accumulated depreciation. Hence, the entire gain is taxed as ordinary income.

2. Section 1245 Recapture, appreciation in asset taxed as Section 1231 gain:—TP sells a machine held long-term in the trade with an original cost of $10 and accumulated depreciation of $7. If the machine is sold for $14, then TP will have a realized gain of $11. TP would characterize this gain as ordinary to the extent of accumulated depreciation ($7). Hence, $7 of gain will be taxed as ordinary income and the remaining $4 of gain will be Section 1231 gain.

3. Section 1250 Recapture and 25% Rate—TP sells a building held long-term in the trade with an original cost of $100 and accumulated depreciation of $45. If the building is sold for $120, then TP will have a realized gain of $65 (TP's adjusted basis is $55). This gain would be taxed as a Section 1231 gain, but $45 of the gain would be taxed at a rate of 25% (assuming all depreciation is straight-line depreciation) whereas the remaining $20 of gain would be eligible for a rate of 15% (0% for lower bracket taxpayers).

---

    5. Recapture for corporations

        a. For Section 1245 property (personalty), the rules for a corporation are the same as for an individual.

        b. For Section 1250 property (buildings) for corporations, the accumulated depreciation claimed in excess of straight-line depreciation is subject to being recaptured as ordinary income.

        c. Section 291 recapture also applies to corporations. Section 291 depreciation recapture applies only to buildings, and is computed as follows:

	Section 1245 recapture IF the property had been Section 1245 property
Less:	The actual Section 1250 recapture
	Excess amount × 20%
	Section 291 recapture

    6. Recapture computation for Partnerships and S Corporations is the same as for individuals.

C. Netting —All Section 1231 gains and Section 1231 losses are netted.

    1. To the extent that Section 1231 gains exceed section 1231 losses, the net gain is treated as a long-term capital gain.

    2. If Section 1231 losses exceed section 1231 gains, the loss is deductible as an ordinary loss (subject to a lookback limit during the previous five years).

    3. The lookback provision states that the net Section 1231 gains must be offset by net Section 1231 losses from the five preceding tax years that have not previously been recaptured. To the extent of these losses, the net Section 1231 gain is treated as ordinary income.

Example:

Taxpayer Z has net Section 1231 gain of $20,000 in 2015. In 2014 she had net Section 1231 gain of $10,000 and net section 1231 loss of $25,000 in 2013. In 2014, the $10,000 gain is taxed as ordinary income since there were Section 1231 losses of $25,000 in the previous year. In 2015, $15,000 of the gain is taxed as ordinary income and the remaining $5,000 is taxed as Section 1231 gain. The Section 1231 loss of $25,000 in 2013 was recaptured in 2014 ($10,000) and 2015 ($15,000).

II. Sales Reporting—Sales of business property, including depreciation recapture, are reported on Form 4797, *Sales of Business Property*.

Section 1231 Assets—Cost Recovery

After studying this lesson, you should be able to:

1. Differentiate between realty and personalty.

2. Utilize the MACRS depreciation rules for realty including the mid-month convention.

3. Apply the MACRS depreciation rules to personalty including the half-year and mid-quarter convention.

4. Compute Section 179 expense for qualifying assets.

5. Identify listed assets and applicable limitations for computing depreciation.

6. Calculate amortization for intangible assets.

Tax Form for this Lesson: Form 4562 (available for download and printing from the lesson overview of your software). MACRS Tables are available at the end of this lesson.

I. **Depreciation**—Depreciation deductions are allowed for assets used to produce income, but the deductions must be calculated using cost recovery rules.

   A. Cost recovery rules—Cost recovery is computed under a uniform method using the class life period (MACRS). The IRS provides tables (MACRS Tables) that show the percentage of the asset's cost basis that can be depreciated each year, based on the asset's classification.

   1. Only business property and income-producing property (e.g., rental real estate) is depreciable. Property used for personal purposes and investment assets are not depreciable.

Example:
TP invests in a large stock portfolio. She has a computer that is used solely for managing her stock portfolio. While the stocks that she owns are not depreciable since they are investment assets, the computer can be depreciated to offset any income from the investment activity.

   2. 200% declining balance or 150% declining balance is used for personalty; straight-line is used for realty.

      a. Definitions—**Realty** is land and other assets affixed thereto (buildings). **Personalty** is any tangible asset that can be moved (not fixed to land).

   3. Recovery for personalty is computed as though assets are purchased at midyear (midyear convention), while recovery for realty uses a mid-month convention. For personalty, depreciation is allowed for half of the year in which it is purchased, regardless of when it is purchased. For realty, depreciation is allowed for half of the month in which it is purchased, regardless of the date it is purchased during the month.

Example:
TP purchased machinery and a building on August 4, 2015. The machinery will be depreciated for 6 months in 2014 and the building will be depreciated for 4.5 months (.5 for August and 4 for September through December).

      a. In the year of purchase, these conventions are already incorporated into the percentages provided in the MACRS tables so no adjustment is necessary to the numbers from the tables.

   4. While there are numerous class lives for personalty, some of the more common are three years (race horses), five years (automobiles, trucks, computers and peripheral equipment, copiers, other office equipment; most assets used in professional services and in retail; appliances and furniture used in rental real estate), and seven years (office furniture and fixtures; agricultural

and other machinery). A 200% declining balance method is used for these classes. Land improvements are included in the 15-year class and are depreciated using the 150% declining balance method.

5. Residential realty (apartments, houses, duplexes, etc.) is depreciated over a 27.5-year straight-line. Nonresidential realty is depreciated over a 39-year straight-line.

6. A disposition of the asset follows the appropriate midyear or mid-month convention. Note that for the year of sale these adjustments are not included in the MACRS tables because it is not known in what year the asset will be sold. Thus, the numbers from the tables must be adjusted as described above.

Example:
TP sells machinery and a building on March 3, 2015. The machinery is eligible for 50% of the depreciation that would have been permitted if the asset had not been sold. For the realty the taxpayer is allowed 2.5 months depreciation (2 for January–February and .5 for March) for 2015.

---

7. Bonus depreciation

    a. At the time of this writing Congress has not extended bonus depreciation to 2015. Bonus depreciation of 50% was allowed for new qualifying property placed in service in 2014.

    b. Note, that for applicable years, bonus depreciation applied unless the taxpayer elected not to do so. Qualifying property was new tangible property with a recovery period of less than or equal to 20 years, computer software, and certain leasehold improvements.

    c. A taxpayer could elect not to use bonus depreciation for a class of property (in which case the election applied to the whole class). The bonus depreciation was allowed for both regular and AMT purposes. No AMT depreciation adjustment was required for any property that uses bonus depreciation.

8. A mid-quarter convention is used for all new personalty (instead of the midyear convention) if more than 40% of personalty acquired during the year is purchased in the last quarter of the year. One-half quarter depreciation is allowed for the quarter the asset is purchased and one-half quarter for the quarter the asset is sold.

Example:
On August 1 of this year TP purchased and placed into service an office building costing $264,000 including $30,000 for the land.

Question: What is TP's MACRS deduction for the office building?

Answer: $234,000 is straight-line depreciated over 39 years, but TP is only entitled to 4.5 months (note that a half month is allowed for August using the mid-month convention) this year. Hence, the cost recovery is $2,250 this year.

B. Section 179 election—There is a Section 179 election to expense a limited amount of tangible **personalty** if used in a trade activity. Note that Section 179 expensing is taken into account before bonus depreciation for years that permitted bonus depreciation. Off-the-shelf computer software also qualifies under Section 179 (Congress has not extended this provision to 2014 at the time of this writing).

    1. The maximum amount expensed in any year is limited to the lesser of business income or $500,000 for 2014. For 2015 this amount is reduced to $25,000 (Congress could increase this for 2015 but has not done so at the time of this writing.)

    2. The Section 179 expense cannot exceed the income from the business, reduced for all expenses except Section 179. Any election to expense in excess of the business income limit is carried forward (indefinitely) and used in a year when income is sufficient.

3. The Section 179 election is phased out (dollar for dollar) if qualified assets purchased exceed $2,000,000 for 2014. For 2015 this amount is reduced to $200,000 (Congress could increase this for 2015 but has not done so at the time of this writing.)

4. A carryforward is not allowed if the Section 179 deduction is reduced due to the excess purchase provision.

5. The taxpayer can revoke the Section 179 election in later years as long as the return is still eligible to be amended.

6. If property for which Section 179 has been collected is converted to nonbusiness use, the Section 179 and MACRS deductions claimed in excess of what would have been allowed if Section 179 had not been elected must be recaptured as income.

Example:
1. TP purchased $2,040,000 (2014) of tangible assets for use in his trade. The Section 179 limit of $500,000 is reduced by $40,000 ($2,040,000 − $2,000,000) to $460,000. There is no carryforward of the amount that is phased out.

2. TP, a self-employed taxpayer, had business income of $15,000 in 2014 prior to deductions associated with cost recovery. This year TP purchased equipment for $25,000.

Question: What is TP's deduction under the election to expense the cost of the machinery?

Answer: TP can elect to expense $25,000, but the deduction is limited to the business income of $15,000. The remaining $10,000 can be carried forward indefinitely and expensed in future years when there is sufficient business income.

3. TP, a self-employed taxpayer, purchased equipment in 2015 for $210,000.

Question: What portion of the cost may TP elect to treat as an expense rather than as a capital expenditure?

Answer: Since $210,000 exceeds the $200,000 trigger by $10,000, the overall limit of $25,000 is reduced to $15,000 ($25,000 − $10,000).

C. Alternatives to MACRS—The taxpayer can elect several alternatives to MACRS.

1. Straight-line can be used for personalty over the MACRS life of the asset. The same MACRS lives and conventions are retained for this method.

2. The alternative depreciation system (ADS) provides for straight-line (for tangible personal property straight-line or 150% declining balance can be used) over an extended life. ADS straight-line must be used for computing earnings and profits, and for listed property not used more than 50% for business purposes.

D. Luxury auto limits—Autos are subject to an annual ceiling on recovery.

1. Special rules limit the amount of depreciation that can be claimed on a passenger automobile (GVW of 6,000 pounds or less). However, these limits are adjusted annually for inflation, so the exact dollar limits do not need to be memorized for the exam. For 2015, first-year depreciation is limited to $3,160 ($3,460 for trucks and vans). For 2014, if bonus depreciated was elected these amounts were increased by $8,000 to $11,160 ($11,460).

2. Trucks, vans, and SUVs (and any other vehicle) that weigh more than 6,000 pounds are exempt from the luxury automobile rule. However, for these heavier vehicles, the Section 179 election is limited to $25,000 (assuming 100% business use). Regular MACRS rules apply for the remaining basis.

3. Note, that the limits mentioned above assume 100% business/investment use (applies to Section 179 also). For mixed-use autos, the limit is multiplied by the percentage of business/investment use.

4. Similar restrictions apply to vehicles leased for business use.

Example:
A taxpayer can claim first year cost recovery of $3,160 (2015) for an auto costing $30,000. However, if the taxpayer uses the auto 30% of the time for personal purposes, then the taxpayer can only claim recovery of $2,212 ($3,160 × 70%).

E. Listed property—Must pass business use test.

Definition:
Listed Property: Includes assets, such as computers and vehicles, that are commonly used for both business and personal purposes. Cell phones are not included as listed property.

1. To use regular MACRS rules, the business use of listed assets must exceed 50% of total use.

2. For purposes of this test, business use is limited to use in the trade/business or for the convenience of the employer. That is, investment use is not considered for meeting the 50% test.

3. Failure to meet the business use test means cost recovery is limited to straight-line (ADS). However, both the business and investment use of the asset may be depreciated. ADS depreciation must be used for the entire depreciable life of the asset, even if the 50% test is met in future years. Additionally, if the 50% test is failed in the current year but accelerated depreciation had been taken in previous years, the excess depreciation from prior years must be recaptured.

   See the following example.

Example:
In Year 1 and Year 2 a computer is used 60% for business use. In Year 3 the business use percentage is 45% and investment use is 12%. For Year 3, ADS straight-line depreciation must be used because the 50% test has been failed, but 57% of the asset's basis can be depreciated. Excess depreciation over straight-line from Years 1 and 2 must be recaptured in Year 3. Additionally, the asset must be depreciated using ADS for the remainder of its depreciable life.

Example:
Comprehensive Example: A new five-year asset is purchased in March 2014 for $650,000. This is the only asset purchased by this calendar year company in 2014. The property is eligible for both bonus depreciation and Section 179 expensing. Note: Section 179 expensing is taken into account before bonus depreciation. Cost recovery is computed as follows:

Section 179 expense	$500,000	
Remaining basis	$150,000	($650,000 − $500,000)
Bonus %	× 50%	
Bonus depreciation	$ 75,000	
Remaining basis	$ 75,000	($650,000 − $500,000 − $75,000)
MACRS %	× 20%	
MACRS expense	$ 15,000	

Total Depreciation:

Section 179	$500,000
Bonus	75,000
MACRS	15,000
	$590,000

II. Amortization and Depletion

A. Depletion—Natural resources are subject to straight-line depletion.

B. Amortization rules

    1. Intangible assets that are **acquired, not created**, can be amortized on a straight-line basis over a **15-year period** beginning with the month in which they are acquired.

    2. Examples include **goodwill**, going concern value, information bases, know-how, government licenses and permits, **franchises, trademarks**, etc.

    3. Other assets (covenants not to compete, computer software, film, sound recordings, video tapes, patents, and copyrights) qualify if acquired in connection with the acquisition of a trade or business.

C. Organization and start-up expenses

    1. Expenses incurred in connection with the **organization of a corporation**.

    2. $5,000 of these expenses may be deducted, but the $5,000 is reduced by the amount of expenditures incurred that exceed $50,000. Expenses not deducted must be **capitalized and amortized** over **180 months** (unless an election is made not to do so), beginning with the month that the corporation begins its business operations. Election must be filed with first corporate tax return.

    3. Same rules apply **for start-up costs**. Start-up costs are expenditures that would be deductible except that the corporation has not yet started its trade or business operation.

    4. **Typical organizational expenses** are legal services incident to organization, accounting services, organizational meetings of directors and shareholders, and fees paid to incorporate. They must be incurred before the end of the taxable year when the business begins (but they do not have to be paid, even if on a cash basis).

    5. Costs of issuing and selling stock (**syndication expenses**) must also be capitalized, but cannot be amortized.

III. Reporting—Depreciation and Amortization are reported on Form 4562, *Depreciation and Amortization*.

See the following MACRS tables.

MACRS Tables

Table 1. General Depreciation System

Applicable Depreciation Method: 200 Percent Declining Balance Switching to Straight Line Applicable Recovery Periods: 3, 5, 7 years Applicable Convention: Half-year

If the Recovery Year is:	3-year	5-year	7-year
		and the Recovery Period is:	
		the Depreciation Rate is:	
1	33.33	20.00	14.29
2	44.45	32.00	24.49
3	14.81	19.20	17.49
4	7.41	11.52	12.49
5		11.52	8.93

6		5.76	8.92
7			8.93
8			4.46

Table 2. General Depreciation System

Applicable Depreciation Method: 200 Percent

Declining Balance Switching to Straight Line

Applicable Recovery Periods: 3, 5, 7 years

Applicable Convention: Mid-quarter (property placed in service in first quarter)

If the		and the Recovery Period is:	
Recovery	3-year	5-year	7-year
Year is:		the Depreciation Rate is:	
1	58.33	35.00	25.00
2	27.78	26.00	21.43
3	12.35	15.60	15.31
4	1.54	11.01	10.93
5		11.01	8.75
6		1.38	8.74
7			8.75
8			1.09

Table 3. General Depreciation System

Applicable Depreciation Method: 200 Percent

Declining Balance Switching to Straight Line

Applicable Recovery Periods: 3, 5, 7 years

Applicable Convention: Mid-quarter (property placed in service in second quarter)

If the		and the Recovery Period is	
Recovery	3-year	5-year	7-year
Year is:		the Depreciation Rate is:	
1	41.67	25.00	17.85
2	38.89	30.00	23.47
3	14.14	18.00	16.76
4	5.30	11.37	11.97
5		11.37	8.87
6		4.26	8.87

7		8.87
8		3.33

Table 5. General Depreciation System

Applicable Depreciation Method: 200 Percent

Declining Balance Switching to Straight Line

Applicable Recovery Periods: 3, 5, 7 years

Applicable Convention: Mid-quarter (property placed in service in fourth quarter)

If the		and the Recovery Period is:	
Recovery	3-year	5-year	7-year
Year is:		the Depreciation Rate is:	
1	8.33	5.00	3.57
2	61.11	38.00	27.55
3	20.37	22.80	19.68
4	10.19	13.68	14.06
5		10.94	10.04
6		9.58	8.73
7			8.73
8			7.64

Table 6. General Depreciation System

Applicable Depreciation Method: Straight Line
Applicable Recovery Period: 27.5 years Applicable
Convention: Mid-month

If the Recovery Year is:	And the Month in the First Recovery Year the Property is Placed in Service is:											
	1	2	3	4	5	6	7	8	9	10	11	12
	the Depreciation Rate is:											
1	3.485	3.182	2.879	2.576	2.273	1.970	1.667	1.364	1.061	0.758	0.455	0.152
2	3.636	3.636	3.636	3.636	3.636	3.636	3.636	3.636	3.636	3.636	3.636	3.636
3	3.636	3.636	3.636	3.636	3.636	3.636	3.636	3.636	3.636	3.636	3.636	3.636
4	3.636	3.636	3.636	3.636	3.636	3.636	3.636	3.636	3.636	3.636	3.636	3.636
5	3.636	3.636	3.636	3.636	3.636	3.636	3.636	3.636	3.636	3.636	3.636	3.636
6	3.636	3.636	3.636	3.636	3.636	3.636	3.636	3.636	3.636	3.636	3.636	3.636
7	3.636	3.636	3.636	3.636	3.636	3.636	3.636	3.636	3.636	3.636	3.636	3.636
8	3.636	3.636	3.636	3.636	3.636	3.636	3.636	3.636	3.636	3.636	3.636	3.636

9	3.636	3.636	3.636	3.636	3.636	3.636	3.636	3.636	3.636	3.636	3.636	3.636
10	3.637	3.637	3.637	3.637	3.637	3.637	3.636	3.636	3.636	3.636	3.636	3.636
11	3.636	3.636	3.636	3.636	3.636	3.636	3.637	3.637	3.637	3.637	3.637	3.637
12	3.637	3.637	3.637	3.637	3.637	3.637	3.636	3.636	3.636	3.636	3.636	3.636
13	3.636	3.636	3.636	3.636	3.636	3.636	3.637	3.637	3.637	3.637	3.637	3.637
14	3.637	3.637	3.637	3.637	3.637	3.637	3.636	3.636	3.636	3.636	3.636	3.636
15	3.636	3.636	3.636	3.636	3.636	3.636	3.637	3.637	3.637	3.637	3.637	3.637
16	3.637	3.637	3.637	3.637	3.637	3.637	3.636	3.636	3.636	3.636	3.636	3.636
17	3.636	3.636	3.636	3.636	3.636	3.636	3.637	3.637	3.637	3.637	3.637	3.637
18	3.637	3.637	3.637	3.637	3.637	3.637	3.636	3.636	3.636	3.636	3.636	3.636
19	3.636	3.636	3.636	3.636	3.636	3.636	3.637	3.637	3.637	3.637	3.637	3.637
20	3.637	3.637	3.637	3.637	3.637	3.637	3.636	3.636	3.636	3.636	3.636	3.636
21	3.636	3.636	3.636	3.636	3.636	3.636	3.637	3.637	3.637	3.637	3.637	3.637
22	3.637	3.637	3.637	3.637	3.637	3.637	3.636	3.636	3.636	3.636	3.636	3.636
23	3.636	3.636	3.636	3.636	3.636	3.636	3.637	3.637	3.637	3.637	3.637	3.637
24	3.637	3.637	3.673	3.637	3.637	3.637	3.636	3.636	3.636	3.636	3.636	3.636
25	3.636	3.636	3.636	3.636	3.636	3.636	3.637	3.637	3.637	3.637	3.637	3.637
26	3.637	3.637	3.637	3.637	3.637	3.637	3.636	3.636	3.633	3.636	3.636	3.636
27	3.636	3.636	3.636	3.636	3.636	3.636	3.637	3.637	3.637	3.637	3.637	3.637
28	1.970	2.273	2.576	2.879	3.182	3.485	3.636	3.636	3.636	3.636	3.636	3.636
29	0.000	0.000	0.000	0.000	0.000	0.000	0.152	0.455	0.758	1.061	1.364	1.667

Like-Kind Exchanges and Involuntary Conversions

Two common areas for which gains and losses may not be recognized are like-kind exchanges and involuntary conversions.

After studying this lesson, you should be able to:

1. Assess whether an exchange qualifies as a like-kind exchange.

2. Compute the deferred gain/loss for a like-kind exchange.

3. Determine how the receipt of boot affects the recognition of gain from an exchange.

4. Evaluate the tax basis of the asset received in the exchange.

5. Appraise whether an event qualifies as an involuntary conversion.

6. Compute the recognized gain/loss from an involuntary conversion.

7. Calculate the basis in the new asset that replaced the converted asset.

Tax Form for this Lesson: Form 8824 (available for download and printing from the lesson overview of your software).

I. **Like-Kind Exchanges**

A. Overview—The deferral provision for direct (like-kind) exchanges is an example of deferral provisions governing transactions for which significant economic changes have not occurred for the taxpayer due to the transaction. In a classic direct exchange, the taxpayer simply exchanges one asset for another, like-kind asset. **Losses are never recognized** from a like-kind exchange. **Recognized gain is the lesser of:**

   1. Realized gain; or

   2. Boot received.

B. Rules are **mandatory**, not elective.

C. Qualifying property—Qualifying property must be exchanged.

   1. Only business and investment property qualifies for deferral.

Definitions:

Business Property: Any property used in a business or held for investment. In contrast, property held for other reasons is referred to as personal-use or "personal" property.

Realty: Land and any property attached thereto (i.e., buildings).

Personalty: Tangible property that is not realty.

 Example:
An apartment building is realty, but a truck is personalty.

---

   2. Exchanges of inventory and receivables do not qualify for deferral.

   3. The property received in the exchange must be "like-kind" property.

Definition:
Like-kind property: This property has the same general character as the property given up.

---

    a. In general, all realty is considered like-kind. So, the exchange of land for an office building is like-kind.

    b. Personalty is divided into broad asset classes, and assets must be within the same class to be like-kind. Examples of asset classes are office furniture, fixtures, and equipment; computer equipment; automobiles; and light-duty trucks. However, an exchange of real property for personalty is NEVER considered like-kind.

    c. Business property can be exchanged for investment property.

Example:
An exchange of a pickup truck for a dump truck may qualify as a like-kind exchange. However, an exchange of an apartment building for a barge cannot be like-kind, because it is an exchange of realty for personalty.

    d. Property located outside the United States will not qualify as like-kind when exchanged for property located inside the United States.

    e. There are special rules that apply to like-kind exchanges when like-kind property is acquired from related taxpayers.

  D. Holding period—Holding period of like-kind property surrendered tacks on to the holding period of like-kind property received.

II. Like-Kind Exchanges and the Receipt of Boot—The receipt of boot triggers gain recognition.

Definition:
Boot: Nonqualifying property received by the taxpayer.

  A. Cash and nonqualifying (not like-kind) property are considered boot.

  B. Note: Mortgage relief is treated as boot received if the taxpayer's mortgage that is assumed is greater than the mortgage that the taxpayer assumes on the new property he or she is receiving. However, if the taxpayer assumes a larger mortgage than he or she gives up, this excess reduces his amount realized, but it does not reduce other boot received.

Example:
TP transfers whiteacre to B in exchange for blackacre. If whiteacre is subject to a mortgage of $100 but blackacre is only subject to a mortgage of $80, then B will have assumed $20 more liabilities than TP. This excess liability will be treated as boot received by TP.

    1. Boot does **not** cause realized losses to be recognized.

    2. The basis of like-kind property received can be computed as follows:

FMV of property received
– Postponed gain
+ Postponed loss
Basis of like-kind property

      a. Basis of non-like-kind property received is the property's FMV, since gain has been recognized to that extent.

Example:

Question: Leker exchanged a van that was used exclusively for business and had an adjusted tax basis of $20,000 for a new van. The new van had an FMV of $10,000, and Leker also received $3,000 in cash. What was Leker's tax basis in the acquired van?

Answer: Leker has a realized loss on this exchange of $7,000 ($13,000 amount realized—$20,000 adjusted basis). He received $3,000 of boot, but boot does not cause realized losses to be recognized. Therefore, the recognized loss is zero and the postponed loss is $7,000. Leker's basis in the acquired van is its FMV ($10,000) plus the postponed loss ($7,000), or $17,000.

III. Involuntary Conversions

A. Overview—The involuntary conversion of property resulting in a realized gain is eligible for deferral.

Exam Tip:
Note, that while the deferral rules for like-kind exchanges are **mandatory**, the rules for involuntary conversions are **elective**. Also, gains and losses are deferred under the like-kind exchange rules, while only gains are deferred for involuntary conversions.

1. This deferral provision does not apply to losses.

2. The deferral provision governing involuntary conversions applies when a gain is generated because an asset is destroyed, stolen, or condemned.

3. Taxpayers may elect to defer gains if the proceeds from the conversion are reinvested in similar property within a reasonable period of time. Hence, after reinvesting in similar property, the taxpayer has no wherewithal to pay the tax, and in addition, no disposition of substance has occurred.

4. Eligible for deferral

   a. Definition of involuntary conversion.

Definitions:
Involuntary Conversion: The result of a casualty (an unexpected, unavoidable outside influence like a storm, fire, or shipwreck), a theft, or a condemnation.

Condemnation: A taking by the government. An imminent threat of condemnation is considered sufficient to trigger an involuntary conversion.

   b. Gains from conversion of any kind of property are eligible for deferral (not just business property; personal use property qualifies also).

Note:
Gains are eligible for deferral because of an involuntary conversion, but losses are recognized (e.g., not postponed).

5. Defer gain—If the taxpayer replaces the converted property with similar property, he or she may elect to defer gain from the transaction.

   a. Replacement property

      i. The replacement property must be similar or related in the service or use made by the taxpayer.

Definition:
The phrase "similar or related in the service or use" means the end use of the replacement property must be similar to the use of the converted property. The determination of whether replacement property qualifies is similar to the process for determining if property qualifies as like-kind. However, this test is generally narrower than the like-kind test, because the properties must also have similar end uses.

    b. Replacement time period

        i. The replacement must be made within two years from the END of the tax year in which the gain is realized.

        ii. The replacement period is extended to three years if the conversion was a condemnation of business realty. The replacement period can also be extended with IRS permission, or if the area of the conversion is declared a disaster area.

    c. Excess proceeds over replacement cost causes recognition of gains.

Amount realized from conversion

– Adjusted basis of old property

========================

Realized gain/loss

========================

Amount realized from conversion

– Cost of replacement property

========================

Recognized gain, limited to realized gain

========================

---

    d. Adjusted basis

        i. The adjusted basis of the new property is its cost reduced by any deferred gain.

Example:
TP's pickup was destroyed in a storm. The pickup has an adjusted basis of $2,000, and TP received $4,500 in insurance proceeds. Thus, TP realized a gain of $2,500 from the conversion of the pickup. If TP only spends $4,300 on a similar pickup within the replacement period, then TP will recognize $200 of gain (the amount of proceeds that were not reinvested). The adjusted basis of the new pickup will be $2,000 ($4,300–$2,300).

  B. Holding period—Holding period of the converted property carries over to the qualified replacement property.

Other Nonrecognition Transactions

This lesson covers several areas for which recognized gains or losses are either excluded or deferred.

After studying this lesson, you should be able to:

1. Determine when and how the wash sale rules defer the recognition of losses.

2. Define related parties and apply the loss disallowance rules.

3. Use the ownership and usage tests to determine who is eligible to exclude gains from the sale of a principal residence.

4. Compute the recognized gain/loss from the sale of a principal residence.

5. Calculate the gain recognized each year from an installment sale obligation.

Tax Forms for this Lesson: Form 6252 (available for download and printing from the lesson overview of your software).

I. Other Loss Disallowances

A. Overview—There are three common provisions that mandate deferral of losses because of opportunities to manipulate taxes. The first, wash sales, are losses from the sales of securities that often occur near year-end. The second provision governs losses from the sale of business/investment property to related parties. In both cases, there is an attempt to recognize a loss without giving up control of the underlying asset. The third area relates to short sales of assets.

B. Wash sales—Losses from the sale of securities are not recognized if similar securities are purchased within 30 days of the sale.

Definition:
A wash sale: A sale that results from the purchase of "substantially identical" stock or securities within a 30-day window around the sale date.

---

1. The taxpayer takes an adjusted basis in the new securities equal to the cost plus the deferred loss from the wash sale.

2. Holding period of the new stock or securities includes the holding period of the old stock or securities.

See the following example.

> **Note:**
> Note that the wash sale rules apply only to losses, not to gains.

Example:
TP sold 100 shares of XYZ stock on December 22 for $1,200. The stock had an adjusted basis of $2,000, and TP realized a loss of $800. If TP purchased 100 shares of XYZ on January 15 of the next year for $1,400, the loss on the December 22 sale would be deferred as a wash sale. The stock held by TP would have a basis of $2,200 ($1,400 plus $800).

> **Note:**
> The "repurchase" of a security can occur either before or after sale of the original security—the 30-day period is a window centered on the sale date. The repurchase period is 61 days, the day of sale plus 30 days before and after this day.

C. Losse—related parties

1. Losses from sales of business/investment property to related parties are not recognized.

Definition:
A related party: for purposes of loss deduction, includes family members—brother, sister, spouse, ancestors, and descendants, and controlled entities (corporations where the taxpayer owns more than 50% of the stock; partnerships where a partner owns more than 50% of the partnership's capital). In addition, beneficiaries of estates and trusts can also be treated as related parties.

2. Deferred losses create a "right of offset" which can be used to reduce a gain upon the ultimate sale of the property to an unrelated taxpayer. However, the right of offset cannot create a loss, nor make a loss greater.

3. Holding period—of the original buyer does not include the holding period of the seller; it begins on the date of purchase of property from a related party.

Note:
In-laws are not considered related parties, although they are eligible to be claimed as dependents; nor are aunts and uncles related parties.

 Example:
TP sold stock to S, his brother, for $1,000. TP had an adjusted basis in the stock of $2,500, but cannot deduct the realized loss of $1,500 because S is a related party. S takes a basis in the stock of $1,000. If S eventually sells the stock to an unrelated third party for $1,800, S can offset the $800 gain with $800 of the deferred loss. The remainder of the deferred loss ($700) is not recognized.

D. Short sale

1. A "short sale" of appreciated stock held by the taxpayer is treated as constructive sale on the date of the short sale.

Note:
The related party rules are not applicable to the sale of personal use property because these losses are not deductible under any circumstances. The only time a loss on personal use property is deductible is if the disposition qualifies as a personal casualty.

Definition:
A short sale: (also called "selling short against the box") A transaction where the taxpayer borrows and sells shares identical to those already owned. This transaction has the effect of eliminating the taxpayer's risk of loss and opportunity for gain potential.

2. The short sale rule causes taxpayers to recognize gains on any short sales even if the sale was not closed through the purchase of additional stock or the delivery of shares previously owned. This rule is referred to as "marking to market," because the gain is measured by the value of the shares at the end of the year.

3. The short sale rule also requires taxpayers to defer losses. Losses are deferred until the short position is actually closed.

II. Sale of Principal Residence

A. Overview—The law provides for an exclusion of gains from a principal residence once every two years.

1. A single taxpayer may exclude realized gains up to $250,000 if the **ownership and use tests** are met.

2. Married couples filing jointly can exclude up to $500,000 on the sale of a residence if:

   a. Either—The taxpayer or spouse meets the **ownership test**.

   b. Both—The taxpayer and spouse meet the **use test**.

   c. For single and married taxpayers, during the two-year period ending on the date of the sale, neither the taxpayer nor spouse excluded gain from the sale of another home (**frequency limit**).

> **Example:**
> TP, a single taxpayer, sold his residence. He had an adjusted basis in the residence of $55,000 and received $415,000 on the sale before commissions. If TP paid sales commissions of $10,000, then he realized a gain of $350,000 on the sale. TP may be eligible to exclude $250,000 of the gain. The remaining gain ($100,000) would be taxed as a capital gain.

    d. Any depreciation taken must be recaptured on the sale (e.g., the gain attributed to the portion of the home depreciated as an office). As long as the business portion is not a separate building, the gain does not need to be allocated between the business and personal portions of the residence.

    e. If the sale occurs not later than two years after the death of a spouse, the surviving spouse may exclude $500,000 of gain. Note, that the rules in "a" and "b" must have been met at the date of death of the deceased spouse for this provision to apply.

> **Example:**
> TP has owned and occupied his residence for the past seven years. In January of this year, TP married S who moved into TP's residence. Immediately prior to the marriage, S sold her residence and excluded the gain. In June, TP and S sold TP's residence. TP qualifies for the exclusion, but S violates the frequency test. Nonetheless, TP can elect to exclude $250,000 of gain on the sale.

    f. The exclusion will not apply to the extent that the property was not used as a principal residence during a portion of the five-year testing period. For example, if during the five-year window the property is rented as a vacation home for two years and then used as a residence for three years, 40% of the gain (two years/five years) cannot be excluded from income. This limitation does not apply if the nonqualified use occurs *after* the home was used as a principal residence.

B. Ownership and use tests

    1. The residence must be owned and used by the taxpayer as a principal residence for at least two of the preceding five years (ownership and use tests).

        a. The amount of time need not be continuous (e.g., ownership and use must only total 730 days during the previous five years).

        b. Short or temporary absences (e.g., vacations) are ignored and use is imputed for taxpayers who are institutionalized (e.g., unable to care for themselves). Additionally, an individual can suspend the running of the five-year test period if serving in the uniformed services, Foreign Service, Peace Corps, or intelligence community.

        c. For married taxpayers, either spouse can meet the ownership test, but both must meet the use test. If only one spouse meets the use test, then that spouse can only claim a $250,000 exclusion.

> **Example:**
> TP has owned and occupied his residence for the past five years. In January of this year, TP married S who moved into TP's residence. In June, TP sold his residence. TP qualifies for the ownership and use test, but S violates the use test. Hence, TP can elect to exclude a maximum of $250,000 of gain on the sale.

C. Other unforeseen circumstances

    1. If a residence is sold prematurely due to changes in employment or health (or other unforeseen circumstances such as a natural disaster, multiple births, or change in wedding plans), then the **maximum** amount of the exclusion is prorated based upon the number of qualifying months (ownership or use) divided by two years (or the equivalent in months or days). The qualifying months are the lesser of the number of ownership/use months or the number of months since the last sale.

> **Example:**
> TP has owned and occupied his residence for the past 18 months. TP was transferred across the country and subsequently sold his residence for a gain of $200,000. TP does not qualify for the exclusion because he has not owned and occupied his residence for two years. Nonetheless, because of the change in employment TP can elect to exclude up to 75% (18/24) of the maximum ($250,000) from the sale. In this situation, TP can exclude $187,500 of the gain ($12,500 will be a taxable gain).

D. Note that the 3.8% tax on net investment income can apply to gain from the sale of a principal residence, but this is unusual since any capital gain up to $250,000 (single) or $500,000 (married) is excluded from taxation if the primary residence is sold. Overall, this means that this tax will not apply to most taxpayers who sell their homes. However, if taxpayers sell their primary home, and the income threshold is met, and capital gains exceed $250,000 for individuals or $500,000 for married couples, the excess realized gain is taxed at 3.8%. A home sale may also result in a capital gain that increases a taxpayer's AGI for purposes of calculating the limits noted above.

> **Example:**
> Mary and Joe have a combined salary of $300,000. They sell their house for $1.4 million, earning a capital gain of $900,000. Their AGI is $300,000 plus $400,000 ($900,000 capital gain minus the $500,000 exclusion) for a total of $700,000. Their AGI exceeds the $250,000 threshold by $450,000. Their net investment income is $400,000 ($900,000 − $500,000 exclusion). The lower of the net investment income or excess AGI is $400,000. The additional tax on net investment income is: $400,000 × 3.8% = $15,200.

III. Installment Sales

A. Overview—The deferral of gains through installment sale is the traditional example of a deferral provision motivated by equitable considerations. The installment sale deferral automatically defers gains (not losses) when payment is made in later periods. Although taxpayers can elect to recognize gains currently, the installment sale treatment prorates the gain recognition according to the proportion of cash received in each year. A sale where one payment is deferred into a future year is eligible for installment treatment.

   1. Taxpayers who are dealers cannot use installment method for sales of inventory.

   2. Even if the installments method is elected all depreciation recapture must be recognized in year one (the year of sale).

B. Recognition of deferred gain—Recognition of deferred gain is triggered by receipt of cash.

   1. A "gross profit percentage" is multiplied by the cash received to determine the gain recognized.

> **Definition:**
> *Gross profit percentage*: The ratio of gain to be recognized to contract price (the total cash to be received).

   2. Gross profit = Sales price less basis of asset sold

      a. Recognized income = Cash collected × (Gross profit/contract price)

      b. Contract price is generally equal to the cash to be received from the sale.

> **Example:**
> TP sells his car (AB=$3) for $12 to be paid in the future. TP expects to receive $2 next year, $4 in the second year, and $6 in the third year (plus interest). Because TP has a realized gain of $9 and a contract price of $12, TP will have a gross profit percentage of 75%. Hence, he will be taxed on a gain of $1.5 next year, $3 in the second year, and $4.5 in the third year. In addition, the interest payments will be taxed as interest income.

   C. Installment obligation

       1. A disposition of the installment obligation will trigger recognition of the deferred gain. The entire gain will be recognized immediately if the installment note is sold or otherwise encumbered.

       2. The installment obligation (note receivable) must have a market interest rate or else a portion of the gain will be treated as imputed interest.

Gross Income—Concepts, Interests, and Dividends

After studying this lesson, you should be able to:

1. Use judicial doctrines to determine income for applicable transactions.

2. Assess the tax effects of interest bearing financial instruments.

3. Compute the tax consequences of the receipt of dividends.

Tax Form for this Lesson: Form 1040 Schedule B (available for download and printing from the lesson overview of your software).

I. General Rules

   A. In general, income is broadly defined, so any realized increases in wealth should be assumed to be included in income unless the tax law provides for a specific exclusion or deferral.

   B. Taxable income differs from accounting income. The purposes of these sets of rules are different so do not confuse them.

   C. Income is not limited to cash receipts. Bartering can also produce income, as can the receipt of property or services in return for services rendered. Bartering is the exchange of property or services. The fair market value of the property or services received must be included in income.

   D. If a taxpayer unexpectedly finds property that she can legally keep, this has increased her net worth and the fair market value of the property is included in her income.

II. Judicial Concepts—The courts have constructed several special rules to address income recognition in unusual circumstances.

   A. Constructive receipt—Constructive receipt requires a *cash basis taxpayer to include the value of property in income in the period in which the right to (or control of) the property is acquired*. The income is not constructively received if substantial restrictions exist on the taxpayer's use of the funds. For example, if the taxpayer would have to forfeit future bonuses to receive the funds then a substantial restriction exists.

   Example:
   TP received a check on December 28 for services this year. He must recognize the income because he has control over the property (the check).

   B. Tax benefit rule—The tax benefit rule requires a taxpayer to include an expense reimbursement in income if the expense was deducted in a prior period and the deduction reduced the taxpayer's taxable income.

   Example:
   TP deducted a $200 business expense last year, but because of limitations the deduction only reduced his taxable income by $120. This year a client reimbursed $150 of the original expense. TP must include $120 of the reimbursement in his income this year.

   C. Claim of right doctrine—The claim of right rule requires the taxpayer to include property in income in the period in which an apparent claim to the property materializes.

      1. A later repayment of the property (because the claim was not valid) generates a deduction, but does not influence the earlier recognition of the income.

Example:
Last year TP was paid a $100 bonus, but this year TP's employer discovered an error and required TP to repay $90 of the bonus. TP should include the $100 bonus in his income last year and claim a $90 deduction for the repayment this year.

D. Assignment of income doctrine—Income is taxed to the individual who earns the income, even if the taxpayer directs that the funds be paid to someone else. Income cannot be assigned for tax purposes to someone other than the party that earned it.

III. Interest Income—

A. General rules

1. Interest is included in income when received (cash basis) or accrued (accrual basis).

2. Common sources of taxable interest that individuals often have are:

   a. United States Treasury notes and bonds

   b. Federal and state tax refunds

   c. Mortgages

3. Special imputed interest rules apply to obligations purchased at a discount or a premium.

4. Prepaid interest income is always taxed when received.

B. Bond premiums—Premiums occur when the amount paid for the bond is more than its face value.

1. If a taxpayer buys a taxable bond at a premium:

   a. An election can be made to amortize the premium.

   b. The amortization reduces the basis of the bond.

   c. The amortization offsets the interest income from the bond.

   d. The amortized bond premium is computed using the constant yield to maturity method.

2. For tax exempt bonds, taxpayers must amortize premiums, but no deduction is available.

C. Bond discounts—Discounts occur when the amount paid for the bond is less than its face value. This difference is known as the discount but basically represents interest income that should be recognized in the future.

1. Individuals amortize bond discounts (as interest income).

2. Original issue discounts must be amortized using the effective interest rate method.

Definition:
Original issue discount: A loan made that requires a payment at maturity exceeding the amount of the original loan. This additional payment is a discount and constitutes interest. These obligations are often non-interest bearing.

Example:
TP purchased a zero coupon (non-interest bearing) obligation for $8,000. It will mature at $10,000 in five years. The $2,000 difference is not a capital gain, but is interest income that must be recognized.

D. Short-term discounts—These are taxed at maturity as ordinary income for cash basis taxpayers. They are reported as earned for accrual basis taxpayers.

1. A short-term obligation has a maturity of one year or less.

2. This rule also applies to original issue discounts for short-term government bonds.

3. In order to defer recognition of the discount, the interest cannot be withdrawn or made available without penalty.

E. Series EE bonds—Interest on Series EE bonds is not paid annually but when the bond matures. The interest is not included in income until maturity unless the taxpayer elects to include the annual increases in the value of the bond as income each year. If the election is made it applies to all future years also. Interest on series EE *savings bonds can be excluded at maturity or when redeemed if the taxpayer uses the proceeds to pay higher education expenses in the year of redemption*.

1. The exclusion is available if the owner of the bond is at least 24 years old (the bond must not be held in a child's name).

2. The interest is excluded in proportion to the educational expenses (tuition and fees) of the taxpayer, spouse, or dependent that are not reimbursed by scholarships.

3. The exclusion is phased out for 2015 when modified AGI exceeds $77,200 ($115,750) (2014) for single (filing jointly) status. The phaseout is proportionate over a range of $15,000 ($30,000 for married-jointly).

IV. **Municipal Interest**—Interest on state or local governmental obligations and obligations of a possession of the United States is excluded.

A. The exclusion does not extend to some special types of municipal bonds, such as "arbitrage" bonds. An arbitrage bond is a bond for which any portion of the proceeds are reasonably expected to be used to acquire higher yielding investments.

B. The exclusion does not mean that interest on municipal bonds cannot be used in other tax calculations, such as in the computation of the alternative minimum tax or the exclusion of social security benefits.

> **Note:**
> *If the state or local bond is sold at a gain, such gain is taxable. Losses are also deductible. The character of the gain/loss is capital since bonds are an investment asset.*

C. For bonds issued after February 17, 2009, or in 2010, certain issuers can elect for the bonds to be treated as Build America Bonds. These are municipal bonds but the election means that the interest on the bonds will be included in income, and the holder will receive a tax credit equal to 35% of the interest.

V. **Interest-Free and Below-Market Loans**

A. If the interest charged for a loan is less than the current market rate (which is based on the Applicable Federal Rates published monthly by the IRS), then special rules may apply. In general, it is assumed that the borrower pays the current market rate of interest to the lender. The borrower will have interest expense and the lender interest income for this hypothetical payment.

1. The lender is then assumed to make a payment to the borrower equal to the hypothetical payment (since the payment was not actually made). The tax consequences to the borrower for this deemed payment are:

a. Compensation income if the borrower is an employee.

b. Dividend income if the borrower is a shareholder.

c. A gift in most other circumstances.

> **Example:**
> Beth works for Publishing, Inc. and receives a $100,000 non-interest bearing loan from Publishing. Assume that the current market rate of interest is 10%. Beth is assumed to pay interest of $10,000 ($100,000 × 10%) to Publishing. The deductibility of this interest is governed by the specific rules related to interest deductions. Publishing recognizes $10,000 of interest income. Since Beth is an employee, she is also deemed to receive $10,000 of compensation income (subject to payroll taxes).

B. Several types of loans are exempt from the below-market rules:

    1. In general loans are excluded if the loan amount does not exceed $10,000 and the borrower does not use the proceeds to purchase investment assets.

    2. If the amount of the loan does not exceed $100,000 and there is not a tax-avoidance motive, the deemed interest paid by the borrower is limited to the borrower's investment income on the loan proceeds. The investment income is deemed to be zero if $1,000 or less.

VI. Dividends on Stock—Generally, distributions of cash or property to shareholders is taxed as dividend income if the distribution is made from the corporation's retained earnings (called **earnings and profits (E&P)** for tax purposes).

> **Definition:**
> *Dividend*: To the extent of earnings and profits, any distribution of cash or property from a corporation to its shareholders is a dividend.

A. The **value** of the property received in a dividend is the amount included in income to the extent the dividend is paid from earnings and profits.

    1. Determining the taxability of dividends is a three-step process:

        a. Dividend income to the extent of earnings and profits;

        b. Then a reduction in the basis of the stock;

        c. Once the basis is exhausted, the excess is capital gain.

    2. Earnings and profits are the tax version of retained earnings.

    3. Dividends are taxed to cash basis taxpayers in the period in which the property is made available (typically when received).

> **Note:**
> *Stock dividends and splits are not taxable events.*

B. Qualified dividend income is taxed at the same rates as long-term capital gains for individuals. It is not taxed (0%) if the taxpayer is in the 10% or 15% bracket. For higher tax brackets, dividend income is taxed at 15% or 20%. To qualify for this lower rate, the dividend must be received from a domestic corporation or a foreign corporation whose stock is tradable on an established U.S. securities market. If the stock was held for 60 days or less during the 121-day period beginning 60 days before the ex-dividend date, then the dividend does not qualify for this lower rate.

    1. A 3.8% net investment income tax applies to taxpayers whose modified AGI exceeds $250,000 if married filing jointly and $200,000 if single or head of household. The 3.8% tax applies to the lesser of (a) net investment income, or (b) the excess of AGI over the AGI thresholds. Dividends are included in net investment income, so the highest tax rate on qualified dividend income is 23.8% (20% + 3.8%). These thresholds are not indexed for inflation.

> **Note:**
> *To be nontaxable, the stock dividend must be paid to **common** stockholders. Either common or preferred stock can be paid to common stock shareholders. A stock dividend paid to **preferred** stockholders is always taxable.*

C. Stock dividends on common stock are not taxable as long as the dividend is proportionate (same percentage for all shareholders). A stock dividend or split requires the taxpayer to adjust the basis of the stock's new number of shares.

> **Example:**
> TP owns 40 shares in XYZ Corporation purchased at a cost of $10 per share ($400 total). TP received an additional 10 shares as a stock dividend. He has realized no income and his shares now have a basis of $8 each ($400 divided by 50 shares).

D. An option to receive cash in lieu of stock (whether or not exercised) triggers recognition of dividend income.

E. Distributions from mutual funds are usually characterized as either ordinary dividends or capital gains. All ordinary dividends are treated as dividend income and the mutual fund will indicate if any of these are qualified dividends taxed at 15% or lower rates. All capital gain distributions are treated as long-term capital gains.

VII. Interest and Dividends Reporting

A. Interest is reported on Lines 1 through 4 and Dividends on Lines 5 through 6 of Form 1040 Schedule B. Schedule B must be used if either interest or dividends exceed $1,500. Otherwise they are reported only on Form 1040.

B. If total interest or dividends exceed $1,500 then Part III must be completed related to foreign accounts.

C. Interest is reported to the taxpayer on Form 1099-INT.

D. Dividends are reported to the taxpayer on Form 1099-DIV.

Gross Income—Other Inclusions

After studying this lesson, you should be able to:

1. Delineate the tax effects of payments related to a divorce.

2. Calculate the tax consequences of payments received for damages and related to insurance benefits.

3. Determine the income recognized from annuity payments.

I. **Wages**—Wages are reported on Form W-2 and are included in income in the year received.

II. **Tip Income**

   A. Only tips received as cash, or on debit and charge cards, must be reported to the employer for purposes of paying and withholding payroll taxes. Tips only have to be reported to the employer if they are greater than or equal to $20 for a month (but all tips must be included in taxable income). Tips can be reported to the employer on Form 4070A or a similar statement and must be signed by the employee. They must be reported by the 10th day of the following month, or the next day after the 10th that is not a Saturday, Sunday, or legal holiday.

   B. A daily tip record should be kept so tips can be reported to the employer and on the tax return.

III. **Alimony**—Alimony is taxed to the recipient and the payor is granted a deduction ("for AGI"). In this way, the income is only taxed once to the ultimate recipient. Payments to a former spouse that do not qualify as alimony are treated as a division of property: nontaxable to the recipient and nondeductible by the payor.

   A. Alimony—Alimony is taxable to the one receiving the payments and deductible by the one making the payments. To qualify as alimony, the payments must be:

      1. **Required** by decree or written agreement and not characterized as something other than alimony;

      2. Made in **cash**;

      3. Paid to or on behalf of **former spouse;**

      4. **Terminate** upon death of recipient; and

      5. Payor and payee cannot be members of the same **household**.

   > **Note:**
   > *It is permissible for alimony to terminate before the spouse's death; it just cannot extend beyond death.*

   B. Child support—Child support is not taxable to the one receiving the payments and is **not deductible** by the one making the payments.

   C. Property transfers—to a former spouse under a divorce decree are **not a taxable event**. The transferor's basis in the property transfers to the transferee.

   D. If the required amount of child support and alimony are not received, payments are first assumed to be child support.

   E. Special front-loading rules require recapture of deductions and income if alimony payments decline more than $15,000 over the first three years after the divorce.

   See the following example.

Example:
The following alimony payments are made: Year 1, $100,000; Year 2, $80,000; and Year 3, $45,000. The alimony recapture is computed as follows:

A. The excess of the Year 2 payments over the Year 3 payments ($80,000 − $45,000 = $35,000) is $20,000 above $15,000. This is the first recapture amount.

> B. Next, reduce the Year 2 payments by the $20,000 from step A, producing $60,000 ($80,000 – $20,000).
>
> C. The Year 2 payments (now $60,000) plus the Year 3 payments ($45,000) equals $105,000. Divide $105,000 by 2 to obtain $52,500.
>
> D. The excess of the Year 1 payments over $52,500 is $47,500 ($100,000 – $52,500 = $47,500) which is $32,500 above $15,000. This is the second recapture amount. The total recapture amount is $20,000 from step A plus $32,500 from step D, which equals $52,500.

IV. Income from Community Property

    A. Community property law divides income into separate property and community property.

        1. Separate property consists of assets owned before marriage or acquired by gift or inheritance while married.

        2. Community property is property acquired during a marriage unless by gift or inheritance.

    B. Allocation of Income

        1. Depending on the state, income from separate property may be either separate property (Idaho, Louisiana, and Texas) or community property (Alaska, Arizona, California, Nevada, New Mexico, Washington, and Wisconsin). If community property, each spouse is taxed on 50% of the income. If separate property, the income is reported by the spouse who owns the property.

        2. Personal service income is usually community property.

V. Damages

    A. Personal injuries—Amounts received to compensate for **physical injury or illness** are not subject to income taxation. Note that worker's compensation is also excluded from income since it is paid due to physical injuries incurred while working.

> **Definition:**
> *Compensation for physical injuries*: Any payment that compensates for damages due to a physical injury or illness. As long as the action generating a payment is due to a physical injury or illness, then all damage payments received, except for punitive damages, are excludible from income. This is the case even if the injured party is being reimbursed for lost wages.

    B. Damages—Received for emotional distress, employment or age discrimination, or injury to reputation must be included in gross income. However, if the emotional distress was caused by an underlying physical injury or illness then the payments are not included in income.

    C. Punitive damages—In general, **must be included** in gross income.

    D. Attorney's fees and costs recovered as part of a judgment must be included in income if the underlying recovery is included in gross income.

> **Example:**
> TP was in an accident caused by Smith. TP received $1,000 to compensate him for medical expenses, $5,000 for emotional distress due to injury, and $2 million for punitive damages. TP is taxed on $2 million but not on the compensation for expenses or emotional distress (it was due to a physical injury).

VI. Annuity Definition

    A. Annuities require an insurance company to make certain payments to a taxpayer for a specified period of time. Annuities are often used as part of a retirement plan.

B. The amount paid for an annuity is the taxpayer's basis in the asset. The basis is recovered over the life of the annuity.

    1. If the annuity is purchased from an insurance company, the taxpayer's basis equals the amount paid.

    2. If the annuity is funded through a retirement plan, the taxpayer only receives tax basis for the contributions to the retirement plan if made from after-tax income.

    3. The taxpayer receives **no basis** for employer contributions and contributions made by the employee that were tax-deductible (e.g., contributions to 401(k) plans).

> **Note:**
> *If a taxpayer receives a judgment or settlement as a result of a discrimination suit, the damages received are typically included in gross income. Attorney's fees and other costs incurred as part of the suit are deductible for AGI, limited to the amount of the proceeds that are included in income.*

VII. Income in Respect of a Decedent (IRD)

A. IRD is income that the decedent had **earned before his death**, but had **not yet recognized** as income because of his method of accounting.

B. IRD must be included in the gross income of the person who receives it, and it has the same character as it would have had if the decedent had recognized it.

C. Some common examples of IRD are **accrued income, accrued interest** on U.S. savings bonds and on savings accounts, and **dividends** for which the record date was before the date of death.

VIII. Jury Duty Pay—Jury duty pay is includible in income. If the jury pay is given to the juror's employer then a deduction for AGI is received to offset this income.

> **Note:**
> *Unemployment compensation is taxable because it is a replacement for wages.*

IX. Unemployment Compensation—This amount is taxable.

Gross Income—Exclusions

This lesson explains the most important exclusions from gross income for taxpayers.

After studying this lesson, you should be able to:

1. Apply rules to determine receipts that can be excluded from income if the proper requirements are met, such as prizes and awards, scholarships, and life insurance benefits received.

2. Distinguish between gifts and inheritances and determine the basis and holding period rules for each.

3. Identify the types of debt forgiveness that can be excluded from income.

4. Compute the tax consequences of the receipt of social security benefits.

Tax Form for this Lesson: Form 1040 (available for download and printing from the lesson overview of your software).

I. Prizes and Awards

A. The **fair market value** of these items must be included in income.

B. Prizes or awards can be **excluded** if they are for civic, **artistic, educational, scientific, or literary achievement** and the recipient is:

  1. Selected without action on his/her part;

  2. Not required to perform services; and

  3. If the amount is paid directly to a tax-exempt or governmental organization.

II. Scholarships

A. Amounts received as scholarships can be **excluded** from income to the extent that the funds are used by a degree seeking student for **tuition, fees, books, supplies**, and equipment required for courses.

B. Amounts received for room and board are treated as **earned income**.

III. Life Insurance Proceeds

A. Proceeds of life insurance received due to the death of the insured are excluded from income. Life insurance proceeds are generally subject to estate tax at the time of the decedent's death. Hence, subjecting the beneficiary to income taxation upon receipt of the proceeds would constitute a double tax on the proceeds.

> **Note:**
> *If the payments from the university are in return for services rendered, the amounts are taxable as wages, even if the services are a condition for receiving the degree, or required of all candidates for the degree.*

  1. The exchange/sale of a life insurance policy for the cash surrender value is treated like a sale and the proceeds in excess of the cost are income.

  2. One exception to this rule is the surrender of a policy or sale of a policy by a terminally ill taxpayer. Accelerated death benefits from a life insurance policy can be excluded from income if the insured taxpayer is terminally or chronically ill. Terminally ill means that a physician has certified that death is likely to occur in 24 months or less. Chronically ill means that the individual cannot perform some common daily activities (e.g., eating, bathing).

B. A life insurance policy purchased (from the insured or the owner of the policy) for consideration is treated like an asset and the proceeds in excess of the cost are income.

> **Example:**
> TP owned a life insurance policy on his spouse, but was short of cash. He sold the policy for $100 to B, an unrelated individual. Upon the death of TP's spouse, B received $500 from the life insurance company. B will be taxed on $400 of income ($100 is return of capital). If TP had not sold the policy, then TP would have received $500 tax-free.

IV. **Gifts and Inheritances**—Gifts and inheritances are taxed under the Federal Estate and Gift Tax law. To avoid the double taxation of these transfers, their value is excluded from the income of the recipient.

A. Gifts—Gifts are excluded if the purpose of the transfer was detached generosity (no quid pro quo or consideration was expected in return for the transfer).

B. Income—Income accrued up to time of gift is still taxed to the donor, whereas income accruing after the gift is taxed to recipient (donee).

V. **Forgiveness of Debt**

A. Generally, the forgiveness of debt results in income to the borrower unless the forgiveness is a gift, or the forgiveness is related to a bankruptcy proceeding.

B. If the taxpayer is bankrupt or insolvent, the debt forgiveness is not taxable. However, the taxpayer must reduce tax attributes such as net operating losses (NOLs), credit carryovers, and then the basis of property. The taxpayer can elect to reduce the basis of property first rather than other tax attributes.

C. A taxpayer that is insolvent, but not bankrupt, can exclude forgiveness of debt only to the extent of the insolvency.

> **Note:**
> *Whether an item is a gift depends on the intent of the donor, not the intent of the donee. For example, S rakes the leaves in T's yard as a gesture of kindness, but T decides to pay her $20 for her work. Even though S did not expect to be paid, S has $20 of income because T's intent was to pay him for the services he rendered.*

> **Example:**
> UNA, Inc. has assets of $500,000 and debts of $750,000. Therefore, their insolvency is $250,000. If creditors forgive $400,000 of debt, the first $250,000 will be excluded from income. The remaining $150,000 will be included as income. UNA will reduce other tax attributes for the $250,000 of excluded income.

D. For cancellation of debt on real property used in a trade or business, no income is recognized even if the taxpayer is not bankrupt or insolvent. However, the taxpayer must reduce the basis of the property by the amount of forgiven debt.

E. For discharges of indebtedness on a taxpayer's principal residence in connection with a debt restructure or foreclosure in 2007–2014, up to $2 million of debt relief may be excluded from income. This debt is limited to indebtedness to acquire, construct, or substantially improve a principal residence. Thus, home equity loans, whose proceeds are not used for these purposes, are not included in this exclusion. Congress has not extended this provision to 2015 at the time of this writing.

VI. **Social Security Benefits**—Generally, SSB are not included in income. However, if the taxpayer's provisional income (PI) exceeds a specified amount, up to 85% of the benefits may be included in income.

PI = AGI + tax-exempt interest + 50% (SSB)

The following base amounts (BA) must be used:

	BA1	BA2
Married taxpayers filing jointly	$32,000	$44,000
Married taxpayers that file separately	$ 0	$ 0
All other taxpayers	$25,000	$34,000

If PI exceeds BA1 but not BA2, then the taxable amount of SSB is the lesser of:

50% × SSB

50% × (PI − BA1)

If PI exceeds BA2, then the taxable amount of SSB is the lesser of:

.85 × SSB, or

.85 × (PI − BA2), plus the lesser of

amount included based on first formula, or

$4,500 (unless married filing jointly, then $6,000).

VII. Foster Child Payments—Payments are excluded from income if they are for reimbursement for expenses incurred to care for the foster child.

VIII. Welfare Payments—Welfare payments received from governmental entities are not included in income.

Note:
If PI is less than $25,000, then none of the SSB is included in income.

Accounting Methods and Periods

After studying this lesson, you should be able to:

1. Apply general rules to determine when income is recognized.

2. Use cash and accrual method of accounting rules to determine income.

3. Utilize inventory rules to compute cost of goods sold for tax purposes.

4. Apply the prepaid tax rules to determine taxable income.

I. **Tax Accounting**—Tax accounting consists of specialized rules for realizing and accounting for income. The accounting rules also apply to expenses, but these rules are described in detail in the section covering deductions. Like financial accounting, the rules used to determine taxable income are premised upon ascertaining net income. Unlike conservative financial accounting rules, the tax rules treat ambiguous circumstances **liberally**, by assuming income is recognized. Thus, the tax rules are normally structured to recognize a larger, rather than smaller, tax liability.

II. **Realization**

Definition:
Realization: The event that triggers the taxation of income. Like realization for financial accounting, realization is difficult to define precisely.

A. Realized income is presumed to be taxable.

1. Realization generally occurs when a transaction results in the receipt of property or a right capable of valuation.

2. Income cannot be realized or recognized if the property received by the taxpayer is not susceptible of valuation. For example, a taxpayer may not be able to value a promise to pay for property based upon future events.

B. Return of capital is not income.

1. Receipts are not recognized as income to the extent the receipts represent the cost of goods or the cost of property sold.

Definition:
Return of capital: The cost of goods or the cost of property sold.

 Example:
SH purchases $10,000 of Motorola stock, and later sells the stock for $13,000. SH is allowed to recover her cost/capital of $10,000 before realizing income. Therefore, her realized income is $3,000 ($13,000 – cost basis of $10,000).

C. Specific exceptions—Congress has enacted specific exceptions for untaxed (unrecognized) income.

1. Nonrecognition provisions may exclude income from taxation or merely defer taxation of the income until a later period.

2. Each type of unrecognized income may be subject to specific, unique limits.

Definition:
Gross income: The amount of realized income after eliminating deferred and excluded income.

D. Corollary—expenses are presumed nondeductible.

    1. Nondeductible expenses do not influence taxable income.

    2. Congress only authorized deductions for a list of specific expenses.

    3. Similar to nonrecognition provisions, each type of deduction may be subject to specific, unique limits.

III. Accounting Methods and Periods

A. Year-ends—Regular corporations do not have restrictions on the year-end that they can choose. However, partnerships and S corporations have significant limitations. These limitations are discussed in the partnership and S corporations sections of the course.

B. Accrual method—The accrual method for taxes is very similar to financial accounting, but exceptions to accrual are usually income increasing.

    1. For tax purposes, unearned (prepaid) income is recognized in the year received, rather than the year earned.

    2. To the extent that accrued expenses are deductible, the deduction can be claimed in the period in which the liability becomes certain (all events test).

C. Cash method—The cash method of accounting recognizes income (and expenses) in the year in which payment is received (or paid).

    1. This rule only addresses the timing of income (and expense), not whether income has been realized.

    2. Under the cash basis, a taxpayer has no accounts receivable because no accounting entry is made for sales on account (no property has been received).

    3. Prepaid expenses are prorated for cash basis taxpayers if recognition of the total expense in the current year would distort taxable income.

> **Note:**
> *A cash basis taxpayer does not need to reduce property to cash to trigger income recognition.*
>
> *A cash basis taxpayer cannot write off accounts receivable but can write off a loan. No entry is made for sales on account, but a loan requires an entry (debit loan receivable and credit cash).*

D. Cash versus accrual accounting—In general, the following entities cannot use the cash method of accounting:

    1. Regular C corporations;

    2. Partnerships that have regular C corporations as partners;

    3. Tax shelters. Note that the exceptions listed below do **not** apply to tax shelters.

> **Definition:**
> *Tax shelter*: An entity other than a C corporation for which ownership interests have been offered for sale in an offering required to be registered with Federal or State security agencies.

    4. Notwithstanding the above, the following entities can use the cash method:

        a. Any corporation (or partnership with C corporation partners) whose annual gross receipts do not exceed $5 million. The test is satisfied for a prior year if the average annual gross receipts for the previous three-year period do not exceed $5 million. Once the test is failed, the entity must use the accrual method for all future tax years;

        b. Certain farming businesses;

        c. Qualified personal service corporations.

> **Definition:**
> *Qualified personal service corporation*: A corporation that exists if 1) substantially all of the activities of the business consist of services in health, law, engineering, architecture, accounting, actuarial science, performing arts, or consulting, and 2) at least 95% of its stock is owned by the employees performing the services.

E. Special inventory rules

1. In general, business with inventories must use the accrual method to report purchases (cost of goods sold) and sales. This method is known as the hybrid method of accounting if other accounts are kept using the cash basis.

2. Taxpayers whose annual gross receipts do not exceed $1 million can also use the cash method for purchase and sales accounts. The test is satisfied for a prior year if the average annual gross receipts for the previous three-year period do not exceed $1 million. Once the test is failed, the entity must use the accrual method for all future tax years.

3. Taxpayers whose annual gross receipts exceed $1,000,000 but are less than $10 million can use the cash method for purchase and sales accounts if their primary business is delivering services (not manufacturing, wholesale, or retail) and they are not a corporation.

4. Manufacturers and retailers

   a. Manufacturers and certain retailers and wholesalers are required to use the **uniform capitalization method** to capitalize all the direct and indirect costs allocable to property they produce and for property bought for resale. These costs are then allocated to ending inventory and property sold during the year, which usually results in an increase in the basis of the inventory.

   b. Property is produced if the taxpayer constructs, builds, installs, manufactures, develops or improves property.

   c. Exceptions to the uniform capitalization method include: small personal property dealers (those with $10 million or less in gross receipts during the preceding three years); long-term contracts; costs incurred in certain farming businesses and in raising and harvesting crops and timber; certain creative expenses and personal property; intangible drilling and development costs; natural gas acquired for resale; and research and experimental expenditures.

5. Costs required to be capitalized

   a. Costs required to be capitalized under the uniform capitalization rules include direct materials and direct labor, and virtually all indirect production (such as utilities, repairs, rent, depreciation) costs must be capitalized for tax purposes.

   b. Marketing, selling, advertising, and distribution expenses are not required to be capitalized under the uniform capitalization rules. General and administrative expenses also do not have to be capitalized.

   c. Storage costs are required to be capitalized to the extent that they can be traced to an off-site storage or warehouse facility. Those storage costs attributed to an on-site facility are not required to be capitalized.

6. Costs can be allocated between ending inventory and cost of goods sold using FIFO, LIFO, weighted average, or specific identification. However, LIFO can be used only if it is also used for financial reporting. During a period of rising prices, LIFO produces a higher cost of goods sold and lower taxable income.

7. Taxpayers can value inventory at the lower of cost or market unless they are using LIFO (in which case cost must be used). Market is defined as replacement cost or reproduction cost.

F. Long-term contracts

1. Special rules apply to recognize income for production projects that generally take more than one year to complete (e.g., aircraft, ships).

2. The general rule is that the percentage of completion method must be used to recognize income, so that the gross profit from the project is recognized over the time period that it takes to complete the project.

3. The completed contract method allows the gross profit from the project to be deferred until the year that the production process is complete. This method may be used by:

   a. Those with $10 million or less in average gross receipts during the preceding three years if the project is expected to last no more than two years.

       b. Home construction contractors.

       c. A contract where less than 10% of the total costs relates to the actual construction of property on the land.

  G. Methods for farming businesses

     1. Income from farming businesses are reported on Schedule F.

     2. The cash method is usually used for farming operations, except the accrual method is required if the farm is organized as a corporation, partnership, or tax shelter.

     3. Inventories can be measured using the following methods: cost, lower of cost of market, farm-price market, and unit-livestock price method.

  H. Changes in accounting methods

     1. Once a taxpayer has selected a particular method of accounting it cannot be changed without the consent of the IRS.

     2. In general, any adjustment to income required due to a voluntary change in accounting method is spread over four years beginning with the year of change. A voluntary change includes changing from an incorrect to a correct method. If the adjustment is less than $25,000, the taxpayer can include all income in the year of change.

     3. If the change in accounting method is initiated due to an IRS examination, any positive adjustment to income is included in the earliest tax year under examination.

IV. Prepaid Items and Long-Term Contracts

  A. Prepaid interest, rents, and royalties—Are usually taxed when received. Lease deposits are not income when received if they can be returned to the lessee at the end of the lease term. They are taxed when the lessor receives an unrestricted right to them.

  B. The taxpayer can elect to include prepaid service income in gross income when received. However, under the deferral method the taxpayer only has to include the payments in gross income in the year of receipt if they are also included in the taxpayer's financial statements. The remaining payments are taxed in the following year (even if not yet earned). The deferral rule also applies to payments received by hotels and other venues where significant services are provided to the lessee.

  C. Revenue from the advanced payment of goods can be deferred until earned as long as the same reporting method is used for financial accounting.

  D. Prepaid dues and subscriptions are reported over the membership or subscription period.

  E. Long-term contracts—Are contracts related to the construction of property for which the property is generally not completed in the year that construction began. Income from long- term contracts is reported under the percentage of completion method. Under the percentage method, the percentage of the contract completed during the tax year is multiplied by the total gross profit from the contract to compute the income inclusion.

     1. Under the completed contract method no income is recognized until the construction process is completed. This method is permitted for home construction contracts and for contracts completed by contractors whose average annual gross receipts for the three preceding year do not exceed $10 million.

  F. Leasehold improvements—The fair value of leasehold improvements is income to the landlord if the improvements are made in lieu of rent.

V. Short-Year Tax Returns—If a corporation files a short-year return for a period less than 12 months (e.g., five months):

  A. The income for that period is first multiplied by 12 months/five months to annualize the income for 12 months.

  B. The corporate tax liability is then computed on this amount for the full 12 months.

  C. That amount is then multiplied by 5/12 to prorate for the short tax year.

Taxation of Employee Benefits

This lesson describes the income implications of benefits that employers often provide their employees.

After studying this lesson, you should be able to:

1. Determine the tax consequences of insurance benefits received from employers.

2. Assess the tax effects of the receipt of other fringe benefits from employers.

3. Compute the income recognized from the receipt and exercise of stock options.

Any benefit received by an employee is included in gross income unless there is a specific provision that excludes the benefit.

I. Insurance Benefits Received

    A. Benefits from taxpayer purchased policies—Health and disability insurance proceeds are excluded if the taxpayer paid the premiums.

        1. Benefits under a policy purchased by the taxpayer are excluded even if payments are a substitute for lost wages.

    B. Benefits from employer purchased policies—

        1. If the employer paid the premium for disability insurance, then proceeds from the disability policy are taxed to the recipient.

        2. Health insurance proceeds may be excluded if the taxpayer's employer paid the premiums. In this case, medical expense reimbursements are excluded:

            a. As long as the expenses reimbursed are for qualified medical expenses (thus, if the reimbursement exceeds the qualified expenses then the excess is income), or

            b. If payment is received for loss of (or the use of) a body part or permanent disfigurement.

            c. These exclusions apply for the employee and the employee's spouse and dependents.

    C. In certain cases members of the armed forces who were injured while performing combat duty do not have to include disability payments in income.

    D. Benefits received from long-term care policies are excluded from income up to $330 per day in 2015, but excess amounts over this limit are not included if the funds were used for actual long-term care services.

Example:
TP was disabled last year. TP's employer-provided health insurance paid his medical expenses of $50,000, and paid TP $40,000 for the wages TP lost while he was disabled. TP may exclude the $50,000, but TP is taxed on the disability proceeds of $40,000 because the employer paid the insurance premiums.

Disability Insurance Summary

• Premiums paid by taxpayer—**not** deductible

• Premiums paid by taxpayer's employer—**excluded** from taxpayer's income; deductible by employer

• Benefits received by the taxpayer from a policy paid for by the taxpayer—**excluded** from income

• Benefits received by the taxpayer from a policy paid for by the employer—**included** in income

II. Fringe Benefits

A. Life insurance premiums—Those paid by an employer are excluded on the basis of group- term life insurance.

1. The limit on this exclusion is the amount of premiums necessary for a $50,000 face value group-term policy.

2. For amounts over $50,000, the insurance benefits are taxable based on the rates in an IRS table. The rates are based on the age of the taxpayer.

3. Note that this exclusion applies only to term life insurance policies. If an employer pays premiums on a whole-life insurance policy for an employee the value of those premiums are included in income.

Example:
UT, Inc. provides life insurance for its employees equal to their annual compensation. T's annual compensation is $80,000 and the includible income per $1,000 of coverage is $1.20 per month (T is 42 years old).

T can exclude payments for the first $50,000 of coverage from income. She is taxed on the excess coverage of $30,000 ($80,000 − $50,000). She has 30 excess increments ($30,000/1,000) each of which is taxed at $1.20 per month, so her income inclusion is $432 (30 × $1.20 × 12).

B. Employer purchased health and long-term care plans

1. Health insurance premiums—Those paid by an employer are excluded.

   a. Corollary—Self-employed individuals can deduct 100% of health insurance premiums paid for coverage of self, spouse, and dependents. However, the deduction cannot exceed the taxpayer's net earnings from self-employment.

2. Employer paid premiums for disability insurance plans and long-term care policies are also excluded from income.

3. Employer paid premiums for wage continuation insurance are included in income, because a wage continuation plan is not considered to be a health plan.

4. For the first plan year beginning on or after Sept. 23, 2010, group health plans and health insurance issuers providing dependent coverage of children generally must continue to provide coverage of children until age 26.

C. Personal expenses paid by employer—If an employer pays the expenses of an employee, the payment is income to the employee because it is compensatory in nature.

Example:
In lieu of additional salary, an employer makes a $200 car payment for an employee. The $200 payment is income to the employee.

D. Food and lodging—The value of food and lodging provided by employer to employees is excluded from the income of the employee if the following conditions are met.

1. The provision must be for the convenience of the employer meaning that the food and lodging must be provided for a non-compensatory reason. For example, a hospital may provide free meals in the hospital's cafeteria for doctors so they will be on call in case an emergency occurs.

2. Employer-provided meals must be provided in kind (i.e., not cash for meals) on the employer's premises.

3. The employer must require the employee to accept lodging as a condition of employment for it to be excluded from income. It must also be provided on employer's premises.

Example:
EE employs TP as a manager of a motel. EE provides lodging worth $2,000 to TP in order to keep TP on call in case of complaints. TP may exclude the value of the lodging if EE requires that TP accept the lodging as a condition of employment.

E. Working condition—Fringe benefits are excluded from the employee's income.

    1. A working condition benefit is a benefit provided by the employer that would be deductible (as an employee business expense) if the employee had instead paid the expense.

Example:
T is an attorney and his law firm reimburses him for his dues to the American Bar Association and his subscription to the *National Law Review*. These reimbursements are excluded from income as working condition fringe benefits

F. De minimus fringes—Are excluded because these benefits are small in value and infrequent. Examples include occasional use of the copy or fax machine, typing services, and free coffee provided in the office.

G. No additional cost services—Are excluded benefits when provided to employee, their spouses, or dependents.

> **Note:**
> *Exclusion applies only to services provided by employers, not to products given to or sold at a discount to employees. If an employee is allowed to take groceries home that have met their expiration date, the value of the groceries would not be excluded since they are a product and not a service.*

    1. These benefits are those provided by employers at no substantial additional cost, such as plane tickets provided to airline employees when there are empty seats.

    2. For businesses with more than one line of business (e.g., operating a hotel and a rental car service), the exclusion only applies for services provided in the business line that the employee works in.

H. Employee discounts—These are excluded if the discount is not excessive (except on realty and marketable securities).

    1. The discount is limited to 20% of the value of services.

    2. The limit on the discount for purchases of merchandise is the average gross profit percentage for the employer.

Example:
T is employed at an office supply store and is allowed to buy a computer that cost the store $900 (offered for sale at $1,300) for $1,000. Since T is paying at least the store's cost, the discount does not exceed the gross profit and is excluded from income.

If the store also provides shipping services for customers, and T is allowed to ship items at a 50% discount, the portion of the discount that exceeds 20% of the value of the services is included in T's income.

I. Nominal gifts—The value of nominal gifts to employees is excluded up to $25 per employee, as long as the gifts are not cash or gift certificates.

Example:
TP is employed by a grocery store that provides all employees with a complimentary turkey for Thanksgiving. If the value of the turkey is less than $25, then the gift is excluded by TP.

J. Safety and length of service achievement awards—Are excluded from income and are subject to a limit of $400 if not a qualified plan, and $1,600 if part of a qualified plan.

1. The award will be taxed if it is made in cash.

2. The award can be given only because of length of service or safety records.

3. The award can be given no more than once every five years.

K. Transportation and parking—Employer reimbursements for mass transit transportation ($130 per month) and parking ($250 per month) are excludible up to the limits shown in 2014.

L. Reimbursement for commuting with a bicycle can be excluded up to $20 (not indexed for inflation) per month. Qualified expenses include the purchase, repair, and storage of the bike if it is regularly used for commuting to work.

Example:
TP is employed by a firm that provides all employees with monthly parking passes. If the value of the parking is less than $250 per month (2014), then this benefit is excluded by TP.

M. Other special benefits—"Qualified" benefits provided by employer may be excluded, including:

1. Employees can **exclude** (up to $5,000; $2,500 if married filing separately) from gross income the value of **child and dependent care services** provided by the employer, if the services are provided so that the **employee can work**.

2. Employees can exclude (up to $5,250) from gross income the value of assistance provided by the employer **for undergraduate and graduate tuition, fees, books, and supplies.**

3. Employees can **exclude** from gross income up to $13,400 (in 2015) of **expenses incurred to adopt a child**, if these expenses are reimbursed by the employer. The exclusion is **phased-out** at AGI levels between $201,010 and $241,010 in 2015.

4. If the adoption expenses are not reimbursed by the employer, the taxpayer receives a **non-refundable credit** for qualified adoption expenses up to the same $13,400 limit per child.

5. Employer reimbursement of moving expenses are excluded, but only if the moving expenses would have been deductible by the employee if he or she had paid for them.

6. Use of athletic facilities provided at a location owned or leased by the employer are excluded. This benefit applies to the employee, the employee's spouse and dependents, as well as retirees.

7. Employer-provided retirement advice is excluded.

8. Qualified tuition reduction by nonprofit educational institutions is excluded and applies to the following: the employee; the employee's spouse and dependents; and undergraduate education, except for graduate students who receive tuition waivers for serving as a graduate assistant.

9. Benefits paid to the family of a deceased employee are included in income.

10. Flexible Spending Accounts (FSAs) are accounts set up by employers to allow their employees to contribute a portion of their salary (pretax funds) to an account. The funds in the account must be used during the tax year to pay for specific expenses of the taxpayer. Specifically, accounts can be created to pay medical, dependent care, or adoption expenses. One drawback of an FSA is that any funds not used by the end of the tax year (may be extended to 2½ months after year-end at option of employer) are forfeited by the employee.

N. Discrimination rules

1. Most of the fringe benefits discussed in this lesson cannot discriminate against non-highly compensated employees. That is, the benefit cannot be extended to only those who are highly compensated.

2. If a benefit is discriminatory, then the highly compensated employees are taxed on the fair market value of the benefit. Non-highly compensated employees are not taxed on the value if it is otherwise excludible.

3. The discrimination rules do not apply to the following fringe benefits (so highly compensated employees would not have to include the value in income):

   a. Health insurance premiums (as long as plan is not self-insured);

   b. Working condition fringe benefits;

   c. Transportation and parking fringe benefits;

   d. Lodging on the employer's premises.

O. Accountable Plans—When employees are reimbursed for business expenses, the determination if this is taxable depends on whether the employee has an accountable plan.

   1. If employee business expenses are reimbursed under an accountable plan, then the reimbursement is not taxable (for FICA or income tax) and the employee gets no deduction for the expense. Technically, the tax law requires the reimbursement to be included as income and the employee's deduction is for AGI. Since this always nets to zero, the IRS allows the income and deduction to not be reported.

   2. If the expenses are reimbursed, but not under an accountable plan, the reimbursement must be included in income (for FICA and income tax) and the deduction is a 2% miscellaneous itemized deduction.

   3. For a plan to be accountable:

      a. It must substantiate all expenses to be reimbursed; and

      b. Excess reimbursements must be returned to the employer.

P. Cafeteria Plans

   1. Under a cafeteria plan, an employee can choose between cash and certain "qualified benefits."

   2. Cash is treated as wages.

   3. Qualified benefits are tax-free benefits if they would have been tax-free if not offered through a cafeteria plan.

   4. Qualified benefits include:

      a. Benefits/coverage under accident or health plans

      b. Long-term or short-term disability coverage

      c. Group-term life insurance coverage

      d. Dependent care assistance programs

      e. Section 401(k) plans

      f. Contributions through health savings accounts

      g. Adoption assistance.

III. **Stock Options**

A. Key dates for stock options

   1. Grant date—Date the option is granted to employee.

   2. Exercise date—Date that the option is exercised and the stock is purchased.

   3. Sale date—Date that the stock is sold.

B. Nonqualified stock options

   1. No income is recognized when the option is granted.

   2. On the exercise date, the employee-recognized ordinary income is equal to:

(FMV of Stock – Exercise Price) × # of shares exercised.

a. The employer receives a salary deduction for this same amount.

b. The employee has a basis in the stock equal to its FMV on the exercise date. When the stock is later sold, this basis is used in computing the gain/loss from the sale.

C. Incentive stock options—**No income** is recognized (except for AMT) when the option is **granted or exercised**. The consequences when the stock itself is later sold vary:

> **Note:**
> *For an ISO, the exercise price cannot be less than the FMV of the stock on the grant date.*

1. The gain on sale is LTCG if acquired stock is:

   a. Held more than one year; and

   b. Not sold until after two years from the date the option was granted.

   c. The employer does not receive a deduction.

2. If these requirements are not met, the option is treated like a **non-qualified stock option**:

> **Note:**
> *Even the tax effects are like those for an NQSO; the timing of the income recognition still takes effect on the date the stock is sold, not the exercise date.*

   a. The gain on the stock sale is ordinary income and the employer receives a deduction equal to the stock's FMV on the exercise date over the exercise price;

   b. The difference in the FMV on the sale date and the FMV on the exercise date is capital gain or loss.

SUMMARY OF TAX EFFECTS OF STOCK OPTIONS		
	INCENTIVE STOCK OPTION	NON-QUALIFIED STOCK OPTION
GRANT DATE	NONE	NONE
EXERCISE DATE	NONE (EXCEPT AMT)	ORDINARY INCOME
SALE DATE	ORDINARY INCOME/CAPITAL GAIN (AMT ADJ. REVERSES)	CAPITAL GAIN

3. The corporation receives a deduction only for the ordinary income portion.

D. Readily Ascertainable Value

1. If a non-qualified stock option has a **readily ascertainable value** on the grant date, the recipient is taxed on the FMV of the option at that time. In that case, there are no other tax consequences until the stock is sold. That is, there are no income tax consequences on the exercise date.

2. To have a readily ascertainable value, generally the option must be traded on an active market. Note that if the recipient cannot trade the option because of a restriction from the employer (which is often the case) then the option's value is considered to be zero on the grant date.

Taxation of Retirement Plans

After studying this lesson, you should be able to:

1. Identify common types of retirement plans including IRAs.

2. Delineate the key differences between traditional and Roth IRAs.

3. Determine the tax consequences of payments made to different types of retirement plans.

4. Assess the income effects of distributions from retirement plans.

I. **Retirement Savings**—Contributions made by an employer (and sometimes the contributions by an employee) to a "qualified" retirement plan are not subject to tax until the contributions are withdrawn from the plan.

   A. Qualified pension plans—Contributions of salary to "qualified" pension plans are deferred until distributions are made from the pension.

      1. For a plan to be "qualified," it must meet nondiscriminatory, funding, vesting, and certain participation/coverage requirements.

      2. Early withdrawals (before age 59½) trigger a penalty in addition to the taxation of the withdrawal.

      3. Employees can also make elective deferrals into certain qualified plans and the deferred amounts are not subject to current taxation. The most common type of elective deferral plans are 401(k)s, SIMPLE plans, 457 plans and 403(b) plans. More explanation of these plans is provided below.

   B. Individual Retirement Accounts (IRAs)—The income earned on contributions made to an individual retirement account is not subject to tax in the current year. The taxation of these contributions varies according to the type of the account—traditional, Roth, or educational.

   C. Traditional IRAs—Provide a deduction for eligible contributions.

      1. Contributions—The limit on any IRA contribution (deductible or nondeductible) is $5,500 (2015), or compensation (an additional $1,000 catch-up contribution is allowed for taxpayers over the age of 50). Hence, for a married couple, the limit on IRA contributions is $11,000, or combined compensation. Excess contributions are subject to a 6% excise tax each year until withdrawn.

      2. IRA deductions -- If the taxpayer is not a participant in a qualified pension plan, the IRA contributions can be deducted for AGI. IRA contributions can also be deducted by taxpayers who are active participants in qualified plans, but this deduction is phased out proportionately over a $10,000 range ($20,000 if married filing jointly) if the taxpayer's modified AGI exceeds the limit below.

Definition:
Modified AGI: Modified AGI is generally computed as: AGI + IRA deduction + Domestic production activities deduction + Student loan interest + Foreign earned income exclusion and housing cost exclusion + Exclusion for employer-provided adoption assistance

Taxable years beginning in	Joint Returns Phaseout range
2015	$98,000–$118,000
Taxable years beginning in	**Single Taxpayers Phaseout range**
2015	$61,000–$71,000

Example:
TP is a single taxpayer who has modified AGI of $63,000. This year (2015), TP is covered by a qualified pension plan, and he made a $5,500 contribution to an IRA. Because of the phaseout, TP loses 20% ($1,100) of the IRA deduction ([$63,000 – $61,000]/ $10,000). Hence, TP deducts $4,400 ($5,500 – $1,100) of the IRA contribution. The remaining $1,100 is a nondeductible contribution.

3. Note, that the phaseout of the IRA deduction is always rounded up to the nearest $10, and the minimum deduction is $200 if the entire deduction is not phased out.

4. A married taxpayer who is not an active participant can deduct contributions even if the taxpayer's spouse is an active participant. However, this deduction is phased out proportionately over a $10,000 range if the joint modified AGI exceeds $183,000 in 2015.

5. Taxpayers who cannot deduct IRA contributions can nonetheless defer the income earned by nondeductible IRA contributions to traditional IRAs. Nondeductible contributions to traditional IRAs are reported on Form 8606. The taxpayer's basis in the IRA is computed on this form.

6. IRA contributions must be made by the original due date of the return, April 15, to be deductible for the previous tax year.

D. Roth IRA—Contributions are not deductible.

1. The limit on contributions to a Roth IRA is the same as those to a traditional IRA (compensation of $5,500, or $6,500 for those 50 or older [$11,000 if married filing jointly]) without consideration of the rule about participation in a qualified pension. The limit on Roth contributions is coordinated with other IRAs so that combined contributions to all IRAs cannot exceed these limits.

2. Covered contributions to a Roth IRA are phased out proportionately if the taxpayer's modified AGI for 2015 exceeds $183,000 for married filing jointly (a $10,000 range) or $116,000 for single taxpayers (a $15,000 range).

E. Conversion of a traditional IRA to a Roth IRA—A traditional IRA can be converted to a Roth IRA, but this is a taxable event.

1. The taxpayer must recognize gain at the time of the conversion to the extent that the conversion amount exceeds the tax basis in the IRA.

2. The same rules apply to conversions of 401(k) plans into Roth plans.

F. Coverdell Education Savings Account—Contributions to a Coverdell Education Savings Account (formerly Education IRA) are not deductible, but income may not be subject to tax.

1. A Coverdell Education Savings Account must be established exclusively to pay higher education costs (tuition, fees, books, and room and board reduced by tax-free scholarships and similar payments, including elementary and secondary school expenses) for a beneficiary who is under age 18 (unless a special-needs student).

2. Contributions to a Coverdell Education Savings Account are limited to $2,000 per beneficiary, per year. The contribution is phased out proportionately if the taxpayer's AGI exceeds $190,000 for married filing jointly (a $30,000 range) or $95,000 for single taxpayers (a $15,000 range).

II. Retirement Distributions

A. Withdrawals from a "traditional" IRA—Are taxed as income in the year of withdrawal.

1. If the taxpayer has made nondeductible contributions to the IRA, then withdrawals are prorated between the total nondeductible contributions and the remaining balance in the account (because the taxpayer has basis for the nondeductible contributions). The portion of withdrawals that constitute nondeductible contributions is not subject to tax.

2. Withdrawals from a traditional IRA may be subject to a penalty tax of 10%. This tax is not imposed if the taxpayer is disabled or age 59½. Withdrawals are also exempt from the penalty when they are used for death or disability expenses or

    a. made in the form of certain periodic payments,

    b. used to pay medical expenses in excess of the allowable percentage of AGI,

    c. used to purchase the health insurance of an individual who is unemployed for at least 12 weeks,

    d. for first-time home buyer expenses (limited to $10,000),

    e. distributed for qualified higher education expenses,

    f. levied by the IRS, or

    g. made by individuals called or ordered to active military duty.

3. Withdrawals from a traditional IRA must begin when the taxpayer reaches age 70½.

4. Up to $100,000 of distributions from an IRA will be tax-free if contributed to a charitable organization by an individual age 70½ or over. At the time of this writing Congress has not extended this provision to 2014.

5. If a taxpayer receives a distribution from an IRA that would be subject to the 10% penalty, the taxpayer can deposit the funds into another eligible retirement plan within 60 days and avoid the penalty. In such a case the distribution would also not be included in income.

B. Withdrawals from a Roth or Coverdell Education Savings Account—May be tax exempt.

1. Withdrawals of contributions from a Roth IRA are not taxed as income. Withdrawals are assumed to be from contributions first, rather than prorated between contributions and accrued income.

2. Withdrawals of income accumulated in a Roth IRA are not taxed as income if the distribution occurred five years or more from the date of the initial contribution, and if it is made on or after an individual attains age 59½. Withdrawals of income are also not taxed if used to pay for the taxpayer's death or disability expenses or if used for first-time home buyer expenses or certain education expenses.

3. Withdrawals of contributions of income from a Coverdell Education Savings Account are not subject to tax if used to pay higher education expenses, or rolled into a Coverdell Education Savings Account for a member of the beneficiary's family.

4. Taxpayers may waive the exclusion for withdrawals from a Coverdell Education Savings Account if they prefer to claim the Hope/Lifetime credits for the educational expenditures.

5. If a withdrawal (or a portion of a withdrawal) from a Coverdell Education Savings Account is not used for education expenses, then the withdrawal is prorated between total contributions and accumulated income. The portion of the withdrawal that constitutes income is subject to tax plus the 10% penalty tax.

6. Withdrawals from a Roth IRA are reported on page 2 of Form 8606.

C. Distribution Rules from Qualified Plans

1. Most taxpayers do not have any basis in their qualified retirement plans, so all distributions are taxable. Basis is not received for employer contributions that are not taxed and for employee contributions that are deducted on the employee's tax return.

2. If a taxpayer made a contribution of his own funds to the plan and did not receive a deduction for the contributions (e.g., after-tax funds were used), basis is received for these contributions.

3. If a taxpayer has basis in the retirement plan, then the annuity rules are used to determine the taxable portion of each payment.

    a. Each payment is part income/part return of capital.

b. Excluded portion = (cost of annuity/expected return) × annual payment.

c. Expected return is annual annuity amount multiplied by life expectancy determined by the IRS table.

d. Exclusion ratio stays the same until the entire cost is fully recovered; additional payments are fully taxable.

e. If the annuitant dies before the total cost is recovered, the unrecovered cost is a deduction on the taxpayer's final return.

Example:
Mr. Kitten purchased an annuity contract for $50,000 from the XYZ Company on March 31, Year 1. He is to receive $1,000 per month starting April 1, Year 1 and continuing for life. He has a life expectancy of 10 years as of March 31, Year 1. Mr. Kitten's reportable annuity income for Year 1 is:

Cost of Annuity ($50,000) / Expected Return (120 months × $1,000 = $120,000) × Pmt. ($9,000) = $3,750

Includible Amount = $9,000 − $3,750 = $5,250

4. The total retirement annuity and the taxable portion of the annuity are reported on Form 1040 each year.

5. Withdrawals from a qualified plan may be subject to a penalty tax of 10%. This tax is not imposed if the taxpayer is at least age 59½. Withdrawals are also exempt from the penalty when:

a. Used for death or disability expenses,

b. Made in the form of certain periodic payments, or

c. Used to pay medical expenses in excess of the applicable percentage of AGI.

D. Tax on Excess Accumulations

1. Distributions from qualified plans must begin by the "required beginning date" and the payment each year must be at least equal to the required minimum distribution.

2. If the required distribution is not made, a tax equal to 50% of the required distribution not made must be paid.

3. The required beginning date is by April 1 of the later of:

a. the year the taxpayer reaches age 70½ or

b. the year the employee retires.

III. Special Retirement Plans—Self-employed taxpayers may make deductible contributions to special retirement plans.

A. Qualified plans for self-employed individuals are called Keogh or HR 10 plans. These plans have the same limits as pension plans, except the maximum percentage limit is based upon self-employment earnings. For 2015, contributions are limited to the lesser of $53,000 or 100% of earned income. Earned income equals net earnings from self-employment less 50% of the self-employment tax less the allowable Keogh contribution.

B. Section 457 plans may be offered by state and local governments and tax-exempt organizations. Employees may defer up to $18,000 in 2015.

C. A 401(k) plan allows voluntary employee contributions to reduce taxable salary up to a maximum of $18,000, plus $6,600 catch-up for those aged 50 and over. A 403(b) plan is similar to a 401(k) plan but is offered by education institutions. The same limits apply for 403(b) plans.

D. A simplified employee pension (SEP) is a plan where the employer may contribute to a SEP- IRA for each employee. Contributions can be limited to employees who (a) are at least 21 years old, (b) have performed service for the employer during at least three of the last five years, and (c) have received compensation from the employer of at least $600 in 2015.

1. Contributions can be discretionary, but must be a uniform percentage of compensation for each employee.

2. Contributions must be 100% vested at all times.

3. Contributions for 2015 to an employee's SEP-IRA are excludable from the employee's income to the extent they do not exceed the lesser of:

   a. 25% of the employee's compensation; or

   b. $53,000.

4. To take a deduction for contributions for a particular year, the contributions made for that year must be made by the due date (including extensions) of the employer's income tax return for that year.

E. Employers establishing a SIMPLE IRA plan make either matching or nonelective contributions. Like SEPs, a SIMPLE IRA plan allows an employer to make contributions toward its employees' retirements, subject to higher limits than those applicable to IRA contributions, without having to deal with the complex compliance and reporting rules that apply to qualified retirement plans.

1. The limit for SIMPLE plans is $12,500 for 2015.

2. SIMPLE IRA plans are available to employers with 100 or fewer employees that receive at least $5,000 of compensation in the prior calendar year. However, employers who have established a SIMPLE IRA plan but who no longer qualify because they exceed the 100-employee limit have a two-year grace period under which they can continue to maintain the plan.

F. Employers may create a Roth 401(k) for their employees. Similar to Roth IRAs, after-tax dollars are contributed to these plans, but all distributions from these plans are tax-exempt.

IV. Health Savings Accounts

A. Qualified taxpayers can contribute funds to a health savings account and receive a deduction for AGI in the year the contributions are made. In 2015, annual contributions are limited to $3,350 for singles and $6,650 for families. Distributions must be used exclusively for qualified medical expenses (health insurance premiums are not qualified).

B. Amounts distributed from an HSA to pay qualified medical expenses of the account beneficiary are not includible in income. Nonqualified distributions are included in gross income and subject to a 20% penalty. Medicine and drugs are qualified only if they are prescription drugs or insulin.

C. To qualify, a taxpayer must be covered only under a high-deductible health plan and may not be entitled to benefits under Medicare. In 2015, a high-deductible health plan must have a deductible of at least $1,300 ($2,600 for family coverage) and annual out-of-pocket expenses cannot exceed $6,450 ($12,900 for family coverage).

V. Section 529 Plans

A. These plans are used to save for college expenses through a vehicle that allows the earnings to be excluded from gross income.

B. Contributions are not deductible, and a beneficiary must be specified for the plan. States typically allow lifetime contributions of as much as $250,000 to the plan.

C. Earnings in the plan are tax-deferred.

D. Distributions from the plans are excluded from income to the extent that the distribution is used to pay for tuition, fees, books, etc., and reasonable room and board costs. Distributions not used for a qualified purpose are subject to income taxation and a 10% penalty.

VI. Non-qualified Deferred Compensation Plans

A. If compensation is deferred but not under a qualified plan, the compensation is taxed currently unless the provisions of Section 409A are met. In general, the employee must agree to defer the compensation before the beginning of the tax year in which the compensation will be earned. At the time of deferral, the employee must specify when the compensation will be paid in the future.

B. If the provisions of Section 409A are not met, then in addition to the compensation being taxed in the year earned, an excise tax equal to 20% of the compensation must also be paid. Interest is also charged on the underpayment at the underpayment rate plus 1%.

C. The business that has the responsibility for paying the deferred compensation cannot deduct it until the year that the employee recognizes the compensation as income.

Deductions—Basic Principles

After studying this lesson, you should be able to:

1. Classify activities as related to trade/business, investment, or personal activities.

2. Apply deductibility rules for each activity type.

3. Recognize expenditures that are not deductible when certain provisions are met.

4. Determine when prepayments are deductible.

I. General Rules

A. Deductions can be divided into two broad categories: **deductions for AGI** and **deductions from AGI** (i.e., itemized deductions).

B. Activities/transactions can be divided into three mutually exclusive categories:

1. Personal

2. Trade/business

3. Investment

C. Expenses related to one's **personal activities cannot be deducted** unless specifically provided for in the IRC (e.g., charitable contributions, mortgage interest).

D. Expenses related to **trade or business activities** are deductible if they are related to the business operations and are **ordinary, necessary, and reasonable**.

E. Expenses related to **investment activities** or other activities that produce income are deductible if **ordinary, necessary, and reasonable**. Expenses related to the **management or maintenance of property** and in connection with the **determination of any tax** are deductible.

Definitions:

Ordinary and Necessary: Interpreted to mean the nature of the expenditure is customary and appropriate under the circumstances.

Reasonable: Interpreted to mean that an expenditure cannot be extravagant in amount.

II. Disallowed Deductions—There are several expenditures for which a deduction is prohibited.

A. No personal expenses are deductible unless specifically allowed, including personal legal expenses (unless the legal expense relates to tax planning or tax preparation services).

B. Expenditures benefiting more than one period must be capitalized rather than expensed.

C. No expenses can be deducted if the expenditure is against public policy. Payments in violation of public policy are not necessary and not deductible. Examples include bribes, fines, and penalties. Expenses of operating an illegal drug business are not deductible. However, cost of goods sold can be deducted for an illegal drug business. The ordinary, necessary, and reasonable expenses of operating other illegal businesses are permitted (as long as the expense itself is not against public policy).

D. No expenses can be deducted if the expense is used to generate tax-exempt income. Thus, a taxpayer (whether an individual or a business) may not deduct life insurance premiums in which the taxpayer is directly or indirectly the beneficiary. However, an employer may deduct the group term life insurance premiums if the insured employee or his/her beneficiaries would receive the insurance proceeds.

E. Lobbying expenses at the state and federal level; deductions are permitted at the city and county government level.

F. For publicly traded companies, executive compensation for the CEO and the four other most highly compensated officers that exceeds $1 million per person is not deductible unless the income is based on a performance-based compensation plan.

G. Specific disallowed deductions from previous exams include life insurance premiums, funeral expenses, and disability insurance premiums.

III. Accounting Methods

A. Expenses are deemed paid under the cash basis when charged to a credit card.

B. Recall from the lesson "Income—Accounting Methods and Periods" that the accrual method must be used to expense inventory sold unless average gross receipts are less than $1,000,000.

C. For prepaid expenses related to a business under the cash method, an immediate deduction can be taken when paid as long as the benefits from the expenditure do not extend beyond the earlier of:

   1. 12 months after benefits first begin *or*

   2. The end of the year after the year in which the payment was made.

   3. If the 12-month rule is not met, the deduction must be spread over the period for which the expenses apply.

D. Notwithstanding the above, prepaid interest must always be amortized over the life of the loan.

E. Under the accrual method of accounting, there are times when it is not clear when economic performance has occurred. Therefore, the following rules have been established:

   1. If there is an obligation to **perform** services or goods in the future (i.e., repairs) the deduction does not occur until the goods or services are provided;

   2. If there is an obligation to **pay** for future goods or services, the deduction does not occur until the recipient has received the goods or services;

   3. The taxpayer can only deduct refunds, rebates, awards, prizes, provision of warranty work or service contracts, taxes, and insurance premiums when actually paid;

   4. If the expenditure is a recurring item, and economic performance occurs within 8½ months after the close of the tax year (or when the return is filed if earlier), then the expenditure can generally be deducted in the year incurred;

   5. Vacation pay and bonuses are deducted only if paid within 2½ months after the close of the tax year.

F. Capital Expenditure versus Repair?

   1. It is sometimes difficult to determine whether a cost should be capitalized as part of the property or expensed as a repair. Expenditures that increase the value of the property or substantially increase the property's useful life are capitalized. Costs are also capitalized if the expenditure adapts the property to a new or different use.

   2. Costs are deducted as repairs if they maintain the normal operating condition of the asset but do not increase its value or lengthen its life.

Example:
TP paints the outside of a factory building. This expenditure would be deducted as a repair, unless it was included as part of a renovation of the entire property.

   3. Costs incurred to place an asset in service are capitalized as part of the cost of the property. This includes taxes that are paid as part of the acquisition and the costs of removing unwanted property.

   4. Small costs that are not material are expensed as an administrative convenience. Examples include items such as pencils, pens, paper, waste baskets, etc.

G. The IRS released new regulations in 2013 that provide guidance on the decision to capitalize or expense a particular expenditure. In general, these regulations apply for tax years beginning in 2014.

1. All costs that are incurred in acquiring or producing a unit of property (UOP) are included in its cost, except for employee compensation and overhead costs. The cost includes all related expenditures incurred before the date the asset is placed in service, even of these expenditures would be repairs if incurred after placed in service.

2. A single UOP includes all components that are functionally interdependent. Thus, a building includes the walls, floors, ceilings, roof, windows, doors, electrical systems, plumbing, heating and air systems, etc. The major exception to this rule is that if a component is treated separately for depreciation purposes, then it will not be grouped into another UOP.

3. The cost of a UOP includes costs incurred to obtain a clean title and investigation costs.

4. The taxpayer can elect to capitalize employee compensation and overhead costs (can elect separately or for both). The election can be made for particular acquisitions.

5. Taxpayers can elect under the de minimis safe harbor election to expense outlays for lower-cost items. The election is irrevocable. This safe harbor applies if the taxpayer:

   a. Has written procedures in place at the beginning of the tax year that provide for the expensing of amounts below a specified dollar amount, or that have a useful life of 12 months or less,

   b. Also expenses the items for its accounting/book records, *and*

   c. Insures that items costing more than $5,000 are capitalized ($500 if the company does not have acceptable (generally meaning audited) financial statements).

6. The de minimis safe harbor election cannot be made for inventory, land, and certain types of spare parts.

7. Routine maintenance to keep UOPs operating efficiently is expensed, such as testing, cleaning, inspecting, and replacing parts. To be routine it must be expected that the expenditure will be needed more than once during the asset's life.

8. An expense cannot be treated as routine maintenance if:

   a. It improves a UOP (treated as a betterment).

   b. A loss has been deducted against the property's basis, or the basis has been reduced as part of a sale/exchange.

   c. The asset has deteriorated to a point that it could not be used and the expenditures restore the UOP to an operating condition.

   d. To adapt a UOP to a new or different use.

   e. It is for maintenance, improvement, or repair of network assets or certain spare parts.

9. A cost is treated as a betterment if it:

   a. Enlarges or increases the capacity of a UOP.

   b. Materially increases the productivity, efficiency, or quality of the UOP.

10. Qualifying small taxpayers (those with $10 million or less average annual gross receipts in the three preceding tax years) can deduct improvements made to an eligible building property (one with an unadjusted basis of $1 million or less). The new safe harbor election applies only if the total amount paid during the tax year for repairs, maintenance, improvements, and similar activities performed on the eligible building does not exceed the lesser of $10,000 or 2% of the building's unadjusted basis.

11. Qualifying small taxpayers (including businesses with less than $10 million in assets) may elect to make these changes in accounting methods on a cut-off basis. This allows the new accounting method to be used solely for amounts paid or incurred, and dispositions, in taxable years beginning after 2013. Since prior years are not affected, no adjustment to income is needed for the change. If elected, these taxpayers will not be required to file Form 3115, *Application for Change in Accounting Method*.

Deductions for AGI

After studying this lesson, you should be able to:

1. Distinguish between deductions for AGI and deductions from AGI.

2. List the most common deductions for AGI and summarize the deductibility requirements, particularly for moving expenses and student loan interest.

Tax Forms for this Lesson: Form 1040 and Schedules C, E, and F (available for download and printing from the lesson overview of your software).

I. **Types of Deductions**—Because the tax laws only allow the deduction of certain specific expenses, it is necessary to identify qualifying expenditures. Each deduction is classified as either for AGI or from AGI. This lesson focuses on deductions for AGI.

Definition:
AGI: This acronym refers to "adjusted gross income." AGI is calculated by subtracting deductions for AGI from gross income.

II. **Deductions for AGI**

   A. Deductions for AGI primarily consist of business-related expenses. These deductions are subject to few(er) limits than itemized deductions.

   B. Business expenses—Associated with a "trade" are deductible for AGI.

Definition:
Trade: An activity with a continuous level of profit seeking, such as in the case of a self- employed taxpayer who depends on the activity for his or her livelihood.

   1. Deductions for AGI are often claimed on separate forms where the deductions serve to directly offset the income generated by the activity.

Example:
Trade expenses offset trade income directly on Schedule C, whereas rental expenses offset rental revenues on Schedule E.

   2. Expenses associated with rental and royalty activities are deducted "for" AGI whether or not the activity is considered a trade.

   C. Nonbusiness deductions—There are several major categories of non-*business deductions, which are deducted for AGI.*

   1. Alimony payments (discussed in the lesson "Gross Income—Other Inclusions").

   2. Half of the self-employment taxes paid by self-employed taxpayers.

   3. 100% of the medical insurance premiums (not exceeding self-employment income) paid by a self-employed taxpayer (including spouse and dependents) for taxpayers (and spouse) who are not eligible to participate in an employer subsidized health plan.

      a. The same applies for premiums paid for long-term care insurance by self-employed individuals who are not eligible to participate in an employer subsidized long-term care plan.

4. Moving expenses.

5. IRA (Keogh) contributions and other contributions to self-employed retirement plans (discussed in the lesson "Taxation of Retirement Plans").

6. Interest on student loans.

7. Contributions to Health Savings Accounts (discussed in the lesson "Taxation of Retirement Plans").

8. Attorney's fees and court costs for discrimination suits.

9. Penalty for early withdrawal of savings.

10. Domestic production activities deduction (discussed in the lesson "Special Corporate Deductions").

11. Other deductions for AGI include forfeited interest on premature withdrawals, repayment of jury pay, and expenses associated with reforestation, clean fuels, and performing artists.

12. Qualified higher education expenses. At the time of this writing Congress has not extended this provision to 2015.

13. Certain educator expenses. At the time of this writing Congress has not extended this provision to 2015.

III. **Moving Expenses**—To be deductible, moving expenses must be associated with a job change or a first job.

   A. The new job location must add 50 miles to the old commute to justify deduction.

   B. The taxpayer must be active in a new job for a substantial period after the move.

> **Definition:**
> *Substantial Period of Employment*: For an employee, this is 39 weeks during the next 12 months. A self-employed taxpayer must meet this requirement, as well as an additional requirement of 78 weeks during the next 24 months.

   C. Qualifying expenses for the move are limited to reasonable amounts paid to move possessions and transportation costs (not meals) for taxpayer and others residing with the taxpayer. If a personal automobile is used, transportation costs are computed at 23 cents per mile (2015). The cost of storing and insuring possessions while being moved is deductible, limited to any consecutive 30-day period after the possessions are moved from the former residence (and before they are delivered to the new residence).

> **Example:**
> TP was transferred from New York to Florida by his employer. TP incurred the following expenses:
>
> | | |
> |---|---|
> | Lodging and travel while moving | $1,000 |
> | Pre-move house hunting | $1,200 |
> | Costs of moving personal effects | $1,800 |
>
> What is the deductible moving expense if TP is employed full-time? Assuming TP meets the employment test after the move, then $2,800 can be deducted for AGI.

IV. **Student Loan Interest**—Interest paid on student loans is deductible.

> **Definitions:**
> *Student Loan*: Is one whose proceeds are used to pay "qualifying" educational expenses of the taxpayer, his or her spouse, or dependents (at the time of the expenditure).
>
> *Qualifying Educational Expenses*: Include tuition, fees, and room and board reduced by educational exclusions (scholarships, education IRAs, education savings bonds, etc.).

A. The deduction is limited to $2,500 of interest that is not otherwise deductible.

B. The deduction is phased out in 2015 proportionately for married taxpayers with an AGI in excess of $1230,000 over a range of $30,000 ($65,000 for unmarried over a range of $15,000).

C. If the parent claims the student as a dependent, the parent can deduct the interest, even if the student paid it. If the student pays the interest and is not a dependent, then the student deducts the interest on her return.

V. Qualified Higher Education Expenses Are Deductible.

(At the time of this writing Congress has not extended this provision to 2015.)

> **Definition:**
> *Qualified Higher Educational Expenses*: Defined the same as expenses under the Hope credit: tuition and academic fees required for enrollment or attendance at a post- secondary educational institution by the taxpayer, spouse, and/or dependents.

A. The deduction is limited to $4,000 of otherwise nondeductible expenses reduced by other tax-free benefits (such as scholarships or Coverdell Education Savings Account distributions). The deduction cannot be claimed for a student if the Hope or Lifetime credit has been claimed with respect to that same student.

B. The deduction is permitted for taxpayers with a modified AGI that does not exceed $65,000 ($130,000 for joint returns). If AGI exceeds these amounts, a deduction of $2,000 is permitted if AGI does not exceed $80,000 ($160,000 for joint returns). If AGI exceeds these higher limits, then no deduction is allowed.

VI. Educator Expenses—An individual who is a teacher in grades kindergarten through grade 12 can deduct, as a deduction for AGI, up to $250 for expenses related to books, equipment, and supplies that are used in the classroom. Any excess over $250 is a 2% miscellaneous itemized deduction. (At the time of this writing Congress has not extended this provision to 2015.)

Itemized Deductions—Medical, Taxes, Interest

After studying this lesson, you should be able to:

1. Compute the standard deduction for taxpayers including special additions if certain requirements are met.

2. Identify allowable medical expenses and compute deductible medical expense.

3. Delineate between the types of taxes that are and are not deductible.

4. Apply the detailed rules for determining the deduction for home mortgage interest.

5. Calculate the deduction for investment interest.

Tax Form for this Lesson: Form 1040 Schedule A (available for download and printing from the lesson overview of your software).

I. **Itemized Deductions (from AGI)**—Itemized deductions consist primarily of non-trade business expenses (employee and investment expenses) and a few personal expenses that can be deducted. These deductions are subject to individual limits, and in the aggregate must exceed the standard deduction before any benefit will be realized.

   A. Personal itemized deductions—Six types of personal expenses may be itemized.

      1. Medical expenses

      2. Interest

      3. Taxes

      4. Charitable contributions

      5. Casualty losses

      6. Miscellaneous deductions

   B. All itemized deductions are reported on Form 1040 Schedule A by the taxpayer.

II. **The Standard Deduction**—The standard deduction may be claimed in lieu of *itemized deductions*.

   A. Standard deduction amounts vary according to filing status (2015) and are indexed for inflation.

Single	$6,300
Head of household	$9,250
Married—jointly	$12,600
Married—separate	$6,300

   B. An additional amount is added to the standard deduction if either the taxpayer or his or her spouse is (1) age 65 or over or (2) blind. In 2015 the amount of the addition is $1,550 for unmarried and $1,250 for married taxpayers. These amounts are indexed for inflation.

   C. Taxpayers choose to itemize if aggregate itemized deductions (after application of limits specific to each individual type of deduction) exceeds the standard deduction.

   D. Spouses filing separately must file consistently (if one elects to itemize, both must itemize).

III. Medical Expenses

A. Uninsured medical expenses are eligible for deduction if the total expense exceeds a limit based upon AGI.

> **Definition:**
> *Medical Expense*: Any expenditure for the care, prevention, cure, or treatment of disease or bodily function. It is deductible for the taxpayer, spouse, and dependent (gross income and joint return tests do not apply for this purpose).

B. Expenses must exceed 10% of AGI to be deductible (7.5% if the taxpayer or taxpayer's spouse has reached age 65 by the end of the tax year).

> **Note:**
> *Medical expenses are the only deductions allowed for payments made on behalf of someone other than the taxpayer (i.e., dependents).*

C. Deductible items include dental, medical, and hospital care; prescription drugs; equipment such as wheelchairs, crutches, eyeglasses, hearing aids, contacts; transportation for medical care; medical insurance premiums; qualified long-term care expenses and insurance; alcohol and drug rehabilitation; weight-reduction programs if as part of medical treatment; stop- smoking programs and prescription drugs for nicotine withdrawal.

D. Non-deductible items include funeral, burial, and cremation expenses; nonprescription drugs (except insulin); bottled water; toiletries; cosmetics; health spas; unnecessary cosmetic surgery.

E. Nursing home expenses qualify if the primary reason for being there is for medical reasons.

F. Capital expenditures may qualify if 1) incurred based on the advice of a physician, 2) the facility is primarily used by the patient alone, and 3) the expense is reasonable. Cost is fully deductible in year incurred. An expense can only be taken to the extent that it exceeds the increase in the value of the property.

G. Qualifying automobile expenses are actual expenses or 23 cents (2015) per mile.

H. Lodging is deductible up to $50 per night; also applies for someone required to travel with a patient. No deduction is allowed for meals, unless part of treatment program.

I. Medical expenses are not deducted until paid, and not until the year in which treatment is received, unless prepayment is required by provider.

> Qualified Medical Expenses
> − Reimbursements from Insurance
> − 10% of AGI
> = Deductible Medical Expense

IV. Taxes—Property taxes and income taxes imposed by state, local, or foreign governments can be deducted as an itemized deduction. For cash basis taxpayers, the taxes are deductible in the year paid or withheld.

A. Personal income taxes—Imposed by state, local, or foreign governments are deductible.

B. Federal taxes, death, excise, and sales taxes are, in general, not deductible.

C. Property taxes—Imposed on personal-use property owned by taxpayer are deductible as an itemized deduction.

1. Property taxes on property used for business purposes can be deducted as a business expense.

2. Property taxes do not include special assessments unless these assessments are for repair or maintenance of the property, or imposed for interest payments.

3. Personal property taxes based on the value of the property (ad valorem) are deductible.

4. Special assessments are not deductible.

5. Fees and licenses (dog, automobile, hunting and fishing, etc.) are not deductible.

D. Taxes are deducted in year withheld or paid, even if payment relates to a different tax year.

V. Interest

A. Home mortgage interest—Interest paid on debt secured by a personal residence can be deducted as an itemized deduction.

1. Interest paid on debt relating to the taxpayer's principal place of abode and second home is eligible for deduction.

a. Interest on a maximum of $1 million of acquisition indebtedness can be deducted if the debt was used to purchase, construct, or improve the residence.

b. Interest on the lower of 1) $100,000 or 2) the equity in the home (FMV—other mortgages) can be deducted regardless of how the proceeds of the debt were used.

2. Points can be deducted if paid by taxpayer in the year of purchase or improvement of the residence.

> **Note:**
> *Taxpayers can **elect to deduct state and local sales taxes** instead of state and local income taxes. If this election is made, the amount of sales taxes can be determined by using actual receipts or by using a table provided by the IRS. The table includes state sales taxes only so an adjustment is required to add local sales taxes. Taxpayers may also add to the table amount sales taxes on major purchases such as cars, motorcycles, motor homes, SUVs, trucks, boats, and airplanes. (Congress has not extended this provision to 2015 at the time of this writing.)*

> **Definition:**
> *Points*: Compensation paid to a lender solely for the use or forbearance of money. Fees paid for services do not qualify as points.

a. Points paid for refinancing are considered prepaid interest that must be amortized over life of loan.

b. Premiums for qualified mortgage insurance related to acquisition indebtedness on a qualified residence are treated as qualified mortgage interest. This deduction phases out if AGI exceeds $100,000. 10% of the deduction is lost for each $1,000 of AGI, or portion thereof, which exceeds $100,000. At the time of this writing Congress has not extended this provision to 2015.

B. Investment interest expense—Is limited to net investment income (investment income less investment expenses).

1. Investment income includes interest, dividends, rents, royalties, and annuities if not derived from a trade/business, a passive activity, or a real estate activity for which there is active participation.

2. Net capital gain attributable to the sale of investment property and qualified dividend income is not included in investment income unless the taxpayer elects to do so. If the taxpayer elects to include this as investment income, this gain must be taxed at ordinary income rates, rather than the preferential capital gain rates.

3. Investment expenses are expenses related to the production of investment income. Note that investment expenses are included in computing net investment income only to the extent that they are deductible after application of the 2% phaseout rule for itemized deductions. Expenses at 2%, other than investment expenses, are applied against the phaseout first.

4. Disallowed investment interest is carried over to future years.

C. Personal interest—That which includes credit card interest, car loan interest, and interest on income tax underpayments, is not deductible.

D. Other interest rules

1. Prepaid interest must be allocated to the years to which the payments relate. Accrual basis taxpayers deduct interest ratably over the life of the loan. Mortgage prepayment penalties are deductible as interest.

2. Not deductible if related to the production of tax-exempt income.

Itemized Deductions—Other

After studying this lesson, you should be able to:

1. Identify permissible charitable contribution deductions.

2. Apply limitations for certain types of contributions including carryover rules.

3. Determine whether an event qualifies as a casualty.

4. Compute the casualty loss deduction for personal use property and business property.

5. Identify which miscellaneous deductions are subject to the 2% rule.

6. Assess when phaseout of itemized deductions is applicable and compute phaseout.

I. **Charitable Contributions**—An itemized deduction is allowed for contributions of cash or property to qualified charities.

    A. Charitable contributions must be made to qualified donees (recipients).

        1. Public (A) charities are government subdivisions, hospitals, churches, schools, and similar institutions operated for religious, scientific, educational, or charitable purposes.

        2. Private (B) charities include fraternal orders, cemetery companies, and private foundations operated for religious, scientific, educational, or charitable purposes.

        3. Political organizations do not qualify as charities.

    B. Contributions can include cash or property, but not services.

        1. All contributions must be reduced by any value or benefit received by the taxpayer.

        2. For **LTCG** property:

            a. **FMV** is deductible.

            b. This deduction is limited to 30% **of AGI**.

            c. The 30% of AGI limitation for capital gain property can be removed if the taxpayer elects to deduct the FMV reduced by the appreciation in the property.

            d. The deduction is limited to the adjusted basis of tangible personal property if the charitable organization does not use the property in a manner that is related to its tax-exempt purpose.

            e. For contributions of tangible personal property exceeding $5,000, if the donee organization sells the property within three years of contribution, the taxpayer must recapture (in the year of sell) the deduction to the extent it exceeded the basis of the property. This recapture can be avoided if the donee organization certifies that the property had been used for an exempt purpose and that this use was substantial.

        3. All other property

            a. The deduction is the fair market value of the property reduced by ordinary income or short-term capital gain that would be recognized if the property was sold.

            b. **Ordinary income property** includes ordinary income due to depreciation recapture.

Example:
Taxpayer owns machinery with a fair market value of $25,000 and adjusted basis of $15,000. Depreciation claimed is $7,000. If the machine was sold, the total gain would be $10,000 ($25,000 – $15,000), of which $7,000 would be recaptured as ordinary income. If this property was contributed to a qualified charitable organization, the deduction would be $18,000 ($25,000 – $7,000).

    c. If the fair market value of the property is less than its adjusted basis, the deduction is limited to the fair market value.

  4. Unreimbursed costs (including $0.14/mile; not indexed for inflation) can be deducted.

  5. For contributions of clothing and household goods, the value of these contributions can be deducted only if the items are in good used condition or better. Deductions may be disallowed for contributions of clothing or household items with minimal value, such as used socks or undergarments. This rule does not apply if the value of a single item exceeds $500 and a qualified appraisal is attached.

  6. Up to $100,000 of distributions from an IRA will be tax-free if contributed to a charitable organization by an individual age 70 or over. This contribution will also not be subject to the 50% or 30% limitations. (Congress has not extended this provision to 2015 at the time of this writing.)

C. Written records of the contribution are required.

  1. No deduction is allowed for a single contribution of **$250 or more** unless the donor has **written acknowledgment** of the amount and purpose of the contribution from the donee organization. A canceled check is not sufficient.

  2. Contributions of cash are not deductible unless the donor has a canceled check, credit card statement, or written statement from the charity.

  3. For property valued at more than $500, a description of the property must be provided.

  4. A qualified appraisal is required for donations of property worth more than $5,000.

  5. For property valued at more than $500,000, the qualified appraisal must be attached to the tax return.

  6. The requirements for property valued at more than $5,000 and $500,000 do not apply to cash, intellectual property, inventory, publicly-traded securities, and qualified vehicles.

  7. Tax reporting

    a. Noncash charitable contributions are reported on Form 8283.

    b. Section A is for property valued at $5,000 or less. Section B is for property valued at more than $5,000.

D. Rule for contributions of autos, etc.—If an auto, boat, or airplane with a claimed value of more than $500 is donated, and the donee sells the vehicle without significant use of the vehicle, the deduction is limited to the gross sales proceeds from the sale of the vehicle. The donee organization must provide substantiation of this amount for the donor to attach to the return.

E. Deduction limitations—*Limitations of the aggregate contribution deduction are based on AGI.*

  1. Deduction is limited to 50% of AGI for aggregate contributions of cash combined with contributions of property.

  2. Deduction for contributions of capital gain property to public ("A") charities is limited to 30% of AGI (ignoring cash contributions).

  3. Deduction for contributions of capital gain property to private ("B") charities is limited to 20% of AGI (ignoring cash contributions).

  4. Contributions in excess of the limits carryforward five years.

  5. The 50% limitation is applied before the 30% limitations. The 30% limitation is applied before the 20% limitation.

II. Casualty Losses—Casualty losses involving personal assets are eligible for deduction if the total unreimbursed loss exceeds a limit based upon AGI. Casualty losses of business assets are deducted as business losses.

A. A casualty loss is calculated by subtracting the adjusted basis of the damaged property from any insurance proceeds.

Definition:
Casualty: A sudden, unexpected event damaging or destroying an asset. A casualty includes the theft of an asset.

B. Amount of casualty loss—For purposes of calculating the casualty loss, the adjusted basis of the damaged property is limited to the lesser of the adjusted basis or the decline in the value of the asset due to the casualty.

> **Note:**
> *Any type of property can generate a casualty loss. However, a casualty of business property qualifies as a business loss. Hence, only casualty losses of personal assets are deducted as itemized deductions.*

    1. This limit does not apply to the complete destruction of a business asset.

    2. The loss is deducted in the year that the casualty occurs or the theft is discovered.

C. For personal casualty losses, the deduction is computed as follows:

> Lower of decline in FMV or AB of property
>
> Insurance Reimbursements
>
>   – $100 per casualty
>
>   – <u>10% × AGI</u>
>
> Casualty loss deduction
>
> ===============================

D. If a gain results from the casualty (insurance reimbursement exceeds property's adjusted basis), then all casualty gains and losses are netted. Note that this netting is done before the 10% of AGI reduction. A net casualty gain is treated as a capital gain.

E. Appraisal fees (to determine fair market value) are a 2% miscellaneous itemized deduction.

III. Miscellaneous Itemized Deductions—Certain business-oriented expenses are not associated with trade activities but are, nonetheless, deductible as itemized deductions. These deductions are referred to as miscellaneous itemized deductions. Some of these expenses are subject to a 2% of the AGI floor, while others are merely added with other itemized deductions.

A. Operation of the 2% of AGI floor limitation.

    1. The floor limit is applied by subtracting 2% of AGI from the aggregate amount of the deductions subject to the floor.

    2. Any excess deductions over the floor are included with other itemized deductions.

Example:
TP has an AGI of $100,000 and miscellaneous itemized deductions subject to the 2% floor of $3,500. TP can include $1,500 of these deductions with his other itemized deductions.

B. There are five major types of miscellaneous deductions subject to the 2% floor.

    1. Employee business expenses not reimbursed under an accountable plan. If reimbursed under an accountable plan, then these expenses are deducted for AGI.

        a. Expenses include job hunting in the same trade or business, specialized clothing used on the job if not suitable for wearing at other times, and other necessary expenses related to one's role as an employee.

    2. Investment expenses (not royalty or rental expenses).

    3. Tax return preparation expenses.

    4. Home office expenses of an employee.

    5. Hobby expenses.

C. Other miscellaneous itemized deductions subject to the floor include appraisal fees to determine casualty loss and legal fees to procure alimony.

D. There are several types of deductions **not** subject to the 2% floor.

    1. Repayments previously included in income under the claim of right doctrine.

    2. Remaining basis of terminated annuity.

    3. Gambling losses to extent of winnings.

    4. Other miscellaneous deductions not subject to the floor include work expenses of handicapped taxpayers, estate taxes related to income in respect of a decedent, short sale expenses, and expenses relating to cooperative housing corporations.

IV. Overall Limitation on Itemized Deductions

A. Taxpayers whose AGI exceeds a threshold must reduce the total amount claimed for itemized deductions. The threshold (2015) is:

Married filing jointly	$309,900
Head of Household	$284,050
Single	$258,250

B. The reduction is 3% of the amount of AGI in excess of the threshold.

C. Itemized deductions **not** subject to the phaseout are medical expenses, investment interest expenses, casualty and theft losses, and gambling losses.

D. The reduction is the lower of:

    1. 3% × (AGI − Threshold), or

    2. 80% × (Taxes + Home mortgage interest + Charitable contributions + 2% Miscellaneous deductions).

Example:

H and W are calendar-year married taxpayers filing a joint return for 2015. The couple has AGI of $800,000 and $25,000 of itemized deductions consisting of $15,000 taxes, $6,000 of contributions, and $4,000 of mortgage interest. The couple's total itemized deduction of $25,000 is reduced by $14,703 to $10,297. The reduction amount is the smaller of (a) or (b) computed as follows:

(a) 3% of excess AGI: $14,703 [3% of $490,100 (i.e., $800,000 AGI less $309,900 threshold)].

(b) 80% of otherwise allowable itemized deductions: $20,000 (i.e., 80% of $25,000).

Allowable itemized deductions is $10,297 ($25,000 − $14,703).

Employee Business Expenses

After studying this lesson, you should be able to:

1. Define accountable plans and contrast tax effects for accountable versus non-accountable plans.

2. Compute deductible travel and entertainment expenses.

3. Evaluate the education expenses that are deductible as a business expenses.

Tax Form for this Lesson: Form 2106 (available for download and printing from the lesson overview of your software).

I. Accountable Plans

A. If employee business expenses are reimbursed under an accountable plan, then the reimbursement is not taxable (for FICA or income tax) and the employee gets no deduction for the expense. Technically, the tax law requires the reimbursement to be included as income and the employee's deduction is for AGI. Since this always nets to zero, the IRS allows the income and deduction to not be reported.

B. If the expenses are reimbursed, but not under an accountable plan, the reimbursement must be included in income (for FICA and income tax), and the deduction is a 2% miscellaneous itemized deduction.

C. If the expenses are not reimbursed by the employer, the employee's deduction is a 2% miscellaneous itemized deduction.

D. For a plan to be accountable:

   1. Must substantiate all expenses to be reimbursed, and

   2. Excess reimbursements must be returned to the employer.

Note:
So how should you answer a question about the deductibility of employee business expenses included under an accountable plan? The context of the question is important. For example, if the question says that the reimbursement has been included in income, then the deduction is for AGI. If the question states that the reimbursement is not included in income, then there is no deduction. The key is that this should have no effect on AGI.

II. Travel Expenses—Deductions for cost of travel are limited to trips with a business purpose.

A. The cost of transportation—Is deductible when the primary purpose is business.

   1. Commuting between the taxpayer's residence and the place of business is never deductible. However, travel from one job or work area to a second job or work area is deductible. Also, travel from home to a "temporary work location" is deductible if the assignment is short-term in nature.

   2. The amount and purpose of the transportation must be substantiated.

   3. Transportation costs include direct costs (airfare, tolls, gas, depreciation of a vehicle, insurance, etc.), or a mileage rate of 57.5 cents (2015) can be claimed for auto use. If the mileage rate is used, the only costs added to this amount are for parking and tolls.

B. Meals and lodging expenses—Can be claimed when the taxpayer is "away from home" overnight.

Definitions:

Away from Home Overnight: Means the trip is of sufficient duration to require the taxpayer to rest.

Home: The taxpayer's principal place of business. If the taxpayer is assigned to a new location for an indefinite period of time or for more than a year, the "tax home" shifts to the new location. Thus, there would be no travel expenses to this location. Rather, this would now be commuting to the new business home.

   1. The cost of meals is reduced by 50%. This reduction applies not just when traveling, but also when entertaining. If an employer reimburses the meal, then the deduction for the meal is

100% because the employer's deduction will be limited to 50%. This rule applies not only to employer/employee relationships, but also to payments between a third party and a payee.

2. For business travel that is mixed with personal travel, the travel to the location is deductible only if more than 50% of the total days are business days. If the 50% test is met, all of the transportation costs to the location are deductible. If not met, then none of the transportation costs are deductible. If Friday and Monday are both business days, then the weekend can also be counted as business days.

3. There are limited circumstances when lodging can be deducted even when not "away from home." For example, a national professional association may have its annual meeting in the city where this employer has its business. If an employer requires an employee to stay overnight at the conference hotel, the lodging is deductible if all the following are met:

   a. The employee is required to stay overnight,

   b. The lodging does not exceed five days and does not occur more than once per quarter.

   c. The employee is required to participate in the event that necessitates the overnight stay.

   d. The lodging is not lavish or extravagant.

4. Even if these requirements are not met, the lodging is deductible if incurred for a valid business reason. For example, a professional football team may stay at a local hotel the night before home football games to prepare for the game. This would be a valid business reason for a deduction.

C. Other travel related limits—Include the following:

1. Travel cannot be a form of business education (e.g., a French teacher travels to France).

2. The cost of a companion is deductible if the companion is an employee of the taxpayer or serves some legitimate business purpose.

3. No deduction is allowed for travel to "investment" seminars.

4. Significant restrictions are placed on deductions for conventions and seminars held on cruise ships or in foreign countries.

III. **Entertainment**—Deductions for the cost of entertainment are closely regulated and limited to 50% of expenditures.

A. Business must be conducted in association with the entertainment or be directly related to the operations of the business.

1. Entertainment must involve a person with a business relation (e.g., customer, client, employee, partner, etc.).

2. A substantial discussion must occur.

3. The discussion must either occur before, during, or after the entertainment on the same business day.

4. No deductions for facilities or club dues.

5. Dues to clubs organized for pleasure or recreation are not deductible. Dues for public service clubs (e.g., Kiwanis), professional organizations, and trade associations are deductible.

6. The deduction for tickets to an entertainment activity is limited to the face value of the ticket (before the 50% disallowance).

7. **Business gifts are limited to $25 per donee**, per year.

B. Contemporaneous written records are required. The record must establish the cost, time, activity, relationship, and business purpose of the entertainment.

C. The cost of deductible meals and entertainment is reduced by 50% (to represent the personal enjoyment of the taxpayer). No reduction is made when the entertainment is provided to employees as compensation, or if provided as a means of advertising or marketing.

Example:
TP provided a Florida vacation to his highest volume salesperson this year. TP can deduct the entire cost of the vacation because it is compensation to the employee.

IV. Education Expenses

A. Education expenses are **not deductible** if:

1. To **meet minimum standards** of a current job or

2. To **qualify the taxpayer for a new trade or business**

B. Education expenses are **deductible** if:

1. To **maintain or improve existing skills** required in a current job

or

2. To **meet the requirements of an employer** or imposed by law to retain employment status

Note:
No deduction is allowed for CPA review courses. Sorry!!

Example:
Law school tuition cannot be deducted because it is required to qualify for a new profession (even if the taxpayer never intends to practice as a lawyer).

V. Employee Business Expenses are Reported on Form 2106

A. Vehicle expenses are computed in Part II of the form and then transferred to Part I.

B. Total employee business expenses are computed in Part 1 and are then transferred to Schedule A as 2% miscellaneous itemized deductions.

C. Form 2106EZ can be used if no reimbursements are received by the employer and if the standard mileage rate is used for vehicle expenses.

Deductions—Losses and Bad Debts

After studying this lesson, you should be able to:

1. List the type of losses deductible for tax purposes.

2. Define worthless assets and related tax consequences.

3. Differentiate between business bad debts and non-business bad debts and apply related tax rules.

4. Compute net operating loss for an individual taxpayer.

I. **Losses**—Losses on the disposition of business assets can generally be deducted, but the deduction of losses from the disposition of personal (non-business) assets is prohibited.

   A. Deductible losses—These are generated with the disposition of business assets.

      1. A disposition occurs with a sale, exchange, or worthlessness of an asset.

      2. The disposition of personal assets will not generate deductible losses unless the disposition qualifies as a personal casualty.

   > **Definition:**
   > *Business Asset*: An asset used in a trade, held for investment, or used by an employee in an employment capacity. A personal asset is an asset used for a motive other than profit seeking (e.g., a personal reason).

      3. An asset that is used partially for business purposes and partially for personal purposes is generally treated as two distinct assets based upon the proportion of time the asset is used for each purpose.

   B. Requirements for deducting the cost of worthless securities

      1. In general, the security must be totally worthless (no residual value).

      2. A worthless asset is treated as being sold for nothing on the last day of the year.

      3. The character of the loss is usually capital. However, if the loss is incurred by a corporation on its investment in an affiliated corporation (80% or more ownership), the loss is generally an ordinary loss.

II. **Bad Debts**—These are deductible if the loan is made in a trade activity.

   A. Loans can only be deducted using a direct write-off method.

   B. Business loans can be deducted to the extent that the loan is partially worthless.

   C. Nonbusiness bad debts are also deductible.

> **Note:**
> *A cash basis taxpayer can deduct losses from worthless loans, but not losses generated by the failure of customers to pay for sales on account. A cash basis taxpayer never establishes a basis for an account receivable (sale on account), whereas a basis for a direct loan is created with the transfer of cash.*

> **Definition:**
> *Non-business Bad Debt*: Any bona fide loan that is not made in a trade capacity, but has a bona fide profit motive.

      1. Whether a loan is bona fide or a disguised gift, depends on facts such as whether interest is charged and collateral is required.

      2. Non-business bad debts are deductible as short-term capital losses in the year of complete worthlessness (no partial worthlessness is allowed).

III. Limitations on Deduction of Losses

A. Losses on the disposition of trade assets are subject to the netting rules under 1231, and losses on investment assets are subject to the netting rules for capital assets. In general, these netting procedures allow deductible losses to offset gains without limit.

B. If capital losses exceed capital gains, then this "net capital loss" is subject to a $3,000 deduction limit for individuals. No deduction is allowed for net capital losses for corporations.

C. Special rules apply if Section 1244 qualifying small corporation stock is sold at a loss or becomes worthless (losses are deductible up to $100,000 as ordinary losses, but gains are still taxed as capital gains). The individual selling the stock must be the original holder of the stock. To qualify as Section 1244 stock, the total capitalization of the corporation cannot exceed $1,000,000 at the time the stock is issued.

IV. Net Operating Losses

A. NOLs must be carried back to the two preceding tax years (beginning with the second prior year) unless an election is made in the year of the NOL to forgo the carryback. The carryover period is 20 years.

B. NOLs are only allowed for business losses and casualty losses. Any nonbusiness losses or expenses must be added back to the taxable loss to determine the NOL. The IRS has stated that losses from rental activity are business losses for purposes of computing the NOL.

C. The net operating loss of a corporation is, in general, equal to its taxable loss for the tax year. A corporation is allowed to include the dividends that received deduction in computing its net operating loss.

D. For an individual, the following cannot create an NOL:

   1. Personal exemptions;

   2. Standard deduction or itemized deductions (except for casualty loss), and other non- business deductions in excess of non-business income;

   3. Excess of non-business capital losses over non-business capital gains (limited to $3,000);

   4. An NOL deduction from another year.

E. In the year to which the NOL is being applied, the NOL is a deduction for AGI for an individual and a regular business deduction for a corporation. For an individual, any deductions that were based on AGI for the carryback year must be recomputed except for the charitable contribution deduction.

Limitations on Certain Business Deductions

After studying this lesson, you should be able to:

1. Identify hobby losses and apply related limitations on deductibility.

2. Determine the deductibility of expenses related to a home office.

3. Distinguish among the three different types of vacation homes for tax purposes and determine deductible expenses for each.

4. Define passive losses and apply limitations on deductibility.

I. Hobby Losses

    A. Hobby expenses may be deducted if the hobby generates revenue.

> **Definition:**
> *Hobby*: An activity that is not primarily profit-oriented because it is primarily undertaken for personal enjoyment.

        1. The expenses from this activity are deductible, but only to the extent the activity generates revenues. In other words, no hobby loss (expenses in excess of revenue) is deductible.

    B. To avoid the hobby designation, the taxpayer must produce evidence that there is a real profit motive in conducting the activity.

> **Example:**
> TP is a wealthy doctor who also owns a ranch in Colorado. TP only visits the ranch during the summer when he uses it to conduct recreational activities. If the ranch is not operated at a profit, then expense deductions are limited to the revenue produced by the ranch.

    C. The deductions associated with a hobby are limited to the gross profit generated by the activity.

        1. Expenses can only be deducted as "2% miscellaneous" itemized deductions. Expenses not allowed due to insufficient income do not carryover to future tax years.

        2. The limitation is imposed by deducting expenses in the following order:

            a. Interest and taxes (fully deductible as itemized deductions)

            b. Cash expenses

            c. Depreciation

            See the following example.

> **Example:**
> TP paints landscapes in the mountains during his summer vacations. This year, TP incurred $400 in airfares and lodging, but only sold $50 in paintings.
>
> **Question:** How much can TP deduct?
>
> **Answer:** TP can deduct hobby expenses up to the amount of hobby income. In this case, TP can deduct $50 as a miscellaneous itemized deduction subject to the 2% of the AGI limit.

D. The burden of proving a lack of profit motive can be shifted to the IRS.

    1. When the activity generates a profit in three out of five consecutive years, the IRS must prove the taxpayer has no profit motive in conducting the activity.

    2. If there are losses in at least three of the previous five years, the taxpayer has the burden to prove that the activity is a business.

II. Business Use of the Home—Deductions associated with a home office or the rental of a personal residence are subject to special limits.

    A. Home office expenses—These can be deducted for a portion of a residence used as an office.

        1. Business use of the office must be exclusive and regular.

        2. The office must be a principal place of business.

        3. If the office is not a principal place of business, then it can still qualify if it is used as the ordinary place for meeting clients or for the administration of the business (There is no other fixed location used for substantial administration).

        4. If the taxpayer is an employee, then the office must be used for the convenience of the employer.

        5. Expenses must be allocated between the portion of the dwelling used as residence and the office.

            a. The IRS provides a simplified method for computing the home-office deduction, which is multiplying the allowable square footage by $5. The maximum square footage under this method is 300, limiting the deduction to $1,500.

        6. Office deductions are limited to income after non-office expenses. Office deductions are applied toward income in the same order as the hobby loss limit (mortgage interest and real estate taxes, cash expenses, depreciation), but excess deductions carryforward and can be used in future years when business income is sufficient.

Example:
TP, a self-employed taxpayer, uses one fourth of his or her apartment exclusively and regularly as an office. TP conducts business only at this location. This year TP received fees of $5,000 and paid rent, utilities, etc., on the apartment of $8,000.

Question: What amount may TP deduct in conjunction with the home office?

Answer: TP may deduct one-fourth of the rent ($2,000) for AGI. This will be reported on Schedule C with other business income and expenses.

    B. Vacation home expenses—These occur when a personal residence is rented.

        1. If rented for less than 15 days a year, it is treated as a **personal residence**. Rent income is excluded and mortgage interest and property taxes are deductible on Schedule A.

        2. If rented for 15 days or more, and if it is not used for personal purposes for **more than the greater of 1) 14 days or 2) 10% of the total days rented**, it is treated as **rental property**. All rent is taxable, net of all regular rental expenses, pro-rated for the percentage of rental days only. A rental loss is allowable.

        3. If rented for 15 days or more, and if it is used for personal purposes for **more than the greater of 1) 14 days or 2) 10% of the total days rented**, it is treated as **personal/rental property**. All regular expenses are pro-rated as above for rental days, but a rental loss is not allowed. Expenses must be deducted in the same order as for a hobby.

Example:
TP owns a duplex. He rents one side of the duplex and lives in the other side. The rental was occupied all year and TP received $7,200 in rent. This year TP paid real estate taxes of $6,400, fire insurance of $600, and TP paid $800 to have the rental painted.

Question: If depreciation on the entire duplex is $5,000, how much will the rental increase TP's adjusted gross income?

Answer: TP's AGI will increase by $400. The $7,200 of revenue will be offset by $3,200 in taxes, $300 in insurance, $800 of maintenance, and $2,500 of depreciation (deducted in that order).

III. **Passive Activity Losses**—Losses from passive activities can offset only passive income. Passive losses cannot offset portfolio income or income from active businesses.

    A. The expenses and revenues from **passive activities** are combined (netted) and the expenses in excess of revenue (the passive loss) are suspended.

Definitions:
Portfolio Income: Investment income such as interest, dividends, capital gains, rents, and royalties.

Passive Activity: A profit-seeking activity in which the taxpayer does not materially participate in its management.

        1. Material participation means being involved in the operation of the activity in a continuous, substantial way. Two specific ways to meet this requirement are to work more than 500 hours in the activity, or to work more than 100 hours if no other individual works more than 100 hours.

        2. All limited partners and most rental activities are considered passive without regard to the taxpayer's participation. Exceptions to this rule are allowed for car rentals, hotels, golf courses, and other activities where the average rental time is seven days or less, or 30 days or less if significant personal services are provided by the owner in connection with the rental.

        3. Real estate professionals are excepted from the limit. A real estate professional must perform more than 50% of his or her personal services in trades or businesses involving real property, and must perform more than 750 hours of services in real property trades or businesses in which he or she materially participates.

> **Note:**
> *The passive loss rules apply to individuals, estates, trusts, personal service corporations, and closely held C corporations.*

    B. Rental real estate—An exception to the limitation of passive losses exists for taxpayers who actively manage rental reality.

Definition:
Active Participation: Occurs for taxpayers who own at least 10% of the property and significantly participate in decision-making. This is a much easier benchmark to meet than material participation.

        1. An active manager can deduct a maximum loss of $25,000 per year.

        2. The exception is phased out for taxpayers with an AGI over $100,000 at the rate of 50% ($1 of deduction for each $2 of AGI over $100,000).

Example:
TP has an AGI of $130,000 and is an active manager in rental realty. If the rental activity generates a loss of $20,000, TP is limited to a deduction of $5,000 ($20 − [($130 − 100) × 50%]).

    C. Suspended losses become deductible in later years if income is generated or the activity is sold.

Personal and Dependency Exemptions

I. **Personal Exemptions**—Most taxpayers can claim an exemption in computing taxable income on their own return.

   A. No personal exemption can be claimed for a taxpayer (or spouse) who is claimed as a dependent by another taxpayer.

      1. Personal exemptions include the taxpayer and spouse if married filing jointly.

   B. A personal exemption can be claimed on the taxpayer's final return even if the taxpayer or spouse dies during the tax year.

   C. If spouses file married filing separate then typically each spouse claims a personal exemption on his/her own return. Note that if one spouse has no gross income and no one else has claimed him/her as a dependent, the other spouse can claim him/her as an exemption on the married filing separate return.

II. **Dependency Exemptions**—The tests for a dependency exemption are applied on the last day of the year, or the last day the dependent was alive (if the dependent died during the year). One must meet all tests to claim an individual as a dependent.

Definition:
Dependency Exemptions: Flat deductions allowed for individuals (other than the taxpayer) who satisfy several specific tests.

   A. One can qualify as a dependent as either a **qualifying child** or a **qualifying relative**.

   B. A qualifying child—Can be claimed as a dependent if the following tests are met:

      1. Relationship test—The dependent must be a natural child, stepchild, adopted child, foster child, sibling, step-sibling, or a descendant of any of these. Note, that this definition includes brothers, sisters, nieces, and nephews.

      2. Residence test—The dependent must have the same principal place of abode as the taxpayer for more than one half of the tax year. Note, that one could live with several individuals who potentially qualify to claim the individual as a dependent (mother, aunt, grandfather) at the same time.

      3. Age test—The dependent must be under the age of 19 at the end of the tax year, or under 24 if a full-time student for at least five months of the tax year. The qualifying child must also be younger than the taxpayer claiming the QC as a dependent. There is no age limitation if the individual is permanently and totally disabled.

      4. Joint return test—A dependent cannot file married-jointly.

         a. A dependent can file jointly to obtain a refund (the dependent is not required to file according to gross income level). Otherwise, a married-jointly taxpayer will not qualify as a dependent despite passing all of the other tests.

5. Citizenship/residency test—A dependent must be a citizen or resident of the U.S., or a resident of Canada or Mexico.

6. Not self-supporting test—To be claimed as a dependent, the individual must not have provided more than 50% of his or her own support.

7. Other requirements—In addition to the above, a qualifying child must be younger than the taxpayer who is claiming the child as a dependent. Also, if a parent is qualified to claim the child as a dependent but declines, no other individual can claim the individual unless that individual's AGI is higher than that of any parent.

C. Tie breaker rules—If more than one individual qualifies to claim the potential dependent, the following rules apply:

1. If one individual is a parent, the parent claims the exemption. If a parent is eligible to claim the qualifying child, the parent cannot allow another eligible individual to claim the child unless the eligible individual has a higher AGI for the tax year than the AGI of any other person eligible to claim the child.

2. If both individuals are parents and they do not file a joint return, the parent with whom the child resided the longest during the tax year claims the exemption.

3. If same as 2. and the child lives with both parents at the same time, the parent with the highest AGI claims the exemption.

4. If none of the individuals is a parent, the taxpayer with the highest AGI claims the exemption.

D. The qualifying relative rule—This rule defines relative very broadly, including all common relatives except for cousins. Step-parents, step-siblings, and in-laws also qualify. The term also includes any person who lives in the taxpayer's home for the entire tax year. A qualifying child cannot also be a qualifying relative. In addition to the relationship test, the following tests must be met to claim a qualifying relative as a dependent:

1. Support test—The taxpayer must provide more than 50% of the dependent's total support. The multiple support agreement provision continues to apply.

> **Definition:**
> *Support*: All necessary living expenses including food, clothes, and other necessities. Support does not include services provided by the taxpayer, but does include the fair market value of housing and food provided by the taxpayer.

   a. The support test traces the source of the funds used to pay for necessities.

   b. Scholarships do not count as support.

2. Gross income test

   a. The dependent's gross income must be less than the exemption amount for the year ($4,000 for 2015). Gross income is defined as only the income that is taxable.

> **Note:**
> *A child under the age of 19 can receive significant amounts of income and not violate the support test. The income would not violate the support test if it was not used to pay for necessities (e.g., the income was placed in savings).*

> **Example:**
> A child of the taxpayer (under age 19) earned $5,000 this year and received a scholarship that paid tuition of $8,000. If the child uses the funds from wages for necessities, the child will still satisfy the support test if the taxpayer provides at least $5,001 of necessities (5,001/10,000 > 1/2).

   b. There are **two exceptions** to this test. These apply for a child/stepchild or for an adopted or a foster child:

        i. That is **under the age of 19** at the end of the tax year. or

        ii. That is **under 24** at the end of the tax year and is **a full-time student** for at least five months during the tax year.

    3. Joint return test—Same as above.

    4. Citizenship/residency test—Same as above.

  E. Additional requirements

III. Other Dependency Rules—There are situations in which individuals may be supported but not meet all tests for a dependency exemption. In two circumstances, multiple support agreements and divorced parents, the law provides for a dependency exemption despite the technical violation of one or more of the tests.

> **Note:**
> *A dependent cannot claim others as a dependent. Additionally, the dependent's social security number must be listed on the return for the exemption to be claimed.*

  A. Multiple support agreements—Allow a group of taxpayers who (together) support an individual more than 50%.

    1. Except for the support test, each individual in the group would otherwise be eligible to claim the individual as a dependent.

    2. The taxpayer claiming the exemption provides over 10% but less than half of the support.

    3. A written agreement allocates the dependency exemption to a member of the group. All members providing more than 10% of the support must sign.

Example:

TP lives alone and has no income. TP is supported by the following people:

	Support	Percent
A (an unrelated friend)	$2,400	40%
B (TP's sister)	2,400	40%
C (TP's son)	720	12%
D (TP's son-in-law)	480	8%

Question: Under a multiple support agreement, who is eligible to claim TP as a dependent?

Answer: Either B or C may claim a dependency exemption for TP (A is not related and D did not provide at least 10% of the total support).

  B. Divorced parents—An exception applies for children who are supported by parents who have been divorced or legally separated for the last six months of the year.

    1. The parent with custody (over half the year) is entitled to dependency exemption in the absence of any written agreement.

    2. The custodial parent can waive the exemption to the other parent by signing Form 8332. The non-custodial parent must attach this form to the return to claim the exemption.

  C. When the taxpayer and spouse file separate returns, the taxpayer only may take an exemption for the spouse when the spouse has no gross income and was not claimed as a dependent on another taxpayer's income tax return.

IV. Phaseout of Exemptions—Exemptions are subject to a phaseout for wealthy taxpayers. The phaseout is triggered by a high AGI, and the amount of the phaseout is determined through a stepwise increment.

  A. The AGI trigger for the phaseout varies by filing status.

Filing Status	AGI—Beginning of Phaseout (2015)	AGI Above Which Exemption Fully Phased Out (2015)
Married Jointly	$309,900	$432,400
Head of Household	$284,050	$406,550
Single	$258,250	$380,750

B. Two percent of total exemptions are lost for each $2,500 increment (or portion) above the trigger AGI.

    1. Each $2,500 increment is called a **step**. Each step is rounded upward and multiplied by two percent. This percent is then multiplied by the total amount of exemptions claimed, and the product is added to taxable income.

Example:
A single taxpayer has AGI that is $48,500 over the trigger. This is 19.4 steps ($48,500/$2,500). The total steps are rounded up to 20 and each step results in a loss of 2% of the exemptions. In other words, the taxpayer will lose 40% of his exemptions. If the taxpayer claimed a personal exemption of $4,000 (2015), the phaseout will be $4,000 × 40% or $1,600.

    2. Shortcut—All exemptions are phased out when AGI is $122,501 over the trigger ($122,501 divided by $2,500 results in 50 steps). Since each step results in a 2% reduction, 100% of the exemptions are lost.

Example:
TP is a single taxpayer who claims two personal (dependency) exemptions. If TP's AGI exceeds the phaseout trigger by $25,300, what portion of the exemptions is subject to a phaseout?

TP's AGI is $25,300 over the trigger, and this translates into 11 steps ($25,300/$2,500). Hence, TP would lose 22% of the exemptions.

See the following formula.

Formula for Tax Calculations

Adjusted Gross Income

less

Itemized Deductions or **Standard Deduction**

and

Personal and Dependent Exemptions

equals

Taxable Income

times

Tax Rates

(determined by Filing Status) equals

Gross Tax

less

Tax Credits

Plus

Additional Taxes

equals

Net Tax

Filing Status

Filing status determines the tax rate to be applied to taxable income. In addition, each filing status has a unique standard deduction. The determination of filing status occurs at year-end (or the death of the taxpayer or spouse). As an aside, it is important to note that most taxpayers are required to calculate their tax using a **tax table** instead of the tax rate schedule.

After studying this lesson, you should be able to:

1. Determine the proper filing status and use it to compute taxable income.

2. Evaluate whether head of household status is required.

3. Apply the requirements to determine if surviving spouse status is available.

4. Compute taxable income for a dependent on another return applying special rules.

5. Apprise whether a child is subject to the kiddie tax, and compute tax liability.

Tax Form for this Lesson: Form 1040 (available for download and printing from the lesson overview of your software).

I. **Married Filing Jointly**—Married taxpayers are treated to wider tax brackets if they choose to file under married-jointly. This election generally means that any tax liability is joint and several. Joint status may be elected by a married couple.

   A. Marital status is determined on the last day of the year, or the last day the taxpayer is alive.

   B. A spouse can avoid joint liability when income is omitted from a joint return if the spouse qualifies as an **innocent** spouse (the spouse has no reason to know of an omission from income and the error can be attributed to the other spouse).

   C. Abandoned spouse—An abandoned spouse is a married taxpayer who is allowed to file as though they are unmarried. An abandoned spouse may file as a head of household. The following requirements must be met:

      1. The taxpayer's spouse has not lived in the home for the last six months of the calendar year.

      2. The taxpayer must provide more than half the cost of maintaining a home for self and a dependent child.

Definition:
Child: A descendant of the taxpayer (e.g., son, daughter, or grandchild), or a stepchild, adopted child, or foster child.

   D. An election can be made to treat a nonresident alien spouse as a U.S. resident for income tax and wage withholding purposes. So married filing jointly can be elected by an individual who is married to a nonresident alien.

II. **Married Filing Separate**—Others, who are married, must file as married-separate.

   A. Married filing separately requires that the spouses divide income and expenses (according to ownership).

   B. Special rules also apply to prevent taxpayers from receiving benefits from filing separately. For example:

      1. If one spouse itemizes, the other spouse must itemize deductions also.

      2. Neither spouse can claim the earned income credit.

3. Neither spouse can claim the child and dependent care credit.

4. Neither spouse can claim an education credit.

5. An expense or credit is not allowed for adoption expenses.

6. The deduction for net capital losses is limited to $1,500 (rather than $3,000).

III. Surviving Spouse—Taxpayers, who are not married, may nonetheless qualify for a more advantageous tax rate schedule if they are a surviving spouse. A surviving spouse is also known as a qualifying widow(er).

A. A **surviving** spouse may use the married-joint rates for two years after the taxpayer's spouse has died. Filing status is Qualifying Widower with Dependent Child. To qualify as a surviving spouse, the taxpayer must provide more than half of the cost of maintaining the household (rent, mortgage interest, taxes, home insurance, repairs, food, utilities, etc.) for a dependent child, a stepchild, or an adopted child. The child's principal place of abode must be with the taxpayer.

> **Note:**
> In determining whether the child is a dependent, the three rules normally used to determine dependency status are ignored: 1) the joint return test; 2) the gross income test for qualifying relatives; and 3) the rule that a dependent cannot also have dependents.

IV. Head of Household—Head of Household status represents a de facto family for certain single taxpayers.

A. The taxpayer must provide more than half of the cost of maintaining the household for a qualifying child or a qualifying relative (a non-relative living in the home for the entire tax year does not qualify). If one is a dependent due to a multiple support arrangement, that also does not qualify. This home must be the qualifying child's or qualifying relative's principal residence for more than half of the tax year.

B. Note that a girlfriend/boyfriend or a child of a girlfriend/boyfriend cannot be a qualifying relative for purposes of the head of household test since non-relatives living in the home for the entire tax year do not qualify.

> **Note:**
> A taxpayer whose spouse dies in the current tax year is usually eligible to file married-joint in the current year regardless of surviving spouse status. The surviving spouse exception applies to the following two tax years during which the taxpayer will use the married-joint rates (despite the absence of a spouse).

C. Two exceptions to these rules:

1. If the **qualifying child** (defined same as for exemption rules) is an unmarried child, the child need not qualify as a dependent. A custodial parent who has released the exemption to the other parent can still file as head of household even though a dependency exemption was not claimed (assuming all other requirements are met). The noncustodial parent cannot file as head of household.

2. If the **qualifying relative** is a parent, the parent need not live with the taxpayer, but the taxpayer must provide more than 50% of the cost of maintaining the parent's home.

V. Single

A. Everyone who is unmarried and does not qualify for surviving spouse or head of household must file single—the default filing status.

B. Shortcut—A taxpayer who resides with a dependent child is most likely to be eligible for some special tax treatment, such as abandoned or surviving spouse status.

VI. Overview of Standard Deduction—The standard deduction is an automatic deduction that reduces the taxable income of most taxpayers.

A. Taxpayers can elect to deduct standard deduction in lieu of itemized deductions, and the amount varies by filing status.

Filing Status	2015 Standard Deduction
Married Individuals Filing Joint Returns and Surviving Spouses	$12,600
Heads of Households	$9,250
Unmarried Individuals (Other than Surviving Spouses and Heads of Households)	$6,300
Married Individuals Filing Separate Returns	$6,300

> **1.** Shortcut—To determine most amounts (limits, cutoffs, etc.) for a taxpayer filing married-separately, divide the amount for married-joint in half.

Study Tip:
For most tax items that vary based on filing status, married taxpayers receive higher amounts than single taxpayers. However, this is not the case for the additional standard deduction.

B. Special adjustments are made to the standard deduction in two instances.

  1. Taxpayer (or spouse if filing jointly) is blind or reaches age 65 at year-end.

  a. In this instance, the standard deduction determined above for 2015 is increased by $1,250 if the taxpayer who is blind, or at least is age 65, is married or is a surviving spouse. Otherwise, the amount of the additional standard deduction is $1,550. Note, that if a taxpayer is 65 and blind, she would receive two additional standard deductions.

  b. These additions do not apply to dependents.

VII. Special Rules for Dependents on Another Return—A taxpayer claimed as a dependent by another is entitled to a "mini" standard deduction and no personal exemption. Amounts are indexed for inflation.

A. The "mini" standard deduction is $1,050 (2015).

  1. A dependent can earn a regular standard deduction by earning income. The amount of the standard deduction is the greater of the mini standard deduction or earned income plus $350 (2015) (limited to the regular standard deduction).

Example:
TP is claimed as a dependent on her parents' return. This year TP received interest of $1,200 and wages of $2,200. TP is eligible for a standard deduction of $2,550, $2,200 + $350 (2015).

Definition:
Earned Income: Income generated by personal services (wages, self-employment income, etc.) as opposed to income generated by property (interest, dividends, etc.).

VIII. Kiddie Tax—The so-called kiddie tax is designed to discourage taxpayers from giving income-generating property to children in order to have the income taxed at the child's low tax rates.

A. The kiddie tax includes all children who are under 18. It also includes children who are 18, or between 19 and 23 who are full-time students, if their earned income does not exceed 50% of their total support for the year. Note that if a child would have his 19th birthday on January 1, he is assumed to turn 19 on the preceding December 31 (same applies for other ages). The tax is reported on Form 8615.

1. Taxable income for the child is divided into net unearned income and other income.

2. Net unearned income is taxed at the parent's tax rate, while other income is taxed at child's tax rate. If the parents are divorced, in general the tax rate of the custodial parent is used.

3. The parents can elect to report the child's income on their tax return and pay the tax if all the following conditions are met. The election is made by attaching Form 8814.

    a. The child is under age 19, or 24 if a full-time student.

    b. The child's income is only from interest, dividends, and capital gain distributions.

    c. The child's gross income is less than $10,000.

    d. The child is not filing a joint return.

    e. No estimated payments, back-up withholding, or prior year refunds can be applied to the tax.

B. Net unearned income is computed by reducing unearned income. Amounts are indexed for inflation.

    1. Taxpayers who don't itemize subtract $2,100 from unearned income (2015).

    2. Taxpayers who itemize subtract $1,050 plus itemized deductions allocated to unearned income (2015).

C. Taxation examples:

Examples:	One	Two	Three
Unearned Income	$2,250	$500	$3,000
Earned Income	250	800	6,100
	2,500	1,300	9,100
Standard Deduction	(1,050)	(1,150)	(6,300)
Personal Exemption	0	0	0
Taxable Income	$1,450	$150	$2,800
Taxed at Parent's Rate	$150	$0	$900
(Unearned Income > $2,000)			
Taxed at Child's Rate	$1,300	$150	$1,900

Alternative Minimum Tax and Other Taxes

After studying this lesson, you should be able to:

1. Compute self-employment tax.

2. Calculate the alternative minimum tax for individual taxpayers.

3. Identify the most common adjustments and preferences when computing the AMT.

Tax Form for this Lesson: Form 6251 (available for download and printing from the lesson overview of your software).

I. **Self-Employment Tax**—The SE tax and the social security tax (OASDI) operate in tandem. Each tax consists of two parts, a retirement rate and a health insurance rate. The retirement rate is capped by a maximum amount of wages and income subject to the tax. If the tax is imposed on wages exceeding the maximum (for example, the taxpayer changed jobs), then the excess tax can be claimed as a refund.

   A. SE tax—The SE tax consists of two parts imposed at twice the OASDI tax rate.

   1. The first part of the SE rate (social security) is 12.4% on the first $118,500 (2015) of SE income (the ceiling).

   2. If wages are earned in addition to SE income, then the ceiling is reduced by the wages subject to OASDI.

   3. The second part of the SE rate (Medicare) is 2.9% on all SE income (no ceiling).

Example:
TP earned $20,900 in wages and $103,600 in self-employment income. While all $124,500 is subject to the 2.9% tax, only $97,600 ($118,500–$20,900 for 2015) of the SE income is subject to the 12.4% tax ($20,900 has already been subjected to FICA).

   B. The SE tax is imposed on income from self-employment.

   1. Self-employment income is gross income from self-employment less deductions associated with the activity. SE income includes director's fees.

      a. The distributive share from a partnership/LLC is self-employment income if the partner is a material participant in the business. The distributive share from an S corporation is never included in self-employment income.

   Note:
   The deductible business expenses incurred by self-employed taxpayers are deductible for AGI.

   2. The last step in calculating the tax is to multiply self-employment income by 92.35%.

   3. Self-employment income × 92.35% must exceed $400 for the SE tax to be assessed.

   4. **Reminder**—One-half of the SE tax is deductible for AGI.

   See the following example.

Example:

   1. TP is a self-employed cash-basis taxpayer who recorded the following this year:

Receipts	$45,000
Dividends (investments)	300

Cost of sales	22,000
Other operating expenses	4,500
State business taxes	950
Federal self-employment tax	1,400

Question: What is TP's net earnings from self-employment?

Answer: $17,550 is SE earnings (the dividends are not earned and the self-employment tax is not deductible in calculating net earnings).

2. TP is a cash-basis self-employed repairman with gross receipts of $20,000 this year. Over the year TP paid the following:

Repair parts	$2,500
Listing in Yellow Pages	2,000
Estimated federal income taxes	1,000
Business long-distance phone calls	400
Charitable contributions	200

Question: What is TP's net self-employment income?

Answer: $15,100 ($20,000 − $2,500 − $2,000 − $400). Note that the charitable contributions are deducted on Schedule A.

3. TP, a retired corporate executive, earned consulting fees of $9,000 and director's fees of $4,000 this year.

Question: What is TP's gross income from self-employment this year?

Answer: $13,000

    C. Nanny tax—Taxpayers, who employ domestic workers, must withhold and pay FICA if cash wages exceeds $1,900 (2015).

    D. Self-employment taxes are reported on Form 1040 Schedule SE.

        1. There is a long-form and short-form Schedule SE.

        2. Most taxpayers can use the short-form unless:

            a. Wages plus self-employment income exceeds the annual wage base limitation for social security taxes *or*

            b. The taxpayer works as a minister, pastor, etc.

II. Payroll Taxes

    A. Social security tax of 6.2% is levied on the first $118,500 of wages in 2015.

    B. Medicare security tax of 6.2% is levied on the first $117,000 of wages in 2015. Tax of 1.45% is levied on all wages paid.

    C. The social security and Medicare tax is matched by the employer.

III. Hospital Insurance Tax—An additional .9% hospital insurance tax applies to wages as follows:

    A. Joint filers with wages > $250,000.

    B. Single and head of household filers with wages > $200,000.

C. Self-employment income above these limits.

D. This tax applies only to employees, not to employers.

IV. Alternative Minimum Tax

A. The alternative minimum tax is a separate tax system that calculates a broader tax base by modifying taxable income for both individuals and corporations. These modifications generally serve to increase taxable income by adding items of income not recognized by regular tax and disallowing deductions that do not necessarily represent economic outlays. The AMT only applies to taxpayers whose net regular liability is less than the tentative tax calculated under the broad AMT rules. This outline covers the individual AMT. The formula shown below follows Form 6251, which is the form for reporting the AMT.

Formula for computing the AMT is as follows:

Regular taxable income

± Adjustments

+ <u>Preferences</u>

AMT Income

− <u>Exemption</u>

AMT Base

× <u>Rate</u>

Tentative Minimum Tax before Foreign Tax Credit

− <u>Certain credits (see discussion below)</u>

Tentative Minimum Tax

− <u>Regular Tax Liability</u>

AMT (if positive)

==================

B. Adjustments—AMT adjustments are specific adjustments that can either increase or decrease taxable income when alternative minimum taxable income is computed. These adjustments often represent income or deductions used to defer the taxation of economic income. Hence, many (but not all) of these adjustments are merely timing differences that will reverse in future periods.

> **Note:**
> *There is no difference between AMT cost recovery and regular cost recovery for real property. Different methods are required only for personalty.*

1. The AMT adjustment applies to MACRS 3-, 5-, 7-, and 10-year property that is depreciated using the 200% declining balance method. For AMT, the 150% declining-balance method is used over the MACRS life.

    a. Note that no AMT adjustments are required for assets purchased in 2008–2014 that use bonus depreciation. For more information on bonus depreciation see the "Section 1231 Assets—Cost Recovery" lesson.

> **Note:**
> *Problems focusing on the accelerated portion of cost recovery will likely give the total amounts for the regular tax and the AMT. You will use this information to compute the AMT adjustment for depreciation.*

2. **Percentage of completion contract** income over completed contract income.

3. For itemized deductions:

    a. The phaseout of itemized deductions is subtracted from taxable income (i.e., phaseout does not apply for AMT).

    b. Medical deduction is allowed only to the extent it exceeds 10% of AGI.

    c. No deduction is allowed for taxes (it must be added back to taxable income).

    d. Two percent miscellaneous deductions are not allowed.

    e. Home mortgage interest is deductible only if the loan proceeds are used to acquire or improve the home.

4. Personal exemptions and the standard deduction (if used) are added back.

5. The compensation element on the exercise date for an incentive stock option.

6. Installment method may not be used by dealers.

C. Preferences—These always increase AMT income. The most common preference items for individuals are:

1. Tax-exempt interest on private activity bonds has been a preference item for many years, but a few recent exceptions have been enacted.

    a. For bonds issued after July 30, 2008, the interest on tax exempt housing bonds is not treated as a preference item if the bonds are for low-income housing developments, mortgage bonds, or mortgage bonds for veterans.

    b. For any private activity bonds issued in 2009 and 2010, the interest earned from these bonds will **not** be included as AMT income.

2. Percentage depletion in excess of cost basis on certain mineral properties.

3. Qualifying Small Business Stock

    a. The general rule for this preference item is that 7% of the gain excluded from income under the qualified small business stock provision (see the "Capital Gain and Losses" lesson for more detail) is a preference item for the AMT. Gain is excluded only if the stock was held for more than five years, so note that stock qualifying for this exclusion that was sold in 2015 would have been purchased before December 31, 2010.

    b. Gain on the sale of qualified small business stock that was acquired after September 27, 2010, and before January 1, 2015, and is sold more than five years after the purchase date will not be subject to the AMT. This gain is also completely excluded from regular tax.

D. AMT exemption—Taxpayers are entitled to an AMT exemption of $83,400 if married filing jointly ($53,600 if not married) in 2015.

1. The exemption is subject to a phaseout triggered by AMTI over $158,900 if married, $119,200 if single (2015).

2. The phaseout rate is 25% of the amount of AMTI over the trigger.

3. For children subject to the kiddie tax, the AMT exemption cannot exceed the sum of the child's earned income plus $7,400 (in 2015).

Example:
For a married taxpayer with AMTI of $254,900, the phaseout is triggered because AMTI exceeds the $158,900 trigger. This taxpayer is $96,000 over the trigger which means that $24,000 of the exemption will be lost ($96,000 × 25%).

4. The AMT has two tax brackets, 26% and 28%.

E. Tax credits

1. The foreign tax credit is allowed for the AMT, as are all personal credits, including:

    a. Child tax credit

    b. Adoption credit

    c. American Opportunity and Lifetime Learning (education) tax credits

    d. Low-income saver's credit

    e. Residential energy efficient property credit

    f. Nonbusiness energy property credit

    g. Credit for the elderly and disabled

    h. Child and dependent care credit

2. The preferential rates on capital gains are available for a net capital gain when calculating the AMT tentative tax.

3. Taxpayers pay the greater of the tentative minimum tax (before credits) or regular tax (before credits).

4. The amount of AMT paid, which is due to timing differences between regular taxable income and AMTI, creates an **AMT credit** that can be used to offset regular tax liability (but not below the tentative minimum tax for a given year) in future years. The AMT credit can be carried forward indefinitely.

Personal Tax Credits

After studying this lesson, you should be able to:

1. Determine when personal tax credits are allowable and list necessary requirements.

2. Compute the following tax credits: 1) child credit; 2) education credits; 3) dependent care credit.

3. Distinguish between refundable and non-refundable credits.

Tax Credit Categories

Personal Credits:

Child Tax Credit

Saver's (IRA) Credit

Education Tax Credits

Dependent Care

Adoption Expense Credit

Elderly Credit

Alternative Motor Vehicle Credit—Residential

Energy Efficient Property Credit—Foreign

Tax Credit

General Business Credits:

Research and Development

Rehabilitation

Miscellaneous

Refundable Credits:

Earned Income

Child Credit (partially refundable)

American Opportunity/Hope Credit (partially refundable)

Health Coverage Tax Credit

I. **Order of Credits**—Credits are applied against the tax liability in a predetermined order.

   A. The order of applying credits against tax is determined by the nature of the credit:

      1. Personal (i.e., nonrefundable) credits are limited to gross tax, and there is no carryover of any excess.

      2. The general business credit is limited to a percentage of gross tax after personal credits, and any excess carries over (back one year and forward 20 years).

      3. Refundable credits (see list above) are applied last because these credits have no limit based upon tax (any excess, or a portion of the excess, is refunded to the taxpayer).

   B. AMT—See the lesson "Alternative Minimum Tax and Other Taxes" for discussion of credits for the AMT.

II. Personal Credits—Personal credits are allowed for a number of activities deemed socially desirable.

    A. Child credit—A $1,000 Child Credit is allowed for each **qualifying child (as defined under the dependency rules)** *under the age of 17.*

        1. Qualifying children's names and social security numbers must be included on the return.

        2. The credit is phased out for married taxpayers with AGI in excess of $110,000 ($75,000 for unmarried). The credit is reduced $50 for each $1,000 (or portion) over the trigger AGI amount. These amounts are not indexed for inflation.

> **Example:**
> TP is married (filing jointly) with two dependent children under the age of 17. This year TP has an AGI of $123,500. TP will be able to claim a credit of $1,300 because TP's gross credit of $2,000 is reduced by $700 (14 × $50).

        3. The additional child tax credit is refundable to the extent of 15% of the taxpayer's earned income in excess of $3,000. Combat pay is treated as earned income for purposes of computing this refundable credit, even though combat pay is not taxable.

III. Education Credits

    A. A Hope credit—Is allowed up to a maximum of $2,500 per year for each eligible student. This credit has been renamed as the American Opportunity Tax Credit (AOTC).

        1. The credit is computed as 100% of the first $2,000 and 25% of the next $2,000 of qualified educational expenses.

        2. Qualified educational expenses are nondeductible tuition and academic fees (reduced by tax-free benefits, such as scholarships) incurred during a student's first **four years** of post-secondary education. The expenses must relate to an academic period beginning in the current tax year, or the first three months of the next tax year. Course materials are also included.

        3. A qualifying student includes the taxpayer, spouse, or any dependent of the taxpayer enrolled at least half time in an institution of higher education. To be eligible, the student must be enrolled in a degree program.

        4. The credit is phased out ratably for single taxpayers with AGI in excess of $80,000 ($160,000 in the case of a joint return). The credit is phased out over a $10,000 range ($20,000 for joint return) and, thus, is completely gone when AGI reaches $90,000 ($180,000 joint return).

        5. The credit can be claimed against the AMT, and 40% of the credit is refundable.

    B. A Lifetime Learning Credit—Is allowed up to a maximum of $2,000 per taxpayer per year.

        1. The credit is computed as 20% of $10,000 of qualified educational expenses incurred for the taxpayer, spouse, or dependent.

        2. Qualified educational expenses are nondeductible tuition and academic fees (reduced by tax-free benefits, such as scholarships) incurred by a taxpayer. Materials and textbooks are qualified expenses only if required to be purchased from the university (this differs from the AOTC). The expenses must be for post-secondary education, but need not relate to a degree program. Student does not need to be at least half-time for expenses to qualify.

        3. The Lifetime Learning Credit is phased out ratably for single taxpayers with an AGI for 2015 in excess of $55,000 ($110,000 in the case of a joint return) and is phased out over a $10,000 range ($20,000 for married-jointly).

        4. The AOTC credit, the Lifetime Learning Credit, and distributions from educational IRAs are **mutually exclusive** in that an educational expenditure can never simultaneously qualify for more than one benefit (i.e., no "double dipping").

Example:
TP spent $3,000 in tuition for his first year in post-secondary education. He was reimbursed $500 through a tax-exempt scholarship, and he recorded AGI of $20,000. TP can use the unreimbursed tuition of $2,500 to claim a $2,125 AOTC credit (100% of $2,000 and 25% of $500).

    a. Shortcut—The two credits differ in the percentage applied to calculating the credit (100% and 25% for the AOTC versus 20% for the Lifetime), the total expenses eligible for the credit ($4,000 per year for the AOTC versus $10,000 total for the Lifetime), and the type of expenses covered by the credit (first four years of post- secondary education in a degree program for the AOTC versus any post-secondary education for the Lifetime). The AOTC applies per student ($2,500 per student), whereas the Lifetime Learning Credit applies per tax return (maximum $2,000 credit per year).

C. A "Saver's Credit"—Is allowed for voluntary contributions to IRA and qualified retirement accounts.

    1. The credit is a maximum of $1,000 (in addition to any exclusion or deduction that would otherwise apply) and is based upon IRA contributions (Roth or Traditional).

    2. The taxpayer must be 18 or older, not a full-time student, nor claimed as a dependent on another return, and cannot receive a distribution from the account.

    3. No credit is allowed for taxpayers with an AGI (2015) in excess of $61,000 ($45,750 for head of household and $30,500 for single taxpayers).

    4. Qualifying taxpayers multiply IRA contributions by 50%, 20%, or 10% depending on the level of AGI (indexed for inflation).

Example:
1. TP is married (filing jointly) and has an AGI of $23,500. If TP contributes $2,000 to an IRA, TP will be able to claim a credit of $1,000 (50% × $2,000) because TP's AGI is below $36,500 (the cut-off level for 50% for married-jointly in 2015). This credit is in addition to a $2,000 IRA deduction.

2. TP is single and has an AGI of $12,000. If TP contributes $3,000 to a Roth IRA, TP will be able to claim a credit of $1,000 (50% × $3,000, limited to a maximum of $1,000) because TP's AGI is below $18,250 (the cut-off level for 50% for single in 2015).

IV. Dependent Care Credit—The dependent care credit is designed to provide a tax credit for a portion of the expenses incurred for care-giving while the taxpayer is employed.

    A. To be eligible for the credit, a person needing care must live with the taxpayer for more than half the year.

        1. A qualifying child or dependent under the age of 13 automatically qualifies (the child can violate the gross income test and still qualify for care).

        2. Other dependents or a spouse will also qualify if they are incapable of self-care (physical or mental disability). This individual must live in the same household as the taxpayer for more than half of the tax year.

    B. Expenditures for household services and care are required for the credit.

        1. Care can be given within the home, but the care-giver cannot be a dependent relative or child of the taxpayer.

        2. The taxpayer must be employed and earn at least as much as the amount of the expenses. If married, then the taxpayer must file jointly (unless abandoned) and the spouse must also be employed.

3. Income is imputed to a full-time student (at least five months per year) or a spouse incapable of self-care ($250 per month for one child; $500 per month for more than one).

4. Other rules include:

   a. Expenses for a child below kindergarten qualify; expenses for before or after school care of a child in kindergarten or higher grade may qualify.

   b. Full amount paid for day camp or similar programs, even if the program specializes in a particular activity.

   c. Summer school and tutoring programs are education and do not qualify.

   d. Sick child centers may qualify for either the credit or a medical expense, but not as both.

   e. For boarding school, amounts paid for food, lodging, clothing, and education must be separated from amounts paid for other goods or services.

   f. Additional cost of providing room and board for a caregiver may qualify if expenses are in addition to normal household expenses.

   g. Cost of overnight expense does not qualify.

   h. Expenses incurred during the specific time of day that the taxpayer was looking for a job also qualify.

C. The credit is calculated by multiplying the qualifying expenditures by the appropriate credit percentage.

   1. The credit percentage begins at 35% if an AGI is less than $15,000, and is reduced by 1% for each $2,000 increment (or part) in an AGI above $15,000. The minimum dependent care credit is 20%.

      a. Shortcut—Taxpayers with an AGI over $43,000 will receive the minimum dependent care credit of 20%.

   2. The maximum amount of expense eligible for the credit is $3,000 ($6,000 if more than one individual qualifies for care) or, if lower, earned income (of the lesser-earning spouse if married).

Example:

1. TP is a single parent with a 10-year-old child at home. This year TP earned $8,000 and paid $2,000 for the care of the child while TP worked. TP qualifies for a dependent care credit of $700 ($2,000 × 35%).

2. TP is a self-employed taxpayer who pays $3,000 for the after-school care of his or her dependent nine-year-old child. TP has an AGI of $86,000.

Question: What amount of the expenses is eligible for the childcare credit?

Answer: For one dependent, the maximum eligible amount is $3,000 or earned income. The credit percentage in this case would be 20%.

V. Adoption Credit

A. The adoption credit is allowed for adoption expenses.

   1. Reasonable expenses up to $13,400 (2015) associated with an adoption qualify for the credit.

   2. A $13,400 (2015) adoption credit is available for children with special needs regardless of actual expenses.

   3. The credit is phased out for taxpayers with an AGI (2015) in excess of $201,010, and is completely phased out for taxpayers with modified adjusted gross income of $241,010.

   4. The credit is limited to the regular tax liability, but any excess credit is carried forward for five years.

VI. The Elderly Credit—This credit is 15% of the difference between an initial (flat) amount and income.

    A. The taxpayer or spouse must be age 65 or totally disabled.

    B. The flat amount is $5,000 if one spouse is eligible or $7,500 for two.

    C. Income is certain types of retirement pay plus one-half of an AGI over $7,500 ($10,000 if joint).

Example:
TP, age 50, is totally and permanently disabled. This year he received social security benefits of $2,000 and had an AGI of $2,500.

Question: Is TP eligible for the elderly credit?

Answer: Yes, taxpayers over age 65, and those who are totally and permanently disabled, are eligible. TP's AGI is low enough to trigger the credit.

VII. Motor Vehicle Credits

    A. Alternative motor vehicle credit

        1. An income tax credit is available for **alternative motor vehicles**. The alternative motor vehicles, to which this credit applies, are **qualified fuel cell motor vehicles** (terminated after 2015).

        2. The alternative motor vehicle credit is also allowed against the AMT.

    B. **Credit for new qualified plug-in electric drive motor vehicles**

        1. A credit is also allowed for purchases of **new** qualified plug-in electric drive motor vehicles. The credit is limited to $5,000 for most passenger cars and trucks, but can go as high as $7,500 for large commercial vehicles. This credit phases out based on the number of vehicles sold during the year.

VIII. Earned Income Credit (EIC)—The earned income credit is a complex method of mitigating employment taxes for low income taxpayers. This is a refundable credit.

    A. The credit is generated by earning income.

        1. The credit percentage increases if the taxpayer maintains a home with qualifying children. The credit percentage is 7.65% for no qualifying children, 34% for one qualifying child, 40% for two qualifying children, and 45% for three or more qualifying children.

        2. The credit is phased out based on earned income or AGI (if greater) exceeding a threshold that also depends upon the number of qualifying children.

            a. **Qualifying child** is defined as it is for the dependency exemption rules; that is, a natural child, stepchild, adopted child, foster child, sibling, step-sibling, or a descendant of any of these. Note that this definition includes brothers, sisters, nieces, and nephews. The descendants must be under the age of 19, full-time students under 24, or permanently disabled dependents; the qualifying child must also be younger than the taxpayer.

            b. The qualifying child also must have lived in the taxpayer's home for more than half of the tax year in the United States.

            c. A qualifying child can only be used by one taxpayer to claim the EIC. If more than one person qualifies to claim the qualifying child, the tie breaker rules are similar to those used for dependency exemptions. Note that the individual who claims the qualifying child as a dependent must be the same individual who claims the EIC.

        3. The credit is disallowed if disqualified income, such as interest, dividends, tax exempt interest, and other investment income exceeds $3,400 (2015).

        4. The most common sources of earned income that qualify for the credit are wages, salaries, tips, and earnings from self-employment. Combat pay can also be included as earned income.

Taxable disability payments from an employer plan qualify as earned income until the taxpayer reaches normal retirement age.

5. A taxpayer cannot claim the credit if she files as married filing separately.

6. The taxpayer must have been a U.S. citizen or resident alien for the entire tax year and must have a valid social security number to claim the credit.

B. Taxpayers between the ages of 25 through 64 without qualifying children are also eligible if they are not claimed as a dependent on another's return and lived in the United States for more than half the year.

C. Information on qualifying children for the earned income credit is reported on Form 1040 Schedule EIC. The amount of the credit is reported on page 2 of Form 1040.

D. A paid preparer must also complete Form 8867 which provides a checklist to insure that the preparer met all due diligence requirements for taking the EIC on the return. There is a $500 penalty for each failure to meet these requirements.

IX. Health Coverage Tax Credit

A. The individual mandate—Beginning in 2014, all individuals are required to buy insurance coverage.

1. Naturally, there are several exceptions to "all." For example, the following categories of people are not penalized for not having health insurance:

a. People who have to pay more than 8% of their income for health insurance (after taking into account employer contributions and tax credits).

b. Members of an Indian tribe.

c. Incarcerated individuals.

d. Undocumented immigrants.

e. People without insurance for less than three months during the year.

f. People whose religion opposes reimbursement from an insurance policy.

g. People with family income below the threshold for filing a federal income tax return.

2. People meet the insurance requirement if they are covered through one or more of the following sources:

a. A plan offered by an employer

b. Medicare

c. Medicaid or Children's Health Insurance Program (CHIP)

d. The veterans' health program

e. TRICARE (covering service members and their families)

f. A grandfathered health care plan in existence before the ACA was enacted

g. A policy purchased by a person through an ACA exchange that is at least Bronze level

3. If people are not in the exempt categories and don't meet the requirement by purchasing insurance, then they are subject to the following penalties:

a. 2014: $95 per adult and $47.50 per child (up to a maximum of $285 per family or 1% of family income, whichever is greater);

b. 2015: $325 per adult and $162.50 per child (up to $975 per family or 2% of family income, whichever is greater);

c. 2016 and beyond: $695 per adult and $347.50 per child (up to $2,085 per family or 2.5% of family income, whichever is greater). After 2016, these numbers will be adjusted for inflation.

B. The Affordable Care Act provides a credit that is designed to make health insurance affordable to individuals with modest incomes who are not eligible for other qualifying coverage, such as Medicare, or eligible employer-sponsored health insurance plans. The credit is available for those whose income is between 100% and 400% of the federal poverty level and who do not otherwise have access to coverage. The credit is advanceable meaning that it can be used to reduce the monthly health care premium during the year. The credit is also refundable.

C. Employer Mandate

    1. Beginning in 2015, a large employer not offering coverage for all its full-time employees and their dependents, offering minimum essential coverage that is unaffordable, or offering minimum essential coverage of less than 60% of medical expenses, is required to pay a penalty.

    2. The annual tax penalty is $2,000 per full-time worker.

    3. If any full-time employee is certified as having purchased health insurance through a state exchange involving a tax credit or cost-sharing reduction paid to the employee, such employers must then absorb an additional $3,000 per employee per year tax penalty, even if the employer already offers health insurance.

X. First-Time Homebuyers Credit

A. In the past a homebuyers credit was allowed for first-time home buyers. This credit still has relevance in 2015 because in some cases it is subject to recapture. For purchases after April 8, 2008, and before 2009, the credit is unusual in that it must be repaid over 15 years on a straight-line basis beginning in the second tax year after the year in which the home is purchased. If sold during the 15-year period, the unrecaptured credit must be added to the tax liability. No repayment is required if the taxpayer dies. Since no interest is charged over the 15 years, the credit is essentially an interest-free loan.

Business Tax Credits

This lesson continues the discussion of tax credits from the previous lesson, Personal Tax Credits.

After studying this lesson, you should be able to:

1. Determine when business and energy tax credits are allowable and list necessary requirements.

2. Compute the foreign tax credit and its effect on the tax liability.

I. **Foreign Tax Credit**—The US taxes income from all sources, including income from foreign countries. The purpose of this credit is to prevent double taxation of foreign income that is subject to income tax in the foreign jurisdiction.

   A. The credit is limited to the lower of the foreign tax paid, or the proportion of U.S. tax allocable to foreign sourced income (known as the foreign tax credit limitation).

      1. The proportion of U.S. tax allocable to foreign sourced income (foreign tax credit limitation) is determined by multiplying U.S. tax times the ratio of foreign taxable income to total taxable income.

Example:
TP records 20% of his income from abroad. TP can claim a foreign tax credit in the amount of the lesser of his foreign tax paid or 20% of the U.S. tax paid.

      2. Excess foreign tax credits carryback one year and forward 10 years. The excess amount is the foreign taxes paid or accrued for a tax year that exceeds the foreign tax credit limitation.

   B. In lieu of a credit, a taxpayer can elect to mitigate foreign taxes in two other ways.

      1. Taxpayers can claim the foreign tax as an itemized deduction.

      2. Taxpayers can elect to exclude income earned (in excess of housing costs) while a bona fide resident in a foreign country. The exclusion is a maximum of $100,800 (2015; adjusted for inflation) if the taxpayer is physically present in the foreign country for at least 330 days in any 12 consecutive months.

Example:
TP earned $99,000 from working 340 days in France in 2015. TP can exclude $93,896 (340/365 × $100,800) because he was in residence more than 330 days.

II. **General Business Credit**—The **General Business Credit** consists of a combination of credits designed to subsidize certain activities. While each credit is calculated independently, the combination of credits is subject to an overall limit.

   A. The overall credit is limited to "net regular" tax.

Definition:
Net Regular Tax Liability: The regular tax less personal credits.

1. The limit is:

> Net regular liability
>
> plus AMT less nonrefundable credits (not including AMT credit)
>
> Less 25% of net regular liability over $25,000.

B. The upshot of the credit is that the business credit cannot offset all of the regular tax if the liability exceeds $25,000.

    1. Unused credits are carried back one year and then forward 20 years.

    2. Credits cannot reduce the regular liability below the "tentative" tax required to be paid under the alternative minimum tax.

Example:
TP has a net regular tax liability of $125,000 this year. TP has a general business tax credit of $70,000 and no other credits.

Question:
What amount of general business tax credit is TP eligible to claim?

Answer:
The maximum credit TP could claim would be $100,000 ($125,000 − ($125,000 − 25,000) × .25,000). Since he has a credit of only $70,000, he can claim the entire credit.

Question:
What if TP also had a tentative minimum tax liability of $105,000?

Answer:
If his tentative tax was $105,000, he could only reduce his regular tax liability to the amount of the tentative tax by claiming a maximum credit of $20,000, because the credit cannot reduce the regular tax liability below the tentative minimum tax for AMT purposes.

III. The Rehabilitation Credit—This is typical of the credits available under the general business credit. There are a number of other credits that are available for specific activities. Each credit has unique requirements and limits, but the rehabilitation credit is a good example.

    A. The rehabilitation credit percentage depends upon the type of expenditure.

        1. Expenditures to rehabilitate property placed in service before 1936 are eligible for a 10% credit.

        2. Expenditures to rehabilitate certified historic structure are eligible for a 20% credit.

    B. Qualifying expenditures are often used to adjust basis, and may be subject to recapture.

        1. The adjusted basis of the property is reduced by the amount of credit.

        2. Rehabilitation credit is recaptured if the building is held less than five years (the recapture rate is 20% per year).

IV. Small Employer Health Insurance Credit

    A. An eligible small employer (ESE) can claim a credit equal to 50% of its nonelective contributions for health insurance for its employees (25% for small tax-exempt employers).

    B. To be eligible for the credit, an ESE has to contribute at least 50% of the cost of the employee's insurance premiums under a contribution arrangement.

    C. The full amount of the credit is available only to an ESE with 10 or fewer full-time equivalent employees and whose employees have average annual full-time equivalent wages of less than

$25,800 (2015). The credit is fully phased out once the number of full-time employees reaches 25 and/or the average wages reach $51,600 (2015).

D. For purposes of the credit, the owner of a business and specified relatives are not treated as employees (and thus, no credit is allowed for the employer contributions for the health insurance of those employees).

E. Any unused credits may be able to be carried back or carried forward.

V. Work Opportunity Tax Credit (WOTC)

(At the time of this writing Congress has not extended this provision to 2015.)

A. This credit is calculated on the amount of wages paid per eligible employee during the first year of employment. The credit is 40% of qualified wages, with a maximum credit of $2,400.

B. The credit is elective.

C. The credit is targeted at certain employee groups, such as veterans.

D. The WOTC reduces the deduction for wages.

VI. Research Credit

(At the time of this writing Congress has not extended this provision to 2014.)

A. Incremental research expenditures are eligible for a 20% credit. The research must be conducted within the U.S. and does not apply to research for commercial production, surveys, or social science research.

B. Taxpayers may elect to use an alternative simplified research credit. This is equal to 14% of the excess of qualified research expenses over 50% of the average research expenses for the last three years.

VII. Miscellaneous Credits—There are many types of business credits designed to subsidize specific activities.

A. The cost of operating employee child care facilities generates a 25% credit for employers up to $150,000 per year.

B. Energy credits are granted for certain solar and geothermal property at a rate of 10%–30% of qualified expenditures. Credits are also allowed for facilities using marine and hydrokinetic renewable energy or wind to produce electricity, as well as biomass, landfill gas, trash, and hydropower.

C. Contractors may claim a credit for each new efficient home, which is used as a residence after sale. The credit is either $1,000 of $2,000 depending on the reduction in energy usage (30% or 50%).

D. Nonbusiness energy credit—This credit is 10% of the amount spent for energy efficiency improvements and residential energy property expenditures, with a lifetime limit of $500. At the time of this writing Congress has not extended this provision to 2015.

E. Other credits include credits for disabled access and low-income housing.

Formation of a Corporation

After studying this lesson, you should be able to:

1. Evaluate whether a corporate formation is eligible for deferral of gain/loss.

2. Compute the basis of stock held by shareholders and assets by corporation after formation.

3. Determine the holding period for stock and assets after the formation.

4. Calculate the effect of liability assumptions by the corporation on gain and basis.

I. **Recognition of Gain or Loss**—The recognition of gain or loss on a contribution of property in exchange for stock is determined by the ownership levels of the contributing shareholders.

II. **Deferral**—Deferral of gain and loss is required for members of the control club.

Definition:
The Control Club: Is the group of individuals, who participate in a transfer of property to a corporation, and are in control of the corporation immediately after the transfer.

    A. To be eligible for membership in the control club, property must be contributed (services rendered to the corporation is not property).

    B. The property must be transferred in exchange for stock.

Definition:
Stock: Is any equity interest except that "nonqualified" preferred stock (NPS) is treated as boot. NPS is preferred stock that is expected to be redeemed within 20 years.

    1. Immediately after the transfer, the transferor(s) are in control, and control is defined as owning at least 80% of the voting and nonvoting stock.

    2. The receipt of boot triggers gain but not loss.

    3. Note: In order to meet the 80% control test, shareholders who contributed services for their stock may also contribute a small amount of property so their stock ownership can contribute to meeting the 80% requirement. However, the IRS has ruled that the value of the property must be equal to at least 10% of the value of the services for the shareholder's stock ownership to be included.

    4. Existing shareholder contributes property so that the group will meet the 80% test. The value of the property contributed by the existing shareholder must be equal to at least 10% of the value of the stock owned by the existing shareholder before the new contribution can be included in the group.

Definition:
Boot: Property received other than stock.

    C. If boot is received, the **gain recognized** to the shareholder is the lower of:

       1. **Realized gain** or

       2. The fair market value of the **boot received**

D. If stock is received in exchange for services:

    1. The transferor has **wage income** equal to the fair market value of the stock received (and basis in the stock equal to that amount).

    2. The **corporation has a salary expense deduction** (unless the services rendered were an organizational expense).

E. Reminder: The corporation does not realize any gain or loss on issuing stock.

III. Basis Issues—The adjusted basis for qualifying property is a carryover basis.

    A. The corporation takes an adjusted basis in the property from the transferor plus any gain recognized by the transferor.

    B. The corporation's basis in the property received is:

> Shareholder's basis in the property + Gain recognized by the shareholder

    C. The shareholder's stock takes the adjusted basis of the transferred property plus any gain recognized less any boot received.

    D. The shareholder's basis in the stock received from the corporation is:

> Basis of all property transferred to the corporation
>
> + Gain recognized by shareholder
>
> − Boot received by shareholder
>
> − Liabilities assumed by corporations

        1. Shortcut—A carryover basis is the fair value of the property less the gain deferred (or plus any loss deferred). This shortcut works only if the value of the property is known.

Example:
TP contributes a building worth $200,000 to a corporation in exchange for 100% of the corporate stock. TP has an adjusted basis of $100,000 in the building, but the property is subject to a $25,000 mortgage. The corporation takes an adjusted basis of $100,000 in the building, but TP takes an adjusted basis of $75,000 in his stock.

    E. Debt assumption—A contribution of encumbered property requires that the transferor reduce the basis of the stock by the amount of debt assumed by the corporation.

    F. Basis adjustment for loss property

        1. If the total basis of the property transferred by a shareholder is greater than the fair market value of the property, a basis adjustment is required to prevent the shareholders and the corporation from both benefiting from this unrealized loss. The downward basis adjustment is allocated proportionately among all assets contributed by the shareholder that had a built-in loss.

        2. Note: If the shareholder and corporation elect, the shareholder's stock basis can be reduced rather than the corporation's assets.

Example:
As part of a corporate formation, TP contributes property with an adjusted basis of $100 and a FMV of $75. The corporation's basis in this property will be reduced to $75, and TP's stock basis will be $100. Alternatively, TP and the corporation could elect to leave the property's basis at $100 and reduce TP's stock basis to $75.

IV. Debt Assumptions—Gain may be recognized in two circumstances if the corporation assumes the shareholders' debt.

    A. If the total liabilities assumed by the corporation exceed the total adjusted basis of property transferred by the shareholder, then gain must be recognized as follows:

> Gain recognized = Liabilities assumed − Basis of property transferred

Example:
Shareholder contributes property to a corporation with a fair market value of $100 and adjusted basis of $60. A liability of $70 is attached to the property and is assumed by the corporation. The shareholder recognizes a gain of $10 ($70 liability − $60 basis). The shareholder's basis in her stock is zero.

    B. If the debt was not incurred by the shareholder for valid business reasons, then the corporate assumption will cause ALL of the debt relief to be treated as boot. This will cause gain to be recognized, but only to the extent of the realized gain.

Example:
Shareholder contributes property to a corporation with a fair market value of $100 and adjusted basis of $60. A liability of $50 is attached to the property and is assumed by the corporation. The liability was not incurred for a valid business reason. Therefore, the $50 debt is treated as boot. The realized gain is $40 ($100 amount realized − $60 basis). The recognized gain is $40, the lower of the boot ($50) or realized gain ($40). The shareholder's basis in her stock is $50 ($60 basis in property − $50 debt relief + $40 gain recognized).

V. Holding Period

    A. The shareholder's holding period—For the stock may or may not include the amount of time the shareholder held the property just given to the corporation.

        1. Capital asset or Section 1231—Asset transferred to corporation—property holding period is tacked on to stock holding period.

        2. All other property—Holding period of property **does not tack** on. Holding period for stock begins on day after the transfer.

    B. The corporation's holding period—In the property received **always includes** the period that the transferor held the property before the exchange.

VI. Debt vs. Equity—Corporate debt can be reclassified as equity, but this is a question of fact.

    A. Debt characteristics are important (instrument, collateral, interest, etc.).

    B. The corporation is not thinly capitalized (debt equity ratio too high).

Corporate Income

Tax Forms for this Lesson: Form 1120, Schedule M-3 (available for download and printing from the lesson overview of your software).

I. Corporate Tax Formula

The Corporate Income Tax Formula

Realized Income

less

Nonrecognition of Income:

Deferrals and Exclusions Cost of Goods Sold

equals

Gross Income

less

Deductions

equals

Taxable Income before Special Deductions

less

Special Deductions

equals

Taxable Income

times

Tax Rates equals **Gross Tax** less

Credits and Payments

plus

Other Taxes

equals

Net Tax

A. The corporate tax calculation is very similar to the formula used to calculate individual taxes. The general income and deduction rules for corporations are the same as those for individuals. For example, the NOL rules for individuals and corporations are generally the same.

> **Definition:**
> *C Corporation*: A corporation subject to the corporate income tax is often referred to as a
> C corporation because the rules governing the corporate tax are contained in
> Subchapter C of the Internal Revenue Code.

B. The corporate formula—Is analogous to the individual formula.

1. Expenses are generally deductible as business deductions (subject to the limits placed on business deductions, such as reasonable, ordinary, etc.).

2. There are categories of special deductions subject to special limitations (see the lesson "Special Corporate Deductions" for more details).

3. Deductible capital losses are offset against recognized capital gains, but there is no deduction for a **net capital loss**. Rather, a net capital loss is carried over (back three years/forward five years) to offset against capital gains in other years.

C. Special rules

1. Corporations can choose a fiscal year unless the corporation makes an "S" election or qualifies as a personal service corporation. Personal service corporations generally must use a calendar year-end.

> **Definition:**
> *Personal Service Corporation*: A corporation whose principal activity is the performance of personal services performed by employees who own substantially all of the stock; for example, a medical corporation whose owners are also the doctors providing the medical services.

2. Accrual accounting is **required** except for small corporations (gross receipts less than $5 million), certain personal service corporations, and S corporations. Recurring expenses, however, must be paid within eight-and-a-half months of the fiscal year-end. Additionally, expenses to certain related taxpayers (e.g., cash basis shareholders) can only be deducted when paid.

3. Multiple tax brackets are not available for members of a "controlled group" (see the lesson "Taxation of Related Corporations") or for personal service corporations (a flat 35% tax rate is employed).

4. Passive loss rules

   a. Passive loss limits do not apply to corporations (except personal service corporations and certain "close" corporations).

   b. Closely held corporations can use passive losses to offset active corporate income but not portfolio income.

   c. Personal service corporations cannot offset passive losses against either active income or portfolio income.

> **Definition:**
> *Closely Held Corporation*: A corporation is a closely held corporation if at any time during the last half of the taxable year more than 50 percent in value of its outstanding stock is owned, directly or indirectly, by or for not more than five individuals.

5. The due date for a corporate return is the 15th day of the third month following the end of the tax year, but there is a six-month extension to file granted upon request. Estimated corporate tax payments are required if the tax liability exceeds $500.

Example:
1. ABC, a calendar-year accrual-basis corporation, received $10,000 of life insurance proceeds due to the death of its controller. ABC was the owner and beneficiary of this policy.

Question:
What amount of taxable income do the proceeds generate?

Answer:
None. Life insurance proceeds are excluded.

2. ABC, a calendar-year accrual-basis corporation, paid $3,000 of insurance premiums on the life of its manager (ABC is the beneficiary of this $100,000 policy) and $4,000 of group term insurance premiums for the corporation's four employees (the employees' spouses are the beneficiaries of these $10,000 policies).

Question:
What amount should ABC deduct for insurance premiums this year?

Answer:
$4,000. The key man premiums are not deductible.

II. **Book Income versus Taxable Income**—Schedule M-1 is a reconciliation of book income to taxable income. Schedule M-1 reconciles to taxable income before the dividends received and net operating loss deductions. Corporations with total assets of $10 million or more are required to file schedule M-3, which provides much more detail than Schedule M-1.

A. Nondeductible expenses are **added** to book income (federal tax expense, net capital loss, expenses in excess of limits, etc.).

B. Income that is taxable but not included in book income is **added** to book income (for example, prepaid income included in taxable income).

C. Nontaxable income that is included in book income is **subtracted** from book income (municipal interest, life insurance proceeds, etc.).

D. Deductions not expensed in book income are **subtracted** from book income (dividends received deduction, election to expense, etc.).

E. Schedule M-3 is divided into three sections.

1. Part I provides certain financial information and reconciles worldwide consolidated net income on the book financial statements to book income for the entities included on the corporate tax return.

2. Part II reconciles the book income computed in Part I to the taxable income shown on the Form 1120. For each reconciling item the effect due to permanent differences and timing differences must be shown.

3. Part III provides a breakdown of the expense/deduction items that affect the reconciliation of book income to taxable income in Part II. This total is carried to Part II and combined with the income items listed in Part II.

4. Certain large S corporations and partnerships must also file Schedule M-3.

Example:

1. Book income of $100 includes a federal tax expense of $22 and municipal interest of $13. The two adjustments to taxable income are identical to reversing entries— add expense of $22 and subtract income of $13 to book income. Hence, taxable income is $109.

2. This year ABC Corporation, an accrual-basis calendar-year corporation, reported book income of $380,000. Included in that amount was $50,000 of municipal bond interest, $170,000 for federal income tax expense, and $2,000 of interest expense on debt incurred to carry the municipal bonds.

Question:
What amount should ABC report as taxable income on Schedule M-1 of Form 1120?

Answer:
$502,000, as calculated by reducing book income by $50,000 and increasing it by $172,000.

3. This year ABC corporation, a calendar-year accrual-basis corporation, had a net book income of $100,000. Included in the computation were the following:

Provision for federal income tax	$26,000
Net capital loss	11,000
Keyman insurance premiums	4,000

Question:
What is ABC's taxable income?

Answer:
$141,000—computed by adding these adjustments to book income.

4. This year ABC corporation reported book income of $140,000. Included in that amount was $50,000 for meals and entertainment expense, and $40,000 for federal income tax expense.

Question:
What amount should be reported as ABC's taxable income in the Form M-1 reconciliation?

Answer:
$205,000—computed by adding back one-half of meals and all of federal taxes to book income.

III. **Net Operating Loss**—A net operating loss (NOL) is negative taxable income carried from other tax years.

A. The carryover period is back two years and forward 20 years.

B. Any carryover from a previous or prior year is not included in calculating the current year NOL (specific for each year).

C. The current year carryover ignores carryovers created in other years. Multiple carryovers to one year are used in a FIFO order.

D. Charitable contributions are not allowed in computing the NOL.

E. NOL carrybacks can be reported on an amended return (Form 1120X), or Form 1139 (*Corporation Application for Tentative Refund*) can be filed by the end of the tax year following the year of loss.

Special Corporate Deductions

There are certain corporate deductions subject to special limitations.

After studying this lesson, you should be able to:

1. Differentiate organizational expenses, start-up costs, and syndication expenses.

2. Compute the deduction for organizational expenses and start-up costs.

3. Compute charitable contribution for corporations.

4. Calculate the dividends received deduction.

5. Determine the applicability of the domestic production deduction.

6. Apply the ordering rules for special corporate deductions.

I. Organizational, Start-Up, and Syndication Expenditures

A. Expenses incurred in connection with the organization of a corporation are organizational expenses. $5,000 of these expenses may be deducted, but the $5,000 is reduced by the amount of expenditures incurred that exceed $50,000. Expenses not deducted must be **capitalized**, and **amortized** over **180 months**, beginning with the month that the corporation begins its business operations, unless an election is filed not to do so.

1. Typical organizational expenses are legal services incident to organization, accounting services, organizational meetings of directors and shareholders, and fees paid to incorporate. They must be incurred before the end of the taxable year that business begins (but they do not have to be paid, even if on the cash basis).

B. An additional deduction is allowed using the same rules as above for start-up costs. Start-up costs are expenditures that would be deductible as regular operating expenses, except that the corporation has not yet started its trade or business operation so they do not meet the criteria for deductibility. For example, if a new restaurant pays waitresses while they are being trained, but before it opens for business, these salary payments are start-up costs.

C. Costs of issuing and selling stock are **syndication expenses**. They must also be capitalized, but cannot be amortized.

II. Charitable Contributions—Can be deducted after the amortization of organizational expenditures.

A. Charitable contribution rules—Are the same as for individuals, with the following exceptions:

1. A corporation's contribution of inventory or depreciables or real property used in its trade or business to charities that use the property in a manner related to the exempt purpose and solely for the care of the ill, needy, or infants, or where the property is used for research purposes under specified conditions, is subject to special rules.

2. The deduction is the lower of:

AB of property + 50% × (FMV − AB),   OR   2 × AB

B. For contributions before 2015, this rule applies for contributions of "wholesome" food inventory by corporations and other businesses to charities that use the food in an appropriate manner. At the time of this writing Congress has not extended this provision to 2015.

C. The corporation can elect to deduct accrued contributions if the contributions are actually paid in the first two-and-a-half months following the year-end.

D. The limit on the deduction is 10% of taxable income (before special deductions for charity, dividends received, and carryovers).

E. Any excess charitable contribution (above the 10% limit) carries forward for five years (there is no carryback).

III. Dividends-Received Deduction—The dividends-received deduction (DRD) is a percentage (%) of domestic dividends.

    A. To be eligible, the stock must be of a domestic corporation held over a 45-day window (90 days for preferred stock). This prevents dividend stripping. The DRD cannot be claimed by S corporations, personal service corporations, and personal holding companies.

    B. The DRD percentage depends on the level of stock owned by the corporation.

        1. Shortcut—If the corporation owns less than 20% of the stock of another corporation, then the dividends-received deduction (DRD) is 70% of the dividends received. If the corporation owns 80% or more, then the DRD is 100% of the dividends received. All ownership levels between these two extremes are entitled to an 80% DRD.

    C. The DRD is limited by taxable income (before the DRD), unless the DRD creates or adds to a net operating loss.

Example:
ABC corporation received $100 in dividends from a domestic corporation (ABC owned less than 20% of the stock). If ABC has taxable income (before the DRD) of $200, then the DRD is $70. If ABC has taxable income (before the DRD) of $90, then ABC is only entitled to a DRD of $63 (70% of $90).

    D. Additional limits are imposed on the DRD if debt is used to finance the investment in stock (DRD is limited to the proportion of dividends that are not financed by debt).

Note:
The dividends-received deduction is not limited by taxable income if the full dividends-received deduction creates or adds to a net operating loss. For example, suppose ABC corporation received $100 in dividends from a domestic corporation (ABC owned less than 20% of the stock). If ABC has taxable income (before the DRD) of $10, then the DRD is $70 because it exceeds taxable income and thereby creates a net operating loss (an NOL of $60).

IV. Domestic Production Deduction (DPD)—Corporations engaged in production activities within the United States qualify for a deduction equal to 9% times the lower of 1) qualified production activity income or 2) taxable income. The DPD is reduced for the production of oil, gas, and related products.

    A. Qualified production activity income is equal to:

        1. Gross receipts from domestic production less:

            a. Cost of goods sold, direct expenses allocated to this income, a pro-rated share of indirect expenses allocated to this income.

    B. This deduction may not exceed 50% of the wages allocable to domestic production income.

Example:
Hanover Company produces computer chips and has the following information:

Gross receipts from qualified production activities	$1,000,000	
Related cost of goods sold	400,000	
Direct costs related to receipts (not including wages)		200,000
Indirect costs related to receipts	100,000	
W-2 wages related to receipts		100,000

40% of the indirect costs relate to the qualified production activities. Hanover Company's taxable income is $350,000.

Hanover's qualified production income is:

Gross receipts from qualified production activities:	$1,000,000
Related cost of goods sold	– 400,000
Direct costs related to receipts (not including wages)	– 200,000
Indirect costs related to receipts	– 40,000
W-2 wages related to receipts	– 100,000
	$ 260,000

Hanover's qualified production activities deduction is:

9% × the lower of   1) QPAI of $260,000

                           2) Taxable income of $350,000

9% × $260,000 = $23,400.

Note that the QPAD cannot exceed 50% of the W-2 wages related to the qualified production income, which is $50,000 ($100,000 × 50%).

V. **Ordering Rules for Corporate Deductions**—The following expenses are deducted in a specific order because each one is limited to the amount of income after reducing taxable income by the prior deduction.

See the following example.

Corporate Tax Formula—Special Deductions

Gross Income

Less: Deductions (except charitable, dividends received, domestic production deduction, NOL carryback, capital loss carryback)

Taxable income for charitable limitation

Less**: Charitable contributions** (<= 10% of above)

Taxable income for Div. Rec'd deduction (however, note that NOL carryforwards are not allowed for computing the DRD limit)

Less: **Dividends received deduction**

Taxable income before carrybacks

Less: **Domestic Production Deduction, NOL carryback, and STCL carryback**

TAXABLE INCOME

Corporate Alternative Minimum Tax

After studying this lesson, you should be able to:

1. Determine whether the AMT rules apply to a particular corporation.

2. Compute the alternative minimum tax for corporations.

3. Identify the most common adjustments and preferences when computing the AMT.

4. Calculate the adjusted current earnings adjustment and its effect on AMTI.

I. **The Corporate AMT Formula**—Is very similar to the individual formula in that taxable income is modified by adding tax preferences and adding or subtracting adjustments to income. The tax is called an alternative tax because it is imposed in lieu of the regular tax when the AMT's "tentative" tax exceeds the regular tax.

II. **Small Corporation Exemption**—The AMT does not apply to small corporations, but other firms need to calculate the AMT to determine if it applies in any given year.

    A. The **corporate AMT doesn't apply to small corporations meeting a gross receipts test.** The tentative minimum tax (TMT) is zero if the corporation's average annual gross receipts for all three-tax-year periods ending before the tax year do not exceed $7,500,000. If a corporation fails this test for any year, then it will be subject to the AMT for ALL future years.

    B. The above gross receipts test is applied by substituting $5,000,000 for $7,500,000 for the first three-year-tax period (or portion thereof) of the corporation that's taken into account under the test. **For new corporations, the TMT is always zero for its first year of operations.** A corporation formed in 2014 would be subject to the following tests:

> 2015—exempt from AMT for first year
>
> 2016—testing period is 2015
>
> 2017—testing period is 2015–16
>
> 2018—testing period is 2015–17

III. **Adjustments and Preferences**—Adjust taxable income (before NOL carryovers) for "tax preferences" and "adjustments" similar to individual formula.

    A. Preferences

> **Definition:**
> *Tax Preferences*: Increase taxable income when computing alternative minimum taxable income (AMTI). They often represent economic income excluded from regular taxable income or excessive deductions.

        1. Tax-exempt interest—On private activity bonds (net of related expenses). Interest from general obligation bonds is not added back. For any private activity bonds issued in 2009 and 2010, the interest earned from these bonds will not be included in AMT income.

        2. Excess of percentage depletion—Deduction over property's adjusted basis.

        3. Excess intangible drilling and development costs.

B. Adjustments

> **Definition:**
> *AMT Adjustments:* Specific adjustments that can either increase or decrease taxable income when computing alternative minimum taxable income. These adjustments often represent income or deductions used to defer the taxation of economic income.

1. The AMT adjustment applies only to MACRS 3-, 5-, 7-, and 10- year property that is depreciated using the 200 percent declining balance method. For AMT, the 150% DBM is used over the MACRS life. Note, that no AMT adjustments are required for assets purchased in 2008–2014 that use bonus depreciation. For more information on bonus depreciation see the "Limitations on Certain Business Deductions" lesson.

   > **Note:**
   > *There is no difference between AMT cost recovery and regular cost recovery for real property. Different methods are required only for personalty.*

2. Differences in gain/loss between regular tax and AMT caused by **different bases in assets** (due to different depreciation methods).

3. Difference in **percentage of completion method income over completed contract method income**.

4. Add regular tax net operating losses in excess of AMT net operating losses.

IV. Adjusted Current Earnings (ACE)—The adjustment for ACE is a recognition that the list of preferences and adjustments contained in the AMT formula was not all-inclusive. Congress addressed this problem by using the adjustments for calculating E&P as a basis for providing a better yardstick for comparing AMTI with economic income.

A. A positive ACE—Represents high pretax economic earnings.

1. To calculate ACE, modify AMTI by adding economic income and adjusting for timing differences analogous to E&P adjustments. Common adjustments are:

   a. Increase for life insurance proceeds less expenses related to policy

   b. Increase in municipal interest income less related expenses

   c. Increase for the 70% dividends received deduction (i.e., deduction is not allowed in ACE)

   d. Adjustment reflecting that installment sales method is not allowed for ACE

   e. Increase for intangible drilling costs

   f. Increase for organizational expense amortization

2. No adjustment is required in computing ACE for:

   a. Excess charitable contributions

   b. Net capital losses

   c. Penalties

   d. Disallowed travel and entertainment

   e. Federal income taxes

   f. 80% and 100% dividends received deduction

   > **Note:**
   > *When answering questions regarding the computation of ACE, you must determine whether the question is asking 1) how an item impacts ACE, or 2) if starting with taxable income, are the items added or subtracted to compute ACE. For example, the 100% dividends received deduction **reduces** ACE. But if the question starts with taxable income and asks what adjustment is required when starting with taxable income for the 100% DRD, **no adjustment** is required since the 100% DRD already reduced taxable income.*

3. If ACE exceeds AMTI (before the ACE adjustment), then 75% of this difference is used as an adjustment for calculating AMTI.

4. Because of timing differences, ACE can also be a negative adjustment, but it is limited to a cumulative amount of prior positive adjustments.

V. Other Items in Corporate AMT Formula—Special characteristics of the corporate AMT formula including the AMT NOL deduction and the corporate AMT exemption.

    A. The AMT NOL deduction is allowed for the carryover of net operating losses under the AMT in prior years, and is limited to 90% of AMTI (before NOL).

    B. The AMT exemption for corporations is $40,000, and it is phased out for AMTI over $150,000 (25% of the amount of AMTI over this trigger).

> **Example:**
> ABC corporation has AMTI of $250,000. ABC will be entitled to claim an exemption of $15,000 ($40,000 less 25% of $100,000).

        1. Shortcut—An exemption for the corporate AMT is completely phased out when AMTI equals $310,000. This is $160,000 over the phaseout trigger of $150,000, and this means that the entire $40,000 exemption is phased out (25% of $160,000).

    C. Corporations pay the greater of the tentative minimum tax or regular tax.

    D. The foreign income tax credit can reduce the AMT liability.

VI. AMT Credit Limitation—In years that the AMT is paid, a credit (minimum tax credit) is generated that can be used in future tax years. The entire AMT amount is available for this credit. This credit is available in a year in which the tentative minimum tax is less than the regular tax. In those years, it can be used to reduce the regular tax but not below the amount of the tentative minimum tax for that year.

VII. Formula for Corporate AMT

See the following illustration.

Formula for Corporate AMT Taxable Income
plus
Tax Preferences
plus or minus
AMT Adjustments
and
ACE Adjustment
equals
Alternative Minimum Taxable Income (AMTI)
minus
Minimum Tax Exemption
equals
Tax Base
times

Tax Rate (20%)

equals

Tentative Tax before Credits

less

Foreign Tax Credit

equals

Tentative Tax

less

Regular Tax

equals

Alternative Minimum Tax (AMT)

Penalty Taxes

After studying this lesson, you should be able to:

1. Compute the accumulate earnings tax.

2. Identify the acceptable reasons for accumulating income.

3. Determine the accumulate earnings credit.

4. Apply the income and ownership tests to determine the applicability of the personal holding company tax.

5. Summarize how dividends impact the applicability of both penalty taxes.

I. **Accumulated Earnings Tax**—Corporations are sometimes used to avoid high individual tax rates. For example, the first $25,000 of corporate taxable income is taxed at only 15%. This use of the corporate form to reduce tax rates only works if the income remains in the corporation. If the income is distributed as dividends, then it is subject to the individual tax and no tax savings is realized. The accumulated earnings tax is designed to mitigate this use of the corporate form. Unnecessarily high levels of accumulated taxable income trigger this penalty tax, and it operates by imposing a penalty tax on any undistributed income. Hence, the accumulated earnings tax can be avoided either by documenting business reasons for accumulating income, or by distributing income as dividends.

   A. An accumulated earnings tax of 20% is imposed on undistributed accumulated taxable income.

      1. Accumulated taxable income is computed by adjusting taxable income to reflect retained economic income.

      2. Dividend distributions reduce accumulated taxable income because income is not accumulated if dividends are paid out to shareholders.

      3. For purposes of the accumulated earnings tax, dividends include **consent dividends** and dividends paid within two-and-a-half months of year-end.

Definition:

Consent Dividend: This dividend is not actually paid to shareholders. Instead, shareholders consent to be taxed as though a dividend (identified in the consent) was paid. The purpose of a consent dividend is to allow a shareholder to avoid a penalty tax by distributing dividends after the year-end.

---

      4. Finally, an accumulated earnings credit is subtracted from any accumulation to represent the "reasonable" accumulation of earnings for business purposes.

         See the following illustration.

The Accumulated Earnings Tax Formula

Taxable Income

plus or minus **Adjustments:**

− corporate income tax

− excess charitable contributions

− net capital loss

> – net capital gain (after tax)
>
> + dividends received deductions
>
> less
>
> **Dividends paid or deemed paid**
>
> less
>
> **Accumulated earnings credit**
>
> equals
>
> **Accumulated Taxable Income**

B. Adjustments—There are six modifications made to taxable income to reflect economic accumulations of income.

    1. Taxable income is reduced by (1) accrued income taxes, (2) excess charitable contributions, (3) net capital loss, (4) net capital gain after tax.

> **Definition :**
> *Excess*: Charitable contributions are the amount of contributions to charity in excess of the corporate deduction limit (10% of taxable income).

        a. Shortcut—The adjustments for net capital loss and net capital gain are mutually exclusive in that only one can occur in any given year. That is, either the corporation will have capital losses in excess of gains (a net capital loss) or vice versa (a net capital gain).

    2. Taxable income is increased by adding back (5) the dividends-received deduction and (6) any net operating loss or capital loss carryovers.

C. Accumulated earnings credit—The accumulated earnings credit is the greater of two numbers related to earnings and profits.

    1. One number is the amount of the **current** earnings and profits needed for the "reasonable needs" of the business.

> **Definition:**
> *Reasonable Needs of a Business:* Are a question of fact, but they have been found to include amounts necessary to finance business expansion (actual or planned), to provide working capital, or to retire liabilities. Reasonable needs, however, do not include amounts retained for unrealistic needs or for loans to shareholders.

    2. A flat $250,000 ($150,000 for service (e.g., health, law, accounting, engineering) corporations) less the **accumulated** earnings and profits at the close of preceding year.

> **Note:**
> *Since this formula is the greater of these two items, there is no maximum on the credit as long as reasonable business needs support it.*

II. Personal Holding Company (PHC) Tax—Corporations are sometimes used to hold investments because corporations are entitled to deduct a portion of dividends received. Hence, taxable income will be less if dividends are received by a corporation rather than an individual. The personal holding company tax is designed to mitigate this use of the corporate form. This penalty tax is triggered by relatively high levels of investment income in a corporation and it operates by imposing a penalty tax on any undistributed income. Hence, the personal holding company tax can be avoided either by keeping investment income levels relatively low, or by distributing income as dividends.

The Personal Holding Company Tax Formula

Taxable Income

plus or minus **Adjustments:**

− corporate income tax

− excess charitable contributions

− net capital gain (after tax)

+ dividends received deduction

+ net operating loss carryover (not previous year)

equals

Adjusted Taxable Income

less

Dividends paid or deemed paid

equals

Undistributed PHC Income

A. A PHC tax of 20% is only imposed on corporations qualifying as a **personal holding company**.

    1. Banks, insurance, and finance companies are exempt from the tax because their business purpose is to manage investments.

    2. The tax base for the PHC tax is taxable income adjusted to reflect retained economic income.

    3. Like the accumulated earnings tax, the PHC tax can be avoided by paying dividends.

> **Note:**
> *A corporation that passes the tests as a personal holding company may be subject to the PHC tax only if it also has undistributed PHC income.*

B. Income and ownership tests—A corporation is a personal holding company if it "passes" two tests: the income test and the ownership test.

    1. The **income** test is met if personal holding company income constitutes 60% of adjusted ordinary gross income (AOGI).

Definitions:

Personal Holding Company Income: This income includes taxable dividends, interest, and sometimes, rents, royalties, and personal service contracts.

Adjusted Ordinary Gross Income (AOGI): Gross income excluding capital and 1231 gains and reduced by expenses associated with the production of rent and royalty income.

---

    2. The **ownership** test is met if more than 50% of the value of the stock is owned directly or indirectly by five or fewer individuals at any time during the last half of the year.

Definition:
Indirect Ownership: Determined by stock "attribution" rules. These rules define ownership to include the stock held by an entity (the portion relating to a corporation, partnership, trust, or estate) or by family members (brothers and sisters, spouse, ancestors, and lineal descendants). An individual will not be considered to be the constructive owner of the stock owned by nephews, cousins, uncles, aunts, and any of his/her spouse's relatives.

      a. Shortcut—A corporation with 10 or more equal and unrelated shareholders would not be a PHC because it will not pass the ownership test.

C. Adjustments—PHC income is taxable income modified by five adjustments. The adjustments to taxable income are designed so that the tax base (undistributed PHC income) reflects retained economic income.

    1. Taxable income is reduced by (1) accrued income tax, (2) excess charitable contributions, and (3) net capital gain (after tax).

    2. Taxable income is increased by adding back (4) the dividends-received deduction and (5) the carryover for net operating losses from year prior to the previous year.

      a. Shortcut—The adjustments for the PHC are similar to those used for the accumulated earnings tax except that there is no adjustment for net capital losses and the adjustment for net operating loss carryovers does not include an NOL from the previous year.

D. PHC tax—The PHC tax is imposed on undistributed PHC income.

    1. To reduce PHC income, dividends must be pro rata (the dividends cannot be paid disproportionately).

    2. For purposes of the PHC tax, dividends include dividends paid during the year, consent dividends, and dividends paid within two-and-a-half months of year-end.

    3. A **deficiency** dividend can also be paid to avoid the PHC tax.

Definition:
Deficiency Dividend: A dividend expressly declared to avoid the tax and is paid within 90 days of tax imposition (the finding of a deficiency due to the PHC tax).

Taxation of Related Corporations

After studying this lesson, you should be able to:

1. Determine whether two or more corporations form an affiliated group.

2. Compute the applicable adjustments for consolidated taxable income.

3. Assess whether two or more corporations form a parent-subsidiary controlled group.

4. Evaluate whether two or more corporations form a brother-sister controlled group.

5. Identify the limitations placed on corporations that are members of a controlled group.

I.   **Overview**—Corporations can be directly related through inter-corporate ownership or indirectly related through common shareholders.

II. **Affiliated Groups**—An "affiliated group" exists when one corporation owns **at least 80% of the voting power** of another corporation **and** holds shares representing at least 80% of its **value**. This test must be met on **every day of the year.**

Example:
P corporation owns 80% of S corporation and 20% of X corporation. S owns 70% of X, but all other shares are held by unrelated individuals. P and S form an affiliated group. Because in aggregate P and S also own more than 80% of the stock of X, this corporation is also included in the affiliated PSX group.

III. **Elect to File**—Eligible affiliated corporations can elect to file a consolidated return.

Note:
*Ownership of a corporation is determined by examining the amount of voting stock, as well as other classes of stock. To qualify as a parent, a corporation must own 80% or more of **each** class. Once a parent and subsidiary exist, then related corporations can be included in the affiliated group if the total ownership (including all corporations within the group) rises to 80% or more.*

   A. **Consolidating permits** the corporations to eliminate intercompany profits and losses, allows the profitable corporation to offset its income against losses of another corporation, and permits net capital losses of one corporation to offset capital gains of another.

   B. Gains and losses on intercompany sales are deferred until disposition outside the group. These gains and losses will be recognized at the time of the eventual disposition outside the consolidated firm but the nature of the gain or loss is determined by the use of the property at the time of the intercompany sale.

   C. Foreign corporations, exempt corporations, S corporations, and insurance companies are not eligible to consolidate.

   D. The election to consolidate must be unanimous and it is binding on future returns (irrevocable) and creates a joint and several tax liability.

   E. The members of the group must conform their tax year to the parent's tax year.

   F. Intercompany dividends are eliminated from consolidated taxable income.

   G. The parent adjusts the basis of the stock of a consolidated subsidiary for allocable portion of income, losses, and dividends.

IV. **Controlled Groups**—Controlled groups are **parent-subsidiary corporations, brother-sister groups, and certain insurance companies**.

   A. A controlled group of corporations is entitled to one $250,000 accumulated earnings tax credit and is limited to taxable income in each of the first two brackets, as though the group were one corporation. A controlled group also receives only one Section 179 expense deduction and one AMT exemption.

Example:
Rather than form a corporation that expects to generate $100,000 of taxable income, a taxpayer might try to form four corporations with $25,000 of taxable income each. This tactic would allow each corporation to be taxed at 15% instead of the higher tax rates imposed on taxable income over $25,000. However, the four corporations would form a controlled group and would only be eligible for one set of tax brackets that could be allocated among the group.

B. The following tests are applied on the **last day of the year**.

C. Parent-Subsidiary—The focus here is on corporate ownership. A parent-subsidiary controlled group exists if:

1. Stock possessing at least 80% of the **voting power** of all *classes of stock entitled to* **vote**, or at least 80% of the total **value** of shares of all *classes of stock* of each of the corporations, except the common parent, is owned by one or more of the other corporations, and

2. The **common parent owns** stock possessing at least 80% of the total combined voting power of all classes of stock entitled to vote, or at least 80% of the total value of shares of all classes of stock of at least one of the other corporations.

D. Brother-Sister—The focus here is on **individual ownership**. A brother-sister controlled group exists if:

1. Two or more corporations are owned by five or fewer persons (individuals, estates, or trusts):

   a. Who have a common ownership of more than 50% of the total combined voting powers of all classes of stock entitled to vote, or more than 50% of the total value of shares of all classes of stock of each corporation, and

   b. Who possess stock representing at least 80% of the total combined voting power of all *classes of stock entitled to vote*, or at least 80% of the total value of shares of all classes of each corporation.

   c. The 80% test does not apply for determining brother-sister corporations in some circumstances. These circumstances include determining corporate tax brackets, the accumulated earnings credit, and the minimum tax exemption.

   See the following example.

Example:
A, B, and C corporations are owned by X and Z (unrelated individuals) as follows:

	Corporations		
Individuals	A	B	C
X	40%	30%	60%
Z	10%	65%	30%

A cannot be a member of a controlled group because it fails the control test (X and Z only own 50%). B and C both meet the total control test (80% or more by five or fewer individuals) and this group also passes the common ownership test (60%). Thus, BC is a controlled group!

2. Shortcut—Set up potential controlled groups in a table like that in the above example. The control test is made by adding down each column. The common ownership test is conducted by adding the smallest percentage in each row as follows:

	Corporations		
Individuals	B	C	Common
X	30%	60%	30%
Y	65%	30%	30%
tests	95%	90%	60%

Distributions from a Corporation

The calculation of earnings and profits is critical to determining whether a corporate distribution is a dividend (taxable to a shareholder) or a return of capital (tax-free up to the shareholder's basis). A distribution qualifies as a dividend if earnings and profits are positive. Hence, earnings and profits is the tax analog to retained earnings.

After studying this lesson, you should be able to:

1. Compute earnings and profits.

2. Differentiate how current and accumulated earnings and profits impact dividend income.

3. Calculate the tax effect of cash distributions to shareholder.

4. Determine the tax effects of property distributions to shareholder and corporation.

5. Evaluate the impact of distributions on earnings and profits.

I. **Earnings and Profits**—To properly classify distributions from a corporation, one must know the corporation's earnings and profits (E&P). To determine earnings and profits, taxable income must be adjusted to represent economic income. Hence, many of the adjustments will be very similar to the reconciling items used to adjust taxable income with book (accounting) income, except the direction of the change will be reversed.

   A. Additions to taxable income—Are made for exempt income or deductions that do not represent an economic outlay.

      1. Municipal interest and life insurance proceeds are added to taxable income because they are economic inflows excluded from taxable income.

      2. The dividends-received deduction does not represent an economic outlay, so it is added back to taxable income in computing E&P.

      3. Deductions claimed for carryovers from previous years (carryforwards) are added back to taxable income.

      4. Domestic production activities deduction.

      5. Proceeds from corporate life insurance policy (less cash surrender value).

   B. Some expenditures are not deductible—But represent economic outlays. These expenditures reduce taxable income in computing E&P.

      1. The amount of federal income tax (net of credits) reduces taxable income in computing E&P because it represents an economic outlay.

      2. Related party losses.

      3. Penalties, fines, lobbying expenses, life insurance premiums for a "key" man, and the disallowed portion of meals and entertainment expenses.

   C. Some modifications to taxable income—Modifications are timing differences and can be positive or negative.

      1. The deferred portion of a gain from a current installment sale (but not other deferrals) is also added to taxable income because it represents an economic inflow. When the gain is recognized in later years, it reduces taxable income because it has already been included in E&P in the year of the sale.

      2. The amount of depreciation deducted in excess of straight-line is viewed as a form of deferral and it is added back to taxable income (like the installment gain, this is a timing adjustment that will reverse in later years).

      3. Section 179 expense.

4. Net capital loss and the excess amount of charitable contributions.

D. Distributions generally reduce E&P

1. Cash distributions reduce E&P.

2. Distributions of property reduce E&P by the greater of the value of the property or the adjusted basis and this amount is then reduced by any liabilities that are assumed by the shareholder.

3. A distribution of **appreciated** property will first increase E&P by the amount of the gain recognized on the distribution.

4. Distributions **cannot create a deficit** in E&P—only losses can create a deficit.

Example:
If Corporation Mouse distributes property with a FMV of $1,000 and a basis of $1,200 to shareholder Cat and Cat assumes a liability attached to the property of $300, E&P is reduced by $900 ($1,200 − $300).

II. **Dividend Treatment**—The taxation of distributions as dividend income to shareholders depends upon the earnings and profits (E&P) accumulated in the corporation prior to distribution. Distributions are:

A. Taxable as **dividend income** to extent of the shareholder's pro-rata share of **E&P**;

B. **Excess is tax-free** to extent of shareholder's **basis** in stock (and reduces the basis);

C. Remaining distribution amount is taxed as a **capital gain**;

D. Both current and accumulated E&P are used to determine whether a distribution is a dividend. There are four possible scenarios.

Note:
Distributions cannot create a deficit in E&P, but E&P can have a negative balance due to net operating losses (negative taxable income).

Definitions:
Current E&P: That which is generated during the year (up to the year-end).

Accumulated E&P: The amount on the first day of the year (ignoring current E&P).

1. Scenario #1—If both current and accumulated E&P are negative, then distributions are a return of capital (tax-free up to adjusted basis—and then capital gain).

2. Scenario #2—If both current and accumulated E&P are positive, then the distribution is taxed as a dividend. Distributions are first taken from current E&P by allocating E&P up to the distribution date. Once current E&P is depleted, then distributions reduce accumulated E&P.

3. Scenario #3—If current E&P is positive but accumulated E&P is negative, then a distribution is a dividend only to the extent of the current E&P.

4. Scenario #4—If accumulated E&P is positive but current E&P is negative, then a distribution is a dividend to the extent of net E&P (accumulated E&P less an allocated portion of the deficit in current E&P) on the date of the distribution.

Note:
*Questions about distributions from E&P will typically use year-end distributions or describe income as **earned ratably** throughout the year. This language simplifies the calculation of the E&P balance on the date of the distribution (necessary to determine whether the distribution is from current or accumulated E&P).*

E&P Status at Time of Distribution	Accumulated E&P is **negative**	Accumulated E&P is **positive**
Current E&P is **negative**	Scenario 1: Distributions are a return of capital	Scenario 4: Dividend income to extent of accumulated E&P after netting against deficit in current E&P
Current E&P is **positive**	Scenario 3: Dividend income to extent of current E&P	Scenario 2: Dividend income to extent of current E&P, then accumulated E&P

E. A deficit in current E&P is allocated ratably during the year based on time, even if there is only one distribution for the year.

Example:
ABC Corp has a deficit in current E&P for the current year of $20,000. A distribution of $10,000 is made on April 1 and that is the only distribution for the year. One-fourth (90 days/365 days) of the current E&P is allocated to the distribution, or $4,932.

F. If more than one distribution is made during the year a **positive** current E&P balance is pro-rated among the distributions based on the amount of the distributions.

G. Accumulated E&P is allocated in chronological order.

III. **Property Distribution**—Distributions of property (in-kind distributions).

A. The value of the property distributed (net of any debt assumed by the shareholder) is the amount eligible for dividend treatment.

B. The distribution of appreciated property causes the corporation to recognize gains (not losses) like a sale of the property.

C. If the liability on the property exceeds the property's fair market value, the FMV is treated as being equal to the liability.

D. Amount distributed = FMV − Liabilities on property

E. Basis of the property to the shareholder is the fair market value.

F. **Constructive dividends** are also treated as distributions.

Definition:
Constructive Dividend: A payment to a shareholder that, although not formally declared as a dividend, is regarded as a dividend. Property distributions to shareholders will often be treated as a constructive dividend.

Example:
TP is the sole shareholder of Green Incorporated. This year, Green paid TP a salary of $200,000 when a reasonable amount of compensation for TP's services would have been $50,000. The excess salary ($150,000) is unreasonable compensation and is not deductible by Green. Instead, this amount is construed as a dividend payment to TP.

Corporate Redemptions and Liquidations

A corporation may engage in two types of transactions that can be viewed as a purchase of the stock held by a shareholder. A corporation may redeem stock by purchasing it from a shareholder. On the other hand, a corporation may dissolve and thereby cause the stock held by shareholders to be liquidated. Unfortunately, these transactions are not always treated as simple sales of stock because these transactions can also be structured to avoid taxes.

After studying this lesson, you should be able to:

1. Contrast the tax implications of dividends and redemptions.

2. Determine when a sale of stock to a corporation qualifies as redemption.

3. Compute the tax effects of redemption to shareholder and to corporation's earnings and profits.

4. Evaluate tax effects to shareholders of corporate liquidation.

5. Calculate effect of liquidation on corporate income, including disallowance of loss rules.

6. Identify requirements for a tax-deferred liquidation of a subsidiary.

I. **Redemptions**—A redemption of stock occurs when a corporation repurchases stock from a shareholder. The redemption is generally treated by the shareholder as a sale of the stock that will trigger recognition of gain or loss. However, a redemption of stock can also be structured to have the identical effect of a dividend distribution. Hence, the tax rules are constructed to assure that redemptions, which have the effect of a dividend, are taxed as dividends rather than sales of stock.

   A. There are two advantages of redemption treatment. First, the shareholder is able to offset stock basis against the redemption proceeds. Second, any resulting gain is treated as capital gain, which is often advantageous as compared to dividend income.

Example:
TP owns 100 shares that constitute 100% of Blue Inc. This year, in lieu of a $100 dividend, Blue redeems one share of stock for $100. This redemption is essentially a disguised dividend because TP remains the sole shareholder of Blue after the redemption.

II. **Three Methods to Qualify**—In order for a redemption to be taxed as a sale, it must qualify under one of three circumstances:

   A. First—A redemption will be treated as a sale, if the distribution is **not essentially equivalent to a dividend (NEED)**.

Definition:
Not Essentially Equivalent to a Dividend (NEED): This phrase has been interpreted to mean that there is a "meaningful" reduction in the shareholder's rights, including voting rights and rights to earnings.

   1. Shortcut—NEED is a question of fact that is very ambiguous.

   B. Second—A **substantially disproportionate** redemption will also qualify as a sale if the shareholder passes two tests: the **control** test and the **reduced interest test**.

Definitions:
Control Test: The shareholder must own less than 50% of the voting shares after the redemption.

Reduced Interest Test: The shareholder must own less than 80% of the shares that were owned prior to the redemption.

>
> **Example:**
> A owns 40 shares of XYZ corporation (one-third of the outstanding stock), and the remaining 80 shares are owned by B. If XYZ redeems 10 of A's shares and 10 of B's shares, the redemption would not be substantially disproportionate for A. Although A owns less than 50% of XYZ shares after the redemption (30/100), his interest has only declined from 33% (40/120) to 30% (30/100). Thus, the redemption would not meet the reduced interest test because A's interest did not decline to 80% of the previous ownership level.

    C. Third—A **complete termination** of the shareholder's interest in the corporation qualifies as a sale.

> **Definition:**
> *Complete Termination*: The shareholder must surrender the stock owned directly and indirectly (through stock attribution).

        1. For complete terminations, family attribution can be waived with the execution of an agreement by the taxpayer to notify the IRS of any subsequent acquisitions of stock for the next 10 years.

III. Attribution—For purposes of the redemption tests, the shareholder's interest includes stock owned direct and indirectly. Indirect or constructive ownership is determined through stock attribution rules.

A. Family attribution

> **Definition:**
> *Family Attribution*: Stock is owned by family members. It is defined to include spouse, children, grandchildren, and parents.

>
> **Example:**
> XYZ corporation is owned equally by TP and his three children. Under the family attribution rules, TP is deemed to own all of the stock of the corporation while each child is only deemed to own TP's shares (no attribution between siblings).

B. Entity attribution—Corporations

> **Definitions:**
> *Stock Attribution*: A taxpayer is deemed to own stock held by other related taxpayers. There are two forms of attribution: attribution to/from an entity and attribution to/from family.
>
> *Entity Attribution*: Stock owned by a corporation, partnership, trust, or estate is deemed to be owned by a taxpayer who is an owner or beneficiary of the entity. Additionally, stock owned by the owner or beneficiary may be deemed to be owned by the entity.

    1. Entity to owner—A shareholder is only subject to entity attribution if the corporation is controlled by the shareholder (owning 50% or more of the value of the stock). In this case, the shareholder is deemed to own a proportionate interest (equal to the ownership interest) of the stock held by the corporation. If the shareholder owns less than 50% of the corporation, then none of the stock owned by the corporation is attributed to the shareholder.

    2. Owner to entity—Stock owned by a 50% or greater shareholder is deemed to be owned in full (100%) by the corporation. If the shareholder owns less than 50% of the corporation, there is no attribution from the shareholder to the entity.

> **Note:**
> *The scope of attribution rules is not uniform across various tax topics. For example, the attribution rules applying to redemptions is narrower than the attribution rules applying to the personal holding companies. The latter rules include siblings (brothers and sisters) who are not included for the redemption rules.*

C. Entity attribution—Partnerships

    1. Entity to owner—Stock owned by a partnership is deemed to be owned by the partner based on her ownership interest in the partnership. Note this attribution applies to all partners, not just partners who own 50% or more.

    2. Owner to entity—Stock owned by a partner is deemed to be owned in full by the partnership. Note that this attribution applies to stock owned by all partners, not just partners who own 50% or more.

D. Entity attribution—Estates and trusts. The attribution rules for estates and trusts are similar to the rules for partnerships.

 Example:
1. A taxpayer owns a 10% interest in a partnership. If the partnership owns 100 shares of a corporation, then the partner is deemed to own 10 shares of the stock (10% of the stock held by a partnership).

2. TP owns 10% in Corporation A. If Corporation A owns 100 share of Corporation R, TP is not attributed any stock of Corporation R. However, if TP owns 60% of Corporation A, then TP would be deemed to own 60 shares (100 × 60%) of Corporation R.

IV. Consequences to Corporation

A. If the corporation distributes appreciated property as part of the redemption, the appreciation is recognized by the corporation. However, the loss in distributed assets that have declined in value is not recognized. If the property has been depreciated, the corporation may have to recognize Section 1245 or Section 1250 recapture.

B. The corporation must reduce its earnings and profits for redemptions. The reduction is the lower of 1) the redeemed stock's proportionate share of E&P, or 2) the amount of the redemption.

    1. If the redemption is actually treated as a dividend, E&P is reduced by the greater of the FMV or adjusted basis of the property distributed, reduced by any liabilities attached to the property.

V. Partial Liquidations

A. A partial liquidation is treated as a sale by noncorporate shareholders, so it is a fourth method to qualify for redemption treatment. There are two tests for partial liquidations, one objective and one subjective.

Definition:
Partial Liquidation: A contraction of the corporate business. Hence, the determination for sale treatment is made by looking for a contraction at the corporate level.

B. The objective test requires that the corporation must completely terminate a **qualifying business** and must continue to operate at least one qualifying business.

Definition:
Qualifying Business: A trade conducted for five years prior to the determination.

C. To meet the subjective test, the distribution must qualify as not essentially equivalent to a dividend in that it results from a genuine contraction of the corporate business, and not just from the sale of excess inventory.

VI. Redemption Used to Pay Death Taxes

A. A redemption used to pay death taxes may also be treated as a sale under two conditions.

B. The death of a shareholder in a valuable closely-held corporation may result in significant death taxes. However, if the corporate stock is the primary asset of the estate, then a redemption may be necessary in order to pay the estate tax. If the stock held by the estate is treated as a sale, no additional tax is usually due because adjusted basis of stock is increased to FMV on date of death.

Note:
Not essentially equivalent to a dividend for purposes of a partial liquidation is different from the definition of NEED for redemptions. The former focuses on the source of the distribution at the corporate level, while the latter examines the effect of the distribution at the shareholder level. However, both definitions are similar in that they are very subjective tests.

    1. The stock held by the decedent must be a large portion of the estate (35% of adjusted gross estate).

    2. The redemption is limited to the amount of federal and state death taxes and funeral and administrative expenses.

VII. Stock Distributions

A. Stock distributions are not taxable to the shareholder if there is no option to receive property in lieu of stock and there is no change in proportionate interests of the shareholders.

B. A **stock bailout** is treated as a dividend to the shareholder to the extent of earnings and profits at the time of the sale or redemption.

> **Definition:**
> *Stock Bailout*: A distribution of nonvoting stock followed by sale (or redemption) of the stock by the corporation.

VIII. Complete Liquidations—A distribution in complete liquidation occurs with the dissolution of a corporation and the distribution of remaining assets. A complete liquidation is similar to a redemption in that the shareholders receive assets in exchange for canceling the shares of stock.

A. Shareholders recognize gain or loss—On the liquidating distribution.

    1. The gain or loss is determined by subtracting the adjusted basis of the stock from the fair market value of the distribution, reduced by any taxes paid by the corporation for the liquidation.

    2. Any gain or loss recognized by the shareholder will generally be a capital gain or loss (depending on whether the stock is a capital asset).

    3. If the distributed property is subject to a liability, then the shareholder reduces the fair market value of the property by the amount of liabilities.

    4. The adjusted basis of the property received in the distribution is its fair market value on the date of distribution, reduced by any taxes paid by the corporation for the liquidation.

> **Example:**
> TP received realty worth $100 in liquidation of XYZ corporation. TP had a basis of $25 in the XYZ stock and the realty was subject to a mortgage of $40. TP will recognize a gain of $35 because the net value received was $60 reduced by an adjusted basis of $25. TP will have an adjusted basis in the realty of $100.

B. A corporation will recognize gain or loss—When it makes a liquidating distribution.

    1. The computation of the gain or loss is computed by subtracting the adjusted basis from the fair market value of the property distributed on the date of distribution.

    2. The nature of the gain or loss depends on the nature of the asset distributed (ordinary, capital, or Section 1231).

    3. If the distributed property is subject to a liability, then the fair market value of the property cannot be less than the amount of liabilities.

Example:
As part of a corporation liquidation, Corporation T distributes land with an FMV of $50,000, adjusted basis of $20,000, and debt attached to the property of $65,000. Corporation T recognizes gain of $45,000 ($65,000 − $20,000).

4. Expenses incurred in the liquidation are deducted on the last corporate return.

Example:
ABC corporation liquidated by distributing inventory worth $200 to its shareholders. If the inventory had an adjusted basis of $70, ABC would recognize ordinary income of $130 on the liquidation.

5. If the corporation realizes a loss on the distribution of property in complete liquidation to a shareholder owning more than 50% in value of the corporation's stock), then the loss is not recognized if:

   a. The distribution of each asset is not pro-rata or

   b. The property distributed is disqualified property (i.e., property acquired by the liquidating corporation in a tax-free incorporation or as a contribution to capital during a five-year period ending on the date of the distribution).

6. Built-in losses will be disallowed on distributions of some disqualified property to any shareholder, if the principal purpose was to recognize loss by the corporation in connection with the liquidation.

   a. Such a purpose is presumed, if the transfer occurs within two years of the adoption of the plan of liquidation, unless a business purpose can be established.

   Note:
   Under the related-party rule, all losses are disallowed. Under the non-related-party rule, only built-in losses are disallowed.

   b. Any decline in value for the property after its contribution to the corporation results in a deductible loss to the liquidating corporation. Only the built-in loss at the time of contribution is disallowed.

C. Subsidiaries—**no gain or loss is recognized**—On the liquidation of a subsidiary by the parent under two conditions. When a controlled subsidiary is liquidated, no real disposition of the assets has occurred. The assets have merely been transferred from one corporate pocket to another. The key to deferring gain and loss is the establishment of control and the timing of the liquidation.

   1. First, the parent must own 80% of the voting stock and other stock of the subsidiary.

   2. Second, the subsidiary must distribute its assets within the tax year (or within three years of the close of the tax year of the first distribution).

   3. The parent corporation takes a carryover basis in the distributed assets and inherits the subsidiary's tax attributes.

   4. Minority shareholders will recognize gain or loss on the liquidation.

Corporate Reorganizations

After studying this lesson, you should be able to:

1. Determine whether a corporate reorganization qualifies as a specific type of tax-deferred transaction.

2. Compute tax effects of a qualifying reorganization to acquiring and target corporations.

3. Evaluate tax effects of a qualifying reorganization to shareholders.

4. Identify the tax attributes that carryover with a qualifying reorganization.

I. **Acquisitions and Reorganizations**—Mergers, stock acquisitions, and asset acquisitions can all qualify for reorganization status if the shareholders of the acquired corporation receive sufficient equity from the acquiring corporations.

   A. Type A reorganization

> **Definition:**
> *Type A Reorganization*: A merger or consolidation under state law (called a statutory merger). Note that Target is exchanging its assets for Acquiring's stock. Once Target dissolves, the shareholders of Target own Acquiring stock.

   1. In a merger, the acquired corporation (target) dissolves into another corporation (the acquiring corporation).

   2. In a consolidation, both the acquired and the acquiring corporations dissolve into a new (surviving) corporation.

   3. At least 50% of the consideration provided to Target by Acquiring must be stock in Acquiring.

   4. The shareholders of the acquired firm can only defer gains and losses to the extent they receive equity of the acquiring corporation. Note, that both voting and/or non-voting stock can be used in Type A reorganization.

   5. Forms of payment that do not qualify as equity, are considered boot.

   6. Acquiring must assume all of the liabilities of Target.

> **Definition:**
> *Boot*: Property that does not qualify for nonrecognition. Boot triggers the recognition of gain, but not the recognition of losses.

> **Example:**
> T corporation merges into B corporation. All T shareholders receive B stock in exchange for their T shares. T shareholders will defer gains and losses on the disposition of their T shares because this transaction qualifies as a reorganization. If B corporation transferred consideration other than voting stock in the acquiring firm, these payments would be considered boot. These payments would not disqualify the merger unless more than 50% of the consideration received by a majority of T shareholders consisted of received boot instead of equity (violation of continuity of interest requirement).

   B. Type B reorganization

> **Definition:**
> *Type B Reorganization*: An acquisition of the stock of the target solely in exchange for voting stock of the acquiring firm. Acquiring exchanges its own stock for stock in Target. Target remains in existence, but it is now owned at least 80% by Acquiring. The former Target shareholders now own stock in Acquiring.

1. The acquiring firm must exchange its own voting stock (or that of its parent company) for the stock of the target. Note that the use of non-voting stock will disqualify the transaction from being a tax-free B reorganization.

2. The acquiring firm must own at least 80% of the stock of the target firm (voting and all other classes of stock) after the most recent acquisition of stock. Note that 80% does not need to be acquired during this acquisition; rather, total ownership must be 80% after the transaction.

3. Any consideration other than voting shares in the acquiring corporation, will violate the requirements of the reorganization.

>
> **Example:**
> B corporation offers B stock to the shareholders of T corporation. If 90% of the T shareholders exchanged their T shares for B shares, then these shareholders would defer any gains or losses on the disposition of their T shares.

C. Type C reorganization

> **Definition:**
> *Type C Reorganization*: An acquisition of "substantially all" of the assets of the target solely in exchange for voting stock of the acquiring firm. Note, that Target is exchanging its assets for Acquiring's stock. The shareholders of Target own Acquiring stock after the reorganization.

1. The target firm then distributes the stock and other assets to its shareholders.

2. **Substantially all of the assets** is defined by the IRS as 90% of net asset value and 70% of gross asset value.

3. The stock that Acquiring transfers to Target can be only voting stock and must be at least 80% of the consideration provided. Other consideration provided (i.e., boot) cannot exceed 20% of the total consideration provided by Acquiring.

   a. If liabilities attached to Target's assets are assumed by Acquiring, this liability relief is not considered as boot (and therefore not subject to the 20% test) unless other boot is also given. If other boot is also given, then the total amount of boot and liability relief cannot exceed 20% of the consideration.

>
> **Example:**
> B corporation transfers B common stock to T corporation in exchange for all of T's assets. T then distributes the B stock to its shareholders. The shareholders of T would defer gains and losses on the cancellation of their T shares. The shareholders would have an adjusted basis in the B shares equal to their adjusted basis in the old T shares.

D. Type D reorganization

> **Definition:**
> *Type D Reorganization*: A divisive reorganization (not acquisitive) in that a corporation (the parent) divides by transferring assets to a subsidiary in exchange for subsidiary shares.

1. The parent then distributes the subsidiary shares to its shareholders (spin-off) or redeems P stock with the S stock (split-off). Alternatively, the parent could be liquidated into two new corporations (a split-up).

2. In all events, the parent corporation must receive and distribute control of the subsidiary in the exchange (80% of the voting and other classes of stock).

Example:
P corporation creates a subsidiary, S corporation, and contributes an office building to S in exchange for all of the S shares. If P then distributes the S shares to its shareholders, this transaction would qualify as a spin-off. The shareholders of P would defer any gains and losses on the distribution and would allocate the adjusted basis of their P stock between their P shares and the S shares.

E. Other reorganizations—Exist to defer gains and losses on specialized transactions.

1. E and F reorganizations are recapitalizations and nominal changes (such as changes in the name of the corporation or the state of incorporation).

2. G reorganizations are related to bankruptcy recapitalizations.

F. In addition to meeting the specific reorganization rules described above, tax-free reorganizations must meet the following judicial principles:

1. The transaction must be motivated by a valid **business purpose**.

2. The **continuity the of business enterprise test** requires that the acquiring corporation must 1) continue the historic business of the target corporation, or 2) use a significant portion of target's assets in the continuing business of acquiring corporation.

3. A merger only qualifies as a reorganization if the **continuity of interest requirement** is met. This test requires that a substantial amount of the consideration that Acquiring gives to Target must be stock in Acquiring. If at least 50% of the consideration is Acquiring stock then this test is definitely met, but the IRS has ruled that 40% can be sufficient also.

4. The **step transaction doctrine** permits multiple steps to be collapsed into a single step when the steps are so interdependent on one another that one would not have occurred without the other(s). Collapsing these steps may lead to a tax result other than that desired by the taxpayer.

II. **Deferral of Gains/Losses and Basis Issues**—Generally, a reorganization does not require income recognition at the **corporate level** (by either the target or the acquiring corporation).

A. Acquiring corporation—In a reorganization, the acquiring corporation does not recognize gain or loss on the transfer of its stock for the acquired corporation.

1. An exception to this rule occurs if the acquiring corporation distributes appreciated property (in addition to stock). The appreciated property will trigger gain recognition to the acquiring corporation just as if the acquiring firm sold the assets.

B. Acquired corporation—In a reorganization, the acquired corporation does not generally recognize gain or loss.

1. A distribution of appreciated property to shareholders in connection with the acquisition will trigger gain recognition by the acquired corporation.

2. The basis that the acquiring corporation takes in the assets received is:

Basis in property to Target + Gain recognized by Target

---

3. Shortcut—Whenever a corporation distributes appreciated property (property with a value in excess of adjusted basis), the corporation will recognize the gain. This applies regardless of whether the distribution is related to a reorganization, a redemption, or a liquidation.

C. Shareholders—No gain or loss is recognized to the shareholders of the corporations involved in a tax-free reorganization if they receive only stock in exchange for property of the acquiring organization.

1. If shareholders receive other property in addition to stock, it is treated as **boot** and **gain is recognized equal to the lower of:**

    a. Boot received *or*

    b. Realized gain.

        i. Any gain recognized will be dividend income to the extent of the shareholder's proportionate share of Target's E&P. Any remaining gain is capital gain.

2. The basis to the shareholder in the **stock received** is:

> Basis in stock surrendered
>
> +   Gain recognized
>
> −   Boot received

III. **Tax Attributes**—The tax attributes of the target firm (such as net operating loss carryovers) survive in reorganizations.

> **Definition:**
> *Tax Attributes*: The tax characteristics of the firm. The most common attributes are the adjusted basis of assets, the earnings and profits of the corporation, carryovers (including net operating loss, capital loss, and excess charitable contributions), accounting methods (including depreciation methods), and tax credit carryovers.

A. If the target firm disappears (in a merger or asset acquisition), then the acquiring corporation is entitled to the target's tax attributes.

>
> **Example:**
> B acquires the assets of T in a merger, which qualifies as a reorganization. The adjusted basis of T's assets does not change even though the assets are now owned by B. In addition, the depreciation methods used on the T assets will continue to be used by B.

B. If the target survives as a subsidiary (e.g., after a stock acquisition), then the tax attributes stay with the target corporation. The acquiring firm can avail itself of a limited amount of the target's attributes through a consolidation with the target. The use of tax attributes by a surviving corporation or a parent is strictly limited through the application of complex provisions designed to limit tax incentives for corporate acquisitions.

C. Specific limitations

1. Earnings and profit of the target firm carries over to Acquiring. However, if Target has a deficit in E&P, that deficit can be used to offset only future earnings of the combined companies (not past E&P of Acquiring).

2. An NOL of Target is limited as follows for Acquiring's first tax return after the reorganization:

> (Income of Acquiring × # of days in year after transfer) / 365 days

3. Additionally, if there is a significant change in the ownership of Target (generally > 50% over a three-year period) the amount of Target's NOL that can be used annually in all future years is strictly limited to:

FMV of Target's stock before the change × the long-term tax-exempt rate

IV. **Other Types of Acquisitions**—The corporate tax consequences of a taxable acquisition (not a reorganization) depend upon the form of the acquisition.

   A. Subsidiaries—If the acquiring firm purchases the stock of the target and operates the target as a **subsidiary**, then neither firm recognizes any gain or loss.

   1. The tax attributes of the target survive, albeit trapped in the target firm.

   2. The acquiring firm uses the purchase price of the target's shares as the adjusted basis of the subsidiary.

   3. The adjusted basis of the target's assets does not change.

   B. Section 338 elections—Under certain conditions in a taxable stock purchase, the acquiring firm can elect to step up the basis of the target's asset to FMV.

   1. This election, referred to as a 338 election, requires the recognition of any gain generated by the difference between the adjusted basis of the target's assets and the fair market value of the stock.

   2. The benefit of the election (step up in the basis of the acquired assets) is generally less than the tax cost triggered by gain recognition. Hence, the election is rarely invoked.

   C. Taxable mergers—If the acquiring firm merges the target or acquires the assets of the target, then the target corporation recognizes gains and losses on the transfer of its assets.

   1. The adjusted basis of the target's assets is their fair market value. Any excess purchase price is allocated to goodwill and amortized over 15 years.

State and Local Taxation

After studying this lesson, you should be able to:

1. List most common taxes levied by state and local governments.

2. Define nexus and describe the process used to determine which states have jurisdiction to tax income.

3. Differentiate between business and nonbusiness income.

4. Describe the apportionment process for computing state income taxes.

I. **Types of State and Local Taxes**—State and local governments levy many different types of taxes. The most common are as follows:

  A. Sales taxes

    1. Levied on tangible personal property and some services.

    2. Exemptions vary by state but usually include items bought for resale and that are used in manufacturing.

  B. Use taxes—Levied on the use of tangible personal property that was not purchased in the state.

  C. Property taxes

    1. *Ad valorem* taxes based on the value of real property (realty taxes) and personal property (personalty taxes).

    2. There are usually exemptions for certain types of property, including those for inventory.

    3. A few states also tax intangible property.

    4. Usually levied for property owned at a specific date.

  D. Franchise tax

    1. Levied on the privilege of doing business in a state.

    2. Based on the value of the capital used in the jurisdiction (common stock, paid-in-capital, and retained earnings).

  E. Excise tax

    1. Levied on the quantity of an item or sales price.

      a. Examples include tax on gasoline, cigarettes, and alcohol.

    2. Can be charged to a manufacturer or consumer.

  F. Unemployment tax

    1. Levied on taxable wages with a limit per employee (usually $7,000).

    2. Rate varies based on experience of employer.

  G. Incorporation fees are charged for incorporating in a state or registering to do business in a state.

II. **Jurisdiction to Tax**—Because many businesses conduct operations in more than one state, a significant issue is determining which states have the authority to levy a tax on a particular business.

Definitions:

Domestic Corporations: Entities incorporated under the laws of a particular state.

Foreign Corporations: Corporations incorporated in another state.

A. Difficult to determine the degree of power to tax foreign corporations.

   B. Supreme Court developed four tests to determine jurisdiction to tax (Complete Auto Transit v. Brady):

      1. Business activity must have substantial nexus with state.

      2. The tax must be fairly apportioned.

      3. The tax cannot discriminate against interstate commerce.

      4. The tax must be fairly related to services that the state provides.

   C. Nexus for taxing a corporation's income does not exist if activity in the state is limited to:

      1. Soliciting sales of tangible personal property that are approved and shipped outside the state

      2. Advertising

      3. Determining reorder needs of customers

      4. Furnishing autos to sales staff

Definition:

Nexus: The degree of the relationship that must exist between a state and a foreign corporation for the state to have the right to impose a tax. The application of nexus to state taxation is governed by Public Law 86-272. This law applies to sales of tangible personal property and does not apply to the sale of services or to the leasing or renting of property. Nexus is determined on a year by year basis.

Example:

Corporation FLY's business domicile is in Texas and it sells widgets to wholesalers in Colorado. The orders are solicited, approved, and shipped from Texas. FLY does not have nexus with Colorado so the sales to Colorado wholesalers are not subject to taxation by Colorado.

   D. The following types of activities are usually sufficient to establish nexus with a state (if these activities occur in the state):

      1. Approving/accepting orders

      2. Hiring/supervising employees other than sales staff

      3. Installation

      4. Maintaining an office or warehouse (an office maintained by an independent contractor does not establish nexus)

      5. Providing maintenance or engineering services

      6. Making repairs

      7. Investigating credit worthiness or collecting delinquent accounts

      8. Providing training for employees other than sales staff

III. State Income Tax Computation—A model law known as the Uniform Division of Income for Tax Purposes Act (UDIPTA) helps to minimize differences among state tax laws.

   A. The starting point for computing state income taxes is federal taxable income, increased by adjustments such as (specific rules depend on state):

      1. Dividends received deduction

      2. Expenses related to interest earned on U.S. bonds

      3. State income taxes

4. Depreciation in excess of that allowed for state

5. Municipal interest taxed for state purposes

B. Decreased by:

1. Federal income taxes paid

2. Expenses related to municipal interest income

3. Interest on U.S. bonds

4. Depreciation in addition to that allowed for federal purposes

C. Business versus nonbusiness income—If more than one state has nexus to tax the income of a business entity then the income must be apportioned among the states. Designating income as business or nonbusiness is very required for this computation.

1. Business income is apportioned among all the states in which the corporation does business.

2. Business income—is generally:

    a. Generated from business's regular operations (**transactional test**), or

    b. From the sale of property that is an integral part of the business (**functional test**).

3. Nonbusiness income—generally includes investment income and income from transactions not part of regular operations. Nonbusiness income is generally allocated to the state of incorporation.

4. If investment income is generated by regular business operations it is business income.

Example:
SMALL Company is domiciled in Oregon. SMALL has invested some of its excess cash reserves with a financial firm in North Carolina. The investment income earned from these investments is taxed in Oregon. Note that if the investment was part of SMALL's regular business operations then the income would be allocated to North Carolina.

D. Apportionment

1. Business income is apportioned among the states in which it is earned based on apportionment factors such as sales, property, and payroll.

2. In general, states have discretion to apply different tax rules to different types of income. The U.S. Supreme Court has allowed states great flexibility to choose an apportioning formula and to tax income of an interstate business.

3. Some states use only one apportionment factor. Others vary in how they weight the factors.

4. Different types of factors are used for financial institutions and service businesses.

5   **Sales factor** is computed as:

Total sales in state / Total sales

a. The state of sale is determined based on the point of delivery.

b. If the business does not have nexus in the state of delivery then the sale is apportioned to the state where the sale originated.

6. **Property factor** is computed as:

Average value of property in state / Value of all property

   a. Property is limited to real property and tangible personal property, but does not include cash. It is valued at cost or book value depending on the state.

   b. Property also includes leased property (usually valued at the annual lease times eight).

   c. Property is included only if used in the production of business income.

7. Payroll factor is computed as:

> Compensation paid or accrued in state / Total compensation paid or accrued

   a. Compensation includes fringe benefits if taxable under federal law.

   b. Payments to independent contractors and paid into Section 401(k) plans are usually not included.

   c. Compensation is included only if related to the production of business income.

8. The Uniform Division of Income for Tax Purposes Act (UDITPA) is a model act adopted by the National Conference of Commissioners on Uniform State Laws (NCCUSL) and the American Bar Association to promote uniformity in state allocation and apportionment rules. Not all states have adopted this Act.

   a. The Act provides that if income-producing activity occurs in more than one state, the receipts are assigned to the state where the greatest cost-of-performance was incurred.

   b. Intangible assets are excluded from the property factor under the standard formula.

   c. To promote fairness across states the Act provides the following:

> If the allocation and apportionment provisions of (UDITPA) do not fairly represent the extent of the taxpayer's business activity in the state, the taxpayer may petition for, or the tax administrator may require, with respect to all or any part of the taxpayer's activity, if reasonable:
>
> a) Separate accounting
>
> b) The exclusion of any one or more of the factors
>
> c) The inclusion of one or more additional factors that will fairly represent the taxpayer's business activity in this state
>
> d) The employment of any other method to effectuate an equitable allocation and apportionment of the taxpayer's income

IV. Filing Requirements for State Income Taxes

  A. Filing approaches vary across states, including:

   1. Each entity reports separately.

   2. Affiliated corporations file a consolidated return.

   3. Members of a unitary group combine their transactions on one return.

Example:
LBJ Corporation owns 100% of LB and BJ Corporations. LBJ has business operations in TN and GA. LB has operations only in TN and BJ only in GA. Under separate entity reporting, LBJ and LB would file separate returns in TN, and LBJ and BJ would file separate returns in GA. If TN required the filing of consolidated returns then LBJ and LB would file a consolidated return in TN.

B. Unitary groups meet the definitional requirements of a specific state. Generally three requirement are evaluated to determine if entities should be combined, including unity of:

   1. Ownership—more than 50%

   2. Operations

   3. Use—centralized management

C. Partnerships may be included in a unitary group.

D. Businesses may be included in a unitary group even if there is not nexus with a state.

E. Note that some states do not recognize the Federal S Corporation election.

F. Some states also tax partnerships at the entity level.

Taxation of Foreign Income

After studying this lesson, you should be able to:

1. Differentiate between foreign source income and U.S. source income.

2. Define controlled foreign corporations and compute constructive dividends to U.S. shareholders of CFCs.

3. Calculate foreign tax credit.

4. Compute foreign earned income exclusion for U.S. individual taxpayers.

I. **General Rules**

   A. Treaties between the United States and other countries generally override the tax provisions in the U.S. tax law or foreign tax law.

   B. Foreign taxpayers are usually taxed only on U.S. source income.

   C. U.S. taxpayers are taxed on all income earned anywhere in the world.

II. **Sourcing of Income and Deductions**—Determining whether income is U.S. source or foreign source is critical for computing the federal income tax.

   A. Earned income is foreign source if earned in a foreign country and U.S. source if earned domestically. This also includes employee benefits.

   B. Unearned income is foreign source if received from a foreign resident or for property that is used in a foreign country.

   C. Income from the sale of personalty is determined based on the residence of the seller, except:

      1. Inventory is sourced where title transfers.

      2. In the case of depreciable property, recapture is sourced where depreciation was claimed. Remaining gain is sourced where title transfers.

   D. Income from the sale of intangibles is sourced where the amortization was claimed. Source of income from the use of intangible property is determined by the country in which the property is used.

   E. Income from the sale or exchange of real property is sourced based on the location of the property. Source of income from the use of tangible real property is determined by the country in which the property is located.

   F. Interest income is U.S. source if received from:

      1. U.S. government

      2. Noncorporate U.S. residents

      3. Domestic corporations

   G. If a U.S. corporation receives 80% or more of its active business income from foreign sources over the previous three years then interest received from that corporation is foreign source.

   H. Dividends from U.S. corporations are U.S. source and from foreign corporations are foreign source.

   I. If a foreign corporation receives 25% or more of gross income from income connected with a U.S. business for the three previous tax years then dividends from that foreign corporation are U.S. source.

   J. Deductions must also be allocated or apportioned as U.S. source or foreign source.

   K. The IRS has the authority to change the allocation of income and deductions if it determines that the taxpayer's methods do not clearly reflect income.

III. Outbound Transactions

A. The transfer of assets from the United States to a foreign country may trigger income (depreciation recapture applies).

B. If assets are used in a trade or business outside the United States, gain is deferred unless the property is:

    1. Inventory or unrealized receivables

    2. Installments obligations

    3. Foreign currency

IV. Controlled Foreign Corporations (CFC)

A. A CFC is a foreign corporation for which more than 50% of the voting power or value of stock is owned by U.S. shareholders (limited to those who own, directly and indirectly, 10% or more of the foreign corporation) on any day of the tax year of the foreign corporation.

Example:
Bottom, Inc., a foreign corporation, is owned by eight U.S. shareholders. One shareholder owns 37% and the other seven shareholders own 9% each. Bottom is not a CFC because only one shareholder owns 10% or more and this shareholderdoes not own more than 50%.

If one of the smaller shareholders increases its ownership interest to 14%, then Bottom would be a CFC since the two shareholders owning 10% or more would own 51% of Bottom.

B. Certain types of income from a CFC are taxed to a U.S. shareholder as a constructive dividend, even if no actual distribution has occurred. This income is referred to as Subpart F income. The main types of income subject to this rule include:

    1. Income that is not connected economically to the country in which the corporation is organized

    2. Income from insuring the risk of loss from outside the county in which the corporation is organized

Example:
Bottom, Inc. is a CFC for the entire tax year. Top, Inc., a U.S. based corporation, owns 75% of Bottom for the entire year. Both are calendar year corporations. Subpart F income is $50,000 and no distributions have been made. What is Top's constructive dividend for the tax year? $50,000 × 75% = $37,500.

V. Worldwide Income—Potential Double Taxation

A. U.S. taxpayers are taxed on all income earned anywhere in the world.

B. Three provisions mitigate the potential double taxation of this income:

    1. Foreign income taxes paid are an itemized deduction for individuals.

    2. Alternatively, a credit may be claimed for foreign taxes paid.

    3. Certain individuals can elect to exclude foreign-earned income.

C. The credit for foreign taxes paid is limited if the U.S. effective tax rate exceeds the foreign effective rate.

Limit = U.S. tax on worldwide income × Foreign source taxable income / Worldwide taxable income

1. Individuals must add personal exemptions to worldwide income.

2. Excess foreign tax credits can be carried back one year and carried forward 10 years.

3. Individuals who have only passive foreign income that does not exceed $300 ($600 for joint returns) can elect to be exempt from the foreign tax credit limitation.

4. A foreign tax credit usually provides a greater benefit than a deduction. The deduction may be preferable when the foreign effective tax rate is high and foreign income, as compared to worldwide income, is small.

D. Qualifying individuals must meet one of two tests to benefit from the foreign-earned income exclusion:

1. During a continuous period that includes an entire tax year, the individual must be a bona fide resident of at least one foreign country.

2. The individual must have a tax home in a foreign country and must have been present in one or more foreign countries for at least 330 days during any 12 consecutive months.

3. Qualifying individuals can exclude:

   a. Foreign-earned income from personal services, limited to $100,800 in 2015.

   b. Employer-provided foreign housing income, limited to $14,112 (14% of the $100,800) for 2015. This exclusion is allowed only to the extent it exceeds 16% × $100,800, or $16,128.

   c. Taxpayers must file an election to take the exclusion, which is binding for future years until revoked.

   d. If a taxpayer was present in a foreign country for at least 330 days but less than the entire year, the exclusion is pro-rated on a daily basis (365 day year).

Example:
J is a bona fide resident of a foreign country and is a U.S. citizen. For 2015 she receives a salary of $110,000 and interest income of $2,500. Of the earned income of $110,000, $100,800 may be excluded and the remaining $9,200 is taxed. The unearned income of $2,500 is not eligible for the exclusion and is taxable.

If J also receives employer-provided housing assistance of $20,000, this may be excluded to the extent it exceeds 16% of $100,800. The excess for J is $3,872 ($20,000 − $16,128). Note that the housing exclusion can never exceed $14,112 in 2015.

VI. Foreign Currency Gains and Losses

A. Foreign currency exchange gains and losses resulting from the normal course of business operations are ordinary.

B. Foreign currency exchange gains and losses resulting from investment or personal transactions are capital.

VII. Transfer Taxes

A. Taxpayers may use transfer pricing to manipulate the amount of income earned in the United States. Assume that BIG Corporation has manufacturing operations in the United States and in a foreign country, and that the U.S. entity sells its product to the foreign entity for the foreign entity to then use in its operations. Clearly, the sales price that BIG sets for the product will determine the amount of gain generated in the United States.

B. If the IRS determines that the price set by BIG does not clearly reflect income, the IRS has broad powers to reallocated income to insure that income is clearly stated.

Tax-Exempt Organizations

After studying this lesson, you should be able to:

1. Summarize filing requirements for tax-exempt organizations.

2. Describe allowable activities for tax-exempt organizations.

3. Define unrelated business income and identify examples.

Tax Form for this Lesson: Form 990 (available for download and printing from the lesson overview of your software).

I. **Tax-Exempt Organizations**—Tax-exempt organizations include **charities, labor organizations, social clubs, pension and profit-sharing trusts, and private foundations**.

   A. Exemption—An exempt organization (EO) may be in the form of a corporation or trust, and it must apply for and receive an exemption from taxation (Form 1023 or Form 1024).

   B. Filing requirements

      1. EO must file an information return (Form 990) if gross receipts exceed $50,000.

         a. This form reports income, expenses, and substantial contributors. It also must include total lobbying and political expenditures.

         b. Churches do not have to file Form 990.

         c. Form 990 must be filed on or before the 15th day of the fifth month after the close of the tax year. An automatic three-month extension is available.

         d. Form 990-EZ can be used unless gross receipts exceed $200,000 (or if total assets exceed $500,000).

      2. Most EOs that are not required to file an information return must file an annual electronic notice with the IRS (**Form 990-N**).

         a. This notice includes demographic information and justifies the continuing basis for tax-exempt status. The EO must also confirm that annual gross receipts are usually $50,000 or less.

         b. The groups that are exempt from the electronic notice requirement include churches, state institutions, and governmental units.

      3. EOs that do not meet these filing requirements for three consecutive years will lose their tax-exempt status.

      4. Most EOs must make their last three years' tax returns and their tax-exempt application available to interested parties.

   C. Private foundations

Definition:
Private Foundations: Tax-exempt organizations that receive less than one-third of their annual support from their members and the general public.

      1. Private foundations file Form 990-PF.

II. **Qualification**—To qualify as an EO the organization must operate exclusively for a tax-exempt purpose.

   A. Many EOs are organized for religious, charitable, scientific, literary, or educational purposes; prevention of cruelty to children or animals; or promoting amateur sports activities.

B. Influencing legislation or political parties is not an acceptable purpose.

1. An excise tax of 5% is imposed on the lobbying expenditures of charitable organizations, and a 5% tax may also be imposed on organization managers who agreed to the expenditures.

2. However, Section 501(c)(3) organizations (e.g., charitable organizations) can participate in lobbying efforts if an election is made and lobbying expenditures do not exceed certain ceilings. This exception does not apply to churches and private foundations.

3. The **lobbying expenditures** cannot exceed the lower of:

   a. $1,000,000 *or*

   b. (20% × first $500,000 paid for exempt purposes) + (15% of the second $500,000) + (10% of the third $500,000) + (5% of any additional expenditures). "Paid" refers to the expenditures incurred in pursuing the tax-exempt activities.

4. The amount spent on grass-roots lobbying to **influence legislation** cannot exceed 25% of the amount determined by this formula.

5. If these limits are exceeded, a 25% excise tax is imposed on the excess expenditures. At certain excess levels a charity can lose its tax exemption.

> **Example:**
> An organization's exempt purpose expenditures for the year are $3 million. If the organization makes the election, it may spend $300,000 ($100,000 (20% of $500,000) + $75,000 (15% of $500,000) + $50,000 (10% of $500,000) + $75,000 (5% of the remaining $1,500,000)) on lobbying for the year, and $75,000 (25% of $300,000) of that amount may be spent on grass roots lobbying.

C. A tax is imposed on non-permitted political expenditures equal to:

1. 10% of the expenditure, charged to the organization, and

2. 2.5% of the expenditure, charged to a manager who agreed to the expenditure (maximum of $5,000 per expenditure).

D. A tax-exempt organization can participate in a joint venture with a for-profit organization if the venture furthers a charitable purpose.

III. Unrelated Business Income—An EO is taxed on its unrelated business income (UBI).

A. To be UBI, income must:

1. Be from a business regularly carried on, *and*

2. Be unrelated to the EO exempt purposes.

B. A business is substantially related only if the activity contributes importantly to the accomplishment of the exempt purposes of the organization.

C. Related income (meaning that the income is not subject to tax) includes:

1. An activity where substantially all work is performed for no compensation

2. A business carried on for the convenience of students or members of a charitable, religious, or scientific organization

3. Sale of merchandise/stock received as contributions

4. In general, investment income

5. Rents received from real property

D. Income from debt-financed property unrelated to the exempt function of the EO is UBI.

E. Income from advertising in journals of the EO is UBI.

F. UBI is taxed (only if it exceeds $1,000) at regular corporate rates if the organization is a corporation; at trust rates if it is a trust.

IV. Disclosure Rules for Deductibility

A. Not all tax-exempt entities qualify for deductibility of contributions. Those that do not qualify must disclose such in a conspicuous format in all fundraising solicitations.

B. Charities eligible to receive tax-deductible contributions that receive contributions greater than $75 must inform the donor that her deduction is limited to the excess of the contribution over the value of the goods or services received from the charity.

Formation and Basis

After studying this lesson, you should be able to:

1. Define partnerships for tax purposes and list the entities taxed as partnerships.

2. Differentiate the characteristics of general and limited partners.

3. Evaluate whether a partnership formation is eligible for deferral of gain/loss.

4. Compute the basis of interest held by partners and assets by partnership after formation.

5. Determine the holding period for partnership interest and assets after the formation.

6. Calculate the effect of liability assumptions by the partnership on gain and basis.

7. Determine the required year-end for partnerships.

I. **Introduction**—A business operated as a partnership is not recognized as a taxable entity under the income tax laws. Instead, the partners divide the income and expenses of the business and report their share on individual returns. The income is taxed to the owners regardless of distributions. Distributions are, in turn, treated as a return of capital. The distinction between partnerships and corporations is important because no tax is imposed on partnerships.

II. **Partnership Definition**

> **Definition:**
> *Partnership*: An association of two or more taxpayers to operate a business that is not taxed as a corporation.

  A. An entity may be exempt from partnership rules if organized for investment purposes.

  B. A partnership must be an **association** of two or more taxpayers with the objective of making a profit. The existence of a partnership is a question of fact, but co-ownership and/or joint use of property does not necessarily constitute a partnership. There must be an active conduct of a business with the intent to share profits.

  C. Certain publicly traded partnerships (i.e., master limited partnerships) are taxed as corporations.

III. **Check-the-Box**—Under the "check-the-box" regulations, unincorporated entities may elect to be taxed as an association (corporation) or a partnership.

  A. Some associations are automatically taxed as corporations and are not eligible to make an election. These *per se* corporations include business entities formed under statutes that refer to the entities as incorporated.

  B. The default entity is a partnership when the business has more than two owners. This default rule typically applies to partnerships and limited liability companies. If an entity does not prefer the default rule, it can elect to be taxed as a corporation.

  C. If an entity has only one owner, then the default classification is that the entity is disregarded for federal income tax purposes. These entities can also elect to be taxed as a corporation.

  D. An election under the check-the-box regulations is effective if filed within the first 75 days of the tax year.

IV. General/Limited Partners

> **Definitions:**
>
> *General partners*: Can participate in management and have joint and several liability for the partnership's debts. All partnerships must have at least one general partner.
>
> *Limited partners*: Are only liable up to their investment, but they cannot participate in management without losing their limited status.

A. A partnership loss will be a passive loss to a limited partner.

B. A partnership loss may be a passive loss to a general partner depending upon whether the partner meets the material participation test. See the "Limitations on Certain Business Deductions" lesson for more detail.

> **Note:**
> *Without specific information (e.g., number of hours of activity for the partner), partnerships engaging in rental activities are most likely passive. See the "Limitations on Certain Business Deductions" lesson for more detail.*

C. Note that owners of limited liability companies are known as members and they also have limited liability.

D. Limited liability partnerships also usually filed as partnerships for federal tax purposes, unless the partners elect differently.

V. Partner Interests—Each partner owns a **capital interest and a profits** interest.

A. The capital-sharing ratio represents each partner's share of partnership capital.

B. Profit and loss (P&L) sharing ratios are each partner's share of profits and losses, respectively.

VI. Formations—The formation of a partnership does not trigger income, but requires that both the partners and the partnership calculate adjusted basis.

A. Contributions to a partnership are not taxable events, but require partners to calculate a substituted basis for their partnership interest.

B. Deferred Gain or Loss—Partners and partnerships recognize no gain or loss on contributions in exchange for a *partnership interest*.

   1. The control club used for corporate contributions is not relevant for partnerships since partnerships are taxed as conduits.

      a. Reminder—The **control club** is the 80% control requirement necessary to provide shareholders with deferral for contributions to a corporation.

   2. No distinction is made between an initial contribution and later additional contributions.

   3. No deferral is available for contributions to a partnership in exchange for property— deferral is only available for exchanges of property for a partnership interest.

C. Exceptions exist for nonrecognition.

   1. Services contributed for a partnership interest create income in the amount of the value of the partnership interest (which also becomes the adjusted basis of the partnership interest).

   2. There is no deferral for contributions that are essentially disguised sales or attempts to diversify stock holdings.

> **Example:**
> **1.** There is no deferral of gain on appreciated stock contributed to an investment partnership.
>
> **2.** TP contributes property ($100 FMV and basis of $20) to partnership PS in exchange for a 5% interest. Five days later, TP withdraws $100 cash. This is a disguised sale, and TP will recognize a gain of $80 on the "contribution" of the property.

VII. Basis Issues at Formation—Each partner calculates his or her personal adjusted basis (outside basis) in the partnership, and the partnership calculates the adjusted basis of the assets (inside basis) held by the partnership.

   A. Partnership—A partnership takes a carryover basis (the adjusted basis of the property in the hands of the partners) for contributed property.

> **Definition:**
> *Inside Basis of Property*: The aggregate basis of assets in the hands of the partnership.

   1. Since the adjusted basis of contributed property carries over from the partners to the partnership, the holding periods and depreciation methods also continue unabated.

   B. Partner—Each partner takes a substituted basis in the partnership interest from the assets contributed to the partnership.

> **Definition:**
> *Outside Basis of Property*: The adjusted basis of each partners' interest in the partnership.

VIII. Holding Period

   A. The holding period in the partnership interest includes the holding period of the contributed asset for contributions of capital assets and Section 1231 assets. For other assets, the holding period starts when the contribution is received by the partnership.

   B. The holding period that the partner has in the asset before contributed always transfers to the partnership, regardless of the type of asset contributed.

   C. The adjusted basis for contributions of services is the value included in the income of the partner.

   D. The adjusted basis for partnership interests purchased from existing partners or interests received as gifts or inheritances are determined like other assets (cost or carryover basis, respectively).

IX. Computation of Basis of Partnership Interest—Partners continually adjust their outside basis for partnership transactions, including the deduction of their share of partnership losses.

   A. Increases—A *partner's basis is increased by contributions of property, income, and increases in liabilities*.

   1. A partner's proportionate share of income includes gains and exempt income.

   2. A partner's proportionate share includes increases in liabilities (treated like a contribution).

   B. Decreases—A *partner's basis is decreased by distributions, expenses, and deemed distributions*.

   1. A partner's proportionate share of expenses, including deductions, losses, and nondeductible expenses (not capital expenditures)

   2. A partner's proportionate share of decreases in liabilities (deemed distributions)

> **Definition:**
> *Deemed Distribution*: Occurs with any decrease in the partnership liabilities.

   3. Reminder—A partner's basis in the partnership cannot be reduced below zero. If the net change in basis in the partnership interest due to debt being assumed by the partnership exceeds the total basis of the assets contributed, the partner must recognize gain equal to that excess to prevent negative basis from occurring.

Example:

Partner R, a 25% partner, contributes property to the partnership with an adjusted basis of $20, FMV of $50, and a liability of $30 which the partnership assumes. R's basis is first increased by $20 for the basis of the property, then decreased by $30 for the debt assumption. However, since the partnership debt increased by $30, and R is responsible for 25% of the debt, or $7.50, his basis is increased by $7.50. The net effect on basis is a decrease of $2.50 (basis of $20 less $22.50 of debt shifted to other partners).

If R's basis before this contribution was $0, he would recognize $2.50 of gain to avoid negative basis. If R's basis before the contribution was $10, his ending basis would be $7.50 ($10 − $2.50).

- **C.** Debt allocations—In the example above, we assumed that Partner R was responsible for 25% of the debt since he was a 25% partner. This is usually a reasonable assumption for the CPA Exam. However, the debt allocation rules are actually much more complex than this.

  - **1.** Recourse debt—For recourse debt, each partner's share of debt is measured by his or her economic risk of loss assuming a **constructive liquidation scenario** occurred. While this material is likely too complex for the exam, you should be aware that limited partners are not allocated any share of recourse debt.

  - **2.** Nonrecourse debt—This is debt for which the lender's only recourse, in the event of default, is to take back the property. As above, the allocation of nonrecourse debt is likely too complex for the exam. However, you should be aware that nonrecourse debt is often allocated based on the partners' profit sharing ratios. Also, contrasted with recourse debt, both **general and limited** partners are allocated nonrecourse debt.

- **D.** Summary—See the following calculation of outside basis.

Initial Basis
Plus:
Additional Contributions
Partner's share of:
Debt Increases
Partnership Income
Exempt Income
Less:
Distributions:
Cash Distributions
Debt Decreases
Asset Distributions
Partner's share of:
Nondeductible Expenses
Partnership Loss

X. Capital Account

- **A.** While basis represents one's investment in a partnership for tax purposes, capital account represents the amount a partner should receive when the partnership is liquidated.

- **B.** Basis and capital account are computed in a similar fashion, except:

1. Liabilities of the partnership do not affect the capital account.

2. The fair market value of contributions and distributions impact the capital account, rather than the tax basis.

XI. Permitted Tax Years—Partners report income in the year that the partnership tax year-ends. A. Since the partnership and the partners may not have the same year-ends, the partners only report income once the partnership closes its books at the partnership year-end.

> **Example:**
> ABC is a partnership with a June 30 fiscal year-end. Partner A, however, has a calendar year-end. This year ABC earned $24,000 for the fiscal year and also earned an additional $9,000 from July through December. If A is an equal partner in ABC, he should report $8,000 of income this year (one-third of $24,000). A's share of the income from July through December will not be taxed until ABC closes its books next year.

B. Required tax year: The required tax year for the partnership is determined as follows:

1. Partnerships use the same year-end as its **majority** interest partner(s) (more than 50% capital and P&L).

2. If the partnership has no single year for the majority, then the partnership uses same year-end as **all** of its principal partners (5% P&L interest or more).

3. If neither the majority interest nor principal partner test is met, the required tax year is determined by using the least aggregate deferral method. This method is computationally intensive, but determines the year-end which will provide the least amount of deferral for the entire partnership group.

C. If a partnership does not want to use the required tax year, the partners can elect a fiscal year-end (with IRS permission) if there is a business purpose; a natural business year can also be used.

> **Definition:**
> *Natural Business Year*: A year in which 25% or more of the gross receipts occur in the last two months of the year (three consecutive years).

D. A second exception to the required tax year is that under Section 444 partnerships may elect a year-end with no more than three months of deferral, but a deposit with the IRS is required to compensate the government for the deferral benefits to the partners (only if the deferral benefit exceeds $500).

E. Partnerships are due on or before the 15th day of the fourth month following the year-end. Partnerships can extend their returns for five months from the due date. This would be September 15 for calendar-year partnerships.

Flow-Through of Income and Losses

After studying this lesson, you should be able to:

1. Define separately stated items for flow-through purposes.

2. Compute partnership income and distributive share to partners.

3. Apply the loss limitation rules for partners.

Tax Form for this Lesson: Form 1065 and 1065K-1 (available for download and printing from the lesson overview of your software).

I.   Allocations of Income

A. Items of income and expense are allocated from the partnership to partners. Partners include these items (known as their distributive share) on the return that includes the year-end of the partnership. Partners modify their adjusted basis in the partnership for these allocations.

B. Allocations—Partners receive a share of income or a (potentially different) share of loss, according to the *partnership agreement*.

1. Any special allocation must pass a judgmental **substantial economic effect** test that ensures that partners with special allocations bear the economic burden or receive the economic benefit of the special allocation.

2. If no special allocation is provided in the partnership agreement, then separately stated items are distributed in the same proportions as income and loss.

II. Distributive Share

A. Partnerships report a share of items of income and expense to each partner.

1. Partnerships are **not** subject to tax, but report taxable income on Form 1065.

2. Profits and losses are allocated to each partner based on each partner's profit and loss sharing ratio.

3. Measuring and reporting partnership income involves a two-step process.

a. All items of income, gain, deduction, loss, or credit that are required to be separately stated, or that are specially allocated, are removed from the partnership's ordinary income or loss determination process. Each partner's proportionate share of these items is reported on Schedule K-1.

b. The remaining items are lumped together to produce the net ordinary income or loss, which is also proportionately reported to each partner.

4. Partnerships report taxable income (ordinary income) and separately stated items to each partner on Schedule K-1.

Definition:
Separately Stated Items: Any tax items (deductions, income, preferences, etc.,) that might affect partners differently—these items retain their character to the owners.

a. Some common examples of separate items are dividends, capital gains and losses, tax-exempt interest, passive losses, charitable contributions, investment income, section 179 expenses. Section 1245 recapture is never separately stated.

b. Qualified dividends (taxed at a maximum rate of 20%) also flow-through to the partner as a separately stated item.

5.   Capital withdrawals do not affect income.

6.   Partnerships may use the cash basis of accounting unless the partnership is a "tax shelter" or at least one partner is a C corporation. Exceptions allow the cash method for farming and where the partnership (or corporate partner) is a small business (average annual gross receipts of $5 million or less for the three prior years ending with the current tax year).

7.   Partnerships may elect to amortize organization and start-up costs.

   a.   Definition: Organization costs relate to organizing the business so they will benefit the business for its entire life, the length of which cannot be estimated. Start-up costs are expenditures of a nature that would usually be deducted in the year incurred, but cannot be deducted since they were incurred before the business began operations (e.g., training costs for employees). Organizational expenses in the amount of $5,000 may be deducted, but the $5,000 is reduced by the amount of expenditures incurred that exceed $50,000.

   b.   Start-up expenses in the amount of $5,000 may be deducted, but the $5,000 is reduced by the amount of expenditures incurred that exceed $50,000.

   c.   Expenses not deducted must be capitalized and amortized over 180 months, beginning with the month that the corporation begins its business operations. An election can be made to not deduct or amortize the expenses.

   d.   **Syndication** expenditures (cost of selling partnership interests) are capitalized and cannot be amortized.

8.   Special simplified reporting (and IRS audit) rules exist for electing large partnerships (non-service partnership with over 100 partners).

9.   General partners' distributive shares are subject to the self-employment tax, whereas limited partners' shares usually are not. However, guaranteed payments for both general and limited partners are subject to the self-employment tax.

10. The extension period for partnerships is five months. Therefore, for calendar year partnerships the extended due date is by September 15.

B.   Family partnerships—Allocations of partnership income related to a partnership interest given to a family member are subject to special limits.

1.   If capital is a material income producing factor, the income allocated to a donated interest cannot exceed the capital percentage.

2.   Partnership income must be adjusted by the value of any services provided by donor family members.

Example:
Dad is a half partner in a partnership where capital is a material income producing factor. Dad gives a 20% interest to his son. This year, the partnership earns $100 of income and Dad provides services worth $10. The son is allocated a partnership income of $18.

C.   Loss limitations

1.   Partners can only deduct losses if all three of the following hurdles are passed (in this order):

   a.   Partners must have enough basis to deduct the loss.

   b.   Partners can deduct losses only to the extent of their at-risk amount. Generally, at-risk equals the partners' basis less the partner's share of nonrecourse debt.

   c.   If the loss is a passive loss, the partner can deduct the loss only to the extent of passive income. Limited partners' losses are passive by definition (for more information see the lesson "Limitations on Certain Business Deductions").

2.   Disallowed losses are carried over and used in future years when the remaining criteria are met.

Transactions with Partners

Despite the status of partnerships as conduit entities, arm's length contracts between a partner and partnership are recognized for tax purposes.

After studying this lesson, you should be able to:

1. Define guarantee payments and apply flow-through rules for these payments.

2. Apply built-in gain/loss rules to sales of property contributed to partnerships.

3. Identify related party transactions involving partnerships that have special tax treatment.

I. **Guaranteed Payments**—Guaranteed payments are those made to partners without regard to partnership income.

    A. Partners are not employees of the partnership, but might receive guaranteed payments for services or capital investment.

    B. Guaranteed payments are ordinary income to the recipients at the partnership year-end.

    C. Guaranteed payments (for deduction purposes) reduce partnership income and thereby reduce each partner's distributive share of such income.

    D. Guaranteed payments are deemed to be paid to the partner on the last day of the partnership's tax year, regardless of when payment was actually made.

II. **Precontribution (Built- In) Gains and Losses**—*These are allocated back to the original contributing partners when the property is sold.*

Definition:
Built-In Gain (or Loss) Property: Property that has appreciated (declined) in value at the time of its contribution to the partnership (the value of gain property is greater than its adjusted basis, whereas the value of loss property is less than its adjusted basis).

    A. The built-in gain or loss is allocated to the contributing partner up to the gain or loss realized on the sale.

    B. The character of the built-in gains and losses is generally determined by the use of the property by the partnership, with two exceptions.

        1. Sales of contributed ordinary income or loss property (e.g., inventory and accounts receivable) generate ordinary income or loss to the contributing partner. The characterization of income or loss as ordinary from a sale of inventory is limited to five years (five years after the property was contributed to the partnership). There is no time limit for the ordinary income characterization for accounts receivables.

            a. Note that **all** gain or loss on the sale is treated as ordinary if the above rule is met. It is not limited to the built-in gain or loss at the time of contribution.

> **Misconception:**
> There is no time limit on the allocation of the amount of built-in gains and losses from sales of property. A time limit (five years) applies to the characterization of these gains and losses as ordinary or capital. Another time limit (seven years) applies to the distribution of built-in gain property (to partners).

Example:
Partner A is an art dealer and a partner in ABC Partners, a consulting firm. A contributes a painting (he held as inventory) to ABC to decorate the ABC office (a Section 1231 asset). The painting has a FMV of $10,000 and an adjusted basis of $6,000. If ABC sells the painting within five years of the contribution, any gain or loss will be allocated to A (up to the built-in gain or loss) and will be characterized as ordinary income. Thus, if the painting is sold four year later for $11,000, the $5,000 gain ($11,000 − $6,000) is characterized as ordinary income. If ABC sells the painting after five years, then the $5,000 gain is Section 1231 gain. Note that in both cases, since the built-in gain was only $4,000 ($10,000 − $6,000), the first $4,000 of gain is allocated to Partner A. The remaining $1,000 of gain is allocated to A and the other partners based on their profit-sharing ratios.

2. Sales of contributed capital assets with built-in capital losses generate capital losses to contributing partners (again only for five years after the contribution). However, for built-in capital losses, the amount of loss that can be recharacterized as capital is limited to the built-in loss at the time the asset was contributed.

Example:
Partner R contributes a capital asset to RST Partnership, which will be used by the partnership as inventory. The asset has a FMV of $10,000 and adjusted basis of $15,000. The built-in loss is $5,000 and, when this asset is sold, the first $5,000 of recognized loss will be allocated to R. If RST sells the asset three years later for $8,000, the recognized loss is $7,000. The first $5,000 of loss is allocated to R and the other $2,000 of loss is allocated to R and the other partners based on their loss-sharing ratios. The $5,000 loss allocated to R is a capital loss (since this was sold within five years), but the remaining $2,000 loss will be characterized based on how the partnership used the asset (inventory = ordinary loss). Note, that only the built-in loss is recharacterized as a capital loss.

III. Related Party Rules

A. Special rules—Partners may contract with the partnership at arm's length with "normal" consequences, but tax avoidance is restricted.

1. No deduction for a payment to a partner can be claimed by an accrual partnership until the cash basis partner includes the payment in income.

2. Losses on sales to partnerships in which the taxpayer is a controlling partner (more than 50% interest) are deferred as related party losses.

3. Sales of capital gain property by a controlling partner (majority interest) to a partnership will be deemed noncapital if the asset is not capital in the hands of the partnership.

4. The above two rules also apply for sales between commonly controlled partnerships (brother-sister partnerships).

Distributions

After studying this lesson, you should be able to:

1. Differentiate between nonliquidating and liquidating distributions.

2. Determine tax consequences for partners of nonliquidating distributions.

3. Compute tax consequences for partners of liquidating distributions.

4. Describe applicability of special rules to certain partnership distributions.

I. Gain/Loss Deferral—*Partnerships generally do not recognize gains or losses on distributions.*

    A. Partners can recognize gains on nonliquidating or liquidating distributions of cash. Cash distributed in excess of outside basis causes gain recognition.

    B. Nonliquidating distributions of property **never** trigger loss recognition, but losses may be recognized on a liquidating distribution.

II. Nonliquidating (or Current) Distributions

Definition:
Nonliquidating Distribution: A distribution to a continuing partner, including a draw by the partner.

    A. Arm's length sales to partners are not distributions.

    B. Basis effects—For partners, non*liquidating distributions are a return of capital that reduces outside basis (in a specific order).*

        1. First, the partner's adjusted basis is allocated to cash distributions and cash deemed distributed (reductions in liabilities).

        2. Second, the partner's adjusted basis is allocated to distributions of unrealized receivables and inventory in an amount equal to the partnership's basis in these assets.

        3. Finally, the partner's adjusted basis is allocated to other assets distributed. Any deficiency in the partner's adjusted basis is allocated to properties with unrealized losses, and any excess basis is allocated to properties with unrealized gains.

        4. Distributed property retains its inside basis (in the hands of the partner) unless the partner runs out of outside basis, then the inside basis of the property is reduced to the outside basis.

        5. If the distributed property consists of multiple assets, then the allocation of basis can be quite complex. A simple approach is to allocate the outside basis by the amount of the inside basis.

Example:
Two parcels of inventory (Parcel A and Parcel B) are distributed to a partner in a nonliquidating proportionate distribution at a time when the partner has an outside basis of \$12. Parcel A has an inside basis of \$6 and Parcel B has an inside basis of \$18. Each parcel is worth \$20. In this situation, one-fourth [(\$6/(\$6 + \$18) × \$12] or \$3 of the outside basis is allocated to parcel A. The remaining three-fourths of the outside basis (\$9) is allocated to parcel B [\$18/(\$6 + \$18) × \$12].

III. Liquidating Distributions—A liquidating distribution may result in gain or loss, and it requires the partner to transfer his or her outside basis to assets received from the partnership.

    A. A liquidating distribution occurs when the entire partnership is liquidated or the interest of one partner is redeemed.

        1. The distribution can be a series of transfers.

        2. The partnership, generally, does not recognize any gains or losses.

B. Basis effect—*Liquidating distributions are treated as a return of capital and the partner's outside basis is substituted for the inside basis of distributed property.*

    1. Like nonliquidating distributions, distributions of cash (and deemed distributions) trigger gain to the extent cash exceeds outside basis.

    2. Distributed property retains its inside basis, but this amount is adjusted (up or down) depending upon the outside basis of the partner. The calculation of this adjustment is complex and unlikely to be tested.

    3. Inventory and receivables must be distributed pro-rata (a non-pro-rata distribution will be disproportionate).

C. Loss recognition—Unlike nonliquidating distributions, partners can recognize losses on liquidating distributions, but only if two conditions are met:

    1. First, the distribution must consist only of cash, inventory, and unrealized receivables.

    2. Second, the outside basis of the partner's interest exceeds the sum of cash plus the inside basis of the receivables and inventory.

IV. Special Issues—Complications are created by built-in gains, deemed distributions, and disproportionate distributions.

A. Deemed distributions (reductions in liabilities) are treated as cash distributions.

B. Distributions of marketable securities (up to the value of the securities less the partner's share of appreciation inherent in the securities) are treated as deemed distributions.

C. Distributions of built-in gain property to other partners (other than the partner who originally contributed the property) within seven years of the original contribution cause gain recognition.

D. "Disproportionate" distributions of **hot assets** can also trigger income recognition.

Definition:
Hot Assets: Generate ordinary income or loss because the partner has not yet been taxed on accrued, but unrealized, income.

E. Hot assets are inventory and unrealized receivable. For distributions, inventory has to be substantially appreciated (FMV > 120% × adjusted basis) for it to be classified as a hot asset.

    1. Unrealized receivables generally are receivables of cash basis taxpayers. Potential section 1245 and section 1250 recapture are also included as an unrealized receivable.

    2. Inventory is defined as any asset other than cash, capital assets, or Section 1231 assets.

Definition:
Disproportionate Distributions: Occur when ordinary income assets (inventory and receivables) are distributed to partners without regard to their proportionate ownership interests. Therefore, if a 12% partner receives 12% of the hot assets, then no special rules need to be applied to those discussed above for distributions.

V. Integrated Review Problem—A, B, and C formed ABC partnership with the following contributions:

	Asset	AB	FMW	Interest
A	Cash	$40,000	$40,000	50%
B	Land	12,000	21,000	20%
C	Inventory	24,000	24,000	30%

A. The land was a capital asset to B and subject to a mortgage of $5,000, assumed by the partnership. Assume that this year the partnership breaks even, but decides to make distributions to each partner.

1. What is B's initial basis? $8,000 (12,000 − 5,000 + (20% × 5,000)).

2. What is C's initial basis? $25,500 (24,000 + (30% × 5,000)).

3. A nonliquidating cash distribution may reduce the recipient partner's basis below zero. False.

4. A nonliquidating distribution of unappreciated inventory reduces the recipient partner's basis in the partnership. True.

5. In a liquidating distribution of property other than money, where the partnership's basis of the distributed property exceeds the basis of the partner's interest, the partner's basis in the distributed property is limited to his or her predistribution basis in the partnership interest. True.

6. Gain is recognized by the partner who receives a nonliquidating distribution of property, where the adjusted basis of the property exceeds his basis in the partnership interest before the distribution. False.

7. In a nonliquidating distribution of inventory, where the partnership has no unrealized receivables or appreciated inventory, the basis of inventory that is distributed to a partner cannot exceed the inventory's adjusted basis to the partnership. True.

8. The partnership's nonliquidating distribution of encumbered property to a partner who assumes the mortgage does not affect the other partners' bases in their partnership interests. False.

Sales and Terminations

After studying this lesson, you should be able to:

1. Define and identify hot assets.

2. Compute tax consequences of sale of partnership interest.

3. Assess when a partnership has terminated for tax purposes.

4. Determine tax effects of partnership terminations.

I. **Sales of Partnership Interests**—A sale of a partnership interest results in a gain or loss calculated in the manner used for other assets, using outside basis to compute the gain or loss. The portion of any gain or loss due to **hot assets** is not eligible for capital gain treatment.

   A. Sales

   1. The sale, exchange, or liquidation of a partner's entire interest closes the partnership's tax year for that partner, but not for other partners or for the partnership as a whole. The income for a partner that dies during the year passes to the partner for the portion of the year that he or she was alive.

   2. The selling partner's amount realized includes the buyer's assumption of the selling partner's share of the partnership liabilities.

   B. Hot assets

   1. If the partnership has hot assets at the time a partnership interest is sold, the selling partner must allocate a portion of the sale proceeds to these assets and recognize ordinary income.

   2. Hot assets are a) unrealized receivables (receivables of a cash basis taxpayer; includes depreciation recapture), and b) inventory.

> **Definition:**
> *Inventory*: All assets other than cash, capital assets, and Section 1231 assets.

   3. The remaining sale proceeds are allocable to the selling partner's capital asset interest and result in a capital gain or loss.

   C. In addition to hot assets, if the partnership owns collectibles or has Section 1250 assets, these items may also impact the gain from the sale of a partnership asset. The selling partners gain will be taxed at 28% to the extent it is due to collectibles, and any unrecaptured Section 1250 gain will be taxed at 25%.

II. **Terminations**—The termination of a partnership requires the closing of the partnership books.

   A. Termination requires a closing of the partnership

   1. Termination requires a closing of the partnership tax-year.

   2. Termination results is a deemed distribution of assets to the partners.

   B. A partnership terminates for tax purposes if either of the following events occur:

   1. No part of the business continues to be carried on by any partner in the partnership form.

> **Example:**
> In a two-person partnership, one partner sells his or her interest to the other partner. This sale terminates the partnership for tax purposes, because it will no longer have two owners (it is now a proprietorship).

2. There is a sale or exchange of at least a 50% interest in both capital and profits within a consecutive 12-month period.

C. Mergers and divisions—Partnerships can merge with or divide from the original partnership continuing as the reporting entity.

    1. In a merger of partnerships, one partnership continues if its old partners also control the new entity (over 50% interest).

    2. In a division of a partnership, one of the new partnerships is a continuation of the old partnership if the partners (in the new partnership) had a controlling interest in the old partnership.

III. Integrated Review Problem—A, B, and C formed ABC partnership with the following contributions:

> **Note:**
> *Generally, partnerships are contracts between the partners that are terminated with the death or withdrawal of any partner. However, the death or withdrawal of a partner doesn't necessarily terminate partnerships for tax purposes. The partnership only determines the share for the decedent partner.*

	Asset	AB	FMW	Interest
A	Cash	$40,000	$40,000	50%
B	Land	12,000	21,000	20%
C	Inventory	24,000	24,000	30%

A. The land was a capital asset to B and subject to a mortgage of $5,000, assumed by the partnership. Assume that this year the partnership breaks even but decides to make distributions to each partner.

    1. What is B's initial basis? $8,000 (12,000 − 5,000 + (20% × 5,000)).

    2. What is C's initial basis? $25,500 (24,000 + (30% × 5,000)).

    3. A nonliquidating cash distribution may reduce the recipient partner's basis below zero. False.

    4. A nonliquidating distribution of unappreciated inventory reduces the recipient partner's basis in the partnership. True.

    5. In a liquidating distribution of property other than money, where the partnership's basis of the distributed property exceeds the basis of the partner's interest, the partner's basis in the distributed property is limited to his predistribution basis in the partnership interest. True.

    6. Gain is recognized by the partner who receives a nonliquidating distribution of property, where the adjusted basis of the property exceeds his basis in the partnership interest before the distribution. False.

    7. In a nonliquidating distribution of inventory, where the partnership has no unrealized receivables or appreciated inventory, the basis of inventory that is distributed to a partner cannot exceed the inventory's adjusted basis to the partnership. True.

    8. The partnership's nonliquidating distribution of encumbered property to a partner who assumes the mortgage does not affect the other partners' bases in their partnership interests. False.

Eligibility, Election, Termination

After studying this lesson, you should be able to:

1. List the tax characteristics of S corporations.

2. Determine if a corporation meets the eligibility requirements to elect S status.

3. Evaluate if election requirements have been met for a valid S election.

4. Assess if an S corporation election has been terminated.

I. **Legal Status**—The S election can only be made by a corporation, and the corporation retains its legal corporate status after the election.

    A. S corporations retain corporate status and their corporate characteristics when:

        1. Shareholders are not liable for corporate debt.

        2. Shares can be freely transferred.

        3. Shareholders can be employees (separation of ownership and management).

    B. Tax characteristics—Unlike C corporations, S corporations act as conduits for taxable income.

        1. Like partners, S shareholders are taxed on portion of income or loss, regardless of distributions.

        2. There is no imposition of the corporate AMT, PHC, or accumulated earnings taxes. Individual (not corporate) tax preferences are allocated to shareholders.

        3. The adjusted basis of shareholders' stock is generally adjusted at year end.

        4. Shareholders recognize gains when the value of distributions (cash or property) exceeds the adjusted basis in the stock.

        5. Partners in a partnership are not eligible to benefit from many fringe benefit exclusions because partners who work for the partnership are not considered to be employees. This same rule applies to S corporation shareholders who own 2% or more of the S corporation.

        6. A 2% or greater S corporation shareholder can deduct premiums paid on health insurance policies issued in his or her own name as a deduction for AGI as long as the shareholder has earned income from the S corporation that exceeds the total of all premiums paid.

        7. Shareholders who work for the S corporation are employees who are subject to payroll taxes (social security and Medicare). However, the distributive share to shareholders is not subject to self-employment taxes.

    C. Default rules for S corporations are the C corporation rules—Despite conceptual similarity to partnerships, corporate rules serve as default rules for S corporations.

        1. There is no special provision for contributions of property to an S corporation. Hence, the "control club" rule prevails for nonrecognition.

        2. S corporations can elect to amortize organizational expenses.

        3. Distributions of property take an outside basis of FMV (rather than inside basis).

        4. Distributions of built-in gain or loss property do not have any special implications for the contributing shareholder.

        5. Distribution of appreciated property causes recognition of gain at the corporate level (passed through to shareholders).

        6. There is no earnings and profits calculation because all earnings are taxed to shareholders, but a special calculation is necessary to distinguish Subchapter S earnings (called accumulated adjustments) from earnings and profits accumulated previously under Chapter C status.

II. **Eligibility Rules**—To qualify for an S election, a corporation must have the requisite ownership structure and be an eligible entity.

   A. Eligibility entity—The corporation must be an eligible entity.

   1. Foreign corporations are not eligible.

   2. Certain members of affiliated groups, parents of subsidiaries, financial institutions, and DISCs are not eligible (certain banks are eligible).

   3. S corporations may own an 80% or more equity interest in a C corporation.

   4. S corporations may own a **qualified** Subchapter S subsidiary.

   > **Definition:**
   > *Qualified Subchapter S Subsidiary*: A corporation that meets all requirements for Subchapter S status and is owned 100% by a parent S corporation.

   B. Shareholder requirements—Shareholders must be eligible.

   1. Nonresident aliens, C corporations, and partnerships are not eligible.

      a. Shortcut—An S corporation can be a parent corporation, but it cannot be a subsidiary of any corporation except another subchapter S corporation.

   2. Estates (bankruptcy or testamentary) can be shareholders.

   3. Trusts can be shareholders, if grantor or testamentary (two-year limit after transfer).

   4. Special stock voting trusts and qualified S trusts can be shareholders (all beneficiaries are qualified and electing shareholders).

   5. Small business electing trusts and exempt entities are allowed as shareholders.

   C. Shareholder limit—An eligible corporation can have no more than 100 shareholders.

   1. All members of a family and their estates are treated as a single shareholder.

   2. Each beneficiary of a shareholding trust is counted as a separate shareholder.

   3. Co-owners of stock each count as one shareholder.

   D. Stock requirements—Only one class of stock is outstanding.

   1. Shares that vary solely in voting rights are not considered two classes of stock.

   2. Convertible debt does not violate the requirement unless and until it is converted into a second class of stock.

   3. Unissued treasury stock does not violate the requirement.

   4. A **safe harbor** exists for shareholder debt to prevent these securities from being interpreted as a second class of equity. The debt must be evidenced by a written promise that is not contingent or convertible. Short-term unwritten loans are sanctioned in amounts under $10,000.

III. **Election Requirements**—The shareholders of the corporation must make a qualifying election to obtain or revoke S status.

   A. Unanimous consent of shareholders is required for election.

   1. The election is valid for the current year, if it is made on or before the 15th day of the third month (Form 2553).

   2. An election that is ineligible for the current year is still valid for the next year (if the circumstance causing ineligibility is corrected).

   3. All current shareholders (and past shareholders for the current year, up to date of election) must consent to election.

   4. Both spouses must consent, if the stock is jointly owned.

   > **Note:**
   > *In its initial year, a corporation must make the S election on or before the 15th day of the third month after commencing business.*

B. Termination requirements—Termination of the election can occur through three circumstances.

1. A voluntary termination occurs through a majority vote (a majority of all shareholders) specifying a prospective year or made before the 15th day of the third month for the current year.

   a. Also note, that if there is a greater than 50% change in the ownership of the S corporation, the new owners must affirm that they wish to continue to S election.

2. An involuntary termination occurs through a violation of an eligibility requirement, and this termination is effective on the date of the violation.

   a. Reminder—The IRS can waive an inadvertent termination.

> **Note:**
> *All shareholders (voting and nonvoting) are entitled to a vote in a voluntary termination of an S election.*

> **Note:**
> *An involuntary termination caused by a violation of an eligibility requirement will generally create a short S year and a short C year.*

> **Definition:**
> *Short Year:* A tax year consisting of less than 12 months.

3. An involuntary termination can occur due to a violation of the limit on passive investment income exceeding 25% of gross receipts for three consecutive years (see discussion of S corporate taxes in the "Income and Basis" and "Distributions and Special Taxes" lessons). This termination is effective on the first day of the fourth consecutive year. This provision only applies if the S corporation has earnings and profits (from previous C corporation years) on its balance sheet.

> **Note:**
> *Once terminated, S status cannot be elected without IRS permission for five years.*

Income and Basis

After studying this lesson, you should be able to:

1. Define separately stated items for flow-through purposes.

2. Compute S corporation income and flow-through allocations to shareholders.

3. Calculate adjusted basis of S corporation stock.

4. Apply the loss limitation rules for S corporation shareholders.

Tax Forms for this Lesson: Form 1120S and Form 1120SK-1 (available for download and printing from the lesson overview of your software).

I. Operating Rules

A. Required year-end—Rather than pay the corporate tax, S corporations report income to shareholders on a year-end consistent with that of the shareholders.

B. A calendar year-end—This is generally the default for S corporations.

  1. S corporations can elect a fiscal year-end (with IRS permission) if there is a business purpose to the election. The most common business purpose is to elect a **natural business year**.

Definition:
Natural Business Year: A year in which 25% or more of the gross receipts occur in the last two months of the year (three consecutive years).

  2. S corporations may elect a year-end under Section 444 with no more than three months of deferral (a deposit with the IRS is required to compensate the government for the deferral benefits to the shareholders if the benefits exceed $500).

II. Reporting Operations—S corporations calculate taxable income (reported on Form 1120S) in a manner similar to partnerships (e.g., no personal deductions).

A. S corporations may use the cash basis of accounting unless the corporation is a tax shelter.

B. An S corporation reports taxable income (ordinary income) and separately stated items for each shareholder on Schedule K-1 whether or not any dividends were declared.

Definition:
Separately Stated Items: Any tax items (deductions, income, preferences, etc.,) that might affect owners differently. These items retain their character to the owners and must, therefore, be reported separately for each owner.

C. S corporations are not entitled to most special corporate deductions, such as the dividends-received deduction.

D. S corporations do not pay alternative minimum tax, personal holding company tax, or accumulated earnings tax.

E. S corporations make most of the tax elections (not shareholders), including the election to amortize organization and start-up costs.

III. Flow-Through to Shareholders—Each shareholder reports income consistent with the period in which the corporate stock was held.

   A. Each shareholder reports income and separately stated items according to pro-rata share of stock ownership.

   1. If relative interests change during the year, each shareholder calculates the share of income on a daily basis.

   2. To calculate the daily share of income prior to (or after) the change in shares, divide annual income (and separately stated items) by the number of days in the year. Next, multiply this amount by (1) number of days prior to (after) the change and (2) the percentage ownership interest.

Example:
As of January 1 of this year, TP1 owned all 100 shares of ABC, a calendar year S corporation. On February 9th (the 40th day of this year), TP1 sold 25 shares to TP2. This year (365 days), ABC reported $73,000 in nonseparately stated income and made no distributions to shareholders. What amount of income should TP1 report from ABC?

TP1 should report income of $56,750 calculated using the daily income ($200 per day) for the 40 days TP1 owned 100% and 75% of the daily income for the 325 days after the sale. Note, that the seller is deemed to own the shares on the day of the sale.

   3. If a shareholder's interest is completely terminated (death or sale), then the share can be calculated by closing the books as of the termination date (an **interim** close). However, all shareholders, including the departing shareholder, must agree to this treatment.

Example:
As of January 1 of this year, TP1 owned half of the 100 shares of ABC, a calendar year S corporation. On February 9th TP1 sold all of his shares to TP2. This year (365 days) ABC reported $73,000 in ordinary income, that accrued ratably throughout the year, and a capital loss of $3,650, which occurred on June 30. What amount of nonseparately stated income should TP1 report from ABC?

Unless the shareholders elect an interim close, TP1 should report ordinary income of $4,000 ($200 per day for the 40 days TP1 owned 50%) and a capital loss of $200 ($10 per day for the 40 days TP1 owned 50%). If all the shareholders elect an interim close, then TP1 still reports the $4,000 of ordinary income (it accrued ratably). TP1 cannot, however, report any of the loss because it occurred after he sold his stock.

IV. Adjusted Stock Basis—Each shareholder has an adjusted basis in his S stock that must be modified by contributions, income, distributions, and expenses.

   A. First, contributions to capital increase the shareholder's adjusted basis.

   B. Second, the shareholder's share of income (including exempt income) increases the shareholder's adjusted basis.

   C. Third, distributions to the shareholder decrease the shareholder's adjusted basis.

   D. Fourth, the shareholder's share of loss (including nondeductible expenses) decreases the shareholder's adjusted basis.

Calculation of S Shareholder's Basis

Initial Basis

Plus: Additional Contributions

> Shareholder's share of: Corporate Income
>
> Exempt Income
>
> Less Distributions from AAA/OAA (in following order):
>
> > Cash
> >
> > Inventory and receivables
> >
> > Other property
> >
> > Nondeductible Expenses
> >
> > Corporate Losses

V. Loss Limitations—*Loss deductions are limited in four ways.*

A. First, the adjusted basis of the stock limits loss deductions because a shareholder's basis cannot be reduced below zero.

B. Second, the adjusted basis of loans to the corporation by the shareholder can be used for loss deductions once the adjusted basis of the stock is exhausted. However, later increases in basis are used to restore the basis of the debt before basis of the stock.

1. Debt basis is created when the shareholder loans his or her own funds to the S corporation.

C. Third, shareholders may only deduct losses to the extent they are "at risk" for investments in the corporation.

D. Fourth, passive loss limits may also limit loss deductions depending upon the nature of the corporate business and the shareholders' participation in management activities.

E. Unused losses (due to inadequate basis) are carried forward indefinitely (until the adjusted basis of the stock increases or the S election is revoked).

F. If an S corporation contributes appreciated property to a charitable organization, the corporation can deduct the fair market value of the property. However, S corporation shareholders can reduce their basis by only the contributed property's basis. Congress has not extended this provision to 2015 at the time of this writing. Thus, for 2015 the basis of the S corporation stock is reduced by the value of the contribution.

See the following examples.

Example:

This year S corporation, an S electing corporation, reported the following:

Gross income	$210,000
Business expenses	283,000
Charitable contributions	14,600

S has two shareholders: PW owns 10% of the stock, and M owns 90%. What amount should PW report this year from S?

S operated at a $73,000 loss, so PW should report $7,300 of loss and $1,460 of charitable contributions. Suppose that PW sold his stock 60 days after the beginning of the year. If PW sold his stock, then (absent a terminating election) the operating loss would be prorated on a daily basis. Hence, S incurred a daily loss of $200 ($73,000/365) and PW's share would be $1,200 ($200 × 60 × 10%). Likewise, the charitable contribution would be $240 ($40 × 60 × 10%).

Example:
ABC, a calendar year S corporation, had an ordinary loss of $36,500 this year. TP owned 50% of ABC for the first 40 days of the year before selling the stock to an unrelated party. TP's basis in the stock was $10,000 and TP was a full-time employee of the corporation. What is TP's share of the loss this year?

The share of the loss is $2,000—calculated by multiplying TP's share (50%) of the daily loss ($100) times the number of days TP held the stock (40).

Distributions and Special Taxes

I. **Distributions**—Distributions may trigger corporate gain, but normally represent a return of capital to shareholders.

   A. Corporate gain—The corporation generates gains by distributing appreciated property.

      1. The gain is passed through to shareholders like other income.

Example:
S Corporation distributes land to its sole shareholder. If the land has a value of $100 and an adjusted basis of $80 on the date of distribution, then S Corporation will recognize $20 of income on the distribution. No tax will be imposed on S Corporation. Instead, the gain will be passed through to the shareholder.

   B. Shareholder income if corporation has no E&P—A distribution creates a gain to the shareholder if the distribution exceeds the shareholder's *adjusted basis in the stock.*

      1. The amount of a distribution is the amount of cash plus the **value** of any property distributed.

      2. Distributions in excess of adjusted basis are taxed as gains from the sale of stock.

      3. Shortcut—Distributions in excess of adjusted basis will most likely be taxed as capital gains because stock will most likely be a capital asset in the hands of the shareholder (an asset held for investment).

   C. Shareholder income if S corporation has E&P—Shareholders of S corporations with accumulated earnings and profits (E&P) from a previous status as a C corporation are subject to a complex distribution system.

      1. Shortcut—An S corporation that has **always** been an S electing corporation will not need to use an accumulated adjustments account unless and until the S election is terminated. In addition, an S corporation, that was previously a C corporation, will not need to use an accumulated adjustments account unless the corporation had earnings and profits from this prior period.

      2. Accumulated undistributed income generated during S status is recorded at the corporate level in the **accumulated adjustments account (AAA).**

      3. AAA is adjusted in the same way as stock basis except (1) no adjustment is made for tax exempt income (and related expenses) and (2) AAA can be negative (only losses can reduce AAA below zero; distributions cannot create a deficit in AAA).

      4. OAA is the **other adjustments account** that tracks tax-exempt income earned by the corporation.

      5. Order of distributions

         a. Distributions follow this order:

            i. First tax-free from AAA (non-taxable; note that distributions from AAA also reduce stock basis)

    ii. Then from E&P (dividend income)

    iii. Next from stock basis, which is a tax-free return of capital

    iv. The remaining distribution is a capital gain

  b. An S corporation can make a **bypass election**, which allows the distribution to first come from E&P and then AAA.

6. Distributions from AAA reduce the balance of AAA (but distributions never reduce AAA below zero—only losses can accomplish this feat).

7. Distributions from AAA and OAA reduce the adjusted basis of the shareholder's stock.

Example:
At the end of this year, ABC corporation (an electing S corporation) has AAA of $100 and E&P of $50. If ABC makes a distribution of $180 to its sole shareholder, the shareholder will report the first $100 as tax-free from the AAA account. Note that this $100 also reduces the basis in the stock. The next $50 is dividend income from the E&P account. The final $30 is a return of capital. If SH had a basis in his ABC stock immediately before the distribution of $120, he would report two sources of income: 1) dividend income of $50 for the distribution from the E&P account, and $10 capital gain (basis of $120 – $100 from AAA – $30 return of capital).

D. Distributions of cash during a minimum one-year period following termination of an S corporation election receive special treatment.

  1. Treated as a tax-free recovery of stock basis to the extent it does not exceed AAA balance.

  2. Since only cash distributions receive this special treatment, the corporation should not distribute property during this post-termination transition period.

II. Built-In Gains Tax—An S corporation can be subject to tax if the corporation sells property that contained a **built-in gain** at the time of the S election.

Definition:
Built-In Gain Property: For purposes of a tax on an S corporation, appreciated property (value in excess of adjusted basis) as of the beginning of the first year of the S status.

A. Shortcut—A built-in gains tax is not imposed on a corporation that has always been an S electing corporation.

B. The tax is imposed at the highest corporate rate (35%) and is limited to the net amount of built-in gain at the time of election.

C. The tax can only be imposed for a period of 10 years after the S election is made.

  1. For assets sold in S Corporation tax years beginning in 2014, the recognition period is reduced to five years from the first day of the first tax year for which the S election was effective. This five-year rule has not been extended to 2015 at the time of this writing.

  2. For assets sold in 2015, the built-in gains tax will not apply if the S election was made on a date in 2004 that is after the date the asset is sold in 2015 (or before). For assets sold in tax years beginning in 2014, the built-in gains tax would not apply if the S election was made in 2008 (or before).

D. In the year of the sell, if property is also sold that had built-in losses at the date of the S election, these built-in losses can offset the built-in gains.

E. The total built-in gain subject to this tax in any given year is also limited to the S corporation's taxable income for that year.

Example:
ABC Corporation made an S election this year and, at the time of the election, it held property with a value of $100 and the basis of $80. ABC will be taxed on this $20 built-in gain (at the highest corporate rate) if the property is sold any time during the next 10 years.

III. **Passive Investment Income Tax**—An S corporation can be subject to the top corporate tax rate if the corporation reports excessive passive investment income and the corporation has E&P from prior status as a C corporation.

Definition:
Passive Income: For purposes of this test includes interest, dividends (except dividends from a subsidiary to the extent the subsidiary is conducting an active trade or business), royalties, and rents (unless substantial extra services are provided).

A. Excessive passive income is passive income over 25% of gross receipts.

B. The IRS may waive this tax if the corporation establishes that it made distributions within a reasonable time of discovering that E&P existed from a prior year.

Example:
ABC Corporation made an S election this year and, at the time of the election, it had E&P. This year ABC will be subject to a tax on excessive passive income if it receives interest of $100 and no other revenue.

C. Shortcut—A corporation that has never been a regular C corporation or does not have E&P from a prior period as a C corporation cannot be subject to the corporate tax on excessive net passive income.

Federal Gift Tax

After studying this lesson, you should be able to:

1. Differentiate between gifts and inheritances.

2. List and define the different forms of joint ownership of property.

3. Identify the key exclusions from the gift tax.

4. Apply the gift splitting rules.

5. Compute the unified credit for gift purposes.

6. Summarize the gift tax formula including deductions.

Tax Forms for this Lesson: Form 709 (available for download and printing from the lesson overview of your software).

I. Gifts and Inheritances—General Definitions

Definition:
Gift: A transfer of property for less than adequate consideration.

A. Transfers, in a business context, are typically for consideration, meaning that they are taxable to the recipient/employee.

B. Transfers for love and affection or marriage are gratuitous.

C. A transfer during the life of the donor (an **inter vivos transfer**) *triggers a gift tax.*

D. A transfer at death (a *testamentary* transfer) triggers the estate tax.

E. The donor or decedent can only transfer their ownership interests and not the interests owned by others. In community property states (Texas and California, among others), property acquired during a marriage is owned one-half by each spouse.

   1. The recipient of a gift is called a **donee**, and the recipient of an inheritance is called an **heir**.

F. The donee or heir is secondarily liable for the transfer tax.

G. The decedent's will directs transfers after the death of the decedent.

H. When a taxpayer transfers property to a trust, the taxpayer has made two gifts, the income interest and the remainder interest (unless the donor retains one of these interests).

   1. The beneficiary of the income interest receives the income from the trust each year.

   2. The beneficiary of the remainder interest receives the property (corpus) of the trust when the trust terminates.

   3. The income and remainder interests are valued using actuarial tables provided by the IRS. The rate used in the valuation is 120% of the applicable Federal midterm rate (published by the IRS) for the month in which the transfer is made.

I. Reminder—Gifts and inheritances are not income to recipients. Under the income tax, most donees assume a carryover basis for a gift and the holding period "tacks" from the donor. For inheritances, the heir takes a step-up basis (the fair market value that was included in the estate) and the holding period is always long-term.

II. The Transfer Must be Complete to be Treated as a Gift

A. The gift must be delivered to the donee.

B. The donor must give up control of the property.

C. The donee must accept the gift; the donee cannot disclaim or refuse the gift or it will be incomplete.

III. Joint Ownership — The creation of a joint *ownership interest without equal consideration from each co-owner is considered a gift of the excess contribution to the owner making a smaller contribution*. Joint ownership is determined under the law of each state, but typically **tenants in common** do not hold property with the right of survivorship. **Tenancy by the entirety** and **joint tenancy with the right of survivorship** hold property with the right of survivorship. **Right of survivorship** means that when one co-owner dies, the property immediately passes to the other co-owners.

A. The creation of a joint interest without adequate consideration creates a gift regardless of the form of ownership (tenancy in common or joint tenancy).

B. Transfers of cash to joint bank accounts do not constitute a complete gift until the donee withdraws the cash.

C. A purchase of a savings bond held jointly in the name of the donee and the donor is not a complete gift.

D. The creation of a joint interest with a spouse (with the right of survivorship) is not taxed because of the marital deduction.

Example:
TP purchases real estate for $50,000 and this property is owned by TP and his son as tenants in common (one-half interest each). TP made a complete gift of $25,000 to his son. If TP had contributed $40,000 and the son contributed $10,000, then the amount of the gift would be $15,000 ($25,000 − $10,000).

E. The termination of joint ownership may also trigger a tax, if the proceeds are not divided according to each owner's interest.

IV. Exclusions from Gift Tax—There are several important exceptions to the taxation of gifts, including the annual exclusion.

A. Certain transfers are not considered gifts

   1. Payment of another individual's medical or educational expenses (tuition and fees only) is not considered a gift. However, these payments must be made directly to the medical provider or the educational institution.

   2. Political contributions are not gifts.

   3. The satisfaction of an obligation is not a gift.

Example:
TP makes a $5,000 child support payment. This is not considered a gift if TP has the obligation to make child support payments.

B. Annual exclusion—An "annual exclusion" of $14,000 (2015 and 2014) eliminates modest gifts from the application of the gift tax.

   1. The annual exclusion is applied per donee per year.

   2. The annual exclusion only applies to a gift of a **present interest**. Thus, if the gift is made in trust and will not benefit the recipient currently, there is no exclusion allowed.

Definition:
A Present Interest: The right to income or to enjoy property currently. A gift to a minor in a trust is considered a present interest if the trustee has the ability to use the funds for the benefit of the minor before the age of 21 (such as for education, medical, etc).

V. Integration of Gift and Estate Tax—The federal gift tax and estate tax are coordinated in order to assure that all transfers are only subjected to one of the two transfer taxes. The transfer taxes are integrated so that taxable gifts affect the tax base for the estate tax.

   A. The two transfer taxes—These were unified after 1976 and hence, special transition rules apply to transfers prior to 1976.

   B. Deductions—For both the estate and gift taxes.

      1. There is an unlimited marital deduction for transfers to a spouse.

      2. There is an unlimited charitable contribution deduction for transfers to charity.

   C. Unified credit—A unified credit provides that the first $5,430,000 (2015; $ 5,340,000 in 2014) of transfers from an estate and/or gifts will not trigger a tax liability

      1. The unified credit applies to taxable transfers by gift or bequest to allow a minimum cumulative amount of tax-free transfers.

      2. Because the unified credit applies to **taxable** transfers, it is not used to offset transfers eligible for a marital deduction (transfers to a spouse) or charitable deduction (transfers to a charity).

VI. Gift Splitting—In community property states, one-half of all property generally belongs to each spouse. Hence, a gift of community property is automatically split between the spouses. To equalize this effect, a gift-splitting election is available.

   A. The purpose of a gift-splitting election—Is to equalize treatment of gifts by spouses with the treatment of gifts in a community property state.

      1. The election is available each year.

      2. The donor must be married at the time of the transfer.

   B. Under the gift-splitting election—A gift is split and treated as being given equally by both spouses.

      1. The value of the gift is divided in two and each spouse is treated as making a gift.

      2. Both spouses can use an annual exclusion for gifts of present interests. Note, that both spouses will need to file a gift tax return so that each can elect gift-splitting.

Example:
TP is married to S and this year made a gift of $50,000 to his son. If TP and S elect to gift splitting, the $50,000 gift is treated as two $25,000 gifts to the son, one gift from TP and one from S. Each gift would be eligible for an annual exclusion of $14,000 (2015), so each spouse would have made a taxable gift of $11,000.

VII. Deductions—Two important deductions are available in calculating the amount of taxable gifts.

   A. A marital deduction—Is allowed for most gifts to a spouse.

      1. Gifts of **terminable interests** generally do not qualify for the deduction.

Definition:
Terminable Interest: An interest in property that terminates upon the death of the recipient. For example, a taxpayer who receives the right to occupy property for the duration of his life has received a terminable interest in that the taxpayer's rights terminate upon his death.

      2. The deduction is unlimited in amount.

      3. The amount of the deduction is the total gift less any excluded portion (if the annual exclusion applies).

      4. The marital deduction does not apply for gifts to a spouse who is not a U.S. citizen, but an annual exclusion of $147,000 (2015; $145,000 in 2014) is permitted.

Examples:

1. H and W became engaged in April, when H gave W a ring with a value of $50,000. In July H and W were married and H gave W a new car worth $75,000.

Question: What amount of annual exclusion may H claim?

Answer: H can claim $14,000 annual exclusion (2015) for the April gift and a $75,000 marital deduction for the new car. The remaining $36,000 for the ring is taxable since H and W were not married at the time of the gift.

2. TP gives Mrs. TP $60,000.

Question: What is the amount of the taxable gift?

Answer: TP can exclude the first $14,000 under the annual exclusion and then claim a marital deduction for the remaining $46,000. No taxable gift was made.

B. A charitable contribution deduction—Is allowed for gifts to charitable organizations.

  1. A charity is defined similarly to income tax (educational, scientific, religious organizations), but includes foreign charities and excludes cemeteries.

  2. There is no limitation on the amount of the deduction.

Example:
TP donated $60,000 to his church.

Question: What is the amount of the taxable gift?

Answer: TP can deduct all $60,000 for gift tax purposes because the church qualifies as a charity. No taxable gift was made.

VIII. Gift Tax Formula—The gift tax calculation includes current gifts and past gifts. The purpose of adding gifts from previous periods is to use prior gifts to determine the gift tax rate (since the rates are progressive) on current gifts. To prevent double taxation of these gifts, the gift tax on prior taxable gifts (not the gift tax paid, but the amount of tax computed ignoring payments) is then subtracted from the total gift tax.

  A. The Federal Gift Tax Formula

Current Gifts

Less: 1/2 of split gifts

Plus: 1/2 of split gifts by spouse

Less: ANNUAL EXCLUSION

<u>Less Marital and Charitable Deductions</u>

Current Taxable Gifts

Prior Taxable Gifts

Cumulative Taxable Gifts

<u>× Tax Rates</u>

<u>Cumulative Tax</u>

less Current Tax on Prior Taxable Gifts

<u>less remaining Unified Credit</u>

<u>Gift Tax Payable</u>

B. There are four steps to calculate the gift tax:

1. First, determine current taxable gifts (gifts reduced by exclusions and deductions).

2. Second, add previous taxable gifts and calculate the total gift tax.

3. Third, reduce the total gift tax by the gift tax computed on taxable gifts from previous periods using the current rates for the unified tax.

4. Fourth, reduce any remaining gift tax by the unused portion of the unified credit.

> **Note:**
> The gift tax on previous gifts is computed using the current tax rate schedule and ignores the use of the unified credit. This amount does not represent the amount of gift tax paid in previous years.

C. Filing requirements—The requirement for filing a return is based upon the annual exclusion.

1. April 15 is the due date for gifts made in the prior year; no fiscal years are allowed.

2. The gift tax return (Form 709) is due if gifts exceed the annual exclusion or if a gift is made of a future interest.

3. No gift tax return is required if a gift to charity exceeds the annual exclusion, as long as the entire value of the transfer qualifies for a charitable contribution.

> **Note:**
> The unused portion of the unified credit is used to reduce the total gift tax. The amount of unified credit used must be tracked from each period because the gift tax on previous periods ignores the amount of gift tax actually paid.

IX. Integrated Review Problem—For each situation, indicate whether the transfer of cash, the income interest, or the remainder interest is a gift of present interest (P), a gift of a future interest (F), or not a completed gift (N).

A. A created a $500,000 trust that provided his mother with an income interest for her life and his sister with the remainder interest at the death of his mother. A expressly retained the power to revoke both the income interest and the remainder interest at any time.

1. The income interest at the trust's creation.

   a. N—incomplete transfer due to power to revoke.

2. The remainder interest at the trust's creation.

   a. N—incomplete transfer due to power to revoke.

B. B created a $100,000 trust to provide her nephew with an income interest until he reaches age 45. When the trust was created, the nephew was age 25 and income distribution was to begin at age 29. The remainder interest, upon the nephew reaching age 45, goes to B's niece.

1. The income interest.

   a. F—no transfer to the nephew for four years.

C. C made a $10,000 cash gift to his son in May of this year and another gift of $12,000 in cash to his son in August of this year.

1. The cash transfers.

   a. P—$14,000 will be excluded (2015).

D. This year D transferred property worth $20,000 to a trust with the income to be paid to his 22-year-old niece. After the niece reaches age 30, the remainder interest is to be distributed to D's brother. The income interest is valued at $9,700 and the remainder interest is valued at $10,300.

1. The income interest.

   a. P—complete transfer because the niece is currently receiving the income. This is a gift of a present interest so the annual exclusion applies to it.

2. The remainder interest.

   a. F—the brother will not receive the gift for another eight years. This gift is a future interest so none of it is excluded by the annual exclusion.

E. E made a $40,000 cash gift to his uncle this year. E was married throughout the year and elected with his spouse to gift split.

   1. The cash transfer.

      a. P—$28,000 will be excluded (2015).

F. This year F created a $1,000,000 trust, which provides his sister with an income interest for 10 years after which the remainder will pass to F's brother. F retained the power to revoke the remainder interest at any time. The income interest is valued at $600,000.

   1. The income interest.

      a. P—complete transfer because the sister is currently receiving the income. This is a gift of a present interest so the annual exclusion applies to it.

   2. The remainder interest.

      a. N—incomplete transfer due to power to revoke. There is no gift tax since it is not a completed gift.

Federal Estate Tax

Tax Form for this Lesson: Form 706 (available for download and printing from the lesson overview of your software).

I. **Gross Estate**—The gross estate includes property owned by the decedent at death and certain property transfers.

Definition:
Estate: A legal entity that comes into existence automatically at the death of a taxpayer (the **decedent**). The **executor** of the estate collects the assets of the decedent, pays the decedent's debts, and distributes the remaining assets to the beneficiaries according to the decedent's will or according to the state law governing inheritances. The estate exists for the period required by the executor to perform his or her duties.

    A. Property owned by the decedent—Property owned at the date of death is included in the probate estate.

Definition:
Probate Estate: This estate includes cash, stocks, and assets such as a residence, clothing, and jewelry. The probate estate is the collection of the decedent's possessions for legal purposes, whereas the gross estate is a measure of the value of these possessions for estate tax purposes.

    B. Property transferred by the decedent at death—Is also included in the gross estate.

        1. Transfer of property occurs without probate through operation of law.

Example:
Property held in joint ownership with right of survivorship passes to the survivor upon the death of the first owner. The interest held in this property by the decedent would be included in his or her gross estate.

        2. Other forms of property that pass by operation of law include retained life estates, revocable gifts, transfers triggered by death (retirement benefits), and life insurance.

    C. Valuation of property—Property is included in the gross estate at the fair market value.

        1. The valuation date is the date of death, or the executor can elect to have the property valued on an alternative valuation date.

Definition:
Fair Market Value: This is a question of fact, but the standard is the amount that a willing buyer and willing seller would agree upon when both are in possession of all relevant information.

2. The alternate valuation date is six months after the date of death or on the date the property is disposed of (if earlier than six months after the date of death).

3. The election to use the alternate valuation date is only available if it causes gross estate and tax payable to decline.

4. An executor can elect to value certain realty used in farming or in connection with a closely held business at a **special use valuation**. The farm or business must continue to be used in that capacity for at least five years during the eight-year period after the date of death.

Definition:
Special Use Valuation: Allows realty to be valued at a current use that does not result in the best or highest fair market value. This election is available when the business is conducted by the decedent's family, constitutes a substantial portion of the gross estate, and the property passes to a qualifying heir of the decedent. Decrease in value cannot exceed $1,100,000 for individuals dying in 2015.

II. **Specific Inclusions in Gross Estate**—Certain property transfers are included in the gross estate because the transfer could be used to avoid the estate tax.

A. Life insurance—Proceeds are included in the gross estate under either of two conditions.

1. The decedent had incidents of ownership (e.g., the right to designate the beneficiary).

2. The decedent's estate or executor is the beneficiary of the insurance policy.

B. Jointly owned property—Is included in the gross estate.

1. The value of the decedent's interest as a tenant in common is included in the gross estate.

2. For jointly owned property by a husband and wife (right of survivorship or tenancy in the entirety), 50% of the value of the property will be included in the estate of the first spouse to die.

3. For jointly owned property with the right of survivorship (unmarried owners), the amount includible is the portion of the property equal to the proportion of the consideration that the decedent provided to acquire the property.

See the following examples.

Examples:
1. TP owns a one-half interest in property worth $100,000. The property was originally acquired for $20,000 and TP provided $5,000 (25%) of the price. If the property is held with the right of survivorship with a person other than TP's spouse, then TP's gross estate will only include $25,000. This is 25% of the value of the property, and this is equal to the portion of the purchase price provided by TP ($5,000/$20,000).

2. Bob furnished 80% of the consideration to buy land and his friend Amy furnished the remaining 20%. The land was titled as joint tenants with right of survivorship.

Question: What amount is included in Bob's estate?

Answer: If Bob dies first, 80% of the value of the property (valued as of Bob's death) will be in Bob's gross estate. If Bob and Amy are husband and wife and Bob dies first, his estate will include 50% of the value of the property.

C. Retained interests—Property transferred where the decedent retained an interest or a power.

1. A retained life estate or the retention of a power to alter, amend, or revoke a transfer are retained interests that cause the property subject to the power to be included in the gross estate.

> **Definition:**
> *Life Interest*: An interest in property that is retained for the life of the transferor. For example, a life interest in a residence means that the residence can be occupied for the life of the owner even though the property itself has already been transferred to another individual.

2. The power to designate possession or enjoyment of property or income (including power created by another that can be exercised in the decedent's favor) will also cause the property to be included in the gross estate.

   a. A general power of appointment allows the taxpayer to designate property to herself, her creditors, or to others. Therefore, if the taxpayer dies while retaining the general power, the property subject to the appointment is included in her gross estate.

   b. A special power or appointment does not allow a taxpayer to designate property to him. Therefore, if the taxpayer dies while retaining the special power, the property subject to the appointment is not included in his gross.

 Example:
Donor transferred property in trust with income to self for life and property to go at donor's death to R (remainderman).

Question: What is included in the donor's estate upon his death?

Answer: The trust property will be in the donor's gross estate.

D. Transfers within three years of death—Certain gifts within three years of death are included in the gross estate of the decedent.

   1. Transfers with retained interests, revocable transfers, and transfers of life insurance are included in the decedent's gross estate if the transfer is made within three years of death.

   2. The property is included at the date of death value.

   3. The gift tax paid on the gift is included in the estate for any gifts made within three years of death (this is the **gross up provision**).

 Example:
Two years ago TP transferred a life insurance policy on his life to S (his son), and paid gift tax on the transfer.

Question: When TP died this year, what was included in his estate?
Suppose that TP also transferred stock to S.

Answer: The value of the insurance and the gift tax paid on the transfer are included in T's gross estate. If TP had transferred stock, only the gift tax would be in his gross estate because TP did not retain any interest and the transfer was not completed by the death of the decedent.

III. **Marital Deduction**—In order to avoid taxing a married couple's estate twice, a deduction is provided for a transfer or bequest to a surviving spouse.

   A. To qualify for the marital deduction, the spouse must receive property outright and be able to control its ultimate destination.

      1. Property that passes to the surviving spouse as a result of joint tenancy qualifies.

      2. Only the net value of property subject to mortgage qualifies.

      3. Property rights that are terminable do not qualify.

Definition:
Terminable Interest: This interest fails due to a contingency or the passage of time. An example of a terminable interest is where the decedent grants the spouse the right to occupy a residence until such time as the spouse remarries.

4. The deduction is unlimited in amount.

B. **Qualified terminable interest property (QTIP)** will qualify for the deduction.

1. An election is made to use the marital deduction for a transfer to a spouse of less than a complete interest in trust.

2. The surviving spouse must receive all of the trust income annually (or more often) for life, but the decedent determines where the property goes at the surviving spouse's death.

3. The property must be included in the surviving spouse's estate at its value when the survivor dies.

C. No marital deduction is allowed for non-citizen spouses.

1. An exception to this rule is a transfer to a **qualified domestic trust**, which assures estate tax imposition upon a non-citizen spouse's death.

Example:
The decedent's will leaves property in trust with income to the surviving spouse for the duration of her life. At her death the property goes to the decedent's daughter by a previous marriage.

Question: Is a marital deduction available for this property?

Answer: The marital deduction may be elected on this transfer under the QTIP rules.

IV. **Other Deductions**—Deductions are allowed for expenses and losses because the taxable estate represents the net amount transferred to beneficiaries.

A. Debts of the estate—These debts, for example mortgages and accrued taxes, are deductible.

B. Final expenses—These expenses are deductible.

Example:
Funeral expenses and administration expenses (e.g., attorneys' and accountants' fees) are examples.

1. The executor has the option of deducting administration expenses on the estate tax return or the estate's income tax return. If deducting on the income tax return the executor must indicate that the deduction will not also be taken on the estate tax return.

C. Casualty and theft losses—Are deductible without any floor limitation.

1. The losses must be incurred during the administration of the estate.

2. The executor has option of deducting casualty and theft losses on the estate tax return or the estate's income tax return.

D. Charitable contributions—Are deductible without any limitation.

1. The same charities as the gift tax (e.g., includes foreign charities, but excludes cemeteries).

V. **Estate Tax Computation**—The estate tax calculation uses the taxable estate increased by adjusted taxable gifts (post 1976). Including gifts results in a higher tax rate applied to the estate property. However, these gifts are not double taxed because gift taxes paid reduce the tax imposed on total transfers.

A. Four steps—There are four steps to calculating the estate tax.

    1. First—The taxable estate is increased by **adjusted taxable gifts** made after 1976.

> **Definition:**
> *Adjusted Taxable Gifts*: Taxable gifts other than gifts already included in the gross estate. Adjusted taxable gifts are included at date of gift values.

> **Example:**
> D had a taxable estate of $5,650,000 and had made adjusted taxable gifts of $800,000 that were not included in the estate. D did not pay any tax on the gifts because he used his unified credit to offset the gift tax.
>
> **Question:** If the unified credit offsets $5,430,000 of taxable transfers (2015), how much of the estate will effectively be subject to the estate tax?
>
> **Answer:** D's estate will owe tax on $1,020,000 ($5,650,000 plus $800,000 less $5,430,000).

    2. Second—Apply current tax rates to total transfers. The maximum tax rate for 2015 is 40%.

    3. Third—Reduce the tentative transfer tax by gift taxes paid or payable (at current rates) on post-1976 gifts.

    4. Fourth—Subtract the unified credit and other credits.

    5. Credits against the estate tax

        a. For 2015, the unified credit will eliminate the tax on a net estate of $5,430,000. Any unused credit from a spouse dying after 2010 may be used in the future by the surviving spouse. Note that an election to use the remaining credit must be made by filing Form 706 even if the estate of the deceased would otherwise not require a return to be filed.

        b. There is a credit for tax on "prior transfers" to adjust for taxes on proximate deaths (deaths within 10 years).

        c. A credit is allowed for all or part of the death taxes paid to a foreign country.

        d. If property gifted before 1977 is included in the transferor's gross estate, a credit is allowed for any gift taxes paid on these gifts equal to the lesser of the gift tax paid or the estate tax attributable to this property.

B. Filing requirement—The requirement for filing a return is based upon whether the gross estate exceeds the exemption equivalent.

    1. The estate tax is levied on the estate, but installment payments of estate taxes is available for closely held business interests.

    2. The estate tax return (form 706) is due nine months after date of death.

    3. An estate tax return must be filed if the gross estate plus adjusted taxable gifts equal or exceed the exemption equivalent.

C. **The Federal Estate Tax Formula**

Property Included in Gross Estate

less Expenses, Debts, and Losses

Adjusted Gross Estate

less Marital and Charitable Deductions

Taxable Estate

plus Adjusted Taxable Gifts (post 1976)

Estate Tax Base

× Tax Rates

Tentative Tax

less: Gift Taxes on post 1976 gifts

Unified Credit

Foreign Death Tax Credit

Taxes on Prior Transfers

Estate Tax Payable

VI. The Generation-Skipping Tax (GST)

Definition:

Generation-Skipping Tax: A supplemental tax, that prevents the avoidance of the transfer taxes by skipping one generation of recipients.

Note:
The unified credit can be looked at in two equivalent ways. For an estate of $6,180,000 in 2015, if the entire unified credit equivalent of $5,430,000 is available, then only $750,000 of the estate is taxable. The tax due would be $300,000 since the estate is in the 40% bracket.
On the actual estate tax return, for an estate of $6,180,000, the tax before the credit is $2,417,800. The unified credit is $2,117,800, which also results in a tax due of $300,000.

A. GST is triggered by the transfer of property to someone who is more than one generation younger than the donor or decedent (e.g., a grandparent transfers property to a grandchild, rather than a child).

B. The GST is not applicable to a transfer of property to someone who is more than one generation younger than donor or decedent, if the persons in the intervening generation are deceased (e.g., a transfer to a grandchild is not subject to the tax if the grandchild's parents are dead).

C. The GST is not widely applicable because most transfers qualify for an annual gift tax exclusion and each donor/decedent is entitled to a large aggregate exemption that is equal to the amount of the unified credit for the estate tax.

Example:
Determine whether the transfer is subject to the generation-skipping transfer tax (A), the gift tax (B), or both taxes (C).

Question: TP's daughter, D, has one child, GD. This year TP made an outright gift of $8,000,000 to GD.

Answer: C—The GST is an addition to the gift tax because a generation (D) was skipped.

Income Taxation of Fiduciaries

After studying this lesson, you should be able to:

1. Compute taxable income for fiduciaries.

2. Define distributable net income.

3. Determine the effect of distributable net income on the income of the fiduciary and beneficiaries.

4. Identify items of income in respect of a decedent.

Tax Form for this Lesson: Form 1041 (available for download and printing from the lesson overview of your software).

I. **Fiduciaries**—Trusts and estates can be taxed on the income that accrues during the administration of the fiduciary. The trust/estate is taxed on income retained by the fiduciary and not distributed currently to beneficiaries. Income distributed to beneficiaries is reported as income during the beneficiary's tax year in which the estate year ends.

II. **Key Definitions**

Definitions:

Trust: A legal entity created by transfer of property from a **grantor**. The purpose of the trust is to hold and administer property for **beneficiaries** according to the terms of the trust instrument. The trust exists for the period determined by the trust instrument and state law.

Terminable Interest: An interest that ends upon the occurrence of a contingency.

Remainderman: A person who receives property after a present interest is terminated.

Contingent Interest: An interest that is created upon the occurrence of a contingency.

A. Single taxation—Income is taxed only once to either the fiduciary or the beneficiary.

   1. A distribution deduction for fiduciary prevents double taxation.

   2. Income taxed to beneficiaries retains its character (a conduit approach).

B. Income computation—Individual income tax rules generally apply to determining the taxable income for fiduciaries.

   1. Fiduciaries get a personal exemption depending on the type of fiduciary: $600 for estates, $300 for simple trusts and for complex trusts that distribute all of their income currently, and $100 for all other complex trusts.

Definitions:

Simple Trust: A trust that (1) must distribute all income currently, (2) make no distributions of corpus currently, and (3) make no current charitable contributions. Any trust that does not qualify as simple must be complex.

Grantor Trust: A trust controlled by the grantor through retained powers or the possibility the property in the trust will revert to the grantor.

   2. A trust may be simple in some years and complex in others.

   3. Fiduciaries get no standard deduction, but can deduct interest, taxes, charitable contributions, and trustee's fees.

4. When income is distributed currently by the fiduciary, then the fiduciary acts as a conduit and the beneficiaries are taxed on the distributed income.

5. Investment advisory fees of nongrantor trusts and estates generally are subject to the 2% of AGI floor as miscellaneous itemized deductions, unless the fees are not "commonly incurred" by individuals.

6. The executor has the option of deducting administration expenses on the estate tax return or the estate's income tax return. If deducting on the income tax return the executor must indicate that the deduction will not also be taken on the estate tax return. The same option applies to casualty losses.

C. Fiduciary accounting rules determine what can be disbursed.

1. Receipts and disbursements of trusts and estates are categorized by the fiduciary instrument or state law as either belonging to income or corpus (principal).

> **Definition:**
> *Corpus:* The principal or property in a trust or estate. The income earned on the principal is distinguished from the principal.

2. Income and deductions are allocated among beneficiaries according to the trust instrument.

D. Deduction for distributions.

1. Fiduciaries are entitled to deduct distributions of **income** to beneficiaries.

2. Fiduciaries pay income taxes, including an alternative minimum tax (when applicable), if the fiduciary has **undistributed** taxable income.

III. Distributable Net Income (DNI)

A. Distributions of income—Create a distribution deduction for the fiduciary.

1. The distribution deduction cannot exceed the distributable net income.

> **Definition:**
> *Distributable Net Income (DNI):* The amount of accounting "income" that's available to be distributed; typically capital gains belong to corpus and are not part of DNI.

2. Property distributions are not generally treated as dispositions of assets, but instead as distributions of DNI.

3. Beneficiaries are taxed on the receipt of distributions (to the extent of DNI).

4. Beneficiaries report income for the beneficiary's tax year in which the estate's or the trust's year-ends.

B. The calculation of DNI—Requires adjusting taxable income.

1. Add back personal exemption, net tax-exempt income, and net capital loss.

2. Subtract net capital gains allocable to corpus (keep net capital gains allocable to income beneficiaries or charity).

3. For estates and complex trusts, there is a two-tier system of allocating income and deductions and a "throwback" rule to discourage tax avoidance by timing trust distributions.

>
> **Example:**
> This year an estate reports $50k of capital gains (allocable to corpus), $100k of interest income, $25k of administrative expenses (allocable to income), and $12k of real estate taxes. Taxable income (before the distribution deduction) is $112,400 ($50,000 + $100,000 − $25,000 − $12,000 − $600). DNI is $63,000 calculated by adding back the personal exemption of $600 and subtracting out the net capital gains of $50k.

4. Shortcut—To calculate DNI, subtract net capital gains from accounting income.

C. Income Tax Formula for Fiduciaries

Gross Income

Less:

    Interest

    Taxes

    Business expenses

    Depreciation

    Charitable contributions

Less Distribution Deduction (maximum is DNI)

<u>Less Personal exemption</u>

Taxable Income

<u>× Tax Rates</u>

equals Gross Tax

Less credits

<u>Plus additional taxes</u>

<u>Tax Payable</u>

IV. Procedural Rules

A. Trusts must use a calendar year, but estates may choose any year-end. Both must file by the 15th day of the fourth month after the year-end (if the 15th falls on the weekend or holiday, the due date is the next business day following the 15th). An automatic extension of five months is allowed to file income tax returns for estates and trusts.

B. Trusts must pay estimated income taxes, but estates need only pay estimated income taxes after their first two tax years of operation.

C. Fiduciaries must file an income tax return (Form 1041) if gross income exceeds $600, if the fiduciary has taxable income, or if a nonresident alien is a beneficiary.

V. Income in Respect of a Decedent

V. Income in Respect of a Decedent—Income in respect of a decedent (IRD) occurs if a decedent was entitled to receive income at the date of death, but the income was not included in the decedent's final tax return. Hence, the income must be taxed as income to the estate (because it has not yet been subjected to any income tax) and also included on the estate tax return (because it is part of the property owned by the decedent at the time of death).

> **Note:**
> *Any estate tax paid due to the IRD is deductible as a miscellaneous itemized deduction (not a 2% itemized deduction) on the individual income tax return.*

A. Income and expenses are reported on a decedent's final individual income tax return up to the date of death.

    1. Income actually and constructively received through the date of death is included on the final return. When the decedent was on the cash basis, some income will not be received until after the date of death.

> **Definition:**
> *Income in Respect of a Decedent*: Income earned by the decedent but not included in the decedent's final return.

> **Example:**
> D died on July 10. D is a cash basis taxpayer who receives a paycheck at the end of each month. The paycheck covering the period up to July 10 is not received until the end of July. It will be income in respect of a decedent.

2. Deductible expenses paid through the date of death are properly claimed in the decedent's final return.

B. Income (or expenses) in respect of a decedent is taxed as income to the estate (or beneficiary if distributed).

> **Definition:**
> *Expenses in Respect of a Decedent*: Deductible expenses paid after the date of death.

C. There is no step up in basis to fair market value for income in respect of decedent. This income has not yet been subject to income tax.

D. The income is included in **both** the estate income tax return and the estate tax return.

E. Accrued expenses paid after the date of death attributed to income in respect of a decedent are deducted on **both** the estate income tax return and the estate tax return.

F. Estates (or beneficiaries) that are taxed on income in respect of a decedent are entitled to deduct the estate tax on this property.

Sources of Tax Authority Research

After studying this lesson, you should be able to:

1. Identify key sources of legislative, administrative, and judicial authority.

2. Describe the process used for creating new tax statutes in Congress.

3. Weight sources of authority in determining relevance for specific tax issues.

4. Summarize the tax research process and key issues for communicating results.

I. **Types of Tax Authority**

   A. There are two types of authority: primary and secondary. Primary authority consists of the original sources of the law, whereas secondary authority is commentary on tax law such as treatises, journals, and commentaries provided by editorial services.

   B. Primary authority comes from each of the three branches of the federal government.

      1. Legislative authority.

      2. Administrative authority.

      3. Judicial authority.

II. **Legislative Authority**—Authority from Congress

   A. Sources of statutory authority include:

      1. The Constitution, as all tax laws must be consistent with the provisions of the Constitution such as the 16th Amendment authorizing an income tax

      2. Internal Revenue Code Statutes (cited as IRC §351)

      3. Treaties

      4. Committee Reports of the House Ways and Means Committee, Senate Finance Committee, and the Joint Conference Committee

   B. The Internal Revenue Code (IRC) is the codification of the tax laws promulgated by Congress. For a tax law to be passed by Congress, it must pass through the following steps:

      1. All tax bills must originate in the House Ways and Means Committee.

      2. The bill, then, must be passed by the House of Representatives.

      3. Afterwards, the House bill moves to the Senate Finance Committee. Note that this committee is free to do as it wills with the House bill, even striking the entire bill and starting anew. However, the Senate Finance Committee can take no action without receiving a bill from the House.

      4. The Senate debates the bill and passes its own version.

      5. The House bill and Senate bill usually differ, so a Joint Conference Committee is created to craft a compromise bill.

      6. Once the Joint Conference Committee passes its bill, this bill must return to the House and Senate for another vote (assuming the compromise bill differs from the original bills).

      7. The President either signs or vetoes the bill.

      8. If vetoed Congress can override a veto with a two-thirds vote.

III. **Administrative Authority**—Authority from the Treasury Department and Internal Revenue Service. While there are many types of pronouncements issued by the Internal Revenue Service, the most significant are as follows. (Examples are provided for how each authority is cited.)

A. Treasury regulations—(Treas. Reg. §1.351-1). Regulations are published in the Federal Register and later in the Internal Revenue Bulletin.

  1. Regulations can be classified as:

   a. Legislative—These regulations have almost as much weight as the statute (IRC), since Congress has authorized the Treasury to develop regulations dealing with a specific issue.

   b. Interpretative—These regulations are written under the general mandate given to Treasury to develop regulations to interpret the laws legislated by Congress.

   c. Procedural—These regulations apply to procedural issues such as the information required to be submitted, the process for submission, etc.

  2. Regulations can also be classified as:

   a. Proposed—Regulations must be issued as proposed regulations for at least 30 days before becoming final, although they may exist in a proposed form for many years. Proposed regulations do not have the effect of law, but they do provide an indication of the IRS's view on a tax issue.

   b. Temporary—These regulations do have the effect of law but only for three years. Temporary regulations are usually issued when taxpayers need immediate guidance on a substantive matter of the law.

   c. Final regulations—Proposed or temporary regulations can later be issued as final regulations which have the effect of law until revoked.

B. Revenue rulings—(Rev. Rul. 2009-12)

  1. Do not have as much weight as regulations

  2. Are limited to a given set of facts

  3. Deal with more specific issues than regulations

C. Private letter rulings—(PLR 200948009)

  1. Request by the taxpayer for the IRS to provide the tax consequences on a specific set of facts.

  2. Transaction cannot have been completed by the taxpayer for the request to be made.

  3. Precedent applies only to the taxpayer making the request. However, PLRs can be used by other taxpayers to establish "substantial authority" for penalty purposes.

  4. IRS does not have to provide a ruling on the request.

D. **Revenue Procedures** (Rev. Proc. 2008-23)—These provide internal management practices of the IRS.

E. Technical advice memoranda—(TAM 201003016)—These are requested by the IRS field agents during an audit. They apply only to the affected taxpayer.

F. Other sources of authority include notices, announcements, and general council memoranda.

IV. Judicial Authority

A. Courts of original jurisdiction—Any tax dispute not resolved between the taxpayer and the IRS that goes to court must begin in a court of original jurisdiction.

  1. U.S. Tax Court

   a. Hears only tax cases.

   b. One court, but the 19 judges travel in smaller groups throughout the country to hear cases. For certain issues all judges may hear the case.

   c. Taxpayer does not have to pay deficiency before trial as long as a petition is filed in a timely manner.

   d. Jury trial is not available.

2. **U.S. District Courts**

   a. Jury trial is possible.

   b. Must pay deficiency first and then sue the IRS for a refund.

   c. Judges are not tax specialists since all types of legal matters are tried.

   d. Many different district courts throughout the country.

3. **The U.S. Court of Federal Claims**

   a. There is only one court in Washington, D.C.

   b. Must pay deficiency first and then sue the IRS for a refund.

   c. 16 judges, who are not tax specialists, since all types of legal matters are tried.

   d. Jury trial is not available.

4. **U.S. Tax Court—Small Cases Division a. $50,000 or less**

   b. No appeal

B. Appellate Courts

1. The U.S. Court of Appeals

   a. Hears appeals from Tax Court and District Court

   b. 11 circuits plus the District of Columbia Circuit

   c. District court must follow the decision/precedent of the Circuit Court of Appeals for the circuit in which the District Court is located

   d. Tax Court will follow previous decisions in the Circuit that will have jurisdiction on appeal (*Golsen rule*).

> **Definition:**
> *Precedent*: The courts must follow previous decisions for future cases with the same controlling set of facts.

2. The U.S. Court of Appeals for the Federal Circuit—Hears appeals from the U.S. Court of Federal Claims.

C. The U.S. Supreme Court

1. Hears very few tax cases

2. Highest court in the United States

V. Weighting of Authority

A. Legislative authority is weighted in the following order. Barring certain exceptions (e.g., constitutional issues), Congress has the last word on what the Federal tax law should be.

1. The highest source of tax authority is the U.S. Constitution.

2. The next highest source is the Internal Revenue Code.

3. If a treaty exists with a foreign country, the provisions of the treaty control the tax consequences of a transaction.

B. Administrative authority

1. Legislative regulations have almost as much weight as the IRC itself.

2. Other types of regulations have very significant authority within the context of administrative authority.

3. Revenue Rulings are the next highest source of authority.

4. Private Letter Rulings apply only to the taxpayer who requested the ruling.

    C. Judicial authority—The weighting of a judicial decision depends on:

        1. Level of court

        2. Legal residence of the taxpayer

        3. Whether the IRS has acquiesced to the decision (meaning that the IRS has indicated that it will follow the decision in the future)

        4. The date of the decision

        5. Whether later decisions have concurred with opinion

VI. Research Process—The following steps should be followed when researching a tax issue:

    A. Identify all relevant facts.

    B. Clearly state problem to be solved.

    C. Locate applicable tax authority.

    D. Evaluate the relevance of the authorities.

    E. Determine alternative solutions.

    F. Determine most appropriate solution.

    G. Communicate results.

VII. Communicating Research—A research memorandum should include the following key procedures:

    A. Document all relevant facts.

    B. Clearly describe the issue investigated.

    C. Report conclusions.

    D. Summarize rationale and authorities that support conclusions.

    E. Summarize key authorities used in research.

Tax Practice and Procedure

After studying this lesson, you should be able to:

1. Describe the key steps in the audit process used by the Internal Revenue Service.

2. Apply the statute of limitations to determine the audit time period for the IRS.

3. Summarize the most important steps in the appeals process when the taxpayer and the IRS do not agree.

4. List the key documents that provide standards of tax practice for CPAs and indicate the significant standards.

I. Audit Process

A. The audit process begins with a review of returns for error and matching information from W-2s, 1099s, etc. This review is applied to all tax returns.

B. All returns are classified by type such as individual, corporation, partnership, fiduciary, etc.

C. Each return is given a score from formulas that are part of the Discriminate Function System (DIF). The DIF score is used to determine which returns to review for possible audit.

D. Statute of Limitations—The IRS can assess additional tax up to three years from the later of:

1. The date the return was filed or

2. The due date for the return, with two exceptions.

   a. The statute of limitations is six years in the formula above if gross income omissions exceed 25% of the gross income stated on the return.

   b. There is no statute of limitations if the taxpayer willfully evaded tax in a fraudulent manner.

E. Audits may be conducted in an IRS office or in the field. Simple audits may be handled through written correspondence.

F. A taxpayer may appoint qualified individuals to represent him or her before the IRS, usually a CPA, attorney, or enrolled agent.

G. The IRS has the power to summon the taxpayer's records and witnesses to testify.

H. IRS reports its findings in an *Income Tax Examination Changes Report*.

I. Disagreements between the taxpayer and IRS may arise from questions of fact or from questions of law.

J. The IRS will take positions consistent with its administrative sources of the tax law.

K. The taxpayer and IRS can negotiate until the issues are resolved.

L. If the taxpayer agrees to the audit changes proposed in the *Revenue Agent's Report* (RAR), he or she cannot pursue tax relief through the appeals process or through the Tax Court. However, note that a signed agreement binds the IRS and taxpayer with regard only to items in the agreement.

M. Nevertheless, once the deficiency is paid the taxpayer can later pursue a claim for refund through the U.S. District Court or U.S. Claims Court.

N. If agreement is not reached through the audit process the taxpayer will receive a copy of the RAR and a **30-day letter**.

O. The IRS encourages the taxpayer to agree to the RAR or request an appellate conference. However, the taxpayer is not required to respond.

P. If the IRS issues a **no change report** after an audit, the IRS generally cannot reopen the examination unless fraud or other similar misrepresentation is involved.

II. Appeals Process

A. To appeal, a written protest must be filed with the request for an appellate conference.

B. The protest must explain the taxpayer's position for each issue and provide the support on which the taxpayer is relying for questions of law.

C. The IRS is not required to grant an appeal in all cases.

D. In general new issues may not be raised by the IRS during the appeal.

E. The appellate conference itself is informal when contrasted to a judicial proceeding.

F. If the case is settled a Form 870-AD is signed, which means that the case will not be reopened unless there is a significant mathematical error or fraud.

G. If a taxpayer does not respond to the 30-day letter or does not reach agreement in the appeals process, a 90-day letter is issued.

H. The **90-day letter** is significant in that this is the time that the taxpayer has to file a petition with the Tax Court. If the petition is not filed in a timely manner then the taxpayer's only judicial recourse is through a U.S. District Court or a U.S. Claims Court, both of which require the deficiency to be paid before the judicial process can begin.

I. Once a petition has been filed with the Tax Court, the IRS cannot issue a notice of deficiency until the court's decision in the matter has been finalized.

III. Other Practice Issues

A. An offer in compromise may be agreed to by the IRS, which allows a taxpayer to settle a tax liability for less than the actual amount owed.

B. The IRS may request the taxpayer to extend the statute of limitations period. While not required to do so, a refusal to extend will usually lead the IRS to assess a tax deficiency.

C. Any communication that would be privileged between a taxpayer and an attorney is also privileged between a taxpayer and any person who is authorized to practice before the IRS.

D. This privilege does **not** apply to criminal tax matters or to corporate tax shelters.

IV. Signing a Return

A. A taxpayer must sign a tax return for it to be complete. Both spouses must sign a joint return. This creates joint and several liability for each spouse, which means that the IRS can collect the entire tax liability from either spouse.

B. A refund cannot be issued unless the return is signed.

C. A taxpayer can use an electronic signature to sign a return that is e-filed.

    1. The taxpayer needs a personal identification number (PIN) to file electronically.

    2. For a married filing jointly return, both spouses need PINs.

    3. A taxpayer can self-select/enter a PIN or have the tax practitioner generate/enter a PIN for him/her.

    4. Note that if a return is filed electronically, no forms or paper need to be mailed to the IRS, not even W-2s.

D. A parent or guardian can sign a child's return as the child's representative.

E. A tax return is signed under the penalty of perjury. If a taxpayer knowingly signs a false tax return, the taxpayer can be subject to civil and/or criminal penalties. See the lesson "Compliance Responsibilities" for more detail.

F. The tax preparer must also sign the tax return and provide a Personal Identification Number (PIN). Failure to do so results in a $50 penalty to the tax preparer for each failure (maximum of $25,000 in any calendar year). The penalty applies separately to the failure to sign and failure to provide a PIN.

V. Standards of Practice

A. Circular 230 describes the rules that one must meet to be eligible to practice before the IRS. The term *practice* in this case relates to representing a client before the IRS. It does not include the preparation of tax returns.

B. In general, only CPAs, attorneys, and enrolled agents can practice before the IRS. Exceptions to this rule include individuals who are employees or officers of an entity. Limited exceptions are also made for registered tax return preparers.

C. Circular 230 provides numerous rules for the standard of conduct that must be met by those who practice before the IRS, including that an individual must:

    1. Advise a client of any noncompliance.

    2. Exercise due diligence in representations.

    3. Not charge an unconscionable fee.

    4. Submit requested records to the IRS.

D. CPAs are also subject to:

    1. AICPA's Code of Professional Conduct.

    2. AICPA's Statements on Standards for Tax Services.

VI. Rules Governing Authority to Practice under Circular 230

A. Who may practice before the IRS—(Individuals may not be under suspension or disbarment.)

    1. Attorneys.

    2. CPAs.

    3. Enrolled agents.

    4. Enrolled actuaries enrolled by the Joint Board for the Enrollment of Actuaries. However, practice is generally limited to issues related to qualified retirement plans.

    5. Enrolled retirement plan agents. However, practice is limited to issues related to employee plans and to IRS forms in the 5300 and 5500 series.

    6. Registered Tax Return Preparers (RTRP).

B. Additional Details for RTRPs—(The judicial system has currently suspended the rules requiring tax preparers to meet the RTRP requirements. The IRS has appealed this decision, so the future of the RTRP requirements is uncertain.)

    1. Practice is limited to preparing and signing tax returns and claims for refund and other documents for submission to the IRS.

    2. An RTRP may represent taxpayers before revenue agents, customer service representatives, or similar officers and employees of the IRS during an examination if the RTRP signed the return or claim for refund under examination.

    3. An RTRP may not represent a client before appeals officers, revenue officers, Counsel or similar officers or employees of the IRS or Treasury Department.

    4. An RTRP can provide tax advice only with regard to the preparation of returns or refund claims submitted to the IRS.

C. Practice before the IRS

    1. Practice before the IRS includes all matters connected with a presentation to the IRS or any of its officers or employees related to a taxpayer's rights, privileges, or liabilities under laws or regulations administered by the IRS.

    2. These presentations include, but are not limited to:

        a. Preparing documents

      b. Filing documents

      c. Corresponding and communicating with the IRS

      d. Rendering written advice with regard to transactions having a potential for tax avoidance or evasion

      e. Representing a client at conferences, hearings, and meetings

3. A power of attorney (Form 2848, *Power of Attorney and Declaration of Representative*) is required for an individual to represent a taxpayer before the IRS.

Compliance Responsibilities

After studying this lesson, you should be able to:

1. Describe the filing requirements and filing deadlines for individual and business returns.

2. Calculate accuracy related penalties for taxpayers.

3. Apply preparer penalties for tax preparers.

4. Define levels of confidence for tax positions.

I. **Filing Requirements**—All taxpayers who have income in excess of a predetermined limit must file an income tax return.

    A. In general, an individual must file an income tax return if his gross income exceeds the standard deduction plus personal exemptions.

        1. This includes the additional standard deduction for one who is age 65 or over (but not the additional deduction for one who is blind). One is considered 65 on the day before her 65th birthday. So if one turns 65 on January 1, 2016 she would be considered 65 on December 31, 2015, and therefore for the 2015 tax year.

Example:
Alvin files as married filing jointly and is age 67. His wife is 59 years old. Their standard deduction (for 2015) is $12,600 + $1,250 (over age 65) = $13,850. Their personal exemptions are $8,000 ($4,000 × 2). Alvin and his wife do not need to file a return unless their gross income exceeds $21,850 ($13,850 + $8,000).

        2. Taxpayers must also file a return if net self-employment income exceeds $400 during the tax year.

> **Note:**
> *The filing requirement includes the standard deduction and the increment for age 65, but does not include the increment to the standard deduction for blind taxpayers.*

II. **Filing Deadlines**

    A. The due date for individual returns is the 15th day of the 4th month after the close of the tax year (April 15, generally). An automatic six-month filing extension (generally October 15) is available to individuals.

    B. The due date for corporate returns is the 15th day of the third month following the close of the tax year. Corporations are entitled to an automatic six-month extension.

    C. Partnerships must file returns by the 15th day of the fourth month following the close of the tax year. Partnerships can receive a five-month extension for filing.

    D. Trusts must file returns by the 15th day of the fourth month following the close of the tax year. Trusts can receive a five-month extension for filing.

    E. In all cases, the estimated tax due must be paid by the original due date of the tax return.

    F. If the due date falls on a weekend or holiday, then the return is due the next business day. See the following table.

SUMMARY OF DUE DATES *		
	Regular Due Date	Extended Due Date
Tax Return	(Months after Year-End)	(Months after Regular Due Date)
Individual	15th day of 4th month	6 months
Corporation	15th day of 3rd month	6 months
S Corporation	15th day of 3rd month	6 months
Partnership	15th day of 4th month	5 months
Fiduciaries (Estates and Trusts)	15th day of 4th month	5 months
Tax-Exempt Organizations	15th day of 5th month	3 months + 3 more months if approved
Estate Tax	9 months after date of death	6 months

*If the due date falls on a weekend or holiday, then the return is due the next business day.

III. **Penalties**—Penalties are imposed on taxpayers under four circumstances. First, a penalty is imposed if the taxpayer fails to file a required tax return. Second, a penalty is imposed if the taxpayer fails to make adequate tax payments during the year (underpayment). Third, a penalty if imposed if the taxpayer fails to pay the tax reflected on the tax return (delinquency). Finally, a penalty is imposed if the taxpayer files an inaccurate tax return.

A. Nonfiling penalty—A nonfiling penalty is imposed on taxpayers (who must file a return) if the return is not filed by the due date.

1. The penalty for late filing is 5% per month (or a portion thereof) of the tax due with the return.

2. The maximum penalty is 25% of the tax due, and the minimum penalty (due if tax is not paid within 60 days of the due date) is the lesser of $135 or the amount of the tax due. If the minimum tax applies and is greater than the maximum tax, then the minimum tax must be paid.

3. If the failure to file is fraudulent (intentional), the penalty is increased to 15% per month up to a maximum of 75% of the tax due with the return.

Note: No penalty is imposed if no tax is due with the return, or the taxpayer is eligible for a refund.

B. Underpayment penalty—An underpayment penalty is imposed for failure to remit taxes during the year (i.e., on the required estimated payment dates).

Definition:
Tax Underpayment: The difference between the tax due and the amount of tax paid on or before the filing of the return plus credits.

1. Required tax payments for individuals

a. Taxes are remitted during the year through withholding or, if withholding is insufficient, through estimated tax payments. Taxpayers must make estimated payments (on the 15th of April, June, September, and January) if the amount of tax owed is at least $1,000 after subtracting withholding and credits.

b. No penalty is imposed if the tax due with the return is less than $1,000.

c. No penalty is imposed if the tax payments during the year were:

i. At least 90% of current year taxes, or

      ii. 100% of last year's taxes. If the taxpayer's AGI exceeds $150,000, then tax payments during the year must be at least 110% of last year's taxes.

    d. The penalty can also be avoided if the annualization exception is met. For this exception the actual income for each quarter is computed, and then each estimated tax payment is based on that income computation.

  2. Required corporate tax payments

    a. Estimated tax payments are due (if annual tax payments are at least $500) on 4/15, 6/15, 9/15, and 12/15 for a calendar-year corporation.

    b. There is no estimated tax underpayment penalty if the payments are at least equal to the lower of:

      i. 100% of current year's tax, or

      ii. 100% of the preceding year's tax.

      iii. The penalty can also be avoided if the annualization exception is met.

    c. A corporation with $1 million or more of taxable income in any of its three preceding tax years can use the preceding year's tax exception only for its first installment. The other installments must be based on the current year's tax to avoid penalty.

    d. If a taxpayer had a net operating loss in the previous tax year, the previous year's tax liability exception cannot be used to avoid anv underpayment penalty.

Example:
TP remitted $8,000 in withholding this year, but his total income tax is $10,000. Hence, $2,000 is due with TP's return. TP will be subject to an underpayment penalty unless his total income tax paid in the preceding year was no more than $8,000 (if his AGI was less than $150,000).

---

  3. Annualization Method

    a. The annualization exception can be used by individuals and corporations.

    b. The amount due with an installment is:

      i. The tax due for the months ending before the due date of the installment, less

      ii. The amount required to be paid for previous installments.

    c. Different exceptions can be used for different installments. For example, the 100% of previous year's tax might be used for the first quarter, and the annualization method for the second quarter.

    d. If a taxpayer determines that the installment under the annualized income method is less than the required installment under the regular method, any reduction in a required installment is recaptured by increasing the amount of the next required installment by the amount of the reduction.

    See the following example.

Example:
The tax due under the annualization method for the first six months of the year is $50,000. Estimated payments and withholding before the second quarter payment are $32,000. Therefore, the required installment for the second quarter is $18,000 ($50,000 − $32,000).

  C. Nonpayment penalties (and interest)—Are imposed if the taxes shown on the return are not paid on the filing date.

1. Interest on late payments starts on the due date for filing and is calculated using the Federal short-term interest rate.

2. Any tax due must be paid at the time of filing, or else a penalty of 0.5% of the underpayment is imposed per month or portion thereof (up to 25% in total).

Example:
TP paid a tax of $1,000 25 days after filing his return. In addition to interest on the underpayment, TP owes $5 ($1,000 × .005) as a delinquency penalty.

3. If both the nonpayment penalty and the non-filing penalty are imposed, the maximum penalty is limited to 5% of the tax due per month.

4. Neither the nonfiling nor the nonpayment penalties are imposed if the taxpayer has a **reasonable cause** for failing to file or failing to pay.

Definition:
Reasonable Cause: A cause outside the control of the taxpayer and not due to neglect, such as irregularities in mail delivery, death or serious illness, unavoidable absence, or disaster. A taxpayer, generally, has the burden of proving that a failure was due to reasonable cause.

Example:
The taxpayer failed to file a timely return and pay taxes because his records were destroyed in a fire. This excuses both penalties, but not the interest on the underpayment.

D. Accuracy penalties—Additional penalties may be imposed if the taxpayer underpays the actual tax because of an **inaccurate position** taken on a tax return.

Definition:
Inaccurate Position: This occurs when a taxpayer disregards the tax rules without reasonable cause.

1. A penalty of 20% of the tax due to the inaccuracy is imposed if the inaccurate position is due to negligence. The penalty is waived if the taxpayer had a reasonable basis for the position taken.

Definition:
Negligence: An intentional disregard of rules and regulations without intent to defraud.

Definition:
Substantial Understatement: For individuals, a substantial understatement results when the additional tax due exceeds the greater of $5,000 or 10% of the total tax on the return. For corporations, a substantial understatement results when the understatement exceeds the lesser of 10% of the tax required to be shown on the return (or $10,000 if that is greater) or $10 million.

3. A penalty is imposed if there is a substantial or gross overstatement of the value or basis of any property. The penalty is 20% of the tax understatement for a **substantial misvaluation** and 40% for a gross misvaluation.

Definitions:
Substantial Misvaluation: This occurs if the property is stated at 150% or more of the correct amount.

Gross Misvaluation: This occurs if the property is stated at 400% or more of the correct amount.

4. The penalty for fraud is 75% of underpayment and an addition of 50% of the interest due on the underpayment.

> **Definition:**
> *Fraud*: A deliberate action by the taxpayer to conceal, misrepresent, or deceive tax authorities about a tax deficiency.

IV. **Statute of Limitations**—The statute of limitations encourages controversies to be settled in a timely way. The statute bars tax disputes after a period of time has elapsed after the filing of the return.

    A. The primary statute of limitations expires after three years from the filing of the return.

        1. The statute begins to run from the due date or filing date, whichever is later.

    B. There are two key exceptions to the three-year rule.

        1. The statute is extended to six years if more than 25% of the gross income is understated on the original tax return.

        2. The statute never expires if the taxpayer commits fraud or fails to file a tax return.

    C. The Statute of Limitation for filing a claim for refund (on form 1040X) is the later of:

        1. Two years from the payment of tax or

        2. Three years from the date the return was filed (or April 15 if filed before the original due date)

    D. Form 1139 is used by corporations to claim refunds based on net operating losses, business credits or capital losses. Form 1045 is used by individuals to claim refunds based on net operating losses, business credits, or capital losses. A claim for refund of erroneously paid income taxes, filed by an individual before the statute of limitations expires, must be submitted on Form 1040X, the amended individual income tax return.

V. **Preparer Penalties**—Penalties may also be imposed on tax preparers. Note that you may want to review Section VI below before continuing to reference definitions of key terms used in this section.

    A. These penalties apply to all tax return preparers, including preparers for estate, gift, employment, excise, and exempt organization returns.

    B. A tax return preparer who prepares a return or refund claim that includes an **unreasonable position** must pay a penalty of the greater of $1,000 or 50% of the income derived by the preparer for preparing the return.

        1. There is an exception to this rule if the position was disclosed and there is a reasonable basis for it. However, this exception applies to reportable transactions and tax shelters only if the position has a **more likely than not** chance of being sustained.

        2. The reasonable cause and good faith exceptions apply.

> **Definition:**
> *Unreasonable Position*: A position is unreasonable if it does not have substantial authority.

    C. If the understated tax liability is due to an unreasonable position and the preparer **willfully attempts** to understate the tax liability or recklessly or intentionally disregards rules or regulations, the penalty is the greater of $5,000 or 50% of the income earned by the tax preparer for preparing the return or claim.

    D. Additional penalties may be imposed on preparers for:

        1. Not signing returns done for compensation.

        2. Not providing a copy of the return for the taxpayer.

        3. Not keeping a list of returns filed.

4. Endorsing or negotiating a refund check.

5. Disclosing information from a tax return, unless for quality or peer review, or under an administrative order by a regulatory agency.

6. A preparer can be fined $500 if he or she does not exercise due diligence in determining if a taxpayer is eligible for the earned income credit.

7. Providers may not base their fees on a percentage of the refund amount or compute their fees using any figure from tax returns.

8. A $500 penalty may be imposed, per I.R.C. §6695(f), on a return preparer who endorses or negotiates a refund check issued to any taxpayer other than the return preparer. The prohibition on return preparers negotiating a refund check is limited to a refund check for returns they prepared.

E. Tax preparers are subject to new penalties related to **knowingly or recklessly** disclosing tax return information. If a tax preparer uses or discloses tax return information without the client's explicit, written consent, each violation could result in a fine of up to $1,000, one year imprisonment, or both.

VI. Summary of Terminology for Penalties

A. Not frivolous = Not patently improper.

B. Reasonable basis = At least one authority that has not been overruled (Treas. Reg. Sec.

   1. 6662-3(b)).

C. Substantial authority = More than a reasonable basis (approximately 40%).

D. More likely than not = More than 50% chance of succeeding.

VII. Uncertain Tax Positions—Corporations that have at least $50 million of assets and uncertain tax positions have to file Schedule UTP if the corporation or a related party has issued audited financial statements. Disclosure requirements include a concise description of each UTP ranked by the current year's relative magnitude based on the financial statement reserve.

VIII. IRS Registration—Effective January 1, 2011, individuals preparing federal tax returns for compensation must register with the IRS and receive a PTIN (Paid Preparer Tax Identification Number).

Tax Planning

After studying this lesson, you should be able to:

1. Determine the marginal tax rate for a taxpayer.

2. Choose appropriate acceleration or deferral of selected tax items based on changes in rates.

3. Explain common tax planning strategies.

4. Describe planning strategies for the alternative minimum tax.

I. Using Tax Rates in Tax Planning

    A. Marginal tax rate is the rate that should be used for decision making.

> **Definition:**
> *Marginal Tax Rate*: The amount of taxes that will be paid on the next dollar of taxable income, or that will be saved on the next dollar of deduction.

> **Example:**
> T is in the 35% tax bracket and itemizes on her tax return. She plans to make a charitable contribution of $1,000 to her alma mater on December 31. The net cost of this contribution to T is $650, since she will save $350 in taxes ($1,000 × marginal tax rate of 35%) because the contribution is deductible.

    B. If rates are increasing in the future, accelerate income and defer deductions.

    C. If rates are decreasing in the future, accelerate deductions and defer income.

    D. Differences in tax rates over time present opportunities for tax planning. These differences can happen for several reasons.

        1. Changing tax brackets based on change in taxable income.

> **Example:**
> B is in the 10% tax bracket in Year 1 but expects to be in a 25% tax bracket in Year 2. B should adopt tax strategies that will accelerate income into Year 1 or defer deductions into Year 2. If he accelerates $10,000 of income into Year 1 his tax savings will be $1,500 ($10,000 × (25% − 10%)).

        2. Time value of money: Note in this example that if the time of value of money is considered, the savings is less than $1,500 since he must pay the $1,000 of taxes ($10,000 x 10%) in Year 1 rather than in Year 2. If he could earn 5% on these funds then he forgoes interest income of $50 ($1,000 × 5%). His net cash savings is $1,450 ($1,500 − $50).

        3. **Caution:** Do not consider the time value of money on the exam unless you are specifically directed to do so in the instructions.

        4. Statutory changes in rates across years.

> **Example:**
> C is in the 40% tax bracket in Year 1 but Congress has decreased her tax bracket to 35% for Year 2. B should adopt tax strategies that will accelerate deductions from to Year 1 or defer income to Year 2. If she defers income of $100,000 until Year 2, her tax savings will be $5,000 ($100,000 × (40% − 35%)).

E. Shift income to lower-bracket taxpayers.

Example:
Mother is in a 50% tax bracket and her 25 year-old son is in a 10% tax bracket. Mother gifts $100,000 of bonds paying 8% interest to Son. The $8,000 of interest income will be taxed at the son's 10% rate, a savings of $3,200 for the family ($8,000 × (50% − 10%)).

F. Differences based on character of income (e.g., long-term capital gain vs. ordinary income).

Example:
Assume that long-term capital gains are taxed at 20% and ordinary income at 40%. Taxpayers should consider strategies to convert ordinary income into long-term capital gains. If taxpayer D sells stocks at a gain of $3,000 that have been owned for 11 months the gain is taxed as ordinary income at the 40% rate (assuming there are no capital losses to net this against). If D had held the stocks for more than one year the gain would be taxed at 20%.

G. Differences based on jurisdiction (e.g., U.S. tax rates versus foreign tax rates).

H. The effective income tax rate for a taxpayer is the federal income tax liability for the year divided by taxable income. This rate should not be used for tax planning, but it does provide an estimate of the overall income tax burden for a taxpayer.

II. **Tax Strategies**—Common tax strategies that may be helpful for solving problems on the exam include:

A. Avoid income by choosing nontaxable fringe benefits over taxable salary.

Example:
Taxpayer F earns a salary of $75,000 per year but does not receive health insurance benefits from his employer. Since health insurance is a tax-free fringe benefit, F should consider having his employer pay his $5,000 of health insurance premiums and reduce his salary to $70,000. This will reduce his taxable salary by $5,000.

B. Defer income by meeting rules such as like-kind exchange rules.

C. Maximize contributions to retirement plans.

D. Recognize capital gains if capital losses have already been recognized which can offset the gains.

Example:
Taxpayer W has $30,000 of capital losses and no capital gains for the current tax year. W will be able to deduct net capital losses of $3,000. If W can generate $27,000 of capital gains, these gains will be offset by the unused capital losses so that no additional tax liability will be due on account of these gains.

E. Generate passive income to offset unused passive losses.

F. Insure that carryforward amounts are used before they expire (e.g., charitable contributions, net operating losses).

III. **Tax Planning for the AMT**

A. Taxpayers should adopt planning strategies to avoid the individual AMT.

1. Reduce adjustments and preferences that increase AMT income, such as certain types of tax-exempt interest and income from the exercise of incentive stock options.

2. Consider the deductions that are not allowed for AMT purposes and minimize those in years when one is subject to the AMT, especially itemized deductions such as:

a. No deduction is allowed for taxes.

b. There is no allowance for 2% miscellaneous deductions.

c. Home mortgage interest is deductible only if the loan proceeds are used to improve the home.

B. If the individual AMT cannot be avoided, it may be advantageous to accelerate income into the AMT year since it will be taxed at a maximum rate of 28%. However, a level of income will eventually be reached where the taxpayer is no longer subject to the AMT but to the regular income tax rates which may be higher than 28%. Income should be accelerated until this level of income is reached.

IV. Tax Planning for Charitable Contributions

A. Gifting appreciated property to a charity avoids recognizing the appreciation as income.

Example:
Taxpayer Z has owned stock for four years that has a basis of $30,000 and fair market value of $100,000. If Z sells the stock she will recognize a long-term capital gain of $70,000. If Z contributes the stock to a charity she will receive a deduction of $100,000 and will avoid recognizing the appreciation of $70,000 as taxable gain.

B. Loss property should not be gifted because the loss is not recognized. Rather, the asset should be sold so the loss can be recognized. The cash from the sale can then be contributed to a charity.

V. Consideration of Non-Tax Factors in Tax Planning

A. Tax effects should never be the only factors considered for a decision.

B. Non-tax factors must also be considered.

C. It is possible that the alternative with the best tax outcome increases costs in other areas for the company.

D. Goal is to maximize after-tax income, not minimize taxes.

See the following example.

Example:
Assume that a corporation is considering two alternative strategies. The revenue, tax savings, and non-tax costs associated with each strategy is as follows:

	Marginal Revenue	Marginal Tax Savings	Marginal Non-Tax Costs
Strategy A	$100,000	($30,000)	$30,000
Strategy B	$100,000	($40,000)	$50,000

Note that the tax-minimizing strategy is Strategy B since it reduces taxes by $40,000 as compared to $30,000 for Strategy A. However, Strategy B increases tax costs by $50,000 which is $20,000 more than the $30,000 increase for Strategy A. The net change in marginal costs is zero for Strategy A and $10,000 for Strategy B, with revenue being the same ($100,000) for both. Therefore, the optimal strategy that maximizes after-tax income is Strategy A (net income is $100,000 for A and $90,000 for B), while the tax minimizing strategy is Strategy B.

Business Entity Choice

After studying this lesson, you should be able to:

1. Identify the legal structures for business entities.

2. Describe the permissible tax entity forms for each business entity type under the check-the-box regulations.

3. Compare and contrast tax entity forms on key characteristics.

4. Explain the advantages and disadvantages of partnership status.

5. List the key similarities and differences of S corporations and partnerships.

I. **Legal Forms**—There are various legal forms that owners can choose for their business, each with certain tax and nontax advantages and disadvantages.

   A. Most common legal forms include:

      1. Sole proprietorships (not a separate entity)

      2. Corporations

      3. General partnerships

      4. Limited partnerships

      5. Limited liability companies

      6. Limited liability partnerships

      7. Business trusts

   B. These legal forms fall into one of the following tax classifications:

      1. Corporations (C and S)

      2. Partnerships

      3. Trusts

      4. Sole proprietorship (individual files on Schedule C)

II. **Check-the-Box Regulations**—Under the check-the-box regulations, unincorporated entities may elect to be taxed as an association (corporation) or a partnership.

   A. Some associations are automatically taxed as corporations and are not eligible to make an election. These *per se* corporations include business entities formed under statutes that refer to the entities as incorporated. These entities are taxed as either S corporations or C Corporations.

      1. *Per se* corporations include:

         a. Entities incorporated under state law

         b. Insurance companies

         c. State-chartered banks, if deposits are insured by FDIC

         d. Publicly-traded partnerships

         e. Specified foreign entities

      2. Certain other entities (such as REITs, tax-exempt organizations, etc.) are also classified as corporations.

   B. For entities not listed as *per se* corporations, the default options for the entity is a partnership when the business has more than two owners. This default rule typically applies to partnerships and limited liability companies. If an entity does not prefer the default classification, it can elect to be taxed as a corporation.

C. If an entity has only one owner, then the default classification is that the entity is "disregarded" for federal income tax purposes. These entities can also elect to be taxed as a corporation.

1. **Disregarded** means that the entity, while clearly a distinct entity for legal purposes, is ignored for federal income tax purposes.

2. An LLC owned 100% by an individual is treated as a sole proprietorship.

3. An LLC owned 100% by a corporation is treated as a division of the corporation on Form 1120.

D. An election under the check-the-box regulations is effective if filed within the first 75 days of the tax year.

E. An election can be changed after five years or with IRS permission.

F. A business trust is taxed as a trust on Form 1041.

III. **Tax Entities Can Be Compared and Contrasted on the Following Characteristics**—Note: Refer to the chart at the end of this lesson for a summary of this material.

A. Limited liability—Corporate shareholders and LLC members have limited liability, as do limited partners.

B. Double taxation—The only entity subject to double taxation is C corporations. Income is taxed to the corporation and then a second time when paid to shareholders as a dividend.

C. Retain income at lower current tax cost—The entity that may be able to retain income at a lower tax cost is the C corporation (this depends on the level of current tax rates for corporations and individuals). This is not possible with flow-through entities since income flows to the owners even if not distributed.

Example:
Assume that the highest corporate/individual tax rate is 40%/70%. C corporations would pay tax at a 40% rate and retain the remaining income. Note that the second level of tax is avoided if dividends are not paid but the funds are used to expand the business. For LLCs, partnerships, and S corporations, the income would flow through to the owners and potentially be taxed at 70%.

D. Tax-deferred contributions—While both corporations and partnerships can be formed in such a manner that realized gains/losses are deferred, the rules are much more favorable for partnerships (and LLCs) since there is no 80% control test requirement for deferrals for partnerships.

E. Distributions—The distributions rules favor partnerships (and LLCs). Gain is recognized on partnership distributions only if the cash distributed exceeds the partner's basis in his or her partnership interest. If a corporation distributes appreciated property as a dividend, redemption, or liquidation, gain will be recognized to the corporation (for the appreciation) and potentially to the shareholder (double taxation) as well.

F. Owner basis for entity level debt—Only partners in a partnership and LLC members can increase their basis in their ownership interest for entity level debt. This benefits the partner/member since losses can be deducted on the owner's tax return only to the extent of basis in the ownership interest. This is the reason that partnerships are often used for tax shelters.

G. Fringe benefits—Partners in a partnership are not eligible to benefit from many fringe benefit exclusions because partners who work for the partnership are not considered to be employees. This same rule applies to S corporation shareholders who own 2% or more of the S corporation.

IV. **Characteristics of Partnerships**

A. Advantages

1. Single taxation.

2. Flexibility—Partners can allocate income, expenses, credits, and all other tax items in any manner as long as the allocation has substantial economic effect.

Example:
Partners A and B agree to share income 50/50 for Year 1 but share losses 70/30. For Year 2 A and B change the income sharing ratio to 40/60. These allocations are permissible because of the flexibility afforded to the allocation of partnership income.

   3. Basis increase for debt.

   4. Tax-deferred contributions/admissions.

   5. Distributions/withdrawals rarely produce gain to the partners.

B. Disadvantages

   1. Unlimited liability for general partners.

   2. Limited partners have limited management rights.

V. Comparison of Partnerships and S Corporations

A. Key similarities

   1. Both are flow-through entities with single taxation.

   2. LLC members, limited partners, and S corporation shareholders have limited liability (but general partners do not),

   3. Both have restrictions on the year-end that must be used for the entity.

B. Key differences

   1. Partners have flexibility with profit and loss sharing ratios. S corporations must allocate all tax items according to the percentage of stock owned by each shareholder.

   2. The built-in gain rules that apply to partnerships do not apply to S corporations.

   3. Income allocations from partnerships to general partners are subject to the self-employment tax. Income allocations from S corporations are not subject to the self- employment tax.

   4. Partners receive a basis increase for partnership debt whereas S corporation shareholders do not.

   See the following table.

COMPARISON OF BUSINESS ENTITIES

Issue	C Corporation	S Corporation	Partnership	Multi-member LLC	Sole Proprietorship
Limited liability	Yes	Yes	No—General; Yes—Limited	Yes	No
Double taxation	Yes	No	No	No	No
Retain income at lower tax loss	Depends on relative tax rates	No	No	No	N/A
Tax-deferred contributions	Possibly—subject to control test	Possibly—subject to control test	Yes	Yes	N/A
Double taxation on distributions	Yes	Possibly	No	No	No
Owner's basis for entity level debt	No	No	Yes	Yes	N/A

Index